THE BOOK OF VIDEO LISTS
1990 EDITION

Thousands of video enthusiasts have already found *The Book of Video Lists* to be the easiest way to discover more movies to enjoy at home. Our exclusive list format provides thousands of suggestions for *every* movie lover . . . because it's organized the way most people shop for videos—by subject and star.

**"Provides very good film information
in a concise format . . ."
—*American Reference Books Annual***

This new 1900 edition is fully updated and expanded. It contains more than 500 lists of movies now available on video—a total of over 4,700 movies—and it includes all of the latest releases! This edition also contains a new chapter entitled Video Extra which includes lists of Oscar-winning movies . . . memorable movie debuts . . . and much more. Plus, there's a special list of the most requested movies that are not yet available on video.

**"Skillfully organized and indexed . . ."
—*Library Journal***

Whether you're looking for a romantic comedy or a World War II drama . . . for a Fred Astaire musical or a John Wayne western . . . for a James Bond thriller or a Walt Disney family film . . . for the latest releases starring Harrison Ford, Eddie Murphy, Meryl Streep or Tom Cruise . . . for films directed by Woody Allen, Alfred Hitchcock, or Martin Scorsese that you somehow missed . . . *The Book of Video Lists* is the only video renter's guide that uncovers so many video treasures in such an organized, practical and fun-to-use format.

**"A handy book . . . Wiener's sound judgment
and thorough knowledge could save you time and money."
—Pat Dowell, *The Washingtonian***

THE BOOK
OF
VIDEO LISTS

1990 EDITION

Tom Wiener

MADISON BOOKS
Lanham • New York • London

Copyright © 1988, 1989 by

Tom Wiener

Madison Books

4720 Boston Way
Lanham, MD 20706

3 Henrietta Street
London WC2E 8LU England

Printed in the United States of America

British Cataloging in Publication Information Available

Cover design by Carlos Aguilar.

Library of Congress Cataloging-in-Publication Data

Wiener, Tom.
The book of video lists: 1990 edition / Tom Wiener.
        p.   cm.
1. Video recordings—Catalogs.   2. Motion pictures—Catalogs.   I. Title.
  PN1992.95.W55   1990   016.79143'75—dc20   89–38204 CIP

ISBN 0–8191–7457–2 (pbk.)

The paper used in this publication meets the minimum requirements of American
National Standard for Information Sciences—Permanence of Paper for Printed Library
Materials, ANSI Z39.48–1984.   ∞

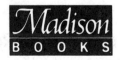

CONTENTS

3 Comedy (CO)   37

4   Cult Films (CU)   **55**

8   Horror (HO)   111

9   Musicals (MU)   123

10   Mystery/Suspense (MY)   133

11   Science Fiction/Fantasy (SF)   143

INTRODUCTION

You know the feeling:

You're in a video store, standing in front of a shelf full of tapes. Some of the films you've seen, a few titles sound familiar, and most you've never heard of. You know what *kind* of a movie you want to rent, but how do you find it? Your hands are sweating, the titles blur together, you're thinking about all the time you've been standing there looking for a movie when you could be home watching one. . . .

That's where *The Book of Video Lists* comes in. This book will make you a smarter video renter, because it provides you with hundreds of suggestions tailored to your tastes in movies, whether you're a fan of classic films, adventure sagas, or horror thrillers, whether your favorite actor is Bette Davis or Robert DeNiro, whether you're looking for a Tom Hanks comedy or a Gene Kelly musical.

Think of this book as a video matchmaker, designed to get you and the right movie together for an evening's entertainment. *The Book of Video Lists,* unlike any other video or movie guide, is organized by subjects and stars, the way most people shop for movies on tape. It's a guide you can use every time you make a trip to the video store.

First, a few words on the contents of this book.

The only place in this Introduction where the word "complete" appears is in this paragraph. No video guide can be complete, because each month dozens of new releases arrive on the market. Nevertheless, the films listed here are as up-to-date as possible, accounting for many recent releases on home video.

There are two types of lists in this book. The subject lists (for example, World War II, Romantic Comedies, Musical Films About Show Biz) are selective. To list every romantic comedy, every WW II drama, every backstage musical available on video would make this book longer than the Manhattan Yellow Pages and a lot less useful. The second type of lists, the Check Lists, are inclusive. More on those under How To Use This Book.

The lists are comprised almost entirely of theatrical films, the most popular form of home video entertainment. I have included a selection of movies originally made for TV if they were of sufficient interest to merit a look on home video.

Every film in this book has been carefully checked for its availability on home video. However, some titles have been "discontinued" by their distributors. When a home video title is discontinued, rental copies can stay in circulation. I've made some judgment calls; if a title was only recently discontinued, there may still be enough rental copies in circulation to justify including the film here.

And finally, don't be disappointed if your video store doesn't carry all 4,700+ titles in this guide. In fact, if your video store *does* carry all the titles in this guide, write me. That's a store I'd like to see.

HOW TO USE THIS BOOK

The first portion of the book contains chapters on categories common to most video stores:

Action-Adventure (AC)	Foreign Films (FF)
Classics (CL)	Horror (HO)
Comedy (CO)	Musicals (MU)
Cult (CU)	Mystery/Suspense (MY)
Drama (DR)	Science Fiction (SF)
Family/Kids (FA)	Westerns (WE)

The two-letter codes after each category are used in the general index. More on that in a moment.

Each chapter contains lists of titles arranged by topic, and numbered in sequence. For example, the first list in the Action-Adventure chapter lists a selection of World War II films (**AC1**). In the Comedy chapter, the seventh list is a collection of movie spoofs (**CO7**). Fans of British mysteries can begin their investigations with the 19th list under Mystery/Suspense (**MY19**).

Each chapter also contains Check Lists of stars, directors, screenwriters, authors whose works have been made into films, and fictional characters. Looking for a James Stewart movie? Try **CL25**. How about a film starring Kathleen Turner? They're listed in **DR46**. Or perhaps you'd prefer a creepy movie based on a Stephen King tale. Look at **HO42**. All Check List names are indexed on page 531.

The Check Lists are intended to be definitive, as of the publication of this book. A few exceptions: when a star appears in a cameo role, that film is usually not included. The litmus test: I assume that a John Wayne fan would not rent *The Greatest Story Ever Told* to see 20 seconds of The Duke. And, in the case of some stars like Wayne, whose prodigious output could practically fill an entire video store, I've been selective.

For the 1990 Edition, I've added two more chapters of lists. Video Extra (**XT**) contains miscellaneous collections of films not confined to one category. There, you'll find Check Lists of all the major Academy Award winners available on videocassette, plus lists of Great Film Debuts, Memorable Final Films, and more.

And finally, there's a long but by no means inclusive list of frequently requested movies still unavailable on videocassette. If you can't find a certain title in this book or in your favorite video store, check this list. Like all lists in this book, it is accurate as of our press time. It's my hope that many of these titles will move into the other chapters of the book for the next edition.

Every film in this book is listed alphabetically in the Index of Titles. Each index entry contains the year of release, color (C) or black & white (B&W), running time, and MPAA rating. Also included are a short description of the film and the code designation for the list or lists that film appears on. For example, *Working Girl* is coded **CO1** (Romantic Comedies), **CO2** (Comedies for Modern Times), **DR10** (Today's Woman), **DR32** (Harrison Ford Check List), **DR75** (Mike Nichols Check List), **DR76** (Sigourney Weaver Check List), and **XT9** (Movies Shot on Location in New York).

On selected titles I offer my own positive ratings: Recommended or Highly Recommended. If you think of movie ratings in terms of stars, Recommended is *** and Highly Recommended is ****.

The Index of Titles can be used in several ways. If you're browsing one of the lists in the first portion of the book and a title is unfamiliar, look it up in the Index. Or, you may want to start in the Index with a title you already know, to check out others on the same subject, or with the same star, by the same director, with the same fictional character, or based on the same author's work.

Some notes on dates, running times, ratings, and recommendations.

On the lists, you'll notice that a title may be designated by a date. Where a date appears alone, it indicates that the same title has been used for more than one film. For instance, there are two movies named

Frantic, a 1958 Jeanne Moreau drama and a 1988 thriller starring Harrison Ford. Where a date appears with the word "version," it's to show that the same story has been filmed more than once. *Hamlet* was filmed in 1948 with Laurence Olivier and in 1969 with Nicol Williamson. In some cases, I've indicated "version" even if a remake (or original) is not available on video, for the sake of clarity.

The dates reflect the film's original theatrical release, its original TV air date, or its release to home video if it never showed in theaters or on TV.

Running times apply to the home video version of the film. Some films have been shortened or lengthened for release on home video, and I've tried to reflect that as faithfully as possible. (See List **CU10** in the Cult Chapter for a collection of movies which have added footage for home video release.)

MPAA ratings are to be used as guidelines, especially by parents. Any entry designated NR has not been rated by the MPAA. This includes most films released before 1968, movies made for broadcast or cable TV, and music performance videos.

The recommendations are my personal choices. My tastes are eclectic enough to embrace both *Tootsie* and *Blue Velvet, The Philadelphia Story* and *Heathers.* If none of those films are to your liking, you may still agree with some of my other recommendations.

This book may have one name below the title but, like a film, it was really a collaboration. Chuck Lean of Madison Books and Ron Castell were present at the creation; their love for good books and good movies nurtured the project. Mike Clark and Stephen Zito, two gentlemen whose writing and love of movies have inspired me, contributed enormously to this book. Pat Dowell, Patrick Sheehan, and Scott Simmon graciously lent advice on various lists.

I want to acknowledge several invaluable sources of published information: Leonard Maltin's *TV Movies and Video Guide* (still the best single volume movie reference at any price), *Variety's Complete Home Video Directory,* National Video Clearinghouse's *The Video Source Book,* and *Video Movie Guide* by Mick Martin and Marsha Porter.

I had support from these people as well: Lauren Malnati, Rich Swope and Liz Godin-Lee, who provided important research assistance; Ray Heinrich of One to One Communications for unsurpassed expertise in all matters technical; Carlos Aguilar and Janet Egolf for brilliant design work; Bill Nuhn, Michael James, and Michelle Lewis, who kept me abreast of new video releases; Mort Zedd, a man of refined tastes; Al Hollin, Mark Miller, Rosemary Prillaman, and Tonda Hernandez for promoting the first edition; Pam Uhl, Roxanne Kavounis, and Jennifer Wyckoff for giving it a spectacular launch; Maureen Humphrys and Louise Millikan for culinary support; and Heidi Diamond for fighting the good fight.

Finally, to Barbara Humphrys, thanks for her insightful suggestions and painstaking proofreading; for her patience, her humor, her love, and doing the dishes on certain nights, I am always grateful.

I welcome comments and corrections from readers. Please address them to me at Madison Books, 4720 Boston Way, Lanham, MD 20706.

—Tom Wiener

Chapter One

ACTION/ADVENTURE
(AC)

WAR MOVIES: WORLD WAR II —————————————————————— AC1

Air Force
Anzio
Attack Force Z
Back to Bataan
Bataan
Battle Cry
Battle of Britain
The Battle of the Bulge
The Big Red One
A Bridge Too Far
The Boat
Bombardier
Cross of Iron
D-Day the Sixth of June
The Dirty Dozen
The Eagle Has Landed
Farewell to the King
Fires on the Plain
Flying Leathernecks
Flying Tigers
The 49th Parallel
From Here to Eternity
The Guns of Navarone
Home of the Brave

The Immortal Sergeant
In Harm's Way
In Which We Serve
The Longest Day
The Malta Story
Midway
The Naked and the Dead
Never So Few
North Star
Patton
Run Silent, Run Deep
The Sands of Iwo Jima
The Sea Wolves
Soldier of Orange
They Were Expendable
Thirty Seconds Over Tokyo
To Hell and Back
Tora! Tora! Tora!
Twelve O'Clock High
A Walk in the Sun
The War Lover
Where Eagles Dare
The Young Lions

WAR MOVIES: WORLD WAR I —————————————————————— AC2

All Quiet on the Western Front
The Blue Max
The Dawn Patrol (1938 version)
A Farewell to Arms (1932 version)
Gallipoli

Hearts of the World
The Lighthorsemen
Paths of Glory
Sergeant York
Wings

WAR MOVIES: KOREAN WAR —————————————————————— AC3

The Bridges at Toko-Ri
Field of Honor
M*A*S*H
Men in War
One Minute to Zero

Pork Chop Hill
Retreat, Hell!
Sergeant Ryker
The Steel Helmet
Torpedo Alley

WAR MOVIES: VIETNAM WAR (AND AFTERMATH) _____ AC4

Apocalypse Now
Bat 21
The Boys in Company C
Braddock: Missing in Action 3
China Gate
Dear America: Letters Home From
   Vietnam
The Deer Hunter
84 Charley Mopic
Fighting Mad (1977)
Full Metal Jacket
Go Tell the Spartans

Good Morning, Vietnam
The Green Berets
Hamburger Hill
The Iron Triangle
Missing in Action
Platoon
Purple Hearts
Rambo: First Blood II
The Siege of Firebase Gloria
Tornado
Uncommon Valor

WAR MOVIES: CIVIL WAR _____ AC5
See also: WE7 Civil War Westerns

The Birth of a Nation
Friendly Persuasion
Gone With the Wind

The Red Badge of Courage
She Wore a Yellow Ribbon
Shenandoah

WAR MOVIES: OTHER CONFLICTS _____ AC6

The Battle of Algiers
The Buccaneer
The Charge of the Light Brigade (1936
   version)
Damn the Defiant!
Drums Along the Mohawk
The Four Feathers

Heartbreak Ridge
Lost Command
Revolution
The Sand Pebbles
Soldiers of Fortune
Zulu
Zulu Dawn

WAR MOVIES: PRISONERS OF WAR _____ AC7

The Bridge on the River Kwai
Grand Illusion
The Great Escape
The Hanoi Hilton
King Rat

Merry Christmas, Mr. Lawrence
Missing in Action 2: The Beginning
POW: The Escape
Stalag 17

URBAN ACTION _____ AC8
See also: AC9 Cops and Robbers

Above the Law
Action Jackson
Angel
Assault on Precinct 13
Avenging Angel
Band of the Hand
China Girl

Cold Sweat
Defiance
Detroit 9000
Die Hard
The Driver
8 Million Ways to Die
Fear City

Gloria
Hard Times
The Hidden
The Hunter
The Killer Elite
Knights of the City
The Mack
Point Blank

Savage Streets
Short Fuse
Streets of Fire
Sweet Sweetback's Badasssss Song
Thief
Tougher Than Leather
The Warriors (1979)

COPS AND ROBBERS _____ AC9
See also: AC8 Urban Action

Across 110th Street
The Anderson Tapes
Badge 373
The Blue Knight
Bullitt
Charley Varrick
City in Fear
Cobra
Code of Silence
Colors
Coogan's Bluff
Crazy Mama
Dead-Bang
Dead Heat
The Dead Pool
Dirty Harry
The Enforcer (1976)
Fatal Beauty
The First Deadly Sin
48HRS.
The French Connection
The French Connection 2
The Gauntlet
The Getaway
Hollywood Vice Squad
The Hot Rock

Hustle
Jackie Chan's Police Force
The January Man
The Laughing Policeman
Lethal Weapon
Madigan
Magnum Force
Nighthawks
Off Limits (1988)
The Presidio
Quiet Cool
Red Heat
Robocop
Running Scared
The Seven-ups
Shakedown
Sharky's Machine
Stick
Sudden Impact
The Taking of Pelham One Two Three
Thunderbolt and Lightfoot
Tightrope
To Live and Die in L.A.
Vice Squad
Walking Tall (series)

HOT WHEELS _____ AC10

Black Moon Rising
Cannonball
The Cannonball Run
Cannonball Run II
Convoy
Death Race 2000
Deathsport
Gone in 60 Seconds
Grand Prix
The Gumball Rally
The Last Chase

Mad Max
Mad Max Beyond Thunderdome
Race With the Devil
Rad
The Road Warrior
Safari 3000
Thunder Road
Vanishing Point
Wheels of Fire
The Wraith

THE WILD BLUE YONDER _____ AC11

The Aviator
Battle of Britain
The Blue Max
Blue Thunder
The Bridges at Toko-Ri
Choke Canyon
The Dawn Patrol (1938 version)
Firefox
Flying Tigers
The Great Waldo Pepper

High Road to China
Iron Eagle
Iron Eagle II
Only Angels Have Wings
The Right Stuff
The Spirit of St. Louis
Top Gun
Twelve O'Clock High
The War Lover
Wings

ADVENTURE IN THE GREAT OUTDOORS _____ AC12

The African Queen
Baby—Secret of the Lost Legend
Beneath the 12 Mile Reef
The Big Blue
The Bounty
A Breed Apart
The Call of the Wild
China Seas
Clan of the Cave Bear
Crusoe
Death Hunt
The Deep
The Eiger Sanction
The Emerald Forest
The Flight of the Eagle
Flight of the Phoenix
Greystoke: The Legend of Tarzan
Hatari!
King Solomon's Mines (1937, 1950 &
   1985 versions)

The Man From Snowy River
The Man Who Would Be King
March or Die
Mogambo
Mutiny on the Bounty (1935 & 1962
   versions)
The Naked Jungle
The Naked Prey
Never Cry Wolf
Quest for Fire
Reap the Wild Wind
The Red Tent
Return to Snowy River, Part II
Shoot to Kill
The Treasure of the Sierra Madre
We of the Never Never
White Dawn
The Wind and the Lion

CLASSIC ADVENTURE _____ AC13
See also: AC14 Romantic Adventure, AC15 Costume Adventure

The Adventures of Robin Hood
Beau Geste (1939 version)
The Black Arrow
The Black Pirate
Captain Blood
Captains Courageous
The Charge of the Light Brigade (1936
   version)
The Corsican Brothers
The Crimson Pirate
Don Q: Son of Zorro
The Flame and the Arrow

The Four Feathers
Gunga Din
The Hurricane (1937 version)
Ivanhoe (1952 version)
Kim
King Solomon's Mines (1937 & 1950
   versions)
Knights of the Round Table
The Last of the Mohicans
The Lives of a Bengal Lancer
The Lost Patrol
The Lost World (1925 version)

Mutiny on the Bounty (1935 version)
Only Angels Have Wings
The Prisoner of Zenda (1937 & 1952 versions)
Reap the Wild Wind
Red Dust
San Francisco
Scaramouche
The Scarlet Pimpernel (1934 version)
The Sea Hawk

The Seven Samurai
Tarzan, the Ape Man (1932 version)
The Thief of Bagdad (1924 & 1940 versions)
Treasure Island (1934 version)
The Treasure of the Sierra Madre
The Vikings
The Wages of Fear
Yojimbo

ROMANTIC ADVENTURE _____ AC14
See also: AC13 Classic Adventure

The African Queen
American Dreamer
The Aviator
The Great Race
High Road to China
Into the Night
Jewel of the Nile
Ladyhawke
Lassiter

Mogambo
The Princess Bride
Raiders of the Lost Ark
Red Dust
Robin and Marian
Romancing the Stone
Time After Time
The Wind and the Lion

COSTUME ADVENTURE _____ AC15
See also: AC13 Classic Adventure

The Four Musketeers
Nate and Hayes
Pirates

The Princess Bride
Robin and Marian
The Three Musketeers (1974 version)

HISTORICAL ADVENTURE _____ AC16
See also: AC1-7 War Movies

Alexander the Great
The Bounty
The Buccaneer
The Charge of the Light Brigade (1936 version)
The Conqueror
El Cid

The Flight of the Eagle
The Hindenburg
Mutiny on the Bounty (1935 & 1962 versions)
The Sicilian
The Wind and the Lion

SUPER HEROES _____ AC17

The Adventures of Buckaroo Banzai Across the 8th Dimension
The Adventures of Hercules
Batman (1966)

Batman (1989)
Conan the Barbarian
Conan the Destroyer
Condorman

Doc Savage: The Man of Bronze
Greystoke: The Legend of Tarzan
Masters of the Universe

Sheena
Supergirl
Superman (series)

SWORD & SORCERY FANTASIES _____ AC18

The Beastmaster
Blademaster
Conan the Barbarian
Conan the Destroyer
Deathstalker
Deathstalker 2
Dragonslayer
Excalibur
Fire and Ice
Flesh and Blood (1985)
Jason and the Argonauts
Krull
Ladyhawke

Legend
The Magic Sword
Metalstorm: The Destruction of Jared-
    Syn
Red Sonja
Robin Hood and the Sorcerer
The 7th Voyage of Sinbad
She (1985 version)
Ulysses (1955)
Warriors of the Wind
Willow
Wizards of the Lost Kingdom

TALES OF REVENGE _____ AC19

Death Wish (series)
The Exterminator
The Exterminator 2
Eye of the Tiger
F/X
Fighting Back
The Final Mission
Fleshburn
Instant Justice
The Killer Elite

The Ladies Club
The Mean Machine
Ms. 45
No Mercy
Point Blank
Rolling Thunder
Steele Justice
Underworld, U.S.A.
Vigilante

MERCENARIES AND OTHER COMBATANTS _____ AC20

American Commandos
Annihilators
Code Name: Wildgeese
Death Before Dishonor
The Delta Force
The Dogs of War
Gold Raiders
Invasion U.S.A.

Let's Get Harry
Night Force
Opposing Force
Red Dawn
Red Scorpion
The Rescue
Toy Soldiers
Uncommon Valor

SOLDIERS OF FORTUNE _____ AC21

Allan Quartermain and the Lost City of
    Gold
Big Trouble in Little China

Escape From New York
Firewalker
High Road to China

Indiana Jones and the Temple of Doom
Jake Speed
Jewel of the Nile
Jungle Raiders
King Solomon's Mines (1937, 1950 &
    1985 version)

The Mines of Kilimanjaro
Raiders of the Lost Ark
Romancing the Stone
Shanghai Surprise
Treasure of the Four Crowns

GANGSTER SAGAS _____ AC22

Al Capone
Angels With Dirty Faces
The Big Heat
Bloody Mama
The Cotton Club
Dillinger
The Godfather
The Godfather, Part II
Hell on Frisco Bay
High Sierra
Lepke
Little Caesar

The Long Good Friday
Lucky Luciano
Mean Frank and Crazy Tony
Once Upon a Time in America
Prime Cut
The Public Enemy
The Roaring Twenties
St. Valentine's Day Massacre
Scarface (1932 & 1983 versions)
The Untouchables
White Heat
The Yakuza

DISASTER STORIES _____ AC23

Airport (series)
Avalanche
Beyond the Poseidon Adventure
City on Fire
The Devil at 4 O'Clock
Earthquake
The Hindenburg
Hurricane (1937 & 1976 versions)

Juggernaut (1974)
Meteor
A Night to Remember (1958)
The Poseidon Adventure
San Francisco
The Towering Inferno
When Time Ran Out

STORIES OF SURVIVAL _____ AC24

Avenging Force
Back From Eternity
Bridge to Nowhere
The Call of the Wild
Certain Fury
Crusoe
Cut and Run
Cyborg
Death Valley
Deliverance
Flight of the Phoenix
Grey Lady Down
Hunter's Blood
Mad Max Beyond Thunderdome
Man Friday

The Most Dangerous Game
The Naked Jungle
The Naked Prey
Never Cry Wolf
Opposing Force
Out of Control
Papillon
Predator
Quest for Fire
The Red Tent
The Road Warrior
Runaway Train
Southern Comfort
The Treasure of the Sierra Madre
White Dawn

ONE-MAN ARMIES _____ AC25

Above the Law
Bullies
Commando
Die Hard
Equalizer 2000
First Blood
Ghost Warrior
Instant Justice
Mad Max
Mad Max Beyond Thunderdome
Nowhere to Hide
Point Blank

Predator
Rambo: First Blood II
Rambo III
Raw Deal
Red Scorpion
The Road Warrior
Robocop
The Soldier
Streets of Fire
The Terminator
Wanted: Dead or Alive

MARTIAL ARTS ACTION _____ AC26
See also: AC33 Chuck Norris, AC34 Bruce Lee Check Lists

American Ninja
American Ninja 2: The Confrontation
American Ninja 3: Blood Hunt
The Big Brawl
Big Trouble in Little China
Billy Jack
Bloodsport
Circle of Iron
Cleopatra Jones
Cleopatra Jones and the Casino of Gold

Cyborg
Gymkata
Jackie Chan's Police Force
Kill and Kill Again
Kill or Be Killed
The Last Dragon
No Retreat, No Surrender
Pray for Death
The Protector
T.N.T. Jackson

STAR CHECK LIST: CLINT EASTWOOD _____ AC27
See also: WE26 Clint Eastwood Check List

Any Which Way You Can
Bird*
City Heat
Coogan's Bluff
The Dead Pool
Dirty Harry
The Eiger Sanction**
The Enforcer (1976)
Escape From Alcatraz
Every Which Way But Loose
Firefox**
The Gauntlet**
Heartbreak Ridge**

Honkytonk Man**
Kelly's Heroes
Magnum Force
Paint Your Wagon
Play Misty for Me**
Sudden Impact**
Thunderbolt and Lightfoot
Tightrope
Where Eagles Dare

*director only
**also director

STAR CHECK LIST: STEVE McQUEEN _____ AC28

Baby, the Rain Must Fall
The Blob

Bullitt
The Cincinnati Kid

An Enemy of the People
The Getaway
The Great Escape
The Hunter
Junior Bonner
Love With the Proper Stranger
The Magnificent Seven
Nevada Smith
Never Love a Stranger
Never So Few

On Any Sunday
Papillon
The Reivers
The Sand Pebbles
Soldier in the Rain
Somebody Up There Likes Me
The Thomas Crown Affair
Tom Horn
The Towering Inferno
The War Lover

STAR CHECK LIST: CHARLES BRONSON _____ AC29

Assassination
Borderline
Breakheart Pass
Breakout
Caboblanco
Chino
Cold Sweat
Death Hunt
Death Wish (series)
The Dirty Dozen
Drum Beat
The Evil That Men Do
The Family (1970)
The Great Escape
Hard Times
Honor Among Thieves
House of Wax
Jubal
Kid Galahad
Kinjite: Forbidden Subjects
Lola
Love and Bullets
The Magnificent Seven

Master of the World
The Mechanic
Messenger of Death
Mr. Majestyk
Murphy's Law
Never So Few
Once Upon a Time in the West
Pat and Mike
Raid on Entebbe
Red Sun
Rider on the Rain
Run of the Arrow
St. Ives
The Sandpiper
Showdown at Boot Hill
Soldiers of Fortune
Someone Behind the Door
The Stone Killer
Telefon
10 to Midnight
This Property Is Condemned
Villa Rides!

STAR CHECK LIST: ARNOLD SCHWARZENEGGER _____ AC30

Commando
Conan the Barbarian
Conan the Destroyer
Predator
Pumping Iron
Raw Deal

Red Heat
Red Sonja
Running Man
Stay Hungry
The Terminator
Twins

STAR CHECK LIST: SYLVESTER STALLONE _____ AC31

Cannonball
Cobra

Death Race 2000
F.I.S.T.

First Blood
The Lords of Flatbush
Nighthawks
Over the Top
Paradise Alley*
Rambo: First Blood II
Rambo III
Rebel (1973)
Rhinestone

Rocky
Rocky II*
Rocky III*
Rocky IV*
Staying Alive **
Victory

*also director
**director only

STAR CHECK LIST: CHUCK NORRIS _____ AC32

Braddock: Missing in Action 3
Breaker! Breaker!
Code of Silence
The Delta Force
An Eye for an Eye
Firewalker
A Force of One
Forced Vengeance
Game of Death
Good Guys Wear Black

Hero and the Terror
Invasion U.S.A.
Lone Wolf McQuade
Missing in Action
Missing in Action 2: The Beginning
The Octagon
Return of the Dragon
Silent Rage
Slaughter in San Francisco

STAR CHECK LIST: BRUCE LEE _____ AC33

Bruce Lee: The Legend
Bruce Lee: The Man/The Myth
The Chinese Connection
Enter the Dragon
Fist of Fear, Touch of Death

Fists of Fury
The Game of Death
The Real Bruce Lee
Return of the Dragon

STAR CHECK LIST: ERROL FLYNN _____ AC34

The Adventures of Captain Fabian
The Adventures of Don Juan
The Adventures of Robin Hood
Against All Flags
Assault of the Rebel Girls (Cuban Rebel
    Girls)
Captain Blood
The Charge of the Light Brigade (1936
    version)
The Dawn Patrol (1938 version)
Dodge City
Gentleman Jim

Kim
Northern Pursuit
The Prince and the Pauper (1937
    version)
The Private Lives of Elizabeth and
    Essex
Santa Fe Trail
The Sea Hawk
Thank Your Lucky Stars
They Died With Their Boots On
The Warriors (1955)

CHARACTER CHECK LIST: JAMES BOND _____ AC35

Casino Royale
Diamonds Are Forever

Dr. No
For Your Eyes Only

From Russia With Love
Goldfinger
Live and Let Die
The Living Daylights
The Man With the Golden Gun
Moonraker
Never Say Never Again

Octopussy
On Her Majesty's Secret Service
The Spy Who Loved Me
Thunderball
A View to a Kill
You Only Live Twice

STAR CHECK LIST: SEAN CONNERY _____ AC36

The Anderson Tapes
Another Time, Another Place
A Bridge Too Far
Cuba
Darby O'Gill and the Little People
Diamonds Are Forever
Dr. No
A Fine Madness
Five Days One Summer
From Russia With Love
Goldfinger
The Great Train Robbery
Highlander
The Longest Day
The Man Who Would Be King
Marnie
Meteor

The Molly Maguires
Murder on the Orient Express
The Name of the Rose
Never Say Never Again
Outland
The Presidio
The Red Tent
Robin and Marian
Shalako
Sword of the Valiant
The Terrorists
Thunderball
Time Bandits
The Untouchables
The Wind and the Lion
Wrong Is Right
You Only Live Twice

STAR CHECK LIST: BURT REYNOLDS _____ AC37

Best Friends
The Best Little Whorehouse in Texas
The Cannonball Run
Cannnonball Run II
City Heat
Deliverance
The End
Everything You Always Wanted To
  Know About Sex
Fuzz
Gator
Heat
Hooper
Hustle
The Longest Yard
Malone
The Man Who Loved Cat Dancing
The Man Who Loved Women (1983
  version)

100 Rifles
Operation C.I.A.
Paternity
Physical Evidence
Rent-a-Cop
Rough Cut
Semi-Tough
Shamus
Shark!
Sharky's Machine
Smokey and the Bandit
Smokey and the Bandit II
Starting Over
Stick
Stroker Ace
Switching Channels
White Lightning

Chapter Two

CLASSICS
(CL)

CLASSICS ILLUSTRATED: LITERARY ADAPTATIONS ——————————— **CL1**

The Adventures of Huckleberry Finn
(1939 version)
Anna Karenina
Barry Lyndon
Billy Budd
The Brothers Karamazov
Caesar and Cleopatra
Camille
Greed
The Heiress
The Hunchback of Notre Dame
The Importance of Being Earnest
Little Women (1933 & 1949 versions)
Madame Bovary
Moby Dick
The Picture of Dorian Gray
Pride and Prejudice
The Prince and the Pauper (1937 & 1978
versions)
Pygmalion
The Red Badge of Courage
Vanity Fair
War and Peace (1956 & 1968 versions)
Wuthering Heights (1939 & 1954
versions)

SHAKESPEARE
As You Like It (1936 version)
Hamlet (1948 & 1969 versions)
Henry V
Julius Caesar (1953 & 1970 versions)
King Lear (1971 & 1987 versions)
Macbeth (1948 & 1971 versions)
A Midsummer Night's Dream (1935
version)
Richard III
Romeo and Juliet (1936 & 1968 versions)
The Taming of the Shrew

DICKENS
A Christmas Carol (1951 version)
David Copperfield
Great Expectations (1946 version)
Little Dorritt
Oliver!
Oliver and Company
Oliver Twist (1922, 1933 & 1948
versions)
Scrooge
Scrooged
A Tale of Two Cities (1935 version)

SCREEN BIOGRAPHIES ———————————————————————— **CL2**

Abe Lincoln in Illinois
Abraham Lincoln
Citizen Kane
Cleopatra
The Diary of Anne Frank
I'll Cry Tomorrow
Joan of Arc
Juarez
Knute Rockne—All American
Lawrence of Arabia
The Life of Emile Zola

Lust for Life
Napoleon (1927)
Pride of the Yankees
The Private Life of Henry VIII
The Private Lives of Elizabeth and
Essex
Sergeant York
Sister Kenny
The Spirit of St. Louis
Young Mr. Lincoln

19

HISTORICAL DRAMA _____ **CL3**

Beau Brummel (1924 version)
The Birth of a Nation
Demetrius and the Gladiators
Desiree
Dr. Zhivago
The Egyptian
The Fall of the Roman Empire
Fire Over England
The Four Horsemen of the Apocalypse
  (1961 version)
Gone With the Wind
Jezebel

Mary of Scotland
Mutiny on the Bounty (1935 version)
A Night to Remember (1958)
Northwest Passage
The Private Lives of Elizabeth and
  Essex
Raintree County
San Francisco
That Hamilton Woman
The Virgin Queen
War and Peace (1956 & 1968 versions)

CLASSIC LOVE STORIES _____ **CL4**

The African Queen
Algiers
Anna Karenina
Back Street
Brief Encounter
Camille
Casablanca
The Clock
Dark Victory
Dr. Zhivago
The Enchanted Cottage
Flesh and the Devil
Gilda
Gone With the Wind
The Heiress

Intermezzo
Letter From an Unknown Woman
Love Is a Many Splendored Thing
Marty
Mayerling (1936 version)
Mr. Skeffington
Notorious
Now, Voyager
The Philadelphia Story
A Place in the Sun
Random Harvest
The Shop Around the Corner
Summertime
Waterloo Bridge
Wuthering Heights (1939 version)

WOMEN'S PICTURES _____ **CL5**
See also: DR10 Today's Woman

Alice Adams
Autumn Leaves
Camille
Christopher Strong
Craig's Wife
I'll Cry Tomorrow
Kitty Foyle
The Letter
Madame Bovary
Madame X (1966 version)

Mildred Pierce
Mr. Skeffington
Morning Glory
Now, Voyager
The Old Maid
Stella Dallas
That Hamilton Woman
The Wind
A Woman Rebels
The Women

CLASSIC TEAR JERKERS _____ CL6
See also: DR2 For a Good Cry

Back Street (1961 version)
Blonde Venus
Casablanca
Dark Victory
The Heiress
Imitation of Life (1959 version)
In Name Only
It's a Wonderful Life
King's Row
Kitty Foyle
Letter From an Unknown Woman

Madame X (1966 version)
Made for Each Other (1939)
Magnificent Obsession (1954 version)
Mildred Pierce
Penny Serenade
A Place in the Sun
The Red Shoes
Stella Dallas
Summertime
Written on the Wind
Wuthering Heights (1939 version)

SHOW BUSINESS STORIES _____ CL7
See also: DR12 Backstage Dramas, MU4 Musical Films About Show Biz

All About Eve
The Bad and the Beautiful
Dancing Lady
A Double Life
A Face in the Crowd
The Great Gabbo
The Greatest Show on Earth
The Last Command
The Lost Squadron
The Red Shoes

The Seven Little Foys
Show People
Stage Door
A Star Is Born (1937 & 1954 versions)
Sunset Boulevard
Sweet Smell of Success
Sweethearts
Swing High, Swing Low
Twentieth Century
Young and Willing

SOCIAL PROBLEM DRAMAS _____ CL8

Bad Day at Black Rock
The Best Years of Our Lives
Black Fury
Crossfire
The Crowd
Dead End
The Defiant Ones (1958 version)
The Grapes of Wrath
Home of the Brave
I Am a Fugitive From a Chain Gang
Inherit the Wind
Judgment at Nuremberg
Knock on Any Door

The Last Angry Man
The Lost Weekend
The Man With the Golden Arm
The Men
Mrs. Miniver
On the Waterfront
Our Daily Bread
A Place in the Sun
The Prisoner
Rebel Without a Cause
They Drive by Night
Till the End of Time
Twelve Angry Men

GREAT COLOR FILMS _____ CL9

The Adventures of Robin Hood
The Barefoot Contessa
Black Narcissus

Black Orpheus
DuBarry Was a Lady
Duel in the Sun

The Far Country
The Four Feathers
Funny Face
The Garden of Allah
The Golden Coach
Heller in Pink Tights
Henry V
Lust for Life
The Phantom of the Opera (1943
  version)

The Pirate
The Quiet Man
The Red Shoes
The River (1951)
The Ten Commandments (1956 version)
The Thief of Bagdad (1940 version)
The Yearling
Yolanda and the Thief

CLASSIC SOUND COMEDIES ⎯⎯⎯⎯⎯⎯⎯⎯⎯⎯⎯⎯ CL10

Adam's Rib
Arsenic and Old Lace
The Awful Truth
Ball of Fire
Born Yesterday
Bringing Up Baby
The Court Jester
Dinner at Eight
Duck Soup
The Great Dictator
His Girl Friday
Holiday
It Happened One Night
It's a Gift
It's in the Bag
Kind Hearts and Coronets
The Lady Eve
The Ladykillers
Mr. Blandings Builds His Dream House

Mister Roberts
My Favorite Wife
My Little Chickadee
My Man Godfrey
Ninotchka
Nothing Sacred
One, Two, Three
The Palm Beach Story
Pat and Mike
The Senator Was Indiscreet
Some Like It Hot
Sons of the Desert
Sullivan's Travels
The Talk of the Town
The Thin Man
To Be or Not to Be (1943 version)
Twentieth Century
Woman of the Year
You Can't Cheat an Honest Man

CLASSIC SILENT COMEDIES ⎯⎯⎯⎯⎯⎯⎯⎯⎯⎯⎯⎯ CL11
See also: C018 Charlie Chaplin Check List, C019 Buster Keaton Check List

The Circus
City Lights
College
The Freshman
The General
The Gold Rush
It

Modern Times
Running Wild
Safety Last
Show People
Steamboat Bill, Jr.
The Three Ages

CLASSIC SILENT DRAMAS ⎯⎯⎯⎯⎯⎯⎯⎯⎯⎯⎯⎯ CL12
See also: CL36 D. W. Griffith Check List, CL53 Erich Von Stroheim Check List

Battleship Potemkin
Beau Brummel (1924 version)
Ben-Hur: A Tale of the Christ

The Birth of a Nation
Blind Husbands
Broken Blossoms

The Crowd
Diary of a Lost Girl
The Docks of New York
Earth
Flesh and the Devil
Foolish Wives
Greed
Intolerance
The Last Command
The Last Laugh
Metropolis (1925 edition)
Napoleon (1927)
Old Ironsides

Pandora's Box
Passion
The Passion of Joan of Arc
Queen Kelly
Sparrows
The Ten Commandments (1923 version)
The Thief of Bagdad (1926 version)
Variety
Way Down East
The Wedding March
The Wind
Wings
A Woman of Paris

RELIGIOUS EPICS _____ CL13

Ben-Hur
Ben-Hur: A Tale of the Christ
The Bible
David and Bathsheba
The Greatest Story Ever Told
Jesus of Nazareth
King of Kings (1961 version)

The Robe
Samson and Delilah
The Silver Chalice
Sodom and Gomorrah
Song of Bernadette
The Ten Commandments (1923 & 1956
   versions)

DELAYED CLASSICS: MOVIES UNAPPRECIATED _____ CL14
IN THEIR OWN TIME

Beat the Devil
Come and Get It
The Devil and Daniel Webster
The Golden Coach
Intolerance
Lola Montes
The Magnificent Ambersons
The Nutty Professor
Once Upon a Time in the West

Petulia
Rio Bravo
The Searchers
Sylvia Scarlett
To Be or Not to Be (1943 version)
Touch of Evil
The Trouble With Harry
Vertigo

MEMORABLE SCREEN TEAMS _____ CL15

Katharine Hepburn & Spencer Tracy
Adam's Rib
Guess Who's Coming to Dinner
Pat and Mike
State of the Union
Woman of the Year

Humphrey Bogart & Lauren Bacall
The Big Sleep
Dark Passage

Key Largo
To Have and Have Not

Fred Astaire & Ginger Rogers
The Barkleys of Broadway
Carefree
Flying Down to Rio
Follow the Fleet
The Gay Divorcee
Roberta

Shall We Dance
The Story of Vernon and Irene Castle
Swing Time
Top Hat

William Powell & Myrna Loy
After the Thin Man
Another Thin Man
The Great Ziegfeld
The Shadow of the Thin Man
Song of the Thin Man
The Thin Man
The Thin Man Goes Home

Richard Burton & Elizabeth Taylor
Cleopatra
Divorce His, Divorce Hers

Doctor Faustus
Hammersmith Is Out
The Sandpiper
The Taming of the Shrew
Under Milk Wood
Who's Afraid of Virginia Woolf?

Nelson Eddy & Jeanette MacDonald
Bitter Sweet
The Girl of the Golden West
I Married an Angel
Maytime
Naughty Marietta
New Moon
Rose Marie (1936 version)
Sweethearts

STAR CHECK LIST: KATHARINE HEPBURN ————————————————— CL16

Adam's Rib
The African Queen
Alice Adams
Bringing Up Baby
Christopher Strong
Dragon Seed
George Stevens: A Filmmaker's Journey
Grace Quigley
Guess Who's Coming to Dinner
Holiday
The Lion in Winter
The Little Minister
Little Women (1933 version)
Long Day's Journey Into Night
Love Among the Ruins
Mary of Scotland

Morning Glory
On Golden Pond
Pat and Mike
The Philadelphia Story
Quality Street
The Rainmaker
Rooster Cogburn
Spitfire (1934)
Stage Door
State of the Union
Suddenly, Last Summer
Summertime
Sylvia Scarlett
The Trojan Women
Woman of the Year
A Woman Rebels

STAR CHECK LIST: JOHN WAYNE ————————————————————— CL17
See also: WE17 John Wayne Check List

Back to Bataan
The Barbarian and the Geisha
Brannigan
Cast a Giant Shadow
Circus World
The Conqueror
Donovan's Reef
The Fighting Seabees
Flying Leathernecks
Flying Tigers
The Green Berets*

Hatari!
The Hell Fighters
In Harm's Way
Lady for a Night
The Lady From Louisiana
The Long Voyage Home
The Longest Day
McQ
The Quiet Man
The Sands of Iwo Jima
Seven Sinners

They Were Expendable
Tycoon
Wake of the Red Witch

Wheel of Fortune
Without Reservations

*also co-director

STAR CHECK LIST: CARY GRANT _____ CL18

Amazing Adventure
Arsenic and Old Lace
The Awful Truth
The Bachelor and the Bobby Soxer
The Bishop's Wife
Blonde Venus
Bringing Up Baby
Charade
Every Girl Should Be Married
Father Goose
The Grass Is Greener
Gunga Din
His Girl Friday
Holiday
Houseboat
The Howards of Virginia
In Name Only
Indiscreet
Mr. Blandings Builds His Dream House
Mr. Lucky
Monkey Business (1952)

My Favorite Wife
Night and Day
None but the Lonely Heart
North by Northwest
Notorious
Once Upon a Honeymoon
Only Angels Have Wings
Operation Petticoat
Penny Serenade
The Philadelphia Story
The Pride and the Passion
She Done Him Wrong
The Sky's the Limit
Suspicion
Sylvia Scarlett
The Talk of the Town
That Touch of Mink
To Catch a Thief
The Toast of New York
Topper
Walk, Don't Run

STAR CHECK LIST: SPENCER TRACY _____ CL19

Adam's Rib
Bad Day at Black Rock
Captains Courageous
The Devil at 4 O'Clock
Dr. Jekyll and Mr. Hyde (1941 version)
Father of the Bride
Father's Little Dividend
Guess Who's Coming to Dinner
A Guy Named Joe
How the West Was Won*

Inherit the Wind
It's a Mad Mad Mad Mad World
Judgment at Nuremberg
The Last Hurrah
Northwest Passage
Pat and Mike
San Francisco
State of the Union
Thirty Seconds Over Tokyo
Woman of the Year

*narrator only

STAR CHECK LIST: HUMPHREY BOGART _____ CL20

The African Queen
Angels With Dirty Faces
The Barefoot Contessa

Beat the Devil
The Big Sleep
The Caine Mutiny

Call It Murder
Casablanca
Dark Passage
Dark Victory
Dead End
Dead Reckoning
The Desperate Hours
The Enforcer (1951)
The Harder They Fall
High Sierra
In a Lonely Place
Key Largo
Knock on Any Door
The Left Hand of God
The Maltese Falcon

Marked Woman
The Oklahoma Kid
Passage to Marseilles
The Petrified Forest
The Roaring Twenties
Sabrina
Sahara
Sirocco
Stand-In
Thank Your Lucky Stars
They Drive by Night
To Have and Have Not
Tokyo Joe
The Treasure of the Sierra Madre
We're No Angels

STAR CHECK LIST: BETTE DAVIS _____ CL21

All About Eve
All This and Heaven, Too
Burnt Offerings
The Corn Is Green (1945 version)
The Dark Secret of Harvest Home
Dark Victory
Death on the Nile
The Disappearance of Aimee
The Empty Canvas
Fashions of 1934
Hell's House
Hush . . . Hush, Sweet Charlotte
Jezebel
Juarez
The Letter
The Little Foxes
Little Gloria . . . Happy at Last
Madame Sin
Marked Woman
Mr. Skeffington

Now, Voyager
Of Human Bondage (1934 version)
The Old Maid
The Petrified Forest
Phone Call From a Stranger
Pocketful of Miracles
The Private Lives of Elizabeth and
  Essex
Return From Witch Mountain
Right of Way
Strangers: The Story of a Mother and
  Daughter
Thank Your Lucky Stars
The Virgin Queen
Watch on the Rhine
The Watcher in the Woods
The Whales of August
What Ever Happened to Baby Jane?
White Mama

STAR CHECK LIST: JAMES CAGNEY _____ CL22

Angels With Dirty Faces
Blood on the Sun
Each Dawn I Die
Footlight Parade
Great Guy
Kiss Tomorrow Goodbye
Love Me or Leave Me
A Midsummer Night's Dream (1935
  version)
Mister Roberts

Never Steal Anything Small
The Oklahoma Kid
One, Two, Three
The Public Enemy
Ragtime
The Roaring Twenties
The Seven Little Foys
Something to Sing About
The Strawberry Blonde
13 Rue Madeleine

The Time of Your Life
What Price Glory (1952 version)

White Heat
Yankee Doodle Dandy

STAR CHECK LIST: CLARK GABLE _____ CL23

China Seas
Dancing Lady
Gone With the Wind
Idiot's Delight
It Happened One Night
The Misfits
Mogambo
Mutiny on the Bounty (1935 version)

No Man of Her Own
The Painted Desert
Possessed
Red Dust
Run Silent, Run Deep
San Francisco
The Tall Men
Teacher's Pet

STAR CHECK LIST: HENRY FONDA _____ CL24

Advise and Consent
Battle Force
The Battle of the Bulge
The Big Street
The Boston Strangler
The Cheyenne Social Club
City on Fire
Drums Along the Mohawk
Fail-Safe
Fort Apache
Gideon's Trumpet
The Grapes of Wrath
The Great Smokey Roadblock
Home to Stay
How the West Was Won
I Dream Too Much
The Immortal Sergeant
In Harm's Way
Jesse James
Jezebel
The Lady Eve
The Last Four Days
The Longest Day
The Mad Miss Manton
Madigan
Meteor
Midway

Mister Roberts
The Moon's Our Home
My Darling Clementine
My Name Is Nobody
Night Flight From Moscow
The Oldest Living Graduate
On Golden Pond
Once Upon a Time in the West
The Ox-Bow Incident
The Red Pony (1973 version)
The Return of Frank James
Rollercoaster
Sometimes a Great Notion
Stage Struck
Summer Solstice
The Swarm
Tentacles
There Was a Crooked Man
The Tin Star
Too Late the Hero
Twelve Angry Men
War and Peace (1956 version)
Warlock
Wings of the Morning
The Wrong Man
You Only Live Once
Young Mr. Lincoln

STAR CHECK LIST: JAMES STEWART _____ CL25

After the Thin Man
Airport '77
Anatomy of a Murder
Bandolero

Bell, Book, and Candle
Bend of the River
The Big Sleep (1978 version)
Broken Arrow

Cheyenne Autumn
The Cheyenne Social Club
Dear Brigitte
Destry Rides Again
The Far Country
Flight of the Phoenix
The Glenn Miller Story
The Greatest Show on Earth
How the West Was Won
It's a Wonderful Life
Made for Each Other (1939)
The Magic of Lassie
The Man From Laramie
The Man Who Knew Too Much (1956 version)
The Man Who Shot Liberty Valance
Mr. Hobbs Takes a Vacation
Mr. Smith Goes to Washington

The Naked Spur
The Philadelphia Story
Pot o' Gold
The Rare Breed
Rear Window
Right of Way
Rope
Rose Marie
Shenandoah
The Shootist
The Shop Around the Corner
The Spirit of St. Louis
Strategic Air Command
Thunder Bay
Two Rode Together
Vertigo
Vivacious Lady
Winchester '73

STAR CHECK LIST: GARY COOPER _____ CL26
See also: WE25 Gary Cooper Check List

Ball of Fire
Beau Geste (1939 version)
Blowing Wild
Cloak and Dagger (1946)
The Court-Martial of Billy Mitchell
A Farewell to Arms (1932 version)
The Fountainhead
Friendly Persuasion
The General Died at Dawn

Good Sam
It
Lives of a Bengal Lancer
Love in the Afternoon
Meet John Doe
Morocco
Pride of the Yankees
Sergeant York
Wings

STAR CHECK LIST: INGRID BERGMAN _____ CL27

Adam Had Four Sons
Arch of Triumph
Autumn Sonata
The Bells of St. Mary's
Cactus Flower
Casablanca
Doctor Jekyll and Mr. Hyde (1941 version)
Europa '51
Fear
From The Mixed-Up Files Of Mrs. Basil E. Frankenweiler
Gaslight
Goodbye Again
Indiscreet

The Inn of the Sixth Happiness
Intermezzo
Joan of Arc
June Night
A Matter of Time
Murder on the Orient Express
Notorious
Spellbound
Stromboli
Swedenhielms
Under Capricorn
Voyage to Italy
A Walk in the Spring Rain
A Woman Called Golda

STAR CHECK LIST: GRETA GARBO _____ **CL28**

Anna Christie
Anna Karenina
Camille
Flesh and the Devil

Grand Hotel
Ninotchka
Wild Orchids

STAR CHECK LIST: MARILYN MONROE _____ **CL29**

All About Eve
The Asphalt Jungle
Bus Stop
Clash by Night
Gentlemen Prefer Blondes
How to Marry a Millionaire
Let's Make Love
Love Happy
The Misfits

Monkey Business (1952)
Niagara
The Prince and the Showgirl
River of No Return
The Seven Year Itch
Some Like It Hot
There's No Business Like Show
   Business

STAR CHECK LIST: AUDREY HEPBURN _____ **CL30**

Breakfast at Tiffany's
Charade
Funny Face
The Lavender Hill Mob
Love in the Afternoon
My Fair Lady
The Nun's Story
Paris When It Sizzles
Robin and Marian

Roman Holiday
Sabrina
Sidney Sheldon's Bloodline
They All Laughed
Two for the Road
The Unforgiven
Wait Until Dark
War and Peace (1956 version)

STAR CHECK LIST: GRACE KELLY _____ **CL31**

The Bridges at Toko-Ri
The Country Girl (1954 version)
Dial M for Murder
High Noon

High Society
Mogambo
Rear Window
To Catch a Thief

STAR CHECK LIST: LAURENCE OLIVIER _____ **CL32**

As You Like It
Battle of Britain
The Betsy
The Bounty
The Boys From Brazil
A Bridge Too Far
Clash of the Titans
Clouds Over Europe
The Divorce of Lady X

Dracula (1979 version)
The Ebony Tower
Fire Over England
The 49th Parallel
Hamlet (1948 version)*
Henry V*
I Stand Condemned
The Jazz Singer (1980 version)
Jesus of Nazareth

The Jigsaw Man
Lady Caroline Lamb
A Little Romance
Love Among the Ruins
Marathon Man
Mr. Halpern and Mr. Johnson
Nicholas and Alexandra
Pride and Prejudice
The Prince and the Showgirl*
Rebecca

Richard III*
The Seven Percent Solution
The Shoes of the Fisherman
Sleuth
Spartacus
That Hamilton Woman
Wagner
Wild Geese II
Wuthering Heights (1939 version)

*also director

STAR CHECK LIST: ELIZABETH TAYLOR _____ CL33

Between Friends
Butterfield 8
Cat on a Hot Tin Roof (1958 version)
Cleopatra
A Date With Judy
Divorce His, Divorce Hers
Doctor Faustus
The Driver's Seat
Father of the Bride
Father's Little Dividend
Giant
Hammersmith Is Out
Ivanhoe
Lassie Come Home
The Last Time I Saw Paris
Life With Father
A Little Night Music
Little Women (1949 version)

Malice in Wonderland
The Mirror Crack'd
National Velvet
Night Watch
A Place in the Sun
Poker Alice
Raintree County
Reflections in a Golden Eye
Return Engagement
The Sandpiper
Secret Ceremony
Suddenly, Last Summer
The Taming of the Shrew
Under Milk Wood
Who's Afraid of Virginia Woolf?
Winter Kills
X, Y, and Zee

DIRECTOR CHECK LIST: JOHN FORD _____ CL34
See also: WE18 John Ford Check List

Arrowsmith
Donovan's Reef
Drums Along the Mohawk
The Grapes of Wrath
How the West Was Won
The Hurricane (1937 version)
The Informer
Judge Priest
The Last Hurrah
The Long Voyage Home

The Lost Patrol
Mary of Scotland
Mister Roberts (co-director)
Mogambo
The Quiet Man
They Were Expendable
This Is Korea/December 7th
Wee Willie Winkie
What Price Glory (1952 version)
Young Mr. Lincoln

DIRECTOR CHECK LIST: HOWARD HAWKS _____ CL35
See also: WE21 Howard Hawks Check List

Air Force
Ball of Fire

The Barbary Coast
The Big Sleep (1946 version)

Bringing Up Baby
Come and Get It (co-director)
The Criminal Code
Gentlemen Prefer Blondes
Hatari!
His Girl Friday
Man's Favorite Sport?

Monkey Business (1952)
Only Angels Have Wings
Scarface (1932 version)
Sergeant York
To Have and Have Not
Twentieth Century

DIRECTOR CHECK LIST: D.W. GRIFFITH _____ CL36

Abraham Lincoln
The Avenging Conscience
The Birth of a Nation
Broken Blossoms
D.W. Griffith Triple Feature
Dream Street
Hearts of the World

Home Sweet Home
Intolerance
Orphans of the Storm
Sally of the Sawdust
The Short Films of D.W. Griffith, Vol. I
True Heart Susie
Way Down East

DIRECTOR CHECK LIST: BILLY WILDER _____ CL37

The Apartment
Buddy Buddy
Double Indemnity
Irma La Douce
The Lost Weekend
Love in the Afternoon
One, Two, Three
The Private Life of Sherlock Holmes

Sabrina
The Seven Year Itch
Some Like It Hot
The Spirit of St. Louis
Stalag 17
Sunset Boulevard
Witness for the Prosecution (1957
 version)

DIRECTOR CHECK LIST: WILLIAM WYLER _____ CL38

Ben-Hur
The Best Years of Our Lives
The Big Country
The Collector
Come and Get It (co-director)
Dead End
The Desperate Hours
Dodsworth
Friendly Persuasion
Funny Girl

The Heiress
Jezebel
The Letter
The Liberation of L.B. Jones
The Little Foxes
Mrs. Miniver
Roman Holiday
These Three
The Westerner
Wuthering Heights (1939 version)

DIRECTOR CHECK LIST: GEORGE CUKOR _____ CL39

Adam's Rib
Born Yesterday
Camille
David Copperfield
Dinner at Eight

A Double Life
Gaslight
Heller in Pink Tights
Holiday
It Should Happen to You

Justine
Les Girls
Let's Make Love
Little Women (1933 version)
Love Among the Ruins
My Fair Lady
Pat and Mike

The Philadelphia Story
Rich and Famous
A Star Is Born (1954 version)
Sylvia Scarlett
A Woman's Face
The Women

DIRECTOR CHECK LIST: FRANK CAPRA _____ CL40

Arsenic and Old Lace
It Happened One Night
It's a Wonderful Life
Lost Horizon

Meet John Doe
Mr. Smith Goes to Washington
Pocketful of Miracles
State of the Union

DIRECTOR CHECK LIST: ORSON WELLES _____ CL41

Citizen Kane*
The Lady From Shanghai*
Macbeth (1948 version)*
The Magnificent Ambersons**
Mr. Arkadin*
The Stranger*
Touch of Evil*
The Trial*

Actor Only
Butterfly
Casino Royale
Catch-22

Journey Into Fear
A Man for all Seasons (1966 version)
Moby Dick
The Muppet Movie
Napoleon (1955 version)
Someone to Love
Start the Revolution Without Me
　(narrator)
The Third Man
Transformers, The Movie (voice)
The Vikings (narrator)
Voyage of the Damned

　*also actor
**also narrator

DIRECTOR CHECK LIST: GEORGE STEVENS _____ CL42

Alice Adams
Annie Oakley
A Damsel in Distress
The Diary of Anne Frank
Giant
The Greatest Story Ever Told
Gunga Din
I Remember Mama
Penny Serenade
A Place in the Sun

Quality Street
Shane
Swing Time
The Talk of the Town
Vivacious Lady
Woman of the Year

Documentary subject
George Stevens: A Filmmaker's Journey

DIRECTOR CHECK LIST: FRITZ LANG _____ CL43

Beyond a Reasonable Doubt
The Big Heat

Clash by Night
Cloak and Dagger (1946)

Contempt*
Destiny
The House by the River
Human Desire
Kriemhilde's Revenge
M
Metropolis
Rancho Notorious
The Return of Frank James

Scarlet Street
Secret Beyond the Door
Siegfried
Spies
The Testament of Dr. Mabuse
While the City Sleeps
The Woman in the Moon
You Only Live Once

*actor only

DIRECTOR CHECK LIST: JOHN HUSTON ———————————————— CL44

The African Queen
Annie
The Asphalt Jungle
The Barbarian and the Geisha
Beat the Devil
The Bible*
Casino Royale (co-directed)
The Dead
Fat City
Key Largo
Let There Be Light
The Life and Times of Judge Roy Bean
The List of Adrian Messenger
The Mackintosh Man
The Maltese Falcon
The Man Who Would Be King
The Misfits
Moby Dick
The Night of the Iguana
Phobia

Prizzi's Honor
The Red Badge of Courage
Reflections in a Golden Eye
The Treasure of the Sierra Madre*
Under the Volcano
The Unforgiven
Victory
Wise Blood

Actor only
Angela
Battle for the Planet of the Apes
Breakout
Cannery Row (narrator)
The Cardinal
Chinatown
Lovesick
Myra Breckenridge
The Wind and the Lion
Winter Kills

*also actor

STAR CHECK LIST: BARBARA STANWYCK ———————————————— CL45

Annie Oakley
Ball of Fire
The Bride Walks Out
Cattle Queen of Montana
Clash by Night
Double Indemnity
Escape to Burma
Executive Suite
Golden Boy
The Lady Eve

Lady of Burlesque
The Mad Miss Manton
The Maverick Queen
Meet John Doe
Roustabout
Sorry, Wrong Number
Stella Dallas
The Strange Love of Martha Ivers
Walk on the Wild Side

STAR CHECK LIST: MYRNA LOY _____ CL46

After the Thin Man
Airport 1975
Another Thin Man
Ants
The April Fools
Arrowsmith
The Bachelor and the Bobby Soxer
The Best Years of Our Lives
Consolation Marriage
The End
The Great Ziegfeld

Just Tell Me What You Want
Lonelyhearts
Midnight Lace
Mr. Blandings Builds His Dream House
The Red Pony (1949 version)
Shadow of the Thin Man
Song of the Thin Man
Summer Solstice
The Thin Man
The Thin Man Goes Home
Vanity Fair

STAR CHECK LIST: MARLENE DIETRICH _____ CL47

Blonde Venus
The Blue Angel
Destry Rides Again
Judgment at Nuremberg
Garden of Allah
Just a Gigolo
Knight Without Armour
Morocco
Paris When It Sizzles
Rancho Notorious

Seven Sinners
The Spoilers
Stage Fright
Touch of Evil
Witness for the Prosecution (1957
 version)

Documentary subject:
Marlene

STAR CHECK LIST: CAROLE LOMBARD _____ CL48

High Voltage
In Name Only
Made for Each Other (1939)
My Man Godfrey
Mr. and Mrs. North
Nothing Sacred

Power (1928)
Racketeer
Swing High, Swing Low
They Knew What They Wanted
To Be or Not to Be (1943 version)
Twentieth Century

STAR CHECK LIST: LILLIAN GISH _____ CL49

The Adventures of Huckleberry Finn
 (1985 version)
The Birth of a Nation
Broken Blossoms
Commandos Strike at Dawn
D.W. Griffith Triple Feature
Duel in the Sun
Follow Me, Boys!
Hambone and Hillie
Hearts of the World
His Double Life

Hobson's Choice (1983 version)
Intolerance
The Night of the Hunter
Orphans of the Storm
Sweet Liberty
True Heart Susie
The Unforgiven
Way Down East
A Wedding
The Whales of August
The Wind

STAR CHECK LIST: JOAN CRAWFORD _____ CL50

Autumn Leaves
Berserk
Dancing Lady
Grand Hotel
Johnny Guitar
Mildred Pierce
Night Gallery

Possessed
Rain
Strait-Jacket
What Ever Happened to Baby Jane?
A Woman's Face
The Women

STAR CHECK LIST: WILLIAM HOLDEN _____ CL51

Alvarez Kelly
Ashanti, Land of No Mercy
Born Yesterday
The Bridge on the River Kwai
The Bridges at Toko-Ri
Casino Royale
The Christmas Tree
The Country Girl (1954 version)
Damien--Omen II
The Dark Past
Dear Wife
The Earthling
Executive Suite
Golden Boy
The Horse Soldiers
The Key
Love Is a Many Splendored Thing

The Moon Is Blue
Network
Our Town
Paris When It Sizzles
Rachel and the Stranger
S.O.B.
Sabrina
Stalag 17
Sunset Boulevard
Texas
The Towering Inferno
Union Station
When Time Ran Out
The Wild Bunch
Wild Rovers
The World of Suzie Wong
Young and Willing

STAR CHECK LIST: EDWARD G. ROBINSON _____ CL52

Barbary Coast
Cheyenne Autumn
The Cincinnati Kid
Double Indemnity
Good Neighbor Sam
Hell on Frisco Bay
I Am the Law
Key Largo
Little Caesar

Mr. Winkle Goes to War
Never a Dull Moment
The Red House
Scarlet Street
Song of Norway
Soylent Green
The Stranger
The Ten Commandments (1956 version)
Thunder in the City

DIRECTOR-STAR CHECK LIST: ERICH VON STROHEIM _____ CL53

Blind Husbands
Foolish Wives
Grand Illusion*
Greed**
Hearts of the World*
Intolerance*

Lost Squadron*
Napoleon (1955 version)*
North Star*
Queen Kelly**
Sunset Boulevard*
The Wedding March

* actor only
** director only

DIRECTOR CHECK LIST: ERNST LUBITSCH _____ **CL54**

Lady Windermere's Fan
The Merry Widow
Ninotchka
Passion

The Shop Around the Corner
That Uncertain Feeling
To Be or Not to Be (1943 version)

DIRECTOR CHECK LIST: JOSEPH L. MANKIEWICZ _____ **CL55**

All About Eve
The Barefoot Contessa
Cleopatra
Julius Caesar (1953 version)

Guys and Dolls
Sleuth
Suddenly, Last Summer
There Was a Crooked Man

DIRECTOR CHECK LIST: JOSEF VON STERNBERG _____ **CL56**

Blonde Venus
The Blue Angel
The Docks of New York
The Last Command

Macao
Morocco
The Shanghai Gesture

DIRECTOR CHECK LIST: FRED ZINNEMANN _____ **CL57**

Behold a Pale Horse
The Day of the Jackal
Five Days One Summer
From Here to Eternity
High Noon
Julia

A Man for all Seasons (1966 version)
The Men
The Nun's Story
Oklahoma!
The Sundowners

DIRECTOR CHECK LIST: ROBERT WISE _____ **CL58**

The Andromeda Strain
Audrey Rose
Blood on the Moon
The Body Snatcher
Born to Kill
Criminal Court
Curse of the Cat People
The Day the Earth Stood Still
Executive Suite
The Haunting

The Hindenburg
I Want to Live!
Rooftops
Run Silent, Run Deep
The Sand Pebbles
The Set-Up
The Sound of Music
Star Trek--The Motion Picture
West Side Story*

* co-director

Chapter Three

COMEDY
(CO)

ROMANTIC COMEDIES —————————————————————— **CO1**

All Night Long
Almost You
American Dreamer
Annie Hall
Arthur
Arthur 2 On the Rocks
Barefoot in the Park
Best Friends
Blind Date (1987)
Blume in Love
Broadcast News
Bull Durham
Cactus Flower
Chances Are
Continental Divide
"Crocodile" Dundee
"Crocodile" Dundee II
Cross My Heart
Crossing Delancey
The Electric Horseman
The Four Seasons
The Goodbye Girl
The Heartbreak Kid
Heartburn
House Calls
It Takes Two
It's My Turn
Manhattan
Micki and Maude
A Midsummer Night's Sex Comedy
Modern Romance

Moonstruck
Murphy's Romance
Never on Sunday
A New Life
Night Shift
The Owl and the Pussycat
Pete 'n' Tillie
Pillow Talk
Play It Again, Sam
Quackser Fortune Has a Cousin in the
   Bronx
Reuben, Reuben
Roxanne
Say Anything
Shampoo
She's Gotta Have It
She's Having a Baby
Skin Deep
Someone to Love
Splash
Starting Over
The Sure Thing
Sweethearts Dance
Switching Channels
10
That Touch of Mink
A Touch of Class
Victor/Victoria
Who Am I This Time?
The Woman in Red
Working Girl

COMEDIES FOR MODERN TIMES ——————————————— **CO2**

After Hours
Annie Hall
Baby Boom
Being There
Between the Lines
Bob & Carol & Ted & Alice

Broadcast News
The Coca-Cola Kid
Creator
Desperately Seeking Susan
Dr. Strangelove: or, How I Learned to
   Stop Worrying and Love the Bomb

Down and Out in Beverly Hills
Earth Girls Are Easy
The Experts
The First Monday in October
The Gods Must Be Crazy
The Graduate
Gung Ho (1986)
Heartburn
I Love You, Alice B. Toklas
It's My Turn
King of Comedy
Little Murders
Local Hero
Lost in America
Making Mr. Right
Manhattan
Max Headroom
Melvin and Howard
The Milagro Beanfield War
Mr. Mom
Moon Over Parador
Mother, Jugs and Speed
A New Life
New York Stories
Night Shift

One, Two, Three
Planes, Trains, and Automobiles
The President's Analyst
Private Benjamin
Putney Swope
Real Genius
Repo Man
The Russians Are Coming! The
   Russians Are Coming!
School Daze
Scrooged
The Secret of My Success
Semi-Tough
Serial
Shampoo
She's Gotta Have It
Something Wild
Stars and Bars
Stay Hungry
Tanner '88
Three Men and a Baby
Tootsie
Whoops Apocalypse
Working Girl

CONTEMPORARY COMEDY TEAMS _____ CO3

All of Me
Armed and Dangerous
Bedazzled
The Best of Times
Big Business
The Blues Brothers
Brewster's Millions
Buddy Buddy
City Heat
The Dream Team
Dirty, Rotten Scoundrels
Feds
A Fine Mess
The In-Laws
Ishtar
Macaroni
9 to 5
The Odd Couple

Outrageous Fortune
Planes, Trains, and Automobiles
Running Scared
See No Evil, Hear No Evil
Silver Streak
Stir Crazy
The Sunshine Boys
The Survivors
Three Amigos
Throw Momma From the Train
Tin Men
Tough Guys
Trading Places
Twins
Vibes
Volunteers
Wise Guys

GROWING UP _____ CO4

American Graffiti
Back to the Future

The Bad News Bears
Big

Breaking Away
Fandango
Fast Times at Ridgemont High
Ferris Bueller's Day Off
Footloose
For Keeps
The Graduate
Heathers
Heaven Help Us
Johnny Be Good
The Joy of Sex
A Little Romance
My Bodyguard
My Life as a Dog
National Lampoon's Animal House

The Night Before
A Night in the Life of Jimmy Reardon
Porky's (series)
Real Genius
Revenge of the Nerds
Rich Kids
Risky Business
Rita, Sue and Bob Too
Say Anything
Sixteen Candles
Some Kind of Wonderful
Teen Wolf
Valley Girl
The World of Henry Orient
You're a Big Boy Now

FUNNY FAMILIES ———————————————————— CO5

Author! Author!
Big Business
Brighton Beach Memoirs
A Christmas Story
Crimes of the Heart
18 Again!
First Family
Garbo Talks
The Great Outdoors
Hannah and Her Sisters
Hope and Glory
The Hotel New Hampshire
I Ought to Be in Pictures
Irreconcilable Differences

Max Dugan Returns
Mr. Mom
Morgan Stewart's Coming Home
National Lampoon's European Vacation
National Lampoon's Vacation
Parents
The Prince of Pennsylvania
Radio Days
Raising Arizona
A Thousand Clowns
Twister
Vice Versa
A Wedding
Where's Poppa?

NUTTY NOSTALGIA ———————————————————— CO6

American Graffiti
Back to the Future
Biloxi Blues
Brighton Beach Memoirs
A Christmas Story
Diner
Good Morning, Vietnam
The Great Race
Hairspray
Harry and Walter Go to New York
Heartbreak Hotel
Hearts of the West
Hope and Glory
How I Won the War
I Wanna Hold Your Hand

In the Mood
M*A*S*H
Mr. North
My Favorite Year
Nadine
The Night They Raided Minsky's
1941
Paper Moon
Parents
Peggy Sue Got Married
A Private Function
Privates on Parade
Radio Days
The Skin Game (1971)
Start the Revolution Without Me

The Sting
Sunset
The Twelve Chairs
Those Lips, Those Eyes

Those Magnificent Men in Their Flying
    Machines
Tin Men

MOVIE SPOOFS _____ CO7

Airplane!
Airplane II: The Sequel
Amazon Women on the Moon
The Big Bus
Blazing Saddles
Bullshot
Casino Royale
Cat Ballou
City Heat
Dead Men Don't Wear Plaid
11 Harrowhouse
High Anxiety
I'm Gonna Git You Sucka
Johnny Dangerously
Love at First Bite
Lust in the Dust
The Man With Two Brains

Monty Python and the Holy Grail
Monty Python's Life of Brian
Movie Movie
Murder by Death
The Naked Gun
Rustler's Rhapsody
Silent Movie
Sleeper
Spaceballs
Take the Money and Run
This Is Spinal Tap
Top Secret!
Transylvania 6-5000
What's Up, Tiger Lily?
Young Frankenstein
Zelig

THE LIGHTER SIDE OF SHOW BIZ _____ CO8

Broadway Danny Rose
Gentlemen Prefer Blondes
Ginger and Fred
Hearts of the West
Hollywood Boulevard
Hollywood or Bust
Hollywood Shuffle
Home Movies
Moon Over Parador
Movers and Shakers
My Favorite Year
The Purple Rose of Cairo
Radio Days
Real Life

Roadie
S.O.B.
Songwriter
Stand-In
Stardust Memories
The State of Things
Sunset
Sweet Liberty
Tapeheads
Those Lips, Those Eyes
Tootsie
Under the Rainbow
Who Framed Roger Rabbit

ACTION COMEDIES _____ CO9
see also: CO10 Crime and Suspense Comedies

Any Which Way You Can
Beverly Hills Cop
Beverly Hills Cop II
The Cannonball Run
Cannonball Run II

"Crocodile" Dundee
"Crocodile" Dundee II
Donovan's Reef
Every Which Way But Loose
Ghostbusters

Ghostbusters II
The Golden Child
The Gumball Rally
Howard the Duck
Innerspace
It's a Mad Mad Mad Mad World

Midnight Run
Raising Arizona
See No Evil, Hear No Evil
Smokey and the Bandit (series)
Speed Zone

CRIME AND SUSPENSE COMEDIES ————————————— CO10
See also: CO9 Action Comedies,
CO26 Peter Sellers Check List (for Pink Panther titles),
MY21 Comic Mysteries

The Black Marble
Burglar
Clue
Compromising Positions
Disorganized Crime
$ (Dollars)
Dragnet (1987)
11 Harrowhouse
A Fish Called Wanda
Fletch
Fletch Lives
Foul Play
Hopscotch
The Hot Rock
The In-Laws
Johnny Dangerously
Jumpin' Jack Flash
The Ladykillers
The Lavender Hill Mob
The Man With One Red Shoe

Married to the Mob
Moonlighting (1985)
Murder by Death
Raising Arizona
Ruthless People
See No Evil, Hear No Evil
Silver Streak
Some Like It Hot
Stakeout
Take the Money and Run
They All Laughed
The Thief Who Came to Dinner
Things Change
Three Fugitives
Throw Momma From the Train
Tough Guys
The Trouble With Harry
Who Framed Roger Rabbit
Who's Harry Crumb?
Wise Guys

SPECIAL EFFECTS FOR LAUGHS ————————————— CO11

Back to the Future
Beetlejuice
Big Top Pee-wee
Explorers
Ghostbusters
Ghostbusters II
The Golden Child
Gremlins
High Spirits
Howard the Duck
The Incredible Shrinking Woman
Innerspace

Max Headroom
Modern Problems
My Demon Lover
My Science Project
My Stepmother Is an Alien
Pee-wee's Big Adventure
Short Circuit
Short Circuit 2
Teen Wolf
Weird Science
Who Framed Roger Rabbit

OFFBEAT COMEDY ————————————————— CO12

The Adventures of Buckaroo Banzai
    Across the 8th Dimension

After Hours
Bagdad Cafe

Being There
Big Top Pee-wee
Bliss
Brewster McCloud
Catch-22
The Coca-Cola Kid
Consuming Passions
A Day in the Death of Joe Egg
Dr. Strangelove: or, How I Learned to
    Stop Worrying and Love the Bomb
Down by Law
The End
Entertaining Mr. Sloane
Grace Quigley
Harold and Maude
Heathers
The Hospital
How I Won the War
I've Heard the Mermaids Singing
King of Comedy
Little Murders
Lolita
Loot . . . Give Me Money, Honey
M*A*S*H

The Magic Christian
Malcolm
Miss Firecracker
My Dinner With Andre
Nasty Habits
Neighbors
A New Leaf
92 in the Shade
Outrageous
Parents
Pee-wee's Big Adventure
Putney Swope
Repo Man
Salvation
Silent Movie
Something Wild
Stranger Than Paradise
Swimming to Cambodia
The Trouble With Harry
UFOria
Used Cars
Where's Poppa?
Zelig

STAR CHECK LISTS: THE ALUMNI OF *SATURDAY NIGHT LIVE* ———————— CO13
see also: CO14 Performance Comics

Dan Aykroyd
The Best of Dan Aykroyd
The Blues Brothers
Caddyshack II
The Couch Trip
Doctor Detroit
Dragnet (1987)
Ghostbusters
Ghostbusters II
The Great Outdoors
It Came From Hollywood
My Stepmother Is an Alien
Neighbors
1941
Spies Like Us
Trading Places
Twilight Zone: The Movie

Jim Belushi
About Last Night
Jumpin' Jack Flash
K-9
The Man With One Red Shoe
The Principal

Real Men
Red Heat
Salvador

John Belushi
The Best of John Belushi
The Blues Brothers
Continental Divide
Goin' South
National Lampoon's Animal House
Neighbors
1941
Old Boyfriends

Chevy Chase
The Best of Chevy Chase
Caddyshack
Caddyshack II
Deal of the Century
Fletch
Fletch Lives
Follow That Bird
Foul Play
Funny Farm

The Groove Tube
Modern Problems
National Lampoon's European Vacation
National Lampoon's Vacation
Oh! Heavenly Dog
Seems Like Old Times
Spies Like Us
Three Amigos
Under the Rainbow

Billy Crystal
Memories of Me
The Princess Bride
Rabbit Test
Running Scared
Throw Momma From the Train

Jane Curtin
How to Beat the High Cost of Living
Suspicion (1987 version)

Garrett Morris
The Anderson Tapes
Critical Condition
The Stuff

Eddie Murphy
Best Defense
The Best of Eddie Murphy: Saturday
   Night Live
Beverly Hills Cop
Beverly Hills Cop II
Coming to America

48HRS.
The Golden Child
Trading Places

Bill Murray
Caddyshack
Ghostbusters
Ghostbusters II
Meatballs
The Razor's Edge (1984 version)
Scrooged
Stripes
Tootsie
Where the Buffalo Roam

Laraine Newman
Invaders From Mars (1986 version)
Perfect!
Wholly Moses

Joe Piscopo
Dead Heat
Johnny Dangerously
Wise Guys

Gilda Radner
The Best of Gilda
First Family
Hanky Panky
Haunted Honeymoon
It Came From Hollywood
Movers and Shakers
The Woman in Red

CHECK LISTS: THE ALUMNI OF *SCTV* _____ CO14

John Candy
Armed and Dangerous
Brewster's Millions
Going Berserk
The Great Outdoors
It Came From Hollywood
National Lampoon's Vacation
Planes, Trains, and Automobiles
Really Weird Tales
Spaceballs
Speed Zone
Splash
Stripes
Summer Rental
Volunteers
Who's Harry Crumb?

Joe Flaherty
Going Berserk
One Crazy Summer
Speed Zone

Eugene Levy
Armed and Dangerous
Club Paradise
Going Berserk
National Lampoon's Vacation
Speed Zone
Splash

Andrea Martin
Black Christmas
Club Paradise

Rick Moranis
Club Paradise
Ghostbusters
Ghostbusters II
Head Office
Little Shop of Horrors (1986 version)
Spaceballs
Strange Brew
Streets of Fire
The Wild Life

Catherine O'Hara
After Hours
Beetlejuice
Really Weird Tales

Harold Ramis
Baby Boom
Caddyshack*

*director only

Club Paradise*
Ghostbusters
Ghostbusters II
National Lampoon's Vacation*
Stripes

Martin Short
Cross My Heart
Innerspace
Really Weird Tales
Three Amigos
Three Fugitives

Dave Thomas
The Experts*
Follow That Bird
Moving
Strange Brew

STARS CHECK LISTS: MONTY PYTHON'S FLYING CIRCUS ———————— CO15

The Troupe
And Now for Something Completely
    Different
Monty Python and the Holy Grail
Monty Python's Flying Circus, Volumes
    1-17
Monty Python's Life of Brian
Monty Python's The Meaning of Life

Individually (but sometimes together)
The Adventures of Baron Munchausen
    (Eric Idle; directed by Terry Gilliam)
All You Need Is Cash (Idle)
Brazil (Michael Palin; directed by
    Gilliam)
Clockwise (John Cleese)
Fawlty Towers, Volumes 1-4 (Cleese)
A Fish Called Wanda (Cleese, Palin)
Jabberwocky (Terry Jones, Palin;
    directed by Gilliam)
Labyrinth (Jones)

The Magic Christian (Graham
    Chapman, Cleese)
The Missionary (Palin)
National Lampoon's European Vacation
    (Idle)
Personal Services (directed by Jones)
The Pied Piper of Hamelin (Idle)
A Private Function (Palin)
Privates on Parade (Cleese)
Ripping Yarns (Jones, Palin)
The Secret Policeman's Other Ball
    (Chapman, Cleese, Jones,
    Palin)
The Secret Policeman's Private Parts
    (Chapman, Cleese, Gilliam, Jones,
    Palin)
Silverado (Cleese)
Time Bandits (Cleese, Palin; directed by
    Gilliam)
Whoops Apocalypse (Cleese)
Yellowbeard (Chapman, Cleese, Idle)

PERFORMANCE COMICS ———————————————————————— CO16
See also: CO29 Richard Pryor Check List

The Andy Kaufman Sound Stage
    Special
The Best of Comic Relief

Bill Cosby: 49
Bill Cosby: Himself
Billy Crystal: A Comic's Line

Billy Crystal: Don't Get Me Started
Carlin at Carnegie
Comic Relief 2
Comic Relief III
Eddie Murphy: Delirious
Eddie Murphy Raw
An Evening With Bobcat Goldthwait:
   Share the Warmth
An Evening With Robin Williams
The First Howie Mandel Special
Gallagher: The Bookkeeper
Gallagher: The Maddest
Gallagher: Melon Crazy
Gallagher: Over Your Head
Gallagher: Stuck in the 60s
Gilda Live
HBO Comedy Club
Jackie Mason on Broadway
The Joe Piscopo Video
The Joe Piscopo New Jersey Special
Jonathan Winters: On the Ledge
Robert Klein: Child of the 60s, Man of
   the 80s
Robert Klein on Broadway
Robin Williams Live!
Rodney Dangerfield: It's Not Easy
   Bein' Me
Steve Martin Live!
Steven Wright Live
Ten From Your Show of Shows
Whoopi Goldberg Live

CLASSIC & CONTEMPORARY BRITISH COMEDY _____ CO17
See also: CO15 Monty Python's Flying Circus Check Lists

Alfie
The Belles of St. Trinian's
Billy Liar
Britannia Hospital
Bullshot
Carry On Doctor
Comfort and Joy
Consuming Passions
A Day in the Death of Joe Egg
Doctor in the House
Eat the Peach
Educating Rita
Entertaining Mr. Sloane
A Fish Called Wanda
Georgy Girl
The Goon Show Movie
The Gospel According to Vic
Gregory's Girl
Gumshoe
Hobson's Choice (1954 version)
Hope and Glory
The Horse's Mouth
How I Won the War
I'm All Right, Jack
Kind Hearts and Coronets
The Ladykillers
The Lavender Hill Mob
Letter to Brezhnev
Local Hero
Loot . . . Give Me Money, Honey!
The Magic Christian
Make Mine Mink
The Man in the White Suit
Morgan: A Suitable Case for Treatment
The Mouse That Roared
Personal Services
Rita, Sue and Bob Too
The Ruling Class
Stars and Bars
That Sinking Feeling
Tom Jones
Two Way Stretch
Waltz of the Toreadors
We Think the World of You
Whisky Galore
Wish You Were Here
Withnail and I
The Wrong Box

FILMMAKER CHECK LIST: CHARLIE CHAPLIN _____ CO18

Short Films
The Chaplin Essanay Book I
The Chaplin Revue
Charlie Chaplin Carnival
Charlie Chaplin Cavalcade
Charlie Chaplin Festival
Charlie Chaplin—The Early Years,
   Vols. I–IV

Charlie Chaplin's Keystone Comedies
The Kid/The Idle Class
Kid's Auto Race/Mabel's Married Life
The Knockout/Dough and Dynamite
The Rink/The Immigrant
The Tramp/A Woman
Work/Police

Feature Films
The Circus

City Lights
The Gold Rush
The Great Dictator
A King in New York
Limelight
Modern Times
Monsieur Verdoux
Tillie's Punctured Romance
A Woman of Paris

FILMMAKER CHECK LIST: BUSTER KEATON _____ CO19

Short Films
The Balloonatic/One Week
The Blacksmith/The Balloonatic
Buster Keaton Festival Vol. I
Buster Keaton Festival Vol. II
Buster Keaton Rides Again/The
  Railrodder

*actor only

Feature Films
College
A Funny Thing Happened on the Way
  to the Forum*
The General
Limelight*
Steamboat Bill, Jr.
The Three Ages

STARS CHECK LIST: LAUREL & HARDY _____ CO20

Atoll K
Block Heads
The Bohemian Girl
Bonnie Scotland
The Bullfighters
A Chump at Oxford
The Fighting Kentuckian*
The Flying Deuces
Great Guns

*Hardy only

Laurel and Hardy Comedy Classics,
  Vols. I-IX
The Music Box/Helpmates
Our Relations
Pack Up Your Troubles
Pardon Us
Saps at Sea
Sons of the Desert
Swiss Miss
Way Out West

STARS CHECK LIST: THE MARX BROTHERS _____ CO21

Animal Crackers
At the Circus
The Big Store
The Cocoanuts
Copacabana*
A Day at the Races
Double Dynamite*
Duck Soup

*Groucho only

A Girl in Every Port*
Go West
Horse Feathers
Love Happy
A Night at the Opera
A Night in Casablanca
Room Service

STAR CHECK LIST: W. C. FIELDS _____ CO22

The Bank Dick
The Barber Shop
The Best of W. C. Fields
David Copperfield
The Dentist
The Fatal Glass of Beer/The Pool Shark
International House
It's a Gift

Mrs. Wiggs of the Cabbage Patch
My Little Chickadee
Never Give a Sucker an Even Break
Running Wild
Sally of the Sawdust
W. C. Fields Comedy Bag
W. C. Fields Festival
You Can't Cheat an Honest Man

STARS CHECK LIST: ABBOTT & COSTELLO _____ CO23

Abbott and Costello in Hollywood
Abbott and Costello Meet Captain Kidd
Abbott and Costello Meet Dr. Jekyll and
   Mr. Hyde
Abbott and Costello Meet Frankenstein
Abbott and Costello Meet the Killer,
   Boris Karloff
Africa Screams

Buck Privates
Hit the Ice
Hold That Ghost
Jack and the Beanstalk (1952 version)
The Naughty Nineties
The Time of Their Lives
Who Done It?

FILMMAKER CHECK LIST: PRESTON STURGES _____ CO24

The Beautiful Blonde From Bashful
   Bend
Christmas in July
The Great McGinty
The Lady Eve
The Miracle of Morgan's Creek

The Palm Beach Story
Paris Holiday*
The Sin of Harold Diddlebock
Sullivan's Travels
Unfaithfully Yours (1948 version)

*actor only

STAR CHECK LIST: JERRY LEWIS _____ CO25

At War With the Army*
The Bellboy**
The Best of Comic Relief
The Big Mouth**
The Caddy*
Cinderfella
Cracking Up
The Disorderly Orderly
Don't Raise the Bridge, Lower the River
The Errand Boy**

The Family Jewels
Hardly Working**
Hollywood or Bust*
Jerry Lewis Live
King of Comedy
The Nutty Professor**
The Patsy**
Slapstick of Another Kind
Which Way to the Front?**

   *with Dean Martin
** also director

STAR CHECK LIST: PETER SELLERS _____ CO26

After the Fox
The Battle of the Sexes
Being There
The Blockhouse
The Bobo
Carlton Browne of the F.O.
Casino Royale
Dr. Strangelove: or, How I Learned to
    Stop Worrying and Love the Bomb
Down Among the Z-Men
The Fiendish Plot of Dr. Fu Manchu
Ghost in the Noonday Sun
The Goon Show Movie
The Great McGonagall
Heavens Above
I Love You, Alice B. Toklas
I'm All Right, Jack
The Ladykillers
Lolita
The Magic Christian
The Mouse That Roared

Murder by Death
The Naked Truth
Never Let Go
The Pink Panther
The Pink Panther Strikes Again
The Prisoner of Zenda (1979 version)
The Return of the Pink Panther
The Revenge of the Pink Panther
A Shot in the Dark
There's a Girl in My Soup
tom thumb
Trail of the Pink Panther
Two Way Stretch
Up the Creek (1958)
Waltz of the Toreadors
What's New Pussycat?
Woman Times Seven
The World of Henry Orient
The Wrong Arm of the Law
The Wrong Box

FILMMAKER CHECK LIST: WOODY ALLEN _____ CO27

Annie Hall
Another Woman*
Bananas
Broadway Danny Rose
Casino Royale**
Everything You Always Wanted to
    Know About Sex But Were Afraid to
    Ask
The Front**
Hannah and Her Sisters
Interiors*
King Lear (1987 version)**
Love and Death

Manhattan
A Midsummer Night's Sex Comedy
New York Stories***
Play It Again, Sam†
The Purple Rose of Cairo*
Radio Days*
September*
Sleeper
Stardust Memories
Take the Money and Run
What's New, Pussycat?†
What's Up, Tiger Lily?
Zelig

*writer-director only
**actor only
***co-director
†writer-actor only

FILMMAKER CHECK LIST: MEL BROOKS _____ CO28

Blazing Saddles
High Anxiety
The History of the World: Part I

The Muppet Movie*
The Producers
Putney Swope*

Silent Movie
Spaceballs
To Be or Not to Be (1983 version)*

The Twelve Chairs
Young Frankenstein

*actor only

STAR CHECK LIST: RICHARD PRYOR _____ CO29

Adios Amigo
The Bingo Long Traveling All-Stars &
   Motor Kings
Blue Collar
Brewster's Millions
Bustin' Loose
California Suite
Car Wash
Critical Condition
Greased Lightning
Jo Jo Dancer, Your Life Is Calling*
Lady Sings the Blues
The Mack
Moving
The Muppet Movie

Richard Pryor: Here and Now
Richard Pryor: Live and Smokin'
Richard Pryor: Live in Concert
Richard Pryor Live on the Sunset Strip
See No Evil, Hear No Evil
Silver Streak
Some Kind of Hero
Stir Crazy
Superman III
The Toy
Uptown Saturday Night
Which Way Is Up?
Wholly Moses
Wild in the Streets
The Wiz

*also director

STAR CHECK LIST: GOLDIE HAWN _____ CO30

Best Friends
Butterflies Are Free
Cactus Flower
$ (Dollars)
The Duchess and the Dirtwater Fox
Foul Play
The Girl From Petrovka
Lovers and Liars
The One and Only, Genuine, Original
   Family Band

Overboard
Private Benjamin
Protocol
Seems Like Old Times
Shampoo
The Sugarland Express
Swing Shift
There's a Girl in My Soup
Wildcats

STAR CHECK LIST: DUDLEY MOORE _____ CO31

Arthur
Arthur 2 On the Rocks
Bedazzled
Best Defense
Foul Play
The Hound of the Baskervilles (1977
   version)
Lovesick
Micki and Maude

Romantic Comedy
Santa Claus, The Movie
Six Weeks
10
30 Is a Dangerous Age, Cynthia
Unfaithfully Yours (1984 version)
Wholly Moses
The Wrong Box

STARS CHECK LIST: CHEECH & CHONG ——————————————————— CO32

After Hours
Born in East L.A.*
Cheech & Chong's Next Movie
Cheech & Chong's The Corsican
  Brothers
Get Out of My Room

It Came From Hollywood
Nice Dreams
Still Smokin'
Things Are Tough All Over
Up in Smoke
Yellowbeard

*Cheech only

STAR CHECK LIST: STEVE MARTIN ——————————————————— CO33

All of Me
Dead Men Don't Wear Plaid
Dirty, Rotten Scoundrels
The Jerk
Little Shop of Horrors (1986 version)
The Lonely Guy
The Man With Two Brains
Movers and Shakers

The Muppet Movie
Pennies From Heaven
Planes, Trains, and Automobiles
Roxanne
Sergeant Pepper's Lonely Hearts Club
  Band
Steve Martin Live!
Three Amigos

WRITER CHECK LIST: NEIL SIMON ——————————————————— CO34
(Based on Simon plays, or original screenplays by Simon, unless noted)

After the Fox
Barefoot in the Park
Biloxi Blues
Brighton Beach Memoirs
California Suite
Chapter Two
The Goodbye Girl
The Heartbreak Kid*
I Ought to Be in Pictures
The Last of the Red Hot Lovers

Max Dugan Returns
Murder by Death
The Odd Couple
Only When I Laugh
The Out of Towners
Plaza Suite
The Prisoner of Second Avenue
Seems Like Old Times
The Slugger's Wife
The Sunshine Boys

*Simon screenplay, based on Bruce Jay Friedman story

CAMPUS COMEDY ——————————————————————— CO35
See also: DR61 School Days

Bedtime for Bonzo
College
Fast Times at Ridgemont High
The Freshman
Getting Straight
Heathers
Heaven Help Us
Horse Feathers

National Lampoon's Animal House
National Lampoon's Class Reunion
The Nutty Professor
Porky's (series)
Real Genius
Revenge of the Nerds
Rock 'n' Roll High School
Summer School

SPORTS FOR LAUGHS _____ CO36
See also: DR22 For Sports Fans

All the Marbles
The Bad News Bears
The Best of Times
The Bingo Long Traveling All-Stars and
    Motor Kings
Bull Durham
The Caddy
Fastbreak
Johnny Be Good

The Longest Yard
Major League
North Dallas Forty
Paper Lion
Pat and Mike
Slap Shot
Stroker Ace
Wildcats

FISH OUT OF WATER: FUNNY TALES OF MISPLACED PERSONS _____ CO37

Adventures in Babysitting
After Hours
All of Me
Back to the Future
Bagdad Cafe
Beverly Hills Cop
Beverly Hills Cop II
Big
Bill and Ted's Excellent Adventure
Chances Are
Coming to America
"Crocodile" Dundee
"Crocodile" Dundee II
Desperately Seeking Susan
Down and Out in Beverly Hills
Dream a Little Dream
The Dream Team

18 Again!
The Experts
Freaky Friday
Howard the Duck
Maxie
Mr. Mom
Moon Over Parador
Moscow on the Hudson
My Man Godfrey
Peggy Sue Got Married
The Secret of My Success
Splash
Sullivan's Travels
Tough Guys
Trading Places
Yentl

UNIFORMLY FUNNY: SERVICE COMEDIES _____ CO38

At War With the Army
Biloxi Blues
Buck Privates
Good Morning, Vietnam
How I Won the War
Kelly's Heroes
M*A*S*H
Off Limits (1953)
Operation Petticoat

Private Benjamin
Privates on Parade
The Secret War of Harry Frigg
Shoulder Arms (in The Chaplin Revue)
Soldier in the Rain
Stripes
Up in Arms
Up the Creek (1958)
The Wackiest Ship in the Army

STAR CHECK LIST: MAE WEST _____ CO39

My Little Chickadee
Sextette

She Done Him Wrong

STAR CHECK LIST: BOB HOPE _____ CO40

Boy, Did I Get a Wrong Number!
Cancel My Reservation
The Great Lover
The Lemon Drop Kid
My Favorite Brunette
Off Limits (1953)
The Paleface
Paris Holiday

The Princess and the Pirate
The Road to Bali
The Road to Rio
Road to Utopia
The Seven Little Foys
Son of Paleface
Sorrowful Jones
They Got Me Covered

STAR CHECK LIST: DANNY KAYE _____ CO41

The Court Jester
Hans Christian Andersen
The Inspector General
The Kid From Brooklyn

The Secret Life of Walter Mitty
Up in Arms
White Christmas
Wonder Man

STAR CHECK LIST: JUDY HOLLIDAY _____ CO42

Adam's Rib
Bells Are Ringing

Born Yesterday
It Should Happen to You

STAR CHECK LIST: ROBIN WILLIAMS _____ CO43

The Adventures of Baron Munchausen
The Best of Comic Relief
The Best of Times
Club Paradise
Comic Relief 2
Comic Relief III
An Evening With Robin Williams

Good Morning, Vietnam
Moscow on the Hudson
Popeye
Robin Williams Live!
Seize the Day
The Survivors
The World According to Garp

STAR CHECK LIST: TOM HANKS _____ CO44

Bachelor Party
Big
The Burbs
Dragnet (1987)
Every Time We Say Goodbye
He Knows You're Alone

The Man With One Red Shoe
The Money Pit
Nothing in Common
Punch Line
Splash
Volunteers

STAR CHECK LIST: MICHAEL KEATON _____ CO45

Batman (1989)
Beetlejuice
Clean and Sober
The Dream Team
Gung Ho (1986)

Johnny Dangerously
Mr. Mom
Night Shift
The Squeeze
Touch and Go (1986)

DIRECTOR CHECK LIST: BLAKE EDWARDS ———————————— CO46

Blind Date (1987)
Breakfast at Tiffany's
The Curse of the Pink Panther
The Days of Wine and Roses
Experiment in Terror
A Fine Mess
The Great Race
The Man Who Loved Women (1983
 version)
Micki and Maude
Operation Petticoat
The Perfect Furlough
The Pink Panther
The Pink Panther Strikes Again

The Return of the Pink Panther
The Revenge of the Pink Panther
S.O.B.
A Shot in the Dark
Skin Deep
Sunset
The Tamarind Seed
10
That's Life!
This Happy Feeling
The Trail of the Pink Panther
Victor/Victoria
Wild Rovers

WRITER-DIRECTOR CHECK LIST: JOHN HUGHES ——————— CO47

The Breakfast Club
Ferris Bueller's Day Off
The Great Outdoors*
Mr. Mom**
Nate and Hayes**
National Lampoon's Class Reunion**
National Lampoon's European
 Vacation**

National Lampoon's Vacation**
Planes, Trains and Automobiles
Pretty in Pink*
She's Having a Baby
Sixteen Candles
Some Kind of Wonderful*
Weird Science

*producer only
**writer only

Chapter Four

CULT FILMS
(CU)

MIDNIGHT MOVIES _____ **CU1**

Angel Heart
Blue Velvet
A Clockwork Orange
Dawn of the Dead
Eraserhead
The Harder They Come
Harold and Maude
King of Hearts
Magical Mystery Tour
Myra Breckenridge
Night of the Living Dead

Outrageous!
Performance
Pink Flamingos
Reefer Madness
Rock 'n' Roll High School
Rude Boy
Sid and Nancy
Something Wild
Stranger Than Paradise
The Texas Chainsaw Massacre
200 Motels

CAMP CULT _____ **CU2**

Beyond the Valley of the Dolls
Bride of the Gorilla
The Conqueror
The Cool and the Crazy
Forbidden Zone
The Fountainhead
Heat (1972)
High School Confidential
Hush . . . Hush Sweet Charlotte
The Killers (1964 version)
The Lonely Lady

Mommie Dearest
Myra Breckenridge
The Private Files of J. Edgar Hoover
Sextette
Shack Out on 101
Sincerely Yours
Strait-Jacket
What Ever Happened to Baby Jane?
The Wicked Lady
The Wild One
The Women

"HEAD" MOVIES _____ **CU3**

Altered States
Cocaine Cowboys
Easy Rider
Head
Performance
The Trip

200 Motels
2001: A Space Odyssey
Up in Smoke
Yellow Submarine
Zabriskie Point

CULT HORROR & SCIENCE FICTION _____ **CU4**

The Abominable Dr. Phibes
Altered States

Android
Andy Warhol's Dracula

Andy Warhol's Frankenstein
Barbarella
Basket Case
A Boy and His Dog
Brazil
The Bride of Frankenstein
The Brood
A Clockwork Orange
Conqueror Worm
Dark Star
Daughters of Darkness
Dawn of the Dead
The Day the Earth Stood Still
Death Race 2000
Fahrenheit 451
Forbidden Planet
Freaks
Glen and Randa
Halloween
The Hills Have Eyes
I Walked With a Zombie
The Incredible Shrinking Man

The Incredibly Strange Creatures Who
   Stopped Living and Became Crazy
   Mixed-Up Zombies
Invasion of the Bee Girls
Invasion of the Body Snatchers (1956 &
   1978 versions)
King Kong (1933 version)
Liquid Sky
The Little Shop of Horrors (1960
   version)
The Man Who Fell to Earth
Martin
Night of the Living Dead
Piranha
Re-Animator
Scanners
The Texas Chainsaw Massacre
Theatre of Blood
Them
The Thing (From Another World)
2001: A Space Odyssey
The Wicker Man
Zardoz

CULT COMEDY _____ CU5

The Adventures of Buckaroo Banzai
   Across the 8th Dimension
After Hours
Beat the Devil
Bedazzled
Bedtime for Bonzo
Brewster McCloud
La Cage aux Folles
Eating Raoul
Get Crazy
Greetings
Harold and Maude
The Heartbreak Kid
Heathers
Hollywood Boulevard

It's a Gift
King of Comedy
King of Hearts
The Ladykillers
Little Murders
Morgan: A Suitable Case for Treatment
My Dinner With Andre
Pee-wee's Big Adventure
Repo Man
The Ruling Class
Something for Everyone
To Be or Not to Be (1943 version)
Used Cars
Where's Poppa?

NOTORIOUSLY SEXY _____ CU6

Angel Heart
Baby Doll
Barbarella
Beyond the Valley of the Dolls
Body Heat
Butterfly
Crimes of Passion

Daughters of Darkness
Devil in the Flesh
Ecstasy
The Fourth Man
Last Tango in Paris
Liquid Sky
The Night Porter

9½ Weeks
Pandora's Box
She's Gotta Have It
Something for Everyone
Summer Lovers

Tales of Ordinary Madness
Thief of Hearts
Two Moon Junction
The Unbearable Lightness of Being

FAMOUS FOR GORE AND VIOLENCE _____ CU7

Across 110th Street
Basket Case
The Brood
Dawn of the Dead
Enter the Dragon
The Evil Dead
Fingers
The Fly (1986 version)
Mad Max
Maniac
Mother's Day

Ms. 45
Night of the Living Dead
Point Blank
Re-Animator
Scanners
Scarface (1983 version)
Shogun Assassin
Taxi Driver
The Texas Chainsaw Massacre
The Warriors
The Wild Bunch

CENSORED OR BANNED MOVIES _____ CU8

Baby Doll
Carnal Knowledge
Ecstasy
Freaks
Hail Mary

North Star
The Outlaw
Peeping Tom
Viridiana

POLITICAL STATEMENTS _____ CU9
See also: DR21 Political Dramas

The Battle of Algiers
Billy Jack
Burn!
The Harder They Come
The Manchurian Candidate
The Parallax View
Potemkin

Salt of the Earth
Strike!
Sympathy for the Devil
Ten Days That Shook the World/
    October
Winter Kills

FOOTAGE ADDED FOR VIDEO _____ CU10

And God Created Woman
Angel Heart
The Bad Sleep Well
Blade Runner
The Bullfighter and the Lady
Crimes of Passion
The Executioner's Song
Frankenstein (1931 version)

Hellbound: Hellraiser II
The Hidden Fortress
Isadora
Johnny Be Good
Lawrence of Arabia
Lost Horizon
Mr. Skeffington
New York, New York

Pat Garrett and Billy the Kid
Scandal
The Sea Hawk
The Sicilian
Star Trek--The Motion Picture
Stealing Heaven
Stop Making Sense
Thief of Hearts

This Is Elvis
Touch of Evil
Two English Girls
The Wedding March
When Time Ran Out
Wild Rovers
The Wizard of Oz

"BAD" MOVIES _____ CU11

Attack of the Killer Tomatoes
Cocaine Fiends
Glen or Glenda?
Plan 9 From Outer Space

Reefer Madness
Robot Monster
Terror of Tiny Town
They Saved Hitler's Brain

BAD TASTE? YOU BE THE JUDGE _____ CU12

Andy Warhol's Bad
Blue Velvet
Desperate Living
Eraserhead
Female Trouble
Flesh
Heat (1972)

Mondo Trasho
Multiple Maniacs
Pink Flamingos
Polyester
Suburbia
Trash
Where's Poppa?

CULT MOVIES BY FAMOUS DIRECTORS _____ CU13

Beat the Devil (John Huston)
The Collector (William Wyler)
Fahrenheit 451 (François Truffaut)
Last Tango in Paris (Bernardo
   Bertolucci)

Rio Bravo (Howard Hawks)
The Searchers (John Ford)
Vertigo (Alfred Hitchcock)

DIRECTORS WHO GOT THEIR STARTS WITH ROGER CORMAN _____ CU14

Boxcar Bertha (Martin Scorsese)
Caged Heat (Jonathan Demme)
Dementia 13 (Francis Ford Coppola)

Hollywood Boulevard (Joe Dante and
   Allan Arkush)
Night Call Nurses (Jonathan Kaplan)

ONE-SHOT DIRECTORS _____ CU15

The Honeymoon Killers (Leonard
   Kastle)
The Night of the Hunter (Charles
   Laughton)

One-Eyed Jacks (Marlon Brando)
The Senator Was Indiscreet (George S.
   Kaufman)

DOCUMENTARIES _____ CU16
See also: MU10 Rock Concert Films, MU11 Rock Documentaries

America at the Movies
Arruza
The Atomic Cafe
Best Boy
Burden of Dreams
Dear America: Letters Home From
 Vietnam
Gates of Heaven
George Stevens: A Filmmaker's Journey
Gizmo!
Harlan County, U.S.A.
Hearts and Minds
The Hellstrom Chronicle
Hotel Terminus
Koyaanisqatsi
Lenny Bruce
Let There Be Light
Louisiana Story
Lulu in Berlin
Marjoe
Marlene

Millhouse: A White Comedy
Nanook of the North
Night and Fog
Olympia
Pumping Iron
Pumping Iron II: The Women
Roger Corman: Hollywood's Wild
 Angel
Say Amen, Somebody
A Sense of Loss
Shoah
The Sorrow and the Pity
Streetwise
Ten Days That Shook the World/
 October
The Thin Blue Line
This Is Korea/December 7
The Times of Harvey Milk
Triumph of the Will
Vernon, Florida
Vietnam: In the Year of the Pig

CULT CASTING _____ CU17

After Hours
Candy Mountain
Casino Royale
Catch-22
The Chase
Dancing Lady
Dinner at Eight
Grand Hotel
Harold and Maude

Into the Night
It's a Mad Mad Mad Mad World
Johnny Guitar
The Last Tycoon
The Magnificent Seven
The Outsiders
Spies Like Us
A Wedding
Winter Kills

REMAKES OF FAMOUS MOVIES _____ CU18
See also: FF36 Foreign Films and Their American Remakes
Note: Remake title is listed first; original title, if different, follows in parentheses.

Against All Odds (1984) (Out of the
 Past)
The Bride (The Bride of Frankenstein)
The Champ
D.O.A.
Diary of a Chambermaid
Farewell, My Lovely (Murder, My
 Sweet)
The Fly
Heaven Can Wait (Here Comes Mr.
 Jordan)

House of Wax (Mystery of the Wax
 Museum)
Invaders From Mars
Invasion of the Body Snatchers
King Kong
The Lady Vanishes
The Man Who Knew Too Much
Mogambo (Red Dust)
Nosferatu the Vampyre (Nosferatu)
The Phantom of the Opera
The Postman Always Rings Twice

Scarface
Silk Stockings (Ninotchka)
Stage Struck (1958) (Morning Glory)
A Star Is Born
Switching Channels (His Girl Friday)

The Thing (The Thing (From Another World))
The 39 Steps
To Be or Not to Be

DIRECTOR CHECK LIST: MICHAEL POWELL _____ CU19
*All co-directed with Emeric Pressburger, except ***

Black Narcissus
The Forty-Ninth Parallel
Ill Met by Moonlight
The Life and Death of Colonel Blimp
One of Our Aircraft Is Missing

Peeping Tom*
Pursuit of the Graf Spee
The Red Shoes
The Spy in Black
Thief of Bagdad (1940 version)*

DIRECTOR CHECK LIST: MAX OPHULS _____ CU20

Caught
The Earrings of Madame De . . .
Letter From an Unknown Woman

Lola Montes
La Ronde

DIRECTOR CHECK LIST: JEAN COCTEAU _____ CU21

Beauty and the Beast (1946 version)

Blood of a Poet

DIRECTOR CHECK LIST: SAMUEL FULLER _____ CU22

The American Friend*
The Baron of Arizona
The Big Red One
China Gate
Hammett*
I Shot Jesse James

Run of the Arrow
Shark!
Slapstick of Another Kind*
The Steel Helmet
Underworld, U.S.A.

* actor only

DIRECTOR CHECK LIST: NICHOLAS RAY _____ CU23

The American Friend*
55 Days at Peking
Flying Leathernecks
In a Lonely Place
Johnny Guitar
King of Kings
Knock on Any Door

The Lusty Men
Rebel Without a Cause
They Live by Night

Documentary subject
Lightning Over Water

* actor only

DIRECTOR CHECK LIST: DOUGLAS SIRK _____ CU24

The First Legion
Imitation of Life (1959 version)
Magnificent Obsession

A Time to Live and a Time to Die
Written on the Wind

DIRECTOR CHECK LIST: ROBERT ALTMAN _____ CU25

Aria (co-director)
Beyond Therapy
Brewster McCloud
Buffalo Bill & the Indians
Come Back to the Five and Dime,
  Jimmy Dean, Jimmy Dean
Countdown
Fool for Love
The James Dean Story (co-director)
M*A*S*H

McCabe and Mrs. Miller
Nashville
O.C. and Stiggs
Popeye
Quintet
Secret Honor
Streamers
That Cold Day in the Park
A Wedding

DIRECTOR CHECK LIST: ALAN RUDOLPH _____ CU26

Choose Me
Endangered Species
Made in Heaven
The Moderns
Premonition

Roadie
Songwriter
Trouble in Mind
Welcome to L.A.

DIRECTOR CHECK LIST: WALTER HILL _____ CU27

Brewster's Millions
Crossroads
The Driver
Extreme Prejudice
48HRS.
Hard Times

The Long Riders
Red Heat
Southern Comfort
Streets of Fire
The Warriors

DIRECTOR CHECK LIST: BRIAN DEPALMA _____ CU28

Blow Out
Body Double
Carrie (1976)
Dressed to Kill
The Fury
Greetings
Home Movies

Obsession
Phantom of the Paradise
Scarface (1983 version)
Sisters
The Untouchables
The Wedding Party (co-director)
Wise Guys

DIRECTOR CHECK LIST: JOHN CARPENTER _____ CU29

Assault on Precinct 13
Big Trouble in Little China

Christine
Dark Star

Escape From New York
The Fog
Halloween
Prince of Darkness

Starman
They Live
The Thing

DIRECTOR CHECK LIST: LARRY COHEN _____ **CU30**

Black Caesar
Deadly Illusion (co-director)
God Told Me To
Hell Up in Harlem
It Lives Again

It's Alive!
The Private Files of J. Edgar Hoover
Q: The Winged Serpent
Special Effects
The Stuff

DIRECTOR CHECK LIST: KEN RUSSELL _____ **CU31**

Altered States
Aria (co-director)
Billion Dollar Brain
Crimes of Passion
The Devils
Gothic
Lair of the White Worm

Lisztomania
Mahler
The Rainbow
Salome's Last Dance
Tommy
Women in Love

DIRECTOR CHECK LIST: JOHN BOORMAN _____ **CU32**

Deliverance
The Emerald Forest
Excalibur
Exorcist II: The Heretic

Hope and Glory
Point Blank
Zardoz

DIRECTOR CHECK LIST: RIDLEY SCOTT _____ **CU33**

Alien
Blade Runner
The Duellists

Legend
Someone to Watch Over Me

DIRECTOR CHECK LIST: NICOLAS ROEG _____ **CU34**

Castaway
Don't Look Now
Eureka
Insignificance

The Man Who Fell to Earth
Performance (co-director)
Track 29

DIRECTOR CHECK LIST: RICHARD LESTER _____ **CU35**

Butch and Sundance: The Early Days
Cuba

Finders Keepers
The Four Musketeers

A Funny Thing Happened on the Way
   to the Forum
A Hard Day's Night
Help!
How I Won the War
Juggernaut (1974)

Petulia
The Ritz
Robin and Marian
Superman II
Superman III
The Three Musketeers (1974 version)

DIRECTOR CHECK LIST: BILL FORSYTH ———————————— CU36

Comfort and Joy
Gregory's Girl
Housekeeping

Local Hero
That Sinking Feeling

DIRECTOR CHECK LIST: TERRENCE MALICK ———————————— CU37

Badlands

Days of Heaven

DIRECTOR CHECK LIST: DAVID LYNCH ———————————— CU38

Blue Velvet
Dune
The Elephant Man

Eraserhead
Zelly and Me*

*actor only

DIRECTOR CHECK LIST: JONATHAN DEMME ———————————— CU39

Caged Heat
Citizens Band
Crazy Mama
Last Embrace
Married to the Mob
Melvin and Howard

Something Wild
Stop Making Sense
Swimming to Cambodia
Swing Shift
Who Am I This Time?

DIRECTOR CHECK LIST: JOE DANTE ———————————— CU40

Amazon Women on the Moon (co-
   director)
The Burbs
Explorers
Gremlins

Hollywood Boulevard (co-director)
The Howling
Innerspace
Piranha
Twilight Zone: The Movie (co-director)

DIRECTOR CHECK LIST: ALLAN ARKUSH ———————————— CU41

Caddyshack II
Deathsport
Get Crazy

Heartbeeps
Hollywood Boulevard (co-director)
Rock 'n' Roll High School

DIRECTOR CHECK LIST: PAUL BARTEL ———————————— **CU42**

Caddyshack II*
Cannonball
Chopping Mall*
Death Race 2000
Eating Raoul**
Hollywood Boulevard*
Killer Party*

The Longshot
Lust in the Dust
Not for Publication
Rock 'n' Roll High School*
Scenes From the Class Struggle in
    Beverly Hills**

* actor only
** also actor

DIRECTOR CHECK LIST: JOHN WATERS ———————————— **CU43**

Desperate Living
Female Trouble
Hairspray*
Mondo Trasho

Multiple Maniacs
Pink Flamingos
Polyester
Something Wild**

* also actor
** only actor

DIRECTOR CHECK LIST: PAUL MORISSEY ———————————— **CU44**

Andy Warhol's Dracula
Andy Warhol's Frankenstein
Flesh
Heat (1972)

The Hound of the Baskervilles (1977
    version)
Mixed Blood
Spike of Bensonhurst
Trash

DIRECTOR CHECKLIST: ED WOOD, JR. ———————————— **CU45**

Bride of the Monster
Glen or Glenda?
Jail Bait
Plan 9 from Outer Space

Revenge of the Dead
The Sinister Urge
The Violent Years

ACTOR CHECK LIST: DENNIS HOPPER ———————————— **CU46**

The American Friend
Apocalypse Now
Black Widow
Blue Velvet
Colors*
Cool Hand Luke
Easy Rider**
Giant
Gunfight at the O.K. Corral

Hang 'Em High
Hoosiers
The Inside Man
King of the Mountain
The Last Movie**
Mad Dog Morgan
My Science Project
O.C. and Stiggs
The Osterman Weekend

Out of the Blue**
The Pick-up Artist
Rebel Without a Cause
Riders of the Storm
Rumblefish
Running Out of Luck

The Sons of Katie Elder
Straight to Hell
The Texas Chainsaw Massacre II
Tracks
The Trip
True Grit

*director only
**also director

ACTOR CHECK LIST: RIP TORN ——————————————— CU47

Baby Doll
The Beastmaster
Beer
Birch Interval
The Cincinnati Kid
City Heat
Coma
Cotter
Cross Creek
Extreme Prejudice
First Family
Flashpoint
Heartland
Hit List
Jinxed

The Man Who Fell to Earth
Misunderstood
Nadine
Nasty Habits
One-Trick Pony
Payday
Pork Chop Hill
The President's Plane Is Missing
The Private Files of J. Edgar Hoover
Rape and Marriage: The Rideout Case
The Seduction of Joe Tynan
Songwriter
A Stranger Is Watching
Summer Rental
You're a Big Boy Now

ACTOR CHECK LIST: WARREN OATES ——————————————— CU48

Badlands
Blue Thunder
The Border
The Brink's Job
Bring Me the Head of Alfredo Garcia
Cockfighter
Crooks and Coronets
Dillinger
Dixie Dynamite
Drum
The Hired Hand
In the Heat of the Night
Major Dundee
1941

92 in the Shade
Race With the Devil
Return of the Seven
Ride the High Country
The Shooting
Sleeping Dogs
Smith!
Stripes
There Was a Crooked Man
The Thief Who Came to Dinner
Tough Enough
White Dawn
The Wild Bunch

ACTOR CHECK LIST: HARRY DEAN STANTON ——————————————— CU49

Alien
The Black Marble
Christine

Cockfighter
Cool Hand Luke
Death Watch

Dillinger
Dream a Little Dream
Escape From New York
Farewell, My Lovely
Fool for Love
The Godfather, Part II
Kelly's Heroes
The Last Temptation of Christ
The Missouri Breaks
Mr. North
One From the Heart
One Magic Christmas
Paris, Texas
Pat Garrett and Billy the Kid
Pretty in Pink

Private Benjamin
The Proud Rebel*
Rafferty and the Gold Dust Twins
Rebel Rousers*
Red Dawn
Repo Man
Ride in the Whirlwind
The Rose
Stars and Bars
Straight Time
Twister
UFOria
Wise Blood
Young Doctors in Love

*billed as Dean Stanton

DIRECTOR CHECK LIST: PHILIP KAUFMAN _____ CU50

Invasion of the Body Snatchers (1979
   version)
The Right Stuff

The Unbearable Lightness of Being
The Wanderers
White Dawn

DIRECTOR CHECK LIST: EROL MORRIS _____ CU51

Gates of Heaven
The Thin Blue Line

Vernon, Florida

Chapter Five

DRAMA
(DR)

ROMANTIC DRAMAS _____ DR1

About Last Night
The Accidental Tourist
Atlantic City
Baby, It's You
Breathless (1983 version)
Children of a Lesser God
Chilly Scenes of Winter
Choose Me
Cocktail
Dangerous Liaisons
Days of Heaven
Dirty Dancing
Everybody's All American
The French Lieutenant's Woman
Fresh Horses
Goodbye, Columbus
A Handful of Dust
Hanover Street
Hard Choices
In a Shallow Grave
Independence Day
Last Tango in Paris
Love With the Proper Stranger
Made in Heaven
Mrs. Soffel

An Officer and a Gentleman
Pete 'n' Tillie
Racing With the Moon
The Rainbow
Robin and Marian
The Roman Spring of Mrs. Stone
The Romantic Englishwoman
The Slugger's Wife
Somewhere in Time
Sophie's Choice
Splendor in the Grass
Starman
The Sterile Cuckoo
Strangers When We Meet
Tender Mercies
Tequila Sunrise
Trouble in Mind
Turtle Diary
Two for the Road
The Unbearable Lightness of Being
Until September
Violets Are Blue
A Walk in the Spring Rain
Winter People
Women in Love

FOR A GOOD CRY _____ DR2
See also: CL6 Classic Tear Jerkers

Beaches
Careful, He Might Hear You
Clara's Heart
Dominick and Eugene
Duet for One
Gaby--A True Story
The Heart Is a Lonely Hunter
Imitation of Life (1959 version)
Love Story
Madame X (1966 version)
Mask
The Natural

Ordinary People
The Other Side of Midnight
Places in the Heart
Project X
Rage of Angels
Resurrection
Six Weeks
Sophie's Choice
Sweet Dreams
Tender Mercies
Terms of Endearment

FORBIDDEN LOVE _____ DR3

American Gigolo
Betrayal
Body Heat
The Collector
Coming Home
Crimes of Passion
Desert Hearts
Every Time We Say Goodbye
Falling in Love
Fatal Attraction
Five Days One Summer
Fool for Love
Georgy Girl
Hanna K.
Hard Choices
Jagged Edge
The Killing of Sister George
Last Tango in Paris
Lianna

Looking for Mr. Goodbar
Making Love
Maurice
Mayerling (1936 version)
My Beautiful Laundrette
Nijinsky
9½ Weeks
The Postman Always Rings Twice (1946
   & 1981 versions)
Prick Up Your Ears
Romeo and Juliet (1936 & 1968 versions)
Ryan's Daughter
Someone to Watch Over Me
Stealing Heaven
Sunday, Bloody Sunday
Swing Shift
Torch Song Trilogy
Two Moon Junction

THE FAMOUS AND NOTORIOUS _____ DR4
See also: MU5 Musical Life Stories

Amadeus
The Amazing Howard Hughes
Bound for Glory
Coal Miner's Daughter
Cross Creek
84 Charing Cross Road
The Elephant Man
Frances
Gandhi
Heart Beat
Heart Like a Wheel
The Incredible Sarah
Isadora
The Jackie Robinson Story
Julia
The Last Emperor
Lenny

MacArthur
The Miracle Worker
The Naked Civil Servant
Nijinsky
Out of Africa
Patton
Prick Up Your Ears
The Private Files of J. Edgar Hoover
Raging Bull
Reds
The Song of Bernadette
Stevie
Sunrise at Campobello
Sweet Dreams
Tucker: The Man and His Dream
Young Winston

HISTORICAL DRAMA _____ DR5

Anne of the Thousand Days
The Assassination of Trotsky
Barry Lyndon
Becket
Bonnie and Clyde
Burke and Wills
Burn!

The Cotton Club
Cromwell
Dangerous Liaisons
Daniel
The Devils
Dreamchild
Eight Men Out

Empire of the Sun
Hannah's War
Haunted Summer
Hester Street
Lady Jane
The Lion in Winter
A Man for all Seasons (1966 & 1988
  versions)
Marat/Sade
Matewan
The Mission
The Moderns
The Molly Maguires
Nicholas and Alexandra
A Night to Remember (1958)
1918

On Valentine's Day
Places in the Heart
Playing for Time
Pretty Baby
Ragtime
The Return of the Soldier
Revolution
Ship of Fools
The Sicilian
Spartacus
Swing Shift
Tai-Pan
Three Sovereigns for Sarah
A Town Like Alice
White Mischief

TRUE-LIFE CONTEMPORARY DRAMA _____ DR6

Act of Vengeance
All the President's Men
Buster
Castaway
Courage (1986)
Cry Freedom
A Cry in the Dark
Dance With a Stranger
Dog Day Afternoon
84 Charing Cross Road
Eleni
The Executioner's Song
The Falcon and the Snowman
Fatal Vision
Gaby--A True Story
Gideon's Trumpet
Gorillas in the Mist
Helter Skelter
The Honeymoon Killers
In Cold Blood
The Killing Fields
Lean on Me
Marie

Mask
Midnight Express
Missing
Mississippi Burning
The Onion Field
Patty Hearst
Prince of the City
Raid on Entebbe
The Right Stuff
Sakharov
Scandal
Serpico
Sid and Nancy
Silkwood
Stand and Deliver
Star 80
The Sugarland Express
Sybil
Talk Radio
10 Rillington Place
The Terry Fox Story
Weeds

MODERN PROBLEMS _____ DR7

About Last Night
Absence of Malice
Alamo Bay
Alice's Restaurant
The Baby Maker
The Big Chill

Birdy
Blue Collar
The Boost
The Border
Cal
Carnal Knowledge

The China Syndrome
Clean and Sober
Coming Home
The Conversation
Country
Cutter's Way
The Day After
The Deer Hunter
Distant Thunder (1988)
Dudes
Easy Rider
End of the Road
Executive Suite
F.I.S.T.
Gardens of Stone
Guess Who's Coming to Dinner
Hanna K.
Hardcore
Iceman
Jacknife
Katherine
Looking for Mr. Goodbar
Medium Cool
Miles From Home
Mississippi Burning
My Beautiful Laundrette

Nightbreaker
El Norte
Petulia
Project X
Promised Land
Return of the Secaucus 7
The River (1984)
Running on Empty
St. Elmo's Fire
Salvador
The Shadow Box
Special Bulletin
Streamers
Street Smart
Talk Radio
Testament
Twilight's Last Gleaming
The Ugly American
The Unbearable Lightness of Being
Under Fire
Wall Street
Wargames
Who'll Stop the Rain?
Windy City
A World Apart
Zabriskie Point

FAMILY TROUBLES _____ DR8

The Accidental Tourist
All My Sons
At Close Range
Bloodbrothers
Clara's Heart
The Color Purple
Country
Da
Dead Ringers
Death of a Salesman (1985 version)
Desert Bloom
Distant Thunder (1988)
Dominick and Eugene
East of Eden
Far North
Field of Dreams
First Born
Five Easy Pieces
The Good Father
The Good Mother
The Great Santini
High Tide
Interiors

Irreconcilable Differences
Islands in the Stream
Kramer vs. Kramer
Light of Day
Long Day's Journey Into Night
Mask
Memories of Me
Misunderstood
The Mosquito Coast
'night, Mother
Nothing in Common
Ordinary People
Out of the Blue
Paris, Texas
Places in the Heart
The Prince of Pennsylvania
Providence
Rain Man
A Raisin in the Sun
The River Niger
Rocket Gibraltar
Running on Empty
See You in the Morning

Shoot the Moon
Shy People
Sometimes a Great Notion
The Stone Boy
Tank

Terms of Endearment
Tribute
Twice in a Lifetime
The World According to Garp
A World Apart

PROBLEM KIDS _____ DR9

All the Right Moves
Bad Boys
The Boy Who Could Fly
The Boys Next Door
The Breakfast Club
The Chocolate War
D.A.R.Y.L.
David and Lisa
Empire of the Sun
The Escape Artist
Footloose
Foxes
Grandview, U.S.A.
The Heart Is a Lonely Hunter
Housekeeping
if . . .
The Karate Kid
The Karate Kid II
Less Than Zero
Lost Angels
Lucas
The Manhattan Project
Mask
The Member of the Wedding
The New Kids

New York Stories
Ordinary People
The Outsiders
Over the Edge
Permanent Record
Pretty in Pink
Rebel Without a Cause
Reckless
River's Edge
Rumblefish
Smooth Talk
Splendor in the Grass
Split Image
Square Dance
Stacking
Stand by Me
Suburbia
Taps
Tex
That Was Then, This Is Now
Ticket to Heaven
Vision Quest
Where the River Runs Black
The Wizard of Loneliness
Zelly and Me

TODAY'S WOMAN _____ DR10
See also: CL5 Women's Pictures

The Accused
Alice Doesn't Live Here Anymore
Anna
Another Woman
Beaches
The Bell Jar
The Burning Bed
Business as Usual
Courage (1986)
Crossing Delancey
Darling
Desert Hearts
Diary of a Mad Housewife
The Dollmaker

Duet for One
Entre Nous
Extremities
First Monday in October
The Good Mother
Gorillas in the Mist
The Group
Hanna K.
High Tide
Housekeeping
I'm Dancing as Fast as I Can
Independence Day
Just Between Friends
Marie

Mystic Pizza
Norma Rae
Nuts
Plenty
Rachel, Rachel
Raggedy Man
The Rain People
Rich and Famous
Shy People

Summer Wishes, Winter Dreams
Swing Shift
Testament
The Turning Point
An Unmarried Woman
Up the Sandbox
Vagabond
Working Girl
Working Girls

GOLDEN OLDSTERS _____ DR11

Cocoon
Cocoon: The Return
Dreamchild
Going in Style
The Grey Fox
Harry and Tonto

Kotch
On Golden Pond
Right of Way
Tough Guys
The Trip to Bountiful
The Whales of August

BACKSTAGE DRAMAS _____ DR12
See also: CL7 Show Business Stories, MU4 Musical Films About Show Biz

Bird
Carny
The Competition
Crossroads
Dancers
The Dresser
Eddie and the Cruisers
Flashdance
The Front
The Gig
Hearts of Fire
Honeysuckle Rose
Honky Tonk Man
I Could Go On Singing
The Idolmaker
The Incredible Sarah
Jo Jo Dancer: Your Life Is Calling
Nashville

Network
New York, New York
Nijinsky
One-Trick Pony
Payday
Pete Kelly's Blues
Punch Line
Purple Rain
The Rose
Round Midnight
Sid & Nancy
Sparkle
Staying Alive
Sweet Dreams
Talk Radio
Tap
Tender Mercies
The Turning Point

INSIDE THE MOVIE BUSINESS _____ DR13

An Almost Perfect Affair
Anna
The Barefoot Contessa
Blow Out
Day for Night
The Day of the Locust
8½

F/X
Frances
The French Lieutenant's Woman
The Goddess
Good Morning, Babylon
The Last Movie
The Last Tycoon

Mommie Dearest
The Oscar
Star 80
A Star Is Born (1937 & 1954 versions)
Strangers Kiss
The Stunt Man

Sunset Boulevard
Targets
The Way We Were
What Ever Happened to Baby Jane?
The Wild Party

BLACK LIFE _____ DR14

Aaron Loves Angela
The Autobiography of Miss Jane
   Pittman
Blue Collar
The Brother From Another Planet
Brother John
The Color Purple
Cornbread, Earl and Me
The Cotton Club
Cry Freedom
The Emperor Jones
For Love of Ivy
Jo Jo Dancer: Your Life Is Calling
Lady Sings the Blues
The Learning Tree

The Liberation of L.B. Jones
Mahogany
The Mark of the Hawk
Native Son
A Raisin in the Sun
The River Niger
School Daze
She's Gotta Have It
The Sky Is Gray
A Soldier's Story
Something of Value
Sounder
Sparkle
Sweet Sweetback's Badasssss Song

LIFE IN THE BIG CITY _____ DR15

Aaron Loves Angela
Addict
Alphabet City
Barfly
Breakfast at Tiffany's
Bright Lights, Big City
The Brother From Another Planet
The Chosen
Colors
Cornbread, Earl and Me
The Cotton Club
Crossing Delancey
Dim Sum: a little bit of heart
Fear City
Five Corners
Flashdance
Fort Apache, The Bronx
Hester Street
House of Games

Mean Streets
Midnight Cowboy
Moscow on the Hudson
New York Stories
On the Nickel
The Pawnbroker
Petulia
The Pope of Greenwich Village
Signal 7
Slaves of New York
Smithereens
Someone to Watch Over Me
Stand and Deliver
Taxi Driver
Turk 182
Urban Cowboy
The Wanderers
The Warriors

LIVES OF CRIME _____ DR16
See also Action/Adventure, Mystery/Suspense Chapters

Against All Odds (1984)
At Close Range

Atlantic City
Badlands

Blood Simple
Bonnie and Clyde
Buster
Chiefs
Cop
Criminal Law
Cruising
Dance With a Stranger
The Executioner's Song
The Falcon and the Snowman
Fatal Vision
Helter Skelter
The Honeymoon Killers
In Cold Blood
Kansas
Last Rites
Mean Streets
Mikey and Nicky

Miles From Home
Mona Lisa
Mrs. Soffel
The Onion Field
Patty Hearst
Performance
Point Blank
Prince of the City
Prizzi's Honor
Serpico
Star Chamber
Straight Time
Suddenly
10 Rillington Place
True Confessions
Wisdom
Witness

COURT'S IN SESSION _____ DR17

The Accused
Anatomy of a Murder
. . . And Justice for All
Criminal Law
A Cry in the Dark
Inherit the Wind
Jagged Edge
Judgment at Nuremberg
Kramer vs. Kramer

Nuts
The Paradine Case
Suspect
To Kill a Mockingbird
Twelve Angry Men
The Verdict
Witness for the Prosecution (1957
   version)

PRISON DRAMAS _____ DR18

Bad Boys
Birdman of Alcatraz
Brubaker
Cool Hand Luke
The Criminal Code
Each Dawn I Die
Escape From Alcatraz
Fast-Walking
I Want to Live! (1958 version)

Kiss of the Spider Woman
The Longest Yard
Midnight Express
On the Yard
Riot in Cell Block 11
Short Eyes
There Was a Crooked Man
Weeds

MODERN FICTION ON FILM _____ DR19

The Accidental Tourist
All the King's Men
Arrowsmith
The Bell Jar
The Bostonians
Bright Lights, Big City
Butterfield 8

Cannery Row
Catch-22
Charly
The Color Purple
Daisy Miller
Daniel
The Day of the Locust

The Dead
Deliverance
Dodsworth
East of Eden (1955 version)
Elmer Gantry
Encore
The End of the Road
The Europeans
A Farewell to Arms (1932 version)
Fat City
From Here to Eternity
The Good Earth
Goodbye, Columbus
The Great Gatsby
The Group
A Handful of Dust
The Heart Is a Lonely Hunter
The Heiress
Housekeeping
Ironweed
Islands in the Stream
Justine
The Killers (1964 version)
The Last Tycoon
Lolita
Lonelyhearts
Lord of the Flies
Maurice
The Milagro Beanfield War
Native Son
The Natural
1984
92 in the Shade
Of Mice and Men (1939 version)
One Flew Over the Cuckoo's Nest

The Outsiders
A Passage to India
A Place in the Sun
Quartet (1949)
The Rainbow
The Razor's Edge (1946 & 1984 versions)
The Red Pony (1949 & 1973 versions)
Reflections in a Golden Eye
The Reivers
Reuben, Reuben
A Room With a View
Rumblefish
Seize the Day
A Separate Peace
Ship of Fools
Slaughterhouse Five
Slaves of New York
Sophie's Choice
Steppenwolf
Studs Lonigan
Tess
The Tin Drum
To Have and Have Not
Tomorrow
Trio
Turn of the Screw
Twister
The Unbearable Lightness of Being
Under the Volcano
The Virgin and the Gypsy
Wise Blood
The Witches of Eastwick
Women in Love
The World According to Garp

PLAYS ON FILM _____ DR20

See also: CL1 Classics
Illustrated: Literary Adaptations (Shakespeare)

Agnes of God
All My Sons
Betrayal
The Boys in the Band
Children of a Lesser God
Crimes of the Heart
Cyrano de Bergerac
Da
Dangerous Liaisons
A Day in the Death of Joe Egg
Death of a Salesman (1985 version)
Deathtrap
Desire Under the Elms
A Doll's House (1973 version)

84 Charing Cross Road
The Emperor Jones
An Enemy of the People
Equus
Extremities
The Glass Menagerie
Long Day's Journey Into Night
Marat/Sade
The Member of the Wedding
The Miracle Worker
Miss Firecracker
'night, Mother
Nuts
Our Town

Plenty
A Raisin in the Sun
The River Niger
The Shadow Box
Sleuth
A Soldier's Story
Streamers

A Streetcar Named Desire
Talk Radio
Torch Song Trilogy
True West
Who's Afraid of Virginia Woolf?
Whose Life Is It Anyway?
Young and Willing

POLITICAL DRAMAS ——————————————————————— DR21
See also: CU9 Political Statements

Advise and Consent
All the King's Men
All the President's Men
Being There
The Candidate
The Manchurian Candidate
No Way Out
The Parallax View

Power
Scandal
The Seduction of Joe Tynan
Seven Days in May
Under Fire
White Nights
Winter Kills
The Year of Living Dangerously

FOR SPORTS FANS ——————————————————————— DR22
See also: CO36 Sports for Laughs

All the Right Moves
American Anthem
American Flyers
Bang the Drum Slowly
Big Wednesday
Bobby Deerfield
Body and Soul (1947 & 1981 versions)
The Boy in Blue
Breaking Away
The Champ (1931 & 1979 versions)
Champion
Chariots of Fire
The Color of Money
The Dirt Bike Kid
Downhill Racer
Easy Living
Eight Men Out
Everybody's All American
Fat City
Field of Dreams
Golden Boy
Grand Prix
The Harder They Fall
Heart Like a Wheel
Hoosiers
Hot Shot
The Hustler
Inside Moves
The Jackie Robinson Story

The Karate Kid
The Karate Kid II
Knute Rockne—All American
The Last American Hero
Long Gone
The Natural
North Shore
On the Edge
One on One
Over the Top
Oxford Blues
Personal Best
Phar Lap
Pride of the Yankees
Raging Bull
Rocky (series)
Running Brave
The Set-Up
Somebody Up There Likes Me
Split Decisions
Streets of Gold
Sylvester
This Sporting Life
Thrashin'
Tiger Town
Vision Quest
Winning
Youngblood

CONTEMPORARY BRITISH DRAMA _____ DR23

Accident
Another Country
Betrayal
Billy Liar
Business as Usual
Cal
Chariots of Fire
Dance With a Stranger
Darling
The Dresser
Gandhi
The Good Father
A Handful of Dust
Heat and Dust
Knights and Emeralds
Little Dorritt
The Long Good Friday
Look Back in Anger
Marat/Sade
Mona Lisa
My Beautiful Laundrette

O Lucky Man!
Pascali's Island
The Ploughman's Lunch
Prick Up Your Ears
The Rainbow
The Romantic Englishwoman
Sammy and Rosie Get Laid
Scandal
Seance on a Wet Afternoon
The Servant
The Shooting Party
Steaming
Stevie
Stormy Monday
Sunday, Bloody Sunday
This Sporting Life
Turtle Diary
Victim
Wetherby
White Mischief
Women in Love

STAR CHECK LIST: JACK NICHOLSON _____ DR24

Batman (1989)
The Border
Broadcast News
Carnal Knowledge
Chinatown
Easy Rider
Ensign Pulver
Five Easy Pieces
Goin' South*
Heartburn
Hell's Angels on Wheels
Ironweed
The Last Detail
The Last Tycoon
The Little Shop of Horrors (1960
    version)
The Missouri Breaks
On a Clear Day You Can See Forever

One Flew Over the Cuckoo's Nest
The Passenger
The Postman Always Rings Twice (1981
    version)
Prizzi's Honor
Psych-Out
The Raven (1963)
Rebel Rousers
Reds
Ride in the Whirlwind
The Shining
The Shooting
Studs Lonigan
Terms of Endearment
The Terror
Tommy
The Wild Ride
The Witches of Eastwick

*also director

STAR CHECK LIST: ROBERT DENIRO _____ DR25

Addict
Angel Heart

Bang the Drum Slowly
Bloody Mama

Brazil
The Deer Hunter
Falling in Love
The Godfather, Part II
Greetings
Jacknife
The King of Comedy
The Last Tycoon
Mean Streets
Midnight Run

The Mission
New York, New York
1900
Once Upon a Time in America
Raging Bull
The Swap
Taxi Driver
True Confessions
The Untouchables
The Wedding Party

STAR CHECK LIST: MERYL STREEP _____ **DR26**

A Cry in the Dark
The Deer Hunter
Falling in Love
The French Lieutenant's Woman
Heartburn
Holocaust
Ironweed
Julia

Kramer vs. Kramer
Manhattan
Out of Africa
Plenty
The Seduction of Joe Tynan
Silkwood
Sophie's Choice
Still of the Night

STAR CHECK LIST: JANE FONDA _____ **DR27**

Agnes of God
Any Wednesday
Barbarella
Barefoot in the Park
California Suite
Cat Ballou
The Chase
The China Syndrome
Comes a Horseman
Coming Home
The Dollmaker
A Doll's House (1973 version)
The Electric Horseman

Fun With Dick and Jane
The Game Is Over
Joy House
Julia
Klute
The Morning After
9 to 5
On Golden Pond
Rollover
Steelyard Blues
They Shoot Horses, Don't They?
A Walk on the Wild Side

STAR CHECK LIST: PAUL NEWMAN _____ **DR28**

Absence of Malice
Buffalo Bill and the Indians
Butch Cassidy and the Sundance Kid
Cat on a Hot Tin Roof
The Color of Money
Cool Hand Luke
The Drowning Pool
Exodus
Fort Apache, The Bronx
The Glass Menagerie*

Harper
Harry and Son**
Hombre
Hud
The Hustler
The Left-Handed Gun
The Life and Times of Judge Roy Bean
The Mackintosh Man
Paris Blues
Quintet

Rachel, Rachel*
The Secret War of Harry Frigg
The Shadow Box*
The Silver Chalice
Slap Shot
Somebody Up There Likes Me
Sometimes a Great Notion**

The Sting
Torn Curtain
The Towering Inferno
The Verdict
When Time Ran Out
Winning
The Young Philadelphians

*director only
**also director

STAR CHECK LIST: ROBERT REDFORD _____ DR29

All the President's Men
Barefoot in the Park
A Bridge Too Far
Brubaker
Butch Cassidy and the Sundance Kid
The Candidate
The Chase
Downhill Racer
The Electric Horseman
The Great Gatsby
The Great Waldo Pepper
The Hot Rock

Jeremiah Johnson
Legal Eagles
The Milagro Beanfield War*
The Natural
Ordinary People*
Out of Africa
The Sting
Tell Them Willie Boy Is Here
This Property Is Condemned
Three Days of the Condor
The Way We Were

*director only

STAR CHECK LIST: DUSTIN HOFFMAN _____ DR30

Agatha
All the President's Men
Death of a Salesman (1985 version)
The Graduate
Ishtar
Kramer vs. Kramer
Lenny
Little Big Man

Madigan's Millions
Marathon Man
Midnight Cowboy
Papillon
Rain Man
Straight Time
Straw Dogs
Tootsie

STAR CHECK LIST: WILLIAM HURT _____ DR31

The Accidental Tourist
Altered States
The Big Chill
Body Heat
Broadcast News

Children of a Lesser God
Eyewitness
Gorky Park
Kiss of the Spider Woman
A Time of Destiny

STAR CHECK LIST: HARRISON FORD _____ DR32

American Graffiti
Apocalypse Now

Blade Runner
The Conversation

Dead Heat on a Merry-Go-Round
The Empire Strikes Back
Force 10 From Navarone
Frantic (1988)
The Frisco Kid
Getting Straight
Hanover Street
Heroes

Indiana Jones and the Temple of Doom
The Mosquito Coast
Raiders of the Lost Ark
Return of the Jedi
Star Wars
Witness
Working Girl

STAR CHECK LIST: MARLON BRANDO _____ DR33

Apocalypse Now
The Appaloosa
Burn!
The Chase
Desiree
The Formula
The Fugitive Kind
The Godfather
Guys and Dolls
Julius Caesar (1953 version)
Last Tango in Paris
The Men
The Missouri Breaks

Morituri
Mutiny on the Bounty (1962 version)
The Nightcomers
On the Waterfront
One-Eyed Jacks
Reflections in a Golden Eye
Sayonara
A Streetcar Named Desire
Superman
The Ugly American
Viva Zapata!
The Wild One
The Young Lions

STAR CHECK LIST: WARREN BEATTY _____ DR34

Bonnie and Clyde
$ (Dollars)
George Stevens: A Filmmaker's Journey
Heaven Can Wait*
Ishtar
Lilith

McCabe and Mrs. Miller
The Parallax View
Reds**
The Roman Spring of Mrs. Stone
Shampoo
Splendor in the Grass

*also co-director
**also director

STAR CHECK LIST: FAYE DUNAWAY _____ DR35

The Arrangement
Barfly
Bonnie and Clyde
Burning Secret
The Champ (1979 version)
Chinatown
The Country Girl (1982 version)
The Disappearance of Aimee
Eyes of Laura Mars
The First Deadly Sin
The Four Musketeers
Little Big Man

Midnight Crossing
Mommie Dearest
Network
Ordeal by Innocence
Supergirl
The Thomas Crown Affair
Three Days of the Condor
The Three Musketeers (1974 version)
The Towering Inferno
Voyage of the Damned
The Wicked Lady

STAR CHECK LIST: SALLY FIELD ———————————————————— DR36

Absence of Malice
Back Roads
Beyond the Poseidon Adventure
The End
Heroes
Home for the Holidays
Hooper
Kiss Me Goodbye
Murphy's Romance

Norma Rae
Places in the Heart
Punch Line
Smokey and the Bandit
Smokey and the Bandit II
Stay Hungry
Surrender
Sybil
The Way West

STAR CHECK LIST: ROBERT DUVALL ———————————————— DR37

Apocalypse Now
Badge 373
The Betsy
Breakout
Bullitt
The Chase
Colors
The Conversation
Countdown
The Eagle Has Landed
The Godfather
The Godfather, Part II
The Great Northfield Minnesota Raid
The Great Santini
The Greatest
Hotel Colonial
Joe Kidd
The Killer Elite

Lady Ice
Let's Get Harry
The Lightship
M*A*S*H
The Natural
Network
The Pursuit of D. B. Cooper
The Rain People
The Seven Percent Solution
The Stone Boy
Tender Mercies
The Terry Fox Story
THX 1138
To Kill a Mockingbird
Tomorrow
True Confessions
True Grit

STAR CHECK LIST: SIDNEY POITIER ———————————————— DR38

The Bedford Incident
Brother John
Buck and the Preacher*
The Defiant Ones (1958 version)
Fast Forward**
For Love of Ivy
Guess Who's Coming to Dinner
Hanky Panky**
In the Heat of the Night
Let's Do It Again*
Lilies of the Field
Little Nikita

The Mark of the Hawk
The Organization
Paris Blues
A Piece of the Action*
A Raisin in the Sun
Shoot to Kill
Something of Value
Stir Crazy**
They Call Me MISTER Tibbs!
To Sir, With Love
Uptown Saturday Night*
The Wilby Conspiracy

* also director
** director only

STAR CHECK LIST: GENE HACKMAN _____ DR39

All Night Long
Another Woman
Bat 21
Bite the Bullet
Bonnie and Clyde
A Bridge Too Far
The Conversation
Doctors' Wives
The Domino Principle
Downhill Racer
Eureka
The French Connection
The French Connection 2
Full Moon in Blue Water
Hawaii
Hoosiers
I Never Sang for My Father
Lilith
March or Die

Marooned
Mississippi Burning
Misunderstood
Night Moves
No Way Out
The Poseidon Adventure
Power
Prime Cut
Reds
Scarecrow
Split Decisions
Superman
Superman II
Superman IV: The Quest for Peace
Target
Twice in a Lifetime
Uncommon Valor
Under Fire
Young Frankenstein

STAR CHECK LIST: DIANE KEATON _____ DR40

Annie Hall
Baby Boom
Crimes of the Heart
The Godfather
The Godfather, Part II
The Good Mother
Harry and Walter Go to New York
Heaven*
I Will, I Will . . . For Now
Interiors
The Little Drummer Girl

Looking for Mr. Goodbar
Love and Death
Lovers and Other Strangers
Manhattan
Mrs. Soffel
Play It Again, Sam
Radio Days
Reds
Shoot the Moon
Sleeper

*director only

STAR CHECK LIST: BURT LANCASTER _____ DR41

Airport
Apache
Atlantic City
Birdman of Alcatraz
Buffalo Bill and the Indians
Control
Conversation Piece
The Crimson Pirate
Elmer Gantry
Executive Action
Field of Dreams

The Flame and the Arrow
From Here to Eternity
Go Tell the Spartans
Gunfight at the O.K. Corral
The Island of Dr. Moreau
Judgment at Nuremberg
The Kentuckian*
The List of Adrian Messenger
Little Treasure
Local Hero
Moses

1900
The Osterman Weekend
The Professionals
The Rainmaker
Rocket Gibraltar
Run Silent, Run Deep
Separate Tables
Seven Days in May
Sorry, Wrong Number
Sweet Smell of Success

The Swimmer
Tough Guys
Trapeze
Twilight's Last Gleaming
Ulzana's Raid
The Unforgiven
Vengeance Valley
Vera Cruz
Zulu Dawn

*also director

STAR CHECK LIST: SHIRLEY MACLAINE _____ DR42

All in a Night's Work
The Apartment
Around the World in 80 Days
Being There
Can-Can
Cannonball Run II
A Change of Seasons
Gambit
Hot Spell
Irma La Douce

Loving Couples
Madame Sousatzka
Some Came Running
Sweet Charity
Terms of Endearment
The Trouble With Harry
The Turning Point
Two Mules for Sister Sara
Woman Times Seven

STAR CHECK LIST: LEE MARVIN _____ DR43

Bad Day at Black Rock
The Big Heat
The Big Red One
The Caine Mutiny
Cat Ballou
The Comancheros
Death Hunt
The Delta Force
The Dirty Dozen
Dog Day
Donovan's Reef
Gorky Park
The Great Scout and Cathouse
   Thursday
Gun Fury

The Killers (1964 version)
The Man Who Shot Liberty Valance
Monte Walsh
Paint Your Wagon
Pete Kelly's Blues
Point Blank
Prime Cut
The Professionals
Raintree County
Sergeant Ryker
Shack Out on 101
Ship of Fools
Shout at the Devil
The Wild One

STAR CHECK LIST: NICK NOLTE _____ DR44

Cannery Row
Death Sentence
The Deep
Down and Out in Beverly Hills

Extreme Prejudice
Farewell to the King
48HRS.
Grace Quigley

Heart Beat
New York Stories
North Dallas Forty
Return to Macon County
The Runaway Barge

Teachers
Three Fugitives
Under Fire
Weeds
Who'll Stop the Rain?

STAR CHECK LIST: PETER O'TOOLE _____ DR45

Becket
The Bible
Caligula
Club Paradise
Creator
Foxtrot
High Spirits
Kidnapped
The Last Emperor
Lawrence of Arabia
The Lion in Winter
Lord Jim
Man Friday

Man of La Mancha
Murphy's War
My Favorite Year
The Night of the Generals
Power Play
The Ruling Class
The Stunt Man
Supergirl
Svengali
Under Milk Wood
What's New, Pussycat?
Zulu Dawn

STAR CHECK LIST: KATHLEEN TURNER _____ DR46

The Accidental Tourist
Body Heat
A Breed Apart
Crimes of Passion
Jewel of the Nile
Julia and Julia

The Man With Two Brains
Peggy Sue Got Married
Prizzi's Honor
Romancing the Stone
Switching Channels

STAR CHECK LIST: DEBRA WINGER _____ DR47

Betrayed
Black Widow
Cannery Row
French Postcards
Legal Eagles
Made in Heaven

Mike's Murder
An Officer and a Gentleman
Slumber Party '57
Terms of Endearment
Thank God, It's Friday
Urban Cowboy

STAR CHECK LIST: MICKEY ROURKE _____ DR48

Angel Heart
Barfly
Body Heat
City in Fear
Diner
Eureka

9½ Weeks
The Pope of Greenwich Village
A Prayer for the Dying
Rape and Marriage: The Rideout Case
Rumblefish
The Year of the Dragon

STAR CHECK LIST: FRANK SINATRA _____ DR49
See also: MU26 Frank Sinatra Check List

The Detective
The Devil at 4 O'Clock
Double Dynamite
The First Deadly Sin
From Here to Eternity
The Man With the Golden Arm
The Manchurian Candidate

The Miracle of the Bells
Never So Few
Ocean's Eleven
The Pride and the Passion
Some Came Running
Suddenly
Von Ryan's Express

DIRECTOR CHECK LIST: DAVID LEAN _____ DR50

Blithe Spirit
The Bridge on the River Kwai
Brief Encounter
Dr. Zhivago
Great Expectations
Hobson's Choice

In Which We Serve (co-director)
Lawrence of Arabia
Oliver Twist (1948 version)
A Passage to India
Ryan's Daughter
Summertime

DIRECTOR CHECK LIST: FRANCIS FORD COPPOLA _____ DR51

Apocalypse Now
The Conversation
The Cotton Club
Dementia 13
Finian's Rainbow
Gardens of Stone
The Godfather
The Godfather, Part II
New York Stories (co-director)

One From the Heart
The Outsiders
Peggy Sue Got Married
The Rain People
Rip Van Winkle
Rumblefish
Tonight for Sure
Tucker: The Man and His Dream
You're a Big Boy Now

DIRECTOR CHECK LIST: MARTIN SCORSESE _____ DR52

After Hours
Alice Doesn't Live Here Anymore
Boxcar Bertha
The Color of Money
King of Comedy
The Last Temptation of Christ
The Last Waltz

Mean Streets
New York, New York
New York Stories (co-director)
Raging Bull
Round Midnight*
Taxi Driver**

*actor only
**also actor

DIRECTOR CHECK LIST: STANLEY KUBRICK _____ DR53

Barry Lyndon
A Clockwork Orange

Dr. Strangelove: or, How I Learned to
Stop Worrying and Love the Bomb

Full Metal Jacket
The Killing
Lolita
Paths of Glory

The Shining
Spartacus
2001: A Space Odyssey

DIRECTOR CHECK LIST: ROMAN POLANSKI — DR54

Chinatown*
Frantic (1988)
Knife in the Water
Macbeth (1971 version)
Pirates

Repulsion
Rosemary's Baby
The Tenant*
Tess

*also actor

DIRECTOR CHECK LIST: ROBERT BENTON — DR55

Bad Company
Kramer vs. Kramer
The Late Show

Nadine
Places in the Heart
Still of the Night

DIRECTOR CHECK LIST: SYDNEY POLLACK — DR56

Absence of Malice
Bobby Deerfield
The Electric Horseman
Jeremiah Johnson
Out of Africa
They Shoot Horses, Don't They?

This Property Is Condemned
Three Days of the Condor
Tootsie*
The Way We Were
The Yakuza

*also actor

DIRECTOR CHECK LIST: MILOS FORMAN — DR57

Amadeus
The Firemen's Ball
Hair

Loves of a Blonde
One Flew Over the Cuckoo's Nest
Ragtime

DIRECTOR CHECK LIST: SIDNEY LUMET — DR58

The Anderson Tapes
Daniel
Deathtrap
Dog Day Afternoon
Equus
Fail-Safe
The Fugitive Kind
Garbo Talks
The Group

Just Tell Me What You Want
Long Day's Journey Into Night
The Morning After
Murder on the Orient Express
Network
The Pawnbroker
Power
Prince of the City
Running on Empty

Serpico
Stage Struck
Twelve Angry Men

The Verdict
The Wiz

DIRECTOR CHECK LIST: ELIA KAZAN _____ DR59

The Arrangement
Baby Doll
East of Eden
A Face in the Crowd
The Last Tycoon

On the Waterfront
Splendor in the Grass
A Streetcar Named Desire
A Tree Grows in Brooklyn
Viva Zapata!

THE WORLD OF BUSINESS _____ DR60

The Amazing Howard Hughes
The Arrangement
The Betsy
Citizen Kane
Executive Suite
F.I.S.T.
The Formula
Giant
The Godfather

The Godfather, Part II
Great Guy
Mr. Arkadin
Nothing in Common
Rollover
Save the Tiger
Tucker: The Man and His Dream
Wall Street

SCHOOL DAYS _____ DR61
See also: CO35 Campus Comedy

Au Revoir, les Enfants
The Chocolate War
The Class of Miss MacMichael
Class of 1984
Dangerously Close
The Devil's Playground
Goodbye, Mr. Chips
if...

Lean on Me
The Paper Chase
The Prime of Miss Jean Brodie
The Principal
To Sir, With Love
Why Shoot the Teacher?
Zero for Conduct

SMALL TOWN LIFE _____ DR62

Blue Velvet
The Chase
Chiefs
The Deer Hunter
East of Eden
Fury
Grandview, U.S.A.
The Heart Is a Lonely Hunter
Independence Day
Murphy's Romance

1918
Our Town
Promised Land
Shadow of a Doubt
Shame (1988)
Signs of Life
Some Came Running
Splendor in the Grass
To Kill a Mockingbird
Vernon, Florida

STAR CHECK LIST: ALEC GUINNESS _____ DR63

The Bridge on the River Kwai
Brother Sun, Sister Moon
The Captain's Paradise
Cromwell
Damn the Defiant!
The Detective (1954)
Dr. Zhivago
The Empire Strikes Back
The Fall of the Roman Empire
Great Expectations
Hitler: The Last Ten Days
The Horse's Mouth
Kind Hearts and Coronets
The Ladykillers
The Lavender Hill Mob
Lawrence of Arabia

Little Dorritt
Little Lord Fauntleroy (1980 version)
Lovesick
The Malta Story
The Man in the White Suit
Murder by Death
A Passage to India
The Prisoner
The Promoter
The Quiller Memorandum
Raise the Titanic!
Scrooge (1970 version)
Star Wars
To Paris With Love
Tunes of Glory

STAR CHECK LIST: JACK LEMMON _____ DR64

Airport '77
The Apartment
The April Fools
Bell, Book and Candle
Buddy Buddy
The China Syndrome
The Days of Wine and Roses
Fire Down Below
Good Neighbor Sam
The Great Race
Irma La Douce
It Should Happen to You
Kotch*

Luv
Macaroni
Mass Appeal
Missing
Mister Roberts
The Odd Couple
The Out-of-Towners
The Prisoner of Second Avenue
Save the Tiger
Some Like It Hot
That's Life!
Tribute
The Wackiest Ship in the Army

*director only

STAR CHECK LIST: VANESSA REDGRAVE _____ DR65

Agatha
Bear Island
Blow Up
The Bostonians
Camelot
Consuming Passions
The Devils
Isadora
Julia
A Man for all Seasons (1966 & 1988
   versions)

Morgan: A Suitable Case for Treatment
Murder on the Orient Express
Playing for Time
Prick Up Your Ears
The Seven Percent Solution
Steaming
Three Sovereigns for Sarah
The Trojan Women
Wagner
Wetherby

STAR CHECK LIST: AL PACINO _____ DR66

...And Justice for All
Author! Author!
Bobby Deerfield
Cruising
Dog Day Afternoon
The Godfather

The Godfather, Part II
Revolution
Scarecrow
Scarface
Serpico

STAR CHECK LIST: JOANNE WOODWARD _____ DR67

A Christmas to Remember
The Drowning Pool
The End
A Fine Madness
The Fugitive Kind
Harry and Son
Paris Blues

Rachel, Rachel
The Shadow Box
The Stripper
Summer Wishes, Winter Dreams
Sybil
They Might Be Giants
Winning

STAR CHECK LIST: SISSY SPACEK _____ DR68

Badlands
Carrie (1976)
Coal Miner's Daughter
Crimes of the Heart
Ginger in the Morning
Heart Beat
Katherine
Marie

Missing
'night, Mother
Prime Cut
Raggedy Man
The River (1984)
Violets Are Blue
Welcome to L.A.

STAR CHECK LIST: MEL GIBSON _____ DR69

Attack Force Z
The Bounty
Gallipoli
Lethal Weapon
Lethal Weapon 2
Mad Max
Mad Max Beyond Thunderdome

Mrs. Soffel
The River (1984)
The Road Warrior
Summer City
Tequila Sunrise
Tim
The Year of Living Dangerously

STAR CHECK LIST: MICHAEL DOUGLAS _____ DR70

The China Syndrome
A Chorus Line
Coma
Fatal Attraction
It's My Turn

Jewel of the Nile
Napoleon and Samantha
Romancing the Stone
The Star Chamber
Wall Street

STAR CHECK LIST: JEFF BRIDGES _____ DR71

Against All Odds (1984)
Bad Company

Cutter's Way
Eight Million Ways to Die

Fat City
Hearts of the West
Heaven's Gate
Jagged Edge
King Kong (1976 version)
Kiss Me Goodbye
The Last American Hero
The Morning After
Nadine

See You in the Morning
Starman
Stay Hungry
Thunderbolt and Lightfoot
Tron
Tucker: The Man and His Dream
Winter Kills
The Yin and Yang of Mr. Go

STAR CHECK LIST: GLENN CLOSE _____ DR72

The Big Chill
Dangerous Liaisons
Fatal Attraction
Jagged Edge

Maxie
The Natural
The Stone Boy
The World According to Garp

STAR CHECK LIST: TOM CRUISE _____ DR73

All the Right Moves
Cocktail
The Color of Money
Legend
Losin' It

The Outsiders
Rain Man
Risky Business
Top Gun

STAR CHECK LIST: JESSICA LANGE _____ DR74

All That Jazz
Country
Crimes of the Heart
Everybody's All American
Far North
Frances

How to Beat the High Cost of Living
King Kong (1976 version)
The Postman Always Rings Twice (1981
     version)
Sweet Dreams
Tootsie

DIRECTOR CHECK LIST: MIKE NICHOLS _____ DR75

Biloxi Blues
Carnal Knowledge
Catch-22
The Day of the Dolphin
The Graduate

Heartburn
Silkwood
Who's Afraid of Virginia Woolf?
Working Girl

STAR CHECK LIST: SIGOURNEY WEAVER _____ DR76

Alien
Aliens
Deal of the Century
Eyewitness
Ghostbusters
Ghostbusters II

Gorillas in the Mist
Half Moon Street
Madman
One Man or Two
Working Girl
The Year of Living Dangerously

Chapter Six

FAMILY/CHILDREN'S
(FA)

DISNEY LIVE ACTION FEATURES ———————————————————————— **FA1**

Action/Adventure
Black Arrow (1984 version)
Condorman
Davy Crockett
Davy Crockett and the River Pirates
The Fighting Prince of Donegal
The Great Locomotive Chase
In Search of the Castaways
The Incredible Journey
Island at the Top of the World
The Journey of Natty Gann
Kidnapped (1960 version)
King of the Grizzlies
The Last Flight of Noah's Ark
The Light in the Forest
Lightning: The White Stallion
Miracle of the White Stallions
Nikki, Wild Dog of the North
Swiss Family Robinson
The Sword and the Rose
Ten Who Dared
Third Man on the Mountain
Toby Tyler
Treasure Island (1950 version)
20,000 Leagues Under the Sea

Comedy
The Absent-Minded Professor
The Barefoot Executive
Blackbeard's Ghost
The Boatniks
Candleshoe
The Cat From Outer Space
The Computer Wore Tennis Shoes
The Devil and Max Devlin
Freaky Friday
Gus
Herbie Goes Bananas
Herbie Goes to Monte Carlo
Herbie Rides Again
The Horse in the Gray Flannel Suit

Lt. Robin Crusoe, USN
Lots of Luck
The Love Bug
The Million Dollar Duck
The Misadventures of Merlin Jones
Monkeys Go Home!
The Monkey's Uncle
Moon Pilot
Never a Dull Moment
No Deposit, No Return
The North Avenue Irregulars
Now You See Him, Now You Don't
The One and Only Genuine Original
    Family Band
The Parent Trap
The Shaggy D. A.
The Shaggy Dog
Snowball Express
Son of Flubber
Superdad
That Darn Cat
The Trouble With Angels
The World's Greatest Athlete

Documentary
The Living Desert
Secrets of Life
The Vanishing Prairie
White Wilderness

Drama
Amy
The Blue Yonder
Charley and the Angel
Follow Me, Boys!
Greyfriars Bobby
Johnny Tremain
The Littlest Horse Thieves
The Littlest Outlaw
Napoleon and Samantha
Night Crossing

Pollyanna
So Dear to My Heart
Summer Magic
Those Calloways

Horror/Mystery/Suspense
Emil and the Detectives
Escape to Witch Mountain
The Moon-Spinners
Return to Witch Mountain
The Watcher in the Woods

Musical
Babes in Toyland
The Happiest Millionaire
Mary Poppins
Pete's Dragon

Science Fiction/Fantasy
Bedknobs and Broomsticks
The Black Hole
Darby O'Gill and the Little People
The Gnome-Mobile
The Three Lives of Thomasina
Tron
Unidentified Flying Oddball

Western
The Adventures of Bullwhip Griffin
The Apple Dumpling Gang
The Apple Dumpling Gang Rides Again
The Castaway Cowboy
Hot Lead and Cold Feet
Old Yeller
Savage Sam
Smith!

DISNEY ANIMATED FEATURES _____ FA2

Alice in Wonderland
Bambi
Cinderella
Dumbo
Lady and the Tramp
The Legend of Sleepy Hollow
Oliver and Company

Pinocchio (1940 version)
Robin Hood
Sleeping Beauty (1959 version)
The Sword in the Stone
The Three Caballeros
The Wind in the Willows

CLASSIC LITERATURE _____ FA3

The Adventures of Huckleberry Finn
  (1939 & 1985 versions)
The Adventures of Tom Sawyer (1938
  version)
Alice in Wonderland (1951 version)
Anne of Green Gables
Captains Courageous
A Connecticut Yankee in King Arthur's
  Court (1949 version)
David Copperfield
Great Expectations
Heidi (1937 version)

Little Lord Fauntleroy (1936 & 1980
  versions)
Mysterious Island
Oliver Twist (1922, 1933, & 1948
  versions)
The Prince and the Pauper (1937 & 1978
  versions)
Tom Brown's School Days (1940
  version)
Treasure Island (1934 & 1950 versions)
20,000 Leagues Under the Sea

FAMILY ADVENTURE _____ FA4

Across the Great Divide
The Adventures of Robin Hood
The Adventures of the Wilderness
  Family

Around the World in 80 Days
Around the World Under the Sea
At the Earth's Core
The Black Pirate

Cold River
The Crimson Pirate
Five Weeks in a Balloon
Gunga Din
Island of the Blue Dolphins
Ivanhoe
Journey of Natty Gann
Journey to the Center of the Earth
The Jungle Book (1942 version)
Kim
King Solomon's Mines (1950 version)
The Life and Times of Grizzly Adams
Lives of a Bengal Lancer
The Man in the Iron Mask
My Pet Monster
Mysterious Island
Never Cry Wolf

The New Adventures of Pippi
   Longstocking
Pippi Longstocking (series)
The Prisoner of Zenda (1937 version)
The Quest
The Railway Children
Return to Oz
Scaramouche
The Scarlet Pimpernel
The Sea Gypsies
Superman (series)
Sword of the Valiant
Tarzan, the Ape Man (1932 version)
The Thief of Bagdad (1940 version)
Wee Willie Winkie
When the North Wind Blows
The Wilderness Family, Part 2
Young Sherlock Holmes

ANIMAL STORIES _____ FA5

All Creatures Great and Small
The Amazing Dobermans
Benji
Benji Takes a Dive at Marineland
Benji, the Hunted
Big Red
Black Beauty (1946 & 1971 versions)
The Black Stallion
The Black Stallion Returns
Blue Fire Lady
Born Free
Casey's Shadow
Charlie, the Lonesome Cougar
The Day of the Dolphin
A Dog of Flanders
For the Love of Benji
The Golden Seal
Goldy: The Last of the Golden Bears
Hambone and Hillie

The Incredible Journey
International Velvet
Lassie Come Home
The Legend of Lobo
Lightning: The White Stallion
Living Free
The Magic of Lassie
Mighty Joe Young
The Miracle of the White Stallions
National Velvet
Nikki, Wild Dog of the North
Oh! Heavenly Dog
Old Yeller
Phar Lap
The Red Pony (1949 & 1973 versions)
Ring of Bright Water
Sylvester
Where the Red Fern Grows
The Yearling

COMEDY _____ FA6
See also: COMEDY Check Lists—CO18 Charlie
Chaplin, CO19 Buster Keaton, CO20 Laurel and Hardy,
CO21 The Marx Bros., CO41 Danny Kaye

Big Top Pee-wee
C.H.O.M.P.S.
A Christmas Story
Cinderfella

Ernest Goes to Camp
Ernest Saves Christmas
The Great Race
Hawmps!

Hollywood or Bust
It's a Mad Mad Mad Mad World
Little Miss Marker (1980 version)
Matilda
Oh God!
Oh God! Book II
Oh God! You Devil

On the Right Track
The Peanut Butter Solution
Pee-wee's Big Adventure
The Prize Fighter
They Went That-a-Way and That-a-Way
Who Framed Roger Rabbit

DRAMAS ABOUT CONTEMPORARY KIDS ————————————— FA7

Big Shots
Birch Interval
Bless the Beasts and Children
The Boy Who Could Fly
Casey's Shadow
The Champ (1979 version)
D.A.R.Y.L.
The Dirt Bike Kid
The Earthling
The Escape Artist
Fast Talking
From the Mixed-Up Files of Mrs. Basil
   E. Frankenweiler
Gregory's Girl

Hot Shot
I Am the Cheese
Jimmy the Kid
The Karate Kid
The Karate Kid II
Lucas
The Peanut Butter Solution
Rad
Savannah Smiles
Tiger Bay
Tiger Town
Where the River Runs Black
Whistle Down the Wind

SCIENCE FICTION/FANTASY ——————————————————— FA8
See also: SF 13 Family Fantasy/Sci-Fi

The Adventures of Baron Munchausen
*batteries not included
Battle for the Planet of the Apes
Beneath the Planet of the Apes
Close Encounters of the Third Kind
Conquest of the Planet of the Apes
The Dark Crystal
The Day the Earth Stood Still
E. T. The Extra-Terrestrial
The Empire Strikes Back
The Enchanted Forest
Escape From the Planet of the Apes
Explorers
Flight of the Navigator
From the Earth to the Moon
The Golden Voyage of Sinbad
Heartbeeps
The Hobbit
The Incredible Shrinking Man
Jason and the Argonauts
King Kong (1933 version)
Labyrinth
The Land of Faraway

Lord of the Rings
Masters of the Universe
The NeverEnding Story
The Phantom Tollbooth
Planet of the Apes
Return of the Jedi
The 7 Faces of Dr. Lao
The 7th Voyage of Sinbad
Sinbad and the Eye of the Tiger
Something Wicked This Way Comes
Star Trek (series)
Star Wars
Thief of Bagdad (1940 version)
Time Bandits
The Time Machine
tom thumb
Tuck Everlasting
The War of the Worlds
The Watcher in the Woods
The Water Babies
Willie Wonka and the Chocolate
   Factory
Willow

MUSICALS _____ FA9

Annie
Bugsy Malone
Camelot
Chitty Chitty Bang Bang
Cinderella (1964 version)
A Connecticut Yankee in King Arthur's
   Court (1949 version)
Doctor Dolittle
Fiddler on the Roof
Follow That Bird
Hans Christian Andersen
A Hard Day's Night
Help!
Jesus Christ Superstar
The King and I
Mary Poppins
Meet Me in St. Louis

The Music Man
My Fair Lady
Oklahoma!
Oliver!
Popeye
1776
Singin' in the Rain
The Sound of Music
South Pacific
State Fair (1962 version)
West Side Story
Willie Wonka and the Chocolate
   Factory
The Wiz
The Wizard of Oz (1939 version)
Yankee Doodle Dandy

NON-DISNEY ANIMATED FEATURES _____ FA10

The Adventures of an American Rabbit
The Adventures of Mark Twain
An American Tail
Animalympics
Bon Voyage, Charlie Brown
A Boy Named Charlie Brown
The Care Bears Movie
Charlotte's Web
The Chipmunk Adventure
Dorothy in the Land of Oz
The Dragon That Wasn't (Or Was He?)
Flight of the Dragons
Gnomes, Vol. 1
Gulliver's Travels (1939 version)
Here Come the Littles
Hey There, It's Yogi Bear
The Hobbit
It's an Adventure, Charlie Brown
Journey Back to Oz

Journey Through Fairyland
The Land Before Time
The Last Unicorn
The Lion, the Witch and the Wardrobe
Lord of the Rings
Mad Monster Party?
My Little Pony: The Movie
Puff the Magic Dragon
Quackbusters
Scruffy
The Secret of NIMH
Shinbone Alley
Snoopy Come Home
Starchaser: The Legend of Orin
Teddy Ruxpin: Teddy Outsmarts
   M.A.V.O.
Transformers: The Movie
Watership Down
The Wizard of Oz (1982 version)

WARNER BROS. CARTOON COLLECTIONS _____ FA11

The Best of Bugs Bunny and Friends
Bugs and Daffy's Carnival of the
   Animals
Bugs Bunny and Elmer Fudd Cartoon
   Festival
Bugs Bunny in King Arthur's Court
Bugs Bunny/Road Runner Movie

Bugs Bunny 3d Movie: 1001 Rabbit
   Tales
Bugs Bunny's Wacky Adventures
Daffy Duck: The Nuttiness
   Continues . . .
Daffy Duck's Movie: Fantastic Island
Elmer Fudd's Comedy Capers

Foghorn Leghorn's Fractured Funnies
The Looney, Looney, Looney Bugs
   Bunny Movie
Pepe Le Pew's Skunk Tales
Porky Pig and Daffy Duck Cartoon
   Festival

Road Runner vs. Wile E. Coyote: The
   Classic Chase
A Salute to Chuck Jones
A Salute to Friz Freleng
A Salute to Mel Blanc

CHECK LIST: FAERIE TALE THEATRE _____ FA12

Aladdin and His Wonderful Lamp
Beauty and the Beast (1984 version)
The Boy Who Left Home to Find Out
   About the Shivers
Cinderella (1984 version)
The Dancing Princesses
The Emperor's New Clothes
Goldilocks and the Three Bears
Hansel and Gretel
Jack and the Beanstalk (1983 version)
The Little Mermaid
Little Red Riding Hood
The Nightingale
The Pied Piper of Hamelin

Pinocchio (1984 version)
The Princess and the Pea
The Princess Who Never Laughed
Puss 'n' Boots
Rapunzel
Rip Van Winkle
Rumpelstiltskin
Sleeping Beauty (1985 version)
The Snow Queen
Snow White and the Seven Dwarfs (1983
   version)
The Tale of the Frog Prince
The Three Little Pigs
Thumbelina

CHRISTMAS STORIES _____ FA13

A Christmas Carol (1951 version)
Christmas in Connecticut
A Christmas Story
A Christmas to Remember
The Christmas Tree
Ernest Saves Christmas
It's a Wonderful Life

Miracle Down Under
Miracle on 34th Street
One Magic Christmas
Santa Claus, The Movie
Scrooge (1970 version)
Scrooged

STAR CHECK LIST: SHIRLEY TEMPLE _____ FA14

Baby, Take a Bow
The Bachelor and the Bobby Soxer
The Blue Bird
Bright Eyes
Captain January
Curly Top
Dimples
Fort Apache
Heidi (1937 version)
Just Around the Corner
The Little Colonel
Little Miss Broadway

The Little Princess
The Littlest Rebel
Miss Annie Rooney
Our Little Girl
Poor Little Rich Girl
Rebecca of Sunnybrook Farm
Stand Up and Cheer
Stowaway
Susannah of the Mounties
To the Last Man
Wee Willie Winkie

STAR CHECK LIST: THE MUPPETS ———————————————————— FA15

Children's Songs and Stories With the
    Muppets
Country Music with the Muppets
Fozzie's Muppet Scrapbook
The Great Muppet Caper
The Kermit and Piggy Story
Muppet Moments

The Muppet Movie
The Muppet Revue
Muppet Treasures
The Muppets Take Manhattan
Rock Music With the Muppets
Rowlf's Rhapsodies With the Muppets

Chapter Seven

FOREIGN FILMS
(FF)

FRANCE ——————————————————————————————————————— **FF1**

See also: FF12 Jean Renoir, FF13 François Truffaut, FF14 Jean-Luc Godard, FF15 Eric Rohmer, FF16 Jacques Tati Check Lists

ACTION/ADVENTURE
L'Addition
La Balance
Bob le Flambeur
Quest for Fire

COMEDY
A Nous la Liberté
Black and White in Color
La Cage aux Folles
La Cage aux Folles II
La Cage aux Folles 3: The Wedding
Cesar
Clean Slate
Les Comperes
Cousin, Cousine
Fanny
Get Out Your Handkerchiefs
Happy New Year (1973 version)
Marius
Mon Oncle d'Amerique
My New Partner
Next Year, If All Goes Well
A Pain in the A—
Pardon Mon Affaire
Le Sex Shop
The Tall Blonde Man With One Black
  Shoe
Three Men and a Cradle
Under the Roofs of Paris
A Very Curious Girl
Zero for Conduct

DRAMA
A Nos Amours
And Now My Love
L'Atalante
Au Revoir, Les Enfants
Bad Girls

Beau Pere
Betty Blue
La Boum
Cesar and Rosalie
Choice of Arms
Deathwatch
Diary of a Chambermaid (1964 version)
Diary of a Country Priest
Entre Nous
The Eternal Return
Forbbiden Games
The Game Is Over
Going Places
The Grand Highway
Heat of Desire
Hiroshima, Mon Amour
I Sent a Letter to My Love
Jean de Florette
Le Jour Se Leve
Last Year at Marienbad
Love Songs
Lumiere
Madame Rosa
A Man and a Woman
A Man and a Woman: 20 Years Later
Manon of the Spring
Mr. Klein
The Moon in the Gutter
Napoleon (1927)
The Passion of Joan of Arc
Providence
Rape of Love
The Return of Martin Guerre
La Ronde
A Simple Story
State of Siege
A Sunday in the Country
Sundays and Cybelle
Swann in Love

Thérèse
La Truite
Vagabond

MUSICALS
Le Bal
The Umbrellas of Cherbourg

MYSTERY/THRILLER
Cat and Mouse
Dear Detective
Diabolique
Diva

Rider on the Rain
Rififi
Sincerely, Charlotte
This Man Must Die
The Wages of Fear
Wedding in Blood
Z

SCIENCE FICTION/FANTASY
Beauty and the Beast (1946 version)
Blood of a Poet
Le Dernier Combat
Fantastic Planet

ITALY _____ **FF2**
See also: FF10 Federico Fellini, FF17 Michelangelo Antonioni, FF18 Bernardo Bertolucci
Check Lists

ACTION/ADVENTURE
Hercules
Mean Frank and Crazy Tony

COMEDY
All the Way, Boys
Big Deal on Madonna Street
Down and Dirty
Joke of Destiny
Love and Anarchy
Lovers and Liars
Macaroni
Malicious
The Seduction of Mimi
Seven Beauties
Sex With a Smile
We All Loved Each Other So Much
Where's Picone?
Wifemistress
Yesterday, Today and Tomorrow

DRAMA
Allonsanfan
The Battle of Algiers
Bellisima
The Bicycle Thief
Brother Sun, Sister Moon
Burn!
Christ Stopped at Eboli
The Damned
Dark Eyes
Death in Venice
Devil in the Flesh
The Eyes, The Mouth
The Family (1987)

The Garden of the Finzi-Continis
General Della Rovere
The Gospel According to St. Matthew
La Grande Bourgeoise
Henry IV
The Inheritance
L'Innocente
Massacre in Rome
The Night of the Shooting Stars
1900
La Nuit de Varennes
Open City
Padre Padrone
Paisan
Romeo and Juliet (1968 version)
Sacco and Vanzetti
Senso
A Special Day
Stromboli
Swept Away
Three Brothers
Time of Indifference
Two Women
Umberto D

HORROR
Beyond the Door
Beyond the Door II

MYSTERY/THRILLER
The Bird with the Crystal Plumage

SCIENCE FICTION/FANTASY
The Tenth Victim

GERMANY _____ FF3
See also: FF19 Werner Herzog, FF20 Rainer Werner Fassbinder, FF21 Wim Wenders Check Lists

ACTION/ADVENTURE
The Boat

COMEDY
Men
Sugarbaby

DRAMA
The Blue Angel
Christiane F.
Coup de Grace
Diary of a Lost Girl
The Inheritors
Kameradschaft
Kamikaze '89
Kricmhilde's Revenge
The Last Laugh
The Lost Honor of Katharina Blum
M
Maedchen in Uniform (1931 version)
A Man Like Eva
Pandora's Box
Passion

Siegfried
Spies
The Tin Drum
Tonio Kroger
Variety
The Wannsee Conference
The White Rose
Westfront 1918
Woman in Flames

HORROR
The Cabinet of Dr. Caligari
The Golem

MUSICAL
The Threepenny Opera

SCIENCE FICTION/FANTASY
Destiny
Metropolis
The NeverEnding Story
The Testament of Dr. Mabuse

JAPAN _____ FF4
See also: FF9 Akira Kurosawa, FF28 Toshiro Mifune Check Lists

ACTION/ADVENTURE
The One-Eyed Swordsman
Shogun Assassin

COMEDY
The Family Game
Tampopo
A Taxing Woman

DRAMA
The Ballad of Narayama
Double Suicide
Fires on the Plain
Floating Weeds
The Forty-seven Ronin, Part One
The Forty-seven Ronin, Part Two
Gate of Hell
The Go Masters
The Golden Demon
Himatsuri
The Human Condition
The Island

The Life of Oharu
Merry Christmas, Mr. Lawrence
Mishima
Odd Obsession
Sansho the Bailiff
Street of Shame
Ugetsu
Woman in the Dunes

HORROR
The Ghost of Yotsuya
Kwaidan

SCIENCE FICTION/FANTASY
Ghidrah, the Three-Headed Monster
Godzilla, King of the Monsters
Godzilla, 1985
Godzilla vs. Megalon
Gorath
The H-Man
The Human Vapor

The Last War
Mothra
The Mysterians

Rodan
Terror of Mechagodzilla

AUSTRALIA _____ **FF5**

ACTION/ADVENTURE
Escape 2000
Fortress
Gallipoli
The Lighthorsemen
Mad Dog Morgan
Mad Max
Mad Max Beyond Thunderdome
The Man From Snowy River
The Odd Angry Shot
The Quest
Razorback
Return to Snowy River, Part II
The Road Warrior
Walk Into Hell
We of the Never Never

COMEDY
Bliss
"Crocodile" Dundee
"Crocodile" Dundee II
Don's Party
Malcolm
Rikky and Pete
Touch and Go (1980)

DRAMA
Breaker Morant
Burke and Wills
Cactus
Caddie
Careful, He Might Hear You
Chain Reaction
A Cry in the Dark
The Devil's Playground
The Fringe Dwellers
The Getting of Wisdom

Ground Zero
Heatwave
High Tide
Kangaroo
The Killing of Angel Street
The Last Wave
Lonely Hearts
Man of Flowers
The Mango Tree
Miracle Down Under
My Brilliant Career
My First Wife
Newsfront
Now and Forever
Picnic at Hanging Rock
Puberty Blues
Rebel (1986)
Shame (1988)
Squizzy Taylor
Storm Boy
Summer City
Tim
A Town Like Alice
Traveling North
Weekend of Shadows
Who Killed Baby Azaria
Winter of Our Dreams
The Year of Living Dangerously

MUSICAL
Starstruck

MYSTERY/THRILLER
Dead Calm
Patrick
The Plumber

LATIN AMERICA _____ **FF6**
See also: FF11 Luis Buñuel Check List

ARGENTINA
Camila
Man Facing Southeast
Miss Mary
The Official Story

BRAZIL
Black Orpheus
Bye Bye Brazil
Doña Flor and Her Two Husbands
Gabriela

Hour of the Star
I Love You
Kiss of the Spider Woman
Pixote

MEXICO
Erendira

NICARAGUA
Alsino and the Condor

OTHER EUROPEAN COUNTRIES & THE SOVIET UNION ———————— **FF7**
See also: FF8 Ingmar Bergman, FF11 Luis Buñuel, FF22 Sergei Eisenstein Check Lists

CZECHOSLOVAKIA
Closely Watched Trains
Ecstasy
The Firemen's Ball
Loves of a Blonde
The Shop on Main Street

DENMARK
Babette's Feast
Pelle the Conqueror

HOLLAND
The Assault
The Fourth Man
Spetters

HUNGARY
Colonel Redl
Mephisto
The Revolt of Job
Time Stands Still

POLAND
Ashes and Diamonds
Kanal
Knife in the Water
Man of Iron
Man of Marble
Moonlighting (1982)
A Year of the Quiet Sun

SOVIET UNION
Moscow Does Not Believe in Tears
Shadows of Forgotten Ancestors
A Slave of Love
War and Peace (1968 version)

SPAIN
El Amor Brujo
Carmen
Dark Habits
Half of Heaven
Law of Desire
The Spirit of the Beehive
What Have I Done to Deserve This!
Women on the Verge of a Nervous
  Breakdown

SWEDEN
The Flight of the Eagle
June Night
The Sacrifice
Swedenhielms

SWITZERLAND
The Boat Is Full

YUGOSLAVIA
Hey Babu Riba
Montenegro

DIRECTOR CHECK LIST: INGMAR BERGMAN ———————— **FF8**

After the Rehearsal
Autumn Sonata
Brink of Life
Cries and Whispers
The Devil's Eye
The Devil's Wanton
Dreams
Fanny and Alexander
From the Life of Marionettes

A Lesson in Love
The Magic Flute
The Magician
Night Is My Future
Persona
Port of Call
Sawdust and Tinsel (The Naked Night)
Scenes From a Marriage
Secrets of Women

The Serpent's Egg
The Seventh Seal
Smiles of a Summer Night
Summer Interlude
Three Strange Loves

Through a Glass Darkly
The Virgin Spring
Wild Strawberries
Winter Light

DIRECTOR CHECK LIST: AKIRA KUROSAWA _____ FF9

The Bad Sleep Well
Dersu Uzala
Dodes'ka-den
Drunken Angel
The Hidden Fortress
High and Low
Ikiru
Kagemusha
The Lower Depths
The Men Who Tread on the Tiger's Tail

Ran
Rashomon
Red Beard
Sanjuro
Sanshiro Sugata
The Seven Samurai
Stray Dog
Throne of Blood
Yojimbo

DIRECTOR CHECK LIST: FEDERICO FELLINI _____ FF10

Amarcord
And the Ship Sails On
The Clowns
La Dolce Vita
8½
Ginger and Fred
Juliet of the Spirits

Love in the City (co-director)
Nights of Cabiria
Satyricon
La Strada
I Vitelloni
The White Sheik

DIRECTOR CHECK LIST: LUIS BUÑUEL _____ FF11

L'Age d'Or
The Brute
Un Chien Andalou (co-director)
The Criminal Life of Archibaldo de la
    Cruz
Diary of a Chambermaid (1964 version)
The Discreet Charm of the Bourgeosie
The Exterminating Angel
Land Without Bread
The Milky Way (1970)

Nazarin
Los Olvidados
The Phantom of Liberty
Simon of the Desert
Susana
That Obscure Object of Desire
Viridiana
A Woman Without Love
Wuthering Heights (1954 version)

DIRECTOR CHECK LIST: JEAN RENOIR _____ FF12

La Bête Humaine*
Boudu Saved From Drowning
A Day in the Country*
Diary of a Chambermaid (1946 version)

The Elusive Corporal
The Golden Coach
Grand Illusion
La Marseillaise

The River (1951)
Rules of the Game*
The Southerner

This Land Is Mine
Toni

*also actor

DIRECTOR CHECK LIST: FRANÇOIS TRUFFAUT _____ FF13

Close Encounters of the Third Kind*
Confidentially Yours
Day for Night**
Farenheit 451
The 400 Blows
The Green Room**
Jules and Jim
The Last Metro
Love on the Run

The Man Who Loved Women (1977 version)
Shoot the Piano Player
Small Change
The Soft Skin
Stolen Kisses
The Story of Adele H.
Two English Girls
The Woman Next Door

*actor only
**also actor

DIRECTOR CHECK LIST: JEAN-LUC GODARD _____ FF14

Alphaville
Aria (co-director)
Band of Outsiders
Breathless (1959 version)
Contempt
First Name: Carmen
Hail, Mary

King Lear (1987 version)
A Married Woman
Masculine-Feminine
My Life to Live
The Oldest Profession (co-director)
Sympathy for the Devil

DIRECTOR CHECK LIST: ERIC ROHMER _____ FF15

The Aviator's Wife
Le Beau Mariage
Boyfriends and Girlfriends
Chloe in the Afternoon
Claire's Knee

Full Moon in Paris
My Night at Maud's
Pauline at the Beach
Summer

DIRECTOR CHECK LIST: JACQUES TATI _____ FF16

Jour de Fête
Mr. Hulot's Holiday
My Uncle

Playtime
Sylvia and the Phantom*

*actor only

DIRECTOR CHECK LIST: MICHELANGELO ANTONIONI _____ FF17

L'Avventura
Blow Up
The Eclipse
Love in the City (co-director)

The Passenger
Red Desert
Zabriskie Point

DIRECTOR CHECK LIST: BERNARDO BERTOLUCCI _____ FF18

The Conformist
The Last Emperor

Last Tango in Paris
1900

DIRECTOR CHECK LIST: WERNER HERZOG _____ FF19

Aguirre, The Wrath of God
Burden of Dreams*
Every Man for Himself and God Against
   All
Fitzcarraldo

Man of Flowers*
Nosferatu the Vampyre
Werner Herzog Eats His Shoe*
Where the Green Ants Dream

*actor only

DIRECTOR CHECK LIST: RAINER WERNER FASSBINDER _____ FF20

Berlin Alexanderplatz
Despair
Fox and His Friends*

Kamikaze '89**
The Marriage of Maria Braun
Querelle

*also actor
**actor only

DIRECTOR CHECK LIST: WIM WENDERS _____ FF21

Alice in the Cities
The American Friend
The Goalie's Anxiety at the Penalty
   Kick
Hammett
Kings of the Road

Lightning Over Water
Paris, Texas
The Scarlet Letter (1980 version)
The State of Things
Wings of Desire
Wrong Move

DIRECTOR CHECK LIST: SERGEI EISENSTEIN _____ FF22

Alexander Nevsky
The General Line
Ivan the Terrible, Parts I and II
Potemkin

Que Viva Mexico!
Strike
Ten Days That Shook the World/
   October

DIRECTOR CHECK LIST: SATYAJIT RAY ———————————— FF23

Distant Thunder (1973)
The Home and the World

Two Daughters
The World of Apu

STAR CHECK LIST: MARCELLO MASTROIANNI ———————— FF24

Allonsanfan
Beyond Obsession
Big Deal on Madonna Street
Blood Feud
Dark Eyes
The Divine Nymph
La Dolce Vita
8½
Gabriela
Ginger and Fred
Henry IV
Lady of the Evening
Lovers and Lunatics

Macaroni
Massacre in Rome
La Nuit de Varennes
Shoot Loud, Louder, I Don't
    Understand
A Slightly Pregnant Man
A Special Day
Stay as You Are
The Tenth Victim
A Very Private Affair
Where the Hot Wind Blows
Wifemistress
Yesterday, Today and Tomorrow

STAR CHECK LIST: LIV ULLMANN ———————————————— FF25

Autumn Sonata
The Bay Boy
A Bridge Too Far
Cold Sweat
Cries and Whispers
Dangerous Moves
Forty Carats
Gaby--A True Story

Leonor
The Night Visitor
Persona
Richard's Things
Scenes From a Marriage
The Serpent's Egg
The Wild Duck

STAR CHECK LIST: JEANNE MOREAU ———————————————— FF26

Diary of a Chambermaid (1964 version)
Frantic (1958)
Going Places
Heat of Desire
Jules and Jim
The Last Tycoon
The Lovers

Lumiere*
Mr. Klein
Monte Walsh
Querelle
The Train
The Trial
Your Ticket Is No Longer Valid

*also director

STAR CHECK LIST: CATHERINE DENEUVE ———————————— FF27

The April Fools
Choice of Arms
Donkey Skin

La Grande Bourgeoise
The Hunger
Hustle

The Last Metro
Love Songs
March or Die
Repulsion

Scene of the Crime
A Slightly Pregnant Man
The Umbrellas of Cherbourg

STAR CHECK LIST: TOSHIRO MIFUNE ———————————— FF28

The Bad Sleep Well
Bushido Blade
The Challenge (1982)
Drunken Angel
The Gambling Samurai
Grand Prix
The Hidden Fortress
High and Low
The Life of Oharu
Love Songs
The Lower Depths
1941
Paper Tiger
Proof of the Man
Rashomon

Red Beard
Red Lion
Red Sun
Rikisha-Man
The Saga of the Vagabonds
Samurai Saga
The Samurai Trilogy
Sanjuro
The Seven Samurai
Stray Dog
Sword of Doom
Throne of Blood
Winter Kills
Yojimbo
Zatoichi Meets Yojimbo

STAR CHECK LIST: GERARD DEPARDIEU ———————————— FF29

La Chèvre
Choice of Arms
Les Comperes
Danton
Get Out Your Handkerchiefs
Going Places
Jean de Florette

The Last Metro
Mon Oncle d'Amerique
The Moon in the Gutter
1900
One Woman or Two
The Return of Martin Guerre
The Woman Next Door

STAR CHECK LIST: KLAUS KINSKI ———————————— FF30

Aguirre, The Wrath of God
Android
Buddy Buddy
A Bullet for the General
Burden of Dreams
Code Name: Wildgeese
Count Dracula
Crawlspace
Creature
Deadly Sanctuary
Fitzcarraldo
For a Few Dollars More

Jack the Ripper
The Little Drummer Girl
Nosferatu the Vampyre
Operation Thunderbolt
The Ruthless Four
Schizoid
The Secret Diary of Sigmund Freud
Shoot the Living, Pray for the Dead
The Soldier
A Time to Love and a Time to Die
Venom

STAR CHECK LIST: SOPHIA LOREN _____ FF31

Aida
Angela
Arabesque
The Black Orchid
Blood Feud
Brass Target
A Breath of Scandal
Courage (1986)
Desire Under the Elms
El Cid
The Fall of the Roman Empire
La Favorita

Firepower
Heller in Pink Tights
Houseboat
The Key
Lady of the Evening
Man of La Mancha
The Pride and the Passion
Sophia Loren: Her Own Story
A Special Day
Two Women
Yesterday, Today and Tomorrow

STAR CHECK LIST: BRIGITTE BARDOT _____ FF32

A Coeur Joie
And God Created Woman (1957 version)
The Bride Is Much Too Beautiful
Contempt
Dear Brigitte
Doctor at Sea
The Legend of Frenchie King

Mademoiselle Striptease
Ms. Don Juan
Ravishing Idiot
Le Repos du Guerrier
Shalako
A Very Private Affair
Voulez-Vous Danser Avec Moi?

STAR CHECK LIST: JEAN-PAUL BELMONDO _____ FF33

Breathless (1959 version)
Casino Royale
High Heels

Le Magnifique
Un Singe En Hiver
Two Women

STAR CHECK LIST: SONIA BRAGA _____ FF34

Doña Flor & Her Two Husbands
Gabriela
I Love You
Kiss of the Spider Woman

Lady on the Bus
The Milagro Beanfield War
Moon Over Parador

DIRECTOR CHECK LIST: CARL DREYER _____ FF35

Day of Wrath
Master of the House
Ordet

The Passion of Joan of Arc
Vampyr

FOREIGN FILMS & THEIR AMERICAN REMAKES _____ FF36

La Bête Humaine/Human Desire
Boudou Saved From Drowning/Down
  and Out in Beverly Hills
Breathless (1959)/Breathless (1982)
Cousin, Cousine/Cousins
Doña Flor and Her Two Husbands/Kiss
  Me Goodbye
Happy New Year (1973)/Happy New
  Year (1987)
The Man Who Loved Women (1977)/
  The Man Who Loved Women (1983)
A Pain in the A--/Buddy Buddy

Pardon Mon Affaire/The Woman in Red
The Seduction of Mimi/Which Way Is
  Up?
The Seven Samurai/The Magnificent
  Seven
The Tall Blonde Man With One Black
  Shoe/The Man With One Red Shoe
Three Men and a Cradle/Three Men and
  a Baby
The Virgin Spring/Last House on the
  Left
Yojimbo/A Fistful of Dollars

Chapter Eight

HORROR
(HO)

CLASSIC HORROR ——————————————————————————————— HO1

The Black Cat
The Body Snatcher
The Bride of Frankenstein
The Cabinet of Dr. Caligari
Cat People (1942 version)
Curse of the Demon
Dead of Night (1945)
The Devil Doll
Dr. Jekyll and Mr. Hyde (1920, 1932 &
    1941 versions)
Doctor X
Dracula (1931 version)
Frankentstein (1931 version)
Frankenstein Meets the Wolf Man
Freaks
The Golem
The Haunting
The Horror of Dracula
House of Wax

I Walked With a Zombie
The Invisible Man (1933 version)
King Kong (1933 version)
M
The Masque of the Red Death
The Mummy (1932 version)
The Mystery of the Wax Museum
Nosferatu
The Phantom of the Opera (1925
    version)
The Picture of Dorian Gray (1945
    version)
Psycho
The Raven (1935)
Son of Dracula
Son of Frankenstein
White Zombie
The Wolf Man

GHOST STORIES ——————————————————————————————— HO2

The Changeling
The Curse of the Cat People
Dead of Night (1945)
The Fog
Ghost Story
The Haunting
The Haunting of Julia
Lady in White
Legend of Hell House

Poltergeist
Poltergeist II
Poltergeist III
The Shining
Sole Survivor
The Supernaturals
13 Ghosts
Turn of the Screw
The Watcher in the Woods

HAUNTED HOUSES ——————————————————————————————— HO3

The Amityville Horror
Amityville II: The Possession
Amityville 3D
Burnt Offerings
The Evil

The Haunting
The Haunting of Julia
House
House on Haunted Hill
House 2: The Second Story

The House Where Evil Dwells
Legend of Hell House
Poltergeist
Poltergeist II

The Shining
13 Ghosts
Twice Dead
The Watcher in the Woods

WEREWOLVES _____ HO4

An American Werewolf in London
The Beast Must Die
The Beast Within
The Company of Wolves
The Curse of the Werewolf
The Howling
The Howling II
Howling III: The Marsupials

The Howling IV
Legend of the Werewolf
Silver Bullet
Teen Wolf
Werewolf of Washington
The Wolf Man
Wolfen

VAMPIRES _____ HO5

Andy Warhol's Dracula
Blacula
The Bloodsuckers
Captain Kronos: Vampire Hunter
Count Yorga, Vampire
Daughters of Darkness
Dracula (1931 & 1979 versions)
Fright Night
Graveyard Shift
The Horror of Dracula
The Hunger
Lair of the White Worm
Lifeforce
The Lost Boys

Love at First Bite
Lust for a Vampire
Mark of the Vampire
Martin
Near Dark
Nosferatu
Nosferatu the Vampyre
The Return of the Vampire
Salem's Lot
Scars of Dracula
Son of Dracula
Vamp
The Vampire Lovers
Vampyr

ZOMBIES _____ HO6

Carnival of Souls
Children Shouldn't Play With Dead
   Things
Dawn of the Dead
Day of the Dead
Dead and Buried
Dead Heat
Deathdream
Hard Rock Zombies
I Walked With a Zombie

Isle of the Dead
Night of the Living Dead
Psychomania
The Return of the Living Dead
Revenge of the Zombies
The Serpent and the Rainbow
The White Zombie
Zombie
Zombie Island Massacre

PEOPLE WITH PSYCHIC POWERS _____ HO7

Cameron's Closet
Carrie (1976)

Creepers
Dark Forces

The Dead Zone
The Evil Mind
Eyes of Laura Mars
The Fury
The Initiation of Sarah

Jennifer
Patrick
Scanners
The Shout
Sweet Sixteen

TALES OF POSSESSION ————————————————————— HO8

The Awakening
Beyond the Door
Beyond the Door 2
The Boogeyman
Child's Play
Dark Places
The Evil Dead

The Evil Dead 2: Dead by Dawn
The Exorcist
Exorcist II: The Heretic
Horror Express
Magic
Mausoleum

PSYCHO KILLERS ———————————————————————— HO9

Alone in the Dark
The Bird With the Crystal Plumage
Blood and Black Lace
The Brute Man
Chamber of Horrors
Deep Red: The Hatchet Murders
Don't Answer the Phone
Eyeball
Eyes of a Stranger
Fade to Black
Halloween
Halloween II
Halloween IV: The Return of Michael
  Myers
Happy Birthday to Me

He Knows You're Alone
The Hitcher
Honeymoon
The Human Monster
Jack the Ripper
The Night Visitor
The Phantom of the Opera (1925 & 1943
  versions)
Psycho
Psycho II
Psycho III
Schizoid
Silent Night, Deadly Night
Slumber Party Massacre

DEAL WITH THE DEVIL ——————————————————————— HO10

Angel Heart
Blood on Satan's Claw
Damien: Omen II
Damn Yankees
The Devil and Max Devlin
The Devil's Rain
The Final Conflict

The Gate
The Mephisto Waltz
The Omen
Rosemary's Baby
To the Devil a Daughter
The Unholy

CULTS ——————————————————————————————— HO11

Because of the Cats
The Believers
The Bloodsuckers

The Brotherhood of Satan
Curse of the Demon
The Dark Secret of Harvest Home

Deadly Blessing
The Devils
The Devil's Rain
The Legacy
Legend of the Minotaur
The Mephisto Waltz

Nomads
Race With the Devil
Rosemary's Baby
Videodrome
The Wicker Man

TEENS IN TROUBLE _____ HO12

April Fool's Day
Black Christmas
Brain Damage
Carrie (1976)
The Final Terror
Friday the 13th (series)
The Funhouse
Graduation Day
Hell Night
Killer Party

Last House on the Left
The Mutilator
A Nightmare on Elm Street (series)
Sleepaway Camp
Sorority House Massacre
Summer Camp Nightmare
Terror Train
The Texas Chainsaw Massacre
Zombie High

SCARY KIDS _____ HO13

Audrey Rose
The Baby
The Bad Seed
The Beast Within
The Brood
Cameron's Closet
Children of the Corn
Damien: Omen II
Evilspeak
The Exorcist
Exorcist II: The Heretic

Firestarter
The Godsend
It Lives Again
It's Alive
Jennifer
The Kindred
The Little Girl Who Lives Down the
   Lane
The Lost Boys
The Omen
Village of the Damned

BAD BLOOD: HORROR STORIES ABOUT FAMILIES _____ HO14
See also: HO15 Evil Twins

The Beast in the Cellar
Crucible of Horror
The Curse
The Curse of the Cat People
Dementia 13
Don't Look Now
Eraserhead
Flowers in the Attic

Hellbound: Hellraiser II
Hellraiser
The Hills Have Eyes
The Oblong Box
Psycho Sisters
Pumpkinhead
Seizure
Whatever Happened to Baby Jane?

EVIL TWINS _____ HO15

Basket Case
The Black Room

Blood Link
Dead Men Walk

Dead Ringers
The Man Who Haunted Himself
The Other

Sisters
Twins of Evil

ANIMALS AND OTHER CREEPY CREATURES _____ HO16

Alligator
Ants
Ben
The Birds
Bug
Child's Play
The Creature From Black Lake
Creepers
Critters
Critters 2: The Main Course
Cujo
Deep Star Six
Dogs of Hell
Dolls
Frogs
Ghoulies
Gremlins
Humanoids From the Deep
In the Shadow of Kilimanjaro
Jaws (series)
King Kong (1933 & 1976 versions)

The Leopard Man
Link
Monkey Shines
The Nest
Nightwing
Of Unknown Origin
Orca
The Pack
Pet Sematary
Pin
Piranha
Q
Razorback
Squirm
Swamp Thing
The Swarm
Trolls
Venom
Willard
Wolfen

MEMORABLE TRANSFORMATIONS _____ HO17

An American Werewolf in London
The Company of Wolves
Demons
Dr. Jekyll and Mr. Hyde (1932 version)

The Fly
The Howling
The Thing
The Wolf Man

GORY HORROR _____ HO18

Basket Case
Blood Feast
Dawn of the Dead
Day of the Dead
Dr. Butcher, M.D.
The Evil Dead
The Evil Dead 2: Dead by Dawn
Friday the 13th (series)

Maniac (1980)
Mother's Day
Night of the Living Dead
A Nightmare on Elm Street (series)
Rabid
Re-Animator
The Return of the Living Dead
Zombie

SCARY BUT NOT BLOODY _____ HO19
See also: HO1 Classic Horror

The Amityville Horror
The Body Snatcher

The Changeling
Coma

Curse of the Demon
The Dead Zone
Don't Look Now
Dracula (1979 version)
Freaks
Fright Night
Ghost Story
The Haunting
The Haunting of Julia
House
House of the Long Shadows

House of Wax
House on Haunted Hill
Lady in White
Link
Magic
Poltergeist
Rosemary's Baby
Something Wicked This Way Comes
Strait-Jacket
13 Ghosts
Turn of the Screw

SCIENCE RUNS AMOK _____ HO20
See also: SF5 Science Gone Wrong

The Abominable Dr. Phibes
Andy Warhol's Frankenstein
The Ape
Atom Age Vampire
The Brain That Wouldn't Die
The Bride
The Bride of Frankenstein
Circus of Horrors
The Curse of Frankenstein
Deadly Friend
Dr. Jekyll and Mr. Hyde (1920, 1932 &
   1941 versions)
Dr. Phibes Rises Again
Fiend Without a Face
The Fly (1958 & 1986 versions)
The Fly II

Frankenstein (1931 & 1973 versions)
From Beyond
Halloween III: Season of the Witch
The Invisible Man
The Island of Dr. Moreau
Link
The Man They Could Not Hang
The Mind Snatchers
Nightmare Weekend
Re-Animator
Scream and Scream Again
Screamers
Son of Frankenstein
Terminal Choice
Watchers

MUTANT MONSTERS _____ HO21

C.H.U.D.
City of the Walking Dead
Class of Nuke 'Em High
The Crazies
The Curse
Cyclops

The Invisible Ray
Mutant
Night of the Creeps
Slithis
Toxic Avenger
Transmutations

MAD MACHINERY _____ HO22

Chopping Mall
Christine
Demon Seed

The Lift
Maximum Overdrive
Videodrome

HORROR ANTHOLOGIES _____ HO23

Asylum
Black Sabbath

Cat's Eye
Creepshow

Creepshow 2
Dead of Night (1945)
Dr. Terror's House of Horrors
From Beyond the Grave
The House That Dripped Blood
The Monster Club
Night Gallery
Nightmares

The Offspring
Tales From the Crypt
Tales of Terror
Torture Garden
Trilogy of Terror
Twice-Told Tales
Twilight Zone - The Movie

HORROR FOR LAUGHS _____ HO24

An American Werewolf in London
Andy Warhol's Dracula
Andy Warhol's Frankenstein
Arnold
Critters
Critters 2: The Main Course
Gremlins
The Little Shop of Horrors (1960
    version)
Love at First Bite
Microwave Massacre
The Monster Squad

Motel Hell
Piranha
The Plumber
Psychos in Love
Return of the Living Dead
Slaughterhouse
The Stuff
Terror at Red Wolf Inn
Theatre of Blood
Toxic Avenger
Vamp

SEXY HORROR _____ HO25

Because of the Cats
Cat People (1982 version)
Demon Seed
The Entity
From Beyond

Gothic
Humanoids From the Deep
Lair of the White Worm
Lust for a Vampire
The Vampire Lovers

HORROR WITH A BRITISH ACCENT _____ HO26

The Abominable Dr. Phibes
And Now the Screaming Starts
Asylum
Bloodbath at the House of Death
Captain Kronos: Vampire Hunter
Circus of Horrors
Conqueror Worm
The Creeping Flesh
The Curse of Frankenstein
The Curse of the Werewolf
Dead of Night (1945)
The Doctor and the Devils
Dr. Phibes Rises Again
Dr. Terror's House of Horrors
The Evil of Frankenstein

From Beyond the Grave
The Ghoul (1933)
The Gorgon
The Haunting of Julia
Horror of Dracula
Horror of Frankenstein
Lust for a Vampire
The Mummy (1959 version)
The Picture of Dorian Gray (1945
    version)
Scars of Dracula
Scream and Scream Again
Tales From the Crypt
Terror in the Wax Museum
Theatre of Blood

To the Devil a Daughter
Turn of the Screw

Village of the Damned
The Watcher in the Woods

STAR CHECK LIST: BORIS KARLOFF _____ HO27

Abbott and Costello Meet Dr. Jekyll and
  Mr. Hyde
Abbott and Costello Meet the Killer,
  Boris Karloff
The Ape
Bedlam
Before I Hang
The Bells
The Black Cat
The Black Room
The Black Sabbath
The Body Snatcher
The Bride of Frankenstein
Cauldron of Blood
Chamber of Fear
Charlie Chan at the Opera
Colonel March of Scotland Yard
Corridors of Blood
The Criminal Code
The Daydreamer (voice only)
Dick Tracy Meets Gruesome
Die, Monster, Die!
Doomed to Die
Frankenstein (1931 version)
Frankenstein 1970

The Ghoul (1933)
The Haunted Strangler
The Invisible Ray
Island Monster
Isle of the Dead
Juggernaut (1937)
The King of the Kongo
The Lost Patrol
Macabre Serenade
Mad Monster Party? (voice only)
The Man They Could Not Hang
Mr. Wong, Detective
Mr. Wong in Chinatown
The Mummy (1932 version)
Old Ironsides
The Raven (1935 & 1963)
Scarface (1932 version)
The Secret Life of Walter Mitty
Sinister Invasion
The Snake People
Son of Frankenstein
Targets
The Terror
You'll Find Out

STAR CHECK LIST: BELA LUGOSI _____ HO28

Abbott and Costello Meet Frankenstein
The Ape Man
Bela Lugosi Meets a Brooklyn Gorilla
  (The Boys From Brooklyn)
The Black Cat
Black Dragons
The Body Snatcher
Bowery at Midnight
Bride of the Monster
Chandu on the Magic Island
The Corpse Vanishes
The Death Kiss
Dracula (1931 version)
Frankenstein Meets the Wolf Man
Ghosts on the Loose
Glen or Glenda?
The Gorilla
The Human Monster

Invisible Ghost
The Invisible Ray
Killer Bats (The Devil Bat)
Mark of the Vampire
The Midnight Girl
Murder by Television
Mysterious Mr. Wong
The Mystery of the *Mary Celeste*: The
  Phantom Ship
Ninotchka
One Body Too Many
The Phantom Creeps
Plan 9 From Outer Space
The Raven (1935)
The Return of Chandu
Return of the Vampire
S.O.S. Coastguard
Scared to Death

Son of Frankenstein
Spooks Run Wild
White Zombie

The Wolf Man
You'll Find Out

STAR CHECK LIST: LON CHANEY, SR. _____ HO29

Flesh & Blood (1922)
The Hunchback of Notre Dame (1923
  version)
Nomads of the North
Oliver Twist (1922 version)

Outside the Law
The Phantom of the Opera (1925
  version)
Shadows
The Shock

STAR CHECK LIST: LON CHANEY, JR. _____ HO30

Abbott and Costello Meet Frankenstein
Behave Yourself!
Bird of Paradise (1932)
Bride of the Gorilla
Casanova's Big Night
Cyclops
The Defiant Ones (1958 version)
Dr. Terror's Gallery of Horrors
Dracula vs. Frankenstein
Frankenstein Meets the Wolf Man
High Noon
Hillbillys in a Haunted House

The Indestructible Man
My Favorite Brunette
Of Mice and Men
The Old Corral
One Million B.C.
Only the Valiant
Passion (1954)
Riders of Death Valley
Son of Dracula
Spider Baby
Undersea Kingdom
The Wolf Man

STAR CHECK LIST: VINCENT PRICE _____ HO31

Abbott and Costello Meet Frankenstein
The Abominable Dr. Phibes
Adventures of Captain Fabian
The Baron of Arizona
Bloodbath at the House of Death
Casanova's Big Night
Champagne for Caesar
Conqueror Worm
Cry of the Banshee
Dangerous Mission
The Devil's Triangle (narrator)
Dr. Phibes Rises Again
The Fall of the House of Usher
The Fly (1958 version)
His Kind of Woman
House of the Long Shadows
House of Wax
House on Haunted Hill
The Last Man on Earth
Laura

The Masque of the Red Death
Master of the World
The Monster Club
The Oblong Box
The Offspring
Pirate Warrior
The Pit and the Pendulum
The Private Lives of Elizabeth and
  Essex
The Raven (1963)
Return of the Fly
Scream and Scream Again
Shock
Snow White and the Seven Dwarfs (1983
  version)
Son of Sinbad
Song of Bernadette
Tales of Terror
The Ten Commandments (1956 version)
Theatre of Blood

The Three Musketeers (1948 version)
Tomb of Ligeia
Tower of London (1962 version)

The Trouble With Girls
Twice Told Tales
While the City Sleeps

STAR CHECK LIST: CHRISTOPHER LEE ——————————— HO32

Against All Odds (1969)
Airport '77
Albino
Bear Island
The Boy Who Left Home to Find Out
    About the Shivers
Caravans
Castle of Fu Manchu
Castle of the Living Dead
Circle of Iron
Corridors of Blood
Count Dracula
The Creeping Flesh
The Crimson Pirate
The Curse of Frankenstein
Dark Places
The Devil's Undead
Dr. Terror's House of Horrors
Dracula and Son
End of the World
An Eye for an Eye
The Four Musketeers
The Girl
The Gorgon
Horror Express
Horror Hotel
Horror of Dracula
The Hound of the Baskervilles (1959
    version)
House of the Long Shadows

The House That Dripped Blood
The Howling II
Jaguar Lives
Jocks
Julius Caesar (1970 version)
The Keeper
Killer Force
The Land of Faraway
The Man With the Golden Gun
The Mummy (1959 version)
1941
The Oblong Box
The Private Life of Sherlock Holmes
Pursuit of the Graf Spee
Return from Witch Mountain
The Return of Captain Invincible
Safari 3000
The Salamander
Scars of Dracula
Scott of the Antarctic
Scream and Scream Again
Scream of Fear
Serial
Shaka Zulu
Theatre of Death
The Three Musketeers (1974 version)
To the Devil a Daughter
The Torture Chamber of Dr. Sadism
The Wicker Man

STAR CHECK LIST: PETER CUSHING ——————————— HO33

Alexander the Great
And Now the Screaming Starts
Asylum
At the Earth's Core
The Beast Must Die
Biggles
Blood Beast Terror
Bloodsuckers
Call Him Mr. Shatter
A Choice of Weapons
The Creeping Flesh

The Curse of Frankenstein
Daleks—Invasion Earth 2150 A.D.
The Devil's Undead
Doctor Phibes Rises Again
Dr. Terror's House of Horrors
Dr. Who and the Daleks
Dynasty of Fear
The Evil of Frankenstein
Fear in the Night
From Beyond the Grave
The Ghoul (1975)

The Gorgon
Hamlet (1948 version)
Horror Express
Horror of Dracula
The Hound of the Baskervilles (1959
    version)
House of the Long Shadows
The House That Dripped Blood
Land of the Minotaur
Legend of the Werewolf
Masks of Death
The Mummy (1959 version)

Scream and Scream Again
Shock Waves
Silent Scream
Star Wars
Sword of the Valiant
Tales from the Crypt
Top Secret!
Torture Garden
Twins of Evil
The Uncanny
The Vampire Lovers

DIRECTOR CHECK LIST: JAMES WHALE _____ HO34

The Bride of Frankenstein
Frankenstein (1931 version)
The Invisible Man

The Man in the Iron Mask (1939
    version)

DIRECTOR CHECK LIST: TOD BROWNING _____ HO35

The Devil Doll
Dracula (1931 version)
Freaks

Mark of the Vampire
Outside the Law

PRODUCER CHECK LIST: VAL LEWTON _____ HO36

Bedlam
The Body Snatcher
Cat People (1942 version)
The Curse of the Cat People

I Walked With a Zombie
Isle of the Dead
The Leopard Man

DIRECTOR CHECK LIST: JACQUES TOURNEUR _____ HO37

Appointment in Honduras
Berlin Express
Cat People (1942 version)
Curse of the Demon
Easy Living
Experiment Perilous

The Flame and the Arrow
Great Day in the Morning
I Walked With a Zombie
The Leopard Man
Out of the Past

DIRECTOR CHECK LIST: GEORGE ROMERO _____ HO38

The Crazies
Creepshow
Creepshow 2
Dawn of the Dead
Day of the Dead

Knightriders
Martin
Monkey Shines
Night of the Living Dead
Season of the Witch

DIRECTOR CHECK LIST: DAVID CRONENBERG ——————————— HO39

The Brood
Dead Ringers
The Dead Zone
The Fly (1986 version)

Rabid
Scanners
They Came From Within
Videodrome

DIRECTOR CHECK LIST: TOBE HOOPER ——————————— HO40

Eaten Alive
The Funhouse
Invaders from Mars (1986 version)
Lifeforce

Poltergeist
Salem's Lot
The Texas Chainsaw Massacre
The Texas Chainsaw Massacre II

AUTHOR CHECK LIST: EDGAR ALLAN POE ——————————— HO41

The Avenging Conscience
The Fall of the House of Usher
The Masque of the Red Death
Murders in the Rue Morgue (1971
  version)
The Oblong Box

The Pit and the Pendulum
The Premature Burial
The Raven (1963)
Tales of Terror
The Tomb of Ligeia
The Torture Chamber of Dr. Sadism

AUTHOR CHECK LIST: STEPHEN KING ——————————— HO42

Based on Works by King
Carrie (1976)
Children of the Corn
Christine
Cujo
The Dead Zone
Firestarter
Maximum Overdrive*

Pet Sematary**
Salem's Lot
The Shining

Original Screenplays
Cat's Eye
Creepshow**
Creepshow 2

  *also director
**also actor

Chapter Nine

MUSICALS
(MU)

MGM MUSICALS MU1

An American in Paris
Anchors Aweigh
Babes in Arms
The Band Wagon
The Barkleys of Broadway
Bells Are Ringing
Brigadoon
Broadway Melody of 1940
Easter Parade
Gigi
Girl Crazy
Good News
The Great Caruso
High Society
Hit the Deck
Invitation to the Dance
Kismet
Kiss Me Kate
Les Girls

Lili
Meet Me in St. Louis
Neptune's Daughter
On the Town
The Pirate
Rose Marie
Royal Wedding
Seven Brides for Seven Brothers
Show Boat (1951 version)
Silk Stockings
Singin' in the Rain
Strike Up the Band
Summer Stock
Three Little Words
Till the Clouds Roll By
The Unsinkable Molly Brown
The Wizard of Oz
Words and Music
Ziegfeld Follies

THE BEST OF BROADWAY MU2

Annie
The Best Little Whorehouse in Texas
Bye Bye Birdie
Cabaret
Camelot
Can-Can
A Chorus Line
Damn Yankees
Fiddler on the Roof
Flower Drum Song
42nd Street
Funny Girl
A Funny Thing Happened on the Way
    to the Forum
Grease
Guys and Dolls
Hair
Hello, Dolly!
How to Succeed in Business Without
    Really Trying

The King and I
Kismet
Kiss Me Kate
A Little Night Music
Mame
Man of La Mancha
The Music Man
My Fair Lady
Oh! Calcutta!
Oklahoma!
Oliver!
The Pajama Game
Purlie Victorious
1776
The Sound of Music
South Pacific
Sweet Charity
West Side Story
The Wiz

GREAT DANCING MUSICALS _____ MU3
See also: MU18 Fred Astaire, MU19 Gene Kelly,
MU20 Busby Berkeley Check Lists

All That Jazz
Best Foot Forward
Carmen
Flashdance
Footloose
Good News
Pennies From Heaven
The Red Shoes

Saturday Night Fever
Seven Brides for Seven Brothers
Stormy Weather
Sweet Charity
Tap
That's Dancing
West Side Story

MUSICAL FILMS ABOUT SHOW BIZ _____ MU4
See also: CL7 Show Business Stories, DR12 Backstage Dramas

All That Jazz
Babes in Arms
The Band Wagon
The Barkleys of Broadway
Breaking Glass
Broadway Melody
Bye Bye Birdie
Carmen
A Chorus Line
Crossover Dreams
Dames
Eddie and the Cruisers
Fame
Footlight Parade
For Me and My Gal
42nd Street
Give My Regards to Broad Street
Gold Diggers of 1933
Holiday Inn
The Idolmaker
The Jazz Singer (1980 version)
Light of Day
New York, New York

Phantom of the Paradise
The Rose
Show Boat (1951 version)
Singin' in the Rain
Sparkle
Springtime in the Rockies
A Star Is Born (1954 & 1976 versions)
Starstruck
Staying Alive
Stormy Weather
The Story of Vernon and Irene Castle
Strike Up the Band
Summer Stock
Swing Time
That'll Be the Day
There's No Business Like Show
 Business
Tonight and Every Night
Wasn't That a Time!
White Christmas
Wonder Man
Young Man With a Horn
Ziegfeld Follies

MUSICAL LIFE STORIES _____ MU5

Amadeus (Mozart)
The Benny Goodman Story
Bird (Charlie Parker)
Bound for Glory (Woody Guthrie)
The Buddy Holly Story
Coal Miner's Daughter (Loretta Lynn)
Deep in My Heart (Sigmund Romberg)
The Fabulous Dorseys
Funny Girl (Fanny Brice)

Funny Lady (Fanny Brice)
The Glenn Miller Story
The Great Caruso
The Great Ziegfeld
Gypsy (Gypsy Rose Lee)
Jolson Sings Again
The Jolson Story
La Bamba (Ritchie Valens)
Lady Sings the Blues (Billie Holiday)

Lizstomania
Love Me or Leave Me (Ruth Etting)
Mahler
Night and Day (Cole Porter)
Seven Little Foys (Eddie Foy)
Song of Norway (Edvard Grieg)
A Song to Remember (Frédéric Chopin)
The Sound of Music (Maria von Trapp)
The Story of Vernon and Irene Castle
Sweet Dreams (Patsy Cline)

This Is Elvis
Three Little Words (Bert Kalmar &
   Harry Ruby)
Yankee Doodle Dandy (George M.
   Cohan)
Till the Clouds Roll By (Jerome Kern)
Wagner
Words and Music (Richard Rodgers &
   Lorenz Hart)

MUSICAL AMERICANA _____ MU6

Bye Bye Birdie
Calamity Jane (1953)
Damn Yankees
Easter Parade
Flower Drum Song
Good News
Guys and Dolls
The Harvey Girls
Holiday Inn
Meet Me in St. Louis
The Music Man
Nashville

New York, New York
Oklahoma!
On the Town
Paint Your Wagon
Seven Brides for Seven Brothers
Show Boat (1951 version)
State Fair (1962 version)
Take Me out to the Ball Game
The Unsinkable Molly Brown
West Side Story
White Christmas
Yankee Doodle Dandy

MUSICALS WHICH WON MAJOR OSCARS _____ MU7

An American in Paris
Broadway Melody
Cabaret
Funny Girl
Gigi
The Great Ziegfeld
The King and I

Mary Poppins
My Fair Lady
Oliver!
The Sound of Music
West Side Story
Yankee Doodle Dandy

FANTASIES AND FAIRY TALES _____ MU8

Brigadoon
Cabin in the Sky
Camelot
Cinderella (1964 version)
A Connecticut Yankee in King Arthur's
   Court
Doctor Dolittle
Finian's Rainbow
Kismet
Little Shop of Horrors (1986 version)

Mary Poppins
On a Clear Day You Can See Forever
Sergeant Pepper's Lonely Hearts Club
   Band
Tommy
The Wiz
The Wizard of Oz
Xanadu
Yellow Submarine
Yolanda and the Thief

ROCK MUSCIALS _____ **MU9**
See also: MU22 Elvis Presley Check List

Absolute Beginners
Beat Street
The Blues Brothers
Body Rock
Breakin'
Breakin' 2: Electric Boogaloo
Breaking Glass
Bye Bye Birdie
Can't Stop the Music
Fame
Get Crazy
The Girl Can't Help It
Give My Regards to Broad Street
Grease
Grease 2
Hair
A Hard Day's Night
The Harder They Come
Head
Help!
The Idolmaker
Jesus Christ, Superstar

Magical Mystery Tour
One-Trick Pony
Phantom of the Paradise
Pink Floyd: The Wall
Purple Rain
Quadrophenia
Roadie
Rock 'n' Roll High School
Rock, Pretty Baby
Rock, Rock, Rock
The Rose
Running Out of Luck
A Star Is Born (1976 version)
Starstruck
Tapeheads
That'll Be the Day
Times Square
Tommy
200 Motels
Wild Style
Yellow Submarine

ROCK CONCERT FILMS _____ **MU10**

The Concert for Bangladesh
Delicate Sound of Thunder
Divine Madness!
Elvis—The 1968 Comeback Special
Gimme Shelter
The Grateful Dead Movie
Heartland Reggae
Jimi Plays Berkeley
Joe Cocker: Mad Dogs and Englishmen
The Last Waltz
Let's Spend the Night Together
The MUSE Concert: No Nukes
Monterey Pop
Motown 25: Yesterday, Today, Forever

Nelson Mandela 70th Birthday Tribute
Rust Never Sleeps
Sign o' the Times
Simon & Garfunkel: The Concert in
   Central Park
Soul to Soul
Stop Making Sense
That Was Rock
U2 Live at Red Rocks "Under a Blood
   Red Sky"
Woodstock
Ziggy Stardust and the Spiders From
   Mars

ROCK DOCUMENTARIES _____ **MU11**

Bring on the Night
Chuck Berry: Hail! Hail! Rock 'n' Roll
The Compleat Beatles
The Decline of Western Civilization
The Decline of Western Civilization II:
   The Metal Years

Don't Look Back
Elvis '56
Elvis on Tour
Elvis—That's the Way It Is
Imagine: John Lennon
Janis

Jimi Hendrix	This Is Elvis
The Kids Are Alright	This Is Spinal Tap
Let It Be	U2: Rattle and Hum
The Song Remains the Same	X, The Unheard Music

FILMS WITH POP STARS IN NON-MUSICAL ROLES _____ MU12

See also: MU18 Fred Astaire, MU25 Bing Crosby, MU21 Judy Garland, MU19 Gene Kelly, MU22 Elvis Presley, DR49 Frank Sinatra, MU27 Barbra Streisand Check Lists

David Bowie
  The Hunger
  Into the Night
  Just a Gigolo
  Labyrinth
  The Last Temptation of Christ
  The Man Who Fell to Earth
  Merry Christmas, Mr. Lawrence
Cher
  Come Back to the Five and Dime,
    Jimmy Dean, Jimmy Dean
  Mask
  Moonstruck
  Silkwood
  Suspect
  The Witches of Eastwick
Kris Kristofferson
  Alice Doesn't Live Here Anymore
  Big Top Pee-wee
  Blume in Love
  Convoy
  Flashpoint
  Heaven's Gate
  The Last Movie
  Pat Garrett and Billy the Kid
  Rollover
  Semi-Tough
  Trouble in Mind
Bette Midler
  Big Business
  Down and Out in Beverly Hills
  Jinxed!
  Outrageous Fortune
  Ruthless People
Sting
  Brimstone and Treacle
  Dune
  Plenty
  Stormy Monday
Others
  The Alamo (Frankie Avalon)
  Barbarosa (Willie Nelson)
  Buster (Phil Collins)
  Captain Newman, M.D. (Bobby Darin)
  Carnal Knowledge (Art Garfunkel)

  Carny (Robbie Robertson)
  Catch-22 (Art Garfunkel)
  Caveman (Ringo Starr)
  Certain Fury (Irene Cara)
  China Gate (Nat King Cole)
  Clue (Lee Ving)
  Coal Miner's Daughter (Levon Helm)
  Conan the Destroyer (Grace Jones)
  Corrupt (John Lydon)
  Desperately Seeking Susan (Madonna)
  Disorganized Crime (Ruben Blades)
  The Dollmaker (Levon Helm)
  Down by Law (John Lurie, Tom Waits)
  Dudes (Lee Ving)
  The Electric Horseman (Willie Nelson)
  Fatal Beauty (Ruben Blades)
  Foxes (Cherie Curie)
  Gunfight (Johnny Cash)
  Hairspray (Ruth Brown, Debby Harry,
    Sony Bono)
  Hamlet (1969 version) (Marianne
    Faithfull)
  The Happy Ending (Robert (Bobby)
    Darin)
  Harry Tracy (Gordon Lightfoot)
  How I Won the War (John Lennon)
  Into the Night (Carl Perkins)
  Ironweed (Tom Waits)
  Jo Jo Dancer, Your Life Is Calling
    (Carmen McRae, Billy Eckstine)
  Let's Get Harry (Glenn Frey)
  Lost Angels (Adam Horovitz)
  Mad Max Beyond Thunderdome (Tina
    Turner)
  McVicar (Roger Daltrey)
  The Milagro Beanfield War (Ruben
    Blades, Freddy Fender)
  Nomads (Adam Ant)
  North to Alaska (Fabian)
  Pat Garrett and Billy the Kid (Bob
    Dylan, Rita Coolidge)
  Plenty (Tracey Ullman)
  The Red Headed Stranger (Willie
    Nelson)
  The Right Stuff (Levon Helm)

Rio Bravo (Rick Nelson)
Runaway (Gene Simmons)
Shanghai Surprise (Madonna)
Short Fuse (Art Garfunkel)
Smooth Talk (Levon Helm)
Straight to Hell (Elvis Costello, Dick
  Rude, Joe Strummer, Grace Jones)
Stranger Than Paradise (John Lurie)
Thief (Willie Nelson)
To Sir, With Love (Lulu, Michael Des
  Barres)

True Grit (Glen Campbell)
Union City (Debby Harry)
Vamp (Grace Jones)
Vibes (Cyndi Lauper)
Videodrome (Debbie Harry)
A View to a Kill (Grace Jones)
The Wackiest Ship in the Army (Rick
  Nelson)
Wanted: Dead or Alive (Gene Simmons)
Who's That Girl (Madonna)

ALL BLACK MUSICALS _____ MU13

Cabin in the Sky
The Duke Is Tops

Lost in the Stars
Stormy Weather

MUSICAL REMAKES OF NON-MUSICAL FILMS _____ MU14

Bundle of Joy
High Society
In the Good Old Summertime
Kiss Me Kate
A Little Night Music
Little Shop of Horrors (1986 version)
Mame

Miss Sadie Thompson
My Fair Lady
Oliver!
Scrooge
Silk Stockings
A Star Is Born (1954 version)
Sweet Charity

MUSICAL REVUES _____ MU15

Glorifying the American Girl
The King of Jazz
Stage Door Canteen
Thank Your Lucky Stars

That's Dancing
That's Entertainment
That's Entertainment 2
Thousands Cheer

STRANGEST MUSICALS _____ MU16

Absolute Beginners
Le Bal
Bugsy Malone
The Fastest Guitar Alive
Forbidden Zone
The Little Prince
Little Shop of Horrors (1986 version)
Murder at the Vanities

One From the Heart
Pennies From Heaven
Pink Floyd: The Wall
Sergeant Pepper's Lonely Hearts Club
  Band
1776
The Umbrellas of Cherbourg

NON-SINGING ACTORS IN MUSICAL ROLES _____ MU17

The Best Little Whorehouse in Texas
  (Burt Reynolds)

Camelot (Richard Harris & Vanessa
  Redgrave)

Doctor Dolittle (Rex Harrison)
Guys and Dolls (Marlon Brando)
Idiot's Delight (Clark Gable)
A Little Night Music (Elizabeth Taylor)
Man of La Mancha (Peter O'Toole &
  Sophia Loren)

My Fair Lady (Rex Harrison)
Paint Your Wagon (Clint Eastwood &
  Lee Marvin)
Yankee Doodle Dandy (James Cagney)

STAR CHECK LIST: FRED ASTAIRE _____ MU18

The Band Wagon
The Barkleys of Broadway*
Belle of New York
Broadway Melody of 1940
Carefree*
Damsel in Distress
Dancing Lady
Easter Parade
Finian's Rainbow
Flying Down to Rio*
Follow the Fleet*
Funny Face
The Gay Divorcee*
Holiday Inn
Let's Dance
Roberta*
Royal Wedding
Second Chorus
Shall We Dance*

Silk Stockings
The Sky's the Limit
The Story of Vernon and Irene Castle*
Swing Time*
That's Dancing
That's Entertainment
That's Entertainment 2
Three Little Words
Top Hat*
Yolanda and the Thief
You Were Never Lovelier
You'll Never Get Rich
Ziegfeld Follies (with Gene Kelly)

NON-MUSIC
The Amazing Dobermans
Ghost Story
On the Beach
The Towering Inferno

* with Ginger Rogers

STAR CHECK LIST: GENE KELLY _____ MU19

An American in Paris
Anchors Aweigh
Brigadoon
Deep in My Heart (guest star)
DuBarry Was a Lady
For Me and My Gal
Hello, Dolly!*
Invitation to the Dance
It's Always Fair Weather**
Les Girls
Let's Make Love
On the Town**
The Pirate
Singin' in the Rain**
Summer Stock
Take Me out to the Ball Game

That's Dancing
That's Entertainment
That's Entertainment 2
Thousands Cheer
Words and Music
Xanadu
Ziegfeld Follies (with Fred Astaire)

NON-MUSIC
The Black Hand
The Cheyenne Social Club*
Forty Carats
Inherit the Wind
Marjorie Morningstar
The Three Musketeers (1948 version)

*director only
**also co-director with Stanley Donen

DIRECTOR/CHOREOGRAPHER CHECK LIST: BUSBY BERKELEY _____ MU20

Babes in Arms
Dames*
Footlight Parade*
For Me and My Gal
42nd Street*
Girl Crazy*
Gold Diggers of 1933*
Jumbo*

Roman Scandals*
Stage Struck
Strike Up the Band
Take Me out to the Ball Game

NON-MUSIC
They Made Me a Criminal

*choreography only

STAR CHECK LIST: JUDY GARLAND _____ MU21

Babes in Arms*
Broadway Melody of 1938
Easter Parade
For Me and My Gal
Girl Crazy*
The Harvey Girls
I Could Go On Singing
In the Good Old Summertime
Meet Me in St. Louis
The Pirate
Presenting Lily Mars
A Star Is Born (1954 version)

Strike Up the Band*
Summer Stock
Thousands Cheer
Till the Clouds Roll By
The Wizard of Oz
Words and Music*
Ziegfeld Follies

NON-MUSIC
The Clock
Judgment at Nuremberg

* with Mickey Rooney

STAR CHECK LIST: ELVIS PRESLEY _____ MU22
See also: MU10 Rock Concerts, MU11 Rock Documentaries

Blue Hawaii
Clambake
Double Trouble
Flaming Star
Follow That Dream
Frankie and Johnny
Fun in Acapulco
G.I. Blues
Girl Happy
Girls! Girls! Girls!
Harum Scarum
It Happened at the World's Fair
Jailhouse Rock
Kid Galahad
King Creole
Kissin' Cousins

Live a Little, Love a Little
Loving You
Paradise, Hawaiian Style
Roustabout
Speedway
Spinout
Stay Away, Joe
Tickle Me
The Trouble With Girls
Viva Las Vegas
Wild in the Country

NON-MUSIC
Change of Habit
Love Me Tender

DIRECTOR CHECK LIST: STANLEY DONEN _____ MU23

Damn Yankees**
Deep in My Heart
Funny Face
It's Always Fair Weather*
The Little Prince
Movie, Movie
On the Town*
The Pajama Game**
Royal Wedding
Seven Brides for Seven Brothers
Singin' in the Rain*

NON-MUSIC
Arabesque
Bedazzled
Blame It on Rio
Charade
The Grass Is Greener
Indiscreet
Saturn 3
Two for the Road

  * with Gene Kelly
** with George Abbott

DIRECTOR CHECK LIST: VINCENTE MINNELLI _____ MU24

An American in Paris
The Band Wagon
Bells Are Ringing
Brigadoon
Cabin in the Sky
Gigi
Kismet
Meet Me in St. Louis
On a Clear Day You Can See Forever
The Pirate
Yolanda and the Thief
Ziegfeld Follies

NON-MUSIC
The Bad and the Beautiful
The Clock
Father of the Bride
Father's Little Dividend
The Four Horsemen of the Apocalypse
  (1961 version)
Lust for Life
Madame Bovary
A Matter of Time
The Sandpiper
Some Came Running

STAR CHECK LIST: BING CROSBY _____ MU25

A Connecticut Yankee in King Arthur's
  Court
High Society
Holiday Inn
The King of Jazz
Let's Make Love
Road to Bali
Road to Rio
Road to Utopia

Robin and the Seven Hoods
White Christmas

NON-MUSIC
The Bells of St. Mary's
The Country Girl (1954 version)
Going My Way
Little Boy Lost

STAR CHECK LIST: FRANK SINATRA _____ MU26
See also: DR49 Frank Sinatra Check List

Anchors Aweigh
Can-Can
Guys and Dolls

High Society
Higher and Higher
On the Town

Robin and the Seven Hoods
Step Lively
Take Me out to the Ball Game

Till the Clouds Roll By
Young at Heart

STAR CHECK LIST: BARBRA STREISAND ———————————— MU27

Funny Girl
Funny Lady
Hello, Dolly!
On a Clear Day You Can See Forever
A Star Is Born (1976 version)
Yentl*

*also director

NON-MUSIC
All Night Long
For Pete's Sake
The Main Event
Nuts
The Owl and the Pussycat
Up the Sandbox
The Way We Were
What's Up, Doc?

DIRECTOR/CHOREOGRAPHER CHECK LIST: BOB FOSSE ———————— MU28

All That Jazz
Cabaret
Damn Yankees*
Kiss Me Kate**
The Little Prince*

The Pajama Game†
Sweet Charity

NON-MUSIC
Lenny
Star 80

  *actor, choreographer only
 **actor only
†choreographer only

Chapter Ten

MYSTERY/SUSPENSE
(MY)

CLASSIC FILM NOIR _____ MY1

The Asphalt Jungle
The Big Combo
The Big Heat
The Big Sleep (1946 version)
Born to Kill
Cat People (1942 version)
Caught
Cornered
Criss Cross
Crossfire
D.O.A. (1949 version)
The Dark Mirror
Dark Passage
Dead Reckoning
Deadline at Dawn
Detour
Double Indemnity
Force of Evil
Gilda
The Glass Key
He Walked by Night
High Sierra
His Kind of Woman
I Wake Up Screaming
Journey Into Fear (1943 version)
Key Largo
The Killing

Knock on any Door
The Lady From Shanghai
Laura (1944)
The Maltese Falcon
Mildred Pierce
Murder My Sweet
The Night of the Hunter
Out of the Past
The Postman Always Rings Twice (1946 version)
Scarlet Street
The Set-Up
Shack Out on 101
Slightly Scarlet
Sorry, Wrong Number
The Strange Love of Martha Ivers
The Stranger (1946)
Suddenly
Sunset Boulevard
T-Men
They Live by Night
They Won't Believe Me
This Gun for Hire
Touch of Evil
While the City Sleeps
White Heat
You Only Live Once

CONTEMPORARY FILM NOIR _____ MY2

Against All Odds (1984)
The American Friend
Angel Heart
The Big Easy
Blade Runner
Blood Simple
Blue Velvet
Body Heat
Bring Me the Head of Alfredo Garcia
Cape Fear

Chinatown
Cutter's Way
D.O.A. (1988 version)
Dance With a Stranger
The Driver
Experiment in Terror
Eyes of Laura Mars
52 Pick-up
Hustle
The Manchurian Candidate

Manhunter
Night Moves
No Way Out (1987)
Performance
Stormy Monday
Taxi Driver

Tequila Sunrise
To Live and Die in L.A.
True Believer
True Confessions
Union City
Who'll Stop the Rain

WOMEN IN DANGER ———————————————————— MY3

Apology
Berserk!
Beware, My Lovely
Charade
The Collector
The Cradle Will Fall
Dead of Winter
Dial M for Murder
Eyes of Laura Mars
Gaslight
The House on Carroll Street
Jack's Back
Jagged Edge
Jamaica Inn (1939 & 1985 versions)
Jane Doe
Klute
Lady in a Cage
Laura
Masquerade

Midnight Lace
The Morning After
Ms. 45
Night Watch
Notorious
The Plumber
Positive I.D.
Rider on the Rain
Scream of Fear
Secret Beyond the Door
See No Evil
Sidney Sheldon's Bloodline
Someone to Watch Over Me
Sorry, Wrong Number
The Spiral Staircase
Suspicion (1941 & 1987 versions)
The Very Edge
Wait Until Dark

TOUGH DAMES ———————————————————————— MY4

Body Heat
The Dark Mirror
Dead Reckoning
Double Indemnity
Gilda

Last Embrace
Niagara
Scarlet Street
To Have and Have Not

SUSPENSE AND ROMANCE —————————————————— MY5

Against All Odds (1984)
Betrayed
The Big Easy
Body Double
Body Heat
Double Indemnity
Dressed to Kill
Eyewitness
The Fourth Man
Jagged Edge
Klute

Laura
Marnie
The Morning After
No Mercy
No Way Out (1987)
Notorious
Obsession
Out of the Past
The Postman Always Rings Twice (1946
    & 1981 versions)
Someone to Watch Over Me

Spellbound
Still of the Night
Suspicion (1941 & 1987 versions)
The Tamarind Seed

They're Playing With Fire
Thief of Hearts
The Thomas Crown Affair
Vertigo

POLITICAL INTRIGUE ———————————————————————— MY6

All the President's Men
The Amateur
Another Country
Arabesque
Billion Dollar Brain
Black Sunday
The Black Windmill
Cornered
A Dandy in Aspic
Dark Journey
The Day of the Jackal
Defense of the Realm
The Eagle Has Landed
The Eiger Sanction
Eye of the Needle
The Falcon and the Snowman
Foreign Correspondent
The Formula
Funeral in Berlin
Gambit
The General Died at Dawn
Gorky Park
Half Moon Street
The Holcroft Covenant
The House on Carroll Street
The Ipcress File
The Jigsaw Man
Journey Into Fear
Keeping Track
The Killer Elite

Last Embrace
The Mackintosh Man
The Man Who Knew Too Much (1934 &
   1955 versions)
The Manchurian Candidate
No Way Out (1987)
Notorious
The Odessa File
The Osterman Weekend
The Parallax View
Philby, Burgess and Maclean: Spy
   Scandal of the Century
The President's Plane Is Missing
The Quiller Memorandum
Sabotage
Saboteur
The Salamander
The Secret Agent
Spy in Black
The Stranger (1946)
The Tamarind Seed
Target
Telefon
The Third Man
The 39 Steps (1935 & 1978 versions)
Three Days of the Condor
Topaz
Torn Curtain
Winter Kills

WRONG MAN THRILLERS ———————————————————————— MY7

The Bedroom Window
Criminal Court
Frenzy
Hit and Run
I Confess
I Wake Up Screaming
Jack's Back
The Man Who Knew Too Much (1934 &
   1955 versions)
Marathon Man
North by Northwest
Out of Bounds

The Paris Express
Pendulum
Saboteur
Star of Midnight
The Stranger on the Third Floor
10 Rillington Place
They Made Me a Criminal
They Won't Believe Me
The 39 Steps (1935 & 1978 versions)
Three Days of the Condor
The Wrong Man
Young and Innocent

TRUE-LIFE SUSPENSE _____ **MY8**
See also: DR6 True-Life Contemporary Drama

Adam
Agatha
Beyond Reasonable Doubt
The Brink's Job
Buster
Dance With a Stranger
Fatal Vision
Hammett

Hide in Plain Sight
Philby, Burgess and Maclean: Spy
   Scandal of the Century
Robbery
10 Rillington Place
The Thin Blue Line
Without a Trace

CAT AND MOUSE GAMES _____ **MY9**

Best Seller
Black Widow
Criminal Law
Deathtrap
Duel
F/X
The Formula

Highpoint
The Last of Sheila
Manhunter
Rope
The Silent Partner
Sleuth
Strangers on a Train

CHARACTER CHECK LIST: SHERLOCK HOLMES _____ **MY10**

The Adventures of Sherlock Holmes
Dressed to Kill (1946)
The Hound of the Baskervilles (1938,
   1959 & 1977 versions)
House of Fear
Masks of Death
Murder by Decree
Pearl of Death
The Private Life of Sherlock Holmes
Pursuit to Algiers
The Scarlet Claw
The Seven Percent Solution
Sherlock Holmes and the Secret
   Weapon

Sherlock Holmes and the Voice of
   Terror
Sherlock Holmes Faces Death
Sherlock Holmes in Washington
The Silver Blaze
The Speckled Band
Spider Woman
A Study in Scarlet
A Study in Terror
Terror by Night
The Triumph of Sherlock Holmes
Without a Clue
The Woman in Green
Young Sherlock Holmes

CHARACTER CHECK LIST: BULLDOG DRUMMOND _____ **MY11**

Bulldog Drummond
Bulldog Drummond at Bay
Bulldog Drummond Comes Back
Bulldog Drummond Escapes
Bulldog Drummond in Africa

Bulldog Drummond Strikes Back
Bulldog Drummond's Bride
Bulldog Drummond's Peril
Bulldog Drummond's Revenge
Bulldog Drummond's Secret Police

CHARACTER CHECK LIST: THE SAINT _____ **MY12**

The Saint in London
The Saint in New York
The Saint Strikes Back

The Saint Takes Over
The Saint's Vacation

CHARACTERS CHECK LIST: NICK & NORA CHARLES _____ MY13

After the Thin Man
Another Thin Man
Shadow of the Thin Man

Song of the Thin Man
The Thin Man
The Thin Man Goes Home

PRIVATE EYES AND OTHER DETECTIVES _____ MY14
See also: MY Character & Author Check Lists

Angel Heart
The Big Fix
Chinatown
Columbo: Prescription Murder
Gotham
In the Heat of the Night

The Kennel Murder Case
Klute
The Late Show
Night Moves
Shamus
An Unsuitable Job for a Woman

AMATEUR SLEUTHS _____ MY15

Blind Date (1984)
Blow Out
Blow Up
Blue Velvet
Coma
The Conversation
Deadline at Dawn
The Detective (1954)
Dressed to Kill (1980)
Gumshoe
Her Alibi

Mike's Murder
The Naked Face
The Name of the Rose
A Night to Remember (1942)
The Parallax View
Rear Window
Rope
Stunts
True Believer
The Velvet Touch

WHODUNITS _____ MY16

And Then There Were None
Appointment With Death
The Body in the Library
Death on the Nile
Evil Under the Sun
Killjoy
The Last of Sheila

The List of Adrian Messenger
Murder at the Vanities
A Murder Is Announced
Murder on the Orient Express
A Pocketful of Rye
Rehearsal for Murder
Ten Little Indians (1975 version)

CRAZY KILLERS _____ MY17

City in Fear
Dressed to Kill (1980)
Fatal Attraction
Frenzy
Jack's Back
The Killer Inside Me
The Lodger
M (1931 version)

Manhunter
No Way to Treat a Lady
Play Misty for Me
The Stepfather
Strangers on a Train
Targets
Ten to Midnight
White of the Eye

SUSPENSE IN THE FAMILY WAY _____ MY18

The Bad Seed
The Cold Room
The Dark Mirror
Don't Look Now
Fatal Attraction
Murder by Natural Causes
Party Line
Reflections of Murder
Road to Salina

Scalpel
Shadow of a Doubt
The Stepfather
Torment
True Confessions
Where Are the Children?
White of the Eye
Winter Kills
Without a Trace

BRITISH MYSTERY/SUSPENSE _____ MY19
See also: MY10 Sherlock Holmes Check List

And Then There Were None
Bellman and True
Candles at Nine
The Cat and the Canary (1977 version)
Dance With a Stranger
The Detective (1954)
Endless Night
The Evil Mind
Gumshoe
Kind Hearts and Coronets
The Lady Vanishes (1938 version)
The Ladykillers
The Lavender Hill Mob
The Long Dark Hall
Number 17
Odd Man Out

Philby, Burgess and Maclean: Spy
   Scandal of the Century
Robbery
Sabotage
Scream of Fear
Seance on a Wet Afternoon
The Secret Agent
Sleuth
The Spy in Black
Stormy Monday
10 Rillington Place
The 39 Steps (1935 version)
Tiger Bay
An Unsuitable Job for a Woman
The Whistle Blower
Young and Innocent

SUSPENSE IN OTHER FOREIGN SETTINGS _____ MY20

The American Friend
Confidentially Yours
Coup de Torchon (Clean Slate)
Dear Detective
Death Watch
Diabolique
Diva
The Fourth Man
Frantic (1958)
Frantic (1988)
Gorky Park
Heatwave

High and Low
The Mighty Quinn
Off Limits (1988)
One Deadly Summer
The Plumber
Rififi
Road Games
Sincerely, Charlotte
The Wages of Fear
Wedding in Blood
Z

COMIC MYSTERIES _____ MY21
See also: CO10 Crime and Suspense Comedies

Arsenic and Old Lace
Bullshot

Clue
Dead Men Don't Wear Plaid

Her Alibi
Kind Hearts and Coronets
Lady of Burlesque
The Ladykillers
The Lavender Hill Mob
Legal Eagles
The Mad Miss Manton
The Man With Bogart's Face
Mr. and Mrs. North

Murder by Death
A Night to Remember (1942)
Scandalous
Star of Midnight
Sunset
The Thin Man (series)
The Trouble With Harry
Who Done It?
Without a Clue

DIRECTOR CHECK LIST: ALFRED HITCHCOCK _____ MY22

The Birds
Blackmail
Dial M for Murder
Easy Virtue
Family Plot
Foreign Correspondent
Frenzy
I Confess
Jamaica Inn (1939 version)
The Lady Vanishes (1938 version)
Lifeboat
The Lodger
The Man Who Knew Too Much (1934 &
   1956 versions)
The Manxman
Marnie
Mr. and Mrs. Smith
Murder
North by Northwest
Notorious
Number 17
The Paradine Case
Psycho

Rear Window
Rebecca
Rich and Strange
Rope
Sabotage
Saboteur
The Secret Agent
Shadow of a Doubt
The Skin Game (1931)
Spellbound
Stage Fright
Strangers on a Train
Suspicion
The 39 Steps (1935 version)
To Catch a Thief
Topaz
Torn Curtain
The Trouble With Harry
Under Capricorn
Vertigo
The Wrong Man
Young and Innocent

AUTHOR CHECK LIST: AGATHA CHRISTIE _____ MY23

And Then There Were None
Appointment With Death
The Body in the Library
Death on the Nile
Endless Night
Evil Under the Sun
Love From a Stranger
The Mirror Crack'd

A Murder Is Announced
Murder on the Orient Express
Ordeal by Innocence
A Pocketful of Rye
Ten Little Indians
Witness for the Prosecution (1957
   version)

AUTHOR CHECK LIST: RAYMOND CHANDLER _____ MY24

The Big Sleep (1946 & 1978 versions)
The Brasher Doubloon

Farewell, My Lovely
Murder My Sweet

AUTHOR CHECK LIST: JAMES M. CAIN _____ **MY25**

Butterfly
Double Indemnity
Mildred Pierce

The Postman Always Rings Twice (1946
   & 1981 versions)
Slightly Scarlet

AUTHOR CHECK LIST: ELMORE LEONARD _____ **MY26**

52 Pick-up
Hombre
Mr. Majestyk

Stick
3:10 to Yuma

AUTHOR CHECK LIST: ROSS MACDONALD _____ **MY27**

The Drowning Pool

Harper

AUTHOR CHECK LIST: DASHIELL HAMMETT _____ **MY28**

The Dain Curse
The Glass Key

The Maltese Falcon
The Thin Man (series)

AUTHOR CHECK LIST: JIM THOMPSON _____ **MY29**

Coup de Torchon (Clean Slate)
The Getaway

The Killer Inside Me

AUTHOR CHECK LIST: MICKEY SPILLANE _____ **MY30**

The Girl Hunters

I, the Jury (1982 version)

AUTHOR CHECK LIST: FREDERICK FORSYTH _____ **MY31**

The Day of the Jackal
The Dogs of War

The Fourth Protocol
The Odessa File

AUTHOR CHECK LIST: ROBERT LUDLUM _____ **MY32**

The Holcroft Covenant

The Osterman Weekend

AUTHOR CHECK LIST: JOHN LECARRE _____ **MY33**

The Little Drummer Girl

The Looking Glass War

HEISTS _____ MY34

The Asphalt Jungle
Bellman and True
Big Deal on Madonna Street
Bob le Flambeur
The Brink's Job
Buster
Dead Heat on a Merry-Go-Round
Diamonds
Disorganized Crime
$ (Dollars)
11 Harrowhouse
A Fish Called Wanda

The Getaway
Going in Style
The Great Train Robbery
The Hot Rock
How to Beat the High Cost of Living
The Killing
The Lavender Hill Mob
Robbery
The Thomas Crown Affair
Thunderbolt and Lightfoot
Topkapi

CHARACTER CHECK LIST: CHARLIE CHAN _____ MY35

Castle in the Desert
Charlie Chan at the Opera
Charlie Chan at the Wax Museum
Charlie Chan in Paris

Charlie Chan in Rio
Charlie Chan's Secret
Murder Over New York

AUTHOR CHECK LIST: DAPHNE DU MAURIER _____ MY36

The Birds
Don't Look Now

Jamaica Inn (1939 & 1985 versions)
Rebecca

Chapter Eleven

SCIENCE FICTION/FANTASY
(SF)

CLASSIC 50S SCI-FI _____ SF1

The Blob
The Brain From Planet Arous
The Crawling Eye
The Creature From the Black Lagoon
The Day the Earth Stood Still
Destination Moon
Earth vs. the Flying Saucers
Fiend Without a Face
The Fly (1958 version)
Forbidden Planet
4D Man
I Married a Monster From Outer Space
The Incredible Shrinking Man

Invaders From Mars (1953 version)
Invasion of the Body Snatchers (1956 version)
It Came From Outer Space
Journey to the Center of the Earth
Kronos
On the Beach
Rocket Ship X-M
The Thing (From Another World)
This Island Earth
Them!
War of the Worlds
When Worlds Collide

CLASSIC PRE-50S SCI-FI/FANTASY _____ SF2

Angel on My Shoulder
Beauty and the Beast (1946 version)
The Bishop's Wife
Blood of a Poet
The Devil and Daniel Webster
Dr. Cyclops
Frankenstein (1931 version)
The Ghost Goes West

Here Comes Mr. Jordan
I Married a Witch
King Kong (1933 version)
Lost Horizon
Metropolis (1926 edition)
The Testament of Dr. Mabuse
Things to Come

OUTER (AND INNER) SPACE TRAVEL _____ SF3

Alien
Aliens
The Angry Red Planet
At the Earth's Core
The Black Hole
Destination Moon
Explorers
Fantastic Voyage
First Men in the Moon
Flight to Mars
Innerspace
Journey to the Center of the Earth
Journey to the Far Side of the Sun

Marooned
Rocket Ship X-M
Saturn 3
Silent Running
SpaceCamp
Spacehunter: Adventures in the Forbbiden Zone
Star Trek (series)
This Island Earth
20,000 Leagues Under the Sea
2001: A Space Odyssey
2010: The Year We Make Contact
Voyage to the Bottom of the Sea

TIME TRAVEL _____ SF4

Biggles
Daleks: Invasion Earth 2150 A.D.
Dinosaurus!
The Final Countdown
Highlander
The Land That Time Forgot
The Lost World (1925 version)
The People That Time Forgot
The Philadelphia Experiment

Slaughterhouse Five
Sleeper
Star Trek IV: The Voyage Home
Time After Time
Time Bandits
The Time Machine
Timerider
Where Time Began

SCIENCE GONE WRONG _____ SF5
See also HO20 Science Runs Amok

Altered States
Android
The Andromeda Strain
The Asphyx
Brainstorm
Coma
Deathwatch
Dr. Cyclops
Dreamscape

The Fly (1958 & 1986 versions)
The Fly II
4D Man
Looker
Metropolis
The Terminal Man
Wargames
X: The Man With the X-Ray Eyes

MAD MACHINES _____ SF6

Colossus: The Forbin Project
Demon Seed
Futureworld
Runaway

Saturn 3
2001: A Space Odyssey
Westworld

SCI-FI DISASTER _____ SF7

The Andromeda Strain
The Day of the Triffids
The Day the Earth Caught Fire
Meteor

The Swarm
War of the Worlds
When Worlds Collide

SURVIVAL ADVENTURES _____ SF8

After the Fall of New York
The Andromeda Strain
Endgame
Enemy Mine
Escape From New York
Exterminators of the Year 3000
Firebird 2015 A.D.
Future-Kill
The Last Starfighter

Logan's Run
Planet of the Apes (series)
Quintet
Soylent Green
W
Warlords of the 21st Century
Warriors of the Wasteland
Zardoz

ALIEN VISITORS   SF9

The Blob
The Brain From Planet Arous
The Brother From Another Planet
Close Encounters of the Third Kind
Cocoon
Cocoon: The Return
The Crawling Eye
The Day the Earth Stood Still
The Day Time Ended
E.T. The Extra-Terrestrial
Earth Girls Are Easy
Earth vs. the Flying Saucers
I Married a Monster From Outer Space
Invaders From Mars (1953 & 1985
   versions)

Invasion of the Body Snatchers (1956 &
   1978 versions)
It Came From Outer Space
The Man Who Fell to Earth
Starman
Strange Invaders
They Live
The Thing
The Thing (From Another World)
This Island Earth
Village of the Damned
War of the Worlds
Wavelength

MUTANT MONSTERS   SF10

Creature From the Black Lagoon
Empire of the Ants
Food of the Gods
Godzilla (series)
Gorgo
The Hideous Sun Demon

It Came From Beneath the Sea
King Kong
Mysterious Island
Prophecy
Them!

FUTURE WARS AGAINST DICTATORS   SF11

Brazil
Dune
The Empire Strikes Back
Escape 2000
Fahrenheit 451
The Last Chase
1984

Return of the Jedi
Rollerball
Running Man
Star Wars
THX 1138
Tron

AFTER THE HOLOCAUST   SF12

After the Fall of New York
Aftermath
A Boy and His Dog
Cyborg
Damnation Alley
The Day After
Glen and Randa
Lord of the Flies

Night of the Comet
On the Beach
Planet of the Apes (series)
The Quiet Earth
Testament
Things to Come
Threads
Virus

FAMILY SCI-FI/FANTASY _____ **SF13**
See also: FA8 Family Sci-Fi/Fantasy

The Adventures of Baron Munchausen
Aurora Encounter
Battle for the Planet of the Apes
Beneath the Planet of the Apes
The Black Hole
The Blue Bird (1940 version)
Conquest of the Planet of the Apes
The Dark Crystal
E.T. The Extra-Terrestrial
The Empire Strikes Back
Escape From the Planet of the Apes
Explorers
From the Earth to the Moon
The Hobbit
Journey to the Center of the Earth
King Kong (1933 version)
The Land of Faraway
Labyrinth
Laserblast
The Last Starfighter
Legend
Lord of the Rings
Making Contact
The Man Who Could Work Miracles

Masters of the Universe
The NeverEnding Story
Planet of the Apes
Return of the Jedi
Return to Oz
The 7 Faces of Dr. Lao
The 7th Voyage of Sinbad
Something Wicked This Way Comes
Space Raiders
Spacehunter: Adventures in the
    Forbidden Zone
Star Trek (series)
Star Wars
Starchaser: The Legend of Orion
The Time Machine
Transformers
Tron
20,000 Leagues Under the Sea
The War of the Worlds
The Watcher in the Woods
Willow
The Wizard of Oz
Wizards

SPECTACULAR SETS _____ **SF14**

The Adventures of Baron Munchausen
Batman (1989)
The Black Hole
Blade Runner
Brazil

Legend
Metropolis
Things to Come
Transatlantic Tunnel

OSCAR-WINNING SPECIAL EFFECTS _____ **SF15**

Alien
Destination Moon
Dr. Cyclops
E.T. The Extra-Terrestrial
The Empire Strikes Back
Fantastic Voyage
Logan's Run
Marooned

Reap the Wild Wind
Star Wars
The Time Machine
tom thumb
20,000 Leagues Under the Sea
2001: A Space Odyssey
When Worlds Collide

SPECIAL EFFECTS MILESTONES _____ **SF16**

An American Werewolf in London
Close Encounters of the Third Kind
The Lost World (1925 version)
King Kong (1933 version)
Metropolis (1926 edition)

Star Wars
2001: A Space Odyssey
Them!
Tron

FUTURE COPS & ROBBERS _____ SF17

Alien Nation
Blade Runner
A Clockwork Orange
The Hidden
The Killings at Outpost Zeta

Outland
Runaway
Space Rage
Trancers

JAPANESE SCI-FI _____ SF18

Ghidrah, the Three-Headed Monster
Godzilla, King of the Monsters
Godzilla, 1985
Godzilla vs. Megalon
Gorath
The H-Man

The Human Vapor
The Last War
Mothra
The Mysterians
Rodan
Terror of Mechagodzilla

SCIENCE FICTION WITH A FOREIGN ACCENT _____ SF19
See also: SF18 Japanese Sci-Fi

Alphaville
The Asphyx
Attack of the Robots
Barbarella
Biggles
Daleks: Invasion Earth 2150 A.D.
The Day of the Triffids
The Day the Earth Caught Fire
Deathwatch
Le Dernier Combat

Dr. Who and the Daleks
Fantastic Planet
Journey to the Far Side of the Sun
The Last Days of Man on Earth
Man Facing Southeast
The Quatermass Conclusion
Village of the Damned
Threads
Zardoz

SCI-FI HORROR _____ SF20

Alien
Alien Predators
Aliens
Altered States
Creature
The Fly (1986 version)
The Fly II
Galaxy of Terror

The Island of Dr. Moreau
Lifeforce
Phase IV
Star Crystal
Terrorvision
The Thing
Xtro

SCI-FI SPOOFS _____ SF21

The Adventures of Buckaroo Banzai
   Across the 8th Dimension
Dark Star
Death Race 2000
Earth Girls Are Easy

Flash Gordon
Galaxina
Heartbeeps
The Ice Pirates
The Incredible Shrinking Woman

Innerspace
The Jet Benny Show
The Last Days of Man on Earth
The Man With Two Brains
Monster in the Closet
Night of the Comet

Really Weird Tales
Simon
Sleeper
Spaceballs
Strange Invaders
The Tenth Victim

SEXY SCI-FI/FANTASY _____ SF22

Barbarella
A Boy and His Dog
Demon Seed

Galaxina
Liquid Sky

SCI-FI CHECK LIST: CLASSIC SERIES _____ SF23

Planet of the Apes
  Planet of the Apes
  Beneath the Planet of the Apes
  Escape From the Planet of the Apes
  Conquest of the Planet of the Apes
  Battle for the Planet of the Apes
Star Trek
  The Motion Picture

  II: The Wrath of Khan
  III: The Search for Spock
  IV: The Voyage Home
Star Wars
  Star Wars
  The Empire Strikes Back
  Return of the Jedi

DIRECTOR CHECK LIST: STEVEN SPIELBERG _____ SF24

Close Encounters of the Third Kind
The Color Purple
Duel
E.T. The Extra-Terrestrial
Empire of the Sun
Indiana Jones and the Temple of Doom

Jaws
Night Gallery (co-director)
1941
Raiders of the Lost Ark
The Sugarland Express
Twilight Zone: The Movie (co-director)

DIRECTOR CHECK LIST: GEORGE LUCAS _____ SF25

American Graffiti
Star Wars

THX-1138

AUTHOR CHECK LIST: H. G. WELLS _____ SF26

Empire of the Ants
First Men in the Moon
Food of the Gods
The Invisible Man
The Island of Dr. Moreau

The Man Who Could Work Miracles
Things to Come
Time After Time
The Time Machine
The War of the Worlds

AUTHOR CHECK LIST: JULES VERNE _____ SF27

Around the World in 80 Days
Five Weeks in a Balloon
From the Earth to the Moon
In Search of the Castaways
Journey to the Center of the Earth

The Light at the Edge of the World
Master of the World
Mysterious Island
20,000 Leagues Under the Sea

Chapter Twelve

WESTERNS
(WE)

WESTERN EPICS _____ WE1

The Alamo
The Big Country
The Big Sky
The Big Trail
Cheyenne Autumn
Cimarron
Duel in the Sun
The Good, the Bad, and the Ugly
Heaven's Gate
How the West Was Won

Little Big Man
Mackenna's Gold
The Magnificent Seven
Once Upon a Time in the West
The Plainsman
Red River
Silverado
The Unforgiven
The Way West

REAL-LIFE WESTERN CHARACTERS _____ WE2

Billy the Kid
Billy the Kid Returns
The Left-Handed Gun
The Outlaw
Pat Garrett and Billy the Kid
Return of the Bad Men
Young Guns

Doc Holliday
Cheyenne Autumn
Gunfight at the O.K. Corral
My Darling Clementine
The Outlaw

Jesse James
Days of Jesse James
The Great Missouri Raid
The Great Northfield Minnesota Raid
I Shot Jesse James
Jesse James
Jesse James at Bay
The Long Riders

Wild Bill Hickok
Calamity Jane
Little Big Man
The Plainsman (1936)

Pony Express
Young Bill Hickok

Wyatt Earp
Cheyenne Autumn
Gunfight at the O.K. Corral
My Darling Clementine
Winchester '73

George Armstrong Custer
Little Big Man
The Plainsman (1936)
Santa Fe Trail
They Died With Their Boots On

William F. Cody (Buffalo Bill)
Annie Oakley
Buffalo Bill and the Indians
The Plainsman (1936)
Pony Express
Young Buffalo Bill

Annie Oakley
Annie Oakley
Buffalo Bill and the Indians
The Plainsman (1936)

LONE GUNFIGHTERS ——————————————————————————— WE3

A Fistful of Dollars
For a Few Dollars More
The Gunfighter
High Noon
High Noon, Part Two: The Return of
    Will Kane
Man Without a Star
Pale Rider

The Red Headed Stranger
Rooster Cogburn
Shane
The Shootist
The Tin Star
True Grit
Warlock
The Westerner

SYMPATHETIC OUTLAWS ————————————————————————— WE4

Barbarosa
The Ballad of Gregorio Cortez
Butch Cassidy and the Sundance Kid
Butch and Sundance: The Early Days
The Good, the Bad, and the Ugly
The Grey Fox
Harry Tracy
Jesse James
The Left-Handed Gun
The Long Riders
Mad Dog Morgan

The Missouri Breaks
Nevada Smith
The Outlaw
The Outlaw Josey Wales
Pat Garrett and Billy the Kid
Stagecoach
Tell Them Willie Boy Is Here
There Was a Crooked Man
Tom Horn
The Wild Bunch

CAVALRY STORIES ——————————————————————————— WE5

Fort Apache
The Horse Soldiers
Rio Grande
She Wore a Yellow Ribbon

Soldier Blue
They Died With Their Boots On
Ulzana's Raid

REVENGE IN THE OLD WEST ——————————————————————— WE6

Cattle Queen of Montana
Coroner Creek
High Plains Drifter
Macho Callahan
My Darling Clementine
Nevada Smith
Once Upon a Time in the West
One-Eyed Jacks

The Outlaw Josey Wales
Pursued
Rancho Notorious
The Red Headed Stranger
The Return of Frank James
The Searchers
The Sons of Katie Elder
Young Guns

CIVIL WAR WESTERNS ——————————————————————————— WE7
See also: AC5 War Movies: Civil War

Alvarez Kelly
Bad Company
The Beguiled
The Comancheros

Dark Command
The Fastest Guitar Alive
Friendly Persuasion
The Good, the Bad, and the Ugly

The Horse Soldiers
How the West Was Won (one segment)
Love Me Tender
Macho Callahan
Major Dundee
Massacre at Fort Holman

The Outlaw Josey Wales
Run of the Arrow
Santa Fe Trail
Shenandoah
The Skin Game (1971)
The Undefeated

INDIANS AS HEROES ———————————————————— WE8

Apache
Broken Arrow
Cheyenne Autumn
Eagle's Wing
Hombre
I Will Fight No More Forever
Little Big Man
A Man Called Horse
Mohawk
Naked in the Sun
100 Rifles
Return of a Man Called Horse

Run of the Arrow
The Searchers
Smith!
Soldier Blue
Tell Them Willie Boy Is Here
Triumphs of a Man Called Horse
Ulzana's Raid
The Unforgiven
The Vanishing American
When the Legends Die
Windwalker

WOMEN OF THE WEST ———————————————————— WE9

Angel and the Badman
Annie Oakley
The Ballad of Cable Hogue
Calamity Jane
Cat Ballou
Cattle Queen of Montana
Comes a Horseman
Destry Rides Again
Duel in the Sun
Girl of the Golden West
Heartland
Heller in Pink Tights
Johnny Guitar

McCabe and Mrs. Miller
The Man Who Loved Cat Dancing
The Maverick Queen
The Misfits
My Darling Clementine
The Plainsman (1936)
Poker Alice
Rachel and the Stranger
The Stalking Moon
Texas Lady
Two Mules for Sister Sara
The Unforgiven

SOUTH OF THE BORDER ———————————————————— WE10

The Americano
Bandolero!
Barbarosa
Bullet for Sandoval
El Condor
A Fistful of Dynamite
Goin' South
100 Rifles

Pancho Villa
The Professionals
Take a Hard Ride
They Came to Cordura
Vera Cruz
Villa Rides
Viva Zapata!
The Wild Bunch

NORTH OF THE BORDER ————————————————— WE11

Blue Canadian Rockies
The Far Country
The Grey Fox
McCabe and Mrs. Miller

North of the Great Divide
North to Alaska
The Spoilers (1942 version)

LAST DAYS OF THE FRONTIER ————————————— WE12

The Ballad of Cable Hogue
Buffalo Bill and the Indians
Butch Cassidy and the Sundance Kid
The Grey Fox
McCabe and Mrs. Miller
The Man Who Shot Liberty Valance

Monte Walsh
Ride the High Country
The Shootist
Tell Them Willie Boy Is Here
Tom Horn
The Wild Bunch

THE CONTEMPORARY WEST ————————————— WE13

Bad Day at Black Rock
Bronco Billy
Coogan's Bluff
Comes a Horseman
Cotter
The Electric Horseman
Giant
Goldenrod
The Great American Cowboy
Hud

Junior Bonner
The Lady Takes a Chance
Last Night at the Alamo
Lonely Are the Brave
The Lusty Men
The Misfits
Three Faces West
Urban Cowboy
When the Legends Die

SPAGHETTI WESTERNS ————————————————— WE14

Beyond the Law
Django
Django Shoots First
A Fistful of Dollars
A Fistful of Dynamite
For a Few Dollars More

The Good, the Bad, and the Ugly
Hang 'Em High
My Name Is Nobody
The Stranger and the Gunfighter
They Call Me Trinity
Trinity Is STILL My Name

WESTERN COMEDIES/SPOOFS ————————————— WE15

Adios Amigo
Along Came Jones
The Beautiful Blonde From Bashful
   Bend
Blazing Saddles
The Brothers O'Toole
Butch and Sundance: The Early Days
Butch Cassidy and the Sundance Kid
Cat Ballou

The Cheyenne Social Club
Destry Rides Again
Draw!
The Duchess and the Dirtwater Fox
The Frisco Kid
Go West (1940)
Goin' South
The Great Scout and Cathouse
   Thursday

The Lady Takes a Chance
The Last Ride of the Dalton Gang
My Little Chickadee
The Paleface
Ruggles of Red Gap
Rustler's Rhapsody
Son of Paleface

Straight to Hell
Support Your Local Sheriff
There Was a Crooked Man
They Call Me Trinity
Trinity Is STILL My Name
Waterhole #3
Way Out West

CULT WESTERNS _____ WE16

Bad Company
The Culpepper Cattle Company
Duel in the Sun
The Great Northfield Minnesota Raid
The Hired Hand
Johnny Guitar
The Life and Times of Judge Roy Bean
McCabe and Mrs. Miller
The Missouri Breaks
The Oklahoma Kid
Once Upon a Time in the West
One-Eyed Jacks
The Outlaw

Pat Garrett and Billy the Kid
Rancho Notorious
Ride in the Whirlwind
Rio Bravo
The Searchers
The Shooting
The Skin Game (1971)
The Terror of Tiny Town
There Was a Crooked Man
3:10 to Yuma
Ulzana's Raid
Wild Rovers
Will Penny

STAR CHECK LIST: JOHN WAYNE _____ WE17
See also: CL17 John Wayne Check List

The Alamo*
Allegheny Uprising
Angel and the Badman
Big Jake
The Big Trail
Cahill: United States Marshall
Chisum
The Comancheros
The Cowboys
Dakota
Dark Command
El Dorado
The Fighting Kentuckian
The Flame of the Barbary Coast
Fort Apache
The Horse Soldiers
How the West Was Won
In Old California
The Lady Takes a Chance

The Man Who Shot Liberty Valance
North to Alaska
Red River
Rio Bravo
Rio Grande
Rio Lobo
Rooster Cogburn
The Searchers
She Wore a Yellow Ribbon
The Shootist
The Sons of Katie Elder
The Spoilers
Stagecoach
Three Faces West
The Train Robbers
True Grit
The Undefeated
War of the Wildcats
The War Wagon

*also director

DIRECTOR CHECK LIST: JOHN FORD ————————————————— WE18
See also CL34 John Ford Check List

Cheyenne Autumn
Fort Apache
The Horse Soldiers
How the West Was Won (co-director)
The Man Who Shot Liberty Valance
My Darling Clementine

Rio Grande
The Searchers
She Wore a Yellow Ribbon
Stagecoach
Two Rode Together
Wagonmaster

DIRECTOR CHECK LIST: SAM PECKINPAH ————————————————— WE19

The Ballad of Cable Hogue
The Deadly Companions
Junior Bonner
Major Dundee
Pat Garrett and Billy the Kid
Ride the High Country
The Wild Bunch

NON-WESTERN
Bring Me the Head of Alfredo Garcia
Convoy
Cross of Iron
The Getaway
The Killer Elite
The Osterman Weekend
Straw Dogs

DIRECTOR CHECK LIST: ANTHONY MANN ————————————————— WE20

Bend of the River
The Far Country
The Man From Laramie
The Naked Spur
The Tin Star
Winchester '73

NON-WESTERN
A Dandy in Aspic
El Cid

The Fall of the Roman Empire
The Glenn Miller Story
God's Little Acre
He Walked by Night (co-director)
Men in War
Railroaded
Strategic Air Command
T-Men
Thunder Bay

DIRECTOR CHECK LIST: HOWARD HAWKS ————————————————— WE21
See also CL35 Howard Hawks Check List

The Big Sky
El Dorado
The Outlaw (co-director)

Red River
Rio Bravo
Rio Lobo

STAR CHECK LIST: RANDOLPH SCOTT ————————————————— WE22

Abilene Town
Badman's Territory
Coroner Creek
Jesse James
The Last of the Mohicans (1936 version)
Man of the Forest

Rage at Dawn
Return of the Badmen
Ride the High Country
The Spoilers
Ten Wanted Men
To the Last Man

NON-WESTERN
Bombardier
Captain Kidd
Follow the Fleet
Gung Ho! (1943)

My Favorite Wife
Rebecca of Sunnybrook Farm
Roberta
Susannah of the Mounties

STAR CHECK LIST: ROY ROGERS _____ WE23

Along the Navajo Trail
Apache Rose
The Arizona Kid
Bad Man of Deadwood
Bells of Coronado
Bells of Rosarita
Bells of San Angelo
The Big Show (with The Sons of the
    Pioneers)
Billy the Kid Returns
Carson City Kid
Colorado
Come on, Rangers
The Cowboy and the Señorita
Dark Command
Days of Jesse James
Don't Fence Me In
Down Dakota Way
Eyes of Texas
The Far Frontier
Frontier Pony Express
Gay Ranchero
The Golden Stallion
Grand Canyon Trail
Hands Across the Border
Heart of the Golden West
Heart of the Rockies
Helldorado
Home in Oklahoma
Idaho
In Old Amarillo
In Old Caliente
Jesse James at Bay
King of the Cowboys
Lights of Old Santa Fe

Man From Cheyenne
My Pal Trigger
Night Time in Nevada
North of the Great Divide
Old Barn Dance (billed as Dick Weston)
The Old Corral
The Ranger and the Lady
Ridin' Down the Canyon
Robinhood of the Pecos
Romance on the Range
Rough Riders Roundup
Saga of Death Valley
Shine on Harvest Moon
Silver Spurs
Son of Paleface
Song of Arizona
Song of Nevada
Song of Texas
South of Santa Fe
Southward Ho!
Springtime in the Sierras
Sunset in the West
Sunset on the Desert
Sunset Serenade
Susanna Pass
Texas Lightning
Trail of Robin Hood
Trigger, Jr.
Under California Stars
Under Nevada Skies
Under Western Stars
The Yellow Rose of Texas
Young Bill Hickok
Young Buffalo Bill

STAR CHECK LIST: GENE AUTRY _____ WE24

The Big Show
The Big Sombrero
Blue Canadian Rockies
Boots and Saddles
Call of the Canyon

Cow Town
Down Mexico Way
Git Along, Little Dogies
Heart of the Rio Grande
The Hills of Utah

In Old Santa Fe
Last of the Pony Riders
The Man From Music Mountain
Man of the Frontier
Melody Ranch
Night Stage to Galveston
The Old Barn Dance
The Old Corral
On Top of Old Smoky
Phantom Empire (serial)
Prairie Moon
Radio Ranch (condensed version of
    Phantom Empire serial)
Ride, Ranger, Ride

Riders of the Whistling Pines
Ridin' on a Rainbow
Robin Hood of Texas
Rootin' Tootin' Rhythm
Round-Up Time in Texas
Saginaw Trail
Sioux City Sue
South of the Border
Valley of Fire
Winning of the West

NON-WESTERN
Manhattan Merry-Go-Round

STAR CHECK LIST: GARY COOPER _____ WE25
See also: CL26 Gary Cooper Check List

Along Came Jones
Distant Drums
Fighting Caravans
High Noon
The Plainsman

They Came to Cordura
Vera Cruz
The Virginian
The Westerner

STAR CHECK LIST: CLINT EASTWOOD _____ WE26
See also: AC27 Clint Eastwood Check List

The Beguiled
Bronco Billy*
A Fistful of Dollars
For a Few Dollars More
The Good, the Bad, and the Ugly
Hang 'Em High

*also director

High Plains Drifter*
Joe Kidd
The Outlaw Josey Wales*
Pale Rider*
Two Mules for Sister Sara

DIRECTOR CHECK LIST: SERGIO LEONE _____ WE27

A Fistful of Dollars
A Fistful of Dynamite
For a Few Dollars More
The Good, the Bad, and the Ugly

Once Upon a Time in the West

NON-WESTERN
Once Upon a Time in America

DIRECTOR CHECK LIST: BUDD BOETTICHER _____ WE28

The Man From the Alamo
A Time for Dying

NON-WESTERN
Arruza
The Bullfighter and the Lady
The Magnificent Matador

AUTHOR CHECK LIST: LOUIS L'AMOUR _____ WE29

Cancel My Reservation
Heller in Pink Tights

The Quick and the Dead
The Sacketts

Chapter Thirteen

VIDEO EXTRA
(XT)

ACADEMY AWARD CHECK LIST: BEST PICTURE ———————————— XT1

1927-28 Wings	1962 Lawrence of Arabia
1928-29 Broadway Melody	1964 My Fair Lady
1929-30 All Quiet on the Western	1965 The Sound of Music
Front	1966 A Man for all Seasons
1930-31 Cimarron	1967 In the Heat of the Night
1931-32 Grand Hotel	1968 Oliver!
1934 It Happened One Night	1969 Midnight Cowboy
1935 Mutiny on the Bounty	1970 Patton
1936 The Great Ziegfeld	1971 The French Connection
1937 The Life of Emile Zola	1972 The Godfather
1939 Gone With the Wind	1973 The Sting
1940 Rebecca	1974 The Godfather, Part II
1942 Mrs. Miniver	1975 One Flew Over the Cuckoo's
1943 Casablanca	Nest
1944 Going My Way	1976 Rocky
1945 The Lost Weekend	1977 Annie Hall
1946 The Best Years of Our Lives	1978 The Deer Hunter
1948 Hamlet	1979 Kramer vs. Kramer
1949 All the King's Men	1980 Ordinary People
1950 All About Eve	1981 Chariots of Fire
1951 An American in Paris	1982 Gandhi
1952 The Greatest Show on Earth	1983 Terms of Endearment
1953 From Here to Eternity	1984 Amadeus
1954 On the Waterfront	1985 Out of Africa
1955 Marty	1986 Platoon
1956 Around the World in 80 Days	1987 The Last Emperor
1957 The Bridge on the River Kwai	1988 Rain Man
1958 Gigi	
1959 Ben-Hur	Note: *Tom Jones*, the 1963 winner, has
1960 The Apartment	been discontinued; copies on
1961 West Side Story	videocassette are difficult to find.

ACADEMY AWARD CHECK LIST: BEST ACTOR ———————————— XT2

1927-28 The Last Command (Emil	1935 The Informer (Victor McLaglen)
Jannings)	1937 Captains Courageous (Spencer
1931-32 (tie) The Champ (Wallace	Tracy)
Beery)	1939 Goodbye, Mr. Chips (Robert
Dr. Jekyll and Mr. Hyde	Donat)
(Fredric March)	1940 The Philadelphia Story (James
1932-33 The Private Life of Henry	Stewart)
VIII (Charles Laughton)	1941 Sergeant York (Gary Cooper)
1934 It Happened One Night (Clark	1942 Yankee Doodle Dandy (James
Gable)	Cagney)

1943 Watch on the Rhine (Paul Lukas)
1944 Going My Way (Bing Crosby)
1945 The Lost Weekend (Ray Milland)
1946 The Best Years of Our Lives
(Fredric March)
1947 A Double Life (Ronald Colman)
1948 Hamlet (Laurence Olivier)
1949 All The King's Men (Broderick
Crawford)
1950 Cyrano de Bergerac (Jose Ferrer)
1951 The African Queen (Humphrey
Bogart)
1952 High Noon (Gary Cooper)
1953 Stalag 17 (William Holden)
1954 On the Waterfront (Marlon
Brando)
1955 Marty (Ernest Borgnine)
1956 The King and I (Yul Brynner)
1957 The Bridge on the River Kwai
(Alec Guinness)
1958 Separate Tables (David Niven)
1959 Ben-Hur (Charlton Heston)
1960 Elmer Gantry (Burt Lancaster)
1961 Judgment at Nuremberg
(Maximilian Schell)
1962 To Kill a Mockingbird (Gregory
Peck)
1963 Lilies of the Field (Sidney
Poitier)
1964 My Fair Lady (Rex Harrison)
1965 Cat Ballou (Lee Marvin)

1966 A Man for all Seasons (Paul
Scofield)
1967 In the Heat of the Night (Rod
Steiger)
1968 Charly (Cliff Robertson)
1969 True Grit (John Wayne)
1970 Patton (George C. Scott)
1971 The French Connection (Gene
Hackman)
1972 The Godfather (Marlon Brando)
1973 Save the Tiger (Jack Lemmon)
1974 Harry and Tonto (Art Carney)
1975 One Flew Over the Cuckoo's
Nest (Jack Nicholson)
1976 Network (Peter Finch)
1977 The Goodbye Girl (Richard
Dreyfuss)
1978 Coming Home (Jon Voight)
1979 Kramer vs. Kramer (Dustin
Hoffman)
1980 Raging Bull (Robert DeNiro)
1981 On Golden Pond (Henry Fonda)
1982 Gandhi (Ben Kingsley)
1983 Tender Mercies (Robert Duvall)
1984 Amadeus (F. Murray Abraham)
1985 Kiss of the Spider Woman
(William Hurt)
1986 The Color of Money (Paul
Newman)
1987 Wall Street (Michael Douglas)
1988 Rain Man (Dustin Hoffman)

ACADEMY AWARD CHECK LIST: BEST ACTRESS _____ XT3

1932-33 Morning Glory (Katharine
Hepburn)
1934 It Happened One Night
(Claudette Colbert)
1936 The Great Ziegfeld (Luise
Rainer)
1937 The Good Earth (Luise Rainer)
1938 Jezebel (Bette Davis)
1939 Gone With the Wind (Vivien
Leigh)
1940 Kitty Foyle (Ginger Rogers)
1941 Suspicion (Joan Fontaine)
1942 Mrs. Miniver (Greer Garson)
1943 The Song of Bernadette (Jennifer
Jones)
1944 Gaslight (Ingrid Bergman)
1945 Mildred Pierce (Joan Crawford)

1947 The Farmer's Daughter (Loretta
Young)
1948 Johnny Belinda (Jane Wyman)
1949 The Heiress (Olivia de Havilland)
1950 Born Yesterday (Judy Holliday)
1951 A Streetcar Named Desire
(Vivien Leigh)
1953 Roman Holiday (Audrey
Hepburn)
1954 The Country Girl (Grace Kelly)
1958 I Want to Live! (Susan Hayward)
1960 Butterfield 8 (Elizabeth Taylor)
1961 Two Women (Sophia Loren)
1962 The Miracle Worker (Anne
Bancroft)
1963 Hud (Patricia Neal)
1964 Mary Poppins (Julie Andrews)

1965 Darling (Julie Christie)
1966 Who's Afraid of Virginia Woolf?
    (Elizabeth Taylor)
1967 Guess Who's Coming to Dinner
    (Katharine Hepburn)
1968 (tie) The Lion in Winter
    (Katharine Hepburn)
    Funny Girl (Barbra Streisand)
1969 The Prime of Miss Jean Brodie
    (Maggie Smith)
1970 Women in Love (Glenda Jackson)
1971 Klute (Jane Fonda)
1972 Cabaret (Liza Minnelli)
1973 A Touch of Class (Glenda
    Jackson)
1974 Alice Doesn't Live Here
    Anymore (Ellen Burstyn)
1975 One Flew Over the Cuckoo's
    Nest (Louise Fletcher)
1976 Network (Faye Dunaway)
1977 Annie Hall (Diane Keaton)

1978 Coming Home (Jane Fonda)
1979 Norma Rae (Sally Field)
1980 Coal Miner's Daughter (Sissy
    Spacek)
1981 On Golden Pond (Katharine
    Hepburn)
1982 Sophie's Choice (Meryl Streep)
1983 Terms of Endearment (Shirley
    MacLaine)
1984 Places in the Heart (Sally Field)
1985 The Trip to Bountiful (Geraldine
    Page)
1986 Children of a Lesser God (Marlee
    Matlin)
1987 Moonstruck (Cher)
1988 The Accused (Jodie Foster)

Note: *Room at the Top* (Simone
Signoret), the 1959 winner, has been
discontinued; copies on videocassette
are difficult to find.

ACADEMY AWARD CHECK LIST: BEST SUPPORTING ACTOR _____ XT4

1936 Come and Get It (Walter
    Brennan)
1937 The Life of Emile Zola (Joseph
    Schildkraut)
1939 Stagecoach (Thomas Mitchell)
1940 The Westerner (Walter Brennan)
1944 Going My Way (Barry Fitzgerald)
1945 A Tree Grows in Brooklyn
    (James Dunn)
1946 The Best Years of Our Lives
    (Harold Russell)
1947 Miracle on 34th Street (Edmund
    Gwenn)
1948 The Treasure of the Sierra Madre
    (Walter Huston)
1949 Twelve O'Clock High (Dean
    Jagger)
1950 All About Eve (George Sanders)
1951 A Streetcar Named Desire (Karl
    Malden)
1952 Viva Zapata! (Anthony Quinn)
1953 From Here to Eternity (Frank
    Sinatra)
1954 The Barefoot Contessa (Edmond
    O'Brien)
1955 Mister Roberts (Jack Lemmon)
1956 Lust for Life (Anthony Quinn)
1957 Sayonara (Red Buttons)
1958 The Big Country (Burl Ives)

1959 Ben-Hur (Hugh Griffith)
1960 Spartacus (Peter Ustinov)
1961 West Side Story (George
    Chakiris)
1963 Hud (Melvyn Douglas)
1964 Topkapi (Peter Ustinov)
1965 A Thousand Clowns (Martin
    Balsam)
1967 Cool Hand Luke (George
    Kennedy)
1969 They Shoot Horses, Don't They?
    (Gig Young)
1970 Ryan's Daughter (John Mills)
1972 Cabaret (Joel Grey)
1973 The Paper Chase (John
    Houseman)
1974 The Godfather, Part II (Robert
    DeNiro)
1975 The Sunshine Boys (George
    Burns)
1976 All the President's Men (Jason
    Robards)
1977 Julia (Jason Robards)
1978 The Deer Hunter (Christopher
    Walken)
1979 Being There (Melvyn Douglas)
1980 Ordinary People (Timothy
    Hutton)
1981 Arthur (John Gielgud)

1982	An Officer and a Gentleman (Louis Gossett, Jr.)	1987	The Untouchables (Sean Connery)
1983	Terms of Endearment (Jack Nicholson)	1988	A Fish Called Wanda (Kevin Kline)
1984	The Killing Fields (Haing S. Ngor)		
1985	Cocoon (Don Ameche)		
1986	Hannah and Her Sisters (Michael Caine)		

Notes: Award debuted in 1936. The 1966 winner, *The Fortune Cookie* (Walter Matthau), has been discontinued; copies on videocassette are difficult to find.

ACADEMY AWARD CHECK LIST: BEST SUPPORTING ACTRESS ————— XT5

1936	Anthony Adverse (Gale Sondergaard)	1966	Who's Afraid of Virginia Woolf? (Sandy Dennis)
1938	Jezebel (Fay Bainter)	1967	Bonnie and Clyde (Estelle Parsons)
1939	Gone With the Wind (Hattie McDaniel)	1968	Rosemary's Baby (Ruth Gordon)
1940	The Grapes of Wrath (Jane Darwell)	1969	Cactus Flower (Goldie Hawn)
1942	Mrs. Miniver (Teresa Wright)	1970	Airport (Helen Hayes)
1944	None but the Lonely Heart (Ethel Barrymore)	1972	Butterflies Are Free (Eileen Heckart)
1945	National Velvet (Anne Revere)	1973	Paper Moon (Tatum O'Neal)
1946	The Razor's Edge (Anne Baxter)	1974	Murder on the Orient Express (Ingrid Bergman)
1948	Key Largo (Claire Trevor)	1975	Shampoo (Lee Grant)
1949	All the King's Men (Mercedes McCambridge)	1976	Network (Beatrice Straight)
1951	A Streetcar Named Desire (Kim Hunter)	1977	Julia (Vanessa Redgrave)
1952	The Bad and the Beautiful (Gloria Grahame)	1978	California Suite (Maggie Smith)
1953	From Here to Eternity (Donna Reed)	1979	Kramer vs. Kramer (Meryl Streep)
1954	On the Waterfront (Eva Marie Saint)	1980	Melvin and Howard (Mary Steenburgen)
1955	East of Eden (Jo Van Fleet)	1981	Reds (Maureen Stapleton)
1956	Written on the Wind (Dorothy Malone)	1982	Tootsie (Jessica Lange)
1957	Sayonara (Miyoshi Umeki)	1983	The Year of Living Dangerously (Linda Hunt)
1958	Separate Tables (Deborah Kerr)	1984	A Passage to India (Peggy Ashcroft)
1959	The Diary of Anne Frank (Shelley Winters)	1985	Prizzi's Honor (Anjelica Huston)
1960	Elmer Gantry (Shirley Jones)	1986	Hannah and Her Sisters (Dianne Wiest)
1961	West Side Story (Rita Moreno)	1987	Moonstruck (Olympia Dukakis)
1962	The Miracle Worker (Patty Duke)	1988	The Accidental Tourist (Geena Davis)
1964	Zorba the Greek (Lila Kedrova)		

Note: Award debuted in 1936.

ACADEMY AWARD CHECK LIST: BEST DIRECTOR ————————— XT6

1929-30	All Quiet on the Western Front (Lewis Milestone)	1934	It Happened One Night (Frank Capra)

1935	The Informer (John Ford)	1969	Midnight Cowboy (John Schlesinger)
1936	Mr. Deeds Goes to Town (Frank Capra)	1970	Patton (Franklin J. Schaffner)
1937	The Awful Truth (Leo McCarey)	1971	The French Connection (William Friedkin)
1939	Gone With the Wind (Victor Fleming)	1972	Cabaret (Bob Fosse)
1940	The Grapes of Wrath (John Ford)	1973	The Sting (George Roy Hill)
1942	Mrs. Miniver (William Wyler)	1974	The Godfather, Part II (Francis Ford Coppola)
1943	Casablanca (Michael Curtiz)		
1944	Going My Way (Leo McCarey)	1975	One Flew Over the Cuckoo's Nest (Milos Forman)
1945	The Lost Weekend (Billy Wilder)		
1946	The Best Years of Our Lives (William Wyler)	1976	Rocky (John G. Avildsen)

1935 The Informer (John Ford)
1936 Mr. Deeds Goes to Town (Frank Capra)
1937 The Awful Truth (Leo McCarey)
1939 Gone With the Wind (Victor Fleming)
1940 The Grapes of Wrath (John Ford)
1942 Mrs. Miniver (William Wyler)
1943 Casablanca (Michael Curtiz)
1944 Going My Way (Leo McCarey)
1945 The Lost Weekend (Billy Wilder)
1946 The Best Years of Our Lives (William Wyler)
1948 The Treasure of the Sierra Madre (John Huston)
1950 All About Eve (Joseph L. Mankiewicz)
1951 A Place in the Sun (George Stevens)
1952 The Quiet Man (John Ford)
1953 From Here to Eternity (Fred Zinnemann)
1954 On the Waterfront (Elia Kazan)
1955 Marty (Delbert Mann)
1956 Giant (Goerge Stevens)
1957 The Bridge on the River Kwai (David Lean)
1958 Gigi (Vincente Minnelli)
1959 Ben-Hur (William Wyler)
1960 The Apartment (Billy Wilder)
1961 West Side Story (Robert Wise)*
1962 Lawrence of Arabia (David Lean)
1964 My Fair Lady (George Cukor)
1965 The Sound of Music (Robert Wise)
1966 A Man for all Seasons (Fred Zinnemann)
1967 The Graduate (Mike Nichols)
1968 Oliver! (Carol Reed)

1969 Midnight Cowboy (John Schlesinger)
1970 Patton (Franklin J. Schaffner)
1971 The French Connection (William Friedkin)
1972 Cabaret (Bob Fosse)
1973 The Sting (George Roy Hill)
1974 The Godfather, Part II (Francis Ford Coppola)
1975 One Flew Over the Cuckoo's Nest (Milos Forman)
1976 Rocky (John G. Avildsen)
1977 Annie Hall (Woody Allen)
1978 The Deer Hunter (Michael Cimino)
1979 Kramer vs. Kramer (Robert Benton)
1980 Ordinary People (Robert Redford)
1981 Reds (Warren Beatty)
1982 Gandhi (Richard Attenborough)
1983 Terms of Endearment (James L. Brooks)
1984 Amadeus (Milos Forman)
1985 Out of Africa (Sydney Pollack)
1986 Platoon (Oliver Stone)
1987 The Last Emperor (Bernardo Bertolucci)
1988 Rain Man (Barry Levinson)

* Wise and choreographer Jerome Robbins shared screen credit for directing; Robbins won a special Oscar for his contribution to the film.

Note: *Tom Jones* (Tony Richardson), the 1963 winner, has been discontinued; copies on videocassette are difficult to find.

ACADEMY AWARD CHECK LIST: BEST FOREIGN LANGUAGE FILM _____ XT7

1949 The Bicycle Thief
1951 Rashomon
1952 Forbidden Games
1954 Gate of Hell
1955 Samurai (The Seven Samurai)
1956 La Strada
1957 Nights of Cabiria
1958 My Uncle
1959 Black Orpheus
1960 The Virgin Spring

1961 Through a Glass Darkly
1962 Sundays and Cybele
1963 8½
1964 Yesterday, Today and Tomorrow
1965 The Shop on Main Street
1966 A Man and a Woman
1967 Closely Watched Trains
1968 War and Peace
1969 Z
1971 The Garden of the Finzi-Continis

1972	The Discreet Charm of the Bourgeoisie	1981	Mephisto
1973	Day for Night	1983	Fanny and Alexander
1974	Amarcord	1984	Dangerous Moves
1975	Dersu Uzala	1985	The Official Story
1976	Black and White in Color	1986	The Assault
1977	Madame Rosa	1987	Babette's Feast
1978	Get Out Your Handkerchiefs	1988	Pelle the Conqueror
1979	The Tin Drum		
1980	Moscow Does Not Believe in Tears		Note: Award debuted in 1947.

ALL IN THE FAMILY: MOVIES FEATURING MOTHERS, FATHERS, SONS, DAUGHTERS, SISTER, BROTHERS ———————————————————— XT8

At Close Range (Sean & Christopher Penn)
Big Wednesday (Barbara Hale & William Katt)
The Chase (Marlon & Jocelyn Brando)
Hearts of the World (Lillian & Dorothy Gish)
Home Sweet Home (Lillian & Dorothy Gish)
Honkytonk Man (Clint & Kyle Eastwood)
The Long Riders (David, Keith & Robert Carradine; Christopher & Nicholas Guest; Stacy & James Keach; Dennis & Randy Quaid)
Nightbreaker (Martin Sheen & Emilio Estevez)

On Golden Pond (Henry & Jane Fonda)
Orphans of the Storm (Lillian & Dorothy Gish)
The Proud Rebel (Alan & David Ladd)
Paper Moon (Ryan & Tatum O'Neal)
That's Life! (Jack & Chris Lemmon; Julie Andrews & Emma Walton)
Thunder Road (Robert & Jim Mitchum)
Tightrope (Clint & Alison Eastwood)
The Treasure of the Sierra Madre (Walter and John Huston)
Tucker: The Man and His Dream (Lloyd & Jeff Bridges)
Wall Street (Martin & Charlie Sheen)
Young Guns (Emilio Estevez & Charlie Sheen)

ON LOCATION: MOVIES THAT MAKE GOOD USE OF MAJOR CITIES ————— XT9

New York
Addict
After Hours
Annie Hall
Barefoot in the Park
Breakfast at Tiffany's
Bright Lights, Big City
Broadway Danny Rose
Coogan's Bluff
"Crocodile" Dundee
"Crocodile" Dundee II
Crossing Delancey
Death Wish
Desperately Seeking Susan
Falling in Love
Fame
Fort Apache, The Bronx

The French Connection
Funny Girl
Garbo Talks
Ghostbusters
Ghostbusters II
Hair
Hannah and Her Sisters
Highlander
It Should Happen to You
Just Tell Me What You Want
Liquid Sky
Love With the Proper Stranger
Manhattan
Married to the Mob
Mean Streets
Midnight Cowboy
Moscow on the Hudson

The Muppets Take Manhattan
New York Stories
The Odd Couple
On the Town
The Out-of-Towners
The Pawnbroker
The Pick-up Artist
Prince of the City
Radio Days
Rooftops
Rosemary's Baby
Saturday Night Fever
Slaves of New York
Smithereens
Someone to Watch Over Me
Splash
The Taking of Pelham One Two Three
Taxi Driver
They All Laughed
A Thousand Clowns
Turk 182
Wall Street
The Warriors
West Side Story
Wolfen
Working Girl
The World of Henry Orient
You're a Big Boy Now

Los Angeles
Against All Odds (1984)
Annie Hall
Beverly Hills Cop
Beverly Hills Cop II
Blue Thunder
California Suite
Chinatown
Colors
The Day of the Locust
Down and Out in Beverly Hills
Night of the Comet
Point Blank
Repo Man
Shampoo
To Live and Die in L.A.
True Confessions
Welcome to L.A.
Zabriskie Point

Chicago
About Last Night
Adventures in Babysitting
The Blues Brothers

Continental Divide
Ferris Bueller's Day off
Medium Cool
Nothing in Common
Red Heat
Risky Business

Washington, D.C.
Advise and Consent
All the President's Men
Born Yesterday
Broadcast News
Chances Are
D.C. Cab
The Day the Earth Stood Still
Earth vs. the Flying Saucers
The Exorcist
First Monday in October
Heartburn
Houseboat
Mr. Smith Goes to Washington
No Way Out
Power (1986)
St. Elmo's Fire
The Seduction of Joe Tynan
Short Fuse
Suspect

San Francisco
Bullitt
The Conversation
The Dead Pool
Dim Sum: a little bit of heart
Dirty Harry
Experiment in Terror
Foul Play
Invasion of the Body Snatchers (1979
    version)
The Laughing Policeman
Petulia
Point Blank
The Presidio
Signal 7
Vertigo
What's Up, Doc?

New Orleans
Angel Heart
The Big Easy
The Cat People (1982 version)
Easy Rider
Pretty Baby
Tightrope

London
Absolute Beginners
An American Werewolf in London
Darling
Frenzy
Georgy Girl
A Hard Day's Night
The Long Good Friday
Look Back in Anger
Midnight Lace
Mona Lisa
My Beautiful Laundrette
Sammy and Rosie Get Laid

Paris
American Dreamer
La Balance
Bob le Flambeur
Breathless (1959 version)
Charade

The Day of the Jackal
Diva
The 400 Blows
Frantic (1988)
French Postcards
Funny Face
Last Tango in Paris
A Little Romance
Masculine-Feminine
Paris Blues
Shoot the Piano Player

Rome
After the Fox
La Dolce Vita
Eclipse
Love in the City
Roman Holiday
The Roman Spring of Mrs. Stone

STUNNING DEBUTS: LEGENDARY FIRST STARRING ROLES ———————— XT10

Adam's Rib (Judy Holliday)
Citizen Kane (Orson Welles)
East of Eden (James Dean)
48HRS. (Eddie Murphy)
Funny Girl (Barbra Streisand)
Golden Boy (William Holden)
Goodbye, Mr. Chips (Greer Garson)
Great Expectations (Alec Guinness)

The Invisible Man (Claude Rains)
Lawrence of Arabia (Peter O'Toole)
Mary Poppins (Julie Andrews)
The Men (Marlon Brando)
Roman Holiday (Audrey Hepburn)
Splendor in the Grass (Warren Beatty)
The Trouble With Harry (Shirley
   MacLaine)

FOND FAREWELLS: MEMORABLE FINAL PERFORMANCES ———————— XT11

Advise and Consent (Charles Laughton)
Enter the Dragon (Bruce Lee)
Giant (James Dean)
Guess Who's Coming to Dinner
   (Spencer Tracy)
The Harder They Fall (Humphrey
   Bogart)
The Misfits (Clark Gable, Marilyn
   Monroe)

Mister Roberts (William Powell)
Network (Peter Finch)
On Golden Pond (Henry Fonda)
Ride the High Country (Randolph Scott)
S.O.B. (William Holden)
Shane (Jean Arthur)
The Shootist (John Wayne)
To Be or Not to Be (1943 version)
   (Carole Lombard)

Chapter Fourteen

UNAVAILABLE ON VIDEOCASSETTE

The following is a selected list of frequently requested titles that were still not on videocassette as of Fall 1989.

A few, such as *American Hot Wax*, are available on videodisc. Some are available in foreign-language versions. For example, a Japanese version of *Rocky Horror Picture Show* has been in circulation.

As with any popular titles, some are available in unauthorized, pirated cassettes whose quality is nearly always suspect.

An Affair to Remember
Alexander's Ragtime Band
All Fall Down
All the Way Home
American Hot Wax
American Pop
The Americanization of Emily
Anastasia
Annie Get Your Gun
Battleground
The Blackboard Jungle
Blithe Spirit (1945 version)
Bread and Chocolate
Cabin in the Cotton
Carmen Jones
Carousel
Carrie (1950)
Cheaper by the Dozen
Claudine
Cooley High
Cover Girl
Cul-de-sac
The Dark at the Top of the Stairs
Design for Living
Desk Set
Drive, He Said
The Effect of Gamma Rays on Man-in-
the-Moon Marigolds
El Topo
F/M
Fantasia
Far From the Madding Crowd
A Farewell to Arms (1957 version)
Force of Evil
Forever Amber

The Gang's All Here
Gentleman's Agreement
The Ghost and Mrs. Muir
Godspell
Gun Crazy
Hail the Conquering Hero
Harvey
Having a Wild Weekend
Heaven Knows, Mr. Allison
Heavy Metal
Hell in the Pacific
Hi, Mom
The High and the Mighty
How Green Was My Valley
The Hucksters
Humoresque
I Walk the Line
The Innocents
Inside Daisy Clover
Jane Eyre (1948 version)
Jet Pilot
The Jungle Book (1967 version)
The King of Marvin Gardens
Land of the Pharoahs
The Last Picture Show
Leave Her to Heaven
Libeled Lady
Lola Montes
The Long, Hot Summer (1958 version)
The Long, Long Trailer
McClintock
The Man in the Grey Flannel Suit
Man of a Thousand Faces
Mourning Becomes Electra
My Cousin Rachel

The Nanny
Nightmare Alley
Of Mice and Men (1939 version)
The Old Man and the Sea
101 Dalmatians
Pal Joey
A Patch of Blue
Peppermint Soda
Peter Pan (1953 version)
Peyton Place
Picnic
Pinky
Play It As It Lays
Porgy and Bess
Portrait of Jennie
Pretty Poison
Rancho Deluxe
Rich Man, Poor Man
The Road to Morocco
The Road to Singapore
The Road to Zanzibar
The Rocky Horror Picture Show
The Rose Tattoo
The Scarlet Empress
The Sea of Grass
Shanghai Express
Shock Corridor
Since You Went Away
The Snake Pit
Snow White and the Seven Dwarfs

The Solid Gold Cadillac
The Song of the South
Sons and Lovers
Sorcerer
Summer and Smoke
A Summer Place
Sunrise
Susan Lennox: Her Rise and Fall
The Swan
Sweet Bird of Youth
The Tall T
Tarzan and His Mate
Tea and Sympathy
The Teahouse of the August Moon
The Thorn Birds
Three Coins in the Fountain
The Three Faces of Eve
Tobacco Road
Two-Faced Woman
Two-Lane Blacktop
Up the Down Staircase
The V.I.P.s
The Valley of Decision
Valley of the Dolls (1967 version)
White Dog
Without Love
A Woman Under the Influence
Yanks
You Can't Take It With You

Discontinued Movies

These titles were made available on videocassette at one time but have been withdrawn from manufacture. Thus, copies are difficult to find. See "How To Use This Book" for further explanation.

Becket
The Day of the Locust
The Fortune Cookie
The King and I
Laura
A Letter to Three Wives (1949 version)

Love Is a Many-Splendored Thing
The Killing of Sister George
Room at the Top
They Shoot Horses, Don't They?
Tom Jones

TITLE INDEX

A Coeur Joie (1967, B&W, 100m, NR)
Brigitte Bardot plays a bored housewife who resumes her career, only to fall in love with another man. **FF32**

A Nos Amours (1984, C, 102m, R)
From France, a drama of a teenaged girl (Sandrine Bonnaire) with a string of lovers and family problems. Directed by Maurice Pialat. **FF1**

A Nous la Liberté (1931, B&W, 87m, NR)
French director René Clair's comic look at how machinery takes over people's lives. **FF1**

Aaron Loves Angela (1975, C, 98m, R)
New York romance between a black Harlem youth (Kevin Hooks) and a Puerto Rican girl (Irene Cara). Moses Gunn co-stars. **DR14, DR15**

Abbott and Costello in Hollywood (1945, B&W, 83m, NR)
Bud and Lou invade the MGM lot and run into plenty of surprise guest stars. **CO23**

Abbott and Costello Meet Captain Kidd (1952, C, 70m, NR)
Charles Laughton hams it up as the notorious pirate in this A&C comedy. **CO23**

Abbott and Costello Meet Dr. Jekyll and Mr. Hyde (1953, B&W, 77m, NR)
Bud and Lou are in London where Lou is accidentally injected with the Mr. Hyde serum. Boris Karloff costars. **CO23, HO27**

Abbott and Costello Meet Frankenstein (1948, B&W, 83m, NR)
Dracula (Bela Lugosi) wants to use Lou's brain in the Frankenstein monster (Glenn Strange) and the Wolf Man (Lon Chaney Jr.) tries to warn him that he's in danger. Vincent Price has a bit at the end as the Invisible Man. **CO23, HO28, HO30, HO31**

Abbott and Costello Meet the Killer, Boris Karloff (1949, B&W, 84m, NR)
Karloff tries to do away with Lou in this A&C comic mystery. **CO2, HO27**

Abe Lincoln in Illinois (1939, B&W, 110m, NR)
Raymond Massey stars as the small-town lawyer who would eventually become our sixteenth President. **CL2**

Abilene Town (1946, B&W, 89m, NR)
Randolph Scott Western set during post-Civil War Kansas, where the townspeople are feuding over land rights. **WE22**

Abominable Dr. Phibes, The (1971, C, 94m, PG)
Vincent Price hams it up in this tongue-in-cheek horror film about a disfigured doctor seeking revenge. **CU4, HO20, HO26, HO31**

About Last Night (1986, C, 113m, R)
Comedy-drama about four young Chicago singles, two of whom think they've found love but aren't sure. Rob Lowe, Demi Moore, Jim Belushi, and Elizabeth Perkins star. Underrated film with some pointed observations about modern romance. **CO13, DR1, DR7, XT9** *Recommended*

Above the Law (1988, C, 99m, R)
Steven Seagall plays a super-agent (martial arts training, multi-lingual, weapons expert) with friends in the Mob. He's on the trail of a C.I.A.-sponsored drug ring. **AC8, AC25**

Abraham Lincoln (1930, B&W, 97m, NR)
Walter Huston stars in director D.W. Griffith's account of the sixteenth President's life. This is the restored version, with slavery sequences once thought lost. **CL2, CL36**

Absence of Malice (1981, C, 116m, PG)
Newspaper reporter tries for big scoop on Miami construction boss and his involvement with crime, only to find out her target is innocent. Sally Field and Paul Newman star; Sydney Pollack directed. **DR7, DR28, DR36, DR56**

Absent-Minded Professor, The (1960, B&W, 97m, G)
Fred MacMurray plays the forgetful inventor who discovers flubber—an amazing substance that raises his Model T and basketball team to new heights in this classic Disney comedy. **FA1**

Absolute Beginners (1986, C, 107m, PG-13)
A stylized musical look at London in the late 1950s, when rock 'n' roll was about to break through and the teenager would become king. David Bowie, Ray Davies, and Sade perform musical numbers. Directed by Julien Temple. **MU9, MU16, XT9** *Recommended*

Accident (1967, C, 105m, NR)
Drama set at a British univeristy, centering on a professor's affair with a lovely young student. Dirk Bogarde, Stanley Baker, Jacqueline Sassard, Delphine Seyrig, and Michael York star. Written by Harold Pinter; directed by Joseph Losey. **DR23** *Recommended*

Accidental Tourist, The (1988, C, 121m, PG)
A guidebook writer who hates to travel, his estranged wife, and a loopy dog trainer are the focus of this drama set in Baltimore. William Hurt, Kathleen Turner, and Oscar winner Geena Davis star, with Amy Wright, Ed Begley, Jr., David Ogden Stiers, and Bill Pullman. Based on Anne Tyler's novel. **DR1, DR8, DR19, DR31, DR46, XT5**

Accused, The (1988, C, 110m, R)
Oscar winner Jodie Foster stars as a woman who's been brutally assaulted in a bar. A determined prosecutor (Kelly McGillis) presses charges against the on-

lookers at the scene of the crime. **DR10, DR17, XT3**

Across 110th Street (1972, C, 102m, R)
Violent crime thriller, with New York police and the Mob in a race to catch freelance robbers who made off with $300,000 of Mob money. Anthony Quinn, Yaphet Kotto, and Anthony Franciosa star. **AC9, CU7**

Across the Great Divide (1977, C, 100m, G)
Family adventure about two orphaned children making the trek over dangerous Rocky Mountain terrain to earn their inherited land in frontier Oregon. **FA4**

Action Jackson (1988, C, 96m, R)
Carl Weathers plays Detroit's most determined police sergeant, Jericho "Action" Jackson. He keeps his cool as a ruthless auto tycoon, a scheming mistress, and his own police force cross his path in this thriller. **AC8**

Adam (1983, C, 100m, NR)
JoBeth Williams and Daniel J. Travanti play the real-life couple whose missing son case stirred controversy and congressional debate. Originally made for TV. **MY8**

Adam Had Four Sons (1941, B&W, 81m, NR)
An intense family drama starring Ingrid Bergman as a French governess for a widower (Warner Baxter) with four boys. Susan Hayward, Fay Wray, Richard Denning, and June Lockhart costar. **CL27**

Adam's Rib (1949, B&W, 101m, NR)
Katharine Hepburn and Spencer Tracy are husband and wife lawyers who wind up on opposing sides of the court. Judy Holliday, in her film debut, is hilarious as the dizzy defendant. Directed by George

Cukor. **CL10, CL15, CL16, CL19, CO42, XT10** *Highly Recommended*

Addict (1971, C, 90m, R)
The life and very hard times of a New York City heroin addict, an ex-hair-dresser, played by George Segal. Karen Black costars; Robert DeNiro has a small part. Original title: *Born To Win*. **DR15, DR25, XT9**

L'Addition (1985, C, 85m, R)
French prison drama, starring Richard Berry and Richard Bohringer. **FF1**

Adios Amigo (1975, C, 87m, PG)
In this western comedy, Fred Williamson (who also wrote and directed) costars with Richard Pryor as the hippest pair of gunslingers ever to ride the range. **CO29, WE15**

Adventures in Babysitting (1987, C, 99m, PG-13)
Shaggy dog tale of teen babysitter dragging her charges off to downtown Chicago to help a stranded friend. Elisabeth Shue stars. **CO37, XT9**

Adventures of an American Rabbit, The (1986, C, 85m, G)
Feature cartoon about Rob Rabbit, a normal bunny transformed into a superhero. **FA10**

Adventures of Baron Munchausen, The (1989, C, 125m, PG)
Spectacular adventure fantasy, based on real German nobleman with a penchant for spinning fabulous and less than credible tales. John Neville stars, with Sarah Polley as his young companion, and Eric Idle, Robin Williams (billed as "Ray Tutto"), Oliver Reed, and Uma Thurman. Directed with great flair by Terry Gilliam. **CO15, CO43, FA8, SF13, SF14** *Recommended*

Adventures of Buckaroo Banzai Across the 8th Dimension, The (1984, C, 103m, PG)
Adventure comedy about a super hero who's a brain surgeon, race car driver, and rock singer—among other talents. Peter Weller stars, with Ellen Barkin, Jeff Goldblum, and John Lithgow. **AC17, CO12, CU5, SF21** *Recommended*

Adventures of Bullwhip Griffin, The (1967, C, 110m, NR)
Disney western comedy, with a novice Bostonian who thinks he can make a bundle during the gold rush days. Roddy McDowall, Suzanne Pleshette, and Karl Malden star. **FA1**

Adventures of Captain Fabian (1951, B&W, 100m, NR)
Errol Flynn swashbuckler has the hero defending Micheline Presle from murder charge. Agnes Moorehead and Vincent Price costar. **AC34, HO31**

Adventures of Don Juan, The (1948, C, 110m, NR)
Costume adventure about history's roguish lover, starring Errol Flynn. Viveca Lindfors and Ann Rutherford costar as his conquests. **AC34**

Adventures of Hercules, The (1984, C, 89m, NR)
Lou Ferrigno plays the well-muscled hero of mythology in this adventure saga. **AC17**

Adventures of Huckleberry Finn, The (1939, B&W, 89m, NR)
Mark Twain's classic of a boy and a runaway slave in a thrilling raft trip down the Mississippi. Mickey Rooney stars. **CL1, FA3**

Adventures of Huckleberry Finn, The (1985, C, 121m, NR)
The most recent version of the Mark Twain classic about adventurous Huck (Patrick Day) rafting down the Mississippi with his runaway friend Jim (Samm-Art Williams). Sada Thompson, Lillian Gish, Richard Kiley, and Butterfly McQueen costar. Originally made for public TV; shown at 240m. **CL49, FA3**

Adventures of Mark Twain, The (1985, C, 90m, G)
The art of claymation is used to capture the likeness of Mark Twain's literary characters (Tom Sawyer, Huck Finn, and Becky Thatcher) in this animated adventure story. **FA10**

Adventures of Robin Hood, The (1938, C, 102m, NR)
Errol Flynn plays the dashing Sherwood Forest outlaw. Olivia de Havilland, Basil Rathbone, and Claude Rains costar in this enchanting classic. **AC13, AC34, CL9, FA4** *Recommended*

Adventures of Sherlock Holmes, The (1939, B&W, 83m, NR)
Sherlock Holmes and Dr. Watson outsmart their arch-rival Professor Moriarity in the first Holmes movie to star Basil Rathbone and Nigel Bruce. **MY10**

Adventures of the Wilderness Family, The (1975, C, 100m, G)
A modern-day family trades in their big-city lifestyle for pioneer life in the West. **FA4**

Adventures of Tom Sawyer, The (1938, C, 77m, NR)
Mark Twain's classic about the Missouri boy whose endless curiosity gets him into all sorts of mischief. Tommy Kelly, Jackie Moran, Walter Brennan, and Victor Jory star. **FA3**

Advise and Consent (1962, B&W, 139m, NR)
From director Otto Preminger comes a drama of Washington political wheeling and dealing over the controversial nomination of a left-wing Senator to become Secretary of State. Henry Fonda stars, with Don Murray, Charles Laughton (in his last film), Walter Pidgeon, Peter Lawford, and Gene Tierney. **CL24, DR21, XT9, XT11**

Africa Screams (1949, B&W, 79m, NR)
Abbott and Costello go on safari with big game hunter Frank Buck. **CO23**

African Queen, The (1951, C, 105m, NR)
Romantic adventure teaming Humphrey Bogart with Katharine Hepburn as the hard-drinking pilot and the uptight spinster who cruise treacherous waters to thwart the Germans in World War I. Directed by John Huston; written by James Agee. **AC12, AC14, CL4, CL16, CL20, CL44, XT2** *Highly Recommended*

After Hours (1985, C, 97m, R)
Ordinary guy finds himself stranded in the middle of the night in an unfriendly New York neighborhood. Offbeat comedy directed by Martin Scorsese with a terrific cast: Griffin Dunne, John Heard, Rosanna Arquette, Catherine O'Hara, Cheech and Chong, Teri Garr, and Linda Fiorentino. **CO2, CO12, CO14, CO32, CO37, CU4, CU17, DR52, XT9** *Recommended*

After the Fall of New York (1985, C, 95m, R)
Adventure saga set in post-holocaust America, where only the strong survive. Michael Sopikow stars. **SF8, SF12**

After the Fox (1966, C, 103m, NR)
Peter Sellers stars in a comedy about a frustrated film director on location in Rome. Victor Mature steals the show as a fading star. Written by Neil Simon. **CO26, CO34, XT9**

After the Rehearsal (1984, C, 72m, R)
Swedish drama from Ingmar Bergman about the intricate relationships of a theater director and his actresses. Erland Josephson, Ingrid Thulin, and Lena Olin star. **FF8**

After the Thin Man (1936, B&W, 113m, NR)
More parties, more hangovers, and more crime for the high-society detective couple Nick and Nora Charles (William Powell, Myrna Loy). James Stewart costars as one of their suspects. **CL15, CL25, CL46, MY13, MY28**

Aftermath (1985, C, 96m, NR)
A trio of astronauts returns to Earth after a long journey to find a nuclear holocaust has ravaged the planet. **SF12**

Against All Flags (1952, C, 83m, NR)
Errol Flynn plays a British soldier who finds his way into a pirate stronghold—and into Maureen O'Hara's heart. Anthony Quinn costars. **AC34**

Against All Odds (1969, C, 93m, NR)
Fu Manchu plans to murder several world leaders by sending slave girls saturated in poison which will kill anyone who kisses them. Christopher Lee stars. Original title: *The Blood of Fu Manchu*. Also known as *Kiss and Kill*. **HO32**

Against All Odds (1984, C, 128m, NR)
An ex-jock (Jeff Bridges), hired to track down the runaway wife of a shady nightclub owner (James Woods), falls in love with her when he finds her. Rachel Ward costars in this remake of *Out of the Past* set in contemporary Los Angeles. **CU18, DR16, DR71, MY2, MY5, XT9**

Agatha (1979, C, 98m, PG)
Vanessa Redgrave portrays mystery writer Agatha Christie in this dramatic account of her 11-day disappearance in 1926. Dustin Hoffman costars as an inquisitive reporter who tracks Christie down. **DR30, DR65, MY8**

L'Age d'Or (1930, B&W, 63m, NR)
Legendary surrealistic film directed by Luis Buñuel, co-written with Salvador Dali. A scandal in its time for its startling imagery. **FF11** *Recommended*

Agnes of God (1985, C, 97m, PG-13)
A young nun is the center of controversy over a murdered newborn infant. Jane Fonda, Anne Bancroft, and Meg Tilly star in this version of John Pielmeyer's play. **DR20, DR27**

Aguirre, The Wrath of God (1972, C, 90m, NR)
Adventure tale of mad conquistador driving his men to destruction in the jungles of South America. Klaus Kinski stars; Werner Herzog directed. **FF19, FF30** *Recommended*

Aida (1953, C, 96m, NR)
Screen version of the famed opera, starring Sophia Loren (with her singing voice dubbed). **FF31**

Air Force (1943, B&W, 124m, NR)
Howard Hawks' World War II drama about bomber crew action in Pearl Harbor, Manila, and the Coral Sea. John Garfield, John Ridgely, Gig Young, and Arthur Kennedy star. **AC1, CL35**

Airplane! (1980, C, 86m, PG)
Spoof of disaster movies (and the *Airport* series in particular), with a joke every 4 seconds, most of them quite funny. Robert Hays and Julie Hagerty star, with Lloyd Bridges, Peter Graves, Robert Stack, Leslie Nielsen, and many guests. **CO7** *Recommended*

Airplane II: The Sequel (1982, C, 85m, PG)
Follow-up to *Airplane!* with same joke ratio, plus Robert Hays, Julie Hagerty, Lloyd Bridges, Peter Graves, and William Shatner. **CO7**

Airport (1970, C, 137m, G)
Original Disaster in the Sky adventure, with snowed-in runways, bomb-crippled planes, cute stowaways, and an all-star cast: Burt Lancaster, Dean Martin, George Kennedy, Helen Hayes (an Oscar winner), Van Heflin, Jacqueline Bisset, and Jean Seberg. **AC23, DR41, XT5**

Airport 1975 (1974, C, 106m, PG)
Second *Airport* film has Charlton Heston at the controls, Karen Black as a stewardess, and a passenger list including Helen Reddy (as a singing nun), Gloria Swanson (as herself), Myrna Loy, and Linda Blair. **AC23, CL46**

Airport '79 *see* The Concorde—Airport '79

Airport '77 (1977, C, 113m, PG)
The third edition of the Unfriendly Skies
finds James Stewart's luxury jet-liner in
the ocean with pilot Jack Lemmon attempting a rescue. Lee Grant, Brenda
Vaccaro, George Kennedy, Joseph Cotten, Olivia de Havilland, Christopher
Lee, and many more appear. **AC23,
CL25, DR64, HO32**

Al Capone (1959, B&W, 105m, NR)
Rod Steiger plays Scarface in this bullet-
riddled film biography. Fay Spain, James
Gregory, and Martin Balsam costar.
AC22

Aladdin and His Wonderful Lamp (1984,
C, 60m, NR)
Robert Carradine is the young man at
odds with a wicked magician (Leonard
Nimoy) until a powerful genie (James Earl
Jones) and a beautiful princess appear
before him. From the Faerie Tale Theatre
series. **FA12**

Alamo, The (1960, C, 161m, NR)
The legendary battle of a small band of
Texans against the Mexican army, di-
rected by and starring John Wayne. With
Richard Widmark, Laurence Harvey,
Chill Wills, and Frankie Avalon. **MU12,
WE1, WE17**

Alamo Bay (1985, C, 98m, R)
Texas fishermen clash with Vietnamese
immigrants trying to make a living in the
same waters. Amy Madigan and Ed Harris star in this topical drama directed by
Louis Malle. **DR7**

Albino (1978, C, 85m, NR)
A murderous albino stalks beautiful
women. Christopher Lee and Trevor
Howard star. **HO32**

Alexander Nevsky (1938, B&W, 107m,
NR)
Stirring historical drama about Russia's
defense in the 13th century against invad-
ing German forces. Directed by Sergei
Eisenstein; music by Sergei Prokofiev.
FF22

Alexander the Great (1956, C, 141m, NR)
Richard Burton plays the great conqueror
in this adventure drama. Fredric March,
Claire Bloom, and Peter Cushing costar;
directed by Robert Rossen. **AC16, HO33**

Alfie (1966, C, 114m, NR)
Michael Caine is a roguish ladies' man in
this British comedy with Jane Asher,
Shelley Winters, and Millicent Martin.
CO17 *Recommended*

Algiers (1938, B&W, 95m, NR)
Classic romance stars Charles Boyer as
Pepe Le Moko, who falls for a spoiled
little rich girl (Hedy Lamarr) on her visit
to the Casbah district of Algiers. **CL4**

Alice Adams (1935, B&W, 99m, NR)
Comedy with Katharine Hepburn as a
social climber who finds true happiness
with a modest young man (Fred Mac-
Murray). Directed by George Stevens.
CL5, CL16, CL42

Alice Doesn't Live Here Anymore (1975,
C, 113m, PG)
A New Mexico housewife who is suddenly widowed decides to move with her
adolescent son to California, where she
can pursue her ambition to be a professional singer. Oscar winner Ellen Burstyn
stars in this comedy-drama, with Kris
Kristofferson, Dianne Ladd, Alfred Lutter III, and Jodie Foster. Directed by
Martin Scorsese. **DR10, DR52, MU12,
XT3** *Recommended*

Alice in the Cities (1974, B&W, 110m, NR)
Drama of the friendship between an
American journalist and an abandoned 9-
year-old German girl. Directed by Wim
Wenders. **FF21**

Alice in Wonderland (1951, C, 75m, G)
Disney animation brings Lewis Carroll's
enchanting classic to life as Alice ven-
tures through the looking glass to discover a world of colorful and frightening
characters. **FA2, FA3** *Recommended*

Alice's Restaurant (1969, C, 111m, PG)
Arlo Guthrie's famed song about a disastrous Thanksgiving Day and his problems with the draft is the basis for this amiable comedy-drama. Guthrie stars, with Pat Quinn and James Broderick. Directed by Arthur Penn. **DR7**

Alien (1979, C, 116m, R)
Science fiction horror classic about life form invading space ship and destroying the crew one by one. Sigourney Weaver stars, with Yaphet Kotto, Ian Holm, Veronica Cartwright, Harry Dean Stanton, and John Hurt. Directed by Ridley Scott; Oscar winner for special effects. **CU33, CU49, DR76, SF3, SF15, SF20** *Recommended*

Alien Nation (1988, C, 89m, R)
In Los Angeles in the near future, a race of aliens resembling humans have become the new minority immigrant problem. An alien cop (Mandy Patinkin) and his human partner (James Caan) team up to uncover a criminal conspiracy within the alien community. **SF17**

Alien Predators (1987, C, 92m, R)
A trio of Americans visiting Spain help a scientist control alien invasion which has taken over a small town. Martin Hewitt, Dennis Christopher, and Lynn-Holly Johnson star. **SF20**

Aliens (1986, C, 137m, R)
Smashing sequel to *Alien,* with survivor Sigourney Weaver returning to hunt down queen mother of creature from first film. Superb blend of action and suspense from director James Cameron. Michael Biehn, Lance Henriksen, and Paul Reiser costar. **DR76, SF3, SF20** *Recommended*

All About Eve (1950, B&W, 138m, NR)
Witty, Oscar-winning look at life in the theater, with ambitious ingenue (Anne Baxter) trying to upstage aging but still formidable veteran (Bette Davis). With Oscar winner George Sanders, Gary Merrill, Celeste Holm, and Marilyn Monroe. Joseph L. Mankiewicz won Oscars for both his direction and original screenplay.

CL7, CL21, CL29, CL55, XT1, XT4, XT6 *Highly Recommended*

All Creatures Great and Small (1974, C, 92m, NR)
Drama adapted from James Herriot's autobiography, following the veterinarian's career from his apprenticeship to an established practice in England's lush countryside. Simon Ward and Anthony Hopkins star. **FA5**

All in a Night's Work (1961, C, 94m, NR)
An office worker is victimized by a misunderstanding involving a respectable businessman. Comedy starring Shirley MacLaine and Dean Martin. **DR42**

All My Sons (1986, C, 122m, NR)
Adaptation of Arthur Miller's play about a family trying to deal with the loss of a son in World War II. James Whitmore, Aidan Quinn, Joan Allen, and Michael Learned star. Originally made for TV. **DR8, DR20**

All Night Long (1981, C, 88m, R)
A middle-aged manager of an all-night drug store falls in love with his neighbor's wife in this wacky romantic comedy starring Gene Hackman, Barbra Streisand, and Dennis Quaid. **CO1, DR39, MU27**

All of Me (1984, C, 93m, PG-13)
A swinging lawyer finds half his body possessed by a ditsy spinster in this frantic comedy. Steve Martin and Lily Tomlin costar, with Victoria Tennant, Richard Libertini, Selma Diamond, and Jason Bernard. **CO3, CO33, CO37** *Highly Recommended*

All Quiet on the Western Front (1930, B&W, 130m, NR)
Harrowing, moving drama of German youth and his disillusionment during World War I combat. Lew Ayres stars; Oscar winner Lewis Milestone directed. An anti-war classic that won the Academy Award for Best Picture. **AC2, XT1, XT6** *Highly Recommended*

All That Jazz (1979, C, 123m, R)
Bob Fosse's autobiographical musical drama about a director-choreographer juggling too many balls in his professional and personal life. Roy Scheider stars, with Ann Reinking, Jessica Lange, Leland Palmer, Cliff Gorman, and Ben Vereen. Sensational dance numbers. **DR74, MU3, MU4, MU28** *Recommended*

All the King's Men (1949, B&W, 109m, NR)
Portrait of a Southern politician whose idealism is corrupted into demagoguery. Oscar winner for Best Picture, Actor (Broderick Crawford), Supporting Actress (Mercedes McCambridge, in her film debut), and Screenplay Adaptation (by director Robert Rossen). Based on Robert Penn Warren's novel, which mirrored the career of Louisiana's Huey Long. **DR19, DR21, XT1, XT2, XT5** *Recommended*

All the Marbles (1981, C, 113m, R)
Raucous comedy set in the world of ladies' professional wrestling, featuring a lovely tag team (Laurene Landon and Vicki Frederick) and their unscrupulous manager (Peter Falk). Robert Aldrich directed. **CO36**

All the President's Men (1976, C, 138m, PG)
Robert Redford and Dustin Hoffman play the real-life *Washington Post* reporters who uncovered the Watergate scandal. With Martin Balsam, Jack Warden, Jane Alexander, Hal Holbrook, and Oscar winner Jason Robards as Ben Bradlee. Directed by Alan J. Pakula. **DR6, DR21, DR29, DR30, MY6, XT4, XT9** *Highly Recommended*

All the Right Moves (1983, C, 90m, R)
In a small town in Pennsylvania, a high school football star breaks with his coach and finds that he's being shut out of a college scholarship—his only way out of the depressed town. Tom Cruise, Craig T. Nelson, and Lea Thompson star. **DR9, DR22, DR73** *Recommended*

All the Way, Boys (1973, C, 105m, PG)
Terence Hill and Bud Spencer star in this Italian comedy about two go-for-broke adventurers flying a decrepit airplane through the Andes. **FF2**

All This and Heaven Too (1940, B&W, 143m, NR)
Drama set in 19th-century France finds Bette Davis as a governess involved in a scandalous relationship with her aristocrat employer (Charles Boyer). **CL21**

All You Need Is Cash (1978, C, 70m, NR)
The Beatles are spoofed in this documentary about a popular British rock group called The Rutles. Eric Idle heads the cast of loonies. Also known as *The Rutles*; originally made for TV. **CO15** *Recommended*

Allan Quartermain and the Lost City of Gold (1986, C, 100m, PG)
Sequel to the latest version of *King Solomon's Mines* has title hero (Richard Chamberlain) on the trail of a legendary city, battling restless natives, hungry crocodiles, and other obstacles. **AC21**

Allegheny Uprising (1939, B&W, 81m, NR)
This action saga of colonial America teams John Wayne with Claire Trevor against a British Army officer. **WE17**

Alligator (1980, C, 94m, R)
A pet alligator is flushed down the toilet; in the sewer system he grows into a monster and begins to terrorize the city. Tongue-in-cheek horror written by John Sayles. Robert Forster stars, with Robin Riker, Michael Gazzo, Dean Jagger, and Jack Carter. **HO16**

Allonsanfan (1974, C, 117m, NR)
Comedy set in early 19th-century Italy about a group of idealists living in the not-so-distant past. Marcello Mastroianni stars; directed by Paolo and Vittorio Taviani. **FF2, FF24**

Almost Perfect Affair, An (1979, C, 93m, PG)
A young American filmmaker, on his first trip to the Cannes Film Festival, has a fling with the bored wife of an Italian producer. Keith Carradine and Monica Vitti star, with Raf Vallone. **DR13**

Almost You (1984, C, 96m, R)
Romantic comedy, with a New York woman questioning her marriage after she's injured in an auto accident. Brooke Adams and Griffin Dunne star. **CO1**

Alone in the Dark (1982, C, 92m, R)
Three psychopaths escape from an asylum and seek revenge on their psychiatrist. Jack Palance, Donald Pleasence, and Martin Landau star. **HO9**

Along Came Jones (1945, B&W, 90m, NR)
A western comedy with Gary Cooper as a cowboy who's the victim of mistaken identity. Loretta Young costars. **WE15, WE25**

Along the Navajo Trail (1945, B&W, 54m, NR)
Roy Rogers and Gabby Hayes ride to protect innocent ranchers. With Dale Evans. **WE23**

Alphabet City (1984, C, 98m, R)
Drama of life on New York's Lower East Side, where the mean streets are lettered—thus, the title. Vincent Spano stars. **DR15**

Alphaville (1965, B&W, 100m, NR)
French science fiction thriller, with Eddie Constantine as a detective trying to rescue a kidnapped scientist. Directed by Jean-Luc Godard. **SF19, FF14**

Alsino and the Condor (1982, C, 89m, R)
From Nicaragua, a drama of a young crippled boy who finds self-esteem fighting with a guerrilla band. Directed by Miguel Littin. **FF6**

Altered States (1980, C, 102m, R)
Scientist lets his experiments in primal research overwhelm him. William Hurt

stars, with Blair Brown, Charles Haid, and Bob Balaban. This science fiction film is packed with dazzling imagery from director Ken Russell. **CU3, CU4, CU31, DR31, SF5, SF20**

Alvarez Kelly (1966, C, 116m, NR)
In this Civil War western, William Holden and Richard Widmark are on opposite sides of the conflict. **CL51, WE7**

Amadeus (1984, C, 158m, PG)
Oscar-winning film portrait of Wolfgang Amadeus Mozart, the brilliant and irritatingly immature composer, as told by his arch-rival Antonio Salieri. Thomas Hulce and F. Murray Abraham star under Milos Forman's direction. Abraham and Forman also won Oscars. Glorious use of Mozart music. **DR4, DR57, MU5, XT1, XT2, XT6** *Recommended*

Amarcord (1974, C, 127m, PG)
Federico Fellini's comic memoir of his youth in a seaside village is full of memorable characters and classic moments. Oscar winner for Best Foreign Film; arguably Fellini's best work. **FF10, XT7** *Highly Recommended*

Amateur, The (1979, C, 111m, R)
A computer operator (John Savage) swears revenge on the terrorists who murdered his girlfriend. **MY6**

Amazing Adventure (1936, B&W, 70m, NR)
On a bet, a wealthy man joins the working class to prove that his skills are worthy of a real job. Cary Grant stars in this British comedy. Original title: *The Amazing Quest of Ernest Bliss*. Released in the U.S. as *Romance and Riches*. **CL18**

Amazing Dobermans, The (1976, C, 94m, PG)
Fred Astaire plays a former con man whose trained dobermans help stop a gang of racketeers. **FA5, MU18**

Amazing Howard Hughes, The (1977, C, 119m, NR)
Dramatization of the life of the aviation pioneer/movie producer/casino owner/legendary lover, starring Tommy Lee Jones, with Ed Flanders as Noah Dietrich and Tovah Feldshuh as Katharine Hepburn. Originally made for TV with a running time of 215m. **DR4, DR60**

Amazing Quest of Ernest Bliss, The
see Amazing Adventure

Amazon Women on the Moon (1987, C, 85m, R)
Catch-all parody of late-night TV movies and commercials, with series of skits featuring lots of stars (Rosanna Arquette, Michelle Pfeiffer, Griffin Dunne, Steve Allen, Henny Youngman, Carrie Fisher). Joe Dante, Carl Gottlieb, Peter Horton, John Landis, and Robert K. Weiss directed. **CO7, CU40**

America at the Movies (1976, C/B&W, 116m, NR)
Compilation of scenes from over 80 movie classics, produced by the American Film Institute. **CU16**

American Anthem (1986, C, 100m, PG-13)
Gymnast Mitch Gaylord stars in this flashy drama about the triumphs and heartbreak of competitive gymnastics. **DR22**

American Commandos (1984, C, 89m, R)
An ex-Green Beret returns to Southeast Asia to carry on the war against deadly drug dealers. **AC20**

American Dreamer (1984, C, 105m, PG)
New Jersey housewife wins trip to Paris, finds herself involved in international intrigue and with a dashing Englishman. JoBeth Williams and Tom Conti star. **AC14, CO1, XT9**

American Flyers (1985, C, 114m, PG-13)
Two estranged brothers are reunited when they enter a grueling bicycle race, only to have one of them fall critically ill. Kevin Costner and David Grant star, with

Alexandra Paul and Rae Dawn Chong. **DR22**

American Friend, The (1977, C, 127m, NR)
From director Wim Wenders comes this suspense story about an innocent German picture framer hired to kill a gangster. Bruno Ganz and Dennis Hopper costar; film directors Nicholas Ray and Samuel Fuller have small roles. **CU22, CU23, CU46, FF21, MY2, MY20**

American Gigolo (1980, C, 117m, R)
Hollywood hustler is set up for murder, turns to the woman he really loves for help. Richard Gere and Lauren Hutton star; Paul Schrader directed. **DR3**

American Graffiti (1973, C, 110m, PG)
Cruising in a small California town, 1962; a nostalgic comedy with a cast full of future stars. Ron Howard, Richard Dreyfuss, Cindy Williams, Charles Martin Smith, Paul LeMat, and Candy Clark star, with Mackenzie Phillips, Harrison Ford, Bo Hopkins, Suzanne Sommers, and Wolfman Jack. George Lucas directed. Wall-to-wall rock soundtrack almost steals the show. **CO4, CO6, CU17, DR32, SF25** *Recommended*

American in Paris, An (1951, C, 113m, NR)
Artist Gene Kelly goes to the City of Light for inspiration and meets a young Parisian dancer (Leslie Caron). Winner of seven Academy Awards, including Best Picture, features an all-Gershwin score. Directed by Vincente Minnelli. **MU1, MU7, MU19, MU24, XT1** *Recommended*

American Ninja (1985, C, 90m, R)
Michael Dudikoff stars in this martial arts adventure about an American battling an international arms dealer and his renegade army. Steve James costars. **AC26**

American Ninja 2: The Confrontation (1987, C, 90m, R)
More martial arts action with Michael Dudikoff and Steve James up against an

army of warriors programmed by a madman. **AC26**

American Ninja 3: Blood Hunt (1989, C, 90m, R)
David Bradley takes over from Michael Dudikoff in this popular martial arts series. This chapter once again takes place at a tournament on a tropical island controlled by a madman (Marjoe Gortner). Steve James costars. **AC26**

American Tail, An (1986, C, 81m, G)
Fievel the mouse emigrates with his family from the Old World to a new life in America. He encounters many adventures along the way in this animated production. **FA10**

American Werewolf in London, An (1981, C, 97m, R)
Two Americans backpacking across the English moors are attacked by a werewolf; one is killed and one becomes a werewolf, in an elaborate transformation scene. David Naughton, Griffin Dunne, and Jenny Agutter star. Directed by John Landis. Ground-breaking makeup effects by Rick Baker. **HO4, HO24, SF16, XT9**
Recommended

Americano, The (1955, C, 85m, NR)
A cowboy (Glenn Ford) travels to Europe with a herd of cattle, unaware that the rancher he's delivering them to has been murdered. **WE10**

Amityville Horror, The (1979, C, 117m, R)
A family moves into their dream house, which turns out to be haunted. Based on an allegedly true story. James Brolin, Margot Kidder, and Rod Steiger star. **HO3, HO19**

Amityville II: The Possession (1982, C, 110m, R)
A prequel to *The Amityville Horror* chronicles the events leading to the possession of the eldest son and his slaughter of the rest of the family. Burt Young and Rutanya Alda star. **HO3**

Amityville 3D (1983, C, 95m, PG)
Two journalists and a parapsychologist inhabit the Amityville house to find out once and for all if the house is haunted. Tony Roberts, Candy Clark, and Tess Harper star. **HO3**

Amor Brujo, El (1987, C, 100m, PG)
Romantic drama with dance from Spain, about two young lovers separated by a twist of fate. Choreographed by Antonio Gades. **FF7**

Amy (1981, C, 100m, G)
In the early 1900s, a headstrong woman decides to leave her husband and embark on a career of teaching handicapped children. Jenny Agutter stars in this Disney drama, with Barry Newman, Kathleen Nolan, and Nanette Fabray. **FA1**

Anatomy of a Murder (1959, B&W, 161m, NR)
James Stewart is a small town lawyer who defends an Army officer (Ben Gazzara) on charges that he murdered the man who raped his wife (Lee Remick). Memorable courtroom drama, with George C. Scott, Eve Arden, Kathryn Grant, and Joseph Welch. **CL25, DR17** *Highly Recommended*

Anchors Aweigh (1945, C, 140m, NR)
Gene Kelly joins Frank Sinatra in a rousing musical about two sailor friends who fall for the same girl (Kathryn Grayson). **MU1, MU19, MU26**

And God Created Woman (1957, C, 92m, NR)
Brigitte Bardot's signature role: the temptress of St. Tropez. Directed by Roger Vadim. Scandalous in its time, relatively tame now. **FF32**

And God Created Woman (1988, C, 100m, R)
Director Roger Vadim offers a remake (in name only) of his erotic drama, this time with Rebecca DeMornay as the free-spirited young woman. Also available in a re-edited, unrated version, with additional

sexy footage added; running time: 98m. **CU10, CU18**

. . . And Justice for All (1979, C, 117m, R) A Baltimore lawyer is asked to defend a corrupt judge on charges that he murdered a prostitute. Al Pacino and John Forsythe star, with Jack Warden and Christine Lahti. **DR17, DR66**

And Now for Something Completely Different (1972, C, 89m, PG) Collection of classic bits by the Monty Python troupe. **CO15** *Recommended*

And Now My Love (1975, C/B&W, 121m, PG) French romantic drama about a wealthy woman (Marthe Keller) and rascal (Andre Dussolier) who manage to come together from widely different backgrounds. **FF1**

And Now the Screaming Starts (1973, C, 87m, R) An aristocratic family is cursed by a disembodied hand which is avenging the rape of a virgin servant girl. Peter Cushing, Ian Ogilvy, and Stephanie Beacham star. **HO26, HO33**

And the Ship Sails On (1984, C, 138m, PG) Federico Fellini parable is set on a luxury liner cruise on the eve of World War I, with the usual assortment of Fellini grotesques and outrageous behavior. **FF10**

And Then There Were None (1945, B&W, 98m, NR) Ten visitors to a lonely island begin to disappear one by one. Barry Fitzgerald and Walter Huston star in this version of the Agatha Christie tale. **MY16, MY23**

Anderson Tapes, The (1972, C, 98m, PG) Thieves plan to rob apartments in a New York building over a summer holiday weekend. Sean Connery and Dyan Cannon star, with Martin Balsam, Christopher Walken, and Garrett Morris. Directed by Sidney Lumet. **AC9, AC36, CO13, DR58**

Android (1982, C, 80m, PG) Low-budget, resourceful, amusing science fiction drama starring Klaus Kinski as a mad scientist and Don Opper as the title creation. Many references to classic film *Metropolis*; directed by Aaron Lipstadt. **CU4, FF30, SF5** *Recommended*

Andromeda Strain, The (1971, C, 130m, G) Deadly virus threatens to trigger nuclear disaster in this science fiction adventure from director Robert Wise. Arthur Hill, David Wayne, James Olson, and Kate Reid star. **CL58, SF5, SF7, SF8**

Andy Kaufman Sound Stage Special, The (1983, C, 60m, NR) An hour of offbeat humor with the very unpredictable comedian, assisted by comic Elayne Boosler. **CO16**

Andy Warhol's Bad (1971, C, 100m, R) Suburban housewife runs a hit man squad out of her home—and that's just for starters in this movie that tries for outrageousness and bad taste at every turn. Caroll Baker, Perry King, Susan Tyrell star. **CU12**

Andy Warhol's Dracula (1974, C, 93m, R) Campy horror film from producer Warhol and director Paul Morissey about vampire who needs virgins to survive. Udo Kier and Joe Dallessandro star. **CU4, CU44, HO5, HO24**

Andy Warhol's Frankenstein (1974, C, 94m, R) Gory update of the mad doctor story, produced by Warhol and directed by Paul Morissey, originally shown in 3-D to disbelieving audiences. Not for viewers with weak stomachs. **CU4, CU44, HO20, HO24**

Angel (1984, C, 92m, R) Orphaned teenager goes to high school by day, but cruises Hollywood Boulevard as a prostitute at night, when she's befriended by a colorful collection of street characters. Donna Wilkes, Cliff Gorman, Susan Tyrell, Dick Shawn, and Rory Calhoun star. **AC7**

Angel and the Badman (1947, B&W, 100m, NR)
Western action and romance as a notorious gunslinger (John Wayne) mends his ways for the affections of a Quaker girl. **WE17**

Angel Heart (1987, C, 113m, R)
Detective thriller stars Mickey Rourke as a private eye hired to track down a missing singer, getting involved in a New Orleans voodoo cult. Robert DeNiro and Lisa Bonet costar. An unrated version is also available, containing a few seconds of footage that nearly got the film an "X" rating. **CU1, CU6, CU10, DR25, DR48, HO10, MY2, MY14, XT9**

Angel on My Shoulder (1946, B&W, 101m, NR)
Fantasy story of dead criminal sent to Earth as a judge and his battles with Satan. Paul Muni stars. **SF2**

Angela (1977, C, 100m, NR)
A middle-aged woman and younger man are attracted to one another, unaware that they're mother and son. Sophia Loren and Steve Railsback star, with John Huston. **CL44, FF31**

Angels With Dirty Faces (1938, B&W, 97m, NR)
Two childhood friends grow apart when one joins the clergy and the other becomes a gangster. James Cagney and Pat O'Brien star, with Humphrey Bogart, Ann Sheridan, and the Dead End Kids. **AC22, CL20, CL22** *Recommended*

Angry Red Planet, The (1959, C, 83m, NR)
Science fiction drama of trip to Mars, starring Gerald Mohr and Nora Hayden. **SF3**

Animal Crackers (1930, B&W, 98m, NR)
The Marx Bros. crash a party. Groucho sings "Hooray for Captain Spaulding." Margaret Dumont is appalled. **CO21**

Animal House *see* National Lampoon's Animal House

Animalympics (1979, C, 79m, NR)
Feature cartoon with various members of the animal kingdom competing in sporting events. Billy Crystal, Gilda Radner, and Harry Shearer are among the actors supplying the voices. **FA10**

Anna (1987, C, 101m, PG-13)
Drama of the relationship (à la *All About Eve*) between an aging Czech film star and her young protegé, both living in New York. Oscar nominee Sally Kirkland and Paulina Porizkova star. **DR10, DR13**

Anna Christie (1930, B&W, 90m, NR)
Adaptation of Eugene O'Neill's classic play finds Greta Garbo as a former prostitute whose past begins to haunt her when she falls for a sailor (Charles Bickford). **CL28**

Anna Karenina (1935, B&W, 95m, NR)
Greta Garbo stars in Tolstoy's tragic love story of a forbidden affair. Fredric March and Freddie Bartholomew costar. **CL1, CL4, CL28**

Anne of Green Gables (1985, C, 195m, NR)
Adaptation of the children's classic about an orphan girl who brings joy to the older couple who adopt her. Megan Follows stars, with Colleen Dewhurst. Originally made for TV. **FA3**

Anne of the Thousand Days (1969, C, 145m, PG)
Historical drama of Henry VIII (Richard Burton) and his wife Anne Boleyn (Genevieve Bujold), who bore him an heir but was still executed. **DR5**

Annie (1982, C, 128m, PG)
Lavish musical, based on the Broadway smash, about comic strip characters—a frizzy-haired orphan and her rich guardian, Daddy Warbucks. Aileen Quinn and Albert Finney star, with support from Carol Burnett, Ann Reinking, Bernadette Peters, and Tim Curry. Directed by John Huston. **CL44, FA9, MU2**

Annie Hall (1977, C, 94m, PG)
Woody Allen's brilliant romantic comedy about an anxious New York comedian and a daffy singer from the Midwest finding—and losing—love. Oscar winner for Best Picture, Director, Actress (Diane Keaton), and Original Screenplay (Allen and Marshall Brickman). With Tony Roberts, Christopher Walken, Colleen Dewhurst, Carol Kane, and Shelley Duvall. Among other attributes, one of the best movies about life in both New York and Los Angeles. **CO1, CO2, CO27, DR40, XT1, XT3, XT6, XT9** *Highly Recommended*

Annie Oakley (1935, B&W, 88m, NR)
George Stevens directed Barbara Stanwyck as the legendary sharpshooter. Preston Foster costars, with Moroni Olsen as Buffalo Bill. **CL42, CL45, WE2, WE9**

Annihilators (1985, C, 87m, R)
A synchronized fighting unit just back from overseas gets some stateside action in a small Southern town overrun with sleazy criminals. Christopher Stone, Andy Wood, and Lawrence Hilton-Jacobs star. **AC20**

Another Country (1984, C, 90m, NR)
Drama set in 1930's Britain about two boarding school chums who eventually became spies for the Soviets. Based on the lives of Guy Burgess and Donald Maclean. Rupert Everett and Colin Firth star. **DR23, MY6**

Another Thin Man (1939, B&W, 105m, NR)
William Powell and Myrna Loy return as detectives Nick and Nora Charles in their third adventure, in which they not only solve another crime but start a family with the birth of Nick, Jr. **CL15, CL46, MY13, MY28**

Another Time, Another Place (1958, B&W, 98m, NR)
Lana Turner melodrama of wartime widow's nervous breakdown. Sean Connery has a small role. **AC36**

Another Woman (1988, C, 84m, PG)
Woody Allen drama, starring Gena Rowlands as a New York academic who becomes involved with the problems of a troubled younger woman (Mia Farrow). Gene Hackman costars. **CO27, DR10, DR39**

Anthony Adverse (1936, B&W, 141m, NR)
Epic saga, based on bestselling novel, of young man's adventures in 19th-century America. Fredric March stars, with Olivia de Havilland, Claude Rains, and Oscar winner Gale Sondergaard. **XT5**

Ants (1977, C, 88m, NR)
An army of killer ants terrorizes a resort. Suzanne Sommers, Myrna Loy, and Lynda Day George star. **CL46, HO16**

Any Wednesday (1966, C, 109m, NR)
A New York executive tries to write off his mistress's apartment as a business expense in this comedy starring Jason Robards and Jane Fonda. **DR27**

Any Which Way You Can (1980, C, 116m, PG)
Sequel to *Every Which Way But Loose* has street brawler Clint Eastwood and his orangutan Clyde mixing it up with comic baddies. Sondra Locke, Geoffrey Lewis, and William Smith costar. **AC27, CO9**

Anzio (1968, C, 117m, PG)
Drama centering on the Allied invasion of a significant Italian beachhead in World War II. Robert Mitchum, Peter Falk, and Robert Ryan star. **AC1**

Apache (1954, C, 91m, NR)
Burt Lancaster stars in this historical account of the bitter battle between the Indians and the U. S. Cavalry. **WE8**

Apache Rose (1947, C, 75m, NR)
Roy Rogers western set on a gambling ship. Dale Evans pilots a tugboat, and Bob Nolan & the Sons of the Pioneers provide the harmonies. **WE23**

Apartment, The (1960, B&W, 125m, NR)
Writer-director Billy Wilder's Oscar-winning comedy about a schnook (Jack Lem-

mon) who lets his bosses borrow his pad for their little one-night stands. Shirley MacLaine and Fred MacMurray costar. **CL37, DR42, DR64, XT1, XT6** *Recommended*

Ape, The (1940, B&W, 62m, NR)
A kindly doctor becomes obsessed with his experiments after the death of his wife and child. He soon resorts to murder disguised as an ape. Boris Karloff stars. **HO20, HO27**

Ape Man, The (1943, B&W, 64m, NR)
Bela Lugosi experiments with a serum derived from ape blood to give humans the power of a gorilla. **HO28**

Apocalypse Now (1979, C, 153m, R)
Director Francis Ford Coppola's nightmare vision of the Vietnam War, starring Martin Sheen, Marlon Brando, and Robert Duvall, with Harrison Ford, Dennis Hopper, Frederic Forrest, Timothy Bottoms, G.D. Spradlin, and Larry Fishburne. Effective use of rock music, brilliant imagery. **AC4, CU46, DR32, DR33, DR37, DR51** *Highly Recommended*

Apology (1986, C, 98m, NR)
Thriller about an artist (Lesley Ann Warren) who solicits confessions by phone, until a serial killer calls for her forgiveness. Peter Weller and John Glover costar. **MY3**

Appaloosa, The (1966, C, 98m, NR)
Western drama starring Marlon Brando as a cowboy who journeys to Mexico to retrieve his stolen horse. John Saxon and Anjanette Comer costar. **DR33**

Apple Dumpling Gang, The (1975, C, 100m, G)
Three frisky kids strike it rich and trigger a wild bank robbery in the gold-mad West. Bill Bixby, Susan Clark, Don Knotts, and Tim Conway star in this Disney western. **FA1**

Apple Dumpling Gang Rides Again, The (1979, C, 88m, G)
Two bumbling outlaws try to go straight, but they can't even seem to get that right

in this Disney western. Tim Conway, Don Knotts, and Tim Matheson star. **FA1**

Appointment in Honduras (1953, C, 79m, NR)
An American and his pals help out a Latin American country. Glenn Ford, Ann Sheridan, and Zachary Scott star. Directed by Jacques Tourneur. **HO37**

Appointment With Death (1988, C, 91m, PG)
Hercule Poirot (Peter Ustinov) solves a murder in 1937 Jerusalem. The suspects in this Agatha Christie whodunit include Lauren Bacall, Piper Laurie, and Carrie Fisher. **MY16, MY23**

April Fools, The (1969, C, 95m, PG)
A married man decides to start his life all over again by running off with a lovely French girl. Jack Lemmon and Catherine Deneuve star, with Charles Boyer and Myrna Loy. **CL46, DR64, FF27**

April Fool's Day (1986, C, 90m, R)
A rich college girl throws a party at her family's home on an island and her guests begin to disappear. Deborah Foreman stars. **HO12**

Arabesque (1966, C, 105m, NR)
Espionage thriller about a college professor (Gregory Peck) lured into political intrigue by a beautiful woman (Sophia Loren). Directed by Stanley Donen. **FF31, MU23, MY6**

Arch of Triumph (1948, B&W, 120m, NR)
Wartime drama stars Ingrid Bergman as a woman in love with an Austrian refugee (Charles Boyer). Charles Laughton costars. **CL27**

Aria (1988, C, 90m, R)
Ten directors concoct short films built around opera arias. Among the filmmakers: Jean-Luc Godard, Ken Russell, Robert Altman, Bruce Beresford, and Julien Temple. The stars include Theresa Russell, Bridget Fonda, Buck Henry, John Hurt, and Beverly D'Angelo. **CU25, CU31, FF14**

Arizona Kid, The (1940, B&W, 54m, NR)
Early Roy Rogers western has him singing and dispensing justice, with Gabby Hayes and Dale Evans along to help. **WE23**

Armed and Dangerous (1986, C, 88m, PG-13)
John Candy and Eugene Levy star in this comedy about pair of inept security guards. **CO3, CO14**

Armored Attack *see* North Star

Arnold (1973, C, 100m, PG)
A rich old man dies but his fiancee goes through with the wedding so she and his family can spend his fortune. Then the members of the family begin to die in strange ways. Stella Stevens, Roddy McDowall, and Elsa Lanchester star. **HO24**

Around the World in 80 Days (1956, C, 178m, G)
Jules Verne tale of an outrageous wager— at least for the late 19th century. David Niven and Cantinflas play the champion travelers; Shirley MacLaine costars, with dozens of familiar faces in bit parts. Oscar winner for Best Picture and Musical Score. **DR42, FA4, SF27, XT1**

Around the World Under the Sea (1966, C, 117m, NR)
Family adventure of special submarine and its record-setting voyage. Lloyd Bridges stars, with Shirley Eaton, David McCallum, and Keenan Wynn. **FA4**

Arrangement, The (1969, C, 120m, R)
Business executive re-examines his life after a failed suicide attempt. Kirk Douglas stars, with Faye Dunaway, Deborah Kerr, and Richard Boone in this drama from director Elia Kazan, based on his novel. **DR35, DR59, DR60**

Arrowsmith (1931, B&W, 99m, NR)
From director John Ford comes the story of a country doctor who travels to the West Indies to study tropical ailments. Ronald Colman and Helen Hayes star, with Myrna Loy. Based on Sinclair Lewis' novel. **CL34, CL46, DR19**

Arruza (1972, C, 75m, NR)
A documentary portrait of Carlos Arruza, one of Mexico's great bullfighters. Directed by Budd Boetticher. **CU16, WE28** *Recommended*

Arsenic and Old Lace (1944, B&W, 118m, NR)
A mystery with plenty of wit, based on the hit play about a couple of sweet, innocent-looking maiden aunts who poison their gentlemen callers. Cary Grant, Raymond Massey, and Peter Lorre star. Directed by Frank Capra. **CL10, CL18, CL40, MY21** *Recommended*

Arthur (1981, C, 97m, PG)
A tipsy millionaire playboy falls in love with a kooky shoplifter, although he's engaged to a socialite. Dudley Moore, Liza Minnelli, and Oscar winner John Gielgud star in this romantic comedy. **CO1, CO31, XT4** *Recommended*

Arthur 2 On the Rocks (1988, C, 113m, PG)
Sequel to *Arthur* finds the tipsy millionaire married to his true love, about to lose his fortune. Dudley Moore, Liza Minnelli, and John Gielgud (in ghostly form) reprise their roles from the first film. **CO1, CO31**

As You Like It (1936, B&W, 96m, NR)
William Shakespeare's comedy explores the many facets of love. Laurence Olivier and Elisabeth Bergner star. **CL1, CL32**

Ashanti: Land of No Mercy (1979, C, 117m, R)
The wife of a British doctor (Michael Caine) is kidnapped by a slave trader (Peter Ustinov). William Holden costars in this adventure set in the Middle East. **CL51**

Ashes and Diamonds (1958, B&W, 96m, NR)
Polish drama set in the immediate aftermath of World War II, when a Resistance youth assassinates the wrong man. Directed by Andrzej Wajda; Zbigniew Cybulski stars. **FF7** *Recommended*

Asphalt Jungle, The (1950, B&W, 112m, NR)
An aging criminal returns from prison to recruit his old gang for one final heist. Sterling Hayden and Sam Jaffe star, with Jean Hagen and Marilyn Monroe. Directed by John Huston. **CL29, CL44, MY1, MY34** *Recommended*

Asphyx, The (1972, C, 96m, PG)
British science fiction drama, set in the 1870s, with a scientist isolating the spirit of death and achieving immortality in the process. Robert Stephens, Robert Powell, and Jane Lapotaire star. **SF5, SF19**

Assassination (1987, C, 88m, PG-13)
A Secret Service agent (Charles Bronson) has reason to believe that the new First Lady (Jill Ireland) is in danger. **AC29**

Assassination of Trotsky, The (1972, C, 103m, R)
Brooding account of the final days of the Soviet leader, living in exile in Mexico. Richard Burton stars, with Alain Delon and Romy Schneider; directed by Joseph Losey. **DR5**

Assault, The (1986, C, 149m, NR)
During the closing days of World War II, a young boy witnesses his family's betrayal to the Nazis and their deportation to the death camps. Oscar-winning drama from Holland. **FF7, XT7**

Assault of the Rebel Girls (1959, C, 68m, NR)
In Errol Flynn's last film, he plays himself in the fight to aid Fidel Castro's revolution. Also known as *Cuban Rebel Girls*. **AC34**

Assault on Precinct 13 (1976, C, 90m, R)
Isolated police station is besieged by vengeful street gangs in this low-budget thriller from director John Carpenter. Emphasis is on suspense rather than violence. **AC8, CU29** *Recommended*

Asylum (1972, C, 92m, PG)
Four scary stories by Robert Bloch are linked together by the conclusion of the fourth story. Peter Cushing stars, with Barbara Parkins, Britt Ekland, and Charlotte Rampling. **HO23, HO26, HO33**

At Close Range (1986, C, 115m, R)
A criminal tries to involve his young sons in his line of work, in this drama based on a true story. Sean and Christopher Penn star, with Christopher Walken and Mary Stuart Masterson. **DR8, DR16, XT8**

At the Circus (1939, B&W, 87m, NR)
The Marx Bros. take over the big top. Groucho sings "Lydia the Tattooed Lady." Margaret Dumont is not amused. **CO21**

At the Earth's Core (1976, C, 90m, PG)
Science fiction adventure, based on Edgar Rice Burroughs story, about scientists burrowing from England into subterranean kingdom of monsters. Peter Cushing, Doug McClure, and Caroline Munro star. **FA4, HO33, SF3**

At War With the Army (1950, B&W, 93m, NR)
Dean Martin and Jerry Lewis join the paratroopers in their first starring feature. **CO25, CO38**

L'Atalante (1934, B&W, 82m, NR)
Classic romance/fantasy about a French couple living on a barge on the Seine, directed by Jean Vigo. **FF1**

Atlantic City (1980, C, 104m, R)
An aging gangster and an aspiring casino dealer are the improbable romantic couple in this offbeat drama set in Atlantic City. Burt Lancaster and Susan Sarandon star; written by John Guare and directed by Louis Malle. **DR1, DR16, DR41** *Recommended*

Atoll K (1950, B&W, 80m, NR)
Laurel & Hardy inherit an island but don't realize they're sitting on top of an uranium mine. Their last film together. Also known as *Utopia*. **CO20**

Atom Age Vampire (1961, B&W, 87m, NR)
A mad doctor fixes a dancer's disfigured face, becomes obsessed with keeping her beautiful, and kills other women for their cells so he can preserve the dancer's looks. **HO20**

Atomic Cafe, The (1982, C/B&W, 88m, NR)
Collection of propaganda film clips from the 1950s about the dangers of nuclear war and how to survive one. Funny and chilling at the same time. **CU16** *Recommended*

Attack Force Z (1981, C, 84m, NR)
Australian-produced World War II drama of commandos on a rescue mission. John Phillip Law, Sam Neill, and Mel Gibson star. **AC1, DR69**

Attack of the Killer Tomatoes (1980, C, 87m, PG)
Cult "bad" movie that tries to spoof science fiction films about marauding giant vegetables and winds up being just plain awful. **CU11**

Attack of the Robots (1966, B&W, 88m, NR)
Combination of science fiction drama and spy thriller, with secret agent out to stop terrorists from programming robots for political assassinations. Shot in France; dubbed into English. Eddie Constantine stars. **SF19**

Au Revoir, les Enfants (1987, C, 103m, PG)
French director Louis Malle's autobiographical drama about a schoolboy befriending a Jewish classmate during the Occupation. **DR61, FF1** *Recommended*

Audrey Rose (1977, C, 113m, PG)
A twelve year old begins having nightmares about being in a fire and an investigation reveals that she is the reincarnation of Audrey Rose, a girl who died in a fiery car crash. Marsha Mason, Anthony Hopkins, and John Beck star. Robert Wise directed. **CL58, HO13**

Aurora Encounter (1986, C, 90m, PG)
A Texas town is the site for a friendly alien's visit in this humorous science fiction tale. Jack Elam stars. **SF13**

Author! Author! (1982, C, 110m, PG)
Domestic comedy starring Al Pacino as a playwright whose wife (Tuesday Weld) leaves him with a brood of children (most of them from her previous marriages). Dyan Cannon costars. **CO5, DR66**

Autobiography of Miss Jane Pittman, The (1974, C, 110m, NR)
Epic story of a black woman's journey from slavery to equality in the modern South, starring Cicely Tyson. Winner of 9 Emmys; originally made for TV. **DR14**

Autumn Leaves (1956, B&W, 108m, NR)
Joan Crawford is the middle-aged woman who finds romance with a man (Cliff Robertson) half her age. Their happiness turns sour when his secret past catches up with him. **CL5, CL50**

Autumn Sonata (1978, C, 97m, PG)
Ingrid Bergman and Liv Ullmann star in this drama of a mother and daughter reunited after seven years, with old wounds opened. Directed by Ingmar Bergman; dialogue in Swedish and English. **CL27, FF8, FF25**

Avalanche (1978, C, 91m, PG)
A new ski resort is about to get more powder than the weather forecasts predicted. Rock Hudson, Mia Farrow, Robert Forster, and Jeanette Nolan star in this disaster adventure. **AC23**

Avenging Angel (1985, C, 93m, R)
Sequel to *Angel,* with prostitute, now in college, gunning for killer of cop who befriended her. Betsy Russell stars, with Rory Calhoun and Susan Tyrell returning from first film. **AC8**

Avenging Conscience, The (1914, B&W, 78m, NR)
This early horror film from D.W. Griffith is based on Edgar Allan Poe's "The Tell-Tale Heart." **CL36, HO41**

Avenging Force (1986, C, 104m, R)
A terrorist group dumps a special agent in the midst of a swamp and forces him to fight for his life. Michael Dudikoff stars. **AC24**

Aviator, The (1985, C, 98m, PG)
Grounded pilot agrees to fly spunky young woman through treacherous territory, and romance develops. Christopher Reeve and Rosanna Arquette star. **AC11, AC14**

Aviator's Wife, The (1981, C, 104m, NR)
French comedy about a young man's disillusionment with his current lover and a chance encounter with a new possibility. Directed by Eric Rohmer. **FF15**

L'Avventura (1960, B&W, 145m, NR)
On a weekend boating trip to a remote island, a woman disappears, prompting the others in her party to examine their lives. Deliberately paced drama from Italian director Michelangelo Antonioni. **FF17**

Awakening, The (1980, C, 102m, R)
An Egyptologist defies a curse and releases the spirit of an evil queen, who then possesses his daughter. Based on a novel by Bram Stoker. Charlton Heston, Susannah York, and Stephanie Zimbalist star. **HO8**

Awful Truth, The (1937, B&W, 92m, NR)
Comedy classic pairs Irene Dunne and Cary Grant as a screwy divorced couple who interfere with one another's love life. Ralph Bellamy costars. Oscar-winning direction by Leo McCarey. **CL10, CL18, XT6** *Recommended*

Babes in Arms (1939, B&W, 96m, NR)
Judy Garland and Mickey Rooney put on a show to raise money for their vaudevillian parents. Directed by Busby Berkeley. **MU1, MU4, MU20, MU21**

Babes in Toyland (1961, C, 105m, NR)
Victor Herbert's music is featured in this Disney fantasy set in the make-believe world of Mother Goose. Annette Funicello, Ray Bolger, Ed Wynn, and Tommy Sands star. **FA1**

Babette's Feast (1987, C, 102m, PG)
Remarkably subtle and rich drama, based on a story by Isak Dinesen: a pair of unmarried sisters in a Norwegian village take in a French woman as a cook and she unexpectedly enriches their lives. Oscar winner as Best Foreign Language Film. Gabriel Axel wrote and directed. **FF7, XT7** *Highly Recommended*

Baby, The (1973, C, 85m, R)
A retarded man is babied by his overprotective mother and sister. When a social worker gets involved with the case, murder soon follows. Anjanette Comer and Ruth Roman star. **HO13**

Baby Boom (1987, C, 110m, PG)
A Manhattan business executive has her single life turned upside-down when she inherits an infant from a relative. Diane Keaton stars in this comedy, with Harold Ramis and Sam Shepard. **CO2, CO14, DR40**

Baby Doll (1956, B&W, 114m, NR)
Tennessee Williams' play about a poor Southern farmer who can't keep his teenaged wife happy. Eli Wallach, Carroll Baker, and Karl Malden star, with Rip Torn. Directed by Elia Kazan. Condemned by the Catholic Church and banned in some cities on its original release. **CU6, CU8, CU47, DR59**

Baby, It's You (1983, C, 105m, R)
Romantic drama involving a Jewish girl and an Italian guy, starting in a New Jersey high school. Rosanna Arquette and Vincent Spano star; John Sayles wrote and directed. **DR1**

Baby Maker, The (1970, C, 109m, R)
An infertile couple hire a free spirit (Barbara Hershey) as a surrogate mother, with predictably complicated results. Written and directed by James Bridges. **DR7**

Baby—Secret of the Lost Legend (1985, C, 92m, PG)
On an expedition in the jungles of Africa, a young couple stumble onto an infant dinosaur and wind up protecting it from a greedy scientist. William Katt and Sean Young star. **AC12**

Baby, Take a Bow (1934, B&W, 76m, NR)
Shirley Temple's first starring role has her helping her ex-con dad (James Dunn) to go straight. **FA14**

Baby, the Rain Must Fall (1965, B&W, 100m, NR)
Just out of prison, a drifter tries to settle down with his wife and child but soon becomes restless. Steve McQueen stars, with Lee Remick and Don Murray. **AC28**

Bachelor and the Bobby-Soxer, The (1947, B&W, 95m, NR)
A playboy (Cary Grant), hauled in for disturbing the peace, is sentenced by a judge (Myrna Loy) to court her younger sister (Shirley Temple). Written by Sidney Sheldon. **CL18, CL46, FA14** *Recommended*

Bachelor Party (1984, C, 106m, R)
Tom Hanks stars as a soon-to-be-married man whose buddies throw him the party of his life. **CO44**

Back From Eternity (1956, B&W, 97m, NR)
Adventure drama of survivors of jungle plane crash, starring Robert Ryan, Anita Ekberg, Rod Steiger, and Phyllis Kirk. **AC24**

Back Roads (1981, C, 94m, R)
Romantic comedy about a pair of drifters who fall in love while traveling the South together. Sally Field and Tommy Lee Jones star. **DR36**

Back Street (1961, C, 107m, NR)
The classic Fannie Hurst soaper about a fashion designer (Susan Hayward) who is hopelessly in love with a married man (John Gavin). Vera Miles costars. **CL4, CL6**

Back to Bataan (1945, B&W, 95m, NR)
John Wayne leads American troops into the Philippines to battle the Japanese. Anthony Quinn costars. **AC1, CL17**

Back to the Future (1985, C, 116m, PG)
A teenager is transported back in time to the 1950s, where he plays matchmaker for his future parents. Michael J. Fox stars, with Christopher Lloyd, Lea Thompson and Crispin Glover. Robert Zemeckis directed. **CO4, CO6, CO11, CO37** *Recommended*

Bad *see* Andy Warhol's Bad

Bad and the Beautiful, The (1952, B&W, 118m, NR)
Hollywood tale of a tough producer (Kirk Douglas) and those who work under his thumb. Lana Turner, Dick Powell, Gloria Grahame (an Oscar winner), and Barry Sullivan costar. Directed by Vincente Minnelli. **CL7, MU24, XT5**

Bad Boys (1983, C, 123m, R)
Prison drama, set in facility for youth offenders, with the new loner taking on the established king of the cell block. Sean Penn and Esai Morales star, with Reni Santoni and Ally Sheedy. **DR9, DR18**

Bad Company (1972, C, 93m, PG)
Jeff Bridges and Barry Brown play a couple of drifters set loose on the frontier during the Civil War. With Jim Davis, David Huddleston, and Ed Lauter. Written by Robert Benton and David Newman; directed by Benton. **DR55, DR71, WE7, WE16** *Highly Recommended*

Bad Day at Black Rock (1955, C, 81m, NR)
Riveting drama of a one-armed stranger (Spencer Tracy) in a contemporary Western town to uncover a mystery. Great supporting cast includes Robert Ryan, Lee Marvin, Ernest Borgnine, Anne Francis, and Dean Jagger. **CL8, CL19, DR43, WE13** *Recommended*

Bad Girls (1968, C, 97m, R)
French romantic triangle involving an aging courtesan, a dissipated playboy, and a lovely street waif. Stephane Audran, Jean-Louis Trintignant, and Jacqueline Sassard star; Claude Chabrol directed. Originally released as *Les Biches* at 104m. **FF1**

Bad Man of Deadwood (1941, B&W, 54m, NR)
Roy Rogers western has him playing a man with a secret past who joins a circus as a sharpshooter. **WE23**

Bad News Bears, The (1976, C, 102m, PG)
An inept Little League team and their beer-guzzling coach are saved from humiliation by a talented young pitcher, who just happens to be a girl. Walter Matthau and Tatum O'Neal star; Michael Ritchie directed. **CO4, CO36** *Recommended*

Bad Seed, The (1956, B&W, 129m, NR)
An innocent-looking little girl (Patty McCormack) holds the terrible secret to a rash of mysterious deaths. **HO13, MY18**

Bad Sleep Well, The (1960, B&W, 152m, NR)
Japanese drama of corporate corruption, directed by Akira Kurosawa, starring Toshiro Mifune. Based on a story by Ed McBain. New video version restores edited footage to the original theatrical running time. **CU10, FF9, FF28**

Badge 373 (1973, C, 116m, R)
Sequel of sorts to *The French Connection* starring Robert Duvall as a New York lawman fighting a lone battle against the Mob. **AC9, DR37**

Badlands (1973, C, 95m, PG)
Cult drama about a young couple's murder spree in the 1950s Midwest, loosely based on the Charles Starkweather-Caril Fugate case. Martin Sheen and Sissy Spacek star, with Warren Oates. Terrence Malick wrote and directed. **CU37, CU48, DR16, DR68** *Recommended*

Badman's Territory (1946, B&W, 97m, NR)
Randolph Scott is a sheriff clashing with outlaws who are out of his jurisdiction. **WE22**

Bagdad Cafe (1988, C, 91m, PG)
Off-center comedy about a German woman stranded in the California desert, and her relationship with a black woman who runs a greasy spoon. Marianne Sagebrecht and CCH Pounder star. **CO12, CO37**

Bal, Le (1982, C, 112m, NR)
One-of-a-kind musical, set in Parisian dance hall, spanning fifty years, told with only music, no dialogue. French lyrics, with English subtitles. Ettore Scola directed. **FF1, MU16**

Balance, La (1982, C, 102m, R)
Cop drama from France about a prostitute and her boyfriend forced to inform on crime boss by a ruthless cop. Nathalie Baye, Philippe Leotard, and Richard Berry star; Bob Swaim directed. **FF1, XT9** *Recommended*

Ball of Fire (1941, B&W, 111m, NR)
To help his research, a language professor (Gary Cooper) and his seven colleagues consult a stripper (Barbara Stanwyck) for her interpretations of slang in this classic comedy. Directed by Howard Hawks; written by Billy Wilder and Charles Brackett. **CL10, CL26, CL35, CL45** *Recommended*

Ballad of Cable Hogue, The (1970, C, 121m, R)
From director Sam Peckinpah comes this gentle, comic tale of an old prospector (Jason Robards), his lady friend (Stella Stevens), and their misadventures in the desert. David Warner and Strother Martin costar. **WE9, WE12, WE19** *Highly Recommended*

Ballad of Gregorio Cortez, The (1982, C, 99m, NR)
Drama based on the famous 1901 manhunt for a Mexican cowhand who, in self-

defense, killed a Texas sheriff and became a folk hero when he tried to escape. Edward James Olmos stars. Originally made for public TV. **WE4**

Balloonatic, The/One Week (1923/1920, B&W, 48m, NR)
A Buster Keaton double feature on one tape. In the first short, he's caught in a runaway hot-air balloon. In the second, Buster and his new bride buy a pre-fab home. **CO19**

Bambi (1942, C, 69m, G)
Classic Disney animated feature about a kind-hearted fawn and his forest friends. **FA2** *Recommended*

Bananas (1971, C, 82m, PG)
Wild Woody Allen comedy, basically a series of sketches starring Woody as Fielding Melish, product tester. Sight gags, puns, in-jokes, political humor—they're all here. Louise Lasser and Howard Cosell costar. **CO27** *Recommended*

Band of Outsiders (1964, B&W, 97m, NR)
French director Jean-Luc Godard at his playful, provocative best, in a tale of theft that turns into a running political and cultural commentary. Anna Karina, Sami Frey, and Claude Brasseur star. **FF14** *Recommended*

Band of the Hand (1986, C, 109m, R)
Five buddies try to stay straight on the mean streets of Miami in this urban action thriller. James Remar and Stephen Lang star. **AC8**

Band Wagon, The (1953, C, 112m, NR)
Fred Astaire plays a fading movie star whose songwriting pals want him for a Broadway show. Cyd Charisse, Jack Buchanan, Oscar Levant, and Nanette Fabray costar. Among the many highlights: the Girl Hunt Ballet. Directed by Vincente Minnelli; written by Betty Comden and Adolph Green. **MU1, MU4, MU18, MU24** *Highly Recommended*

Bandolero! (1968, C, 106m, PG)
James Stewart and Dean Martin are two fugitive brothers who take Raquel Welch hostage from Texas to Mexico. **CL25, WE10**

Bang the Drum Slowly (1973, C, 97m, PG)
A star pitcher tries to help his roommate, a third-string catcher, face up to a fatal illness. Michael Moriarty and Robert DeNiro star in this drama. **DR22, DR25**

Bank Dick, The (1940, B&W, 74m, NR)
W.C. Fields gets a job as a bank guard, and a robber decides to make his move. Grady Sutton and Franklin Pangborn costar. **CO22** *Recommended*

Barbarella (1968, C, 98m, PG)
Science fiction spoof, with spacey heroine (Jane Fonda) experiencing all kinds of adventures. Considered sexy at the time of its release, but check the rating. **CU4, CU6, DR27, SF19, SF22**

Barbarian and the Geisha, The (1958, C, 105m, NR)
Historical drama starring John Wayne as a diplomat who helps open 19th-century Japan to the West. Directed by John Huston. **CL17, CL44**

Barbarosa (1982, C, 90m, PG)
Willie Nelson plays an aging outlaw who teaches a naive farmboy survival skills to carry on his legend. Gary Busey costars. **MU12, WE4, WE10**

Barbary Coast (1935, B&W, 90m, NR)
Miriam Hopkins plays a saloon singer in the Gold Rush days of San Francisco, fending off the advances of her ruthless boss (Edward G. Robinson). Howard Hawks directed. **CL35, CL52**

Barber Shop, The (1933, B&W, 21m, NR)
Classic W.C. Fields short, with Bill playing a barber with a very sharp razor. **CO22**

Barefoot Contessa, The (1954, C, 128m, NR)
Humphrey Bogart stars as manipulative director who promotes his protege (Ava Gardner) into stardom, with the help of a cynical press agent (Oscar winner Edmond O'Brien). Striking color photography; directed by Joseph L. Mankiewicz. **CL9, CL20, CL55, DR13, XT4**

Barefoot Executive, The (1971, C, 95m, G)
Disney comedy finds Kurt Russell as a young employee at a struggling television network; with the help of a clever chimpanzee, he goes from the mailroom to executive row in no time. **FA1**

Barefoot in the Park (1967, C, 105m, NR)
Neil Simon's romantic comedy about a young couple's struggles to make a life in New York, starring Jane Fonda and Robert Redford. Charles Boyer and Mildred Natwick offer fine support. **CO1, CO34, DR27, DR29, XT9**

Barfly (1987, C, 99m, R)
Two skid-row alcoholics strike up a friendship of sorts, based on their mutual love of the bottle. Mickey Rourke and Faye Dunaway star in this comedy-drama based on the writings of Charles Bukowski. **DR15, DR35, DR48** *Recommended*

Barkleys of Broadway, The (1949, C, 109m, NR)
Fred Astaire and Ginger Rogers play famous dancing partners who marry, separate, and then reunite. **MU1, MU18**

Baron of Arizona, The (1950, B&W, 90m, NR)
Vincent Price stars as a landgrabbing villain in 19th-century Arizona. Directed by Sam Fuller. **CU22, HO31**

Barry Lyndon (1975, C, 183m, PG)
Stanley Kubrick's epic about an 18th-century Irish scoundrel. Based on William Makepeace Thackeray's classic novel. Exquisitely photographed by John Alcott. Ryan O'Neal and Marisa Berenson star. **CL1, DR5, DR53** *Recommended*

Basket Case (1982, C, 89m, NR)
Horror story of separated Siamese twins, one a deformed monster, both seeking revenge on the doctors who separated them. Has well-deserved cult reputation. **CU4, CU7, HO15, HO18** *Recommended*

Bat 21 (1988, C, 88m, R)
An American soldier, stranded behind enemy lines during the Vietnam War, has as his only hope a courageous chopper pilot. Gene Hackman and Danny Glover star. **AC4, DR39**

Bataan (1943, B&W, 114m, NR)
Classic World War II drama of brave Americans holding out against impossible odds. Robert Taylor, George Murphy, and Thomas Mitchell star. **AC1**

Batman (1966, C, 105m, NR)
Adventure starring the Caped Crusader from the comics, spun off from the popular TV series of the mid-1960s. Adam West and Burt Ward repeat their roles as Batman and Robin; comic villains are played by Burgess Meredith, Cesar Romero, and Lee Meriwether. **AC17**

Batman (1989, C, 126m, PG-13)
Michael Keaton is the Caped Crusader, Jack Nicolson is the Joker in this extravagantly produced adventure of the comic book hero. Eye-popping sets. Tim Burton directed. **AC17, CO45, DR24, SF14** *Recommended*

*batteries not included (1987, C, 107m, PG)
A group of tenants in a New York slum apartment house scheduled for demolition get some unusual help from an army of tiny aliens. Jessica Tandy and Hume Cronyn head the cast of this family fantasy drama. **FA8**

Battle Cry (1955, C, 149m, NR)
World War II drama, taking Marine outfit through training and into combat. Based on Leon Uris's novel; directed by Raoul Walsh. Van Heflin, Tab Hunter, and Dorothy Malone star. **AC1**

Battle for the Planet of the Apes (1973, C, 92m, PG)
Fifth and final in the *Apes* series, featuring clips from earlier installments. Roddy McDowall, Paul Williams, and John Huston star. **CL44, FA8, SF8, SF13, SF23**

Battle Force (1978, C, 97m, NR)
Drama traces the lives of two families, one German and the other American, up to World War II. Henry Fonda and Stacy Keach star. Also known as *The Great Battle*. **CL24**

Battle of Algiers, The (1965, B&W, 123m, NR)
Documentary-style drama of Algerian resistance to French colonialism during the 1950s. Powerful political film directed by Gillo Pontecorvo. **AC6, CU9, FF2** *Recommended*

Battle of Britain (1969, C, 132m, G)
All-star British cast enlivens this account of aerial combat over British soil during World War II. Michael Caine, Christopher Plummer, Laurence Olivier, Ralph Richardson, Harry Andrews, and Trevor Howard appear. **AC1, AC11, CL32**

Battle of the Bulge, The (1965, C, 141m, NR)
Henry Fonda, Robert Shaw, Robert Ryan, and Dana Andrews star in this account of the 1944 battle for Belgium against desperate German forces. Original running time: 163m. **AC1, CL24**

Battle of the Sexes, The (1960, B&W, 88m, NR)
Peter Sellers plays an auld Scot with murder in his heart in this wacky British comedy. **CO26**

Battleship Potemkin *see* Potemkin

Bay Boy, The (1984, C, 107m, R)
Coming-of-age drama set in rural Canada during the Depression, starring Kiefer Sutherland, Liv Ullmann, and Peter Donat. **FF25**

Beaches (1988, C, 123m, PG-13)
The lifelong friendship of two women (Bette Midler, Barbara Hershey) is put to the test when one falls fatally ill. An unabashedly sentimental drama. Midler performs several songs. **DR2, DR10**

Bear Island (1980, C, 118m, PG)
Adaptation of the Alistair MacLean novel about the race for a Nazi submarine loaded with gold, trapped under the Arctic ice. Donald Sutherland, Vanessa Redgrave, and Christopher Lee star. **DR65, HO32**

Beast in the Cellar, The (1970, C, 87m, R)
Two spinster sisters hide their maniacal brother in the basement in this British horror story. Beryl Reid and Flora Robson star. **HO14**

Beast Must Die, The (1974, C, 93m, PG)
A wealthy man believes one of his friends is a werewolf. He installs surveillance cameras throughout his home, then invites his friends for the weekend. Peter Cushing stars. **HO4, HO33**

Beast Within, The (1982, C, 98m, R)
A woman, raped on her wedding night by a deformed fiend, gives birth to a son who never misbehaves, until his 17th birthday. Ronny Cox, Bibi Besch, and Paul Clemens star. **HO4, HO13**

Beastmaster, The (1982, C, 118m, PG)
Sword and sorcery adventure, featuring a hero who communicates with animals, a lovely slave girl, and an evil priest. Marc Singer, Tanya Roberts, and Rip Torn star. **AC18, CU47**

Beat Street (1984, C, 106m, PG)
Inner city kids put on a show in this breakdancing musical, starring Rae Dawn Chong and Guy Davis. **MU9**

Beat the Devil (1954, B&W, 89m, NR)
Humphrey Bogart and Jennifer Jones head the cast of this unusual spoof of spy films. Written by Truman Capote and John Huston (who also directed). Gina Lollobrigida, Robert Morley, and Peter

Lorre costar. Misunderstood on its initial release, now a cult classic. **CL14, CL20, CL44, CU5, CU13**

Beau Brummel (1924, B&W, 92m, NR)
Silent historical drama of the famed ladies' man who led a life of dissolution after seeing his true love married off to a nobleman he despised. John Barrymore stars, with Mary Astor and Willard Louis. **CL3, CL12**

Beau Geste (1939, B&W, 114m, NR)
Classic Foreign Legion tale of three brothers surviving desert hardships, tribal warfare. Gary Cooper, Ray Milland, Robert Preston, and Brian Donlevy star. **AC13, CL26**

Beau Marriage, Le (1982, C, 97m, R)
From French director Eric Rohmer, a comedy about a determined young woman who decides it's time she got married—even though her intended has no idea of her plans. **FF15**

Beau Pere (1981, C, 120m, NR)
French comedy-drama about a man's relationship with his teenaged stepdaughter blossoming into romance after the death of her mother. Patrick Dewaere and Ariel Besse star; Bertrand Blier directed. **FF1**

Beautiful Blonde From Bashful Bend, The (1949, C, 77m, NR)
Comic western about a woman gunslinger who's mistaken for a proper lady. Betty Grable stars, with Cesar Romero, Rudy Vallee, and Sterling Holloway. Directed by Preston Sturges. **CO24, WE15**

Beauty and the Beast (1946, B&W, 92m, NR)
From French director Jean Cocteau, the classic fable of an impossible romance. Jean Marais and Josette Day star. **CU21, FF1, SF2**

Beauty and the Beast (1984, C, 60m, NR)
Love is in the eye of the beholder—as the beauty (Susan Sarandon) brings out the best in the beast (Klaus Kinski) in a romantic fantasy adventure from Faerie Tale Theatre. **FA12**

Because of the Cats (1973, C, 95m, R)
A gang of wealthy kids fall into a bizarre murder cult. Sylvia Kristel stars. **HO11, HO25**

Becket (1964, C, 148m, NR)
Grand historical drama of clash between England's King Henry II (Peter O'Toole) and the Archbishop of Canterbury, Thomas à Becket (Richard Burton). **DR5, DR45**

Bedazzled (1967, C, 107m, NR)
Comedy of nerdy man who makes several deals with the Devil to be near the woman he loves. Dudley Moore and Peter Cook star; Stanley Donen directed. **CO3, CO31, CU5, MU23** *Recommended*

Bedford Incident, The (1965, B&W, 102m, NR)
An aggressive U.S. naval captain tries to attack a Soviet submarine in international waters. Richard Widmark stars, with Sidney Poitier and Martin Balsam. **DR38**

Bedknobs and Broomsticks (1971, C, 117m, G)
An amateur witch (Angela Lansbury) helps the British win a few World War II battles in this Disney fantasy. **FA1**

Bedlam (1946, B&W, 79m, NR)
Val Lewton produced this horror story about a young lady (Anna Lee) who tries to reform conditions at an insane asylum and finds herself being committed. Boris Karloff stars. **HO27, HO36**

Bedroom Window, The (1987, C, 112m, R)
A wrong-man thriller in the Hitchcock mold. An innocent man (Steve Guttenberg) is accused of murder when he covers for the witness—his lover and his boss' wife. Isabelle Huppert and Elizabeth McGovern costars. **MY7**

Bedtime for Bonzo (1951, B&W, 83m, NR)
Comedy about a professor who takes a chimp into his house as an experiment. Ronald Reagan's name at the top of the cast has made this a cult comedy. **CO35, CU5**

Beer (1985, C, 82m, R)
A female ad executive comes up with a tasteless campaign to sell suds—and, of course, it works. Satire starring Sally Kellerman, with Rip Torn, Kenneth Mars, and Dick Shawn. **CU47**

Beetlejuice (1988, C, 92m, PG)
A pair of friendly ghosts can't scare away the obnoxious family that's moved into their house, so they call on a legendary "bio-exorcist" for help. Alec Baldwin, Geena Davis, and Michael Keaton star, with Catherine O'Hara and Jeffrey Jones in this comedy packed with wild special effects. Directed by Tim Burton. **CO11, CO14, CO45** *Recommended*

Before I Hang (1940, B&W, 71m, NR)
A doctor working on a rejuvenation serum becomes a killer when he uses the blood of a murderer. Boris Karloff and Evelyn Keyes star. **HO27**

Beguiled, The (1971, C, 109m, R)
Clint Eastwood plays a wounded Confederate soldier who seeks shelter in a girls' school, with disastrous results. Geraldine Page and Elizabeth Hartman costar. **WE7, WE26** *Recommended*

Behave Yourself! (1951, B&W, 81m, NR)
A couple is chased by a criminal gang after witnessing a crime. Farley Granger and Shelley Winters star, with Lon Chaney, Jr. in this thriller played for laughs. **HO30**

Behold a Pale Horse (1964, B&W, 118m, NR)
Drama of post-Civil War Spain, with exiled guerrilla Gregory Peck deciding to return to his homeland, in the face of certain death at the hands of an old enemy (Anthony Quinn). Fred Zinnemann directed. **CL57**

Being There (1980, C, 124m, PG)
A reclusive gardener is set loose on the world when his boss dies, and his cryptic remarks are mistaken for profound political observations. Peter Sellers stars in this satire adapted from Jerzy Kosinski's novel. Shirley MacLaine, Oscar winner Melvyn Douglas, Jack Warden, and Richard Dysart costar. **CO2, CO12, CO26, DR21, DR42, XT4** *Recommended*

Bela Lugosi Meets a Brooklyn Gorilla (1952, B&W, 74m, NR)
Duke Mitchell and Sammy Petrillo are shipwrecked on an island where a mad doctor (Bela Lugosi) is conducting bizarre experiments. Also known as *The Boys From Brooklyn.* **HO28**

Believers, The (1987, C, 114m, R)
A widowed police psychiatrist discovers his son has been chosen as the next sacrifice to a voodoo cult operating out of Harlem. Martin Sheen stars, with Helen Shaver, Robert Loggia, and Harley Cross. Directed by John Schlesinger. **HO11**

Bell, Book, and Candle (1958, C, 103m, NR)
Kim Novak plays a contemporary witch who casts a love spell on her next-door neighbor (James Stewart) in this comedy. Jack Lemmon, Elsa Lanchester, Ernie Kovacs, Hermione Gingold costar. **CL25, DR64**

Bell Jar, The (1979, C, 107m, R)
Drama set in the early 1950s about a sensitive college student's breakdown, based on the novel by Sylvia Plath. Marilyn Hasset stars, with Julie Harris, Anne Jackson, and Barbara Barrie. **DR10, DR19**

Bellboy, The (1960, B&W, 72m, NR)
Jerry Lewis stars in this series of comic sketches set in a plush Miami Beach hotel. Lewis's character never speaks; his first film as a director. **CO25** *Recommended*

Belle of New York, The (1952, C, 82m, NR)
This musical set in the gay 90s has Fred Astaire as a society playboy pursuing a missionary, played by Vera-Ellen. **MU18**

Belles of St. Trinians, The (1955, B&W, 90m, NR)
Classic British comedy set in a girls school run by a zany headmistress, whose bookie brother would like to use the students as part of his operation. Alastair Sim stars (in two roles), with Joyce Grenfell, George Cole, and Hermione Baddeley. **CO17**

Bellisima (1951, B&W, 112m, NR)
An overbearing mother pushes her daughter into a stage career in this Italian drama starring Anna Magnani. Luchino Visconti directed. **FF2**

Bellman and True (1988, C, 112m, R)
Bank robbers enlist the aid of a mild-mannered computer expert, threatening his son if he doesn't cooperate. Bernard Hill stars in this British thriller. **MY19, MY34** *Recommended*

Bells, The (1926, B&W, 108m, NR)
Silent drama of an innkeeper who murders a traveler and is tormented by his conscience. Lionel Barrymore stars, with Boris Karloff. **HO27**

Bells Are Ringing (1960, C, 127m, NR)
Musical comedy about an answering service operator and a ladies' man. Judy Holliday (in her last film) stars with Dean Martin. Vincente Minnelli directed. Songs include "Just in Time" and "The Party's Over." **CO42, MU1, MU24**

Bells of Coronado (1950, B&W, 67m, NR)
Roy Rogers stars in this contemporary western about an insurance agent out to thwart a uranium deal with foreign agents. **WE23**

Bells of Rosarita (1945, B&W, 68m, NR)
Roy Rogers gallops to the rescue of a young girl. **WE23**

Bells of St. Mary's, The (1945, B&W, 126m, NR)
Sequel to *Going My Way,* with Father O'Malley (Bing Crosby) in a new parish with a wise Sister Superior (Ingrid Bergman). **CL27, MU25**

Bells of San Angelo (1947, B&W, 54m, NR)
Roy Rogers takes on evildoers who want to snatch a young girl's ranch. With Dale Evans. **WE23**

Ben (1972, C, 94m, PG)
A sequel to *Willard* has the lead rat, Ben, befriend a sick young boy. Lee Harcourt Montgomery and Joseph Campanella star. Michael Jackson sings the title song. **HO16**

Ben-Hur (1959, C, 217m, G)
Winner of a record eleven Academy Awards, this religious epic is wholesome family entertainment. Charlton Heston and Stephen Boyd star as former friends, now rivals in a spectacular chariot race. Heston, director William Wyler, and supporting actor Hugh Griffith won Oscars. **CL13, CL38, XT1, XT2, XT4, XT6**

Ben-Hur: A Tale of the Christ (1926, B&W/C, 148m, NR)
Silent classic, shot with then-record budget, about rival charioteers in the time of Christ. Ramon Novarro and Francis X. Bushman star. Video version includes original tinted and Technicolor sequences. **CL12, CL13**

Bend of the River (1952, C, 91m, G)
Wagon train saga set in 1840s Oregon, starring James Stewart and Rock Hudson. Directed by Anthony Mann. **CL25, WE20**

Beneath the Planet of the Apes (1970, C, 95m, PG)
Second *Planet of the Apes* story features the simian heroes battling human mutants who somehow survived the holocaust. James Franciscus, Kim Hunter, and Charlton Heston star. **FA8, SF8, SF13, SF23**

Beneath the 12 Mile Reef (1953, C, 102m, NR)
The scenery's the star in this adventure of a Florida family of sponge divers. Robert Wagner and Terry Moore star. **AC12**

Benji (1980, C, 87m, G)
Benji, the Laurence Olivier of the dog world, stars in his first adventure story. **FA5**

Benji Takes a Dive at Marineland (1984, C, 60m, NR)
America's canine hero takes a tour of Marineland—and comes up swimming in this family adventure. **FA5**

Benji the Hunted (1987, C, 88m, G)
The lovable mutt uses his wits in the wilderness to protect some lion cubs in this adventure from the Disney studios. **FA5**

Benny Goodman Story, The (1955, C, 116m, G)
Film bio of America's premier jazz clarinetist, with Steve Allen as the King of Swing. Benny's great sidemen Gene Krupa, Lionel Hampton, and Teddy Wilson appear as themselves. **MU5**

Berlin Alexanderplatz (1980, C, 931m, NR)
Epic portrait of Berlin during the 1920s from director Rainer Werner Fassbinder, adapted from novel by Alfred Doblin. Originally produced for German TV in 13 episodes. Gunter Lamprecht, Hanna Schygulla, and Barbara Sukowa star. **FF20**

Berlin Express (1948, B&W, 86m, NR)
In Berlin after World War II, several Allied agents attempt to free a German government offical kidnapped by members of the Nazi underground. Merle Oberon, Robert Ryan, and Paul Lukas star. Directed by Jacques Tourneur. **HO37**

Berserk! (1967, C, 96m, NR)
A circus owner (Joan Crawford) becomes frantic when a series of murders occur under her big top. **CL50, MY3**

Best Boy (1979, C, 111m, NR)
Oscar-winning documentary about filmmaker Ira Wohl's retarded cousin, a 52-year-old man named Philly. **CU16**

Best Defense (1984, C, 94m, R)
Comedy about the arms race, featuring two related stories. In one, Dudley Moore bumbles through the development of a super tank, and in the other, Eddie Murphy plays a soldier stationed in the Middle East who has to employ the weapon. **CO13, CO31**

Best Foot Forward (1943, C, 95m, NR)
Big Broadway star decides to pay a visit to a small town in this musical comedy. Lucille Ball stars; several good dance numbers. **MU3**

Best Friends (1982, C, 108m, PG)
When a screenwriting team changes their status from Living Together to Married, their love life suffers. Burt Reynolds and Goldie Hawn star, with Ron Silver and Richard Libertini. **AC37, CO1, CO30**

Best Little Whorehouse In Texas, The (1982, C, 114m, R)
The hit Broadway musical about a sheriff (Burt Reynolds) who tries to close down the infamous Chicken Ranch, run by his girlfriend (Dolly Parton). **AC37, MU2, MU17**

Best of Bugs Bunny and Friends, The (1986, C, 53m, NR)
Collection of Warner Bros. classic cartoon stars features *Duck Soup to Nuts, A Feud There Was,* and *Tweetie Pie.* Bugs' costars include Daffy Duck, Tweetie Pie, and Porky Pig. **FA11**

Best of Chevy Chase, The (1987, C, 60m, NR)
Chevy's brief stint on *Saturday Night Live* yields this hour of comedy, featuring

his Gerald Ford impression and his "Weekend Update" bits. **CO13**

Best of Comic Relief, The (1986, C, 120m, NR)
Highlights of a benefit show to help homeless people, hosted by Robin Williams, Billy Crystal, and Whoopi Goldberg. Among the comics featured are Jay Leno, Garry Shandling, Howie Mandel, Bobcat Goldthwait, and Jerry Lewis. **CO16, CO25, CO43** *Recommended*

Best of Dan Aykroyd, The (1986, C, 60m, NR)
Classic Aykroyd bits from *Saturday Night Live,* including the Bass-o-matic salesman, Richard Nixon, and the Coneheads. **CO13**

Best of Eddie Murphy: Saturday Night Live, The (1989, C, 79m, NR)
Eddie's memorable bits from Saturdays gone by, including Mr. Robinson's Neighborhood, Little Richard Simmons, James Brown, Bill Cosby, and Buckwheat. **CO13** *Recommended*

Best of Gilda, The (1989, C, 59m, NR)
Highlights from Gilda Radner's skits on *Saturday Night Live*, featuring Roseanne Roseannadanna, Baba Wawa, Emily Litella, Lisa Loobner, and more. **CO13**

Best of John Belushi, The (1985, C, 60m, NR)
The Killer Bees, Samurai Everything, Joe Cocker—they're all here on this collection of Belushi highlights from *Saturday Night Live*. **CO13**

Best of Times, The (1986, C, 105m, PG-13)
A pair of former high school football teammates get a chance to redeem themselves in a 20-year anniversary rematch of the Big Game they lost. Robin Williams and Kurt Russell star in this comedy, with Pamela Reed and Holly Palance. **CO3, CO36, CO43**

Best of W. C. Fields, The (1930, B&W, 58m, NR)
Three of Fields' early short comedies, produced by Mack Sennett. **CO22**

Best Seller (1987, C, 110m, R)
A former hit man for a corporation turns to a bestselling novelist (and former cop) to write his life story. James Woods and Brian Dennehy star in this cat-and-mouse thriller. **MY9**

Best Years of Our Lives, The (1946, B&W, 170m, NR)
Three World War II veterans (Dana Andrews, Oscar winners Fredric March and Harold Russell) adjust to life back home in this heartfelt drama. Oscar winner for Best Picture and Director (William Wyler). With Myrna Loy, Hoagy Carmichael, Teresa Wright, and Virginia Mayo. **CL8, CL38, CL46, XT1, XT2, XT4, XT6** *Recommended*

Bête Humaine, La (1938, B&W, 106m, NR)
French drama of a railway worker's obsession with a married woman, who tries to persuade him to kill her husband. Jean Renoir directed; Jean Gabin, Simone Simon, and the director star. U.S. remake: *Human Desire*. **FF12, FF36**

Betrayal (1983, C, 95m, R)
Harold Pinter's play about a romantic triangle begins at the very end of the affair, flashing back in stages to the beginning. Jeremy Irons, Ben Kingsley and Patricia Hodge star. **DR3, DR20, DR23** *Recommended*

Betrayed (1988, C, 127m, R)
An inexperienced F.B.I. agent (Debra Winger) is assigned to go undercover to investigate a white supremacist group. What she doesn't count on is falling in love with one of the group's leaders (Tom Berenger). With John Heard and John Mahoney; Costa-Gavras directed. **DR47, MY5**

Betsy, The (1978, C, 125m, R)
Laurence Olivier stars as the head of a family-owned auto manufacturing plant. Trashy drama from Harold Robbins. Blockbuster cast includes Robert Duvall, Katharine Ross, Tommy Lee Jones, Jane Alexander, Lesley-Anne Down, and Edward Herrmann. **CL32, DR37, DR60**

Betty Blue (1986, C, 121m, NR)
Erotic story of a writer's affair with a free-spirited young woman, whose mental instability begins to threaten their lives. Jean-Hughes Anglade and Beatrice Dalle star; Jean-Jacques Beneix directed. **FF1**

Between Friends (1983, C, 100m, NR)
Elizabeth Taylor and Carol Burnett play middle-aged women who offer each other moral support as they begin a new life in the singles world. Originally made for cable TV. **CL33**

Between the Lines (1977, C, 101m, R)
An alternative newspaper in Boston is the setting for this charming comedy about a group of idealistic friends. Outstanding cast of young performers: Lindsay Crouse, John Heard, Jeff Goldblum, Jill Eikenberry, Gwenn Welles, Bruno Kirby, and Stephen Collins. Directed by Joan Micklin Silver. **CO2** *Recommended*

Beverly Hills Cop (1985, C, 105m, R)
Eddie Murphy plays Axel Foley, a Detroit cop who travels to California to investigate the murder of a friend. Action comedy costarring Lisa Eichorn, Judge Reinhold, Ronny Cox, and John Ashton. **CO9, CO13, CO37, XT9**

Beverly Hills Cop II (1987, C, 103m, R)
The further adventures of Axel Foley; this time, he's on the trail of a gang of murderous thieves. Eddie Murphy stars, with Ronny Cox, John Ashton, Judge Reinhold, Brigitte Nielsen, Dean Stockwell, and Jurgen Prochnow. **CO9, CO13, CO37, XT9**

Beware, My Lovely (1952, B&W, 77m, NR)
A lonely woman (Ida Lupino) hires a handyman (Robert Ryan), only to discover that he's a psychopath. **MY3**

Beyond a Reasonable Doubt (1956, C, 80m, NR)
Mystery, based on true story, of a usually peaceful New Zealand town that turns violent when an innocent farmer is charged with double murder. Fritz Lang directs. **CL43, MY8**

Beyond Obsession (1984, C, 116m, NR)
Marcello Mastroianni and Tom Berenger star in this thriller, set in Marrakesh, about an Italian ex-diplomat and an American and their mutual interest in the same woman. **FF24**

Beyond the Door (1974, C, 94m, R)
Horror film from Italy about the possession of a young girl, with *Exorcist* overtones. Juliet Mills and Richard Johnson star. **FF2, HO8**

Beyond the Door 2 (1979, C, 92m, R)
A little boy is possessed by the soul of his dead father seeking revenge on his wife. Horror drama from Italy, directed by Mario Bava. **FF2, HO8**

Beyond the Law (1968, C, 91m, NR)
Lee Van Cleef plays an outlaw who decides to go straight when he learns that, as sheriff, he can claim a silver mine. **WE14**

Beyond the Poseidon Adventure (1979, C, 122m, PG)
Sequel to *The Poseidon Adventure* about a race to recover treasure from the capsized ship before it sinks. Michael Caine, Sally Field, Telly Savalas, Slim Pickens, and Shirley Knight star. **AC23, DR36**

Beyond the Valley of the Dolls (1970, C, 109m, R)
Spoofy "sequel" to famous trash story of three casualties of wicked Hollywood, with all-girl rock band clawing and sleeping their way to the top. Directed by Russ

Meyer; written by Roger Ebert. **CU2, CU6**

Beyond Therapy (1987, C, 93m, R)
Comedy of two souls trying for romance but thwarted by their respective therapists. Julie Hagerty and Jeff Goldblum star, with Glenda Jackson, Tom Conti, and Christopher Guest; Robert Altman directed. **CU25**

Bible, The (1966, C, 174m, NR)
Religious epic detailing many familiar stories from the first book of Genesis. John Huston directed and stars as Noah; also in the cast: Michael Parks (as Adam), George C. Scott (as Abraham), plus Peter O'Toole, Ava Gardner, and Richard Harris. **CL13, CL44, DR45**

Biches, Les *see* Bad Girls

Bicycle Thief, The (1949, B&W, 90m, NR)
Classic Italian drama of a poor man and his son searching the streets of Rome for their stolen bicycle. Vittorio De Sica directed; winner of a special Oscar. **FF2, XT7**

Big (1988, C, 102m, PG)
Tom Hanks stars in this comedy of a 12-year-old boy who wakes up one morning in the body of a 30-year-old man. With Elizabeth Perkins, Robert Loggia, and John Heard. **CO4, CO37, CO44** *Recommended*

Big Blue, The (1988, C, 118m, PG)
Adventure story of a pair of rival French free divers (men who use no equipment in their underwater diving), one of whom falls in love with an American woman. Rosanna Arquette stars, with Jean-Marc Barr and Jean Reno. **AC12**

Big Brawl, The (1980, C, 95m, R)
Martial arts star Jackie Chan is featured in this action drama set in 1930s gangster-era Chicago. Lots of action and not a few laughs. **AC26**

Big Bus, The (1976, C, 88m, PG)
Spoof of disaster movies set on a mammoth bus making an accident-prone cross-country trip. Stockard Channing, Joseph Bologna, John Beck, Lynn Redgrave, and Ned Beatty head the cast. **CO7**

Big Business (1988, C, 97m, PG)
Comedy starring Bette Midler and Lily Tomlin as two sets of twins mismatched at birth. One set grows up to run a New York corporation; the other grows up poor in rural West Virginia. Trouble starts when the country sisters travel to New York and run into you-know-who. **CO3, CO5, MU12**

Big Chill, The (1983, C, 103m, R)
A group of college friends from the 1960s are reunited when one of their group commits suicide. Slick portrait of a generation, starring William Hurt, Glenn Close, Kevin Kline, JoBeth Williams, Mary Kay Place, Tom Berenger, and Jeff Goldblum, with Meg Tilly. **DR7, DR31, DR72**

Big Combo, The (1955, B&W, 89m, NR)
A cop (Cornel Wilde) takes on the mob with the help of a gangster's ex-girlfriend. **MY1**

Big Country, The (1958, C, 166m, NR)
From director William Wyler comes an epic tale of the Old West, with a land battle erupting between settlers. Gregory Peck and Charlton Heston head the cast, which also includes Oscar winner Burl Ives, Jean Simmons, Carroll Baker, and Chuck Connors. **CL38, WE1, XT4**

Big Deal on Madonna Street (1956, B&W, 91m, NR)
Classic Italian comedy about an inept band of crooks and their bungling attempts to pull off a heist. Vittorio Gassman and Marcello Mastroianni star. **FF2, FF24, MY34** *Recommended*

Big Easy, The (1987, C, 101m, R)
A thriller set in New Orleans, with an easy-going police detective (Dennis Quaid) trying to solve a series of drug-related murders and a nosey district attor-

ney (Ellen Barkin) getting in his way. **MY2, MY5, XT9**

Big Fix, The (1978, C, 108m, PG)
Richard Dreyfuss plays Moses Wine, a hippie turned private eye. He's on the trail of fellow former activist. **MY14**

Big Heat, The (1953, B&W, 90m, NR)
An ex-cop becomes obsessed with a case when his wife is killed by a car bomb meant for him. Glenn Ford, Gloria Grahame, and Lee Marvin star. Directed by Fritz Lang. **AC22, CL43, DR43, MY1** *Recommended*

Big Jake (1971, C, 110m, PG)
John Wayne swings into action to save his grandson's life. Richard Boone, Maureen O'Hara, and Wayne's real-life son Patrick costar in this western drama. **WE17**

Big Mouth, The (1967, C, 107m, NR)
Jerry Lewis comedy about a treasure hunt and its unscrupulous participants. **CO25**

Big Red (1962, C, 89m, NR)
Disney drama of a young boy's adventures with one very special Irish setter. **FA5**

Big Red One, The (1980, C, 113m, PG)
World War II drama of tough sergeant (Lee Marvin) pushing his young recruits through several European campaigns. Mark Hamill costars; Samuel Fuller directed. **AC1, CU22, DR43** *Recommended*

Big Shots (1987, C, 91m, PG-13)
A pint-sized version of *The Sting*, with streetwise Darius McCrary and his newfound suburban pal Ricky Busker hustling their way through the streets of Chicago. **FA7**

Big Show, The (1936, B&W, 70m, NR)
Gene Autry plays two roles, a conceited movie cowboy and his look-alike stunt man, in this musical western. The Sons of the Pioneers (with Roy Rogers, billed as Leonard Slye) do some harmonizing. **WE23, WE24**

Big Sky, The (1952, B&W, 122m, NR)
Kirk Douglas and a rowdy band of 1830s furtrappers set out on a back-breaking expedition up the Missouri River. Howard Hawks directed. **WE1, WE21**

Big Sleep, The (1946, B&W, 114m, NR)
Private eye Philip Marlowe (Humphrey Bogart) falls for the lovely sister (Lauren Bacall) of a girl he's hired to protect in Raymond Chandler's classic thriller. Howard Hawks directed. **CL15, CL20, CL35, MY1, MY24** *Recommended*

Big Sleep, The (1978, C, 100m, R)
Robert Mitchum plays Philip Marlowe in an updated version of Raymond Chandler's novel, closer to the actual story than the Bogart version, although the setting is London. With Sarah Miles, Candy Clark, Oliver Reed, Richard Boone, and James Stewart. **CL25**

Big Sombrero, The (1949, C, 77m, NR)
Gene Autry comes to the aid of a lovely señorita whose fiance is in cahoots with a swindler. **WE24**

Big Store, The (1941, B&W, 80m, NR)
The Marx Bros. go shopping at a department store. Margaret Dumont is not buying any of their nonsense. **CO21**

Big Street, The (1942, B&W, 88m, NR)
A Damon Runyon story about a shy busboy (Henry Fonda) who idolizes an embittered former show girl (Lucille Ball) who is wheelchair-bound. **CL24**

Big Top Pee-wee (1988, C, 86m, PG)
Pee-wee Herman finds a circus in his farm yard and he decides to join the action, especially when he catches sight of a lovely trapeze artist. With Kris Kristofferson and Valeria Golino. Silly family fun. **CO11, CO12, FA6, MU12**

Big Trail, The (1930, B&W, 110m, NR)
An epic western featuring John Wayne in one of his first starring roles, as a giant-sized, tender-hearted cowboy. Originally filmed in 70mm. **WE1, WE17**

Big Trouble in Little China (1986, C, 99m, PG-13)
A truck driver agrees to help his Chinese-American pal rescue the guy's fiancee from a cult operating beneath the streets of Chinatown. Kurt Russell stars in this action adventure from director John Carpenter. **AC21, AC26, CU29**

Big Wednesday (1978, C, 120m, PG)
Three surfing buddies from the 1960s find that the passing years aren't kind to them. Jan-Michael Vincent, Gary Busey, and William Katt star, with Barbara Hale (Katt's real-life mother); John Milius wrote and directed. **DR22, XT8**

Biggles (1986, C, 100m, PG)
Time travel drama, with British man (Alex Hyde-White) moving between 1986 New York and World War I Europe, where he assists an aviator. With Neil Dickson and Peter Cushing. **HO33, SF4, SF19**

Bill and Ted's Excellent Adventure (1989, C, 90m, PG)
Time-travel comedy featuring a pair of lame-brained high school buddies (Keanu Reeves and Alex Winter) who get a crash course in history, thanks to a hip dude of a wizard (George Carlin). **CO37**

Bill Cosby: 49 (1987, C, 67m, NR)
The comedian holds forth on his impending middle age, his family, and a host of other topics, all grist for his comic mill. **CO16**

Bill Cosby: Himself (1981, C, 104m, NR)
An extended Cosby concert, filmed in Canada, featuring his observations on fatherhood and other modern dilemmas. **CO16**

Billion Dollar Brain (1967, C, 111m, NR)
Michael Caine plays international spy Harry Palmer in this drama of espionage set in Scandinavia. Based on a Len Deighton novel; directed by Ken Russell. **CU31, MY6**

Billy Budd (1962, B&W, 112m, NR)
Terence Stamp, Robert Ryan, and Peter Ustinov star in this version of Herman Melville's classic novel about a naive sailor's court martial. Directed by Ustinov. **CL1** *Recommended*

Billy Crystal: A Comic's Line (1984, C, 59m, NR)
The *Saturday Night Live* alumnus leaves no comic stone unturned in this concert tape. **CO16**

Billy Crystal: Don't Get Me Started (1986, C, 60m, NR)
Plenty of Billy's best bits, plus a "documentary" on his life and a screamingly funny spoof of a 1950s kiddie TV show. **CO16**

Billy Jack (1971, C, 114m, PG)
Pacifist schoolteacher is harassed by bullies at her school for Indians; karate expert shows up to help her out. Cult movie that preaches non-violence, starring Tom Laughlin and Delores Taylor. **AC26, CU9**

Billy Liar (1963, B&W, 96m, NR)
British comedy-drama about a young man who prefers fantasies of heroic action to his drab everyday life. Tom Courtenay and Julie Christie star; John Schlesinger directed. **CO17, DR23**

Billy Rose's Jumbo *see* Jumbo

Billy the Kid Returns (1938, B&W, 60m, NR)
Roy Rogers is mistaken for the legendary outlaw. **WE2, WE23**

Biloxi Blues (1988, C, 106m, PG-13)
Neil Simon comedy, a sequel to *Brighton Beach Memoirs*, with Eugene Jerome (Matthew Broderick) now in the U.S. Army. Christopher Walken costars. Mike Nichols directed. **CO6, CO34, CO38, DR75**

Bingo Long Traveling All-Stars & Motor Kings, The (1976, C, 110m, PG)
The comic adventures of a black baseball team barnstorming the countryside in the

1930s. Billy Dee Williams, James Earl Jones, and Richard Pryor star. **CO29, CO36**

Birch Interval (1977, C, 104m, PG)
Drama of an 11-year-old girl who is sent to live with relatives in Pennsylvania's Amish community. Eddie Albert, Rip Torn, Ann Wedgeworth, and Susan McClung star. **CU47, FA7**

Bird (1988, C, 161m, R)
The life of pioneering jazz musician Charlie Parker, marked by artistic triumphs and personal setbacks, leading to his death at age 34. Forest Whitaker stars, with Diane Venora as Parker's wife, Chan. Clint Eastwood directed. **AC27, DR12, MU5** *Recommended*

Bird of Paradise (1932, B&W, 80m, NR)
A soldier of fortune falls in love with a native woman. Joel McCrea and Dolores Del Rio star, with Lon Chaney, Jr. Directed by King Vidor. **HO30**

Bird with the Crystal Plumage, The (1969, C, 98m, PG)
An American writer in Rome witnesses a Jack the Ripper style murder, tries to help the police, but finds himself involved with the case. Tony Musante and Suzy Kendall star. **FF2, HO9**

Birdman of Alcatraz (1962, B&W, 143m, NR)
True story of Charles Strouse, a convicted murderer confined to the famed maximum security prison and how he became an expert on birds. Burt Lancaster stars. **DR18, DR41** *Recommended*

Birds, The (1963, C, 120m, NR)
Alfred Hitchcock's classic chiller finds a coastal California community terrorized by thousands of birds. Rod Taylor, Tippi Hedren, Jessica Tandy, and Suzanne Pleshette star. Based on a story by Daphne du Maurier. **HO16, MY22, MY36**

Birdy (1984, C, 120m, R)
Two boyhood friends go to Vietnam and come back shattered, one with his face disfigured, the other retreating into his boyhood fantasies of being a bird. Matthew Modine and Nicolas Cage star. **DR7**

Birth of a Nation, The (1915, B&W, 159m, NR)
D.W. Griffith's controversial account of the Civil War and Reconstruction from the South's perspective. Lillian Gish, Henry B. Walthall, Mae Marsh, and Miriam Cooper star. A landmark in film history. **AC5, CL3, CL12, CL36, CL49** *Highly Recommended*

Bishop's Wife, The (1947, B&W, 108m, NR)
David Niven plays a bishop in need who's visited by a charming angel (Cary Grant). Loretta Young costars in this classic fantasy. **CL18, SF2**

Bite the Bullet (1975, C, 131m, PG)
Western drama of an epic horse race, starring Gene Hackman, James Coburn, Ben Johnson, Jan-Michael Vincent, and Candice Bergen. **DR39**

Bitter Sweet (1940, C, 94m, NR)
Nelson Eddy and Jeanette MacDonald teamed up for the sixth time in this musical drama set in turn-of-the-century Vienna, with songs by Noel Coward. **CL15**

Black and White in Color (1976, C, 90m, NR)
Frenchmen living in Africa at the outbreak of World War I decide to attack a nearby German fort. This droll comedy won an Oscar for Best Foreign Language Film. **FF1, XT7**

Black Arrow, The (1948, B&W, 76m, NR)
Robert Louis Stevenson swashbuckling adventure set in England follows the exploits of a young soldier (Louis Hayward) out to solve his father's murder. George MacReady is the villain, Janet Blair the lady fair. **AC13**

Black Arrow (1984, 93m, C, NR)
Remake of the 1948 film of an exiled archer who returns to England and swears revenge on the villain (Oliver

Reed) who drove him from his homeland. Disney swashbuckler made for cable TV. **FA1**

Black Beauty (1946, B&W, 74m, NR)
Mona Freeman stars as the young girl who develops a very special bond with a wild horse. Based on Anna Sewell's famed novel. **FA5**

Black Beauty (1971, C, 105m, G)
This version of Anna Sewell's classic tale takes a dramatic stand for animal rights. Mark Lester and Walter Slezak star. **FA5**

Black Caesar (1973, C, 96m, R)
Fred Williamson stars in this violent gangster melodrama directed by Larry Cohen. With Art Lund, Julius W. Harris, and Gloria Hendry. **CU30**

Black Cat, The (1934, B&W, 65m, NR)
The bizarre home of an architect who is also a devil worshipper is the setting for this tale about a man who seeks vengeance for the death of his wife. Boris Karloff and Bela Lugosi star in this horror classic that is genuinely scary without resorting to on-screen gore. Not based on Edgar Allan Poe's story; directed by Edgar G. Ulmer. **HO1, HO27, HO28** *Recommended*

Black Christmas (1974, C, 100m, R)
Sorority sisters prepare for their Christmas holiday while a madman stalks them. Margot Kidder, Olivia Hussey, and Keir Dullea star, with Andrea Martin. **CO14, HO12**

Black Dragons (1949, B&W, 62m, NR)
Japanese agents sabotage the American war effort. Bela Lugosi and Clayton Moore star. **HO28**

Black Fury (1935, B&W, 92m, NR)
Paul Muni plays a coal miner who attempts to improve conditions for his fellow laborers in this classic social drama. **CL8**

Black Hand, The (1950, B&W, 93m, NR)
In a rare dramatic role, Gene Kelly plays a young man in turn-of-the-century New York who avenges his father's murder by a secret society. **MU19**

Black Hole, The (1979, C, 97m, PG)
Disney science fiction adventure of distant space travelers encountering title phenomenon. Maximillian Schell and Anthony Perkins star. **FA1, SF3, SF13, SF14**

Black Marble, The (1980, C, 113m, PG)
Romance blossoms between cops Paula Prentiss and Robert Foxworth when they're assigned to the case of a dognapper. Harry Dean Stanton costars in this adaptation of Joseph Wambaugh's novel. **CO10, CU49**

Black Moon Rising (1985, C, 100m, R)
A high-tech car is the bone of contention between an organized car theft ring and a freelance thief. Tommy Lee Jones, Linda Hamilton, and Robert Vaughn star. **AC10**

Black Narcissus (1946, C, 99m, NR)
Drama set in the Himalayas finds three nuns (Deborah Kerr, Jean Simmons, Flora Robson) faced with overwhelming obstacles when they try to set up a hospital. Breathtaking color photography by Jack Cardiff; directed by Michael Powell. **CL9, CU19**

Black Orchid, The (1959, B&W, 96m, NR)
A businessman and a widow fall in love, but she must persuade her children that the marriage will make them happy, too. Anthony Quinn and Sophia Loren star. **FF31**

Black Orpheus (1959, C, 98m, NR)
Oscar-winning drama from Brazil is based on Greek myth, transferred to Rio at Carnival time. Colorful imagery, with memorable music by Luis Bonfa and Antonio Carlos Jobim. **FF6, CL9, XT7** *Recommended*

Black Pirate, The (1926, B&W, 132m, NR)
Douglas Fairbanks' silent swashbuckler classic. Billie Dove and Donald Crisp co-

star in this adventure for the entire family. **AC13, FA4**

Black Room, The (1935, B&W, 75m, NR)
Boris Karloff plays cursed twins, one of whom is literally a ladykiller. When he's suspected of the murders, he kills the good brother and impersonates him. **HO15, HO27**

Black Sabbath (1964, C, 99m, NR)
A compilation of three horror stories. *The Drop of Water* is about a nurse who steals a ring from a corpse, which comes back to haunt her through her tap. *The Telephone* is about a prostitute who receives mysterious phone calls. *The Wurdalak* features a Russian vampire who infects his whole family. Boris Karloff stars. Directed by Mario Bava. **HO23, HO27**

Black Stallion, The (1980, C, 118m, G)
Walter Farley's magical tale of the famed black horse and the boy who loved him. Mickey Rooney, Kelly Reno, Teri Garr, and Hoyt Axton star. Directed by Carroll Ballard, lovingly photographed by Caleb Deschanel. **FA5** *Highly Recommended*

Black Stallion Returns, The (1983, C, 103m, PG)
The young hero of *The Black Stallion* is off to Morroco when his best friend is horsenapped. Kelly Reno, Vincent Spano, and Teri Garr star. **FA5**

Black Sunday (1977, C, 143m, R)
Arab terrorists plot to kill the President at the Super Bowl. Bruce Dern stars, with Marthe Keller and Robert Shaw. **MY6**

Black Widow (1986, C, 103m, R)
An offbeat thriller about a woman who's been widowed by wealthy men so many times that she's aroused the suspicions of a government investigator. Theresa Russell and Debra Winger star in this cat-and-mouse thriller. With Sami Frey, Nicol Williamson, and Dennis Hopper. **CU46, DR47, MY9**

Black Windmill, The (1974, C, 106m, PG)
A secret agent (Michael Caine) investigates the kidnapping of his son. Directed by Don Siegel. **MY6**

Blackbeard's Ghost (1980, C, 106m, G)
Dean Jones conjures up the spirit of the famed pirate (Peter Ustinov) to protect his descendants' home from racketeers. Suzanne Pleshette costars in this Disney comedy-adventure. **FA1**

Blackmail (1929, B&W, 85m, NR)
Alfred Hitchcock's first talking picture, about a woman who kills a man in self-defense and then has to prove her innocence when she's trapped between her detective boyfriend and a blackmailer. Originally shot as a silent film. **MY22**

Blacksmith, The/The Balloonatic (1922/1923, B&W, 57m, NR)
Two Buster Keaton comedy shorts on one tape. In the first, he's the apprentice to the village smithy. In the second, he's trapped on a runaway hot-air balloon. **CO19** *Recommended*

Blacula (1972, C, 92m, PG)
An African prince is transformed into a vampire, imprisoned in a coffin, then unleashed in modern Los Angeles. William Marshall and Vonetta McGee star. **HO5**

Blade Master, The (1984, C, 92m, PG)
Adventure saga featuring the title character, who leads the forces of good against the evil ones who would possess the Sword of Knowledge. Miles O'Keefe and Lisa Foster star. **AC18**

Blade Runner (1982, C, 123m, R)
Harrison Ford plays a cop hunting down criminal androids in Los Angeles of the next century. With Rutger Hauer, Sean Young, and Daryl Hannah. Ridley Scott directed; spectacular sets almost steal the show. Video contains some scenes of violence not shown in theaters. **CU10, CU33, DR32, MY2, SF14, SF17** *Recommended*

Blame It on Rio (1984, C, 90m, R)
Comedy about two married men on holiday in Rio with their daughters and the trouble that develops when one man begins an affair with his pal's daughter. Michael Caine, Joseph Bologna, Demi Moore, and Michelle Johnson star. Directed by Stanley Donen. **MU23**

Blazing Saddles (1974, C, 93m, R)
Mel Brooks takes a satirical look at Westerns in this free-for-all, starring Gene Wilder, Cleavon Little, Harvey Korman, and Madeline Kahn. **CO7, CO28, WE15**
Recommended

Bless the Beasts and Children (1972, C, 109m, PG)
At a summer camp, six city youths plan to save a herd of buffalo from their demise. Directed by Stanley Kramer. **FA7**

Blind Date (1984, C, 100m, R)
A blind man (Joseph Bottoms), obsessed that a psychopathic killer be brought to justice, implants a sight-giving computer chip in his head. Kirstie Alley costars. **MY15**

Blind Date (1987, C, 95m, PG-13)
A young executive is fixed up with an unpredictable woman for an important business dinner, with wildly comic results. Bruce Willis and Kim Basinger star, with John Laroquette and William Daniels. Directed by Blake Edwards. **CO1, CO46**

Blind Husbands (1919, B&W, 98m, NR)
Erich von Stroheim stars in and directed this controversial silent drama about a military man who falls for a doctor's wife. **CL12, CL53**

Blind Man's Bluff *see* Cauldron of Blood

Bliss (1985, C, 93m, R)
From Australia, a dark comedy about a successful businessman who suffers a nearly fatal heart attack and recovers with a new perspective on his greedy lifestyle and uncaring family. Barry Otto stars. **CO12, FF5**

Blithe Spirit (1945, C, 96m, NR)
Rex Harrison stars in this comic fantasy about a man haunted by the ghost of his first wife, who tries to ruin his second marriage. Margaret Rutherford costars; David Lean directed. **DR50**

Blob, The (1958, C, 86m, NR)
Jelly-like mass from outer space begins devouring everything—and everyone—in a small town, whose teens rush to the rescue. Classic 1950s science fiction, starring Steve McQueen. **AC28, SF1, SF9**

Block Heads (1938, B&W, 55m, NR)
Laurel and Hardy comedy, with Stanley still thinking World War I is on, Ollie having to bring him out of the trenches. **CO20**

Blockhouse, The (1973, C, 90m, NR)
Drama of men trapped in an underground bunker during the D-Day invasion. Peter Sellers stars, with Per Oscarsson and Charles Aznavour. **CO26**

Blonde Venus (1932, B&W, 97m, NR)
Marlene Dietrich becomes the sole provider when her husband becomes ill; she returns to her career as a nightclub singer until a suave playboy (Cary Grant) makes her an irresistible offer. Directed by Josef von Sternberg. **CL18, CL28, CL47, CL56**
Recommended

Blood and Black Lace (1964, C, 90m, NR)
A man becomes a psychopathic killer when he can no longer hide his desire for beautiful women. Cameron Mitchell and Eva Bartok star. Directed by Mario Bava. **HO9**

Blood Beast Terror (1969, C, 81m, NR)
An entomologist conducts experiments on his own daughter, turning her into a bloodthirsty insect. Peter Cushing stars. **HO33**

Blood Feast (1963, C, 75m, PG)
An Egyptian preparing to bring a goddess to life needs body parts and organs from various women to complete the ritual. One of the first horror films to use explicit

gore; directed by Herschell Gordon Lewis. **HO18**

Blood Feud (1979, C, 112m, NR)
Drama set in Sicily in the 1920s, with widow (Sophia Loren) romanced by two men (Marcello Mastroianni, Giancarlo Giannini). Directed by Lina Wertmuller. **FF24, FF31**

Blood Link (1986, C, 98m, R)
A doctor begins to have a recurring dream that he is committing a murder. He discovers that he was once a Siamese twin and that his brother is still alive and deranged. Michael Moriarty stars. **HO15**

Blood of a Poet (1930, B&W, 55m, NR)
French director Jean Cocteau's meditation on an artist's inner world is a study in striking imagery, but not for every taste. **CU21, FF1, SF2**

Blood of Fu Manchu, The *see* Against All Odds (1969)

Blood on Satan's Claw (1970, C, 93m, R)
A farmer unearths the corpse of a half man/half beast and evil takes hold of the community, eventually possessing a young girl. Linda Hayden and Patrick Wymark star. **HO10**

Blood on the Moon (1948, B&W, 88m, NR)
Western drama starring Robert Mitchum and Robert Preston as rivals in a land fraud scheme. Robert Wise directed. **CL58**

Blood on the Sun (1945, B&W, 98m, NR)
James Cagney stars in this drama about an American living in Japan during the 1930s and foreseeing that country's war plans. **CL22**

Blood Simple (1984, C, 97m, R)
A jealous husband hires a seedy private detective to murder his wife and her lover. Contemporary cult thriller, written by Joel and Ethan Coen, directed by Joel. John Getz, Frances MacDormand, M. Emmet Walsh, and Dan Hedaya star. **DR16, MY2**

Bloodbath at the House of Death (1983, C, 92m, NR)
A British spoof of horror films, about a group of paranormal researchers setting up shop in a house which has been the scene of many murders. Kenny Everett, Pamela Stephenson, and Vincent Price star. **HO26, HO31**

Bloodbrothers (1978, C, 116m, R)
Young New Yorker is torn between following his father and uncle into construction work and following his own dream of becoming a teacher. Richard Gere stars, with Paul Sorvino and Tony LoBianco. Based on Richard Price's novel. **DR8**

Bloodline *see* Sidney Sheldon's Bloodline

Bloodsport (1987, C, 92m, R)
Martial arts drama of American who enters the Kumite, a secret fighting contest. Jean Claude Van Damme stars; based on a true story. **AC26**

Bloodsuckers, The (1970, C, 87m, R)
An Oxford don visiting Greece takes up with a mysterious woman who leads him into black magic and vampirism. Patrick Mower stars, with Peter Cushing. **HO5, HO11, HO33**

Bloody Mama (1970, C, 90m, R)
Shelley Winters plays the notorious Ma Barker, the gangster who included her sons in her criminal affairs. Robert De-Niro, Don Stroud, Pat Hingle, and Bruce Dern costar. Directed by Roger Corman. **AC22, DR25**

Blow Out (1981, C, 107m, R)
From director Brian De Palma comes a suspense thriller about a sound effects engineer (John Travolta) who becomes involved in a political conspiracy. With Nancy Allen, John Lithgow, and Dennis Franz. **CU28, DR13, MY15**

Blowing Wild (1953, B&W, 90m, NR)
Barbara Stanwyck romances two men: oil tycoon husband (Anthony Quinn) and a wildcatter (Gary Cooper). **CL26**

Blowup (1966, C, 100m, NR)
An innocent London photographer takes snapshots of a couple which later, when enlarged, expose what appears to be a murder. Michelangelo Antonioni directed; David Hemmings stars, with Vanessa Redgrave and Sarah Miles. **DR65, FF17, MY15, XT9** *Recommended*

Blue Angel, The (1930, B&W, 103m, NR)
German classic about an aging professor's pathetic infatuation with a heartless nightclub singer. Marlene Dietrich and Emil Jannings star; Josef von Sternberg directed. **FF3, CL47, CL56** *Recommended*

Blue Bird, The (1940, C, 83m, NR)
Classic fantasy about the search for the special bird which will bring happiness. Shirley Temple stars. **FA14, SF13**

Blue Canadian Rockies (1952, B&W, 58m, NR)
Gene Autry's boss sends him to Canada on a personal expedition to discourage his daughter's marriage to a fortune hunter. **WE11, WE24**

Blue Collar (1978, C, 114m, R)
A trio of auto workers discover their union has been ripping off its workers, and they decide to get even. Hard-bitten drama from director Paul Schrader, starring Richard Pryor, Yaphet Kotto, and Harvey Keitel. **CO29, DR7, DR14** *Recommended*

Blue Fire Lady (1983, C, 96m, NR)
Family drama of a girl's love for horses and her training an obstinate mare, Blue Fire Lady, for racing. Cathryn Harrison stars. **FA5**

Blue Hawaii (1961, C, 101m, NR)
Elvis Presley musical has The King as a cashiered soldier working in a tourist agency in Honolulu. Angela Lansbury co-stars. **MU22**

Blue Knight, The (1973, C, 103m, NR)
Veteran cop, about to retire, wants to bring in one more criminal. William Holden stars in this adaptation of the Joseph Wambaugh novel. Originally made for TV. **AC9**

Blue Max, The (1966, C, 156m, NR)
Drama of aerial combat during World War I, starring George Peppard, James Mason, and Ursula Andress. **AC2, AC11**

Blue Thunder (1983, C, 110m, R)
Los Angeles police develop super-helicopter for crowd control, but political conspiracy has other ideas. Roy Scheider stars, with Daniel Stern, Malcolm McDowell, Warren Oates, and Candy Clark. **AC11, CU48, XT9**

Blue Velvet (1986, C, 120m, R)
A nightmarish, disturbing film from director David Lynch about a naive young man's discovery of the dark side of a small American town. Kyle MacLachlan, Dennis Hopper, and Isabella Rossellini star, with Laura Dern, Dean Stockwell, and Brad Dourif. **CU1, CU12, CU38, CU46, DR62, MY2, MY15** *Recommended*

Blue Yonder, The (1985, C, 89m, NR)
Disney drama of a young boy (Huckleberry Fox) who travels back in time to share flying adventures with his grandfather (Peter Coyote), an ace aviator. Originally made for cable TV. **FA1**

Blues Brothers, The (1980, C, 113m, R)
John Belushi and Dan Aykroyd extend their *Saturday Night Live* routine into a gargantuan musical comedy, featuring a great array of black performers, including Aretha Franklin, James Brown, Ray Charles, Cab Calloway, and many more. The streets of Chicago take a pounding in this grand finale car chase. **CO3, CO13, MU9, XT9**

Blume in Love (1973, C, 117m, R)
A lawyer's brief indiscretion has his wife packing her bags and has him pleading to get her back. Sharp romantic comedy-drama from director Paul Mazursky, starring George Segal and Susan Anspach, with Kris Kristofferson, Marsha Mason,

and Shelley Winters. **CO1, MU12** *Recommended*

Boat, The (1981, C, 145m, R)
Stunning World War II drama set aboard a German submarine, starring Jurgen Prochnow, directed by Wolfgang Petersen. This is the dubbed version of the original German-language film. **AC1, FF3** *Recommended*

Boat Is Full, The (1983, C, 104m, NR)
German refugees fleeing the Nazis are turned away by neutral Swiss officials in this drama produced in Switzerland. **FF7**

Boatniks, The (1970, C, 99m, G)
Disney comedy has an accident-prone Coast Guard ensign (Robert Morse) tangling with a band of jewel thieves. Phil Silvers, Stephanie Powers, Norman Fell, Wally Cox, and Don Ameche costar. **FA1**

Bob & Carol & Ted & Alice (1969, C, 104m, R)
A California couple are happily married until they meet a "modern" husband and wife, who believe in getting in touch with one's real inner feelings. Hilarious satire directed by Paul Mazursky, starring Robert Culp & Natalie Wood & Elliott Gould & Dyan Cannon. **CO2** *Recommended*

Bob le Flambeur (1955, B&W, 102m, PG)
A middle-aged Parisian gambler decides to pull off a casino heist in this first-rate crime story directed by Jean-Pierre Melville. Roger Duchesne and Isabel Corey star. **FF1, MY34, XT9** *Recommended*

Bobby Deerfield (1977, C, 124m, PG)
Drama of a race car driver and his love for a German woman who is afflicted with a terminal disease. Al Pacino and Marthe Keller star; Sydney Pollack directed. **DR22, DR56, DR66**

Bobo, The (1967, C, 105m, NR)
Peter Sellers plays an aspiring singing matador who tries to seduce a lovely but remote senorita (Britt Ekland). **CO26**

Body and Soul (1947, B&W, 104m, NR)
John Garfield stars in the classic boxing drama of man who cuts every corner on his way to the championship. Written and directed by Robert Rossen. **DR22**

Body and Soul (1981, C, 100m, R)
Remake of the John Garfield classic, with Leon Isaac Kennedy as the hard-driving fighter. **DR22**

Body Double (1984, C, 109m, R)
From director Brian DePalma comes the story of an unemployed actor whose spying on a voluptuous neighbor involves him in a twisted plot. Craig Wasson and Melanie Griffith star. **CU28, MY5**

Body Heat (1981, C, 113m, R)
A sexy, steamy thriller starring William Hurt and Kathleen Turner (her film debut). A lawyer and a married woman plot to murder her wealthy husband. Richard Crenna and Mickey Rourke costar. Written and directed by Lawrence Kasdan. **CU6, DR3, DR31, DR46, DR48, MY2, MY4, MY5** *Recommended*

Body in the Library, The (1984, C, 153m, NR)
Miss Marple, Agatha Christie's elderly sleuth, investigates the murder of a young woman whose corpse is found in a stately mansion. Joan Hickson stars. Originally made for British TV. **MY16, MY23**

Body Rock (1984, C, 93m, PG-13)
Breakdancing musical about a group of "downtown" kids showing the folks at an "uptown" club what good music and dancing is all about. Lorenzo Lamas stars. **MU9**

Body Snatcher, The (1945, B&W, 77m, NR)
A Val Lewton production about the macabre relationship between a doctor and the grave robber who steals bodies for the doctor's experiments. Boris Karloff stars, with Bela Lugosi in a supporting role. **HO1, HO19, HO27, HO28, HO36**

Bohemian Girl, The (1936, B&W, 70m, NR)
Laurel and Hardy adopt an abandoned girl who turns out to be the heir to a throne. **CO20**

Bombardier (1943, B&W, 99m, NR)
Randolph Scott plays a fighter cadet being trained for battle during air raids over World War II Japan. **AC1, WE22**

Bon Voyage, Charlie Brown (1980, C, 76m, G)
The *Peanuts* comic strip gang go overseas as exchange students in this feature-length animated film. **FA10**

Bonnie and Clyde (1967, C, 111m, NR)
Brilliant, controversial portrait of Depression-era outlaws who became folk heroes. Warren Beatty, Faye Dunaway, and Gene Hackman star, with Oscar winner Estelle Parsons, Michael J. Pollard, and Gene Wilder. Written by Robert Benton and David Newman; directed by Arthur Penn. **DR5, DR16, DR34, DR35, DR39, XT5** *Highly Recommended*

Bonnie Scotland (1935, B&W, 80m, NR)
Laurel and Hardy are a pair of Scots assigned to a military outpost in the desert. **CO20**

Boogeyman, The (1980, C, 86m, R)
A boy kills his mother's lover but is witnessed by his sister. Years later the girl returns to the scene of the crime to confront her fears. **HO8**

Boost, The (1989, C, 95m, R)
A young couple find that sudden success in business has exacted a heavy price— they've become cocaine addicts. James Woods and Sean Young star. **DR7**

Boots and Saddles (1937, B&W, 59m, NR)
A young Englishman becomes a real western rancher after Gene Autry shows him the ropes. **WE24**

Border, The (1982, C, 107m, R)
Jack Nicholson plays a Tex-Mex border cop who begins taking bribes to let ille-gals in and becomes involved with a desperate Mexican woman and her child. Valerie Perrine, Warren Oates, and Harvey Keitel costar. Music by Ry Cooder. **CU48, DR7, DR24**

Borderline (1980, C, 105m, PG)
Charles Bronson plays a Border Patrol officer tracking a dangerous killer. Bruno Kirby, Bert Remsen, and Kenneth McMillan costar. **AC29**

Born Free (1966, C, 96m, NR)
Drama based on the true story of Joy Adamson, the wife of a British game warden living in Kenya who raised a lioness as a pet in the wilds of Africa. **FA5**

Born in East L.A. (1987, C, 84m, R)
Cheech Marin stars in a comedy about a legal resident of Los Angeles who's rounded up with a group of illegals and deported to Mexico. Paul Rodriguez, Daniel Stern, and Jan-Michael Vincent costar. **CO32**

Born To Kill (1947, B&W, 92m, NR)
Film noir about a man who marries a woman for her money, but is really attracted to her divorced sister. Lawrence Tierney, Claire Trevor, Walter Slezak, and Audrey Long star. Directed by Robert Wise. **CL58, MY1**

Born To Kill (1974) *see* Cockfighter

Born To Rock *see* That Was Rock

Born To Win *see* Addict

Born Yesterday (1950, B&W, 103m, NR)
George Cukor directed Garson Kanin's Broadway comedy about a wisecracking girl (Oscar winner Judy Holliday) in need of some polish. Her sugar daddy (Broderick Crawford) hires a tutor (William Holden) to smooth over her rough edges. Some scenes shot on location in Washington, D.C. **CL10, CL39, CL51, CO42, XT3, XT9** *Recommended*

Boston Strangler, The (1968, C, 120m, NR)
Intense, gripping drama based on the exploits of the crazed killer who terrorized Boston for over a year. Henry Fonda and Tony Curtis star, with George Kennedy. **CL24**

Bostonians, The (1984, C, 120m, NR)
In 19th-century New England, feminists have a new young spokeswoman. She's also the center of a tug-of-war between a Southern reporter and one of her colleagues in the movement. Vanessa Redgrave, Christopher Reeve, and Madeleine Potter star in this version of Henry James's novel. **DR19, DR65**

Boudu Saved From Drowning (1932, B&W, 87m, NR)
French comedy from director Jean Renoir about a tramp rescued by a book dealer and the havoc he wreaks on the man's household. Michel Simon stars. American remake: *Down and Out in Beverly Hills*. **FF12, FF36**

Boum, La (1981, C, 100m, PG)
A teenaged girl tries to stay out of the way of her quarreling parents in this comedy-drama from France. Claude Brasseur, Brigitte Fossey, and Sophie Marceau star. **FF1**

Bound for Glory (1976, C, 147m, PG)
Superb portrait of folk music composer and singer Woody Guthrie, concentrating on his life during the Great Depression. David Carradine stars and sings Guthrie's music; Ronny Cox, Melinda Dillon, and Randy Quaid costar. Directed by Hal Ashby; photographed by Haskell Wexler. **DR4, MU5** *Recommended*

Bounty, The (1984, C, 130m, PG)
Latest version of the *Mutiny on the Bounty* story, with Mel Gibson as Fletcher Christian and Anthony Hopkins as Captain Bligh. Laurence Olivier has a small role. **AC12, AC16, CL32, DR69**

Bowery at Midnight (1942, B&W, 63m, NR)
A killer is stalking the inhabitants of the Bowery. Bela Lugosi stars. **HO28**

Boxcar Bertha (1972, C, 97m, R)
Trashy tale of Depression-era train robbers, starring David Carradine and Barbara Hershey, directed by Martin Scorsese. Produced by Roger Corman. **CU14, DR52**

Boy and His Dog, A (1975, C, 87m, R)
A post-nuclear wasteland is the setting for this cult science fiction tale of a young hustler and his "dog" robot. Don Johnson stars. **CU4, SF12, SF22**

Boy, Did I Get a Wrong Number! (1966, C, 99m, NR)
Bob Hope comedy, costarring Phyllis Diller and Elke Sommer, with Ol' Ski Nose a fast-talking real estate man helping to conceal a fugitive movie star. **CO40**

Boy in Blue, The (1986, C, 98m, R)
True story of 19th-century rowing champion Ned Hanlon, starring Nicolas Cage, with Christopher Plummer and David Naughton. **DR22**

Boy Named Charlie Brown, A (1969, C, 85m, G)
Movie debut of the "Peanuts" gang, with Charlie Brown going for the grand prize in a national spelling bee. **FA10**

Boy Who Could Fly, The (1986, C, 108m, PG)
Story of a 14-year-old boy whose fantasy is to soar away from his unhappy home life. Jay Underwood, Lucy Deakins, and Bonnie Bedelia star. **DR9, FA7**

Boy Who Left Home to Find Out About the Shivers, The (1981, C, 60m, NR)
Brothers Grimm tale about a boy (Peter MacNichol) who's fearless until he's put to a test against the Evil Sorcerer. Christopher Lee and Dana Hill costar in this Faerie Tale Theatre production. **FA12, HO31**

Boyfriends and Girlfriends (1988, C, 102m, PG)
The concluding chapter in French director Eric Rohmer's six-film "Comedies and Proverbs" series. It's about a quartet of young people in the throes of romantic angst in a Paris suburb. **FF15**

Boys From Brazil, The (1978, C, 123m, R)
Gregory Peck stars in this bizarre tale of an army of Hitler-cloned youth intended for use in a neo-Nazi takeover. Laurence Olivier costars as a Nazi hunter. **CL32**

Boys From Brooklyn see Bela Lugosi Meets a Brooklyn Gorilla

Boys in Company C, The (1977, C, 127m, R)
Tough Army sergeant trains young recruits for Vietnam combat. Stan Shaw, Andrew Stevens, and Craig Wasson star. **AC4**

Boys in the Band, The (1970, C, 119m, R)
Mart Crowley's play about a group of homosexual friends at a birthday party, starring Kenneth Nelson, Peter White, Leonard Frey, Cliff Gorman, and Laurence Luckinbill. **DR20**

Boys Next Door, The (1985, C, 90m, R)
Disturbing drama of two seemingly normal teenagers who go on a crime spree on the eve of their graduation. Charlie Sheen and Maxwell Caulfield star; Penelope Spheeris directed. **DR9**

Braddock: Missing in Action 3 (1988, C, 103m, R)
Chuck Norris returns once again to Vietnam as former POW Colonel Braddock, this time to rescue his long-lost Vietnamese wife and their son. **AC4, AC32**

Brain Damage (1988, C, 94m, R)
From Frank Henenlotter, the director of *Basket Case*, a horror story of a teenager plagued by a monstrous parasite which acts like a narcotic. **HO12**

Brain From Planet Arous, The (1958, B&W, 70m, NR)
Title creature inhabits scientist John Agar's head, while the brain of a cop occupies Agar's dog in this low-budget science fiction drama. **SF1, SF9**

Brain That Wouldn't Die, The (1963, B&W, 81m, NR)
A doctor keeps alive the head of his decapitated fiancee while he searches for a body. **HO20**

Brainstorm (1983, C, 106m, PG)
Research scientists discover a telepathic device; the military can't wait to use it for a weapon. Christopher Walken, Louise Fletcher, and Natalie Wood (in her last film) star. **SF5**

Brannigan (1975, C, 111m, PG)
A tough Chicago detective (John Wayne) is off to England to bring home a fugitive. Richard Attenborough costars. **CL17**

Brasher Doubloon, The (1947, B&W, 72m, NR)
Raymond Chandler's detective mystery stars George Montgomery as Philip Marlowe, who's after some rare coins linked to a series of murders. **MY24**

Brass Target (1978, C, 111m, PG)
World War II drama that imagines General Patton was murdered to cover up a gold theft by his men. John Cassavetes, Sophia Loren, and George Kennedy star. **FF31**

Brazil (1985, C, 131m, R)
Futuristic tale of a bureaucrat mistakenly targeted as a terrorist, brilliantly directed by Terry Gilliam. Jonathan Pryce stars, with Robert DeNiro, Kim Greist, Bob Hoskins, and Michael Palin. Eye-filling sets, special effects. **CU4, CO15, DR25, SF11, SF14** *Highly Recommended*

Breaker! Breaker! (1977, C, 86m, PG)
Trucker uses his CB to rescue son from a crooked judge. Chuck Norris stars. **AC32**

Breaker Morant (1979, C, 107m, PG)
Edward Woodward stars in this Australian drama set during the Boer War, about the court-martial of several soldiers on questionable charges. Directed by Bruce Beresford. **FF5**

Breakfast at Tiffany's (1961, C, 115m, NR)
Romantic comedy stars Audrey Hepburn as Holly Golightly, a small town girl transformed into a hip New Yorker. With George Peppard, Patricia Neal, Buddy Ebsen, Mickey Rooney, and Martin Balsam. Based on Truman Capote's story; directed by Blake Edwards. **CL30, CO46, DR15, XT9** *Recommended*

Breakfast Club, The (1985, C, 92m, R)
Five high school students, confined to the school for a Saturday detention, become fast friends, despite their outward differences. Emilio Estevez, Molly Ringwald, Ally Sheedy, Anthony Michael Hall, and Judd Nelson star; written and directed by John Hughes. **DR9, CO47**

Breakheart Pass (1976, C, 95m, PG)
Western drama about secret agent (Charles Bronson) on the trail of gunrunners. Action takes place mostly on a train; good supporting cast includes Ben Johnson, Richard Crenna, Charles Durning, Ed Lauter, Archie Moore, and Jill Ireland. **AC29**

Breakin' (1984, C, 90m, PG)
A waitress hopes to crash the show business world as a break dancer. Lucinda Dickey stars in this musical drama. **MU9**

Breakin' 2: Electric Boogaloo (1984, C, 94m, PG)
Lucinda Dickey and her break dancing partners are back for more musical numbers in this sequel to *Breakin'*. **MU9**

Breaking Away (1979, C, 100m, PG)
A Midwestern teenager trains for a major bike race in this warm comedy-drama starring Dennis Christopher, Dennis Quaid, and Paul Dooley. **CO4, DR22** *Recommended*

Breaking Glass (1980, C, 104m, PG)
British musical drama of a singer (Hazel O'Connor) determined to make it with her own style of punkish music. Phil Daniels, Jon Finch, and Jonathan Pryce costar in this look behind the scenes of the music business. **MU4, MU9**

Breakout (1975, C, 96m, PG)
True-life action drama of an American held in Mexican prison and a helicopter pilot's attempts to spring him. Charles Bronson, Robert Duvall, Randy Quaid, and John Huston star. **AC29, CL44, DR37**

Breath of Scandal, A (1960, C, 98m, NR)
Costume drama starring Sophia Loren as a princess wooed by an American (John Gavin). Maurice Chevalier and Angela Lansbury costar. **FF31**

Breathless (1959, B&W, 89m, NR)
A petty thief and an American girl find romance and death on the streets of Paris. Historic French film from director Jean-Luc Godard. Jean-Paul Belmondo and Jean Seberg star. U.S. remake released in 1982. **FF14, FF33, FF36, XT9** *Recommended*

Breathless (1983, C, 100m, R)
American remake of the French classic; this time the drifter is an American who's enthralled with rock music and comic books and his lover is a French exchange student. Richard Gere and Valerie Kaprisky star. **DR1, FF36**

Breed Apart, A (1984, C, 95m, R)
Adventure drama of a couple living in the mountains of North Carolina, protecting a rare species of bird. Enter a mysterious stranger, with orders to capture the bird. Kathleen Turner, Rutger Hauer, and Powers Boothe star. **AC12, DR46**

Brewster McCloud (1970, C, 101m, R)
Offbeat comedy about a young man who believes he's a bird and tries to fly in the Houston Astrodome. Packed with absurd bits and throwaway gags; a real cult film. Directed by Robert Altman; Bud Cort stars, with Sally Kellerman, Michael Mur-

phy, Shelley Duvall, Stacy Keach, and Margaret Hamilton. **CO12, CU5, CU25** *Recommended*

Brewster's Millions (1985, C, 97m, PG)
Frequently film comic story about a man who must spend $30 million in 30 days in order to inherit $300 million. Richard Pryor and John Candy star; Walter Hill directed. **CO3, CO14, CO29, CU27**

Bride, The (1985, C, 113m, PG-13)
Remake of *The Bride of Frankenstein,* starring Sting as the mad doctor and Jennifer Beals as his creation. **CU18, HO20**

Bride Is Much Too Beautiful, The (1958, B&W, 90m, NR)
Brigitte Bardot plays a simple farm girl whose life is turned upside-down when she's recruited to become a fashion model. Louis Jourdan costars. **FF32**

Bride of Frankenstein, The (1935, B&W, 75m, NR)
Masterful follow-up to the first great Frankenstein film, with Boris Karloff "wed" to Elsa Lanchester. Colin Clive and Ernest Thesiger play the matchmakers; James Whale directed. **CU4, HO1, HO20, HO27, HO34** *Highly Recommended*

Bride of the Gorilla (1951, B&W, 76m, NR)
Camp classic about a newlywed who discovers that her husband is regularly transformed into a hairy beast. Raymond Burr, Barbara Payton, and Lon Chaney, Jr. star. **CU2, HO30**

Bride of the Monster (1955, B&W, 69m, NR)
Inept horror film from the king of inept movies, Ed Wood, Jr. Bela Lugosi stars as a mad scientist; Tor Johnson is his immense assistant Lobo. Must be seen to be believed. **CU45, HO28**

Bride Walks Out, The (1936, B&W, 81m, NR)
Romantic comedy starring Barbara Stanwyck and Gene Raymond as a young couple trying to make ends meet. **CL45**

Bridge on the River Kwai, The (1957, C, 161m, NR)
British prisoners of war are forced to construct a bridge vital to the Japanese; meanwhile, commandos are sent to destroy it. Seven Oscars, including Best Picture, Director (David Lean), and Actor (Alec Guinness). William Holden, Sessue Hayakawa, and Jack Hawkins costar. **AC7, DR50, CL51, DR63, XT1, XT2, XT6** *Highly Recommended*

Bridge to Nowhere (1986, C, 82m, NR)
Five city kids head into trouble on a hike in the country when they trespass on a madman's property. **AC24**

Bridge Too Far, A (1977, C, 175m, PG)
World War II epic about ill-fated Allied attempt to surround German forces in Holland. Among the many stars: Dirk Bogarde, James Caan, Michael Caine, Sean Connery, Edward Fox, Gene Hackman, Laurence Olivier, Robert Redford, Ryan O'Neal, and Liv Ullmann. Richard Attenborough directed; Joseph E. Levine produced. **AC1, AC36, CL32, DR29, DR39, FF25**

Bridges at Toko-Ri, The (1954, C, 103m, NR)
Korean war drama focusing on fighter pilot and his qualms about the U.S. involvement. William Holden, Grace Kelly, Fredric March, and Mickey Rooney star. **AC2, AC11, CL31, CL51**

Brief Encounter (1945, B&W, 85m, NR)
Classic romance finds Celia Johnson and Trevor Howard in World War II England as ordinary, middle-aged people who have a bittersweet affair. Directed by David Lean. **CL4, DR50** *Recommended*

Brigadoon (1954, C, 108m, NR)
Lerner and Loewe Broadway hit, with Gene Kelly and Van Johnson as two

Americans discovering a magical Scottish village. Directed by Vincente Minnelli. **MU1, MU8, MU19, MU24**

Bright Eyes (1934, B&W, 90m, NR)
Shirley Temple sings "On the Good Ship Lollipop" in this sentimental story of a custody battle. With Shirley's fellow child star Jane Withers. **FA14**

Bright Lights, Big City (1988, C, 110m, R)
Portrait of young New Yorker coming apart at the seams, as his partying and drug habit take their toll on his marriage and job at a prestitigious magazine. Michael J. Fox stars, with Kiefer Sutherland, Phoebe Cates, Tracy Pollan, and Jason Robards. Based on Jay McInerney's novel. **DR15, DR19, XT9**

Brighton Beach Memoirs (1986, C, 110m, PG-13)
Nostalgic comedy about growing up in Brooklyn in the 1940s, written by Neil Simon from his Broadway hit. Jonathan Silverman, Bob Dishy, Blythe Danner, and Judith Ivey star. **CO5, CO6, CO34**

Brimstone and Treacle (1982, C, 85m, R)
Bizarre tale of strange young man who moves in uninvited with a couple whose teenaged daughter is in a coma from an auto accident. Sting stars, with Denholm Elliot, Joan Plowright, and Suzanna Hamilton. **MU12**

Bring Me the Head of Alfredo Garcia (1974, C, 112m, R)
Director Sam Peckinpah's story of honor and revenge, with Warrern Oates as a lowly piano player who tangles with a greedy Mexican. **CU48, MY2, WE19**

Bring on the Night (1985, C, 97m, PG-13)
Documentary about rock star Sting and his formation of a jazz-rock band. **MU11**

Bringing Up Baby (1938, B&W, 102m, NR)
Classic screwball comedy featuring a socially inept zoologist, a ditsy heiress, and her Baby—a pet leopard. Katharine Hepburn and Cary Grant star; Howard Hawks

directed. **CL10, CL16, CL18, CL35** *Recommended*

Brink of Life (1958, B&W, 84m, NR)
Drama from director Ingmar Bergman about the lives of three women in a maternity ward. Eva Dahlbeck, Ingrid Thulin, and Bibi Andersson star. **FF8**

Brink's Job, The (1978, C, 103m, PG)
Seriocomic version of the famed 1950 robbery of armored car offices in Boston by a motley crew, played by Peter Falk, Peter Boyle, Allen Goorwitz, and Warren Oates. **CU48, MY8, MY34**

Britannia Hospital (1982, C, 115m, R)
British comedy, set in an ineptly run hospital, takes swipes at socialized medicine, quack medical research, corrupt unions. Malcolm McDowell stars; Lindsay Anderson directed. A loose continuation of the McDowell/Anderson film, *O Lucky Man.* **CO17**

Broadcast News (1987, C, 131m, R)
Romantic comedy set in a Washington, D.C., TV newsroom, involving a dynamo producer (Holly Hunter) and two reporters (William Hurt, Albert Brooks) who both love her. Jack Nicholson has a small role as a network anchorman. James L. Brooks wrote and directed. **CO1, CO2, DR24, DR31, XT9** *Recommended*

Broadway Danny Rose (1983, C, 85m, PG)
A luckless New York talent agent gets mixed up with a mobster's wife. Woody Allen and Mia Farrow star in this gentle comedy about the less glamorous side of show business. **CO8, CO27, XT9** *Recommended*

Broadway Melody (1929, B&W, 104m, NR)
A pair of sisters try to break into show biz and fall for the same entertainer. The first musical to win the Best Picture Oscar. Bessie Love and Anita Page star. **MU4, MU7, XT1**

Broadway Melody of 1938 (1937, B&W, 110m, NR)
Eleanor Powell stars as a dancer torn between two men (Robert Taylor and George Murphy). Judy Garland and Sophie Tucker costar. **MU21**

Broadway Melody of 1940 (1940, B&W, 102m, NR)
Fred Astaire and George Murphy are dance partners and rivals for dancing star Eleanor Powell. Songs by Cole Porter. **MU1, MU18**

Broken Arrow (1950, C, 93m, NR)
Classic western drama of the Apache Indian chief Cochise and his struggle to make peace with white settlers. James Stewart and Jeff Chandler star. **CL25, WE8**

Broken Blossoms (1919, B&W, 95m, NR)
D.W. Griffith's silent tragedy, with Lillian Gish as an abused child who's befriended by a gentle Chinaman. **CL12, CL36, CL49**

Bronco Billy (1980, C, 119m, PG)
A Wild West Show entrepreneur (Clint Eastwood) leads his ragged troupe from one improbable adventure to the next. **WE13, WE26**

Bronze Venus *see* The Duke Is Tops

Brood, The (1979, C, 90m, R)
David Cronenberg directed this gory story of a genetic experiment gone wrong. Like many of his films, this has a cult following, but the faint of heart should beware. **CU4, CU7, HO13, HO39**

Brother From Another Planet, The (1984, C, 109m, NR)
Dark-skinned alien fugitive lands in Harlem, where he's treated like just another strange dude. Science fiction with its tongue in its cheek; written and directed by John Sayles, who also plays a small role. Joe Morton stars. **DR14, DR15, SF9**

Brother John (1972, C, 94m, PG)
Sidney Poitier stars in this story of the return of the Messiah in the form of a black man, who can't get anyone to believe him. Will Geer, Beverly Todd, and Paul Winfield costar. **DR14, DR38**

Brother Sun, Sister Moon (1973, C, 121m, PG)
Italian director Franco Zeffirelli's portrait of Francis of Assisi, starring Graham Faulkner and Judi Bowker, with Alec Guinness. Music by Donovan. **DR63, FF2**

Brotherhood of Satan (1971, C, 92m, PG)
A coven of witches takes over a small town and three outsiders fight for their lives. Strother Martin stars. **HO11**

Brothers Karamazov, The (1958, C, 146m, NR)
Dostoyevsky's classic tragedy, an exploration of good, evil, and faith involving a father and his three sons. Lee J. Cobb, Yul Brynner, Richard Basehart, and William Shatner star. **CL1**

Brothers O'Toole, The (1973, C, 94m, NR)
This western comedy follows the misadventures of two drifters who ride into a broken-down 1890s mining town. **WE15**

Brubaker (1980, C, 132m, R)
An idealistic warden at a Southern prison farm uncovers massive corruption. Robert Redford stars, with Yaphet Kotto, Jane Alexander, Brian Keith, Morgan Freeman, and Tim McIntire. **DR18, DR29**

Bruce Lee: The Legend (1984, C, 88m, NR)
Documentary about the great martial arts star, with rare footage and out-takes, plus interviews with Steve McQueen and other friends of Lee. **AC33**

Bruce Lee: The Man/The Myth (1984, C, 90m, PG)
Dramatizd biography of the martial arts star, featuring real footage of Lee in action. **AC33**

Brute, The (1952, B&W, 81m, NR)
To break a tenants' strike, a slumlord hires an ignorant slaughterhouse worker, who falls into an affair with the slum-

lord's wife. Luis Buñuel directed this drama filmed in Mexico. Katy Jurado and Pedro Armendariz star. **FF11**

Brute Man, The (1946, B&W, 60m, NR)
A college football hero is disfigured by a lab accident, which turns him into the Creeper, a psychopathic killer. Rondo Hatton stars. **HO9**

Buccaneer, The (1958, C, 121m, NR)
Drama set during the War of 1812, with Andrew Jackson (Charlton Heston) teaming up with pirate Lafitte (Yul Brynner) to fight the bloody British. Produced by Cecil B. DeMille; directed by Anthony Quinn. **AC6, AC16**

Buck and the Preacher (1972, C, 102m, PG)
Sidney Poitier stars in and directed this western about a couple of con men. Harry Belafonte and Ruby Dee costar. **DR38**

Buck Privates (1941, B&W, 84m, NR)
Abbott and Costello's first starring roles, in a wacky service comedy. The Andrews Sisters sing "Boogie Woogie Bugle Boy." **CO23, CO38**

Buddy Buddy (1981, C, 96m, R)
A suicidal man and a hit man wind up in the same hotel room in this comedy starring Jack Lemmon and Walter Matthau. Billy Wilder directed; Klaus Kinski costars. Remake of French comedy *A Pain in the A—*. **CO3, CL37, DR64, FF30, FF36**

Buddy Holly Story, The (1978, C, 113m, PG)
The short but brilliant life of rock music pioneer Buddy Holly, portrayed with gusto by Gary Busey, who also performs Holly's ground-breaking music. Don Stroud and Charlie Martin Smith costar. **MU5** *Recommended*

Buffalo Bill and the Indians (1976, C, 120m, PG)
A moody portrait of the Hero of the Plains in his final days, when he ran a traveling Wild West Show. Paul Newman and Burt Lancaster star, with Geraldine

Chaplin, Frank Considine, Harvey Keitel, and Will Sampson. Directed by Robert Altman. **CU25, DR28, DR41, WE2, WE12** *Recommended*

Bug (1975, C, 100m, PG)
An earthquake lets loose a swarm of insects capable of setting anything on fire. Bradford Dillman stars. **HO16**

Bugs and Daffy's Carnival of the Animals (1976, C, 26m, NR)
Bugs Bunny and Daffy Duck combine their talents with a live orchestra conducted by Michael Tilson Thomas in this fantasy based on Camille St. Saens' title composition. Directed by Chuck Jones; originally made for TV. **FA11** *Recommended*

Bugs Bunny and Elmer Fudd Cartoon Festival (1984, C, 54m, NR)
Seven classic Bugs and Elmer shorts, including *Wabbit Twouble, Stage Door Cartoon,* and *The Big Snooze.* **FA11**

Bugs Bunny in King Arthur's Court (1977, C, 25m, NR)
That wascally wabbit and his pals retell Mark Twain's *Connecticut Yankee in King Arthur's Court.* Directed by Chuck Jones; originally made for TV. **FA11**

Bugs Bunny/Road Runner Movie, The (1979, C, 90m, G)
Warner Bros. classic cartoon compilation features Bugs, Daffy Duck, Elmer Fudd, The Road Runner, Wile E. Coyote, Porky Pig, and Pepe Le Pew. **FA11**

Bugs Bunny 3rd Movie: 1001 Rabbit Tales (1982, C, 74m, G)
A collection of old and new Warner Bros. favorites. Voices by Mel Blanc. **FA11**

Bugs Bunny's Wacky Adventures (1957, C, 59m, NR)
Eight prized tales featuring that wascally wabbit. **FA11**

Bugsy Malone (1976, C, 93m, G)
Jodie Foster heads the all-child cast in a musical which spoofs gangster films. Mu-

sic by Paul Williams; directed by Alan Parker. **FA9, MU16**

Bull Durham (1988, C, 108m, R)
A veteran catcher, wrappping up his career in the minor leagues, befriends a goofy young pitcher with great talent but no brains for the game, while the team's most devoted female fan makes a play for both men. Kevin Costner, Tim Robbins, and Susan Sarandon star in this sensational comedy from writer-director Ron Shelton. **CO1, CO36** *Recommended*

Bulldog Drummond (series)
Bulldog Drummond (1929, B&W, 85m, NR)
Bulldog Drummond at Bay (1937, B&W, 62m, NR)
Bulldog Drummond Comes Back (1937, B&W, 64m, NR)
Bulldog Drummond Escapes (1937, B&W, 65m, NR)
Bulldog Drummond in Africa (1938, B&W, 60m, NR)
Bulldog Drummond Strikes Back (1947, B&W, 65m, NR)
Bulldog Drummond's Bride (1939, B&W, 55m, NR)
Bulldog Drummond's Peril (1938, B&W, 66m, NR)
Bulldog Drummond's Revenge (1937, B&W, 60m, NR)
Bulldog Drummond's Secret Police (1939, B&W, 56m, NR)
The exploits of Hugh "Bulldog" Drummond, a high-flying ex-British officer with dashing good looks who always got his man with the help of his constant companion Algy. Ronald Colman stars in the first film; John Howard appears in all others in the series. **MY11**

Bullet for Sandoval, A (1970, C, 96m, PG)
A Civil War veteran swears revenge on those who caused the death of his son. Western action starring Ernest Borgnine. **WE10**

Bullet for the General, A (1967, C, 115m, NR)
Italian-made western with American gunfighter joining marauding Mexicans for mayhem. Gian Maria Volonte, Lou Castel, and Klaus Kinski star. **FF30**

Bullfighter and the Lady (1951, B&W, 125m, NR)
To impress a lovely lady, an American finds a Mexican matador to teach him bullfighting. Robert Stack and Gilbert Roland star. Budd Boetticher directed. New video version adds footage to restore film to original running time. **CU10, WE28**

Bullfighters, The (1945, B&W, 61m, NR)
Laurel and Hardy comedy, with Stanley mistaken for a famed matador and forced into the ring. **CO20**

Bullies (1986, C, 96m, R)
A clan of mountain rednecks terrorize a small community, with only a teenaged boy to stand up to them. **AC25**

Bullitt (1968, C, 113m, PG)
Modern classic cop drama, with Steve McQueen the cool San Francisco detective caught up in political machinations, trying to protect a criminal witness. With Robert Vaughn, Jacqueline Bisset, and (in a small part) Robert Duvall. Memorable car chase sequence. **AC9, AC28, DR37, XT9** *Recommended*

Bullshot (1983, C, 85m, PG)
Send-up of Bulldog Drummond detective series, adapted from a play by Alan Shearman, Diz White, and Ron House, who all star as well. **CO7, CO17, MY21**

Bundle of Joy (1956, C, 98m, NR)
Debbie Reynolds takes custody of an abandoned baby, creating problems with fiance Eddie Fisher, in this remake of *Bachelor Mother.* **MU14**

Burbs, The (1989, C, 103m, PG)
Tom Hanks plays a suburbanite who's suspicious of his new neighbors in this comedy from director Joe Dante. **CO44, CU40**

Burden of Dreams (1982, C, 94m, NR)
Documentary about the filming of *Fitzcarraldo,* a movie plagued by physical

hardships, a feuding star (Klaus Kinski) and director (Werner Herzog), and remote locations. Directed by Les Blank. **CU16, FF19, FF30** *Highly Recommended*

Burglar (1987, C, 103m, R)
A bookshop owner who moonlights as a cat burglar witnesses a murder and can't go to the police with her story. Whoopi Goldberg stars in this comedy with Bobcat Goldthwait. **CO10**

Burke and Wills (1986, C, 140m, PG-13)
Historical drama, set in 1860 Australia, of the first two men to cross that continent. Jack Thompson, Nigel Havers, and Greta Scacchi star. **DR5, FF5**

Burn! (1969, C, 112m, PG)
Marlon Brando stars in this political drama of British meddling on an 18th-century Caribbean island. Superb political drama from Italian director Gillo Pontecorvo; dialogue in English. **CU9, DR5, DR33, FF2** *Recommended*

Burning Bed, The (1984, C, 100m, NR)
An abused wife reaches the breaking point and sets fire to the bed in which her husband is sleeping. Farrah Fawcett and Paul LeMat star in this harrowing true-life story. Originally made for TV. **DR10**

Burning Secret (1988, C, 107m, R)
Post-World War I Vienna is the setting for this romantic drama starring Faye Dunaway as an American woman seduced by a dashing nobleman (Klaus Maria Brandauer). **DR35**

Burnt Offerings (1976, C, 115m, PG)
There's something spooky about the summer house Karen Black and Oliver Reed have rented for their family. Bette Davis costars. **CL21, HO3**

Bus Stop (1956, C, 96m, NR)
Marilyn Monroe stars as a small-town singer bound for Hollywood who has a boisterous rodeo cowboy (Don Murray) in love with her. **CL29**

Bushido Blade, The (1979, C, 104m, R)
In 19th-century Japan, Commander William Peary attempts to recover a valuable stolen sword. Action adventure starring Richard Boone, James Earl Jones, and Toshiro Mifune. **FF28**

Business As Usual (1988, C, 89m, PG)
British drama of a sexual harassment suit, starring Glenda Jackson and Cathy Tyson. **DR10, DR23**

Buster (1988, C, 94m, R)
Pop star Phil Collins plays the mastermind behind Britain's 1962 Great Train Robbery. Julie Walters costars as Buster's wife. **DR6, DR16, MU12, MY34**

Buster Keaton Festival Vol. I (1923, B&W, 55m, NR)
Three classic comedy shorts: *The Boat, The Frozen North,* and *The Electric House.* **CO19** *Recommended*

Buster Keaton Festival Vol. II (1920/1923, B&W, 54m, NR)
Three more great silent comedy shorts: *Daydreams, The Balloonatic,* and *The Garage.* **CO19** *Recommended*

Buster Keaton Rides Again/The Railrodder (1965, B&W, 81m, NR)
The Railrodder is one of Keaton's last films; shot in Canada, it tries to recreate his classic style, as Buster travels cross-country on a railroad handcar. *Rides Again* is a documentary on the making of *The Railrodder,* with revealing footage about Keaton's working methods. **CO19** *Recommended*

Bustin' Loose (1981, C, 94m, R)
Richard Pryor plays an ex-con who's hustled into driving a school bus full of ornery kids to a camp. Cicely Tyson costars in this comedy. **CO29**

Butch and Sundance: The Early Days (1979, C, 110m, PG)
Prequel to *Butch Cassidy and the Sundance Kid* shows the formative years of the famous outlaw duo. Tom Berenger

and William Katt star. Directed by Richard Lester. **CU35, WE4, WE15**

Butch Cassidy and the Sundance Kid (1969, C, 112m, PG)
Paul Newman and Robert Redford play the legendary outlaws in this comic western. With Katharine Ross, Strother Martin, and Ted Cassidy. Written by William Goldman; directed by George Roy Hill. **DR28, DR29, WE4, WE12, WE15**

Butterfield 8 (1960, C, 110m, NR)
Elizabeth Taylor won an Oscar as the call girl of John O'Hara's novel. She's attracted to a married client (Laurence Harvey) and counseled by her best friend (Eddie Fisher). **CL33, DR19, XT3**

Butterflies Are Free (1972, C, 109m, PG)
Romance blossoms between a young blind man (Edward Albert) and his goofy neighbor (Goldie Hawn), despite the interference of his mother (Oscar winner Eileen Heckart). **CO30, XT5**

Butterfly (1981, C, 107m, R)
Sexy young woman seduces a man who may be her father in this trashy version of the James M. Cain story. Pia Zadora, Stacy Keach, and Orson Welles star. **CL41, CU6, MY25**

Bye Bye Birdie (1963, C, 112m, NR)
Musical about rock star, loosely modeled on Elvis, coming to small town just before he's drafted. Janet Leigh, Dick Van Dyke, Ann-Margret, and Paul Lynde star. **MU2, MU6, MU9**

Bye Bye Brazil (1980, C, 110m, R)
A troupe of entertainers tour the Brazilian countryside in this comedy-drama. **FF6**

C.H.O.M.P.S. (1979, C, 89m, G)
The title means: Canine HOMe Protection System. A young inventor perfects a mechanical guard dog in this family comedy starring Wesley Eure and Valerie Bertinelli. **FA6**

C.H.U.D. (1984, C, 90m, R)
Derelicts who live in the New York sewer system are turned into flesh eating mutants, Cannabilistic Humanoid Underground Dwellers, by nuclear waste. John Heard, Daniel Stern, and Kim Greist star. **HO21**

Cabaret (1972, C, 128m, PG)
Hit Broadway musical, set in the early days of the Third Reich, about a decadent Berlin nightclub featuring an American singing star (Liza Minnelli) and nasty emcee (Joel Grey). Minnelli, Grey, and director Bob Fosse won three of the film's 8 Oscars. **MU2, MU7, MU28, XT3, XT4, XT6** *Recommended*

Cabin in the Sky (1943, B&W, 100m, NR)
Black musical fantasy about one man's struggle with the forces of good and evil. Eddie "Rochester" Anderson is the man, and the musical stars include Lena Horne, Ethel Waters, and Louis Armstrong. Directed by Vincente Minnelli. **MU8, MU13, MU24**

Cabinet of Dr. Caligari, The (1919, B&W, 69m, NR)
Silent German classic about an evil doctor and his zombie-like creation. Sensational sets and imagery. Werner Krauss stars; Robert Wiene directed. **FF3, HO1** *Recommended*

Caboblanco (1980, C, 87m, R)
Intrigue set in wartime South America, with bartender Charles Bronson keeping an eye on Nazi Jason Robards and other characters. Dominique Sanda and Fernando Rey costar. **AC29**

Cactus (1986, C, 95m, NR)
Love story involving a blind man (Robert Menzies) and a woman who is losing her sight (Isabelle Huppert). Australian Paul Cox directed. **FF5**

Cactus Flower (1969, C, 103m, PG)
Goldie Hawn won an Oscar for her role as the kookie girl friend of a swinging middle-aged dentist (Walter Matthau). Ingrid Bergman plays Matthau's nurse, who

breaks out of her shell when she realizes she's in love with him. **CL27, CO1, CO30, XT5**

Caddie (1976, C, 107m, NR)
Helen Morse stars in this true story of an Australian woman trying to raise two children and manage a career during the 1920s. **FF5**

Caddy, The (1953, B&W, 95m, NR)
Martin and Lewis comedy set on the golf links, with Donna Reed and guest appearances by several golf pros. **CO25, CO36**

Caddyshack (1980, C, 90m, R)
Comic shenanigans at a snooty country club, starring Rodney Dangerfield, Ted Knight, Bill Murray, and Chevy Chase. Directed by Harold Ramis. **CO13, CO14**

Caddyshack II (1988, C, 98m, PG)
More hijinks at Bushwood Country Club, featuring Jackie Mason, Dyan Cannon, Robert Stack, Paul Bartel, and "guest appearances" by Chevy Chase and Dan Aykroyd. Directed by Allan Arkush. **CO13, CU41, CU42**

Caesar and Cleopatra (1946, C, 134m, NR)
Rendition of George Bernard Shaw's play with Claude Rains and Vivien Leigh as the mighty conqueror and his young Egyptian queen. **CL1**

Cage aux Folles, La (1978, C, 91m, R)
French comedy about a gay couple (Ugo Tognazzi, Michel Serrault), one with a son about to be married, both trying to keep their private lives secret from the future in-laws. **CU5, FF1**

Cage aux Folles II, La (1981, C, 100m, R)
More misadventures with the popular gay couple (Ugo Tognazzi, Michel Serrault), this time involving espionage and multiple mistaken identities. **FF1**

Cage aux Folles 3: The Wedding, La (1985, C, 88m, PG-13)
In the third chapter, the oddest couple are about to land an inheritance, but only if one of them is married. **FF1**

Caged Heat (1974, C, 84m, R)
Women-in-prison drama, directed by Jonathan Demme, produced by Roger Corman, has Barbara Steele as warden confined to a wheelchair, the usual shower scenes, etc. **CU14, CU39**

Cahill: United States Marshal (1973, C, 103m, PG)
John Wayne plays a lawman whose son is tempted by a life of crime. **WE17**

Caine Mutiny, The (1954, C, 125m, NR)
Humphrey Bogart stars in the Herman Wouk story of Navy officers who join forces to relieve their captain of his ship when they find him mentally unfit. Jose Ferrer, Van Johnson, Fred MacMurray, E. G. Marshall and Lee Marvin costar. **CL20, DR43**

Cal (1984, C, 102m, R)
An Irish youth who was involved in the murder of a British policeman falls in love with his widow. John Lynch and Helen Mirren star. Produced by David Puttnam; music by Mark Knopfler. **DR7, DR23**

Calamity Jane (1953, C, 101m, NR)
Doris Day plays the Wild West sharpshooter. Howard Keel costars; features the Oscar winning song "Secret Love." **MU6, WE2, WE9**

California Suite (1978, C, 103m, PG)
A series of comic sketches, all set in the Beverly Hills Hotel. The cast features Jane Fonda, Richard Pryor, Bill Cosby, Maggie Smith (an Oscar winner), Michael Caine, Elaine May, Walter Matthau, and Alan Alda. Written by Neil Simon. **CO29, CO34, DR27, XT5, XT9**

Caligula (1980, C, 156m, NR)
Lavish, violent, exceptionally sexy portrait of ancient Rome from *Penthouse* magazine publisher Bob Guccione, star-

ring Malcolm McDowell, Peter O'Toole, and John Gielgud. Also available in a R-rated version with a running time of 105m. **DR45**

Call Him Mr. Shatter (1976, C, 90m, R)
Stuart Whitman plays a hit man in Hong Kong who's had enough. Peter Cushing costars. **HO33**

Call It Murder (1934, B&W, 80m, NR)
Humphrey Bogart stars in a mystery about a jury foreman's daughter who gets the death penalty when she's romantically linked to a gangster. Also known as *Midnight*. **CL20**

Call of the Canyon (1942, B&W, 71m, NR)
Gene Autry and his radio ranch are caught under hoof when a crooked meat packer starts a stampede. **WE24**

Call of the Wild, The (1972, C, 100m, PG)
The Jack London adventure tale of gold fever in the turn-of-the-century Klondike, starring Charlton Heston. **AC12, AC24**

Camelot (1967, C, 178m, NR)
Broadway musical of the Knights of the Round Table, featuring Vanessa Redgrave, Richard Harris, and Franco Nero as Guinevere, King Arthur, and Sir Lancelot. **DR65, FA9, MU2, MU8, MU17**

Cameron's Closet (1988, C, 86m, R)
Horror tale of a psychic child whose powers cause the deaths of those who would control him. Cotter Smith, Mel Harris, and Tab Hunter star. **HO7, HO13**

Camila (1984, C, 105m, NR)
Romantic drama, based on true events, of a young socialite's love for a priest. This Argentinean film was nominated for an Oscar for Best Foreign Language Film. **FF6**

Camille (1936, B&W, 108m, NR)
Greta Garbo, Robert Taylor, and Lionel Barrymore star in Alexandre Dumas' story of the tragic heroine who is thwarted in her desire for the man she

truly loves. Directed by George Cukor. **CL1, CL4, CL5, CL28, CL39**

Can-Can (1960, C, 131m, NR)
Gay Nineties setting for this lavish musical featuring Cole Porter music. Frank Sinatra, Shirley MacLaine, Maurice Chevalier, Louis Jourdan, and Juliet Prowse star. **DR42, MU2, MU26**

Cancel My Reservation (1972, C, 99m, G)
Bob Hope comedy of a New York talk show host, on vacation in Arizona, becoming implicated in murder. Based on a novel by Louis L'Amour. **CO40, WE29**

Candidate, The (1972, C, 109m, PG)
A novice office seeker suddenly finds himself the front-runner in a Senatorial race against a veteran incumbent. Sharp observations on the media-dominated political climate in contemporary America. Robert Redford stars, with Don Porter, Melvyn Douglas, and Peter Boyle. Oscar-winning screenplay by Jeremy Larner. **DR21, DR29** *Recommended*

Candles at Nine (1944, B&W, 84m, NR)
In order to inherit her late uncle's estate, an innocent showgirl must first live a month in his home, which his other relatives have booby-trapped. Jessie Matthews stars in this British thriller. **MY19**

Candleshoe (1977, C, 101m, G)
Jodie Foster stars as an orphan pawn in a con man's swindle to steal heiress Helen Hayes's fortune. Disney comedy costars David Niven. **FA1**

Candy Mountain (1987, C, 91m, PG)
Unusual tale of musician's search for legendary guitar maker, with several prominent pop musical figures playing roles, including Dr. John, Tom Waits, Leon Redbone, Joe Strummer, and David Johansen (Buster Poindexter). Directed by photographer Robert Frank and writer Rudolph Wurlitzer. **CU17**

Cannery Row (1982, C, 120m, PG)
An adaptation of John Steinbeck's story about opposites who attract: a marine

biologist Nick Nolte meets a goofy drifter Debra Winger in Monterey, California, in the 1930s. John Huston narrates this sweet tale of love. **CL44, DR19, DR44, DR47** *Recommended*

Cannonball (1976, C, 93m, R)
Low-budget road race movie starring David Carradine, Veronica Hamel, and Robert Carradine. Directed by Paul Bartel; watch for Roger Corman, Sylvester Stallone, Martin Scorsese, and others in bit parts. **AC10, AC31, CU42**

Cannonball Run, The (1981, C, 95m, PG)
Burt Reynolds and pals race across country in vehicles of all makes and descriptions. Roger Moore, Farrah Fawcett, Dom DeLuise, Dean Martin, Sammy Davis, Jr., and many more guest drivers and pedestrians show up. **AC10, AC37, CO9**

Cannonball Run II (1984, C, 108m, PG)
More road racing action with Burt Reynolds and friends, this time including Dom DeLuise, Shirley MacLaine, and Marilu Henner. Look quickly for Frank Sinatra. **AC10, AC37, CO9, DR42**

Can't Stop the Music (1980, C, 118m, PG)
Rock musical featuring The Village People, with Valerie Perrine, Bruce Jenner, and Steve Guttenberg on hand for dramatic flourishes. **MU9**

Cape Fear (1962, B&W, 105m, NR)
An ex-convict, out for revenge, terrorizes the family of the attorney who convicted him. Robert Mitchum and Gregory Peck star. **MY2**

Captain Blood (1935, B&W, 99m, NR)
Doctor turns pirate but doesn't ignore a certain attractive damsel. Errol Flynn's first swashbuckler; Olivia de Havilland and Basil Rathbone costar. **AC13, AC34**

Captain January (1936, B&W, 76m, NR)
Shirley Temple drama of a kindly lighthouse keeper (Guy Kibbee) and his charge. Buddy Ebsen and Shirley trip the light fantastic. **FA14**

Captain Kidd (1945, B&W, 89m, NR)
Adventures on the high seas with the notorious pirate (Charles Laughton) in search of treasure. Randolph Scott costars. **WE22**

Captain Kronos: Vampire Hunter (1974, C, 91m, R)
From Britain's Hammer Studios, a spoof of horror and adventure serials, with a caped superhero and his two sidekicks who travel the world searching for vampires to kill. **HO5, HO26**

Captain Newman, M.D. (1963, C, 126m, NR)
Army psychiatrist (Gregory Peck) counsels patients, does battle with military brass in this comedy-drama. Angie Dickinson, Tony Curtis, and Bobby Darin costar. **MU12**

Captains Courageous (1937, B&W, 116m, NR)
Classic family adventure about a spoiled little rich kid (Freddie Bartholomew) whose attitude improves when he falls from a cruise ship and into the custody of a very wise Portuguese fisherman (Spencer Tracy). Tracy won an Oscar for his role. Based on Rudyard Kipling's novel. **AC13, CL19, FA3, XT2**

Captain's Paradise, The (1953, B&W, 77m, NR)
Alec Guinness stars in this British comedy about a sea captain with wives in two ports. Yvonne de Carlo and Celia Johnson are his mates. **DR63**

Car Wash (1976, C, 97m, PG)
Multi-character comedy set at an inner-city car wash. Richard Pryor and Franklin Ajaye head the cast; fine rock soundtrack. **CO29**

Caravans (1978, C, 123m, PG)
Adventure tale of the search in the Middle East for a U.S. Senator's daughter. Anthony Quinn and Jennifer O'Neill star, with Michael Sarrazin, Christopher Lee, and Joseph Cotten. **HO32**

Cardinal, The (1963, C, 175m, NR)
From director Otto Preminger comes the epic story of a priest's rise to power in the Catholic Church. Tom Tryon stars, with Romy Schneider, Carol Lynley, and John Huston. **CL44**

Care Bears Movie, The (1985, C, 75m, G)
Those roly-poly, lovable little bears are on a mission to help people share their feelings and to prevent evildoers like Professor Coldheart from taking over the world. **FA10**

Carefree (1938, B&W, 80m, NR)
Fred Astaire plays a psychiatrist, with Ginger Rogers as his patient, in this Irving Berlin musical. **CL15, MU18**

Careful, He Might Hear You (1983, C, 116m, PG)
Moving drama from Australia, based on Sumner Locke Elliott novel of a young boy caught in a bitter custody battle between two aunts. Wendy Hughes, Robyn Nevin, and Nicholas Gledhill star. **DR2, FF5** *Recommended*

Carlin at Carnegie (1983, C, 60m, NR)
Comedian George Carlin in concert at New York's venerable Carnegie Hall. **CO16**

Carlton Browne of the F.O. (1959, B&W, 88m, NR)
The British Foreign Office discovers a forgotten island that's still part of the Commonwealth and dispatches a bumbling diplomat to take charge. Terry-Thomas and Peter Sellers star. Also known as *Man in a Cocked Hat*. **CO26**

Carmen (1983, C, 102m, R)
Spanish troupe rehearses for dance interpretation of the famed opera, with the choreographer and his female star playing out the story backstage. Antonio Gades and Laura Del Sol star; Carlos Saura directed. Brilliant dance numbers. **FF7, MU3, MU4** *Recommended*

Carnal Knowledge (1971, C, 96m, R)
Drama of two college friends who treat women as objects and don't understand why they can't find love. Jack Nicholson, Art Garfunkel, Ann-Margret, and Candice Bergen star. Banned in at least one state and subject of a famous trial. Directed by Mike Nichols; written by Jules Feiffer. **CU8, DR7, DR24, DR75, MU12**

Carnival of Souls (1962, B&W, 80m, NR)
A woman is pursued by a zombie-like man after an accident in which she was involved. **HO6**

Carny (1980, C, 107m, R)
Life behind the scenes at a traveling carnival, with young runaway (Jodie Foster) getting a liberal education from barker (Robbie Robertson) and his pal (Gary Busey). **DR12, MU12** *Recommended*

Carrie (1976, C, 97m, R)
High school wallflower gets even with her tormentors and her strict mother by using her telekinetic powers. Horror shocker directed by Brian DePalma, based on a story by Stephen King. Sissy Spacek stars, with Piper Laurie, William Katt, Nancy Allen, Amy Irving, and John Travolta. **CU28, DR68, HO7, HO12, HO42** *Recommended*

Carry On Doctor (1968, C, 95m, NR)
British comedy in the long-running *Carry On . . .* series, with hospital setting and the usual bedpan humor. **CO17**

Carson City Kid (1940, B&W, 54m, NR)
Roy Rogers cleans up yet another Western town and gets in a few tunes as well. With Dale Evans and Gabby Hayes. **WE23**

Casablanca (1943, B&W, 102m, NR)
The Oscar-winning classic romantic movie that just gets better and better. Humphrey Bogart and Ingrid Bergman make the perfect pair of war-torn lovers. Sydney Greenstreet, Dooley Wilson, Claude Rains, and Paul Henreid costar. Director Michael Curtiz also won an

Academy Award. **CL4, CL6, CL20, CL27, XT1, XT6** *Recommended*

Casanova's Big Night (1954, C, 86m, NR)
Joan Fontaine mistakes Bob Hope for the infamous Casanova (Vincent Price) and havoc ensues throughout Venice. Lon Chaney, Jr. costars. **HO30, HO31**

Casey's Shadow (1978, C, 117m, PG)
A free-wheeling horse trainer has to raise three sons when his wife leaves him. Walter Matthau stars in this family drama. **FA5, FA7**

Casino Royale (1967, C, 130m, NR)
Anything-for-a-laugh spoof of James Bond movies with amazing cast (Peter Sellers, Woody Allen, David Niven, Ursula Andress, Orson Welles, William Holden, Deborah Kerr, Jean-Paul Belmondo) and plenty of sight gags, including explosive finale in Monte Carlo casino. Co-directed by John Huston. **AC35, CL41, CL44, CL51, CO7, CO26, CO27, CU17, FF33**

Cast a Giant Shadow (1966, C, 142m, NR)
True-life drama about Mickey Marcus, Israeli freedom fighter. Kirk Douglas stars, with Angie Dickinson and many guest stars in bit parts. **CL17**

Castaway (1987, C, 118m, R)
True story of middle-aged man and young woman who intentionally set themselves up on a desert island for a year. Oliver Reed and Amanda Donohoe star; Nicolas Roeg directed. **DR6, CU34**

Castaway Cowboy, The (1974, C, 91m, G)
Cowboy James Garner goes Hawaiian to help a farm widow (Vera Miles). Robert Culp costars as the bad guy in this tropical Disney western. **FA1**

Castle in the Desert (1942, B&W, 62m, NR)
It's the crafty detective Charlie Chan (Sidney Toler) up against a modern version of the Borgia clan in this mystery. **MY35**

Castle of Fu Manchu (1968, B&W, 92m, PG)
Fu Manchu and his minions are out to create havoc in the world one more time. Christopher Lee stars. **HO32**

Castle of the Living Dead (1964, B&W, 90m, NR)
A mysterious nobleman turns his vistors into mummies. Christopher Lee stars, with Donald Sutherland. **HO32**

Cat and Mouse (1975, C, 107m, PG)
Comic mystery from France about a murdered husband whose less-than-faithful ways leave a long list of suspects. Michele Morgan and Serge Reggiani star; Claude Lelouch directed. **FF1**

Cat and the Canary, The (1978, C, 96m, NR)
British remake of the classic tale finds a group of guests visiting a mansion on your basic dark and stormy night, victims of a series of bizarre pranks. Michael Callan, Carol Lynley, Olivia Hussey star. **MY19**

Cat Ballou (1965, C, 96m, NR)
Comic Western featuring Jane Fonda as a cowgirl avenging her father's murder and Oscar winner Lee Marvin in two roles. **CO7, DR27, DR43, WE9, WE15, XT2**

Cat From Outer Space, The (1978, C, 104m, G)
An extraterrestrial feline crashes on Earth, creating mayhem with the U.S. government. Disney comedy starring Ken Berry, Sandy Duncan, Harry Morgan, and McLean Stevenson. **FA1**

Cat on a Hot Tin Roof (1958, C, 108m, NR)
Elizabeth Taylor and Paul Newman star in this drama of a deceptive Southern family who cozy up to their dying patriarch (Burl Ives), hoping to get a piece of his inheritance. Based on Tennessee Williams's play. **CL33, DR28**

Cat People (1942, B&W, 73m, NR)
Producer Val Lewton's first horror film is about a mysterious bride obsessed with a curse that will transform her into a deadly panther. Directed by Jacques Tourneur. **HO36, HO37, MY1**

Cat People (1982, C, 118m, R)
An erotic remake of the 1942 Val Lewton classic, set in New Orleans. Nastassja Kinski, Malcolm McDowell, John Heard, and Annette O'Toole star. Directed by Paul Schrader. **HO25, XT9**

Catch-22 (1970, C, 121m, R)
Joseph Heller's darkly comic view of World War II, with pilot Alan Arkin frustrated and near a breakdown. Incredible supporting cast includes Martin Balsam, Bob Newhart, Buck Henry, Jon Voight, Orson Welles, Art Garfunkel, Martin Sheen, Charles Grodin, Anthony Perkins, and Paula Prentiss. Directed by Mike Nichols. **CL41, CO12, CU17, DR19, DR75, MU12** *Recommended*

Cat's Eye (1985, C, 93m, PG13)
A trio of Stephen King short stories are linked by a cat involved in all three. James Woods, Drew Barrymore, and Robert Hays star. **HO23, HO42**

Cattle Queen of Montana (1954, C, 88m, NR)
Ronald Reagan's an undercover federal agent investigating cattle thievery. Barbara Stanwyck costars. **CL45, WE6, WE9**

Caught (1949, B&W, 88m, NR)
A young woman (Barbara Bel Geddes) trapped in a miserable marriage to a millionaire finds happiness with a struggling doctor. James Mason and Robert Ryan costar; directed by Max Ophuls. **MY1, CU20** *Recommended*

Cauldron of Blood (1967, C, 97m, PG)
A blind sculptor uses skeletons provided by his murderous wife. Boris Karloff, Viveca Lindfors, and Jean-Pierre Aumont star. **HO27**

Caveman (1981, C, 92m, PG)
Comedy of life in prehistoric times, featuring Ringo Starr as a lovable Neanderthal. Barbara Bach, John Matuszak, Shelley Long, and Dennis Quaid costar. **MU12**

Certain Fury (1985, C, 88m, R)
Two girls, accused of a crime they didn't commit, are on the run from both police and hoods. Tatum O'Neal and Irene Cara star. **AC24, MU12**

Cesar (1933, B&W, 170m, NR)
Third in classic trilogy of life in France's Provence region, with Fanny's son learning the true identity of his father. Preceded by *Marius* and *Fanny*. Raimu, Pierre Fresnay, and Orane Demazis star. Marcel Pagnol wrote and directed. **FF1**

Cesar and Rosalie (1972, C, 110m, R)
Yves Montand, Romy Schneider, and Sami Frey star in this French drama of a woman's longtime love for two men. **FF1** *Recommended*

Chain Reaction (1980, C, 87m, NR)
An accident at a nuclear power plant forces a worker to confront the dangers of nuclear power. Australian drama starring Steve Bisley. **FF5**

Challenge, The (1982, C, 112m, R)
An American boxer visiting Japan becomes embroiled in a feud between two brothers. Scott Glenn and Toshiro Mifune star; John Frankenheimer directed. **FF28**

Chamber of Fear (1968, C, 88m, NR)
A madman tortures all those who visit his castle. Boris Karloff and Isela Vega star. Also known as *The Fear Chamber*. **HO27**

Chamber of Horrors (1940, B&W, 80m, NR)
A charming man (Leslie Banks) is secretly a killer of beautiful women and he has already selected his next victim (Lili Palmer). **HO9**

Champ, The (1931, B&W, 87m, NR)
Wallace Beery won an Oscar for his portrayal of a broken-down boxer trying to keep custody of his son (Jackie Cooper). A classic three-hankie movie. Remade in 1979. **CL6, DR22, XT2**

Champ, The (1979, C, 121m, PG)
An ex-fighter (Jon Voight) may lose custody of his son (Ricky Schroder) in this tear-jerker remake of the 1931 film. Faye Dunaway costars. **CU18, DR22, DR35, FA7**

Champagne for Caesar (1950, B&W, 99m, NR)
This comedy poking fun at television game shows has Ronald Colman winning big prizes and the show's worried sponsor (Vincent Price) trying to distract him. **HO31**

Champion (1949, B&W, 90m, NR)
Kirk Douglas plays the ultimate boxing machine in this drama of an overly ambitious fighter. Marilyn Maxwell and Arthur Kennedy costar. **DR22**

Chances Are (1989, C 108m, PG-13)
A Washington widow (Cybill Shepherd) has a new man in her life—a young man to whom her daughter is attracted. The real complication: he's her late husband reincarnated. Robert Downey, Jr., Mary Stuart Masterson, and Ryan O'Neal costar. **CO1, CO37, XT9**

Chandu on the Magic Island (1940, B&W, 67m, NR)
Chandu the magician travels to a lost island to battle an evil cult of devil worshippers. Bela Lugosi stars. **HO28**

Change of Habit (1969, C, 93m, G)
Elvis Presley stars in this drama with no musical numbers about an inner-city physician and his relationship with a nun (Mary Tyler Moore). **MU22**

Change of Seasons, A (1980, C, 102m, R)
A professor takes one of his students for a lover, and his wife retaliates by taking up with a younger man, too. Anthony Hopkins, Shirley MacLaine, Bo Derek, and Michael Brandon star in this comedy. **DR42**

Changeling, The (1979, C, 107m, R)
A composer who has lost his wife and child in an accident rents an old house, discovers it is haunted by the ghost of a murdered child, then sets out to solve the murder. George C. Scott, Trish Van Devere, and Melvyn Douglas star. **HO2, HO19**

Chaplin Essanay Book I, The (1915, B&W, 51m, NR)
Collection of Charlie Chaplin's early short films, including *The Tramp* and *The Champion*. **CO18** *Recommended*

Chaplin Revue, The (1958, B&W, 121m, NR)
Charlie Chaplin personally assembled this collection in 1958 of his early silent shorts, including *Shoulder Arms* (1918) and *The Pilgrim* (1922). **CO18, CO38** *Recommended*

Chapter Two (1979, C, 124m, PG)
Neil Simon's autobiographical drama of a writer trying to get over the death of his wife and falling all too quickly in love with another woman. James Caan and Marsha Mason star. **CO34**

Charade (1963, C, 114m, NR)
A young widow finds that several men are interested in a secret that killed her husband. Audrey Hepburn and Cary Grant star in this romantic mystery set in Paris, with Walter Matthau, George Kennedy, and James Coburn. Directed by Stanley Donen. **CL18, CL30, MU23, MY3, XT9** *Recommended*

Charge of the Light Brigade, The (1936, B&W, 116m, NR)
Adventure tale of fateful British maneuver during the Crimean War, starring Errol Flynn and Olivia de Havilland. Directed by Michael Curtiz. **AC6, AC13, AC16, AC34**

Chariots of Fire (1981, C, 123m, PG)
Oscar-winning drama, based on a true story, of rival runners in the 1924 Olympics. Ben Cross, Ian Charleson, Ian Holm, and Alice Krige star, with guest appearances by John Gielgud and Lindsay Anderson. Directed by Hugh Hudson; produced by David Puttnam. **DR22, DR23, XT1**

Charley and the Angel (1973, C, 93m, G)
Fred MacMurray learns a heavenly lesson from a wise angel (Harry Morgan): shape up his strict ways with his family or he'll be shipped off to the hereafter. Drama from the Disney studios. **FA1**

Charley Varrick (1973, C, 111m, PG)
Robber of small town bank gets more than he bargained for when he learns the loot is laundered Mob money. Walter Matthau stars, with Joe Don Baker, Felicia Farr, John Vernon, and Andy Robinson. First-rate action drama directed by Don Siegel. **AC9** *Recommended*

Charlie Chan at the Opera (1936, B&W, 68m, NR)
An opera singer (Boris Karloff) seems the perfect suspect for the sleuthing of Chan (Warner Oland). William Demarest co-stars as a rival detective. **HO27, MY35**

Charlie Chan at the Wax Museum (1940, B&W, 64m, NR)
An escaped killer vows vengeance against the wily detective (Sidney Toler) who put him behind bars. **MY35**

Charlie Chan in Paris (1935, B&W, 72m, NR)
On the trail of forged bank bonds, Chan (Warner Oland) is soon caught up in a murder investigation in the City of Light. **MY35**

Charlie Chan in Rio (1941, B&W, 62m, NR)
A suspected murderess is herself found dead, and Chan (Sidney Toler) sets out to find the real killer. **MY35**

Charlie Chan's Secret (1936, B&W, 72m, NR)
A seance turns deadly, and Chan (Warner Oland) must divine the killer's identity. **MY35**

Charlie Chaplin Carnival (1916, B&W, 80m, NR)
This collection of silent comedy classics includes *The Vagabond, The Fireman, The Count,* and *One A.M.* **CO18** *Recommended*

Charlie Chaplin Cavalcade (1916, B&W, 81m, NR)
Includes these silent shorts: *One A.M., The Pawnshop, The Floorwalker,* and *The Rink.* **CO18** *Recommended*

Charlie Chaplin Festival (1917, B&W, 80m, NR)
More Chaplin classics: *The Cure, The Adventurer, The Immigrant,* and *Easy Street.* **CO18** *Recommended*

Charlie Chaplin—The Early Years, Volumes I-IV (1916-1917, B&W, approx. 60m each, NR)
Gems from Chaplin's first years in Hollywood. Volume I includes *The Immigrant* and *Easy Street.* Volume II features *The Pawnshop* and *One A.M.* Volume III has *The Cure* and *The Vagabond.* Volume IV: *The Rink* and *The Fireman.* **CO18** *Recommended*

Charlie Chaplin's Keystone Comedies (1914, B&W, 59m, NR)
Six one-reelers that helped to introduce Chaplin to the world: *Making a Living* (Chaplin as a villain), *Kid's Auto Races, A Busy Day, Mabel's Married Life, Laughing Gas,* and *The New Janitor.* **CO18** *Recommended*

Charlie, the Lonesome Cougar (1968, C, 75m, G)
Disney's animal adventure-comedy stars a likable cougar who befriends a rugged logger. **FA5**

Charlotte's Web (1972, C, 94m, G)
E.B. White's famous story of Wilbur the pig and his friendship with Charlotte the spider is transformed into a cartoon musical for the whole family. **FA10**

Charly (1968, C, 103m, NR)
Through a scientific experiment, a retarded man is given powers of superintelligence. Oscar winner Cliff Robertson and Claire Bloom star. Based on Daniel Keyes' story, "Flowers for Algernon." **DR19, XT2**

Chase, The (1966, C, 135m, NR)
Delirious melodrama, with super cast, about a small Texas town awaiting the return of a notorious escaped convict. Marlon Brando, Robert Redford, Jane Fonda, Robert Duvall, Angie Dickinson, E.G. Marshall, James Fox, and Janice Rule star, with Jocelyn Brando, Paul Williams, and Martha Hyer. Written by Lillian Hellman; directed by Arthur Penn. **CU17, DR27, DR29, DR33, DR37, DR62, XT8** *Recommended*

Cheech & Chong's Next Movie (1980, 95m, R)
The second set of adventures featuring that stoned L.A. comedy team. **CO32**

Cheech & Chong's The Corsican Brothers (1984, C, 90m, R)
C&C play three roles each in this broad spoof of the swashbuckler adventures. Rae Dawn Chong (Tommy's daughter) costars. **CO32**

Chevre, La (1986, C, 91m, NR)
French comedy starring Pierre Richard and Gerard Depardieu as a pair of inept detectives on the trail of a kidnapped businessman's daughter. Also known as *The Goat*. **FF29**

Cheyenne Autumn (1964, C, 154m, NR)
Director John Ford's last western tells the epic story of the Cheyenne tribe's relocation by the U.S. government. Richard Widmark stars, with Carroll Baker, Edward G. Robinson, Karl Malden, Delores

Del Rio, and James Stewart. **CL25, CL52, WE1, WE2, WE8, WE18**

Cheyenne Social Club, The (1970, C, 103m, PG)
Comic western has James Stewart inheriting a house of ill repute, running it with the help of Henry Fonda. Directed by Gene Kelly. **CL24, CL25, MU19, WE15**

Chiefs (1983, C, 200m, NR)
A murder in a small Southern town goes unsolved from 1924 to 1962, until the town's first black chief takes a personal interest in the case. Charlton Heston, Billy Dee Williams, Brad Davis, and Keith Carradine star in this epic drama. Originally made for TV. **DR16, DR62**

Chien Andalou, Un (1928, B&W, 20m, NR)
Surrealistic film, directed by Luis Buñuel and Salvador Dali, is a series of memorable images. A preview of things to come from both artists. **FF11** *Recommended*

Children of a Lesser God (1986, C, 119m, R)
A teacher at a school for the deaf and one of his most difficult pupils embark on a tempestuous affair. William Hurt and Oscar winner Marlee Matlin star, with Piper Laurie. Based on Mark Medoff's play. **DR1, DR20, DR31, XT3**

Children of the Corn (1984, C, 93m, R)
Stephen King short story is the basis for this tale of a young couple passing through a small Midwestern town, discovering that the children are murderers. Linda Hamilton and Peter Horton star. **HO13, HO42**

Children Shouldn't Play With Dead Things (1973, C, 91m, PG)
An acting company goes to a burial island to shoot a movie. When the director tries to raise the dead to use in his film, he succeeds too well. **HO6**

Children's Songs and Stories With the Muppets (1985, C, 56m, NR)
The Muppets are joined by guest stars Julie Andrews, Judy Collins, John Denver, Brooke Shields, and Twiggy in a treasure trove of songs and stories. **FA15**

Child's Play (1988, C, 87m, R)
An innocent-looking toy doll is possessed by the soul of a mass killer, who continues his crime spree. Chris Sarandon, Catherine Hicks, and Alex Vincent star. **HO8, HO16**

Chilly Scenes of Winter (1979, C, 96m, PG)
A determined young man tries to win back his former sweetheart in this adaptation of Ann Beattie's novel. John Heard and Mary Beth Hurt star, with Peter Riegert, Kenneth McMillan, and Gloria Grahame. Also known as *Head Over Heels.* **DR1**

China Gate (1957, B&W, 95m, NR)
In one of the first films to deal with the Vietnam War, French soldiers attack a communist outpost. Gene Barry, Angie Dickinson, and Nat King Cole star. Samuel Fuller directed. **AC4, CU22, MU12**

China Girl (1987, C, 90m, R)
Gang warfare breaks out between hot-headed youths in the adjoining New York neighborhoods of Chinatown and Little Italy. An interracial couple is caught in the crossfire. Directed by Abel Ferrara. **AC8**

China Seas (1935, B&W, 90m, NR)
Clark Gable takes to the high seas as the captain of a shipping vessel bound for the Orient, with pirates and a deadly typhoon to contend with. **AC12, CL23**

China Syndrome, The (1979, C, 123m, PG)
A TV news reporter and her cameraman learn that officials at a nuclear power plant are covering up certain details of an accident. Jane Fonda, Michael Douglas, and Jack Lemmon star. **DR7, DR27, DR64, DR70** *Recommended*

Chinatown (1974, C, 131m, R)
Director Roman Polanski's tale of love and mystery in Depression-era Los Angeles. A moody, hard-boiled detective, (Jack Nicholson) is hired to find the missing husband of a shady lady (Faye Dunaway). John Huston costars. Written by Robert Towne. **CL44, DR24, DR35, DR54, MY2, MY14, XT9** *Highly Recommended*

Chinese Connection, The (1980, C, 107m, R)
Bruce Lee martial arts saga of young man avenging the death of his instructor. **AC33**

Chino (1976, C, 98m, PG)
Western drama starring Charles Bronson as a half-breed whose ranch is under attack from prejudiced locals. **AC29**

Chipmunk Adventure, The (1987, C, 76m, G)
Alvin, Simon, and Theodore take to the skies in their full-length animated feature. **FA10**

Chisum (1970, C, 111m, G)
A cattle baron (John Wayne) wages war on local political corruption. **WE17**

Chitty Chitty Bang Bang (1968, C, 142m, G)
Dick Van Dyke portrays an eccentric inventor whose wild imagination takes him, his two children, and a beautiful woman named Truly Scrumptious (Sally Ann Howes) into a mystical world—all in a magical car. Family musical fun. **FA9**

Chloe in the Afternoon (1972, C, 97m, NR)
Eric Rohmer directed this French comedy of a married man's obsession with a store clerk. Bernard Valery and Zouzou star. **FF15**

Chocolate War, The (1988, C, 103m, R)
At a Catholic boys' school, a freshman defies both the stern principal and a secret student society known as The Vigils. Ilan Mitchell-Smith, John Glover, and Wally Ward star in this drama based on

Robert Cormier's novel. **DR9, DR61** *Recommended*

Choice of Arms (1983, C, 114m, NR)
Yves Montand and Gerard Depardieu are the antagonists in this French drama of a retired mobster and a young punk who threatens him and his wife (Catherine Deneuve). **FF1, FF27, FF29**

Choice of Weapons, A (1976, C, 88m, NR)
A man's investigation into the death of his father leads him to a society of modern-day knights. David Birney, Barbara Hershey, Donald Pleasance and Peter Cushing star. Also known as *Dirty Knight's Work*. **HO33**

Choke Canyon (1986, C, 95m, PG)
Scientist attempts to keep ruthless conglomerate out of protected wilderness area. Plenty of high-flying aerial action. Bo Svenson and Stephen Collins star. **AC11**

Choose Me (1984, C, 106m, R)
Romantic drama set largely in a big-city bar run by a loveless woman (Lesley Ann Warren) who is attracted to a smooth-talking newcomer (Keith Carradine). Genevieve Bujold and Rae Dawn Chong costar; Alan Rudolph directed. **CU26, DR1**

Chopping Mall (1986, C, 76m, R)
Horror story of shopping mall's automated security robots going haywire, with quartet of shoppers trapped inside after hours. Russell Todd and Barbara Crampton star, with Paul Bartel. **CU42, HO22**

Chorus Line, A (1985, C, 118m, PG-13)
Film version of Broadway's long-running musical, the backstage tale of a group of dancers auditioning for a show that may give them their first break. Michael Douglas stars, with Alyson Reed, Audrey Landers, Janet Jones, and Nicole Fosse. Directed by Richard Attenborough. **DR70, MU2, MU4**

Chosen, The (1981, C, 108m, G)
In 1940s Brooklyn, two Jewish boys, one Hassidic, the other Americanized, strike up a wary friendship. Robby Benson and Barry Miller star, with Rod Steiger and Maximillian Schell. **DR15**

Christ Stopped at Eboli (1979, C, 120m, NR)
Italian drama of an anti-Fascist writer living in exile at a small village during the 1930s. Gian Maria Volonte stars; Francesco Rosi directed. **FF2**

Christiane F. (1981, C, 124m, R)
A teenager enters Berlin's seamy underworld of prostitution and drug addiction in this disturbing German drama based on true events. Nadja Brunkhorst stars; David Bowie concert appearance is included. **FF3**

Christine (1983, C, 111m, R)
A 1958 Plymouth Fury turns into a killing machine in this adaptation of the Stephen King novel, directed by John Carpenter. Keith Gordon stars, with Alexandra Paul and Harry Dean Stanton. **CU29, CU49, HO22, HO42**

Christmas Carol, A (1951, B&W, 86m, NR)
Charles Dickens' classic story of the nasty, stingy Scrooge; he learns a few of life's lessons through the help of the ghost of his late partner, Marley, and the ghosts of Christmas Past, Present, and Future. Alistair Sim stars. **CL1, FA13**

Christmas in Connecticut (1945, B&W, 101m, NR)
Barbara Stanwyck stars in this comedy about a recipe author who's really at a loss in the kitchen, and her attempts to host a lonely sailor without a place to go for the holidays. Dennis Morgan and Sydney Greenstreet costar. **FA13**

Christmas Story, A (1983, C, 98m, PG)
Nostalgic holiday story, set in the Midwest of the early 1950s, about a boy whose only wish is to have a Red Ryder BB gun for Christmas. Peter Billingsley

stars, with Darren McGavin and Melinda Dillon. Written and narrated by Jean Shepherd. **CO6, FA6, FA13** *Recommended*

Christmas to Remember, A (1978, C, 100m, NR)
During the Depression, an elderly farm couple is visited by their grandson for the holidays. Jason Robards, Eva Marie Saint, and Joanne Woodward star. Originally made for TV. **FA13, DR67**

Christmas Tree, The (1969, C, 110m, G)
Sentimental tale of a wealthy man's reconciliation with his dying young son. William Holden stars. Also known as *When Wolves Cry*. **FA13, CL51**

Christopher Strong (1933, B&W, 77m, NR)
A female aviator (Katharine Hepburn) goes into a tailspin over a married man (Colin Clive). **CL5, CL16**

Chuck Berry: Hail! Hail! Rock 'n' Roll (1987, C, 120m, PG)
Documentary about one of rock's Founding Fathers intersperses interview material with footage from a historic concert in Berry's hometown, St. Louis. Performers include Keith Richards, Eric Clapton, Linda Ronstadt, Etta James, and Robert Cray; interviewees include Bruce Springsteen, Little Richard, Bo Diddley, the Everly Brothers, and Jerry Lee Lewis. **MU11** *Highly Recommended*

Chump at Oxford, A (1940, B&W, 63m, NR)
Laurel and Hardy matriculate at England's most prestigious university. **CO20**

Cimarron (1931, B&W, 124m, NR)
Oscar-winning western epic of a family settling the frontier, based on Edna Ferber's novel. Richard Dix stars, with Irene Dunne and Estelle Taylor. **WE1, XT1**

Cincinnati Kid, The (1965, C, 113m, NR)
Steve McQueen stars as a poker playing ace who challenges rich Edward G. Robinson to a high-stakes game. Ann-Margret, Tuesday Weld, Rip Torn, Karl Malden, and Joan Blondell costar. **AC28, CL52, CU47**

Cinderella (1950, C, 75m, G)
Disney's full-length animated fairy tale finds a beautiful maiden dominated by an evil stepmother and ugly stepsisters until her fairy godmother and Prince Charming come to her rescue. **FA2** *Recommended*

Cinderella (1964, C, 77m, NR)
Musical version of the famed fairy tale, with Lesley Ann Warren, Ginger Rogers, Celeste Holm, and Walter Pidgeon, plus a Rodgers and Hammerstein score. Originally made for TV. **FA9, MU8**

Cinderella (1984, C, 60m, NR)
Jennifer Beals is the over-worked, under-loved maiden, Matthew Broderick is the charming prince, Jean Stapleton plays her fairy godmother, and Eve Arden is the wicked stepmother in this Faerie Tale Theatre presentation. **FA12**

Cinderfella (1960, C, 91m, NR)
Jerry Lewis spoofs the famed fairy tale as an orphaned boy who has to cook and clean for his evil step*brothers*. **CO25, FA6**

Circle of Iron (1979, C, 102m, R)
Martial arts combines with fantasy in this tale of an American searching for perfect peace and Zen awareness. David Carradine, Jeff Cooper, Roddy McDowall, and Christopher Lee star. Based on an idea by James Coburn and Bruce Lee. **AC26, HO32**

Circus, The (1928, B&W, 72m, NR)
Charlie Chaplin classic silent comedy finds him charmed by the circus owner's stepdaughter. Also available on a tape which includes Chaplin's 33-minute short, *A Day's Pleasure*, about a family's mishaps during a day set aside for fun and games. **CL11, CO18** *Recommended*

Circus of Horrors (1960, C, 89m, NR)
A plastic surgeon and his nurse try hiding in an unusual circus to escape a patient

they once disfigured. Donald Pleasence stars. **HO20, HO26**

Circus World (1964, C, 135m, NR)
After a fifteen-year absence, a circus owner attempts to locate his ex-lover, who's also the mother of the child he's raised. John Wayne and Rita Hayworth star. **CL17**

Citizen Kane (1941, B&W, 120m, NR)
The story of publishing tycoon Charles Foster Kane is the basis for this stunning Hollywood debut by Orson Welles, who stars and also co-wrote, directed, and produced. Joseph Cotten, Agnes Moorehead, Everett Sloane, Dorothy Commingore, and Ruth Warrick are among the supporting players. **CL2, CL41, DR60, XT10** *Highly Recommended*

Citizens Band (1977, C, 98m, PG)
Comedy focusing on activities of CB enthusiasts in a small town, full of rich characters. Paul LeMat stars, with Candy Clark, Ann Wedgeworth, Marcia Rodd, Charles Napier, and Bruce McGill. Directed by Jonathan Demme. Also known as *Handle With Care*. **CO2, CU39**

City Heat (1984, C, 94m, PG)
Spoof of 1930s gangster films starring Clint Eastwood as a cop and Burt Reynolds as his pal, a private eye. Rip Torn is the villain; Richard Roundtree, Madeline Kahn, Jane Alexander, and Irene Cara head the supporting cast. **AC27, AC37, CO3, CO7, CU47**

City in Fear (1980, C, 150m, NR)
David Janssen plays a reporter on the trail of a psycho killer who's terrorizing a city. Robert Vaughn, Perry King, and Mickey Rourke costar. Originally made for TV. **AC9, DR48, MY17**

City Lights (1931, B&W, 86m, NR)
Charlie Chaplin is the poor tramp whose sudden fortune brings sight to a blind girl in this delightful silent classic. **CL11, CO18** *Highly Recommended*

City of the Walking Dead (1983, C, 92m, R)
Zombies come to life in search of humans to feast on. Mel Ferrer stars. **HO21**

City on Fire (1979, C, 101m, R)
Disaster story of a city endangered by a blaze set by an embittered refinery worker. Barry Newman, Henry Fonda, Ava Gardner, Shelley Winters, and Susan Clark star. **AC23, CL24**

Claire's Knee (1971, C, 103m, PG)
A groom-to-be develops an obsession with the daughter of a friend, or more specifically, the knee of a daughter of a friend. Comedy from French director Eric Rohmer. **FF15**

Clambake (1967, C, 97m, NR)
Elvis Presley musical, with El as a rich boy who wants to be treated just like everyone else. Set in Miami; Shelley Fabares costars. **MU22**

Clan of the Cave Bear (1985, C, 100m, R)
Prehistoric adventure saga, based on Jean M. Auel novel, starring Daryl Hannah, Pamela Reed, and James Remar. **AC12**

Clara's Heart (1988, C, 108m, PG-13)
A Jamaican housekeeper brings a young boy out of his emotional shell in this sentimental drama starring Whoopi Goldberg. Neil Patrick Harris, Kathleen Quinlan, and Michael Ontkean costar. **DR2, DR8**

Clash by Night (1952, B&W, 105m, NR)
Barbara Stanwyck plays a restless woman who finally settles down with a fisherman (Paul Douglas), but she's hooked on her husband's best friend (Robert Ryan). Marilyn Monroe has a small part; Fritz Lang directed. **CL29, CL43, CL45**

Clash of the Titans (1981, C, 118m, PG)
Fantasy adventure retells ancient Greek mythology with the help of contemporary special effects by Ray Harryhausen. Laurence Olivier stars as Zeus, with Harry Hamlin, Maggie Smith, Claire

Bloom, Ursula Andress, and Burgess Meredith. **CL32**

Class of Miss MacMichael, The (1978, C, 99m, R)
Glenda Jackson is the teacher of a class of disadvantaged rebels in this schoolroom drama. Oliver Reed costars. **DR61**

Class of 1984 (1982, C, 93m, R)
Violent melodrama of a lone teacher (Perry King) confronting a vicious gang of "students." Timothy Van Patten leads the truants; watch for Michael J. Fox. **DR61**

Class of Nuke 'Em High (1986, C, 81m, R)
A New Jersey high school becomes a nuclear waste dump and the students are transformed into obnoxious mutants. **HO21**

Clean and Sober (1988, C, 121m, R)
Absorbing drama of an investment counselor (Michael Keaton) and his battle against alcohol abuse and drug addiction. With Morgan Freeman, Kathy Baker, and M. Emmet Walsh. **CO45, DR7** *Recommended*

Clean Slate (1981, C, 128m, NR)
French black comedy, set in colonial Africa, about a police chief who gains revenge on everyone who has mistreated him. Philippe Noiret, Stephane Audran, and Isabelle Huppert star; Bertrand Tavernier directed. Based on a novel by Jim Thompson. Also known as *Coup de Torchon*. **FF1, MY20, MY29** *Recommended*

Cleopatra (1963, C, 243m, G)
The legendary film that made Elizabeth Taylor and Richard Burton the celebrity couple of our time and nearly bankrupt one movie studio. Rex Harrison costars, with Roddy MacDowall and Martin Landau. Joseph L. Mankiewicz directed. Also available in a 194m. version. **CL2, CL15, CL33, CL55**

Cleopatra Jones (1973, C, 89m, PG)
Tamara Dobson stars as a secret agent skilled in the martial arts in this adventure

saga. Shelley Winters plays her nemesis. **AC26**

Cleopatra Jones and the Casino of Gold (1975, C, 96m, R)
Second chapter in Cleo saga, with Tamara Dobson squaring off against dragon lady Stella Stevens. **AC26**

Cloak and Dagger (1946, B&W, 106m, NR)
Gary Cooper plays a professor caught up in espionage on his way to Germany. Fritz Lang directed. **CL26, CL43**

Clock, The (1945, B&W, 90m, NR)
Classic romance between soldier on leave in New York and an office worker. Robert Walker and Judy Garland star, with James Gleason and Keenan Wynn. Directed by Vincente Minnelli. **CL4, MU21, MU24**

Clockwise (1986, C, 96m, PG)
A British schoolmaster who prides himself on his punctuality encounters a series of comic disasters on the most important day of his career. John Cleese stars. **CO15**

Clockwork Orange, A (1971, C, 137m, R)
In the ultra-violent future, Alex and his droogs (gang members) lead merry lives of crime until the authorities catch him and subject him to a gruesome form of rehabilitation. Malcolm McDowell stars in director Stanley Kubrick's version of Anthony Burgess's novel. **CU1, CU4, DR53, SF17** *Recommended*

Close Encounters of the Third Kind (1977, C, 135m, PG)
Steven Spielberg's science fiction drama of aliens landing in Wyoming, tipping off their arrival ahead of time to Earthlings. Richard Dreyfuss and Melinda Dillon star, with François Truffaut. This is the Special Edition, which contains footage added for the film's theatrical rerelease. **FA8, FF13, SF9, SF16, SF24** *Recommended*

Closely Watched Trains (1966, B&W, 89m, NR)
Oscar-winning comedy-drama from Czechoslovakia about a young railway worker's first brush with sex. Set during the Nazi occupation; directed by Jiri Menzel. **FF7, XT7**

Clouds Over Europe (1939, B&W, 78m, NR)
Laurence Olivier stars with Ralph Richardson in a light-hearted mystery about a test pilot and British inspector assigned to unravel a case of missing bombers. Also known as *Q Planes*. **CL32**

Clowns, The (1971, C, 90m, NR)
Documentary from Federico Fellini about the merry men and women of the circus, with some serious commentary on the human condition as well. **FF10**

Club Paradise (1986, C, 104m, PG-13)
A Chicago fireman moves to a Caribbean island with hopes of opening a swank resort for swingin' singles. Robin Williams stars, with Jimmy Cliff, Peter O'Toole, Andrea Martin, Rick Moranis, and Eugene Levy. Directed by Harold Ramis. **CO14, CO43, DR45**

Clue (1985, C, 96m, PG)
Comic mystery, based on the popular board game, starring Tim Curry, Eileen Brennan, Madeline Kahn, Martin Mull, Michael McKean, Christopher Lloyd, Lesley Ann Warren, and Lee Ving among the suspects. Released theatrically with three different endings; all are featured on the video version. **CO10, MU12, MY21**

Coal Miner's Daughter (1980, C, 125m, PG)
Oscar winner Sissy Spacek stars as country music queen Loretta Lynn in this drama about her roller-coaster life and career. Tommy Lee Jones plays her husband, Beverly D'Angelo is Patsy Cline, Levon Helm is Lynn's father. Both actresses do their own singing. **DR4, DR68, MU5, MU12, XT3** *Recommended*

Cobra (1986, C, 88m, R)
Sylvester Stallone is the take-no-prisoners police detective who's after a gang of vicious killers. Brigitte Nielsen costars. **AC9, AC31**

Coca-Cola Kid, The (1985, C, 94m, R)
Charming, offbeat comedy about a brash American marketing expert sent to the Australian outback to push the title product. Eric Roberts and Greta Scacchi star. Directed by Dusan Makavejev. **CO2, CO12** *Recommended*

Cocaine Cowboys (1979, C, 87m, R)
Andy Warhol produced this comedy about a rock band that doubles as dope smugglers. Jack Palance, Tom Sullivan, and Warhol star. **CU3**

Cocaine Fiends (1937, B&W, 74m, NR)
Serious ''message'' film from the distant past warning audiences of the consequences of cocaine use (prostitution, suicide) is now regarded a camp ''bad'' movie. **CU11**

Cockfighter (1974, C, 83m, R)
Warren Oates plays a man who drifts through the rural South, training fighting birds, in this cult film adapted from Charles Willeford's novel. With Harry Dean Stanton, Troy Donahue, and Millie Perkins. Also known as *Born To Kill*. **CU48, CU49**

Cocktail (1988, C, 104m, R)
Tom Cruise stars in this light romantic drama about a young man whose claim to fame in New York is his considerable bartending skills. Bryan Brown plays his mentor, Elisabeth Shue his girlfriend. **DR1, DR73**

Cocoanuts, The (1929, B&W, 96m, NR)
The Marx Brothers' debut film, about phony land sales in Florida, adapted from their Broadway hit. **CO21**

Cocoon (1985, C, 117m, PG-13)
Senior citizens in Florida and aliens disguised as humans collide in this comedy-drama starring Hume Cronyn, Wilford

Brimley, Jessica Tandy, Maureen Stapleton, Gwen Verdon, Steve Guttenberg, Brian Dennehy, and Oscar winner Don Ameche. Directed by Ron Howard. **DR11, SF9, XT4** *Recommended*

Cocoon: The Return (1988, C, 102m, PG)
This sequel to the story of alien visitors and oldsters in Florida reunites virtually the entire cast of the first film for more adventures. **DR11, SF9**

Code Name: Wildgeese (1984, C, 101m, R)
Action in the jungles of Southeast Asia, as a hand-picked mercenary force lays siege to a major opium smuggling operation. Lee Van Cleef, Klaus Kinski, and Ernest Borgnine star. **AC20, FF30**

Code of Silence (1985, C, 100m, R)
Chicago police detective is shunned by his colleagues when he turns in a crooked cop, and is also caught between warring gangs. Chuck Norris and Henry Silva star. **AC9, AC32**

Cold River (1982, C, 94m, PG)
Family adventure of a brother and sister stranded in the wilderness when their father suffers a fatal heart attack. Filmed on location in the Adirondack Mountains; set in 1932. **FA4**

Cold Room, The (1984, C, 95m, NR)
A German vacation for a father (George Segal) and his college daughter (Amanda Pays) turns into a series of bizarre incidents when a mysterious man is found hiding out in her hotel room. Originally made for cable TV. **MY18**

Cold Sweat (1971, C, 94m, PG)
Charles Bronson plays an American expatriate in France who gets involved with drug dealing. James Mason, Liv Ullmann, and Jill Ireland costar. **AC8, AC29, FF25**

Collector, The (1965, C, 119m, NR)
A shy young man (Terence Stamp) wins a fortune in a football pool and buys an estate, where he keeps a beautiful girl (Samantha Eggar) captive in hopes that she'll fall in love with him. Directed by

William Wyler. **CL38, CU13, DR3, MY3** *Recommended*

College (1927, B&W, 65m, NR)
Buster Keaton goes out for the football team to impress a sweet coed. **CL11, CO19, CO35**

Colonel Redl (1985, C, 144m, R)
Klaus Maria Brandauer stars in this Hungarian drama about an army officer's rise to power in the days before World War I. Istvan Szabo directed. **FF7**

Color of Money, The (1986, C, 117m, R)
Sequel to *The Hustler*, set 25 years later, with Paul Newman's Eddie Felson training a hot new young prospect (Tom Cruise). Mary Elizabeth Mastrantonio and Helen Shaver costar. Newman won an Oscar under Martin Scorsese's direction. **DR22, DR28, DR52, DR73, XT2** *Recommended*

Color Purple, The (1985, C, 152m, PG-13)
Drama of two black sisters and their painful separation and enduring love for one another. Whoopi Goldberg stars, with Danny Glover, Oprah Winfrey, Margaret Avery, Rae Dawn Chong, and Adolph Caesar. Steven Spielberg directed; based on Alice Walker's novel. **DR8, DR14, DR19, SF24**

Colorado (1940, B&W, 54m, NR)
Roy Rogers and partner Gabby Hayes saddle up and head out for the wilds of Colorado. **WE23**

Colors (1988, C, 120m, R)
On the streets of Los Angeles, two police officers (Robert Duvall, Sean Penn) try to keep the peace amid warring gangs. Directed by Dennis Hopper; some brief footage added for video release. **AC9, CU46, DR15, DR37, XT9**

Colossus: The Forbin Project (1970, C, 100m, PG)
Science fiction tale of a super-computer that begins to develop a mind of its own, overriding all attempts to thwart it. Eric

Braeden and Susan Clark star. Also known as *The Forbin Project*. **SF6**

Columbo: Prescription Murder (1967, C, 99m, NR)
The disarming sleuth in the rumpled raincoat, Lt. Columbo (Peter Falk), is on the trail of a philandering psychiatrist. Originally made for TV; pilot for the successful series. **MY14**

Coma (1978, C, 113m, PG)
A doctor discovers a horrifying secret when her patients begin to suffer major brain damage after relatively minor surgery. Genevieve Bujold stars, with Michael Douglas and Rip Torn. **CU47, DR70, HO19, MY15, SF5**

Comancheros, The (1961, C, 107m, NR)
A Texas ranger (John Wayne) goes undercover in an attempt to halt the sale of guns and liquor to the Comanches. Lee Marvin costars. **DR43, WE7, WE17**

Come and Get It (1936, B&W, 99m, NR)
Frances Farmer plays dual roles in this adventure story set in Wisconsin timber country. Edward Arnold and Joel McCrea star as the men in her life; Oscar winner Walter Brennan costars. A cult favorite, mainly for Farmer's amazing performance. Co-directed by Howard Hawks and William Wyler. **CL14, CL35, CL38, XT4** *Recommended*

Come Back to the Five and Dime, Jimmy Dean, Jimmy Dean (1982, C, 110m, NR)
A reunion of women who hung around the set of Dean's last film in a small Texas town is shaken up by the arrival of a stranger. Cher, Sandy Dennis, and Karen Black star; Robert Altman directed this drama. **CU25, MU12**

Come On, Rangers (1938, B&W, 54m, NR)
Roy Rogers and Gabby Hayes demonstrate the cowboy way in this musical western. **WE23**

Comes a Horseman (1978, C, 118m, PG)
A cattle baron plots to rustle up the land in his territory, but there's a feisty woman in his way. James Caan, Jane Fonda, Jason Robards star in this modern western. **DR27, WE9, WE13** *Recommended*

Comfort and Joy (1984, C, 93m, PG)
Disarmingly charming comedy about a Scottish disc jockey who looks for "meaning" in his life after his girlfriend leaves him; he gets involved in a feud between local ice cream truck companies. Bill Paterson stars; Bill Forsyth directed. **CO17, CU36** *Recommended*

Comic Relief 2 (1987, C, 120m, NR)
More great bits from the comedians' benefit concert to aid the homeless, hosted by Robin Williams, Billy Crystal, and Whoopi Goldberg. **CO16, CO43**

Comic Relief III (1989, C, 120m, NR)
More stand-up comedy from Billy Crystal, Whoopi Goldberg, Robin Williams, and friends in a benefit concert to aid the homeless. Among the guests: Bobcat Goldthwait, Arsenio Hall, Shelley Long, Garry Shandling, and Steven Wright. **CO16, CO43**

Coming Home (1978, C, 127m, R)
In the late 1960s, a crippled Vietnam vet, now opposed to the war, has an affair with the wife of a gung-ho Marine. Oscar winners Jon Voight and Jane Fonda star, with Bruce Dern, Penelope Milford, and Robert Carradine. **DR3, DR7, DR27, XT2, XT3**

Coming to America (1988, C, 116m, R)
Eddie Murphy comedy about an African prince who decides to look for a bride in the land of the brave and the home of the free. Arsenio Hall heads the supporting cast; he and Murphy play several character parts in disguises. With James Earl Jones, Madge Sinclair, John Amos, and Shari Headley. **CO13, CO37**

Commando (1985, C, 90m, R)
Former fighting man (Arnold Schwarzenegger) swings into action when nasties kidnap his daughter. A one-man army movie if ever there was one. Rae Dawn Chong costars. **AC25, AC30**

Commandos Strike at Dawn (1942, B&W, 96m, NR)
A Norwegian comes to the aid of British soldiers when Nazis invade his homeland. Paul Muni stars, with Anna Lee and Lillian Gish. **CL49**

Company of Wolves, The (1984, C, 95m, R)
Fantasy about a granny (Angela Lansbury) who tells various werewolf stories to her granddaughter (Sarah Patterson), which culminate in an erotic twist on the Little Red Riding Hood fairy tale. **IIO4, HO17**

Comperes, Les (1985, C, 109m, PG)
A French comedy about two bachelors with an ex-lover in common whose missing child may be one of theirs. Gerard Depardieu and Pierre Richard star. **FF1, FF29**

Competition, The (1980, C, 129m, PG)
Richard Dreyfuss and Amy Irving play rival pianists at a classical contest who fall in love. **DR12**

Compleat Beatles, The (1982, C, 120m, NR)
Documentary portrait of the four lads from Liverpool, packed with familiar and rare footage of their performances and fans. Narrated by Malcolm McDowell. **MU11** *Recommended*

Compromising Positions (1985, C, 99m, R)
Long Island housewife turns sleuth when her lecherous dentist is murdered. A suspense comedy starring Susan Sarandon, with Raul Julia, Judith Ivey, and Mary Beth Hurt. **CO10**

Computer Wore Tennis Shoes, The (1970, C, 91m, G)
A riotous Disney comedy with Kurt Russell as Dexter Riley, a college student who accidentally gets zapped by a computer and then has gangsters, gamblers, and college deans fighting for his knowledge. **FA1**

Conan the Barbarian (1982, C, 115m, R)
Arnold Schwarzenegger plays Robert Howard's pulp hero in this tale of his origins and battle against Thulsa Doom (James Earl Jones). With Max von Sydow and Sandahl Bergman; John Milius directed. **AC17, AC18, AC30**

Conan the Destroyer (1984, C, 101m, PG)
Arnold Schwarzenegger returns for more sword-wielding action. Grace Jones and Wilt Chamberlain costar. **AC17, AC18, AC30, MU12**

Concert for Bangladesh, The (1972, C, 90m, G)
Documentary of 1971 rock concert in Madison Square Garden to benefit victims of famine in Asia. George Harrison (who organized) performs, along with Bob Dylan, Leon Russell, and Ringo Starr. **MU10** *Recommended*

Concorde, The—Airport '79 (1979, C, 123m, PG)
Fourth *Airport* adventure has more mid-air disasters with an entirely new lineup of stars, featuring Robert Wagner, Alain Delon, Susan Blakely, Sylvia Kristel, John Davidson, and Martha Raye. **AC23**

Condorman (1981, C, 90m, PG)
A cartoonist is transformed into a super hero to help a lovely Russian spy to defect. Michael Crawford, Oliver Reed, and Barbara Carrera star; produced by the Disney studios in Britain. **AC17, FA1**

Confidentally Yours (1983, B&W, 110m, PG)
A French comedy-mystery about a wrong man framed for murder, while his devoted secretary tries to prove his innocence. Director François Truffaut's last film.

Based on Charles Williams' *The Long Saturday Night*. **FF13, MY20**

Conformist, The (1971, C, 115m, R)
In the 1930s, an Italian fascist is ordered to murder his former professor in this chilling drama from director Bernardo Bertolucci. Jean-Louis Trintignant, Dominique Sanda, and Stefania Sandrelli star. **FF18** *Recommended*

Connecticut Yankee in King Arthur's Court, A (1949, C, 107m, NR)
Bing Crosby plays Mark Twain's resourceful hero in this musical version of the time-travel tale. Rhonda Fleming, William Bendix, and Cedric Hardwicke costar. **FA3, FA9, MU8, MU25**

Conqueror, The (1956, C, 111m, NR)
John Wayne portrays the mighty warlord Genghis Khan in this adventure drama which has acquired a cult following. Susan Hayward costars. **AC16, CL17, CU2**

Conqueror Worm (1968, C, 98m, NR)
Horror tale set in Cromwell's England, about a lustful witchfinder (Vincent Price). Edgar Allan Poe's title poem is quoted, but the story is unrelated. A cult horror film directed by Michael Reeves. **CU4, HO26, HO31**

Conquest of the Planet of the Apes (1972, C, 87m, PG)
Fourth in the *Apes* series is a flashback story to the origin of the famed planet, and how the apes took control. Roddy McDowall stars. **FA8, SF8, SF13, SF23**

Consolation Marriage (1931, B&W, 82m, NR)
Drama of a couple who marry when their respective lovers desert them. Years later, they face a tough decision when their ex-lovers return. Pat O'Brien and Irene Dunne star, with John Halliday and Myrna Loy. **CL46**

Consuming Passions (1988, C, 98m, R)
Dark British comedy of a candy firm which discovers success with its new flavor—created when several workers accidentally fall into a vat of chocolate. Based on a play by Monty Python's Michael Palin and Terry Jones. Vanessa Redgrave and Jonathan Pryce star. **CO12, CO17, DR65**

Contempt (1963, C, 103m, NR)
Director Jean-Luc Godard's wry comedy about modern filmmaking, with respectable writer selling out to write a potboiler version of *The Odyssey*. Jack Palance stars, with Brigitte Bardot, Michel Piccoli, and Fritz Lang. **CL43, FF14, FF32** *Recommended*

Continental Divide (1981, C, 103m, PG)
A Chicago reporter and a Colorado ornithologist manage to find love on a disastrous hiking expedition in the Rockies. John Belushi and Blair Brown star. **CO1, CO13, XT9**

Control (1987, C, 83m, NR)
Fifteen people volunteer to be confined to a fallout shelter in an experiment. They're trapped when a real nuclear emergency occurs. Burt Lancaster stars, with Kate Nelligan and Ben Gazzara. **DR41**

Conversation, The (1974, C, 113m, PG)
Gene Hackman plays a professional surveillance man who thinks he's heard a couple plotting a murder. With John Cazale, Robert Duvall, Harrison Ford, Cindy Williams and Frederic Forrest. Brilliantly directed by Francis Ford Coppola on location in San Francisco. **DR7, DR32, DR37, DR39, DR51, MY15, XT9** *Highly Recommended*

Conversation Piece (1976, C, 112m, R)
A middle-aged professor becomes involved with a woman, her wild children, and her young lover. Burt Lancaster, Silvana Mangano, and Helmut Berger star; directed by Luchino Visconti. **DR41**

Convoy (1978, C, 110m, R)
A big rig driver (Kris Kristofferson), accompanied by his good buddies of the road, form the world's longest truck es-

cort. Directed by Sam Peckinpah. **AC10, MU12, WE19**

Coogan's Bluff (1968, C, 100m, R)
A modern-day sheriff pursues his quarry from the West to the streets of New York. Clint Eastwood stars, with Don Stroud and Susan Clark. Directed by Don Siegel. **AC9, AC27, WE13, XT9** *Recommended*

Cool and the Crazy, The (1958, B&W, 78m, NR)
1950s version of *Reefer Madness*, with high school kids "turned on" to marijuana, suffering dire consequences. **CU2**

Cool Hand Luke (1967, C, 126m, NR)
A rebellious prisoner on a Southern chain gang becomes a folk hero to his fellow cons. Paul Newman stars, with Oscar winner George Kennedy, Strother Martin, Harry Dean Stanton, Wayne Rogers, Clifton James, Joe Don Baker, Ralph Waite, Dennis Hopper, J.D. Cannon, and Jo Van Fleet. **CU46, CU49, DR18, DR28** *Highly Recommended*

Cop (1987, C, 110m, R)
James Woods plays a policeman at the breaking point in this intense drama, co-starring Lesley Ann Warren, Charles Durning, and Charles Haid. **DR16**

Copacabana (1947, B&W, 92m, NR)
Comedy about the mix-ups that occur at a famous New York nightclub when a girl applies for two different jobs. Groucho Marx and Carmen Miranda costar (their only film together), with Abel Green and Earl Wilson. **CO21**

Corn Is Green, The (1945, B&W, 114m, NR)
Bette Davis plays a middle-aged teacher who devotes much of her time and attention to one of her star pupils. **CL21**

Cornbread, Earl and Me (1975, C, 95m, R)
A black youth's idolization of a neighborhood basketball star is shattered when the older boy is accidentally shot by a policeman. Moses Gunn, Bernie Casey, Rosal-

ind Cash, and Keith (Jamal) Wilkes star. **DR14, DR15**

Cornered (1945, B&W, 102m, NR)
Thriller staring Dick Powell, who's on a manhunt in Buenos Aires chasing his wife's killer. Directed by Edward Dmytryk. **MY1, MY6**

Coroner Creek (1948, C, 93m, NR)
Randolph Scott western has him seeking revenge for the murder of his fiancée. **WE6, WE22**

Corpse Vanishes, The (1942, B&W, 64m, NR)
A scientist kidnaps young women to use in his rejuvenation serum for his elderly wife. Bela Lugosi stars. **HO28**

Corridors of Blood (1958, B&W, 86m, NR)
A 19th-century doctor experiments with a way to anesthetize patients, becomes addicted to one of the drugs he tries, and resorts to robbing graves to maintain his experiments. Boris Karloff stars, with Christopher Lee. **HO27, HO32**

Corrupt (1983, C, 99m, PG)
A New York cop (Harvey Keitel) finds himself immersed in illegal activities in order to catch a killer. Rock singer John Lydon costars, with Nicole Garcia and Sylvia Sidney. **MU12**

Corsican Brothers, The (1941, B&W, 112m, NR)
Classic swashbuckler, based on the Dumas tale of separated twins. Douglas Fairbanks, Jr. stars. **CL13**

Cotter (1973, C, 94m, NR)
An Indian rodeo clown returns to his small town to pick the pieces of his life after a tragic accident. Don Murray stars, with Rip Torn, Carol Lynley, and Sherry Jackson. **CU47, WE13**

Cotton Club, The (1984, C, 124m, R)
Colorful tale of Harlem's famed night spot, where gangsters and movie stars mingled to watch the likes of Duke Ellington and Cab Calloway perform. Richard

Gere, Diane Lane, Gregory Hines, Bob Hoskins, Fred Gwynne, and James Remar head the cast. Directed by Francis Ford Coppola. **AC22, DR5, DR14, DR15, DR51**

Couch Trip, The (1988, C, 98m, R)
Dan Aykroyd stars in this comedy about an escaped mental patient who takes over the radio call-in show of a vacationing therapist. Charles Grodin, Walter Matthau, and Donna Dixon costar. **CO13**

Count Dracula (1970, C, 98m, R)
Christopher Lee plays the vampire with an eye for ladies' necks. Klaus Kinski costars. **HO32, FF30**

Count Yorga, Vampire (1970, 90m, PG)
A vampire in modern Los Angeles holds seances as a way of attracting women into his lair. Robert Quarry stars. **HO5**

Countdown (1968, C, 101m, NR)
Drama centering on the approaching launch of a manned satellite, starring Robert Duvall and James Caan. Directed by Robert Altman. **CU25, DR37**

Country (1984, C, 109m, PG)
An embattled farm couple struggle to hold on to their land against overwhelming economic pressures. Jessica Lange and Sam Shepard star. **DR7, DR8, DR74**

Country Girl, The (1954, B&W, 104m, NR)
Drama of aging alcoholic singer trying for a comeback. Bing Crosby and Oscar winner Grace Kelly star; William Holden plays a director with a professional interest in Crosby and personal one in Grace. **CL31, CL51, MU25, XT3**

Country Girl, The (1982, C, 137m, NR)
Remake of the 1954 drama of an aging alcoholic actor (Dick Van Dyke), his younger wife (Faye Dunaway), and their director friend (Ken Howard). Originally made for TV. **DR35**

Country Music with the Muppets (1985, C, 55m, NR)
Compilation of favorite country music highlights from *The Muppet Show* feature Johnny Cash, Roy Clark, Crystal Gayle, and Roger Miller. **FA15**

Coup de Grace (1976, C, 96m, NR)
German drama of a countess pining for the love of a no-good military officer. Margarethe von Trotta stars; her husband, Volker Schlöndorff, directed. **FF3**

Coup de Torchon *see* Clean Slate

Courage (1986, C, 141m, NR)
In this true-life drama, Sophia Loren plays an American housewife who becomes a drug agent after she discovers that her own son is an addict. Billy Dee Williams costars. Originally made for TV. **DR6, DR10, FF31**

Court Jester, The (1956, C, 101m, NR)
Danny Kaye impersonates a clown; soon the joke's on him when a band of outlaws ask him to dethrone their nasty king. Glynis Johns, Basil Rathbone and Angela Lansbury costar in this comedy classic. **CL10, CO41**

Court-Martial of Billy Mitchell, The (1955, C, 100m, NR)
Gary Cooper stars as the Army officer whose obstreperous ways landed him in trouble with the brass in 1925. Charles Bickford, Ralph Bellamy, and Rod Steiger costar; directed by Otto Preminger. **CL26**

Cousin, Cousine (1975, C, 95m, R)
French comedy about an affair between two people who have become cousins by marriage. Marie-Christine Barrault and Victor Lanoux star. American remake: *Cousins*. **FF1, FF36**

Cousins (1989, C, 110m, R)
American remake of French romantic comedy *Cousin, Cousine*, with married man and woman falling in love at a wedding which is about to make them cousins. Ted Danson and Isabella Rossellini

star, with William Petersen, Sean Young, Lloyd Bridges, and Norma Aleandro. **CO1, FF36**

Cow Town (1950, B&W, 70m, NR)
Gene Autry's homesick on the range when ranchers take stake in their land with a fence war to protect it from cattle rustlers. **WE24**

Cowboy and the Señorita, The (1944, B&W, 56m, NR)
Roy Rogers finds a missing girl and wins the love of her cousin (Dale Evans). **WE23**

Cowboys, The (1972, C, 128m, PG)
A veteran cattleman is forced to employ a group of young boys on his 400-mile cattle drive. John Wayne stars, with Bruce Dern as a dastardly villain. **WE17**

Cracking Up (1983, C, 83m, PG)
Jerry Lewis comedy, a series of skits revolving around stories told by a suicidal patient to his shrink. With Herb Edelman, Dick Butkus, Sammy Davis, Jr., and Foster Brooks. Directed by Lewis; originally titled *Smorgasbord*. **CO25**

Cradle Will Fall, The (1983, C, 100m, NR)
Thriller about a desperate woman (Lauren Hutton) who can't convince her family and friends that she witnessed a murder. Ben Murphy and James Farentino costar. Originally made for TV. **MY3**

Craig's Wife (1936, B&W, 75m, NR)
Rosalind Russell plays a material girl who loves her possessions more than her man (John Boles). **CL5**

Crawling Eye, The (1958, B&W, 85m, NR)
A small town in the Swiss Alps is plagued by an immobile cloud and a series of gruesome murders. A psychic discovers that the cloud is an alien invader that resembles a large eye. **SF1, SF9**

Crawlspace (1986, C, 80m, R)
A landlord spies on his female tenants from an elaborate network in the ceilings of their apartments. Klaus Kinski stars in this horror drama. **FF30**

Crazies (1973, C, 103m, R)
A strange plague transforms and controls the inhabitants of a small town. Directed by George Romero. **HO21, HO38**

Crazy Mama (1975, C, 82m, R)
Crime saga, set in the 1950s, about a grandmother, mother, and daughter as they wend their way from California to Arkansas. Ann Sothern, Cloris Leachman, and Linda Purl star. Directed by Jonathan Demme. **AC9, CU39**

Creator (1985, C, 108m, R)
Peter O'Toole stars in this comedy-drama about a scientist who preserves some of his late wife's tissue in the hopes that he can recreate her in his laboratory. Mariel Hemingway, Vincent Spano, and Virginia Madsen costar; Ivan Passer directed. **CO2, DR45**

Creature (1985, C, 97m, R)
Science fiction horror drama about an expedition to one of Saturn's moons making a gruesome and deadly discovery. Stan Ivar and Klaus Kinski star. **FF30, SF20**

Creature From Black Lake, The (1976, C, 97m, PG)
Two men come across Bigfoot in a Louisiana swamp. Jack Elam stars. **HO16**

Creature From the Black Lagoon (1954, B&W, 79m, NR)
Trip to Amazon results in find of Gill-Man who lives underwater. Classic 1950s science fiction starring Richard Carlson, Julia Adams, Richard Denning, and Ricou Browning as the Creature. **SF1, SF10**

Creepers (1985, C, 82m, R)
A psychopath stalks a young girl who can communicate with insects via telepathy. Donald Pleasence and Jennifer Connelly star. Directed by Dario Argento. **HO7, HO16**

Creeping Flesh, The (1972, C, 91m, PG)
A scientist injects his daughter with an experimental serum which turns out to be the essence of evil. Peter Cushing and Christopher Lee star. **HO26, HO32, HO33**

Creepshow (1982, C, 120m, R)
Five tales of revenge by Stephen King filmed in the style of the old E.C. comic books. Hal Holbrook, Adrienne Barbeau, Leslie Nielsen, Ted Danson, and King star. Directed by George Romero. **HO23, HO38, HO42**

Creepshow 2 (1987, C, 89m, R)
George Romero adapted three Stephen King short stories for this sequel to *Creepshow*. Lois Chiles and George Kennedy stars. **HO23, HO38, HO42**

Cries and Whispers (1972, C, 106m, R)
Stunning drama from Ingmar Bergman about four women: three sisters (one of whom is dying) and their servant. Harriet Andersson, Liv Ullmann, Ingrid Thulin, and Kari Sylwan star. Oscar-winning photography by Sven Nykvist. **FF8, FF25** *Recommended*

Crimes of Passion (1984, C, 101m, R)
Successful businesswoman moonlights as a prostitute, runs into trouble from a crazed preacher. Kathleen Turner and Anthony Perkins star; Ken Russell directed. (An unrated version of the film is also available, containing more explicit sexual material.) **CU6, CU10, CU31, DR3, DR46**

Crimes of the Heart (1986, C, 105m, PG-13)
A trio of Southern sisters (Diane Keaton, Sissy Spacek, Jessice Lange) muddle through life in this adaptation of Beth Henley's play. Sam Shepard and Tess Harper costar. **CO5, DR20, DR40, DR68, DR74**

Criminal Code, The (1931, B&W, 98m, NR)
From director Howard Hawks comes the story of a young man convicted of manslaughter and sent off to prison. Walter

Huston, Phillips Holmes, Boris Karloff, and Constance Cummings star. **CL35, DR18, HO27** *Recommended*

Criminal Court (1946, B&W, 63m, NR)
A lawyer involved in a murder trial knows the defendant is innocent—because he committed the crime. Robert Wise directed this thriller starring Tom Conway. NOTE: Packaged on videocassette with *The Saint Strikes Back*. **CL58, MY7**

Criminal Law (1989, C, 113m, R)
After a young attorney successfully defends his client on a murder charge, he begins to suspect that the man really is a killer. Gary Oldman and Kevin Bacon star. **DR16, DR17, MY9**

Criminal Life of Archibaldo de la Cruz, The (1955, B&W, 91m, NR)
Offbeat drama from director Luis Buñuel of a man fascinated by death as a result of a childhood trauma. Also known as *Ensayo de un Crimen (Rehearsal of a Murder)*. **FF11**

Crimson Pirate, The (1952, C, 104m, NR)
Exhilirating pirate classic, with Burt Lancaster and former fellow acrobat Nick Cravat swinging, climbing, and somersaulting their way across the Mediterranean in this high-seas adventure. **AC13, DR41, FA4, HO32** *Highly Recommended*

Criss Cross (1949, B&W, 87m, NR)
Moody thriller with Burt Lancaster as a loser whose fatal flaw is his devotion to his deceitful ex-wife (Yvonne de Carlo). Tony Curtis's film debut. **MY1**

Critical Condition (1987, C, 99m, R)
A convict in the hospital for treatment finds himself mistaken for a doctor during a power failure. Richard Pryor stars in this comedy, with Rachel Ticotin, Ruben Blades, and Garrett Morris. **CO13, CO29**

Critters (1986, C, 86m, PG-13)
Hairy little aliens crashland in Kansas and proceed to eat all the humans they can. A little boy and two intergalactic hunters try to save the day. Dee Wallace

Stone and Scott Grimes star. **HO16, HO24**

Critters 2: The Main Course (1988, C, 87m, PG-13)
More chompin' by those furry little demons from outer space. Scott Grimes and Liane Curtis try to stay out of the sauce. **HO16, HO24**

"Crocodile" Dundee (1986, C, 102m, PG-13)
Romantic comedy with an international twist: an American journalist travels to Australia to interview a rough-and-tumble bush guide. He then comes to New York and learns how to "survive" in the urban jungle. Paul Hogan and Linda Kozlowski star. **CO1, CO9, CO37, FF5, XT9**

"Crocodile" Dundee II (1988, C, 110m, PG)
Sequel to the romantic comedy about an Australian bush guide (Paul Hogan) and his American sweetheart (Linda Kozlowski). This time, the couple's adventures begin in New York and continue Down Under. **CO1, CO9, CO37, FF5, XT9**

Cromwell (1970, C, 145m, G)
Richard Harris plays the British rebel soldier in this historical epic, with Alec Guinness, Robert Morley, Frank Finlay, and Timothy Dalton. **DR5, DR63**

Crooks and Coronets (1969, C, 106m, PG)
Telly Savalas and Warren Oates are con artists at work on an elderly English lady (Edith Evans) in this comedy. Also known as *Sophie's Place*. **CU48**

Cross Creek (1983, C, 122m, PG)
True story of author Marjorie Kinan Rawlings, who moved away from Long Island society in the 1920s to homestead in a Florida swamp and become a writer. Mary Steenburgen stars, with fine support from Rip Torn, Alfre Woodard, and Dana Hill. **CU47, DR4**

Cross My Heart (1987, C, 90m, R)
Comic chronicle of a modern couple's "crucial" third date, starring Martin Short and Annette O'Toole. **CO1, CO14**

Cross of Iron (1977, C, 119m, R)
Director Sam Peckinpah's first war film follows the lives of German officers (James Coburn and Maximilian Schell) amidst World War II. With James Mason. **AC1, WE19**

Crossed Swords *see* The Prince and the Pauper (1978)

Crossfire (1947, B&W, 86m, NR)
One of the first postwar films to explore the issue of bigotry. A Jewish man is beaten to death, and three soldiers are held for questioning. Robert Young stars, with Robert Mitchum and Robert Ryan. **CL8, MY1** *Recommended*

Crossing Delancey (1988, C, 97m, PG)
A New York woman finds herself the object of an arranged courtship in this romantic comedy-drama starring Amy Irving and Peter Riegert, with Reizl Bozyk, Jeroen Krabbe and Sylvia Miles. **CO1, DR10, DR15, XT9** *Recommended*

Crossover Dreams (1985, C, 86m, NR)
Musical drama about a salsa singing star (Ruben Blades) who gets a swelled head over his forthcoming album. **MU4**

Crossroads (1986, C, 100m, R)
Young guitar player journeys the Mississippi back roads in search of someone to teach him authentic blues licks. Ralph Macchio and Joe Seneca star; Walter Hill directed. Music by Ry Cooder. **DR12, CU27**

Crowd, The (1928, B&W, 104m, NR)
Classic silent drama from director King Vidor about the triumphs and tragedies of an "ordinary" couple living in New York. Eleanor Boardman and James Murray star. **CL8, CL12** *Recommended*

Crucible of Horror (1971, C, 91m, PG)
A man murdered by a member of his family comes back to haunt them. **HO14**

Cruising (1980, C, 106m, R)
A New York cop goes undercover to solve a series of murders in the gay community. Al Pacino stars. **DR16, DR66**

Crusoe (1989, C, 95m, PG-13)
The classic adventure tale of a marooned man, this time portrayed as an American slave trader (Aidan Quinn). Written by Walon Green; directed by Caleb Deschanel. **AC12, AC24** *Recommended*

Cry Freedom (1987, C, 157m, PG)
True drama of South African activist Steven Biko and his friendship with white reporter Donald Woods, who smuggled the story of Biko's torture and death to the outside world. Denzel Washington and Kevin Kline star; Richard Attenborough directed. **DR6, DR14**

Cry in the Dark, A (1988, C, 122m, PG-13)
Australian fact-based drama about the sensational case of Lindy Chamberlain, a mother accused of murdering her infant baby (whom she claimed was carried off by a wild dog). Meryl Streep and Sam Neill star. Directed by Fred Schepisi. **DR6, DR17, DR26, FF5** *Recommended*

Cry of the Banshee (1970, C, 87m, PG)
A witch and a satanist seek revenge against a nobleman who is on a witch hunt. Vincent Price stars. **HO31**

Cuba (1979, C, 121m, PG)
Love story set against the downfall of dictator Batista and rise of Castro, starring Sean Connery and Brooke Adams. Directed by Richard Lester. **AC36, CU35** *Recommended*

Cuban Rebel Girls *see* Assault of the Rebel Girls

Cujo (1983, C, 91m, R)
Stephen King story about a woman and her son who are being terrorized by a rabid dog. Dee Wallace stars. **HO16, HO42**

Culpepper Cattle Company, The (1972, C, 92m, PG)
A western cult favorite about a 16-year-old boy who quickly becomes a man when he joins a cattle drive through violent post-Civil War Texas. Gary Grimes stars, with Billy "Green" Bush, Luke Askew, and Bo Hopkins. **WE16**

Curly Top (1935, B&W, 75m, NR)
Shirley Temple classic finds the greatest child star of them all playing matchmaker and singing "Animal Crackers in My Soup." **FA14**

Curse, The (1987, C, 90m, PG-13)
A meteorite lands on a farm in Tennessee, and soon everyone in the family, except the young son, is acting strangely. Wil Wheaton and John Schneider star. **HO14, HO21**

Curse of Frankenstein, The (1957, C, 83m, NR)
The first horror film from Britain's Hammer Studios, about Mary Shelley's doctor who becomes obsessed by his experiments and his creation. Peter Cushing, Christopher Lee, and Hazel Court star. **HO20, HO26, HO32, HO33**

Curse of the Cat People, The (1944, B&W, 70m, NR)
A lonely little girl is befriended by the ghost of her father's first wife in this sequel to *Cat People*. Produced by Val Lewton; directed by Robert Wise. **CL58, HO2, HO14, HO36**

Curse of the Demon (1957, B&W, 82m, NR)
An American professor (Dana Andrews) comes face to face with the dark side of the occult when he tries to solve the mysterious death of a colleague. Directed by Jacques Tourneur. **HO1, HO11, HO19, HO37**

Curse of the Pink Panther (1983, C, 109m, PG)
The final Pink Panther film, made after Peter Sellers' death, with Ted Wass playing Inspector Clouseau. Cameo appear-

ances by Panther alumni David Niven, Herbert Lom, Bert Kwouk, and Capucine. Directed by Blake Edwards. **CO46**

Curse of the Werewolf, The (1961, C, 91m, NR)
A servant girl is raped and eventually gives birth to a son who, when he reaches adulthood, discovers that strange things happen to him when the moon is full. Oliver Reed stars. **HO4, HO26**

Cut and Run (1985, C, 87m, R)
A pair of ambitious reporters stumble onto a big scoop when they travel to South America in search of an evil disciple of Jim Jones. Lisa Blount, Willie Aames, and Karen Black star. **AC24**

Cutter's Way (1981, C, 105m, R)
A moody mystery set in Santa Barbara, California, involving a cynical, crippled Vietnam vet (John Heard), his alcoholic girl friend (Lisa Eichorn), and their beach bum pal (Jeff Bridges). They set out to prove that a local pillar of society is involved in a sordid murder case. **DR7, DR71, MY2** *Recommended*

Cyborg (1989, C, 85m, R)
Martial arts star Jean Claude Van Damme plays the title role in this post-apocalyptic tale of revenge. **AC24, AC26, SF12**

Cyclops (1957, B&W, 75m, NR)
An expedition discovers the man they are searching for has been transformed into a monster by a radiation blast. Gloria Talbott, Lon Chaney, Jr., and Tom Drake star. Directed by Bert I. Gordon. **HO21, HO30**

Cyrano de Bergerac (1950, B&W, 112m, NR)
Jose Ferrer won an Oscar for his portrayal of the long-nosed romantic of Edmond Rostand's play. **DR20, XT2**

D.A.R.Y.L. (1985, C, 99m, PG)
A young boy (Barrett Oliver) baffles his parents because he is too "perfect." He soon becomes the most popular kid around—wanted even by the government.

Michael McKean and Mary Beth Hurt costar. **DR9, FA7**

D.C. Cab (1983, C, 99m, R)
Amiable comedy about a wacked-out collection of cabbies cruising the streets of Our Nation's Capital. Adam Baldwin stars, with Max Gail, Gary Busey, Mr. T, and Irene Cara. **XT9**

D-Day the Sixth of June (1956, C, 106m, NR)
Dramatic recreation of the Normandy invasion, starring Robert Taylor and Richard Todd as, respectively, American and British officers. **AC1**

D.O.A. (1949, B&W, 83m, NR)
A man is given poison—he has a few days to find his killer. Edmond O'Brien stars in this classic thriller. **MY1**

D.O.A. (1988, C, 96m, R)
Remake of the film noir classic, with Dennis Quaid as the poisoning victim trying to track down his killer. Meg Ryan costars. **CU18, MY2**

D.W. Griffith Triple Feature (1913, B&W, 50m, NR)
A trio of short films from the movies' first great director: *The Battle of Elderbush Gulch, Iola's Promise,* and *The Goddess of Sagebrush Gulch.* Lillian Gish, Mary Pickford, and Mae Marsh are among the stars. **CL36, CL49**

Da (1988, C, 102m, PG)
An Irish-American playwright returns to his homeland when his father dies. The old man's ghost confronts his son as they recall their good and bad times together. Martin Short and Barnard Hughes star; based on Hugh Leonard's play. **DR8, DR20**

Daffy Duck: The Nuttiness Continues . . . (1956, C, 59m, NR)
Daffy's very own collection of cartoon classics, including *Beanstalk Bunny, Deduce You Say, Dripalong Daffy,* and *The Scarlet Pumpernickel.* **FA11**

Daffy Duck's Movie: Fantastic Island (1983, C, 78m, G)
Collection of ten classic Warner Bros. cartoon features Speedy Gonzales, Bugs Bunny, Porky Pig, Sylvester, Tweety, Pepe Le Pew, Pirate Sam, Foghorn Leghorn, and of course, Daffy Duck, who provides linking storyline that spoofs TV's *Fantasy Island*. **FA11**

Dain Curse, The (1978, C, 118m, NR)
James Coburn and Jean Simmons star in this Dashiell Hammett thriller. A private eye assigned to a relatively easy case of theft uncovers a series of complex murders in the process. Originally made for TV. **MY28**

Daisy Miller (1974, C, 91m, G)
Cybill Shepherd stars as the heroine of Henry James's comic novel about a headstrong American girl touring the Continent. With Barry Brown, Cloris Leachman, Mildred Natwick, and Eileen Brennan. Directed by Peter Bogdanovich. **DR19**

Dakota (1945, B&W, 82m, NR)
John Wayne battles land grabbers in this western saga. Vera Miles costars. **WE17**

Daleks: Invasion Earth 2150 A.D. (1966, C, 81m, NR)
Dr. Who travels to London 2150 A.D. and helps out a small band of resistance fighters in their battle against the Daleks, robots who want to kill all humans. Peter Cushing and Bernard Cribbens star. **HO33, SF4, SF19**

Dames (1934, B&W, 90m, NR)
Busby Berkeley's film about a millionaire who tries to prevent the opening of a Broadway show. Dick Powell and Ruby Keeler costar. **MU4, MU20**

Damien: Omen II (1978, C, 110m, R)
Sequel to *The Omen* opens seven years later, with Damien a student at a military academy where he discovers his true identity as the anti-christ. William Holden and Lee Grant star as Damien's uncle and aunt, who are now his legal guardians. **CL51, HO10, HO13**

Damn the Defiant! (1962, C, 101m, NR)
Adventure of sea battles during Napoleonic wars, with Dirk Bogarde and Alec Guinness on opposing sides. **AC6, DR63**

Damn Yankees (1958, C, 110m, NR)
Musical fantasy of baseball fan who makes deal with the Devil to be a young star who will help his Washington Senators beat the hated New York Yankees. Tab Hunter, Ray Walston, and Gwenn Verdon star. Directed by Stanley Donen and George Abbott. Choreography by Bob Fosse. **HO10, MU2, MU6, MU23, MU28** *Recommended*

Damnation Alley (1977, C, 91m, PG)
Five survivors of a nuclear holocaust travel the wasteland in search of other human life. Jan-Michael Vincent, George Peppard, Dominique Sanda, Paul Winfield, and Jackie Earle Haley star. **SF12**

Damned, The (1969, C, 146m, R)
A dark portrait from Italian director Luchino Visconti of a decadent family of German arms merchants and their ties to the Third Reich. Dirk Bogarde, Ingrid Thulin, Helmut Griem, Helmut Berger, and Charlotte Rampling star in this controversial drama, originally rated "X." **FF2**

Damsel in Distress, A (1937, B&W, 101m, NR)
George Gershwin musical comedy stars Fred Astaire as a London dancer who pursues Joan Fontaine. George Burns and Gracie Allen costar. George Stevens directed. **CL42, MU18**

Dance With a Stranger (1985, C, 101m, R)
The true story of Ruth Ellis (Miranda Richardson), a divorced woman who killed her younger lover (Rupert Everett) and was hanged for her crime—the last woman in Britain to be executed. Ian Holm costars. **DR6, DR16, DR23, MY2, MY8, MY19** *Recommended*

Dancers (1987, C, 97m, PG)
Mikhail Baryshnikov stars in this drama about the ballet world, with a pair of dancers imitating in real life the love story they're performing on stage. Directed by Herbert Ross. **DR12**

Dancing Lady (1933, B&W, 94m, NR)
Clark Gable romances dancer Joan Crawford in this backstage musical that also features Fred Astaire in his film debut and comic relief from the original Three Stooges. **CL7, CL23, CL50, CU17, MU18**
Recommended

The Dancing Princesses (1984, C, 60m, NR)
A princess (Lesley Ann Warren) teaches her overly strict father a lesson when his daughters break out of their locked rooms and into their dancing slippers with the help of a handsome prince (Peter Weller). From The Faerie Tale Theatre series. **FA12**

Dandy in Aspic, A (1968, C, 107m, NR)
A Russian double agent (Laurence Harvey) tires of his dangerous profession but can see no way out. With Tom Courtenay and Mia Farrow. Director Anthony Mann died during production; Harvey finished the film. **MY6, WE20**

Dangerous Liaisons (1988, C, 120m, R)
Intrigue in 18th-century France, with villainous schemers John Malkovich and Glenn Close plotting to divest innocent wife Michelle Pfeiffer of her virtue. With Uma Thurman, Keanu Reeves, and Swoosie Kurtz; Christopher Hampton adapted his play. **DR1, DR5, DR20, DR72**
Recommended

Dangerous Mission (1954, C, 75m, NR)
A witness to a gangland killing flees across country with the killers in hot pursuit. Piper Laurie and Vincent Price star. **HO31**

Dangerous Moves (1984, C, 95m, PG)
Oscar-winning drama from Switzerland about an international chess match and the behind-the-scenes machinations that accompany it. Michel Piccoli, Leslie Caron, and Liv Ullmann star. **FF25, XT7**

Dangerously Close (1986, C, 95m, R)
Melodrama of a society of high school vigilantes bullying kids who don't fit their clean-cut standards. John Stockwell stars. **DR61**

Daniel (1983, C, 130m, R)
Drama about a brother and sister whose parents were executed as spies in the 1950s and how that event still haunts them years later. Timothy Hutton and Amanda Plummer star, with Lindsay Crouse, Mandy Patinkin, Ed Asner, and Ellen Barkin. Based on E.L. Doctorow's novel, *The Book of Daniel;* directed by Sidney Lumet. **DR5, DR19, DR58**

Danton (1982, C, 136m, PG)
Drama in French from Polish director Andrzej Wajda, about the stormy days of the French Revolution. Gerard Depardieu stars in the title role. **FF29**

Darby O'Gill and the Little People (1959, C, 90m, G)
Deep in the emerald forest of Ireland, a weaver of tall tales falls into the land of leprechauns in this Disney fantasy. An early role for Sean Connery. **AC36, FA1**

Dark Command (1940, B&W, 94m, NR)
In Civil War Kansas, John Wayne is the town marshal who clashes with local vigilante leader Walter Pidgeon. With Claire Trevor, Gabby Hayes, and Roy Rogers. **WE7, WE17, WE23**

Dark Crystal, The (1983, C, 93m, PG)
Fantasy adventure from director Jim Henson and producer George Lucas, about the quest to replace the missing shard in the all-powerful Dark Crystal. Family entertainment, packed with unique creatures. **FA8, SF13**

Dark Eyes (1987, C, 118m, NR)
Marcello Mastroianni stars in this comedy-drama about a faded Italian aristocrat who takes one last, mad fling at love. **FF2, FF24**

Dark Forces (1980, C, 96m, PG)
An updating of the Rasputin story, about a faith healer who gains access into a Senator's family by apparently curing the son, then developing a psychic power over the Senator. Robert Powell stars. **HO7**

Dark Habits (1984, C, 116m, NR)
Irreverent comedy by Spanish director Pedro Almodóvar: a singer on the lam hides out in convent. Christina Pascual, Julieta Serrano, and Carmen Maura star. **FF7**

Dark Journey (1937, B&W, 82m, NR)
Romantic suspense with Vivien Leigh as a World War I British spy who gets involved with a German intelligence officer (Conrad Veidt) while in Stockholm. **MY6**

Dark Mirror, The (1946, B&W, 85m, NR)
Twin sisters, one evil and the other good, are implicated in a murder case. Olivia de Havilland plays both sisters. **MY1, MY4, MY18**

Dark Passage (1947, B&W, 106m, NR)
An escaped convict (Humphrey Bogart) undergoes plastic surgery to cover up his identity while a beautiful girl (Lauren Bacall) tries to prove his innocence. **CL15, CL20, MY1**

Dark Past, The (1948, B&W, 75m, NR)
Hostage tale of a psycho killer and a psychologist. William Holden and Lee J. Cobb star. **CL51**

Dark Places (1973, C, 91m, PG)
Three people out to defraud a man of his inheritance are haunted by the ghost of a murderer. Christopher Lee and Joan Collins star. **HO32**

Dark Secret of Harvest Home, The (1978, C, 200m, NR)
A New York City family moves to a small town in New England. A mysterious old woman (Bette Davis) slowly draws the wife and daughter into her circle while the husband tries to solve some mysteri-

ous happenings. Originally made for TV. **CL21, HO11**

Dark Star (1974, C, 83m, PG)
Low-budget science fiction adventure from director John Carpenter that pokes fun at sci-fi epics such as *2001*. **CU4, CU29, SF21**

Dark Victory (1939, B&W, 106m, NR)
A young woman (Bette Davis) with a fatal disease decides to live her last few months to the fullest in this classic love story. George Brent and Humphrey Bogart costar, with Geraldine Fitzgerald and Ronald Reagan. **CL4, CL6, CL20, CL21**

Darling (1965, C, 122m, NR)
Drama of a successful London fashion model and her inability to find real love or meaning in her life. Oscar winner Julie Christie stars, with Dirk Bogarde and Laurence Harvey. Written by Frederic Raphael; directed by John Schlesinger. **DR10, DR23, XT3, XT9** *Recommended*

Date With Judy, A (1948, C, 113m, NR)
Comedy with music revolving around two mischievous teenagers and their families. Wallace Beery, Jane Powell, Elizabeth Taylor, and Carmen Miranda star. **CL33**

Daughters of Darkness (1971, C, 87m, R)
Horror film with a cult following about a pair of lesbian vampires who prey on honeymooning couples. Filmed in France; Delphine Seyrig stars. **CU4, CU6, HO5**

David and Bathsheba (1951, C, 116m, NR)
Gregory Peck and Susan Hayward play the title roles in this religious drama of the Biblical king and his consort. **CL13**

David and Lisa (1963, B&W, 94m, NR)
Two mentally disturbed young people meet in a therapy session and develop a friendship that slowly blossoms into romance. Keir Dullea and Janet Margolin star, with Howard Da Silva. Written by Eleanor Perry; directed by Frank Perry. **DR9**

David Copperfield (1935, B&W, 130m, NR)
An all-star production of the life and times of Charles Dickens' character in Victorian England. Directed by George Cukor. Freddie Bartholomew, Frank Lawton, W.C. Fields, Lionel Barrymore, Roland Young, Basil Rathbone, Maureen O'Sullivan, and many more star. **CL1, CL39, CO22, FA3** *Recommended*

Davy Crockett (1955, C, 88m, G)
Disney portrait of the King of the Wild Frontier (Fess Parker), as he takes on wild bears and nasty Indians before making his last stand at the Alamo. Buddy Ebsen costars. **FA1**

Davy Crockett and the River Pirates (1956, C, 81m, G)
Two episodes from the Disney TV series: Davy and riverboat king Mike Fink (Jeff York) square off in a boat race; Davy and his sidekick George Russell (Buddy Ebsen) take on some pesky Indians. **FA1**

Dawn of the Dead (1979, C, 126m, NR)
Gruesome and darkly funny sequel to *Night of the Living Dead* finds a quartet of humans holed up in an abandoned shopping mall besieged by flesh-eating zombies. George Romero directed. **CU1, CU4, CU7, HO6, HO18, HO38** *Recommended*

Dawn Patrol, The (1938, B&W, 82m, NR)
World War I drama of brave pilots on the edge of collapse from exhaustion, starring David Niven and Errol Flynn. **AC2, AC11, AC34** *Recommended*

Day After, The (1983, C, 126m, NR)
Controversial portrait of America undergoing nuclear attack and the attendant devastation. Jason Robards, JoBeth Williams, Steve Guttenberg, and John Lithgow star. Nicholas Meyer directed; originally made for TV. **DR7, SF12**

Day at the Races, A (1937, B&W, 111m, NR)
The Marx Bros. invade a race track. Chico sells tutti-frutti ice cream and hot tips on the ponies. Margaret Dumont tries to ignore him. **CO21**

Day for Night (1973, C, 120m, PG)
Loving look at filmmaking from director François Truffaut, who also plays the director of a romantic comedy with behind-the-scenes crises, affairs, hopes, and dreams. Jean-Pierre Leaud, Jacqueline Bisset, Jean-Pierre Aumont, and Valentina Cortese costar. Oscar winner for Best Foreign Film. **DR13, FF13, XT7** *Recommended*

Day in the Country, A (1936, B&W, 36m, NR)
French director Jean Renoir's short film, about a family's outing, suggests some of the inspirations for the Impressionist painters like his father. A mini-classic. **FF12** *Recommended*

Day in the Death of Joe Egg, A (1972, C, 106m, R)
Darkly comic story of a British couple trying to deal with their severely handicapped daughter. Alan Bates and Janet Suzman star in this adaptation of Peter Nichols' play. **CO12, CO17, DR20**

Day of the Dead (1985, C, 91m, NR)
The third of the . . . *Dead* trilogy that began with *Night of the Living* and continued with *Dawn of the* has the zombies in control of everything and the last of the humans in a bunker waiting for the final battle. Directed by George Romero. **HO6, HO18, HO38**

Day of the Dolphin, The (1973, C, 104m, PG)
A marine biologist uses his trained dolphins to thwart an assassination plot. George C. Scott stars; Mike Nichols directed. **DR75, FA5**

Day of the Jackal, The (1973, C, 141m, PG)
Thriller based on the Frederick Forsyth bestseller about a young British assassin's plot to kill DeGaulle in Paris and French officials' desperate race to catch him. Edward Fox stars; directed by Fred

Zinnemann. **CL57, MY6, MY31, XT9**
Recommended

Day of the Locust, The (1975, C, 144m, R)
Drama about the dark underside of Hollywood in the 1930s, with an impressionable painter meeting a gallery of grotesque show-biz characters. Adapted from Nathanael West's classic novel. William Atherton stars, with Donald Sutherland, Karen Black, Burgess Meredith, and Geraldine Page. **DR13, DR19, XT9** *Recommended*

Day of the Triffids, The (1963, C, 95m, NR)
Science fiction drama about blinding meteor showers and invasion of mutant monsters. Howard Keel stars in this British production. **SF7, SF19**

Day of Wrath (1943, B&W, 110m, NR)
From Danish director Carl Dreyer, a tale of 16th-century superstition and revenge. An old woman, accused of witchcraft, places a curse on the clergyman who fingered her. **FF35**

Day the Earth Caught Fire, The (1962, B&W, 99m, NR)
The Earth comes dangerously close to the sun in this British science fiction drama starring Edward Judd and Leo McKern. **SF7, SF19**

Day the Earth Stood Still, The (1951, B&W, 92m, NR)
Classic 1950s science fiction drama, with spaceship landing in Washington, D.C., alien trying to warn Earth of its disastrous nuclear arms race. Michael Rennie, Sam Jaffe, Patricia Neal, Billy Gray, and "Gort" star. Robert Wise directed. **CL58, CU4, FA8, SF1, SF9, XT9** *Highly Recommended*

Day Time Ended, The (1980, C, 79m, PG)
Family living in the desert experience a strange alien visitation. Jim Davis, Dorothy Malone, and Christopher Mitchum star. Also known as *Time Warp*. **SF9**

Daydreamer, The (1966, C, 98m, NR)
Live action mixes with animation in this tale of a young Hans Christian Andersen thinking of the fairy tale characters he will later write about. Jack Gilford and Margaret Hamilton star, with the voices of Boris Karloff and Tallulah Bankhead. **HO27**

Days of Heaven (1978, C, 95m, PG)
Romantic drama, set in Texas wheatfields at the turn of the century, about a farm owner who woos an itinerant worker, only to find that her "brother" is really her lover. Stunning photography by Nestor Almendros and Haskell Wexler won an Oscar. Richard Gere, Brooke Adams, Sam Shepard, and Linda Manz star. Directed by Terrence Malick; music by Ennio Morricone. **CU37, DR1** *Highly Recommended*

Days of Jesse James (1939, B&W, 63m, NR)
Roy Rogers plays the notorious outlaw in one of his early films. **WE2, WE23**

Days of Wine and Roses, The (1962, B&W, 117m, NR)
Drama of an alcoholic couple and how they ruin their lives before one of them makes a recovery. Jack Lemmon and Lee Remick star; Blake Edwards directed. **CO46, DR7, DR64** *Recommended*

Dead, The (1987, C, 82m, PG)
James Joyce's short story is the basis for this drama of family life in turn-of-the-century Dublin, centering around a holiday party and the memories it evokes. Anjelica Huston stars; her father, John, directed—his last film. **CL44, DR19**

Dead and Buried (1981, C, 92m, R)
A sheriff looks into a series of bizarre murders and discovers that some of his neighbors are actually zombies. James Farentino, Melody Anderson, and Jack Albertson star. **HO6**

Dead-Bang (1989, C, 105m, R)
Don Johnson stars in a crime saga of a relentless police detective whose pursuit

of a cop killer uncovers a nest of verminous white supremacists. **AC9**

Dead Calm (1989, C, 96m, R)
Australian suspense drama has a couple on a yacht encountering a stranger on another boat who, they belatedly discover, has murdered all on board. Sam Neill, Nicole Kidman, and Billy Zane star. Phillip Noyce directed. **FF5**

Dead End (1937, B&W, 93m, NR)
Drama set on New York's Lower East Side during the Depression. Sylvia Sidney, Joel McCrea, and Humphrey Bogart star, with the film debut of The Dead End Kids, later The Bowery Boys. Directed by William Wyler. **CL8, CL20, CL38** *Recommended*

Dead Heat (1988, C, 86m, R)
Buddy-cop/horror story, with a pair of detectives (Joe Piscopo, Treat Williams) on the trail of a mad doctor who's reviving criminals from the dead. **AC9, CO13, HO6**

Dead Heat on a Merry-Go-Round (1966, C, 107m, NR)
Heist drama centering on the robbery of an airport bank. Plenty of twists and double crosses. James Coburn stars, with Camilla Sparv, Aldo Ray, and Ross Martin. Harrison Ford makes a brief appearance, in his first film. **DR32, MY34**

Dead Men Don't Wear Plaid (1982, B&W, 91m, PG)
A comedy thriller starring Steve Martin as a private detective with a very bizarre assortment of suspects. Includes scenes from many film noir classics of the 1940s skillfully woven into the story. Directed by Carl Reiner. **CO7, CO33, MY21**

Dead Men Walk (1943, B&W, 64m, NR)
An evil twin involved with the black arts resorts to vampirism to get back at his good brother. **HO15**

Dead of Night (1945, B&W, 102m, NR)
An architect discovers that the cottage he is to redesign and its occupants are ex-

actly the same as in his recurring nightmare. His story prompts the other guests to tell of their own brushes with the supernatural. Highlight: the tale of the nervous ventriloquist and his independent dummy, featuring Michael Redgrave. **HO1, HO2, HO23, HO26**

Dead of Night (1973) *see* Deathdream

Dead of Winter (1987, C, 100m, R)
An aspiring actress (Mary Steenburgen) is lured to a remote farmhouse with the promise of a movie role. Once there, she finds herself trapped by a bizarre game of deception. Roddy MacDowall costars. **MY3**

Dead Pool, The (1988, C 91m, R)
Clint Eastwood's fifth outing as Dirty Harry has him trailing a killer with a hit list of San Francisco celebrities—a list which includes Harry. **AC9, AC27, XT9**

Dead Reckoning (1947, B&W, 100m, NR)
A World War II veteran (Humphrey Bogart) attempts to solve the murder of a fellow officer. **CL20, MY1, MY4**

Dead Ringers (1988, C, 117m, R)
Disturbing psychological study of twin doctors who share an apartment, a gynecological practice—and more. Jeremy Irons stars as both twins, with Genevieve Bujold. Brilliantly directed by David Cronenberg; based loosely on a true story. **DR8, HO15, HO39** *Recommended*

Dead Zone, The (1983, C, 104m, R)
An accident victim comes out of a coma after five years and discovers he now has psychic powers. Christopher Walken, Martin Sheen, Brooke Adams, and Tom Skerritt star. Directed by David Cronenberg; based on a novel by Stephen King. **HO7, HO19, HO39, HO42**

Deadline at Dawn (1946, B&W, 83m, NR)
A mystery with Susan Hayward as an aspiring actress who tries to clear the name of a sailor accused of murder. Written by Clifford Odets. **MY1, MY15**

Deadly Blessing (1981, C, 102m, R)
A young couple move to a farm that borders the compound of a community called The Hittites. A series of strange murders begins. Maren Jenson and Lisa Hartman star. Directed by Wes Craven. **HO11**

Deadly Companions, The (1961, C, 90m, NR)
Brian Keith plays a tough gunfighter who accidentally kills the son of a dance hall girl (Maureen O'Hara). Director Sam Peckinpah's first film. **WE19**

Deadly Friend (1987, C, 91m, R)
A teenaged genius has two friends—the girl next door and his special robot. When the girl dies, he pushes his experiments into a deadly realm. Directed by Wes Craven. **HO20**

Deadly Illusion (1987, C, 87m, R)
A detective is framed for murder in this thriller starring Billy Dee Williams, with Vanity, Morgan Fairchild, and John Beck. Written and co-directed by Larry Cohen. **CU30**

Deadly Sanctuary (1970, C, 93m, R)
Horror drama focusing on the writings of the Marquis De Sade (Klaus Kinski), starring Jack Palance, Sylvia Koscina, and Mercedes McCambridge. **FF30**

Deal of the Century (1983, C, 99m, PG)
Chevy Chase stars in this satire on the arms race; he plays a fast-talking salesman of high-tech military hardware. Gregory Hines and Sigourney Weaver costar. **CO13, DR76**

Dear America: Letters Home From Vietnam (1987, C/B&W, 87m, NR)
Moving documentary composed of TV news footage and home movies of the war in Vietnam, with a soundtrack of actual letters written by servicemen and nurses (read by such stars as Robin Williams, Robert DeNiro, Kathleen Turner), plus well-chosen pop and rock music of the period. Originally made for cable TV. **AC4, CU16** *Recommended*

Dear Brigitte (1965, C, 100m, NR)
James Stewart stars in a comedy about an 8-year-old boy's infatuation with French "sex kitten" Brigitte Bardot. Glynis Johns and Fabian costar; Bardot makes a guest appearance. **CL25, FF32**

Dear Detective (1977, C, 105m, NR)
A French thriller starring Annie Girardot as a detective who takes time out from several murder investigations for a little romance with a college professor. Also known as *Dear Inspector*. **FF1, MY20**

Dear Inspector *see* Dear Detective

Dear Wife (1949, B&W, 88m, NR)
William Holden stars in this comedy about an aspiring politician competing against a much older man (Edward Arnold) for state office. **CL51**

Death Before Dishonor (1986, C, 95m, R)
A Marine sergeant (Fred Dryer) and his elite unit track down a terrorist in the Middle East. **AC20**

Death Hunt (1981, C, 97m, R)
A Mountie (Lee Marvin) pursues a trapper (Charles Bronson) accused of murder across the frozen Canadian landscape. **AC12, AC29, DR43**

Death in Venice (1971, C, 130m, PG)
Italian drama, based on Thomas Mann novel, of a composer's final days in Venice, as he struggles to come to terms with his homosexuality and art. Dirk Bogarde stars; Luchino Visconti directed. **FF2**

Death Kiss, The (1933, B&W, 75m, NR)
During the filming of a movie, an actor is murdered. Bela Lugosi and David Manners star. **HO28**

Death of a Salesman (1985, C, 150m, NR)
Dustin Hoffman plays Willy Loman in the latest adaptation of the classic Arthur Miller play. Kate Reid, John Malkovich, Stephen Lang, and Charles Durning costar. Directed by Volker Schlöndorff. Originally made for TV. **DR8, DR20, DR30**

Death on the Nile (1978, C, 140m, PG)
An all-star production of the Agatha Christie novel, in which the famed Hercule Poirot (Peter Ustinov) must determine who killed an heiress aboard ship. Bette Davis, Angela Lansbury, and David Niven star. **CL21, MY16, MY23**

Death Race 2000 (1975, C, 78m, R)
Low-budget science fiction adventure about a road race that awards points for hitting pedestrians. David Carradine, Sylvester Stallone, and Mary Woronov star; Paul Bartel directed. Sequel: *Deathsport.* **AC10, AC31, CU4, CU42, SF21**

Death Sentence (1974, C, 78m, NR)
A juror discovers that the wrong man is on trial for murder when her husband is revealed as a killer. Cloris Leachman stars, with Nick Nolte. Originally made for TV. **DR44**

Death Valley (1982, C, 87m, R)
A young boy visiting Arizona is witness to a murder and flees for his life from a psychotic killer. Paul LeMat, Catherine Hicks, Peter Billingsley, and Stephen McHattie star. **AC24**

Death Wish (series)
Death Wish (1974, C, 93m, R)
Death Wish II (1982, C, 89m, R)
Death Wish III (1985, C, 100m, R)
Death Wish IV: The Crackdown (1987, C, 100m, R)
Charles Bronson plays Paul Kersey in these violent action melodramas. In the first film, his wife is killed and his daughter brutally assaulted by street thugs, and he goes on a vigilante-style killing spree. Subsequent chapters have him in both New York and Los Angeles, dealing out his brand of justice to criminals. **AC19, AC29, XT9** (first film)

Deathdream (1973, C, 90m, PG)
A veteran is discovered to be responsible for a series of murders because he is a zombie in need of human blood. Directed by Bob Clark. Also known as *Dead of Night.* **HO6**

Deathsport (1978, C, 82m, R)
Sequel to *Death Race 2000,* with deadly road race featuring killer cycles. David Carradine and Claudia Jennings star; Allan Arkush directed. **AC10, CU41**

Deathstalker (1984, C, 80m, R)
Sword and sorcery saga featuring a lovely princess (Barbi Benton), who's the prize for the bravest warrior of them all. **AC18**

Deathstalker 2 (1987, C, 85m, R)
Name-only sequel in this adventure tale of a brave fighting man. Monique Gabrielle and John Terlesky star. **AC18**

Deathtrap (1982, C, 118m, PG)
A complicated thriller about a burned-out playwright, his smothering wife, and an ambitious student who's written a very good play. Michael Caine, Dyan Cannon, and Christopher Reeve star. Based on Ira Levin's hit play; directed by Sidney Lumet. **DR20, DR58, MY9**

Deathwatch (1980, C, 128m, R)
A dying woman is followed by a TV reporter who has a camera imbedded in his head, with her story transmitted on national TV. Romy Schneider, Harvey Keitel, and Harry Dean Stanton star in this science fiction drama from France, with English dialogue. Directed by Bertrand Tavernier. **CU49, FF1, MY20, SF5, SF19**

Decline of Western Civilization, The (1981, C, 100m, NR)
Documentary of the Los Angeles punk music scene, directed by Penelope Spheeris, featuring such household names as Black Flag, Fear, X, and Catholic Discipline. **MU11**

Decline of Western Civilization Part II: The Metal Years, The (1988, C, 90m, R)
Director Penelope Spheeris follows up her documentary on the punk music scene with a look at the heavy metal artists who've made it (Ozzy Osbourne, Joe Perry, Steve Tyler, Gene Simmons) and the younger generation of musicians looking for the same kind of fame. **MU11**

Deep, The (1977, C, 123m, PG)
Couple on an innocent skindiving expedition in Caribbean wind up finding treasure and drugs. Nick Nolte, Jacqueline Bisset, and Robert Shaw star. **AC12, DR44**

Deep in My Heart (1954, C, 132m, NR)
Jose Ferrer plays Sigmund Romberg in this biographical musical which features guest stars Gene Kelly, Ann Miller, and Tony Martin. Directed by Stanley Donen. **MU5, MU19, MU23**

Deep Red: The Hatchet Murders (1975, C, 98m, R)
A man who witnessed an ax murder and a journalist set out to investigate a series of similar killings. David Hemmings and Daria Nicolodi star. Directed by Dario Argento. **HO9**

Deep Star Six (1988, C, 103m, R)
An underwater expedition encounters a sea monster in this high-tech horror story. Greg Evigian, Cindy Pickett, and Taurean Blacque star. **HO16**

Deer Hunter, The (1978, C, 183m, R)
Drama of small-town buddies whose experiences in Vietnam shatter their lives. Robert DeNiro, Christopher Walken, John Savage, John Cazale, and Meryl Streep star. Directed by Michael Cimino. Oscar winner for Best Picture, Director, and Supporting Actor (Walken). **AC4, DR7, DR25, DR26, DR62, XT1, XT4, XT6**

Defense of the Realm (1985, C, 96m, PG)
A journalist's story forces a British officer to resign. When the writer learns of the result, he attempts to uncover the entire story. **MY6**

Defiance (1980, C, 102m, PG)
Urban loner (Jan-Michael Vincent) takes on New York street gangs. Art Carney, Theresa Saldana, and Danny Aiello co-star. **AC8**

Defiant Ones, The (1958, B&W, 97m, NR)
Tony Curtis and Sidney Poitier play two escaped cons who must look past the color of their skin to survive. With Lon Chaney, Jr. **CL8, DR38, HO30**

Delicate Sound of Thunder (1989, C, 100m, NR)
Concert film of rock group Pink Floyd's Momentary Lapse of Reason tour, featuring four songs not on the album of the same name. **MU10**

Deliverance (1972, C, 109m, R)
Four men on a canoe trip down an isolated stretch of river encounter disaster. Burt Reynolds, Jon Voight, Ned Beatty, and Ronny Cox star. John Boorman directed this adaptation of James Dickey's novel. **AC24, AC37, CU28, DR19** *Recommended*

Delta Force, The (1986, C, 125m, R)
When terrorists commandeer an airliner and its terrified passengers, a special squad of fighting men swing into action. Chuck Norris and Lee Marvin are the rescuers; Shelley Winters and Martin Balsam are among the hostages. **AC20, AC32, DR43**

Dementia 13 (1963, B&W, 81m, NR)
Low-budget thriller about murders in and around an Irish castle. Directed by Francis Ford Coppola; produced by Roger Corman. **CU14, DR51, HO14**

Demetrius and the Gladiators (1954, C, 101m, NR)
Saga of ancient Rome, with Victor Mature the stalwart hero, Susan Hayward his royal lover, and a flamboyant Jay Robinson as the emperor Caligula. **CL3**

Demon *see* God Told Me To

Demon Seed (1977, C, 94m, R)
Computer goes mad, attacks scientist's wife for purposes of reproduction in this science fiction thriller. Julie Christie and Fritz Weaver star; Donald Cammell directed. **HO22, HO25, SF6, SF22**

Demons (1986, C, 89m, R)
An audience watching a slasher film is terrorized by a demonic army and trans-

formed into hideous creatures. Directed by Lamberto Bava. **HO17**

Dentist, The (1932, B&W, 22m, NR)
W.C. Fields stars in this comedy short about a man with a mission for removing molars. **CO22**

Dernier Combat, Le (1984, B&W, 90m, R)
After the apocalypse, a survivor wanders a bizarre landscape and encounters equally strange characters. French film with no dialogue, only music and sound effects. Directed by Luc Besson. **FF1, SF19**

Dersu Uzala (1975, C, 124m, G)
Oscar-winning drama from Japan's Akira Kurosawa about the friendship between a Japanese guide and a Russian explorer in turn-of-the-century Siberia. Slow-moving, but worthwhile. **FF9, XT7** *Recommended*

Desert Bloom (1986, C, 106m, PG)
Sensitive portrait of a teenager with family problems in 1950s Las Vegas, at the time of A-bomb testing. Annabeth Gish stars, with Jon Voight, JoBeth Williams, and Ellen Barkin. **DR8** *Recommended*

Desert Hearts (1986, C, 96m, R)
In the 1950s, a female professor in Reno to get a divorce falls in love with another woman. Helen Shaver and Patricia Charbonneau star. **DR3, DR10**

Desire Under the Elms (1958, B&W, 114m, NR)
Drama based on Eugene O'Neill play set in 19th-century New England. Mother loves stepson, family bickers over land. Sophia Loren, Anthony Perkins, and Burl Ives star. **DR20, FF31**

Desiree (1954, C, 110m, NR)
Marlon Brando plays Napoleon, Jean Simmons his love object, Merle Oberon Empress Josephine in this historical drama. **CL3, DR33**

Despair (1979, C, 119m, R)
A Russian emigré starts a successful business in Germany, only to see the Nazis come to power and ruin his life. Dirk Bogarde stars in this version of Vladimir Nabokov's book. Written by Tom Stoppard and directed by Rainer Werner Fassbinder. **FF20**

Desperate Hours, The (1955, B&W, 112m, NR)
Humphrey Bogart stars in this drama of an escaped convict and his gang hiding out in the house of a middle-class family. Fredric March, Arthur Kennedy, and Martha Scott costar. William Wyler directed. **CL20, CL38**

Desperate Living (1977, B&W, 87m, NR)
Baltimore's gift to movies, director John Waters, strikes again with this story of a murderous housewife (Mink Stole), her accomplice maid (Jean Hill), and other not-of-this-earth characters. Edith Massey and Liz Renay costar. Don't say you weren't warned. **CU12, CU43**

Desperately Seeking Susan (1985, C, 104m, PG-13)
New Jersey housewife and New York con artist get their identities switched in this madcap, modern comedy. Rosanna Arquette and Madonna star, with Aidan Quinn. **CO2, CO37, MU12, XT9** *Recommended*

Destination Moon (1950, C, 91m, NR)
Early example of postwar science fiction, with rocketship making perilous trip to the moon. Oscar-winning special effects; co-written by Robert Heinlein. **SF1, SF3, SF15**

Destiny (1921, B&W, 122m, NR)
Early film from German director Fritz Lang, a fantasy of a woman's desperate attempt to rescue her lover from the hands of death. **FF3, CL43**

Destry Rides Again (1939, B&W, 94m, NR)
One of the great western comedies, with sheriff James Stewart trying to clean up

the town—without resorting to violence. Marlene Dietrich costars. **CL25, CL47, WE9, WE15** *Recommended*

Detective, The (1954, B&W, 91m, NR)
Alex Guinness stars as Father Brown, the cleric-turned-detective created by G.K. Chesterton. **DR63, MY15, MY19**

Detective, The (1968, C, 114m, NR)
Frank Sinatra plays a police detective who's overzealous in his search for a killer and sends the wrong man to the electric chair. Al Freeman, Jr. and Lee Remick costar. **DR49**

Detour (1945, B&W, 69m, NR)
A hitchhiker gets involved in a murder after he encounters a mysterious woman. A low-budget classic, starring Tom Neal and Ann Savage, directed by Edgar G. Ulmer. **MY1** *Recommended*

Detroit 9000 (1973, C, 106m, R)
Jewel thieves and cops shoot it out on the streets of Motown. Alex Rocco, Hari Rhodes, and Vonetta McGee star. **AC8**

Devil and Daniel Webster, The (1941, B&W, 85m, NR)
Fantasy about a young farmer who meets up with the Devil. A flop in its original release, now a cult favorite. Edward Arnold and Walter Huston star. **CL14, SF2**

Devil and Max Devlin, The (1981, C, 96m, PG)
Deceased Max Devlin (Elliott Gould) bargains with the Devil (Bill Cosby) for another chance at life—in exchange, he'll provide three souls. Comedy from the Disney studios. **FA1, HO10**

Devil at 4 O'Clock, The (1961, C, 120m, NR)
Spencer Tracy plays a priest sent to rescue sickly children from the shadow of an erupting volcano. Frank Sinatra costars. **AC23, CL19, DR49**

Devil Bat, The *see* Killer Bats

Devil Doll, The (1936, B&W, 80m, NR)
A madman shrinks humans to the size of small dolls and gets them to carry out various crimes. Lionel Barrymore and Maureen O'Sullivan star. Directed by Tod Browning. **HO1, HO35**

Devil in the Flesh (1986, C, 110m, R)
Sexually explicit drama of a young woman who's torn between her terrorist lover and a younger man. Maruschka Detmers, Federico Pitzalis, and Riccard de Torrebruna star. Italian filmmaker Marco Bellochio directed. Also available in an unrated version which contains footage that earned the film its original "X" rating. **CU6, FF2**

Devils, The (1971, C, 109m, R)
Religious hysteria grips a convent in 17th-century France, and a lecherous priest attempts to aid the delirious nuns. Ken Russell directed this controversial drama starring Oliver Reed and Vanessa Redgrave. **CU31, DR5, DR65, HO11**

Devil's Eye, The (1960, B&W, 90m, NR)
Director Ingmar Bergman's drama of the Devil's emissary sent to take a young woman's virginity. Jarl Kulle and Bibi Andersson star. **FF8**

Devil's Playground, The (1976, C, 107m, NR)
Life at an Australian Catholic boys' school, whose students and teachers are wrestling with sexual problems. Fred Schepisi directed. **DR61, FF5** *Recommended*

Devil's Rain, The (1975, C, 86m, PG)
Ernest Borgnine is the reincarnation of a 17th-century witch who is to deliver souls to the Devil. He and his coven melt everyone who gets in his way. William Shatner costars. **HO10, HO11**

Devil's Triangle, The (1978, C, 59m, NR)
Vincent Price narrates this documentary about the strange occurrences in the Bermuda Triangle area. **HO31**

Devil's Undead, The (1972, C, 90m, PG)
A satanic cult who yearn for immortality try to project their souls into children. Christopher Lee, Peter Cushing, and Diana Dors star. **HO32, HO33**

Devil's Wanton, The (1949, B&W, 72m, NR)
Ingmar Bergman drama of an unhappy prostitute and her love affair with a writer. Doris Svenlund stars. Released in the U.S. in 1962. **FF8**

Diabolique (1955, B&W, 107m, NR)
Classic French thriller about a wife and mistress who murder a heartless schoolteacher—and the surprising aftermath. Simone Signoret and Vera Clouzot star; Henri-Georges Clouzot directed. **FF1, MY20** *Recommended*

Dial M for Murder (1954, C, 105m, NR)
A faithless husband (Ray Milland) plots the murder of his wealthy, adulterous wife (Grace Kelly). Robert Cummings co-stars. Directed by Alfred Hitchcock. **CL31, MY3, MY22**

Diamonds (1975, C, 101m, PG)
Heist drama, with Robert Shaw playing two roles: the lead crook and his twin brother, the designer of the target vault's security system. Richard Roundtree, Shelley Winters, and Barbara Seagull (Hershey) costar. Filmed in Israel. **MY34**

Diamonds Are Forever (1971, C, 119m, PG)
James Bond travels to Las Vegas, but it's not to catch any of the shows or play the slots. Sean Connery stars, with Jill St. John and Charles Gray in support. Car chases galore. **AC35, AC36**

Diary of a Chambermaid (1946, C, 81m, NR)
Jean Renoir directed this English-language drama about a disruptive servant (Paulette Goddard). Written by and co-starring Burgess Meredith. Original running time: 98m. **FF12**

Diary of a Chambermaid (1964, B&W, 97m, NR)
A French maid (Jeanne Moreau) discovers a world of hypocrisy and corruption when she takes a job with a country family during the Nazi Occupation. Luis Buñuel directed this remake of Jean Renoir's film. **CU18, FF1, FF11, FF26**

Diary of a Country Priest (1950, B&W, 120m, NR)
French director Robert Bresson paints a moving portrait of a young idealist assigned to a rural parish. **FF1**

Diary of a Lost Girl (1929, B&W, 104m, NR)
Silent classic from Germany starring Louise Brooks as a woman whose life is a virtual catalogue of tragedy, from rape to residence in a bordello. Directed by G.W. Pabst. **CL12, FF3**

Diary of a Mad Housewife (1970, C, 94m, R)
A Manhattan woman, fed up with her status-seeking husband, tries to find solace in an affair with an actor. Carrie Snodgress stars, with Richard Benjamin and Frank Langella. **DR10**

Diary of Anne Frank, The (1959, C, 150m, NR)
The true account of a Jewish family's hiding out from the Nazis, as told by a teenaged daughter in her diary. Millie Perkins stars, with Oscar winner Shelley Winters, Joseph Schildkraut, Richard Beymer, and Ed Wynn. George Stevens directed. **CL2, CL42, XT5**

Dick Tracy Meets Gruesome (1947, B&W, 65m, NR)
Dick Tracy is on the trail of master criminal Gruesome, who is using a gas to freeze people in the middle of his bank robberies. Ralph Byrd stars, with Boris Karloff. **HO27**

Die Hard (1988, C, 131m, R)
Riveting, breathlessly paced thriller set in a Los Angeles high-rise office building, with a terrorist gang holding hostages and

battling a lone New York cop trapped inside. Bruce Willis stars, with Alan Rickman, Alexander Gudonov, and Bonnie Bedelia. **AC8, AC25** *Recommended*

Die, Monster, Die! (1965, C, 80m, NR)
Boris Karloff stars in this British-made horror story of a hermit who's given strange powers by a fallen meteor. Based on an H. P. Lovecraft story. **HO27**

Dillinger (1973, C, 96m, R)
Portrait of America's most notorious Depression-era gangster, played with roguish charm by Warren Oates. Costarring Ben Johnson (as Melvin Purvis), Cloris Leachman (as the Lady in Red), Richard Dreyfuss (as Baby Face Nelson), Michelle Phillips, and Harry Dean Stanton. Directed by John Milius. **AC22, CU48, CU49** *Recommended*

Dim Sum: a little bit of heart (1984, C, 89m, PG)
Drama set in San Francisco's Chinatown, focusing on the relationship between a mother with her Old World ways, and her more modern, Americanized daughter. Directed by Wayne Wang. **DR15, XT9**

Dimples (1936, B&W, 78m, NR)
Shirley Temple classic finds the child star taking on the burden of her father's financial difficulties to help ease his mind. Songs include: "Oh Mister Man Up In the Moon," "What Did the Bluebird Say." **FA14**

Diner (1982, C, 110m, R)
Baltimore in the late 1950s is the setting for this nostalgic comedy about five young men reluctant to get on with their adult lives. Mickey Rourke, Daniel Stern, Kevin Bacon, Steve Guttenberg, Paul Reiser, and Timothy Daly star, with Ellen Barkin. Written and directed by Barry Levinson. **CO6, DR48** *Highly Recommended*

Dinner at Eight (1933, B&W, 113m, NR)
Comedy classic from George Cukor stars Lionel Barrymore and Billie Burke as a highfalutin' couple who throw swell par-

ties, where guests open up to reveal deep-dark secrets. All-star MGM cast also includes Wallace Beery, Jean Harlow, Lee Tracy, John Barrymore, Jean Hersholt, Marie Dressler, and many more. **CL10, CL39, CU17** *Recommended*

Dinosaurus! (1960, C, 85m, NR)
Science fiction adventure about a pair of cavemen and a dinosaur discovered on a remote tropical island. **SF4**

Dirt Bike Kid, The (1986, C, 90m, PG)
Peter Billingsley plays a precocious teen with an unusual bike that rides him right into mischief. **DR22, FA7**

Dirty Dancing (1987, C, 100m, PG-13)
Romantic drama, set in the summer of 1963 at a mountain resort hotel, where a 16-year-old girl blossoms under the eye of a handsome dance instructor. Jennifer Grey and Patrick Swayze star. **DR1**

Dirty Dozen, The (1967, C, 150m, NR)
Allies recruit 12 convicts for nasty job behind Nazi lines. Lee Marvin trains the misfits, who include Charles Bronson, Jim Brown, John Cassavetes, Telly Savalas, and Clint Walker; Robert Ryan and Ernest Borgnine also star. Directed by Robert Aldrich. **AC1, AC29, DR43** *Recommended*

Dirty Harry (1971, C, 102m, R)
The first film in the series about the San Francisco cop (Clint Eastwood) who makes his own rules—whatever it takes to keep the streets clean. A psychotic killer (Andy Robinson) is terrorizing the city, and Harry Callahan is ordered to bring him in. Directed by Don Siegel. **AC9, AC27, XT9** *Recommended*

Dirty Knight's Work *see* Choice of Weapons, A

Dirty, Rotten Scoundrels (1988, C, 110m, PG)
A pair of hustlers who romance wealthy women wager on a common target—the one who succeeds first has the French Riviera to himself. Steve Martin and Mi-

chael Caine are the title characters. **CO3, CO33**

Disappearance of Aimee, The (1976, C, 110m, NR)
Faye Dunaway and Bette Davis star in this drama, set in the 1920s, about the much-publicized disappearance and reappearance of the evangelist Aimee Semple McPherson. Originally made for TV. **CL21, DR35**

Discreet Charm of the Bourgeoisie, The (1972, C, 100m, R)
Straight-faced comedy about the inability of a group of well-to-do friends to conclude a dinner party. Director Luis Buñuel's film deservedly won the Oscar for Best Foreign Film. Dialogue in French. **FF11, XT7** *Highly Recommended*

Disorderly Orderly, The (1964, C, 90m, NR)
Jerry Lewis comedy set in a nursing home. Directed by Frank Tashlin. **CO25**

Disorganized Crime (1989, C, 101m, R)
A quartet of inept crooks, waiting for their leader to show up for a big heist, manage to create plenty of havoc in the meantime. Fred Gwynne, William Russ, Ruben Blades, and Lou Diamond Phillips are the crooks; Corbin Bernsen is their leader. **CO10, MU12, MY34**

Distant Drums (1951, C, 101m, NR)
Gary Cooper is swamped by Seminole Indians in 19th-century Florida. **WE25**

Distant Thunder (1973, C, 100m, NR)
Indian director Satyajit Ray presents a devastating drama of the great 1942 famine in Bengal. Soumitra Chatterji stars. **FF23**

Distant Thunder (1988, C, 114m, R)
A Vietnam veteran, living in isolation in a woodsy retreat since the war, confronts his teenaged son, whom he abandoned 16 years before. John Lithgow and Ralph Macchio star. **DR7, DR8**

Diva (1982, C, 123m, R)
Contemporary French thriller, set in Paris, about a young courier's obsession with an opera singer and his accidental possession of a valuable tape recording. Stylish fun, directed by Jean-Jacques Beneix. **FF1, MY20, XT9** *Recommended*

Divine Madness (1980, C, 95m, R)
Concert film featuring Bette Midler, in all her campy glory. **MU10**

Divine Nymph, The (1979, C, 90m, R)
Costume drama starring Marcello Mastroianni, Laura Antonelli, and Terence Stamp as points of a love triangle. **FF24**

Divorce His—Divorce Hers (1972, C, 144m, NR)
Richard Burton and Elizabeth Taylor play a husband and wife who offer two sides to the story behind a marriage breakup. Originally made for TV. **CL15, CL33**

Divorce of Lady X, The (1938, C, 91m, NR)
A British debutante (Merle Oberon) pretends she's married to trick her lawyer (Laurence Olivier). **CL32**

Dixie Dynamite (1976, C, 89m, PG)
After their father is killed by a deputy sheriff, two lovely sisters arm for revenge. Jane Anne Johnstone and Kathy McHaley star, with Warren Oates and Christopher George. **CU48**

Django (1968, C, 90m, PG)
A south-of-the-border western finds a group of Americans feuding with Mexican bandits. **WE14**

Django Shoots First (1974, C, 96m, NR)
In this spaghetti western, a cowboy is out to avenge the murder of his father. Glenn Saxon stars. **WE14**

Doc Savage: The Man of Bronze (1975, C, 100m, G)
Pulp hero created by author Kenneth Robeson makes his movie debut in this adventure about a super scientist/muscle

man and his five colleagues. Ron Ely stars. **AC17**

Docks of New York, The (1928, B&W, 76m, NR)
Classic silent drama about a man who falls for the emotionally unstable woman he's just saved from drowning. Directed by Josef von Sternberg. **CL12, CL56**

Doctor and the Devils, The (1985, C, 93m, R)
Two grave robbers provide corpses to a dedicated surgeon who needs them for practice. Based on a screenplay written in the 1940s by Dylan Thomas. Timothy Dalton, Jonathan Pryce, and Twiggy star. **HO26**

Doctor at Sea (1955, C, 93m, NR)
British comedy-drama of young doctor signing on to work a freighter. Dirk Bogarde and Brigitte Bardot star. **FF32**

Dr. Butcher, M.D. (1980, C, 88m, NR)
An investigation of mutilated corpses leads a doctor and scientist to an island where cannibalism is practiced. They find a mad doctor experimenting with strange transplants and creating a race of monstrous zombies. **HO18**

Dr. Cyclops (1940, C, 75m, NR)
A mad scientist in the Peruvian jungle transforms a quartet of colleagues into miniaturized humans. Oscar-winning special effects highlight this classic fantasy. **SF2, SF5, SF15**

Doctor Detroit (1983, C, 89m, R)
A college professor finds himself involved with pimps, prostitutes, and other low-lifes in this comedy starring Dan Aykroyd and Howard Hesseman. **CO13**

Doctor Dolittle (1967, C, 144m, NR)
Rex Harrison is the magical doctor who can talk to the animals, in this musical based on Hugh Lofting's children's stories. Samantha Eggar and Anthony Newley costar. **FA9, MU8, MU17**

Doctor Faustus (1968, C, 93m, NR)
Richard Burton stars in this drama based on Christopher Marlowe's play of an embittered scholar in need of some soul searching. Elizabeth Taylor appears briefly as Helen of Troy. **CL15, CL33**

Doctor in the House (1954, C, 92m, NR)
Classic British comedy about medical students majoring in female anatomy. Dirk Bogarde stars. **CO17**

Dr. Jekyll and Mr. Hyde (1920, B&W, 63m, NR)
A silent version of Robert Louis Stevenson's story about a doctor (John Barrymore) who is experimenting with a way to separate the good half and the evil half in humans. **HO1, HO20**

Dr. Jekyll and Mr. Hyde (1932, B&W, 82m, NR)
Superb version of the Robert Louis Stevenson tale, with an Oscar-winning performance by Fredric March, solid support from Miriam Hopkins, excellent direction by Rouben Mamoulian. The transformation scenes are especially effective. **HO1, HO17, HO20, XT2** *Recommended*

Dr. Jekyll and Mr. Hyde (1941, B&W, 114m, NR)
Spencer Tracy and Ingrid Bergman star in this version of Robert Louis Stevenson's classic tale. Lana Turner and Donald Crisp costar. **CL19, CL27, HO1, HO20**

Dr. No (1963, C, 111m, PG)
The first film appearance of James Bond (Sean Connery), as he battles a sinister mastermind (Joseph Wiseman) in the Caribbean. Ursula Andress costars. **AC35, AC36** *Recommended*

Dr. Phibes Rises Again (1972, C, 89m, PG)
The sequel to *The Abominable Dr. Phibes* has Phibes going to Egypt to perform a ritual that will bring his wife back to life. Vincent Price, Robert Quarry, and Peter Cushing star. **HO20, HO26, HO31, HO33**

Dr. Strangelove or: How I Learned to Stop Worrying and Love the Bomb (1964, B&W, 93m, NR)
Landmark black comedy about a crazy Air Force general who orders U.S. planes to bomb the Soviet Union, triggering frantic actions by the President to save the world. Peter Sellers stars in three roles, with Sterling Hayden, George C. Scott, Keenan Wynn, Slim Pickens and Peter Bull in support. Directed by Stanley Kubrick. **CO2, CO12, CO26, DR53** *Highly Recommended*

Dr. Terror's Gallery of Horrors (1967, C, 90m, NR)
Five-part horror anthology featuring John Carradine as a warlock, Lon Chaney, Jr., as a mad doctor, and more. **HO30**

Doctor Terror's House of Horrors (1964, C, 98m, NR)
Five tales are linked together by the mysterious Dr. Schreck, foretelling the futures of five people on a train. Peter Cushing, Christopher Lee, and Donald Sutherland star. **HO23, HO26, HO32, HO33**

Dr. Who and the Daleks (1965, C, 85m, NR)
Science fiction adventure, inspired by popular British TV character, with Dr. Who and his friends on another planet with robot-like creatures. Peter Cushing and Jennie Linde star. **HO33, SF19**

Doctor X (1932, C, 77m, NR)
The path of a murderer is traced back to a mysterious doctor. Lionel Atwill and Fay Wray star. **HO1**

Dr. Zhivago (1965, C, 197m, NR)
An epic of the Russian Revolution and the people whose lives it changed. Omar Sharif and Julie Christie star, with Geraldine Chaplin, Rod Steiger, Alec Guinness, and Tom Courtenay. Based on Boris Pasternak's novel; directed by David Lean. **CL3, CL4, DR50, DR63**

Doctors' Wives (1971, C, 100m, R)
Trashy drama about the murder of a wife who had been cheating on her physician husband. Gene Hackman stars, with Richard Crenna and Rachel Roberts. **DR39**

Dodes'ka-den (1970, C, 140m, NR)
Japanese drama centering on the lives of shanty dwellers in a Tokyo slum is both funny and terribly moving. Directed by Akira Kurosawa. **FF9** *Recommended*

Dodge City (1939, C, 105m, NR)
Western saga starring Errol Flynn as a two-fisted marshal. Olivia de Havilland, Ann Sheridan, Bruce Cabot, Alan Hale, and Ward Bond costar. **AC34**

Dodsworth (1936, B&W, 101m, NR)
A middle-aged American couple discover on a European holiday that their marriage is no longer solid. Walter Huston, Ruth Chatterton, and Mary Astor star in this excellent version of Sinclair Lewis's novel, directed by William Wyler. **CL38, DR19** *Recommended*

Dog Day (1983, C, 101m, NR)
French drama starring Lee Marvin as a U.S. traitor on the run who bargains with some farmers for refuge. **DR43**

Dog Day Afternoon (1975, C, 130m, R)
True-life drama of a bank robbery in summertime New York that goes awry, with the desperate thieves holding hostages. Taut suspense mixed with humor. Al Pacino and John Cazale star, with John Forsythe and Chris Sarandon. Directed by Sidney Lumet. **DR6, DR58, DR66** *Recommended*

Dog of Flanders, A (1959, C, 96m, NR)
A badly abused dog is cared for and loved back to good health by a Dutch boy and his grandpa in this animal story. **FA5**

Dogs of Hell (1983, C, 90m, R)
The U.S. Army trains a pack of Rottweilers to be the perfect killing machines. The dogs escape and terrorize a nearby town. Earl Owensby stars. **HO16**

Dogs of War, The (1981, C, 109m, R)
Frederick Forsyth's bestseller about a band of ruthless mercenaries who try to overthrow a sadistic African dictator. Christopher Walken and Tom Berenger star, with JoBeth Williams. **AC20, MY31**

Dolce Vita, La (1960, B&W, 175m, NR)
Exuberant, sobering, one-of-a-kind look at contemporary Rome from director Federico Fellini. Marcello Mastroianni stars as a jaded journalist who thinks he's seen it all, but really hasn't. Anita Ekberg heads the supporting cast of this drama filmed on many well-known locations in Rome. **FF10, FF24, XT9** *Recommended*

$ (Dollars) (1972, C, 119m, R)
Comic tale of elaborate heist, with wild chase sequence. Warren Beatty and Goldie Hawn star in this caper film shot in Germany. **CO10, CO30, DR34, MY34**

Dollmaker, The (1984, C, 140m, NR)
Drama of woman's struggle to keep her family together when they move from the rural South to Detroit in search of work. Jane Fonda won an Emmy for her performance; Levon Helm costars as her husband. Originally made for TV. **DR10, DR27, MU12**

Dolls (1987, C, 77m, R)
A family and a couple of hitchhikers are forced by a storm to take refuge in a mysterious house owned by an old couple who make dolls that can kill. Directed by Stuart Gordon. **HO16**

Doll's House, A (1973, C, 103m, G)
Jane Fonda stars in this adaptation of the Henrik Ibsen play about a 19th-century housewife's fight for independence. David Warner, Trevor Howard, Delphine Seyrig, and Edward Fox costar. **DR20, DR27**

Dominick and Eugene (1988, C, 111m, PG-13)
Sentimental tale of two Pittsburgh brothers (Tom Hulce, Ray Liotta), one a slow-witted, well-meaning child-man, the other an aspiring doctor. Trouble arises when the intern must continue his studies in another city. **DR2, DR8**

Domino Principle, The (1977, C, 97m, R)
Thriller about a man recruited by a political conspiracy to be an assassin. Gene Hackman stars, with Candice Bergen, Richard Widmark, and Mickey Rooney. **DR39**

Don Q: Son of Zorro (1925, B&W, 148m, NR)
Douglas Fairbanks stars in this silent classic about the Mexican swordsman and his offspring, who is determined to follow in his father's famous footsteps. **AC13**

Doña Flor and Her Two Husbands (1977, C, 105m, R)
Brazilian comedy about a lovely young widow who remarries, then has to satisfy her sex-starved husband's ghost. Sonia Braga stars. U.S. remake: *Kiss Me Goodbye*. **FF6, FF34, FF36**

Donkey Skin (1971, C, 90m, NR)
Comic fairy tale starring Catherine Deneuve as a princess whose mother's dying request leads to a rather delicate situation with her father. **FF27**

Donovan's Reef (1963, C, 109m, NR)
Classic action comedy stars John Wayne as an ex-Navy man living the island high-life in the South Pacific until a prudish New England girl arrives in search of her dad. With Elizabeth Allen, Lee Marvin, Jack Warden, Cesar Romero, and Mike Mazurki. John Ford directed. **CL17, CL34, CO9, DR43** *Recommended*

Don's Party (1976, C, 91m, NR)
Australian comedy about an election-night bash featuring heated political debates and some sexual escapades as well. Bruce Beresford directed; John Hargreaves heads the splendid cast. **FF5** *Recommended*

Don't Answer the Phone (1980, C, 94m, R)
A psychopath stalks and attacks the patients of a beautiful talk show psycholo-

gist. James Westmoreland and Flo Gerrish star. **HO9**

Don't Fence Me In (1945, B&W, 71m, NR)
Roy Rogers plays a singin' cowpoke who can't be tied down. **WE23**

Don't Look Back (1967, B&W, 96m, NR)
Unsparing, often very funny documentary about singer Bob Dylan's tour of England in 1965. Incisive portrait of a brilliant, difficult subject. Directed by D. A. Pennebaker. **MU11** *Highly Recommended*

Don't Look Now (1973, C, 110m, R)
Julie Christie and Donald Sutherland star in a gripping thriller about a couple who try to make contact with their dead child. Directed by Nicolas Roeg; adapted from a Daphne du Maurier story. **CU34, HO14, HO19, MY18, MY36** *Recommended*

Don't Raise the Bridge, Lower the River (1968, C, 99m, NR)
Jerry Lewis plays an American living in England whose free-spending ways are financed by his get-rich-quick schemes. **CO25**

Dorothy in the Land of Oz (1981, C, 60m, NR)
Animated musical based on the popular Wizard of Oz tales, with old friends and some new members added to the Oz family. **FA10**

Dorritt's Story *see* Little Dorritt

Double Dynamite (1951, B&W, 80m, NR)
Frank Sinatra stars in this comedy about a bank clerk mistakenly accused of embezzlement. Jane Russell and Groucho Marx costar. **CO21, DR49**

Double Indemnity (1944, B&W, 106m, NR)
Classic film noir with Barbara Stanwyck the ultimate femme fatale, Fred MacMurray the ultimate sap in this murder for love story. Edward G. Robinson costars. Billy Wilder directed and wrote the screenplay with Raymond Chandler,

based on the James M. Cain novel. **CL37, CL45, CL52, MY1, MY4, MY5, MY25** *Highly Recommended*

Double Life, A (1947, B&W, 104m, NR)
A serious actor (Oscar winner Ronald Colman) finds he can't separate his work from his personal life when he takes on the role of Othello. Directed by George Cukor. **CL7, CL39, XT2**

Double Suicide (1969, B&W, 105m, NR)
Japanese drama of ill-fated affair between a merchant and a prostitute. Directed by Masahiro Shinoda. **FF4**

Double Trouble (1967, C, 90m, NR)
Elvis Presley musical about a pop star (guess who) and one of his teen fans in Britain. Annette Day and John Williams costar. **MU22**

Down Among the Z-Men (1952, B&W, 70m, NR)
Britain's Goon Show radio team stars in this comedy about an inept gang of crooks trying to steal a secret formula. Harry Secombe, Spike Milligan, and Peter Sellers star. Also known as *Stand Easy*. **CO26**

Down and Dirty (1976, C, 115m, NR)
Italian comedy, directed by Lina Wertmuller, about a poverty-stricken family and their ribald adventures in a Rome slum. Nino Manfredi stars. **FF2**

Down and Out in Beverly Hills (1985, C, 103m, R)
Homeless man tries to commit suicide in Beverly Hills swimming pool, is rescued and moves in with nutsy family. Comic look at modern lifestyles starring Nick Nolte, Richard Dreyfuss, Bette Midler, and Little Richard. Directed by Paul Mazursky, who plays a small role. Remake of French classic, *Boudu Saved From Drowning*. **CO2, CO37, DR44, FF36, XT9** *Recommended*

Down by Law (1986, B&W, 90m, R)
A trio of jailbirds escape from a Louisiana pokey for a series of comic adventures.

John Lurie, Tom Waits, and Robert Benigni star; Jim Jarmusch directed this offbeat comedy. **CO12, MU12**

Down Dakota Way (1949, B&W, 67m, NR)
Roy Rogers is on the trail of the bad guys when he learns of his friend's death. Dale Evans costars. **WE23**

Down Mexico Way (1941, B&W, 78m, NR)
Gene Autry and sidekick Smiley Burnette wind up among a ring of thieves. **WE24**

Downhill Racer (1969, C, 102m, PG)
Cocky ski champ and his coach clash all the way to the Olympics. Robert Redford and Gene Hackman star; Michael Ritchie directed. **DR22, DR29, DR39**

Dracula (1931, B&W, 85m, NR)
Bela Lugosi recreates his famous stage role as the mysterious nobleman who only comes out at night and lives to drink human blood. Costarring Dwight Frye; directed by Tod Browning. **HO1, HO5, HO28, HO35** *Recommended*

Dracula (1979, C, 109m, R)
Frank Langella plays the famous vampire in this version of Bram Stoker's novel, which gives the old count a sexier appeal. Laurence Olivier costars. **CL32, HO5, HO19**

Dracula and Son (1979, C, 90m, PG)
Dracula's boy just wants to play football and date girls; he won't bite anyone, even when his father punishes him. Christopher Lee stars. **HO32**

Dracula vs. Frankenstein (1971, C, 90m, PG)
Dracula (Lon Chaney, Jr.) goes to see Dr. Frankenstein (J. Carroll Naish) to arrange for a continuous blood supply. **HO30**

Dragnet (1987, C, 106m, PG-13)
Dan Aykroyd stars as the nephew of TV's Sgt. Joe Friday in this continuation of that show's tight-lipped traditions, with a few contemporary comic touches. Tom Hanks costars, with Dabney Coleman,

Alexandra Paul, Christopher Plummer, and Harry Morgan. **CO10, CO13, CO44**

Dragon Seed (1944, B&W, 145m, NR)
A Chinese town bands together to ward off a Japanese invasion in this classic drama based on Pearl Buck's novel. Katharine Hepburn and Walter Huston star. **CL16**

Dragon That Wasn't (Or Was He?), The (1983, C, 96m, NR)
An animated feature about Ollie B. Bear, a jolly bruin who raises a baby dragon he finds on his doorstep. **FA10**

Dragonslayer (1981, C, 108m, PG)
Sorcerer's apprentice (Peter MacNicol, not Mickey Mouse) learns his craft well when he takes on an enormous dragon. Caitlin Clark and Ralph Richardson costar in this adventure tale with dazzling special effects. **AC18**

Draw! (1981, C, 98m, NR)
Kirk Douglas and James Coburn play a couple of has-been outlaws in this old-fashioned Western comedy. Originally made for cable TV. **WE15**

Dream a Little Dream (1989, C, 114m, PG-13)
A smitten teenager exchanges personalities with an old man in this comedy-drama starring Corey Feldman and Jason Robards. With Meredith Salenger, Piper Laurie, and Harry Dean Stanton. **CO37, CU49**

Dream Street (1921, B&W, 138m, NR)
D.W. Griffith's silent drama looks at London's seamy lower depths, where two brothers are both in love with the same girl. **CL36**

Dream Team, The (1989, C, 113m, PG-13)
A quartet of psychiatric patients are set adrift in New York City when their doctor is injured during a field trip. Comedy starring Michael Keaton, Christopher Lloyd, Peter Boyle, and Stephen Furst. **CO3, CO37, CO45**

Dreamchild (1985, C, 94m, PG)
Imaginative drama of elderly English woman who, as a little girl, was the inspiration for Lewis Carroll's *Alice in Wonderland,* now coming to New York to attend a program honoring the late author. Coral Browne stars, with Ian Holm (as Carroll), Peter Gallagher, and Nicola Cowper. Written by Dennis Potter. **DR5, DR11** *Recommended*

Dreams (1955, B&W, 86m, NR)
Drama from Ingmar Bergman about a model and the head of her photo agency, their problems with men and their careers. Eva Dahlbeck and Harriet Andersson star. **FF8**

Dreamscape (1984, C, 99m, PG-13)
A research project into dreams is secretly used for sinister political purposes in this science fiction thriller. Dennis Quaid, Kate Capshaw, and Max von Sydow star. **SF5**

Dressed to Kill (1946, B&W, 72m, NR)
Super sleuth Sherlock Holmes uncovers a music box with some valuable hints as to a theft at the Bank of England. Basil Rathbone and Nigel Bruce star. **MY10**

Dressed to Kill (1980, C, 105m, R)
Brian DePalma's thriller finds an adulterous wife (Angie Dickinson) brutally murdered. Her son launches his own investigation by seeking out a prime witness. Michael Caine, Keith Gordon, and Nancy Allen costar. **CU28, MY5, MY15, MY17**

Dresser, The (1983, C, 118m, PG)
In postwar Britain, the temperamental star of a traveling troupe is tended to by his loyal valet. Albert Finney and Tom Courtenay star, with Edward Fox. **DR12, DR23**

Driver, The (1978, C, 90m, R)
Stripped-down thriller (characters have no names) about a getaway man (Ryan O'Neal), a detective (Bruce Dern), and a lovely lady (Isabelle Adjani). Directed by Walter Hill. **AC8, CU27, MY2**

Driver's Seat, The (1973, C, 101m, R)
Thriller, made in Italy, stars Elizabeth Taylor as a psychotic on a rendezvous with death. **CL33**

Drowning Pool, The (1976, C, 108m PG)
Paul Newman plays private eye Lew Harper in Ross MacDonald's mystery about the murder of a businessman. Joanne Woodward costars. **DR28, DR67, MY27**

Drum (1976, C, 110m, R)
Sequel to *Mandingo,* with further adventures of fighting slaves, lusting massas, and their women. Warren Oates, Ken Norton, and Pam Grier star. **CU48**

Drum Beat (1954, C, 111m, NR)
Alan Ladd western about Indian wars. Audrey Dalton costars; watch for Charles Bronson in a small role. **AC29**

Drums Along the Mohawk (1939, C, 103m, NR)
Henry Fonda and Claudette Colbert star in this drama of settlers living in upstate New York during the colonists' fight against the British. Directed by John Ford. **AC6, CL24, CL34**

Drunken Angel (1948, B&W, 108m, NR)
A young gangster (Toshiro Mifune) is treated by a kindly doctor (Takashi Shimura) for a bullet wound and learns that he has tuberculosis. Japanese drama from director Akira Kurosawa. **FF9, FF28**

DuBarry Was a Lady (1943, C, 101m, NR)
Red Skelton plays a patsy who dreams he's in the court of Louis XIV with co-stars Lucille Ball and Gene Kelly. Outstanding color photography and sets. **CL9, MU19**

Duchess and the Dirtwater Fox, The (1976, C, 103m, PG)
Western comedy teams George Segal and Goldie Hawn; he's a bumbling cardsharp and she's a kooky dance hall girl. **CO30, WE15**

Duck Soup (1933, B&W, 70m, NR)
The Marx Bros. take over a country called Freedonia. Zeppo's last appearance with Groucho, Chico, and Harpo. Margaret Dumont acts offended. A classic satire on politics, perhaps the best Marxist movie. **CL10, CO21** *Highly Recommended*

Duck, You Sucker *see* A Fistful of Dynamite

Dudes (1988, C, 90m, R)
On a cross-country trip, a trio of punk rockers from New York are harassed by a gang of rednecks. Jon Cryer, Daniel Roebuck, Catherine Mary Stewart, and Lee Ving star; Penelope Spheeris directed. **DR7, MU12**

Duel (1971, C, 90m, NR)
Steven Spielberg directed this terrifying tale of a businessman (Dennis Weaver) being stalked on the highway by an unseen truck driver. Originally made for TV. **MY9, SF24** *Recommended*

Duel in the Sun (1946, C, 130m, NR)
Producer David O. Selznick's colorful western saga, with Jennifer Jones a hot-blooded half-breed caught between brothers Gregory Peck and Joseph Cotten. The supporting cast includes Lionel Barrymore, Walter Huston, Lillian Gish, and Butterfly McQueen. **CL9, CL49, WE1, WE9, WE16** *Recommended*

Duellists, The (1977, C, 101m, PG)
A pair of feuding soldiers carry their grudge through many years and campaigns in this drama set in the Napoleonic era. Harvey Keitel and Keith Carradine star; Ridley Scott directed. **CU33** *Recommended*

Duet for One (1987, C, 110m, R)
A concert violinist is struck with a debilitating disease, throwing her shaky marriage onto the rocks, forcing her into therapy. Julie Andrews stars, with Alan Bates, Max von Sydow, and Rupert Everett. **DR2, DR10**

Duke Is Tops, The (1938, B&W, 80m, NR)
All-black musical about a girl trying for her first break in show business. Lena Horne stars, in one of her first screen appearances. Also known as *Bronze Venus*. **MU13**

Dumbo (1941, C, 63m, G)
Disney animation brings this poignant tale of the tiny elephant with oversized ears to life. **FA2** *Highly Recommended*

Dune (1984, C, 137m, PG-13)
Science fiction epic, based on Frank Herbert's classic novel, about intergalactic war and intrigue in the distant future. David Lynch directed; Kyle MacLachlan stars, with Jürgen Prochnow, Sting, Francesca Annis, Sean Young, Kenneth McMillan, Brad Dourif, and Linda Hunt. **CU38, MU12, SF11**

Dynasty of Fear (1973, C, 93m, NR)
The wife and assistant of a headmaster at a boys school conspire to murder him. Peter Cushing, Joan Collins, and Ralph Bates star. **HO33**

E.T. The Extra-Terrestrial (1982, C, 115m, PG)
Box-office champion about friendly visitor and the kids who protect him from uncaring adults. Directed by Steven Spielberg, with Oscar-winning special effects. Henry Thomas, Drew Barrymore, Robert McNaughton, Peter Coyote, and Dee Wallace star. **FA8, SF9, SF13, SF15, SF24**

Each Dawn I Die (1939, B&W, 92m, NR)
James Cagney prison drama, with our hero a framed man trying to prove his innocence. George Raft and George Bancroft costar. **CL22, DR18**

Eagle Has Landed, The (1977, C, 133m, PG)
World War II espionage drama about an attempt to kidnap Winston Churchill. Michael Caine, Donald Sutherland, Robert Duvall, Jenny Agutter, and Donald Pleasence star. Based on the Jack Higgins novel. **AC1, DR37, MY6**

Eagle's Wing (1979, C, 100m, PG)
An Indian renegade and a white trapper come to blows over a white stallion in this British-made western. Martin Sheen, Sam Waterston, and Harvey Keitel star. **WE8**

Earrings of Madame de . . . , The (1954, B&W, 105m, NR)
Elegant costume drama of wealthy woman's gift passing from hand to hand and eventually ruining her marriage. Danielle Darrieux, Charles Boyer, and Vittorio De Sica star; Max Ophuls directed. **CU20**

Earth (1930, B&W, 63m, NR)
Russian silent classic dealing with the formation of a peasant farm in the Ukraine. **CL12**

Earth Girls Are Easy (1989, C, 99m, PG)
Comedy with musical numbers about a manicurist (Geena Davis) living in the San Fernando Valley and her close encounter with three handsome aliens (Jeff Goldblum, Jim Carrey, Damon Wayans). With Julie Brown and Michael McKean. Julien Temple directed. **CO2, SF9, SF21**

Earth vs. the Flying Saucers (1956, B&W, 82m, NR)
Unfriendly aliens come out of the skies in this 1950s science fiction classic starring Hugh Marlowe and Joan Taylor. Finale featuring the destruction of Washington, D.C. is not to be missed. **SF1, SF9, XT9** *Recommended*

Earthling, The (1980, C, 102m, PG)
Family drama of an orphaned boy (Ricky Schroder) and a terminally ill man (William Holden) learning the ways of the bush country. **CL51, FA7**

Earthquake (1974, C, 129m, PG)
Los Angeles is hit by a catastrophic quake in this all-star disaster drama. Charlton Heston, Ava Gardner, Lorne Greene, Genevieve Bujold, Marjoe Gortner, Richard Roundtree, George Kennedy, and (in a bit part) Walter Matthau try to keep their balance. **AC23**

East of Eden (1955, C, 115m, NR)
Two brothers become rivals for the love of their father in John Steinbeck's transplanting of the Cain and Abel story to early 1900s California. James Dean's starring debut won him an Oscar nomination. Raymond Massey, Julie Harris, and Oscar winner Jo Van Fleet costar. Elia Kazan directed. **DR8, DR19, DR59, DR62, XT5, XT10** *Recommended*

East Side Kids Meet Bela Lugosi *see* Ghosts on the Loose

Easter Parade (1948, C, 103m, NR)
MGM musical, with tunes by Irving Berlin, about a dancer (Fred Astaire) caught between his current partner (Judy Garland) and his old one (Ann Miller). **MU1, MU6, MU18, MU21**

Easy Living (1949, B&W, 77m, NR)
An aging football star (Victor Mature) can't face his impending retirement or his nagging wife (Lizabeth Scott) until the team secretary (Lucille Ball) comes up with her own strategy. Directed by Jacques Tourneur. **DR22, HO37**

Easy Rider (1969, C, 94m, R)
Two California bikers hit the road for New Orleans with money from a drug deal. Legendary ''head'' movie starring Dennis Hopper (who directed), Peter Fonda, and Jack Nicholson. Superb rock soundtrack. **CU3, CU46, DR7, DR24, XT9** *Recommended*

Easy Virtue (1927, B&W, 79m, NR)
Early film from Alfred Hitchcock, a silent melodrama about a married woman whose husband is an alcoholic and whose lover commits suicide. Based on a play by Noel Coward. **MY22**

Eat the Peach (1987, C, 95m, NR)
Comedy about two friends who come up with a plan to break away from their Irish village by forming a daring motorcycle act. **CO17**

Eaten Alive (1976, C, 96m, NR)
A demented hotel owner keeps a live crocodile in his front yard and feeds it any troublesome guests. Neville Brand, Carolyn Jones, and Mel Ferrer star in this horror film from director Tobe Hooper. **HO40**

Eating Raoul (1982, C, 87m, R)
Strange comedy about a couple who murder swingers for their money to pay for a new restaurant. Paul Bartel and Mary Woronov star; Bartel directed. **CU5, CU42**

Ebony Tower, The (1983, C, 80m, NR)
An aging artist living in a country house with two young women hosts an art critic, who begins a romance with one of the women. Laurence Olivier, Roger Rees, and Greta Scacchi star. Based on a novel by John Fowles. Originally made for cable TV. **CL32**

Eclipse, The (1962, B&W, 123m, NR)
From Italian director Michelangelo Antonioni, a drama of doomed love between a young Roman translator and a handsome broker, starring Monica Vitti and Alain Delon. **FF17, XT9**

Ecstasy (1933, B&W, 88m, NR)
Notorious film, banned for many years in some states, mainly for brief nude swimming and suggestive love-making scenes. The story is of a bored young wife (Hedy Lamarr) and her affair with a workman. **CU6, CU8, FF7**

Eddie and the Cruisers (1983, C, 90m, PG)
A rock group's debut album is a smash hit, but their leader disappears with the tapes for their follow-up record. Years later, a journalist opens an investigation of the mystery. Tom Berenger, Michael Pare, and Ellen Barkin star. **DR12, MU4**

Eddie Murphy: Delirious (1983, C, 60m, NR)
This live concert, taped at Washington, D.C.'s Constitution Hall, features some of Murphy's most outrageous routines, with no-holds-barred language and wit. **CO16**

Eddie Murphy Raw (1987, C, 91m, R)
More concert comedy featuring the outrageous humor of Eddie Murphy, filmed at New York's Madison Square Garden. Directed by Robert Townsend. **CO16**

Educating Rita (1983, C, 110m, PG)
A young wife (Julie Walters) who works as a hairdresser wants to improve her life, and she selects an alcoholic professor (Michael Caine) to do the job. **CO17**

Egyptian, The (1954, C, 140m, NR)
Elaborate historical drama set in ancient Egypt, centering on a physician to the Pharoah and his love affairs. Edmund Purdom stars, with Victor Mature, Michael Wilding, Jean Simmons, and Peter Ustinov. **CL3**

Eiger Sanction, The (1975, C, 128m, R)
Clint Eastwood directed and stars in this drama of a professor who moonlights as a CIA agent. He leads a mountain-climbing expedition designed to expose a traitorous agent. **AC12, AC27, MY6**

8 1/2 (1963, B&W, 135m, NR)
Oscar-winning film from Federico Fellini about a film director unsure what his next project is to be. This autobiographical film has had an enormous influence on many other movies. Marcello Mastroianni, Claudia Cardinale, and Anouk Aimee star. **DR13, FF10, FF24, XT7** *Highly Recommended*

Eight Men Out (1988, C, 120m, PG-13)
Superbly detailed recreation of the major league scandal that forever changed the sport, when players on the 1919 Chicago White Sox conspired to "fix" the World Series. John Cusack, David Strathairn, D.B Sweeney, and Charlie Sheen star, with Christopher Lloyd, Clifton James, and Studs Terkel. Written and directed by John Sayles, who plays sportswriter Ring Lardner. **DR5, DR22** *Highly Recommended*

8 Million Ways to Die (1986, C, 115m, R)
Urban action drama of an alcoholic ex-cop (Jeff Bridges) involved with a prostitute (Rosanna Arquette) and her vicious pimp (Andy Garcia). With Alexandra Paul. **AC8, DR71**

18 Again! (1988, C, 100m, PG)
A teenager (Charlie Schlatter) recovers from an accident to find that the mind of his lively grandfather (George Burns) has taken over his body. **CO5, CO37**

84 Charing Cross Road (1987, C, 100m, PG)
Drama about New York writer Helene Hanff and her twenty-year correspondence with a London bookseller. A small gem of a film starring Anne Bancroft and Anthony Hopkins. **DR4, DR6, DR20** *Recommended*

84 Charley Mopic (1989, C, 95m, R)
Vietnam War drama, presenting events as seen through the eyes (and lens) of a documentary filmmaker. Written and directed by Patrick Duncan. **AC4** *Recommended*

El Cid (1961, C, 184m, R)
The story of the legendary eleventh-century Christian hero (Charlton Heston) who freed Spain from Moorish invaders. Directed by Anthony Mann; Sophia Loren costars. **AC16, FF31, WE20**

El Condor (1970, C, 102m, R)
Western tale set in Mexico, with two cowpokes searching for a cache of gold. Jim Brown and Lee Van Cleef star. **WE10**

El Dorado (1967, C, 126m, NR)
From director Howard Hawks comes this tale of an aging gunslinger (John Wayne) who stands up to a land-grabbing cattle baron. Robert Mitchum costars. **WE17, WE21**

Electric Horseman, The (1979, C, 120m, PG)
A reporter (Jane Fonda) rounds up a rodeo star (Robert Redford) for a scoop, but she winds up with more than she bargained for. Willie Nelson costars; Sydney Pollack directed this romantic comedy. **CO1, DR27, DR29, DR56, MU12, WE13**

Eleni (1985, C, 116m, PG)
Drama based on New York reporter Nicholas Gage's search for the man who executed Gage's mother in war-torn Greece in the late 1940s. John Malkovich and Kate Nelligan star. **DR6**

Elephant Man, The (1980, B&W, 125m, PG)
The life of John Merrick, a Victorian-age Briton who suffered from a terrible, deforming disease. John Hurt and Anthony Hopkins star; David Lynch directed. **CU38, DR4** *Recommended*

11 Harrowhouse (1974, C, 98m, PG)
Spoof of heist movies, written by and starring Charles Grodin as a diamond merchant who decides to pull off the ultimate jewel theft. Candice Bergen and James Mason costar. **CO7, CO10, MY34**

Elmer Fudd's Comedy Capers (1957, C, 57m, NR)
Cartoon comedy at its finest, including *The Rabbit of Seville, Hare Brush,* and *What's Opera, Doc?* **FA11** *Recommended*

Elmer Gantry (1960, C, 145m, NR)
Burt Lancaster won an Oscar as the smooth-talking tent preacher of Sinclair Lewis's novel. Jean Simmons and Oscar winner Shirley Jones costar as the women in Elmer's life—and his downfall. Richard Brooks directed. **DR19, DR41, XT2, XT5**

Elusive Corporal, The (1962, B&W, 108m, NR)
From French director Jean Renoir, the story of a World War II P.O.W. and his attempts to escape. **FF12**

Elvis '56 (1987, C, 61m, NR)
Documentary, narrated by Levon Helm, focuses on the year when Elvis rocked the nation with stunning performances in concert and on national television. Directed by Alan and Susan Raymond; originally made for cable TV. **MU11** *Highly Recommended*

Elvis—1968 Comeback Special (1968, C, 76m, NR)
This live television broadcast marked the King's return to the concert stage. **MU10** *Highly Recommended*

Elvis on Tour (1972, C, 93m, NR)
Elvis Presley, on-stage and off, on one of his cross-country tours. **MU11**

Elvis: That's the Way It Is (1970, C, 97m, NR)
Behind the scenes with Elvis, as he prepares for his debut on the Las Vegas stage. **MU11**

Emerald Forest, The (1985, C, 113m, R)
Adventure tale, based on fact, of an American father looking in the Amazon jungles for his long-lost son, who was actually kidnapped and raised by natives. Powers Boothe and Charley Boorman star; John Boorman directed. **AC12, CU32**

Emil and the Detectives (1964, C, 99m, NR)
Disney adventure about a young boy who is robbed and enlists the help of his detective friends to catch the thief. **FA1**

Emperor Jones, The (1933, B&W, 72m, NR)
Paul Robeson stars in this adaptation of the Eugene O'Neill play about a black fugitive who escapes a chain gang and becomes the king of a Caribbean island. **DR14, DR20**

Emperor's New Clothes, The (1984, C, 60m, NR)
This story from the Faerie Tale Theatre collection features Art Carney and Alan Arkin as two con men who pull the invisible wool over the eyes of a vain king (Dick Shawn). **FA12**

Empire of the Ants (1977, C, 90m, PG)
Vacationers on an island are attacked by monster ants in this loose adaptation of an H.G. Wells story. Joan Collins and Robert Lansing star. **SF10, SF26**

Empire of the Sun (1987, C, 152m, PG)
A British boy living in Shanghai when Japanese invade in the 1930s finds himself separated from his parents and on his own during the war. Steven Spielberg directed; Christian Bale and John Malkovich star. **DR5, DR9, SF24**

Empire Strikes Back, The (1980, C, 124m, PG)
The first sequel to *Star Wars* features a developing romance between Han Solo (Harrison Ford) and Princess Leia (Carrie Fisher), while Luke Skywalker (Mark Hamill) meets the kindly sage Yoda. Billy Dee Williams and Alec Guinness costar. Special effects won an Oscar. **DR32, DR63, FA8, SF11, SF13, SF15, SF23** *Recommended*

Empty Canvas, The (1964, B&W, 118m, NR)
Bette Davis plays the mother of a model who is the obsession of a young French artist. Horst Bucholz and Catherine Spaak costar. **CL21**

Enchanted Cottage, The (1945, B&W, 91m, NR)
Dorothy McGuire and Robert Young portray two misfits who fall in love in a magical New England cottage. **CL4**

Enchanted Forest, The (1945, C, 78m, NR)
Fantasy of a young boy who learns about life from his visits to an old man who lives in the forest. Edmund Lowe stars. **FA8**

Encore (1952, B&W, 89m, NR)
Sequel to *Quartet* and *Trio* presents three more tales by W. Somerset Maugham, with Anthony Pelissier, Nigel Patrick, and Glynis Johns heading the cast. **DR19**

End, The (1978, C, 100m, R)
Burt Reynolds stars in this black comedy about a terminally ill man whose friends and relatives can't seem to deal with his imminent demise. Sally Field, Dom DeLuise, Joanne Woodward, Myrna Loy, Pat O'Brien, and Kristy McNichol costar. **AC37, CL46, CO12, DR36, DR67**

End of the Road, The (1969, C, 110m, R)
Basic drama of a romantic triangle in college community is a springboard for commentary on variety of late-1960s social issues in this bizarre film. Stacy Keach, Harris Yulin, Dorothy Tristan, and James Earl Jones star; based on John Barth's novel. **DR7, DR19**

End of the World (1977, C, 87m, PG)
Christopher Lee plays two roles: a priest and his grotesque, murderous double in this science fiction drama about alien invaders. **HO32**

Endangered Species (1982, C, 97m, R)
New York cop on vacation stumbles onto mystery in small Wyoming town involving cattle mutilations. Robert Urich, Jo-Beth Williams, Paul Dooley, and Hoyt Axton star. Alan Rudolph directed. **CU26**

Endgame (1985, C, 98m, PG-13)
Science fiction adventure set in a vaguely post-apocalyptic world, with survival the name of the game. Al Cliver and Moira Chen star. **SF8**

Endless Night (1971, C, 99m, NR)
A chauffeur marries an heiress (Hayley Mills), and they move into a mysterious old house. Based on an Agatha Christie novel. **MY19, MY23**

Enemy Mine (1985, C, 108m, PG-13)
When an astronaut crashes on a remote planet, he is forced to join with an alien to survive various hardships. Dennis Quaid and Louis Gossett, Jr. star. **SF8**

Enemy of the People, An (1977, C, 103m, G)
Steve McQueen stars in this version of Henrik Ibsen's 19th-century drama about a doctor warning a small town of the dangers of water pollution. Bibi Andersson and Charles Durning costar. **AC28, DR20**

Enforcer, The (1951, B&W, 87m, NR)
Humphrey Bogart stars as a crusading district attorney determined to put a syndicate boss (Everett Sloane) behind bars. **CL20**

Enforcer, The (1976, C, 96m, R)
Third in the *Dirty Harry* series, with Clint Eastwood taking on a female partner (Tyne Daly), as they hunt down terrorists who have kidnapped the mayor of San Francisco. **AC9, AC27**

Ensayo de un Crimen (Rehearsal of a Murder) *see* Criminal Life of Archibaldo de la Cruz, The

Ensign Pulver (1964, C, 104m, NR)
This sequel to *Mister Roberts* follows the shenanigans of Ensign Pulver (Robert Walker, Jr.) as he tries to save the captain (Burl Ives), who has been washed overboard. Notable for early screen appearances of Jack Nicholson and Larry Hagman. **DR24**

Enter the Dragon (1973, C, 90m, R)
Martial arts classic, with cult following, starring Bruce Lee in his last finished film. He's invited to a fighting tournament on an island stronghold run by a criminal kingpin. Exciting action sequences. **AC33, CU7, XT11** *Highly Recommended*

Entertaining Mr. Sloane (1970, C, 94m, NR)
In this offbeat comedy based on the Joe Orton play, a handsome young criminal becomes sexually involved with both a widow and her brother. Beryl Reid, Harry Andrews, and Peter McEnery star. **CO12, CO17**

Entre Nous (1983, C, 110m, PG)
Drama of two women whose friendship for each other over a 20-year span proves stronger than what they feel for their husbands. Isabelle Huppert and Miou-Miou star; Diane Kurys directed. **DR10, FF1** *Recommended*

Equalizer 2000 (1986, C, 85m, R)
In a post-apocalypse world, only Slade, the one-man army, will take on the brutal dictatorship of The Ownership. Richard Norton and Corinne Wahl star. **AC25**

Equus (1977, C, 138m, R)
A psychiatrist (Richard Burton) tries to unravel the problems of a stable boy (Peter Firth) who intentionally blinds horses. Based on the Peter Shaffer play; directed by Sidney Lumet. **DR20, DR58**

Eraserhead (1978, B&W, 90m, NR)
Director David Lynch's legendary cult film about a reclusive young man (John Nance), the deformed baby he fathers, and his bizarre imaginary life. A midnight-screening favorite. **CU1, CU12, CU38, HO14**

Erendira (1983, C, 103, NR)
Offbeat drama, based on a story by Gabriel Garcia Marquez, about a woman who travels the countryside with a carnival starring her young granddaughter as a sexual slave. Irene Papas stars; filmed in Mexico. **FF6**

Ernest Goes to Camp (1987, C, 93m, PG)
Ernest P. Worrell, world's most inept human, gets his wish when he envisions himself as a camp counselor. Jim Varney stars in this silly family comedy. **FA6**

Ernest Saves Christmas (1988, C, 89m, PG)
Jim Varney stars as Ernest P. Worrell, the good-natured hayseed who's out to fill in when Santa can't make his annual trip. **FA6, FA13**

Errand Boy, The (1961, B&W, 92m, NR)
Star Jerry Lewis directed this tale of a nutty young nerd set loose in a movie studio. **CO25**

Escape Artist, The (1982, C, 96m, PG)
Young magician tries to follow in his late father's footsteps in this offbeat drama starring Griffin O'Neal, with Teri Garr, Raul Julia, Joan Hackett, and Desi Arnaz. Directed by Caleb Deschanel. **DR9, FA7** *Recommended*

Escape From Alcatraz (1979, C, 112m, PG)
Clint Eastwood stars as bank robber Frank Morris, who led the only escape from the famed maximum security prison in which no one was caught. Directed by Don Siegel. **AC27, DR18** *Recommended*

Escape From New York (1981, C, 99m, R)
In the near-future, Manhattan has become a maximum-security prison for the worst criminal elements. When the President's plane crashes there, the government hires a soldier of fortune to rescue him. John Carpenter directed; Kurt Russell, Lee Van Cleef, Harry Dean Stanton, and Adrienne Barbeau star. **AC21, CU29, CU49, SF8**

Escape From the Planet of the Apes (1971, C, 98m, PG)
Third in the *Apes* series of science fiction adventures, with the ape characters in contemporary Los Angeles. Roddy McDowall, Kim Hunter, and Bradford Dillman star. **FA8, SF8, SF13, SF23**

Escape to Burma (1955, C, 87m, NR)
Barbara Stanwyck's the tough mistress of a tea plantation who's confronted by a desperate fugitive (Robert Ryan). **CL45**

Escape to Witch Mountain (1975, C, 97m, G)
Two children with mysterious powers are the object of a villain's plans in this Disney adventure. Ray Milland, Eddie Albert, and Donald Pleasence costar. **FA1**

Escape 2000 (1981, C, 92m, R)
Futuristic action drama about a society where criminals are hunted down like animals. Filmed in Australia; Steve Railsback and Olivia Hussey star. **FF5, SF11**

L'Ete Meurtrier *see* One Deadly Summer

Eternal Return, The (1943, B&W, 100m, NR)
French drama, based on the Tristan and Isolde legend, starring Jean Marais. Jean Cocteau contributed to the screenplay. **FF1**

Eureka (1981, C, 130m, R)
Offbeat drama set on a Caribbean island, about a wealthy ex-prospector, his daughter and her shady lover, and a pair of hit men. Gene Hackman, Theresa Russell,

Rutger Hauer, and Mickey Rourke star; Nicolas Roeg directed. **CU34, DR39, DR48**

Europa '51 (1951, B&W, 110m, NR)
Ingrid Bergman stars in a drama of a wealthy woman's search for peace after the death of her son. Roberto Rossellini, then Bergman's husband, directed. Also known as *The Greatest Love*. **CL27**

Europeans, The (1979, C, 90m, NR)
A staid American family living in 19th-century New England tries to cope with the arrival of two foreign cousins. Ismail Merchant produced and James Ivory directed this drama, based on the Henry James novel. Lee Remick stars. **DR19**

Even More Ripping Yarns *see* Ripping Yarns (series)

Evening With Bobcat Goldthwait, An: Share the Warmth (1987, C, 83m, NR)
The comedian whom one critic called "a cross between Joe Cocker and a serial killer" performs in concert. **CO16**

Evening With Robin Williams, An (1982, C, 92m, NR)
The fastest funny man in America goes wild in this energetic comedy special. **CO16, CO43**

Every Girl Should Be Married (1948, B&W, 85m, NR)
Comedy about a determined girl (Betsy Drake) who sets out to capture the affections of a bachelor (Cary Grant). **CL18**

Every Man for Himself and God Against All (1975, C, 110m, NR)
German drama, based on fact, about a strange, child-like man who appeared one day in 19th-century Nuremberg. Directed by Werner Herzog. Also known as *The Mystery of Kasper Hauser*. **FF19** *Recommended*

Every Time We Say Goodbye (1987, C, 97m, PG-13)
An American soldier recuperating in a Jerusalem hospital falls in love with a

Jewish girl, and her family opposes the romance. Tom Hanks and Christine Marsillach star in this drama set during World War II. **CO44, DR3**

Every Which Way But Loose (1978, C, 114m, PG)
Clint Eastwood plays a two-fisted truck driver who travels the country with his pet orangutan Clyde in pursuit of a country and western singer (Sondra Locke). Beverly D'Angelo and Ruth Gordon co-star in this action comedy. **AC27, CO9**

Everybody's All American (1988, C, 127m, R)
Dennis Quaid and Jessica Lange star in a romantic drama of a college football star and homecoming queen who marry and then have to deal with his post-sports career problems. With Timothy Hutton and John Goodman. **DR1, DR22, DR74**

Everything You Always Wanted to Know About Sex But Were Afraid to Ask (1972, C, 87m, R)
Writer-director Woody Allen stars in this compilation of seven comic sketches, each answering a valid question about sexuality. With Gene Wilder, John Carradine, Burt Reynolds, and Tony Randall. The last bit, "What Happens During Orgasm?", is particularly funny. **AC37, CO27** *Recommended*

Evil Dead, The (1982, C, 85m, NR)
Gruesome horror film about five college pals on a woodsy vacation in a remote cabin and how they're possessed by spirits of the dead. **CU7, HO8**

Evil Dead 2: Dead by Dawn (1987, C, 85m, X)
The remaining survivior from *The Evil Dead* returns to the sight of the murders, where supernatural demons once again take over. **HO8**

Evil Mind, The (1934, B&W, 80m, NR)
A phony clairvoyant begins to predict events which do happen. Claude Rains and Fay Wray star. **HO7, MY19**

Evil of Frankenstein (1964, C, 98m, NR)
The baron tries to manipulate his monster with the help of a hypnotist, but the monster runs amok. Peter Cushing stars in this British-made film. **HO26, HO33**

Evil That Men Do, The (1984, C, 89m, R)
Charles Bronson action thriller, with the hero tracking down a doctor who advises dictators on torture techniques. Joseph Maher plays the villain. **AC29**

Evil Under the Sun (1982, C, 102m, PG)
Hercule Poirot (Peter Ustinov) investigates a murder at a resort hotel. Based on the Agatha Christie novel; Jane Birkin, James Mason, Sylvia Miles, Diana Rigg, and Maggie Smith costar. **MY16, MY23**

Evilspeak (1982, C, 90m, R)
An orphan at a military academy uses black magic on the cadets who have tormented him. **HO13**

Excalibur (1981, C, 140m, R)
The King Arthur legend, starring Nigel Terry, Helen Mirren, Nicol Williamson, and Cherie Lunghi; directed by John Boorman. **AC18, CU32**

Executioner's Song, The (1982, C, 157m, NR)
Dramatic account of murderer Gary Gilmore and his fight to be executed by the state of Utah. Emmy winner Tommy Lee Jones costars with Rosanna Arquette; Norman Mailer adapted his own book. Originally made for TV; video version contains footage not shown in original broadcast. **CU10, DR6, DR16**

Executive Action (1973, C, 91m, PG)
Burt Lancaster stars in this thriller claiming a conspiracy was behind President Kennedy's assassination. Robert Ryan costars in one of his last screen appearances. **DR41**

Executive Suite (1954, B&W, 104m, NR)
High-powered corporate soap opera, with all-star cast: William Holden, June Allyson, Barbara Stanwyck, Fredric March, Walter Pidgeon, and Shelley Winters. Di-

rected by Robert Wise. **CL45, CL51, CL58, DR7, DR60**

Exodus (1960, C, 213m, NR)
Paul Newman and Eva Marie Saint star in this epic drama of the birth of the modern state of Israel and the Palestinean war that resulted. Ralph Richardson, Sal Mineo, John Derek, and Jill Haworth costar. Directed by Otto Preminger; based on Leon Uris's novel. **DR28**

Exorcist, The (1973, C, 122m, R)
A young girl is possessed by the devil and a special priest is called in to perform a horrifying ritual of exorcism. Linda Blair, Ellen Burstyn, Max von Sydow, and Jason Miller star in this modern horror classic based on the bestseller by William Peter Blatty, set in Washington, D.C.. **HO8, HO13, XT9** *Recommended*

Exorcist II: The Heretic (1977, C, 110m, R)
Delirious sequel to *The Exorcist*, with Linda Blair the subject of experiments by priest Richard Burton and researcher Louise Fletcher. Directed by John Boorman. **CU32, HO13**

Experiment in Terror (1962, B&W, 123m, NR)
An F.B.I. agent (Glenn Ford) tracks a killer who has terrorized a bank teller (Lee Remick) into embezzlement by kidnapping her sister. Directed by Blake Edwards on location in San Francisco. **CO46, MY2, XT9**

Experiment Perilous (1944, B&W, 91m, NR)
An unsuspecting wife (Hedy Lamarr) is tormented by her overbearing husband (Paul Lukas), who is set on driving her mad. Directed by Jacques Tourneur. **HO37**

Experts, The (1989, C, 94m, PG-13)
Comedy adventures of a pair of hip (but not too bright) dudes who travel from New York to what they think is a Nebraska town to open a night club. In reality, they're in a mock American town

inside the Soviet Union, unwittingly teaching pop culture to Russian agents masquerading as Americans. John Travolta and Arye Gross star, with Charlie Martin Smith and Kelly Preston. Directed by Dave Thomas. **CO2, CO14, CO37**

Explorers (1985, C, 109m, PG)
A young science fiction buff gets his wish for space travel in a scheme concocted by his friend. Joe Dante directed this special effects comedy. **CO11, CU40, FA8, SF3, SF13**

Exterminating Angel, The (1962, B&W, 95m, NR)
Surrealistic masterwork from director Luis Buñuel: a party of well-to-do friends suddenly find they cannot leave a room. Silvia Pinal stars. **FF11** *Highly Recommended*

Exterminator, The (1980, C, 101m, R)
Robert Ginty plays a Vietnam veteran with vengeance on his mind when his buddy is blown away by the Mob. This extremely violent action thriller was directed by James Glickenhaus. **AC19**

Exterminator 2, The (1984, C, 88m, R)
Star Robert Ginty and director James Glickenhaus return for more adventures of the man with the blowtorch. **AC19**

Exterminators of the Year 3000 (1983, C, 101m, R)
Science fiction adventure with the world gone dry from years without rain and warring factions fighting for every precious drop of water. **SF8**

Extreme Prejudice (1987, C, 104m, R)
Violent action drama about boyhood friends who grow up on opposite sides of the law and on opposite sides of the Tex-Mex border. Nick Nolte is the Texas Ranger, Powers Boothe the drug kingpin. With Maria Conchita Alonso and Rip Torn. Walter Hill directed. **CU27, CU47, DR44**

Extremities (1986, C, 89m, R)
A woman is nearly raped in her home but turns the tables on her attacker and holds him prisoner, trying to decide how to dispense justice. Farrah Fawcett stars. **DR10, DR20**

Eye for an Eye, An (1981, C, 106m, R)
Chuck Norris is a cop whose partner is killed by drug dealers. He swears vengeance and singlehandedly takes on the gang leader (Christopher Lee) and his men. **AC32, HO32**

Eye of the Needle (1981, C, 112m, R)
Donald Sutherland is a German spy stranded on a British island during World War II. He seduces a lonely woman (Kate Nelligan) in hopes of using her to effect his plans. **MY6**

Eye of the Tiger (1986, C, 88m, R)
A newcomer to a small town battles local corruption, goes on a rampage when his wife and child are murdered. Gary Busey and Yaphet Kotto star. **AC19**

Eyeball (1977, C, 87m, R)
Horror story of a psychopathic murderer and his particularly gruesome calling card. **HO9**

Eyes of a Stranger (1980, C, 85m, R)
A newswoman is on the trail of a psychopathic killer after she finds that her sister, a blind and deaf young girl, could be his next victim. **HO9**

Eyes of Laura Mars (1978, C, 103m, R)
A fashion photographer (Faye Dunaway) has premonitions of brutal murders, but she can't persuade anyone to believe her. Tommy Lee Jones costars in this stylish thriller. **DR35, HO7, MY2, MY3**

Eyes of Texas (1948, B&W, 54m, NR)
Roy Rogers turns his ranch into a camp for boys orphaned by World War II. With Andy Devine. **WE23**

Eyes, the Mouth, The (1982, C, 100m, R)
A young man tries to come to grips with his twin brother's suicide in this drama

from Italian director Marco Bellochio. Lou Castel stars. **FF2**

Eyewitness (1981, C, 102m, R)
A janitor (William Hurt) pretends he has access to evidence in a baffling murder case, just to get acquainted with a TV news reporter (Sigourney Weaver) he admires. With Christopher Plummer, James Woods, and Pamela Reed. **DR31, DR76, MY5**

F.I.S.T. (1978, C, 145m, PG)
Sylvester Stallone plays a union boss who unsuccessfuly attempts to resist corruption in this drama based loosely on the life of Jimmy Hoffa. With Rod Steiger, Peter Boyle, and Melinda Dillon. **AC31, DR7**

F/X (1986, C, 106m, R)
A movie special effects expert is hired to stage the phony killing of a government witness against the Mob. When the man actually dies, the effects man realizes he has been set up. Bryan Brown stars, with Jerry Orbach and Mason Adams. **AC19, DR13, MY9**

Fabulous Dorseys, The (1947, B&W, 88m, NR)
Biography of those great bandleaders and musicians, Tommy and Jimmy Dorsey, with the brothers playing themselves. Musicians Art Tatum and Charlie Barnet appear in one memorable jam session. **MU5**

Face in the Crowd, A (1957, B&W, 125m, NR)
Andy Griffith portrays a country bumpkin who rises to sudden fame as a television star and develops dangerous political ambitions. Patricia Neal and Walter Matthau costar, with Lee Remick making her film debut. Written by Budd Schulberg; directed by Elia Kazan. **CL7, DR59** *Recommended*

Fade to Black (1980, C, 100m, R)
A lonely young man who fantasizes about movies begins dressing up like famous

film villains and eliminating his tormentors. Dennis Christopher stars. **HO9**

Fahrenheit 451 (1967, C, 111m, NR)
In a future society, firemen start fires, urged by a dictatorship to burn books and keep the population ignorant. Oskar Werner and Julie Christie (playing two roles) star; François Truffaut directed. **CU5, CU13, FF13, SF11**

Fail-Safe (1964, B&W, 111m, NR)
A U.S. Air Force plane is accidentally ordered to bomb the Soviet Union, which could start a nuclear war. Henry Fonda stars; Sidney Lumet directed. **CL24, DR58**

Falcon and the Snowman, The (1985, C, 131m, R)
True story of two boyhood friends (Timothy Hutton, Sean Penn) who grow up to become spies and sell American secrets to the Russians. **DR6, DR16, DR26, MY6**

Fall of the House of Usher, The (1960, C, 79m, NR)
A beautiful young girl is brought to her fiance's mysterious house, where the skeletons come out of the closets with hairraising results. Vincent Price stars; Roger Corman directed this first of his eight films based on the works of Edgar Allan Poe. Also known as *House of Usher*. **HO31, HO41**

Fall of the Roman Empire, The (1964, C, 153m, NR)
From director Anthony Mann comes an epic of Livius, the renegade general (Stephen Boyd) who's torn between his country and his lover (Sophia Loren). Costars Alec Guinness, James Mason, Christopher Plummer, and Omar Sharif. **CL3, DR63, FF31, WE20**

Falling in Love (1984, C, 106m, PG-13)
Robert DeNiro and Meryl Streep star as two married Manhattan-bound commuters who strike up a friendship that develops into something more serious. **DR3, DR25, DR26, XT9**

Fame (1983, C, 134m, R)
New York City's High School for the Performing Arts is the backdrop for this story of aspiring students who struggle to make it in show business. Directed by Alan Parker. **MU9, XT9**

Family, The (1970, C, 100m, R)
An ex-con seeks retribution against the man who framed him and stole his girl friend while he was in prison. Charles Bronson stars, with Jill Ireland and Telly Savalas. **AC29**

Family, The (1987, C, 127m, PG)
Drama of eighty years in the life of one family in Rome, directed by Ettore Scola. Vittorio Gassman stars, with Fanny Ardant, Philippe Noiret, and Stefania Sandrelli. **FF2**

Family Game, The (1984, C, 107m, NR)
Comedy centering on Japanese family who hires a tutor for one its sons and winds up being totally dominated by the teacher. Directed by Yoshimitsu Morita. **FF4**

Family Jewels, The (1965, C, 100m, NR)
Jerry Lewis plays seven outrageously different roles, as potential guardians to a little heiress. **CO25**

Family Plot (1976, C, 120m, PG)
Alfred Hitchcock's final film is about a phony psychic who, along with her private-eye boyfriend, tries to find a missing heir. Barbara Harris, Bruce Dern, William Devane, and Karen Black star. **MY22**

Fandango (1985, C, 91m, PG)
Five college friends decide to go off for one last fling before they're drafted to fight in the Vietnam War. Judd Nelson and Kevin Costner star. **CO4**

Fanny (1932, B&W, 120m, NR)
Second part of famed trilogy by French writer-director Marcel Pagnol (*Marius* is first, *Cesar* is last). Fanny (Orane Demazis) is abandoned by her true love Marius (Pierre Fresnay). **FF1**

Fanny and Alexander (1983, C, 197m, R)
Oscar-winning family epic from director Ingmar Bergman, a mixture of comedy and drama set in turn-of-the-century Sweden. The point of view is that of a young boy and his sister, as they witness their beloved father's death and their mother's remarriage to a stern minister. **FF8, XT7**
Recommended

Fantastic Planet (1973, C, 72m, NR)
From France, an animated science fiction adventure about a planet where men are slaves to gigantic mechanical creatures. **FF1, SF19**

Fantastic Voyage (1966, C, 100m, NR)
Team of scientists is miniaturized and injected into the body of a patient in need of advanced micro-surgery. Oscar-winning special effects highlight this science fiction adventure. Donald Pleasence, Stephen Boyd, Raquel Welch, and Edmond O'Brien star. **SF3, SF15**

Far Country, The (1955, C, 97m, NR)
Western tale about a cattleman (James Stewart) in search of a boomtown on the Alaskan tundra. Directed by Anthony Mann. **CL9, CL25, WE11, WE20**

Far Frontier, The (1948, B&W, 67m, NR)
Roy Rogers rides to the rescue of a kidnapped Border Patrol agent. With Andy Devine. **WE23**

Far North (1988, C, 88m, PG-13)
Sam Shepard wrote and directed this drama of a woman's struggle to reconcile herself with her father. Jessica Lange and Charles Durning star, with Anne Wedgeworth. **DR8, DR74**

Farewell, Friend *see* Honor Among Thieves

Farewell, My Lovely (1975, C, 97m, R)
Robert Mitchum plays Philip Marlowe, Raymond Chandler's famous detective, who is hired to find an ex-con's sweetheart. With Charlotte Rampling, John Ireland, and Harry Dean Stanton. Filmed in

1944 as *Murder My Sweet*. **CU18, CU48, MY24**

Farewell to Arms, A (1932, B&W, 78m, NR)
Tragic love story, based on the Ernest Hemingway novel, about an affair between an army nurse (Helen Hayes) and a young soldier (Gary Cooper) during World War I. **AC2, CL26, DR19**

Farewell to the King (1989, C, 117m, PG-13)
During World War II, a renegade American soldier successfully leads natives on a South Pacific island against the Japanese. Nick Nolte stars in this action drama from writer-director John Milius. **AC1, DR44**

Farmer's Daughter (1947, B&W, 97m, NR)
Loretta Young gave an Academy Award-winning performance in this comedy of a Swedish housemaid and her boss, a Washington politician. With Joseph Cotten, Ethel Barrymore, and Charles Bickford. **XT3**

Fashions of 1934 (1934, B&W, 78m, NR)
Bette Davis plays a fashion designer who, along with a con man (William Powell), conquers the Paris fashion world. **CL21**

Fast Break (1979, C, 107m, PG)
A New York City basketball coach accepts a position in the Midwest and brings his street-wise players with him. Gabe Kaplan stars. **CO36**

Fast Forward (1985, C, 110m, PG)
Eight teenagers from a small town in Ohio venture to New York City to enter a national dance contest. Directed by Sidney Poitier. **DR38**

Fast Talking (1986, C, 93m, NR)
A bright 15-year-old from a broken home uses his wits to wriggle out of sticky situations. Family comedy-drama stars Steve Bisley. **FA7**

Fast Times at Ridgemont High (1982, C, 92m, R)
Sean Penn stars as Spicoli, the ultimate party animal, in this comedy about high school life. Jennifer Jason Leigh, Phoebe Cates, and Judge Reinhold are his less laid-back classmates. Directed by Amy Heckerling. **CO4, CO35** *Recommended*

Fast-Walking (1982, C, 116m, R)
James Woods portrays Fast-Walking Miniver, a cynical prison guard who is ordered to assassinate a new black con (Robert Hooks) but can't resist an offer of $50,000 to help the same man escape. With Tim McIntire and Kay Lenz. **DR18** *Recommended*

Fastest Guitar Alive, The (1968, C, 88m, NR)
Civil War western starring rock star Roy Orbison. He's the leader of a band of Confederate soldiers trying to return money they stole just before the end of the conflict. Title refers to Orbison's instrument, which converts to a gun; he does sing several songs. **MU16, WE7**

Fat City (1972, C, 100m, PG)
John Huston directed this story of a small time boxer trying to pass on some of his ring savvy to a young fighter. Stacy Keach and Jeff Bridges star. Written by Leonard Gardner; based on his novel. **CL44, DR19, DR22, DR71** *Recommended*

Fatal Attraction (1987, C, 102m, R)
A family man (Michael Douglas) has a weekend fling with a young woman (Glenn Close), who turns murderously possessive, threatening to ruin his entire life. Anne Archer costars; directed by Adrian Lyne. **DR3, DR6, DR70, DR72, MY17, MY18**

Fatal Beauty (1987, C, 105m, R)
Whoopi Goldberg goes undercover to track the dealers of a dangerous drug, Fatal Beauty. She gets help from a bodyguard (Sam Elliott) whom she suspects of knowing more about distribution of the drug than he admits. Ruben Blades costars. **AC9, MU12**

Fatal Glass of Beer, The/Pool Shark, The
(1933/1915, B&W, 29m, NR)
Two classic shorts starring W.C. Fields.
In the first, Fields is in the frozen North
battling the elements. In the second, one
of his early silent films, Fields gets involved in a duel over a beautiful girl; no
pistols or swords are brandished, only
pool cues. **CO22**

Fatal Vision (1984, C, 200m, NR)
True story about an army doctor accused
of killing his wife and two daughters. His
father-in-law is sure of his guilt, and pursues the case in a bitter trial. Karl Malden, Gary Cole, and Andy Griffith star.
Originally made for TV. **DR16, MY8** *Recommended*

Father Brown *see* The Detective (1954)

Father Goose (1964, C, 115m, NR)
Cary Grant plays a beach bum on a South
Pacific island during World War II. He
winds up protecting a teacher (Leslie Caron) and her girl students, who are fleeing
the Japanese. **CL18**

Father of the Bride (1950, B&W, 93m, NR)
Spencer Tracy is the father, Elizabeth
Taylor is the bride in this warm comedy
about preparations for a wedding. Vin-
cente Minnelli directed. **CL19, CL33,
MU24** *Recommended*

Father's Little Dividend (1951, B&W, 82,
NR)
Sequel to *Father of the Bride* has Spencer
Tracy adjusting to the idea of becoming a
grandfather. Elizabeth Taylor costars;
Vincente Minnelli directed. **CL19, CL33,
MU24**

Favorita, La (1952, B&W, 82m, NR)
Film version of the opera, with Sophia
Loren in an early supporting role. **FF31**

Fawlty Towers, Volumes 1-4 (1975, C, approx. 75m. each, NR)
Each of these four volumes contains three
episodes of the hilarious British TV series
starring John Cleese as the hyperbolic
owner of a slightly rundown seaside hotel.

Prunella Scales and Connie Booth costar;
Cleese and Booth wrote the scripts. **CO15**
Highly Recommended

Fear (1954, B&W, 84m, NR)
Ingrid Bergman stars as a woman who
begins to collapse from the everyday
pressures of life. Directed by Roberto
Rossellini, then her husband. **CL27**

Fear Chamber, The *see* Chamber of Fear

Fear City (1984, C, 96m, R)
Tom Berenger and Jack Scalia plays the
owners of a New York talent agency that
specializes in "exotic dancers." They're
looking for a killer who has been eliminating their clients. Billy Dee Williams, Melanie Griffith, and Rae Dawn Chong costar. **AC8, DR15**

Fear in the Night (1972, C, 94m, NR)
Peter Cushing and Joan Collins star in
this tale of a tormented wife whose fear
drives her to the brink of insanity. **HO33**

Feds (1988, C, 83m, PG-13)
A pair of female recruits (Rebecca De-
Mornay, Mary Gross) bungle their way
through training at the F.B.I. Academy.
CO3

Fellini Satyricon *see* Satyricon

Female Trouble (1975, B&W, 95m, NR)
Director John Waters' follow-up to *Pink
Flamingos* stars Divine as a girl gone
wrong who finally suffers for her sins in
the electric chair. Camp or crude? It's up
to the viewer. **CU12, CU43**

Ferris Bueller's Day Off (1986, C, 103m,
PG-13)
A high school senior (Matthew Broderick)
with a knack for ducking trouble takes a
day off from school with two pals. Writ-
ten and directed by John Hughes. Mia
Sara and Alan Ruck costar, with Jeffrey
Jones, Jennifer Grey, and Charlie Sheen.
CO4, CO47, XT9

Fiddler on the Roof (1971, C, 184m, G)
Popular Broadway musical about a humble Ukrainian farmer at the turn of the century who has no dowries for his five unwed daughters. Great family viewing. **FA9, MU2** *Recommended*

Field of Dreams (1989, C, 106m, PG)
An Iowa farmer (Kevin Costner) builds a baseball diamond in his corn field, where the spirits of long-gone baseball stars like Shoeless Joe Jackson (Ray Liotta) come to play. Sentimental drama also features Amy Madigan, James Earl Jones, and Burt Lancaster. **DR8, DR22, DR41**

Field of Honor (1986, C, 93m, R)
Drama of a Dutch soldier's horrifying experiences in the Korean War. Based on a true story; Everett McGill stars. **AC3**

Fiend Without a Face (1958, B&W, 74m, NR)
Great special effects enhance this gruesome tale of a scientist whose thoughts materialize in the form of invisible creatures. These creatures then seek out victims to feed on their brains. **HO20, SF1**

Fiendish Plot of Dr. Fu Manchu (1980, C, 108m, PG)
Peter Sellers' last film casts him in two roles: Fu Manchu and his nemesis, Inspector Nayland Smith. As Fu Manchu tries to conquer the world, his bumbling enemy tries to stop him. **CO26**

55 Days at Peking (1963, C, 150m, NR)
Epic account of events in China surrounding the 1900 Boxer Rebellion, starring Charlton Heston, Ava Gardner, and David Niven. Directed by Nicholas Ray. **CU23**

52 Pick-up (1986, C, 114m, R)
A self-made businessman (Roy Scheider) is blackmailed by three creeps who know he has been cheating on his wife (Ann-Margret). John Glover and Clarence Williams III costar. Based on an Elmore Leonard novel. **MY2, MY26** *Recommended*

Fighting Back (1982, C, 98m, R)
A deli owner in South Philadelphia organizes his neighbors into a vigilante group to fight local thugs, with unexpected results. Tom Skerritt stars, with Patty LuPone, Michael Sarrazin, and Yaphet Kotto. **AC19**

Fighting Caravans (1932, B&W, 80m, NR)
Gary Cooper takes to the great outdoors in this western based on a Zane Grey story. **WE25**

Fighting Kentuckian, The (1949, B&W, 100m, NR)
John Wayne comes to rescue of homesteaders in colonial Kentucky. Oliver Hardy costars in a rare dramatic role. **CO20, WE17**

Fighting Mad (1977, C, 96m, R)
A soldier in Vietnam is left to die by his company, only to be captured by Japanese troops who think that World War II is still on. James Iglehart, Jayne Kennedy, and Leon Isaac Kennedy star. **AC4**

Fighting Prince of Donegal, The (1966, C, 112, NR)
Disney swashbuckler has the new head of an Irish family in the 16th century fighting for his people against British troops. **FA1**

Fighting Seabees, The (1944, B&W, 100m, NR)
John Wayne and Dennis O'Keefe are soldiers stationed in the South Pacific, both fighting for the same woman (Susan Hayward). **CL17**

Final Conflict, The (1981, C, 108m, R)
This third and final chapter of *The Omen* saga follows anti-christ Damien Thorn to adulthood, as he moves toward the Presidency. **HO10**

Final Countdown, The (1980, C, 104m, PG)
Modern aircraft carrier passes through a time warp to Pearl Harbor on the eve of the Japanese attack. Kirk Douglas and Martin Sheen star in this science fiction adventure. **SF4**

Final Mission, The (1984, C, 101m, NR)
A Vietnam veteran, now a policeman, gets a chance for revenge against a man who betrayed him in Southeast Asia. **AC19**

Final Terror, The (1983, C, 82m, R)
A psychopathic killer stalks teenagers in a forest. Daryl Hannah and Rachel Ward star. **HO12**

Finders Keepers (1984, C, 96m, PG)
Frantic comedy, set mostly on a train, involving con men, coffins, hired killers, and a fortune in stolen money. Michael O'Keefe, Beverly D'Angelo, and Louis Gossett, Jr. star; Richard Lester directed. **CU35**

Fine Madness, A (1966, C, 104m, NR)
Sean Connery plays an iconoclastic poet in this comedy-drama about society's attempts to tame a misfit. Joanne Woodward and Jean Seberg costar. **AC36, DR67**

Fine Mess, A (1986, C, 88m, PG)
Comedy about a pair of bumblers (Ted Danson, Howie Mandel) who overhear plans to fix a horse race, and wind up with the Mob and the police on their trail. Directed by Blake Edwards. **CO3, CO46**

Fingers (1978, C, 91m, R)
Cult movie with exceptionally violent scenes about a young man torn between career as a concert pianist and loyalty to his father, a numbers runner. Harvey Keitel stars, with Michael V. Gazzo and Jim Brown. James Toback directed. **CU7**

Finian's Rainbow (1968, C, 145m, NR)
Musical starring Fred Astaire as an Irishman whose leprechaun comes to life in the American South. Francis Ford Coppola directed this sly commentary on racism. **DR51, MU8, MU18**

Fire and Ice (1983, C, 81m, PG)
Animated adventure saga based on Frank Frazetta's dungeon & dragons characters, directed by Ralph Bakshi. **AC18**

Fire Down Below (1957, C, 116m, NR)
Shipboard romantic triangle, with Robert Mitchum and Jack Lemmon in conflict over Rita Hayworth on a tramp steamer. **DR64**

Fire Over England (1936, B&W, 89m, NR)
Vivien Leigh and Laurence Olivier portray young lovers in the court of Queen Elizabeth during the British-Spanish conflict. **CL3, CL32**

Firebird 2015 A.D. (1981, C, 97m, PG)
In this science fiction adventure, cars have been banned because of an oil shortage. Darren McGavin and Doug McClure star. **SF8**

Firefox (1982, C, 124m, PG)
An American undercover agent steals a super-secret plane from the Russians and heads for the border with Soviet aircraft in pursuit. Clint Eastwood stars; he also directed. **AC11, AC27**

Firemen's Ball, The (1968, C, 73m, NR)
Comedy from Czechoslovakia about a volunteer firemen's dance that turns into a full-scale disaster. Directed by Milos Forman. **DR57, FF7**

Firepower (1979, C, 104m, R)
Action drama, set in the Caribbean, starring Sophia Loren as a woman seeking revenge for the murder of her husband. James Coburn, O.J. Simpson, and Eli Wallach costar. **FF31**

Fires on the Plain (1959, B&W, 105m, NR)
Japanese war drama focuses on the suffering of several soldiers during the final days of World War II. Directed by Kon Ichikawa. **AC1, FF4**

Firestarter (1984, C, 115m, R)
Drew Barrymore plays a child who inherits the ability to start fires at a glance. Based on the Stephen King bestseller; George C. Scott and Martin Sheen costar. **HO13, HO42**

Firewalker (1986, C, 96m, R)
Tongue-in-cheek adventure story, with
Chuck Norris and Louis Gossett, Jr. as
two bumbling soldiers of fortune. **AC21,
AC32**

First Blood (1982, C, 97m, R)
Sylvester Stallone's first appearance as
John Rambo, the Vietnam vet with a chip
on his shoulder. Here, he's harassed by a
small town sheriff and he leads law enforcement officials and a National Guard
company on a wild backwoods chase.
With Richard Crenna and Brian Dennehy.
AC25, AC31

First Born (1984, C, 100m, PG-13)
A teenager is suspicious of his divorced
mother's new boyfriend, especially when
he finds evidence that the man is dealing
drugs. Christopher Collet, Teri Garr, and
Peter Weller star in this underrated
drama. **DR8** *Recommended*

First Deadly Sin, The (1980, C, 112m, R)
Frank Sinatra stars as a New York City
cop who tracks a psycho. Faye Dunaway,
Brenda Vaccaro, and James Whitmore
costar. **AC9, DR35, DR49**

First Family (1980, C, 104m, R)
This political satire casts Bob Newhart as
a President bumbling through life trying
to deal with his wife (Madeline Kahn) and
sex-crazed daughter (Gilda Radner). With
Rip Torn, Richard Benjamin, and Harvey
Korman. Written and directed by Buck
Henry. **CO5, CO13, CU47**

First Howie Mandel Special (1983, C, 53m,
NR)
The star of T.V.'s *St. Elsewhere* gives it
all he's got in this energetic comedy performance. **CO16**

First Legion, The (1951, B&W, 86m, NR)
A priest is skeptical of events surrounding
a miracle in his town. Charles Boyer stars
in this drama directed by Douglas Sirk.
CU24

First Men in the Moon (1964, C, 85m, NR)
H.G. Wells tale of space explorers, with
outstanding special effects by Ray Harryhausen. Edward Judd, Martha Hyer,
and Lionel Jeffries star. **SF3, SF26**

First Monday in October (1981, C, 98m,
R)
This light comedy concerns the first female member of the Supreme Court lock-
ing horns with a fellow justice. Jill Clayburgh and Walter Matthau star. **CO2,
DR10, XT9**

First Name: Carmen (1983, C, 85m, NR)
French director Jean-Luc Godard's meditation on the Carmen story, with updating to make the heroine a terrorist/film-
maker. Maruschka Detmers stars;
Godard plays her "Uncle Jean," a has-
been director. **FF14**

Fish Called Wanda, A (1988, C, 108m, R)
British caper comedy featuring a gang
composed of one thick-headed macho
American (Oscar winner Kevin Kline),
his sexy girl friend (Jamie Lee Curtis),
and a stuttering accomplice (Michael
Palin)—all mixed up with a confused barrister (John Cleese). Co-written by
Cleese. Small dog or tropical fish lovers,
beware. **CO10, CO15, CO17, MY34, XT4**
Recommended

Fist of Fear, Touch of Death (1980, C, 90m,
R)
Drama set at a karate championship at
Madison Square Garden, starring Fred
Williamson and Ron Van Clief. Bruce Lee
appears in a short segment. **AC33**

Fistful of Dollars, A (1964, C, 96m, NR)
A mysterious gunfighter (Clint Eastwood)
is caught between two feuding families in
this classic spaghetti western directed by
Sergio Leone. Remake of Japanese samurai drama, *Yojimbo*. **FF36, WE3, WE14,
WE26, WE27**

Fistful of Dynamite, A (1972, C, 138m, R)
A peasant thief (Rod Steiger) and an explosives mastermind (James Coburn) join
forces during the Mexican Revolution.

From director Sergio Leone. Also known as *Duck, You Sucker.* **WE10, WE14, WE27**

Fists of Fury (1972, C, 103m, R)
Bruce Lee's first feature film has him playing a martial arts student out to avenge his teacher's death. **AC33**

Fitzcarraldo (1982, C, 157m, NR)
Epic drama from German director Werner Herzog about an obsessed man's attempt to build an opera house in the midst of the Amazon jungles. Klaus Kinski stars in this bold, memorable drama. **FF19, FF30** *Recommended*

Five Corners (1988, C, 92m, R)
In 1964, a Bronx neighborhood is shaken by the return of an ex-con looking for revenge. A young idealist (Tim Robbins) agrees to protect a girl (Jodie Foster) from the criminal. Written by John Patrick Shanley; directed by Tony Bill. **DR15**

Five Days One Summer (1983, C, 93m, PG)
A middle-aged man and his young female companion travel in 1930s Switzerland posing as man and wife—although their relationship is secretly quite different. Sean Connery and Betsy Brantley star; Fred Zinnemann directed. Original running time: 108m. **AC36, CL57, DR3**

Five Easy Pieces (1970, C, 96m, R)
Breakthrough role for Jack Nicholson in this tale of a drifter who chooses a blue-collar job rather than follow his family of classical musicians. Written by Carol Eastman (under the name Adrien Joyce) and directed by Bob Rafelson. Karen Black and Susan Anspach costar, with Billy "Green" Bush, Lois Smith, Toni Basil, and Helena Kallianotes. **DR8, DR24** *Highly Recommended*

Five Weeks in a Balloon (1962, C, 101m, NR)
Jules Verne adventure about a hot air balloon expedition to Africa. Red Buttons, Barbara Eden, and Fabian star. **FA4, SF27**

Flame and the Arrow, The (1950, C, 88m, NR)
Burt Lancaster stars as a swashbuckler in medieval Italy who leads his people to victory against the Hessians. Virginia Mayo and Nick Cravat costar; Jacques Tourneur directed. **AC13, DR41, HO37**

Flame of the Barbary Coast (1945, B&W, 91m, NR)
John Wayne western with the Duke competing for the hand of a saloon singer (Ann Dvorak). **WE17**

Flaming Star (1960, C, 92m, NR)
Elvis Presley plays a half-breed who must choose sides when an Indian uprising threatens his family. **MU22**

Flash Gordon (1980, C, 110m, PG)
The hero of the old movie serials gets a big-budget, tongue-in-cheek treatment in this spoofy adventure. Sam J. Jones, Max von Sydow, Ornella Muti, Melody Anderson, Topol, and Timothy Dalton star. Music by Queen. **SF21**

Flashdance (1983, C, 96m, R)
A young female welder moonlights as an exotic dancer, although she aspires to audition for a ballet company. Jennifer Beals stars; music by Giorgio Moroder. **DR12, DR15, MU3**

Flashpoint (1984, C, 94m, R)
A pair of border cops stumble onto some evidence that will help solve an old mystery. Kris Kristofferson and Treat Williams star, with Rip Torn. **CU47, MU12**

Flesh (1968, B&W, 90m, NR)
Paul Morissey directed and Andy Warhol produced this cult comedy about a male hustler (Joe Dalessandro) and his many conquests. **CU12, CU44**

Flesh & Blood (1922, B&W, 74m, NR)
A lawyer goes to jail for 15 years for a crime he didn't commit. Lon Chaney, Sr. stars in this silent melodrama. **HO29**

Flesh & Blood (1985, C, 126m, R)
Adventure tale of lovely young princess captured by a band of roving thieves, with her intended in hot pursuit. Rutger Hauer, Jennifer Jason Leigh, and Tom Burlinson star; Paul Verhoeven directed. **AC18**

Flesh and the Devil (1927, B&W, 103m, NR)
Greta Garbo silent drama in which she plays the ultimate temptress, breaking up the friendship of John Gilbert and Lars Hanson. **CL4, CL12, CL28**

Fleshburn (1984, C, 91m, R)
Confined to an asylum for five years, a Vietnam veteran escapes and seeks revenge against the doctors who had him committed. **AC19**

Fletch (1985, C, 96m, PG)
Chevy Chase plays a wise-guy reporter who relies on disguises to get the scoop on a drug ring. **CO10, CO13**

Fletch Lives (1989, C, 95m, PG-13)
Chevy Chase returns as the investigative reporter and master of disguises. Here, he inherits a Southern mansion and a mystery that goes with the house. **CO10, CO13**

Flight of Dragons, The (1982, C, 98m, NR)
Enter a world of dragons, dungeons and castles, and mysterious happenings in this full-length animated feature. **FA10**

Flight of the Eagle, The (1982, C, 139m, NR)
Swedish adventure story, based on historical events, about a daring hot-air balloon trip to the North Pole in 1897. Max von Sydow stars. **AC12, AC16, FF7**

Flight of the Navigator (1986, C, 90m, PG)
Fantasy about a 12-year-old boy who leaves earth on an alien spacecraft, but returns as a 12-year-old boy eight years later. Veronica Cartwright and Joey Cramer star. **FA8**

Flight of the Phoenix (1966, C, 147m, NR)
Tense tale of survival, starring James Stewart as the leader of a squadron whose plane crashes in the Arabian desert. Richard Attenborough, Peter Finch, and Ernest Borgnine costar. **AC12, CL25** *Recommended*

Flight to Mars (1951, C, 72m, NR)
Low-budget science fiction adventure about trip to the Red Planet and discovery of a lost civilization. **SF3**

Floating Weeds (1959, C, 119m, NR)
From Japan, a drama about an actor visiting his illegitimate son and ex-lover after many years' absence. Directed by Yasujiro Ozu. **FF4**

Flower Drum Song (1961, C, 133m, NR)
Rodgers and Hammerstein musical about life in San Francisco's Chinatown. Nancy Kwan, James Shigeta, and Miyoshi Umeki star. **MU2, MU6**

Flowers in the Attic (1987, C, 95m, PG-13)
A widowed mother of four is desperate to be reinstated in her father's good graces—and in his will. She and her kids move into his house, where she keeps the children confined to one room. Based on the novel by V. C. Andrews. **HO14**

Fly, The (1958, B&W, 94m, NR)
An experiment turns into a disaster as a scientist's machine mixes some of his molecules with those of a fly. Vincent Price, Herbert Marshall, and David Hedison star. **HO20, HO31, SF1, SF5**

Fly, The (1986, C, 96m, R)
Remake of the horror science fiction film about an experiment gone terribly wrong, with much more explicit and gruesome detail. Jeff Goldblum and Geena Davis star; David Cronenberg directed. **CU7, CU18, HO17, HO20, HO39, SF5, SF20** *Recommended*

Fly II, The (1989, C, 105m, R)
Follow-up to 1986 remake of the sci-fi horror classic has the son of the scientist/insect following in his father's fateful

footsteps. Eric Stoltz and Daphne Zuniga star. **HO20, SF5, SF20**

Flying Deuces (1939, B&W, 65m, NR)
Laurel and Hardy join the foreign legion to forget Ollie's recent lost love. **CO20**

Flying Down to Rio (1933, B&W, 89m, NR)
Fred Astaire and Ginger Rogers dance "The Carioca" in their first screen teaming. Dolores Del Rio costars. **CL15, MU18**

Flying Leathernecks (1951, C, 102m, NR)
John Wayne and Robert Ryan play two Marine officers who argue over Wayne's treatment of his troops during World War II. Nicholas Ray directed. **AC1, CL17, CU23**

Flying Tigers (1942, B&W, 102m, NR)
World War II action over China, starring John Wayne. **AC1, AC11, CL17**

Fog, The (1980, C, 91m, R)
An old fisherman in a California coastal town creates havoc when he tells a ghost story to a group of young children. John Carpenter directed; Jamie Lee Curtis and John Houseman star. **CU29, HO2**

Foghorn Leghorn's Fractured Funnies (1986, C, 58m, NR)
Collection of classic Warner Bros. cartoons featuring the best of Foghorn Leghorn's adventures. Included are *Lovelorn Leghorn, The Leghorn Blows at Midnight,* and *Leghorn Swaggled.* **FA11**

Follow Me, Boys! (1966, C, 131m, NR)
Disney drama set in 1930s Midwest, with Fred MacMurray starting a Boy Scout troop in a small town. With Vera Miles, Lillian Gish, and Kurt Russell. **CL49, FA1**

Follow That Bird (1985, C, 88m, G)
Big Bird, *Sesame Street*'s favorite giant, is placed in a foster home, and slowly works his way back to the gang at Sesame Street. Many guest stars include Dave Thomas, John Candy, and Chevy Chase.

Also known as *Sesame Street Presents Follow That Bird.* **CO13, CO14, FA9**

Follow That Dream (1962, C, 110m, NR)
Elvis Presley muscal about a young man whose family moves to Florida and is not accepted by the local townspeople. **MU22**

Follow the Fleet (1936, B&W, 110m, NR)
Fred Astaire dances his way through the Navy to Irving Berlin tunes. Ginger Rogers and Randolph Scott costar. **CL15, MU18, WE22**

Food of the Gods (1976, C, 88m, PG)
H.G. Wells tale of animals growing to gigantic proportions after eating an unusual substance. Marjoe Gortner, Pamela Franklin, and Ida Lupino star. **SF10, SF28**

Fool for Love (1985, C, 118m, R)
Two lovers meet at a desert motel and try to sort out their past in this drama written by and starring Sam Shepard, with Kim Basinger, Harry Dean Stanton, and Randy Quaid. Robert Altman directed. **CU25, CU49, DR3**

Foolish Wives (1922, B&W, 107m, NR)
Erich Von Stroheim directed and stars in this classic silent movie about a corrupt man who poses as a Russian count. **CL12, CL53**

Footlight Parade (1933, B&W, 104m, NR)
Classic backstage musical about the difficulty of putting on a show. James Cagney, Ruby Keeler, and Dick Powell star, with choreography by Busby Berkeley. **CL22, MU4, MU20** *Recommended*

Footloose (1984, C, 106m, PG)
A young high school student (Kevin Bacon) shakes up a town where dancing has been outlawed by a powerful minister. Lori Singer and John Lithgow costar. **CO4, DR9, MU3**

For a Few Dollars More (1965, C, 130m, PG)
In this sequel to *A Fistful of Dollars,* Clint Eastwood is a cigar-smoking bounty hunter out to track down a vicious bandit.

Lee Van Cleef costars, with Klaus Kinski. Directed by Sergio Leone. **FF30, WE3, WE14, WE26, WE27**

For Keeps (1988, C, 98m, PG-13)
In this comedy, Molly Ringwald plays a high school senior whose unplanned pregnancy forces her to postpone college. **CO4**

For Love of Ivy (1968, C, 102m, NR)
A brother and sister fix up their family's black maid with a trucking company owner in this romantic comedy. Sidney Poitier and Abbey Lincoln are the lovers; Beau Bridges and Lauri Peters are the matchmakers. **DR14, DR38**

For Me and My Gal (1942, B&W, 104m, NR)
Gene Kelly made his film debut opposite Judy Garland in this musical about a vaudeville couple's attempts to hit the big time. Busby Berkeley directed. **MU4, MU19, MU20, MU21**

For Pete's Sake (1974, C, 90m, PG)
Barbra Streisand stars as the well-intentioned wife of a cab driver (Michael Sarrazin); her schemes to help him make money immerse them in comic misadventures. **MU27**

For the Love of Benji (1977, C, 84m, G)
The lovable canine stars in his second adventure; this time, he's running through the streets of Athens, dodging criminals who want a formula tattoed on his paw. **FA5**

For Your Eyes Only (1981, C, 127m, PG)
James Bond adventure, with the usual exotic locales and sinister villains, but less emphasis on gadgetry and gimmicks. Roger Moore stars, with Carole Bouquet, Chaim Topol, and Lynn-Holly Johnson. **AC35**

Forbidden Games (1951, B&W, 87m, NR)
Oscar-winning French film about an orphan girl and her stepbrother retreating into their own world. Brigitte Fossey stars; Rene Clement directed. **FF1, XT7**
Recommended

Forbidden Planet (1956, C, 98m, NR)
Classic 1950s science fiction drama about astronauts discovering planet occupied by wicked scientist and his lovely daughter. A loose version of Shakespeare's *Tempest*, starring Walter Pidgeon, Anne Francis, and Leslie Nielsen. **CU4, SF1**
Recommended

Forbidden Zone (1980, C, 76m, R)
This unusual, campy musical deals with an underground kingdom set in the sixth dimension. Herve Villechaize stars. **CU2, MU16**

Forbin Project, The *see* Colossus: The Forbin Project

Force of Evil (1948, B&W, 78m, NR)
A small-time attorney (John Garfield) gives up his ideals to find success working for a racketeer. Classic film noir, written and directed by Abraham Polonsky. **MY1**

Force of One, A (1979, C, 90m, PG)
Chuck Norris stars in this karate-kicking sequel to *Good Guys Wear Black,* about a small California town overrun by drug dealers and the man who would stop them. **AC32**

Force 10 From Navarone (1978, C, 118m, PG)
This sequel to *The Guns of Navarone* features Harrison Ford and Robert Shaw as members of a force out to blow up a bridge that is vital to the Nazis. **DR32**

Forced Vengeance (1982, C, 90m, R)
In Hong Kong, a Vietnam War veteran, now the head of security at a casino, tangles with some gangsters. Chuck Norris stars. **AC32**

Foreign Correspondent (1940, B&W, 119m, NR)
Joel McCrea is a journalist who falls for a British girl and uncovers a spy ring headed by her father. Directed by Alfred Hitchcock. **MY6, MY22**

Formula, The (1980, C, 117m, R)
A Los Angeles cop investigates the murder of his friend and discovers a conspiracy involving a formula for synthetic fuel. Marlon Brando and George C. Scott star. **DR33, DR60, MY6, MY9**

Fort Apache (1948, B&W, 127m, NR)
John Ford directed this classic western about cavalrymen (John Wayne and Henry Fonda) who protect the frontier from the Indians. Shirley Temple, Victor McLaglen, and Ward Bond costar. **CL24, FA14, WE5, WE17, WE18** *Recommended*

Fort Apache, The Bronx (1981, C, 125m, R)
Paul Newman plays a weary, streetwise cop trying to do his job against often impossible odds in a dangerous neighborhood. Ed Asner, Ken Wahl, Pam Grier, and Danny Aiello costar. **DR15, DR28, XT9**

Fortress (1985, C, 89m, NR)
Australian action drama of kidnapping of a teacher and her students in the Austrlian outback. Rachel Ward stars. **FF5**

Forty Carats (1973, C, 110m, PG)
Liv Ullmann is a middle-aged divorced woman who falls in love with a man half her age. Gene Kelly and Edward Albert costar in this comedy. **FF25, MU19**

48HRS. (1982, C, 97m, R)
Eddie Murphy made his screen debut in this action/thriller about a weary cop (Nick Nolte) who gets a con (Murphy) out of jail for two days to help track a deranged killer. Directed by Walter Hill. **AC9, CO13, CU27, DR44, XT10**

49th Parallel, The (1941, B&W, 105m, NR)
When a Nazi U-boat is sunk in Canadian waters, its survivors struggle to reach neutral territory. Suspense from director Michael Powell, starring Anton Walbrook, Eric Portman, Leslie Howard, and Laurence Olivier. **AC1, CL32, CU19**

42nd Street (1933, B&W, 89m, NR)
The star of a Broadway show gets sick, and a naive girl (Ruby Keeler) is picked to go on in her place. Great songs, including "Shuffle Off to Buffalo," and superb choreography by Busby Berkeley. **MU4, MU20** *Recommended*

Forty-Seven Ronin, The
   Part One (1941, B&W, 113m, NR)
   Part Two (1942, B&W, 112m, NR)
Epic Japanese historical drama about a group of royal retainers out to avenge the honor of their lord. Directed by Kenji Mizoguchi. **FF4**

Foul Play (1978, C, 116m, PG)
Suspense comedy, set in San Francisco, about a woman caught in a murder plot. No one will believe her, except a detective who happens to be falling in love with her. Goldie Hawn and Chevy Chase star, with support from Dudley Moore. **CO10, CO13, CO30, CO31, XT9**

Fountainhead, The (1949, B&W, 114m, NR)
Gary Cooper plays an idealistic architect who won't compromise his designs for the company he works for, or for the woman he loves (Patricia Neal). Cult camp based on the Ayn Rand novel. **CL26, CU2**

4D Man (1959, C, 85m, NR)
Science fiction drama of a scientist whose experiments give him the power to pass through solid matter. Robert Lansing and Lee Meriwether star. **SF1, SF5**

Four Feathers, The (1939, C, 115m, NR)
A cowardly British officer decides to prove his prowess when he helps fellow soldiers in the Sudan uprising. Ralph Richardson and C. Aubrey Smith star in this Technicolor saga. **AC6, AC13, CL9**

Four Horsemen of the Apocalypse (1961, C, 153m, NR)
Vincente Minnelli directed this remake and updating of the silent classic about the break-up of a family whose members fight on opposite sides during World War

II. Glenn Ford and Charles Boyer star. **CL3, MU23**

400 Blows, The (1959, B&W, 99m, NR)
Stunning account of a young Parisian boy's desperate search for affection in a loveless household. Jean-Pierre Léaud stars in this first of several films about the same character, Antoine Doinel; François Truffaut directed. **FF13, XT9** *Highly Recommended*

Four Musketeers, The (1975, C, 108m, PG)
Sequel to 1974 version of *The Three Musketeers* (filmed at the same time), with grand cast indulging in more swordplay and double-dealing. Oliver Reed, Faye Dunaway, Frank Finlay, Michael York, and Richard Chamberlain star, with Christopher Lee, Charlton Heston, Raquel Welch, and Roy Kinnear. Brilliantly directed by Richard Lester. **AC15, CU35, DR35, HO32** *Highly Recommended*

Four Seasons, The (1981, C, 107m, PG)
Three middle-aged couples vacation together during each of the seasons of the year. Alan Alda directed and stars, with Carol Burnett, Rita Moreno, and Jack Weston. **CO1**

Fourth Man, The (1979, C, 104m, NR)
A bisexual writer begins an affair with a seductive young woman, but is more attracted to her current boyfriend. Then he learns that the woman's three husbands all died mysteriously. Dutch film with cult reputation for its sexy explicitness. **CU6, FF7, MY5, MY20** *Recommended*

Fourth Protocol, The (1987, C, 119m, R)
A British spy (Michael Caine) tries to stop a Russian plot to sever ties between England and America. Pierce Brosnan and Joanna Cassidy costar as the Russian agents. Based on a Frederick Forsyth novel. **MY31**

Fox and His Friends (1975, C, 123m, NR)
German drama of a gay carnival worker who is exploited by his wealthy lover. Rainer Werner Fassbinder directed himself in the title role. **FF20**

Foxes (1980, C, 106m, R)
The trials and tribulations of four teenaged girls growing up fast in the San Fernando Valley, starring Jodie Foster, Cherie Curie, Marilyn Kagan, and Kandice Stroh, with Scott Baio, Sally Kellerman, and Randy Quaid. **DR9, MU12**

Foxtrot (1976, C, 91m, R)
Peter O'Toole stars in this drama about a wealthy couple who flee Europe in the late 30s to escape the approaching madness of World War II. They settle on an island off the coast of Mexico. With Charlotte Rampling and Max von Sydow. **DR45**

Fozzie's Muppet Scrapbook (1985, C, 58m, NR)
Milton Berle, Raquel Welch, and Beverly Sills join Sesame Street's lovable Fozzie Bear in some of his greatest adventures. **FA15**

Frances (1982, C, 140m, R)
Jessica Lange plays Frances Farmer, the Hollywood actress of the 1930s whose brushes with the law and conflicts with her domineering mother cut short her career. Kim Stanley and Sam Shepard costar. **DR4, DR13, DR74** *Recommended*

Frankenstein (1931, B&W, 71m, NR)
The definitive Man-Made Monster movie, with Boris Karloff the creation of mad scientist Colin Clive. Video version restores footage not seen since the original release. Directed by James Whale. **CU10, HO1, HO27, HO34, SF2** *Recommended*

Frankenstein (1973, C, 200m, NR)
Made-for-television version of the Mary Shelley story features Michael Sarrazin as the creation, more a dashing rogue than a monster. Robert Foxworth and James Mason costar. **HO20**

Frankenstein Meets the Wolf Man (1943, B&W, 72m, NR)
Summit meeting of film monsters, starring Bela Lugosi and Lon Chaney, Jr. **HO1, HO28, HO30**

Frankenstein—1970 (1958, B&W, 83m, NR)
This version of the classic horror story stars Boris Karloff as a mad scientist and takes more of a science fiction approach to the familiar material. **HO27**

Frankie and Johnny (1966, C, 87m, NR)
Elvis Presley plays a riverboat gambler caught in a love triangle. **MU22**

Frantic (1958, B&W, 90m, NR)
A man and woman plan to murder her husband, but the plan backfires, and the man gets accused of murders he didn't commit. Jeanne Moreau stars; Louis Malle directed. **FF26, MY20**

Frantic (1988, C, 120m, R)
Thriller starring Harrison Ford as an American whose wife is kidnapped while they're vacationing in Paris. With Emmanuelle Seigner and Betty Buckley. Directed by Roman Polanski. **DR32, DR54, MY20, XT9** *Recommended*

Freaks (1932, B&W, 66m, NR)
Classic horror film, banned for many years in Britain, about circus troupe, starring real "human oddities." Directed by Tod Browning. **CU4, CU8, HO1, HO19, HO35** *Recommended*

Freaky Friday (1977, C, 95m, G)
This Disney comedy features Barbara Harris and Jodie Foster as a mother and daughter who switch personalities for a day. **CO37, FA1**

French Connection, The (1971, C, 104m, R)
Oscar winner Gene Hackman plays Popeye Doyle, a hard-driving New York City detective on the trail of a heroin smuggling ring. Oscars for Best Picture and Director (William Friedkin). Roy Scheider and Fernando Rey costar. **AC9, DR39, XT1, XT2, XT6, XT9** *Recommended*

French Connection 2, The (1975, C, 119m, R)
Popeye Doyle travels to France in an attempt to locate the drug kingpin who

eluded him in New York. Gene Hackman and Fernando Rey star; John Frankenheimer directed. **AC9, DR39**

French Lieutenant's Woman, The (1981, C, 123m, R)
Screen version of John Fowles' story of ill-fated Victorian love affair adds a parallel modern story about actor and actress shooting a film and becoming lovers. Meryl Streep and Jeremy Irons star; written by Harold Pinter and directed by Karel Reisz. **DR1, DR13, DR26**

French Postcards (1979, C, 92m, PG)
A group of American teenagers studying in Paris get involved in many misadventures. Early screen appearances for Debra Winger, Mandy Patinkin, and Blanche Baker. **DR47, XT9**

Frenzy (1972, C, 116m, R)
Alfred Hitchcock directed this tale of a London strangler known as The Necktie Murderer, and the innocent man who is suspected of the killer's crimes. Jon Finch and Barry Foster star, with Barbara Leigh-Hunt, Anna Massey, Alec McCowen, and Vivien Merchant. **MY7, MY17, MY22, XT9** *Recommended*

Fresh Horses (1988, C, 104m, PG-13)
A soon-to-be-married young man has second thoughts when he meets a sensual young woman, although they're from very different backgrounds. Andrew McCarthy and Molly Ringwald star in this romantic drama. **DR1**

Freshman, The (1925, B&W, 70m, NR)
In this silent comedy classic, Harold Lloyd plays a college freshman who will do anything to be accepted by his fellow students. **CL11, CO35**

Friday the 13th (series)
Part I (1980, C, 90m, R)
Part II (1981, C, 87m, R)
Part III (1982, C, 96m, R)
The Final Chapter (1984, C, 91m, R)
Part V: A New Beginning (1985, C, 102m, R)
Part VI: Jason Lives (1986, C, 87m, R)

Part VII: The New Blood (1988, C, 90m, R)
This horror series portrays a mad, seemingly indestructible killer named Jason, who masquerades behind a hockey mask, murdering innumerable teenagers at a summer camp. **HO12, HO18**

Friendly Persuasion (1956, C, 140m, NR)
A family of Quakers hold fast to their faith during the Civil War. Gary Cooper and Dorothy McGuire star. William Wyler directed. **AC5, CL26, CL38, WE7**

Fright Night (1987, C, 105m, R)
A teenager hires a TV horror movie host to kill a new neighbor, whom he suspects of being a vampire. Chris Sarandon and Roddy McDowall star. **HO5, HO19**

Fringe Dwellers, The (1986, C, 98m, PG)
Australian drama about an aborigine family moving into a white, middle-class neighborhood, with expected problems. Directed by Bruce Beresford. **FF5**

Frisco Kid, The (1979, C, 122m, PG)
A wild western about a Polish rabbi (Gene Wilder) who sets out on the 1850s frontier to meet his San Francisco congregation. Harrison Ford costars. **DR32, WE15**

Frogs (1972, C, 91m, PG)
Ray Milland stars as a man who destroys the natural wildlife near his home only to have his family threatened by an onslaught of avenging reptiles. **HO16**

From Beyond (1986, C, 85m, R)
A scientist's insatiable search for a sixth sense eventually drives his staff to insanity. Based on a H.P. Lovecraft tale; exceptionally gory. **HO20, HO25**

From Beyond the Grave (1973, C, 97m, PG)
Four horror stories centering on a British antique shop, where the mysterious owner (Peter Cushing) helps his customers meet terrible fates. Margaret Leighton, Diana Dors, and David Warner costar. **HO23, HO26, HO33**

From Here to Eternity (1953, B&W, 118m, NR)
The James Jones story of army life in Pearl Harbor, just before the Japanese attack, starring Burt Lancaster, Deborah Kerr, Montgomery Clift, and Oscar winners Frank Sinatra and Donna Reed. Winner of six other Academy Awards, including Best Picture and Director (Fred Zinnemann). **AC1, CL57, DR19, DR41, DR49, XT1, XT4, XT5, XT6** *Highly Recommended*

From Russia With Love (1963, C, 118m, NR)
The second James Bond adventure, and one of the very best, with Sean Connery sparring with lovely Soviet spy Daniela Bianchi. Robert Shaw and Lotte Lenya make an especially colorful pair of villains. **AC35, AC36** *Highly Recommended*

From the Earth to the Moon (1958, C, 100m, NR)
Jules Verne's fantasy adventure about man's first voyage to the moon, starring George Sanders, Debra Paget, and Cedric Hardwicke. **FA8, SF13, SF27**

From the Life of the Marionettes (1980, C/ B&W, 104m, R)
Drama from director Ingmar Bergman about a respectable businessman involved in the murder of a prostitute. Robert Atzorn stars. **FF8**

From the Mixed-Up Files of Mrs. Basil E. Frankenweiler (1973, C, 105m, NR)
Two children hide out in New York City's Metropolitan Museum and befriend a reclusive woman (Ingrid Bergman). **CL27, FA7**

Front, The (1976, C, 94m, PG)
Woody Allen stars as a restaurant cashier who fronts for a group of blacklisted television writers in 1950s New York. He slowly becomes a celebrity as he accepts the praise and recognition for their work. Directed by Martin Ritt. **CO27, DR12**

Frontier Pony Express (1939, B&W, 54m, NR)
Roy Rogers and Trigger ride into action to round up Pony Express bandits. **WE23**

Fugitive Kind, The (1959, B&W, 122m, NR)
A drifter (Marlon Brando) arrives in a Southern town and begins romancing two women (Joanne Woodward and Anna Magnani). Tennessee Williams drama directed by Sidney Lumet. **DR33, DR58, DR67**

Full Metal Jacket (1987, C, 117m, R)
After a grueling basic training period, a cynical young army journalist (Matthew Modine) is plunged into combat in Vietnam. A gritty, violent tale from director Stanley Kubrick. Vincent D'Onofrio, Lee Ermey, and Adam Baldwin costar. **AC4, DR53** *Recommended*

Full Moon in Blue Water (1988, C, 96m, R)
Gene Hackman plays the owner of a rundown seaside bar whose bad fortune is reversed by the arrival of a young woman (Teri Garr). **DR39**

Full Moon in Paris (1984, C, 102m, R)
French comedy about an independent young woman juggling three lovers. Pascale Ogier stars; Eric Rohmer directed. **FF1, FF15**

Fun in Acapulco (1963, C, 97m, NR)
Elvis Presley plays a lifeguard by day and nightclub entertainer at night in this musical set in Mexico. **MU22**

Fun With Dick and Jane (1977, C, 95m, PG)
Jane Fonda and George Segal play an upwardly mobile couple who turn to robbery when he loses his job. Ed McMahon costars in this comedy about modern lifestyles. **DR27**

Funeral in Berlin (1966, C, 102m, NR)
Michael Caine's second film as British spy Harry Palmer; here he arranges for the defection of a Russian officer. **MY6**

Funhouse, The (1981, C, 96m, R)
Four teenagers decide to spend the night in a carnival funhouse, where they are terrorized by an unknown assailant. Directed by Tobe Hooper. **HO12, HO40**

Funny Face (1957, C, 103m, NR)
Fred Astaire is a fashion photographer who takes a plain Audrey Hepburn and turns her into a beautiful Paris model, all set to Gershwin music. **CL9, CL30, MU18, MU23, XT9**

Funny Farm (1988, C, 101m, PG)
Chevy Chase is a sportswriter looking for a rural retreat—and finding nothing but trouble. Madolyn Smith costars. **CO13**

Funny Girl (1968, C, 151m, G)
Barbra Streisand, in her debut film, won an Academy Award for recreating her Broadway success as Fanny Brice, the comedy legend who rose to stardom in the Ziegfeld Follies. Directed by William Wyler. **CL38, MU2, MU5, MU7, MU27, XT3, XT9, XT10**

Funny Lady (1975, C, 137m, PG)
This sequel to *Funny Girl* portrays Fanny Brice (Barbra Streisand) at the peak of her career, married to showman Billy Rose (James Caan). **MU5, MU27**

Funny Thing Happened on the Way to the Forum, A (1966, C, 99m, NR)
Zero Mostel portrays a sly slave in ancient Rome with a yearning to be free. Based on the Broadway musical, with costars Buster Keaton, Jack Gilford, and Michael Crawford; directed by Richard Lester. **CO19, CU35, MU2**

Fury (1936, B&W, 94m, NR)
An innocent man (Spencer Tracy) becomes a criminal after he's almost lynched by a small town mob. Fritz Lang directed this classic tale of prejudice. **CL8, CL19, CL43, DR62** *Recommended*

Fury, The (1978, C, 118m, R)
Young girl and boy with telekinetic powers are united against evil American agents. Brian DePalma directed; Kirk

Douglas, Amy Irving, John Cassavetes, and Andrew Stevens star. **CU28, HO7**

Future-Kill (1985, C, 83m, R)
Science fiction action with a band of rowdy fraternity boys taking on anti-nuclear activists in a city wasteland. Edwin Neal and Marilyn Burns star. **SF8**

Futureworld (1976, C, 104m, PG)
Sequel to *Westworld*, with that film's robots hatching a Take Over the World scheme. Science fiction drama starring Peter Fonda, Blythe Danner, and Yul Brynner. **SF6**

Fuzz (1972, C, 92m, PG)
Cop drama, with moments of dark humor, about Boston policemen and their attempts to stay sane amid the chaos of big city life. Burt Reynolds stars, with Raquel Welch, Yul Brynner, Jack Weston, Tom Skeritt, and Peter Bonerz. **AC37**

G.I. Blues (1960, C, 104m, NR)
Elvis Presley stars as a guitar-playing soldier in Germany who romances a leggy dancer (Juliet Prowse). **MU22**

Gabriela (1983, C, 102m, R)
Barkeeper takes on lovely young woman as a cook, and romance follows. Marcello Mastroianni and Sonia Braga costar in this Brazilian film. **FF6, FF24, FF34**

Gaby—A True Story (1987, C, 110m, R)
True-life drama of a young woman afflicted with cerebral palsy, struggling to overcome her handicap and her parents' overprotectiveness to become a bestselling writer. Rachel Levin stars, with Liv Ullmann, Robert Loggia, and Norma Aleandro. **DR2, DR6, FF25**

Galaxina (1980, C, 95m, R)
Science fiction spoof of both *Star Wars* and *Star Trek* movies, starring Avery Schreiber and sexy Dorothy Stratten. **SF21, SF22**

Galaxy of Terror (1981, C, 80m, R)
Astronauts confront monsters while on a rescue mission in this science fiction/hor-

ror tale. Edward Albert, Erin Moran, and Ray Walston star. **SF20**

Gallagher (series) (1984-85, C, approx. 60m ea., NR)
Stand-up comic Gallagher, appears in this series of five separate performances: *The Bookkeeper, The Maddest, Melon Crazy, Over Your Head,* and *Stuck in the 60s.* **CO16**

Gallipoli (1981, C, 110m, PG)
World War I drama, starring Mel Gibson and Mark Lee as two naive young recruits thrown into fierce battle. Directed by Peter Weir. **AC2, DR69, FF5**

Gambit (1966, C, 109m, NR)
A crook (Michael Caine) wants to steal a valuable statue, and he hires a kooky young woman (Shirley MacLaine) to help him do the job. **DR42, MY6**

Gambling Samurai, The (1960, C, 93m, NR)
Toshiro Mifune stars in this tale of a wandering warrior. **FF28**

Game Is Over, The (1966, C, 96m, NR)
French drama of a woman's marriage to a wealthy man and her affair with his son. Jane Fonda stars; Roger Vadim directed. **DR27, FF1**

Game of Death (1979, C, 102m, R)
Bruce Lee finished twenty minutes of fighting scenes for this film before he died; a story was composed around those sequences to take advantage of his phenomenal popularity. Chuck Norris, Kareem Abdul-Jabbar, Gig Young, and Hugh O'Brian costar. **AC32, AC33**

Gandhi (1982, C, 200m, PG)
Ben Kingsley won an Oscar for his portrayal of India's modern spiritual leader, whose courage inspired his countrymen to reject British colonial rule. John Gielgud, Edward Fox, and Martin Sheen costar; the film and director Richard Attenborough also won Academy Awards. **DR4, DR23, XT1, XT2, XT6** *Recommended*

Garbo Talks (1984, C, 103m, PG-13)
A son works to grant his mother's dying wish—she wants to meet Greta Garbo, who is living in seclusion in New York City. Anne Bancroft and Ron Silver star, with Carrie Fisher, Catherine Hicks, Steven Hill, Howard da Silva, Dorothy Loudon, and Harvey Fierstein. Directed by Sidney Lumet. **CO5, DR58, XT9**

Garden of Allah (1936, C, 86m, NR)
Charles Boyer and Marlene Dietrich star in this romance set in the Algerian desert. Lovely color photography. **CL9, CL47**

Garden of the Finzi-Continis, The (1971, C, 95m, R)
Oscar-winning drama from Italy about an aristocratic Jewish family in wartime Italy oblivious to the Holocaust until it is too late to escape. Vittorio De Sica directed; Dominique Sanda stars. **FF2, XT7**

Gardens of Stone (1987, C, 112m, R)
Title refers to Arlington National Cemetery, scene of this drama set during the early days of the Vietnam War. An army company that buries the dead welcomes a young recruit yearning for combat experience. James Caan, James Earl Jones, Anjelica Huston, and D.B. Sweeney star; Francis Ford Coppola directed. **DR7, DR51**

Garry Shandling: Alone in Vegas (1984, C, 52m, NR)
The popular guest host of *The Tonight Show* and his own cable series is shown in a live performance in Las Vegas. **CO16**

Gaslight (1944, B&W, 114m, NR)
Ingrid Bergman won an Academy Award for playing a tormented woman whose husband (Charles Boyer) is slowly driving her insane. **CL27, CL39, MY3, XT3**

Gate, The (1987, C, 92m, PG-13)
A young boy is grounded, and he and a friend discover the gate to hell in his back yard. **HO10**

Gate of Hell (1954, C, 89m, NR)
Japanese drama of a 12th century samurai who falls in love with a married woman, then discards her. Oscar winner for Best Foreign Language Film. **FF4, XT7**

Gates of Heaven (1978, C, 85m, NR)
Documentary about pet cemeteries, the people who use them, the people who run them. Directed by Errol Morris. A movie that manages to be both funny and touching. **CU16, CU51** *Recommended*

Gator (1976, C, 116m, PG)
Good ol' boy Burt Reynolds teams up with the feds to get the goods on a crooked politican in this sequel to *White Lightning*. **AC37**

Gauntlet, The (1977, C, 109m, R)
A cop is assigned to escort a prostitute, set to testify against the Mob, from Las Vegas to Phoenix; both are unaware they've been set up for assassination. Clint Eastwood and Sondra Locke star. **AC9, AC27**

Gay Divorcee, The (1934, B&W, 107m, NR)
Fred Astaire and Ginger Rogers dance to Cole Porter music. Also includes the first Oscar-winning song, "The Continental." **CL15, MU18**

Gay Ranchero, The (1947, B&W, 53m, NR)
Roy Rogers and sidekick Andy Devine go searching for a downed airplane in this contemporary western. **WE23**

General, The (1927, B&W, 74m, NR)
Buster Keaton plays a man trying to steal a train during the Civil War, with riotous results. One of the truly great comedies. **CL11, CO19** *Highly Recommended*

General Della Rovere (1960, B&W, 129m, NR)
Vittorio De Sica stars in a drama of an Italian impersonating a general during World War II and beginning to believe his ruse. Roberto Rossellini directed. **FF2**

General Died at Dawn, The (1936, B&W, 97m, NR)
Gary Cooper stars in this tale of romance and intrigue in the mysterious East, with Madeleine Carroll as the agent he falls for, Akim Tamiroff his wily adversary. **CL26, MY6**

General Line, The (1929, B&W, 90m, NR)
Soviet director Sergei Eisenstein's silent drama of a rural woman's struggle to start a collective. **FF22**

Gentleman Jim (1942, B&W, 104m, NR)
Errol Flynn plays Jim Corbett, the famed heavyweight boxing champion of the early 20th century, in this colorful drama. Alexis Smith, Jack Carson, and Alan Hale costar. **AC34**

Gentlemen Prefer Blondes (1953, C, 91m, NR)
Marilyn Monroe and Jane Russell are two showgirls who set out to find themselves husbands in this vibrant adaptation of the Broadway musical. Monroe proves that "diamonds are a girl's best friend." Directed by Howard Hawks. **CL29, CL35, CO8**

George Stevens: A Filmmaker's Journey (1984, C, 110m, NR)
Katharine Hepburn, Ginger Rogers, and Warren Beatty are three of the performers who add insight to this documentary of director Stevens' films. Includes scenes from *Alice Adams, Giant,* and *A Place In the Sun.* Directed by George Stevens, Jr. **CL16, CL42, CU16, DR34** *Recommended*

Georgy Girl (1966, B&W, 100m, NR)
Lynn Redgrave is an ugly duckling London girl who's romanced by a wealthy older gentleman (James Mason). Alan Bates and Charlotte Rampling costar. **CO17, DR3, XT9**

Get Crazy (1983, C, 90m, NR)
A theater owner plans to stage the biggest rock concert ever on New Year's Eve, but everything goes wrong. Cult comedy with many characters resembling real-life rock stars, lots of in-jokes about the music business. Daniel Stern stars, with Malcolm McDowell, Ed Begley, Jr., Lou Reed, Bobby Sherman, and Fabian Forte. Directed by Allan Arkush. **CU5, CU41, MU9** *Recommended*

Get Out of My Room (1985, C, 53m, NR)
Cheech and Chong perform in this compilation of four crazy comedy and music videos, including *Love Is Strange* and *Born in East L.A.* **CO16**

Get Out Your Handkerchiefs (1978, C, 109m, R)
Dark comedy from France about a man so desperate to keep his wife happy that he urges her to take a lover. Gerard Depardieu, Patrick Dewaere, and Carole Laure star. Oscar winner for Best Foreign Langauge Film. **FF1, FF29, XT7**

Getaway, The (1972, C, 122m, PG)
Sam Peckinpah's modern-day Bonnie & Clyde tale about a bank robber and his wife (Steve McQueen and Ali McGraw) who lead a corrupt politician and the police on a wild chase across Texas. With Ben Johnson, Al Letieri, Sally Struthers, Dub Taylor, John Bryson, and Slim Pickens. Based on a novel by Jim Thompson. **AC9, AC28, MY29, MY34, WE19** *Recommended*

Getting of Wisdom, The (1977, C, 100m, NR)
Australian drama of a girl from the outback holding her own at a stuffy boarding school. Directed by Bruce Beresford. **FF5**

Getting Straight (1970, C, 124m, R)
A graduate student (Elliott Gould) is caught between his loyalty to his studies and the student activist movement taking place on campus. Candice Bergen costars; watch for Harrison Ford in a small role. **CO35, DR32**

Ghidrah, the Three-Headed Monster (1965, C, 85m, NR)
Monster movie from Japan, with Godzilla, Mothra, and Rodan battling the title character. **FF4, SF18**

Ghost Goes West, The (1936, B&W, 82m, NR)
The new owner of a castle finds it's haunted by the ghost of a playboy. Eugene Pallette and Robert Donat costar; Rene Clair directed. **SF2**

Ghost in the Noonday Sun (1973, C, 89m, NR)
Pirate comedy starring Peter Sellers, Tony Franciosa, Spike Milligan, and Peter Boyle. **CO26**

Ghost of Yotsuya, The (1950, C, 100m, NR)
Japanese horror film about a man tortured by an evil spirit. **FF4**

Ghost Story (1981, C, 104m, R)
Four elderly men are tormented by an event which took place 50 years before. Fred Astaire, Melvyn Douglas, Douglas Fairbanks, Jr., John Houseman, and Patricia Neal star in this horror tale. **HO2, HO19, MU18**

Ghost Warrior (1984, C, 86m, R)
A samurai warrior found frozen in modern-day Japan is brought to Los Angeles. When he thaws out and someone tries to steal his sword, all hell breaks loose on the streets. **AC25**

Ghostbusters (1984, C, 107m, PG)
A trio of nutty paranormal researchers (Bill Murray, Dan Aykroyd, Harold Ramis) decide to start their own business, flushing out ghosts in New York. Dazzling special effects and a brilliant comic performance by Murray. With Sigourney Weaver, Ernie Hudson, Rick Moranis, William Atherton, and Annie Potts. **CO9, CO11, CO13, CO14, DR76, XT9** *Highly Recommended*

Ghostbusters II (1989, C, 102m. PG)
Return of the spook-chasing trio and their associates, with stars from first installment reprising their roles. **CO9, CO11, CO13, CO14, XT9**

Ghosts on the Loose (1943, B&W, 65m, NR)
A honeymooning couple has to spend the night in a haunted house, and the East Side Kids go there pretending to haunt the place. Bela Lugosi and Ava Gardner, in one of her first roles, star. Also known as *East Side Kids Meet Bela Lugosi*. **HO28**

Ghoul, The (1933, B&W, 73m, NR)
British horror tale, with Boris Karloff as a man buried with jewels from an Egyptian tomb, resurrected when they're stolen. With Cedric Hardwicke, Ernest Thesiger, and (in his film debut) Ralph Richardson. **HO26, HO27**

Ghoul, The (1975, C, 88m, NR)
Innocent people are accosted by the monster of a wealthy man (Peter Cushing). John Hurt costars. **HO26, HO33**

Ghoulies (1984, C, 81m, PG-13)
On his 18th birthday, a young man inherits a rambling mansion and an ability to conjure up evil spirits. **HO16**

Giant (1956, C, 201m, G)
Elizabeth Taylor, Rock Hudson, and James Dean (in his last film) star in Edna Ferber's sprawling story of Texas cattlemen who strike it rich with oil. With Mercedes McCambridge, Dennis Hopper, Carroll Baker, Chill Wills, Jane Withers, and Sal Mineo. Directed by Oscar winner George Stevens. **CL33, CL42, CU46, DR60, WE13, XT6, XT11**

Gideon's Trumpet (1980, C, 104m, NR)
Henry Fonda plays a convict whose battle for his basic rights became a landmark Supreme Court decision. Jose Ferrer costars; originally made for TV. **CL24, DR6**

Gig, The (1986, C, 95m, NR)
An amateur group of jazz musicians get their first big break—but aren't sure if they can handle the pressures. Wayne Rogers and Cleavon Little star. **DR12**

Gigi (1958, C, 119m, NR)
Winner of nine Academy Awards, including Best Picture, here's the story of a young Parisian girl (Leslie Caron) who chooses marriage over becoming a courtesan. Louis Jourdan, Maurice Chevalier, and Hermione Gingold costar; directed by Oscar winner Vincente Minnelli. **MU1, MU7, MU24, XT1, XT6**

Gilda (1946, B&W, 110m, NR)
Rita Hayworth's most famous role, a woman married to a wealthy South American casino owner, whose right-hand man (Glenn Ford) is a love from her past. **CL4, MY1, MY4**

Gilda Live (1980, C, 90m, NR)
Former *Saturday Night Live* regular Gilda Radner recreates many of her characters in this filmed version of her Broadway show. **CO16**

Gimme Shelter (1970, C, 91m, NR)
This stunning documentary of The Rolling Stones' 1969 concert tour of America includes footage from their tragic appearance at Altamount, where an audience member was murdered. Directed by Albert and David Maysles, with Charlotte Zwerin. **MU10** *Recommended*

Ginger and Fred (1986, C, 126m, PG-13)
A couple of small-time Italian entertainers who once imitated Astaire and Rogers are reunited thirty years later for a television show. Giulietta Masina and Marcello Mastroianni star; directed by Federico Fellini. **CO8, FF10, FF24**

Ginger in the Morning (1973, C, 89m, PG)
Love story between an unlikely pair: a lonely traveling salesman (Monte Markham) and a free-spirited hitch-hiker (Sissy Spacek). **DR68**

Girl, The (1986, C, 104m, R)
A wealthy attorney's affair with a teenager soon leads to murder in this thriller starring Franco Nero and Christopher Lee. **HO32**

Girl Can't Help It, The (1956, C, 99m, NR)
A gangster hires an agent to promote his girlfriend, who wants to be a singer. Edmond O' Brien, Tom Ewell, and Jayne Mansfield are the leads, but the real stars are the rock performers (Little Richard, Eddie Cochran, Gene Vincent) who appear in concert segments. Directed by Frank Tashlin. **MU9** *Recommended*

Girl Crazy (1943, B&W, 99m, NR)
Mickey Rooney plays a hypochondriac who moves from New York to Arizona, where he falls for a local girl (Judy Garland). Directed by Busby Berkeley, with songs by George and Ira Gershwin. **MU1, MU20, MU21**

Girl From Petrovka (1974, C, 104m, PG)
A Russian ballerina (Goldie Hawn) falls in love with an American correspondent (Hal Holbrook). **CO30**

Girl Happy (1965, C, 96m, NR)
Elvis Presley chaperones a gangster's daughter (Shelley Fabares) to Ft. Lauderdale. **MU22**

Girl Hunters, The (1963, B&W, 103m, NR)
Author Mickey Spillane wrote and starred in this tale of detective Mike Hammer, who travels to Europe to find his missing secretary. **MY30**

Girl in Every Port, A (1952, B&W, 86m, NR)
Groucho Marx and William Bendix star in a comedy about two sailors who hide a racehorse aboard ship. **CO21**

Girl of the Golden West, The (1938, B&W, 121m, NR)
Jeanette MacDonald and Nelson Eddy star in a musical western about a desperado and the woman who loves him. Walter Pidgeon, Leo Carillo, and Buddy Ebsen head the supporting cast. **CL15, WE9**

Girls! Girls! Girls! (1962, C, 106m, NR)
Elvis Presley musical about a man with
women on his mind. El sings "Return to
Sender;" Stella Stevens costars. **MU22**

Git Along, Little Dogies (1937, B&W, 60m,
NR)
Gene Autry sings his heart out for a bank-
er's daughter. **WE24**

Give My Regards to Broad Street (1984, C,
109m, PG)
A rock star (Paul McCartney) searches
for his stolen master recordings. Paul
plays some new tunes, as well as a few
ditties he wrote when he was with a band
called The Beatles. **MU4, MU9**

Gizmo! (1977, C/B&W, 77m, G)
Documentary tribute to inventors and
their wacky creations, directed by Howard Smith. **CU16**

Glass Key, The (1942, B&W, 85m, NR)
An unscrupulous politician calls on his
right-hand man to clear him of a murder
frameup in this version of the Dashiell
Hammett novel. Brian Donlevy, Alan
Ladd, and Veronica Lake star. **MY1,
MY28**

Glass Menagerie, The (1987, C, 135m, PG)
Paul Newman directed this adaptation of
the Tennessee Williams play about a timid
cripple (Karen Allen), her faded Southern
belle mother (Joanne Woodward), her
shiftless brother (John Malkovich), and
the dream worlds they live in. **DR20,
DR28**

Glen and Randa (1971, C, 94m, R)
Science fiction drama with cult following
about the end of the world and a surviving
couple (Steven Curry, Shelley Plimpton).
Directed by Jim McBride. **CU4, SF12**

Glen or Glenda? (1953, B&W, 61m, NR)
Contender for title of Worst Movie Ever,
with (naturally) a cult following. Serious
attempt to document one man's struggle
with sexuality winds up a hilarious comedy. Bela Lugosi "hosts;" directed by Ed
Wood, Jr. **CU11, CU45, HO28**

Glenn Miller Story, The (1954, C, 116m,
G)
A sentimental musical biography that fol-
lows the life of the legendary big band
leader. James Stewart stars; Anthony
Mann directed. **CL25, MU5, WE20**

Gloria (1980, C, 121m, R)
A feisty New York woman takes a young
Puerto Rican boy under her protection
after his parents are rubbed out by mob-
sters. Gena Rowlands stars, with John
Adames, Buck Henry, and Julie Carmen.
John Cassavetes directed. **AC8**

Glorifying the American Girl (1929, B&W,
87m, NR)
Flo Ziegfeld produced this musical revue
featuring the top talent of the day, including Helen Morgan, Rudy Vallee, and
Eddie Cantor. **MU15**

Gnome-Mobile, The (1967, C, 90m, NR)
Disney adventure starring Walter Brennan as an elderly businessman who, along
with his grandchildren, discovers gnomes
in a forest. The three try to protect them
from being captured by freak show owners. **FA1**

Gnomes, Vol. 1 (1980, C, 52m, NR)
This animated feature introduces the
Gnomes, tiny creatures who battle the
Trolls, who are trying to ruin a Gnome
wedding. **FA10**

Go Masters, The (1982, C, 123m, NR)
Japanese-Chinese production traces relationship of two families, one from each
country, from the 1920s to the 1950s.
Title refers to chess-like game played by
various members of each clan. **FF4**

Go Tell the Spartans (1978, C, 114m, R)
Vietnam War drama starring Burt Lancaster as a commander during the early
days of that conflict. Craig Wasson and
Marc Singer costar. **AC4, DR41**

Go West (1940, B&W, 81m, NR)
The Marx Brothers take a hilarious train
ride through the Old West. **CO21, WE15**

Goalie's Anxiety at the Penalty Kick, The (1971, C, 110m, NR)
German drama about a soccer player's depression over a crucial misplay and his subsequent breakdown. Directed by Wim Wenders; adapted from a Peter Handke story. **FF21**

Goat, The see Chevre, La

God Told Me To (1977, C, 95m, R)
Horror film about normal New Yorkers driven to unexplained acts of madness. Larry Cohen directed. Also known as *Demon*. **CU30**

Goddess, The (1958, B&W, 105m, NR)
Drama, loosely based on Marilyn Monroe story, of Hollywood star at the breaking point. Kim Stanley and Lloyd Bridges star; screenplay by Paddy Chayevsky. **DR13**

Godfather, The (1972, C, 175m, R)
Sensational adaptation of Mario Puzo's look into the world of a Mafia chieftain (Marlon Brando) in 1930s New York City. The supporting cast includes James Caan, Diane Keaton, Robert Duvall, and Al Pacino. Winner of three Oscars, including Best Picture and Actor (Brando). Masterfully directed by Francis Ford Coppola. **AC22, DR33, DR37, DR40, DR51, DR60, DR66, XT1, XT2** *Highly Recommended*

Godfather, Part II, The (1974, C, 200m, R)
Sequel to *The Godfather* combines two stories: the rise to power of the Corleones' youngest son, Michael (Al Pacino), and the struggles of his young immigrant father (Robert DeNiro) in early 20th-century New York City. Winner of six Oscars, including Best Picture, Best Director (Francis Ford Coppola), and Best Supporting Actor (DeNiro). With Diane Keaton, John Cazale, Robert Duvall, Talia Shire, Lee Strasberg, Michael V. Gazzo, Harry Dean Stanton, and, in one flashback scene, James Caan. **AC22, CU49, DR25, DR37, DR40, DR51, DR60, DR66, XT1, XT4, XT6** *Highly Recommended*

God's Little Acre (1958, B&W, 110m, NR)
A Georgia farmer (Robert Ryan) destroys his land in search of sunken treasures in this version of the Erskine Caldwell novel. Directed by Anthony Mann. **WE20**

Gods Must Be Crazy, The (1981, C, 108m, PG)
Comedy, set in South Africa, with two intertwining tales: a community of Bushmen encounter civilization in the form of a soft drink bottle, and a clumsy scientist romances a pretty schoolteacher. **CO2**

Godsend, The (1979, C, 93m, R)
Horror story of a couple who take in a little girl left with them by a strange woman, and the death and destruction she brings to their lives. **HO13**

Godzilla, King of the Monsters (1956, B&W, 80m, NR)
The film that started the cycle of Japanese monster movies, featuring that Tokyo-stomping behemoth. Raymond Burr co-stars. **FF4, SF10, SF18**

Godzilla, 1985 (1985, C, 91m, PG)
The big guy returns and is reunited—more or less—with Raymond Burr. **FF4, SF10, SF18**

Godzilla vs. Megalon (1976, C, 80m, G)
Godzilla, now a good guy, joins forces with a robot monster to square off against Megalon and his buddy in a monster tag-team match. **FF4, SF10, SF18**

Goin' South (1978, C, 109m, PG)
Jack Nicholson stars in this romantic Western comedy about an outlaw who ties the knot to save his neck. Film debuts for John Belushi and Mary Steenburgen. Nicholson directed. **CO13, DR24, WE10, WE15**

Going Berserk (1983, C, 85m, R)
John Candy plays a scatter-brained chauffeur who saves his future father-in-law from a religious cult. Joe Flaherty and Eugene Levy costar. **CO14**

Going in Style (1979, C, 96m, PG)
Touching comedy-drama about a trio of elderly men (George Burns, Art Carney, Lee Strasberg) who decide to rob a bank for the hell of it. Directed by Martin Brest. **DR11, MY34** *Recommended*

Going My Way (1944, B&W, 126m, NR)
Bing Crosby and Barry Fitzgerald play parish priests with different approaches to their flock in this touching classic. Oscars went to both actors, writer-director Leo McCarey, and the film. **MU25, XT1, XT2, XT4, XT6**

Going Places (1974, C, 117m, R)
French drama, with darkly comic overtones, of two drifters (Gerard Depardieu, Patrick Dewaere) and their determinedly carefree lifestyle. Brigitte Fossey and Jeannne Moreau costar; directed by Bertrand Blier. **FF1, FF26, FF29**

Gold Diggers of 1933 (1933, B&W, 96m, NR)
Busby Berkeley choreographed this musical about a songwriter (Dick Powell) who can't finance his extravaganza until some spunky showgirls (Ginger Rogers, Ruby Keeler) save the day. **MU4, MU20**

Gold Raiders (1983, C, 106m, NR)
A plane carrying $200 million in gold is shot down over Laos and a commando squad tries to retrieve the precious cargo. Robert Ginty stars. **AC20**

Gold Rush, The (1925, B&W, 72m, NR)
Charlie Chaplin classic set in the Yukon gold rush days. Georgia Hale and Mack Swain costar. **CL11, CO18** *Highly Recommended*

Golden Boy (1939, B&W, 99m, NR)
A would-be musician turns to boxing to make a living in this Clifford Odets classic. William Holden made his screen debut opposite Barbara Stanwyck. With Lee J. Cobb and Adolphe Menjou. **CL45, CL51, DR22, XT10**

Golden Child, The (1986, C, 96m, PG-13)
A youth with magical powers is kidnapped by a cult, and it's up to Eddie Murphy to rescue him in this adventure comedy packed with special effects. **CO9, CO11, CO14**

Golden Coach, The (1952, C, 105m, NR)
French director Jean Renoir's classic drama of a theatrical troupe in 18th-century Peru, starring Anna Magnani as a lady of many affairs. Superb color photography. **CL9, CL14, FF12**

Golden Demon, The (1953, C, 95m, NR)
From Japan, a drama about a young man in love with the daughter of his adopted parents. His frustration grows when she is given in an arranged marriage to a wealthy businessman. **FF4**

Golden Seal, The (1983, C, 93m, PG)
Family drama about a young boy who befriends a seal. Steve Railsback, Penelope Milford, and Michael Beck star. **FA5**

Golden Stallion, The (1949, B&W, 67m, NR)
Roy Rogers' horse, Trigger, gets most of the spotlight in this western, as he tries to set a small mare free from her nasty owners. **WE23**

Golden Voyage of Sinbad, The (1974, C, 104m, G)
John Phillip Law stars as the swashbuckling pirate in this adventure/fantasy which features great special effects. **FA8**

Goldenrod (1977, C, 100m, NR)
A rodeo champion (Tony LoBianco) reevaluates his life after a debilitating accident. Originally made for TV. **WE13**

Goldfinger (1964, C, 111m, NR)
Third James Bond adventure has 007 foiling plan to rob Fort Knox. Sean Connery stars, but Gert Fröbe, Harold Sakata, and Honor Blackman steal the show as Goldfinger, Odd Job, and Pussy Galore. **AC35, AC36** *Highly Recommended*

Goldilocks and the Three Bears (1985, C, 60m, NR)
Tatum O'Neal stars as the little girl who invades the lives of three bears in this Faerie Tale Theatre adventure. John Lithgow, Alex Karras, and Carole King co-star. **FA12**

Goldy: The Last of the Golden Bears (1984, C, 91m, NR)
An orphaned child adopted by a prospector goes on an incredible adventure to rescue a golden bear from the circus. **FA5**

Golem, The (1920, B&W, 118m, NR)
Classic silent horror film about a legendary robot-like creature created to save German Jewish peasants from persecution. **FF3, HO1**

Gone in 60 Seconds (1974, C, 103m, PG)
A professional car thief eludes police with his incredible driving skills. This action drama features a 40-minute car chase. Written and directed by H.B. Halicki. **AC10**

Gone With the Wind (1939, C, 222m, G)
Civil War epic of Scarlett O'Hara (Vivien Leigh) and her tempestuous romance with Rhett Butler (Clark Gable). Winner of 10 Oscars, including Best Picture, Best Actress, Best Supporting Actress (Hattie McDaniel), and Best Director (Victor Fleming). Olivia de Havilland and Leslie Howard costar. **AC5, CL3, CL23, XT1, XT3, XT5, XT6** *Highly Recommended*

Good Earth, The (1937, B&W, 138m, NR)
Oscar winner Luise Rainer costars with Paul Muni in Pearl Buck's story of Chinese peasants coming to ruin over greed. **DR19, XT3**

Good Father, The (1987, C, 90m, R)
An embittered man whose marriage has just broken up takes out his frustrations by interfering in the domestic problems of a friend. Anthony Hopkins stars in this British drama. **DR8, DR23**

Good Guys Wear Black (1979, C, 96m, PG)
Karate action drama with Chuck Norris, featuring his incredible stunt of leaping through the windshield of a moving car. Anne Archer costars. **AC32**

Good Morning, Babylon (1987, C, 115m, NR)
Two Italian stonemasons emigrate to American in search of work, wind up laboring on the sets of D.W. Griffith's silent film epic, *Intolerance*. Vincent Spano and Joaquim de Almeida star; Charles Dance plays Griffith. Dialogue in Italian and English. **DR13**

Good Morning, Vietnam (1987, C, 120m, R)
Robin Williams stars as a zany disc jockey who shakes up Armed Forces Radio during the Vietnam War. Forest Whitaker costars; Barry Levinson directed. **AC4, CO6, CO38, CO43** *Recommended*

Good Mother, The (1988, C, 104m, R)
Diane Keaton plays a divorced woman locked in a bitter battle for custody of her young daughter. With Liam Neeson, Jason Robards, Ralph Bellamy, and Teresa Wright. **DR8, DR10, DR40**

Good Neighbor Sam (1964, C, 130m, NR)
A young advertising executive out to impress a new client gets caught up in a complicated masquerade involving a lovely neighbor who's mistaken for his wife. Jack Lemmon stars, with Edward G. Robinson, Romy Schneider, and Dorothy Provine. **CL52, DR64**

Good News (1943, C, 93m, NR)
A college football star (Peter Lawford) won't graduate unless he passes his French exam in this musical set in the Roaring Twenties. June Allyson costars. **MU1, MU3, MU6**

Good Sam (1948, B&W, 128m, NR)
A good samaritan (Gary Cooper) creates tension in his homelife when he overdoes his generosity. Ann Sheridan costars. **CL26**

Good, the Bad, and the Ugly, The (1967, C, 161m, NR)
Three unscrupulous men (Clint Eastwood, Lee Van Cleef, Eli Wallach) hunt for a treasure while the Civil War rages around them. Directed by Sergio Leone. **WE1, WE4, WE7, WE14, WE26, WE27** *Highly Recommended*

Good to Go *see* Short Fuse

Goodbye Again (1961, B&W, 120m, NR)
Ingrid Bergman stars in the melodrama of a lonely woman's affair with a younger man (Anthony Perkins). Yves Montand costars. **CL27**

Goodbye, Columbus (1969, C, 105m, R)
Romantic comedy-drama of a naive young Jewish man falling for snobbish girl, getting involved with her family. Richard Benjamin and Ali MacGraw star; based on Philip Roth's short novel. **DR1, DR19**

Goodbye Girl, The (1977, C, 110m, PG)
An aspiring actor (Oscar winner Richard Dreyfuss) shares an apartment with a divorced woman (Marsha Mason) and her precocious daughter (Quinn Cummings) in this Neil Simon comedy. **CO1, CO34, XT2**

Goodbye, Mr. Chips (1939, B&W, 114m, NR)
Robert Donat won an Oscar for his portrayal of a devoted schoolmaster in this classic drama. Greer Garson costars in her film debut. **DR61, XT2, XT10**

Goon Show Movie, The (1953, B&W, 75m, NR)
The zany antics of Britain's Goon Show are presented in this collection of their sketches. Spike Mulligan, Harry Secombe, and Peter Sellers star. Also known as *Stand Easy*. **CO17, CO26**

Gorath (1964, C, 77m, NR)
Japanese science fiction drama about a meteor forcing scientists to change Earth's orbit. **FF4, SF18**

Gorgo (1961, C, 78m, NR)
A baby sea monster is captured and placed in a London zoo, and its giant parent comes to the rescue. Bill Travers stars in this science fiction drama from Britain. **SF10**

Gorgon, The (1964, C, 83m, NR)
After she is possessed by an evil spirit, a beautiful girl's gaze turns people to stone. Peter Cushing, Christopher Lee, and Barbara Shelley star. **HO26, HO32, HO33**

Gorilla, The (1939, B&W, 66m, NR)
The Ritz Brothers play detectives who investigate a series of murders that take place at the stroke of midnight. Bela Lugosi costars. **HO28**

Gorillas in the Mist (1988, C, 129, PG-13)
Sigourney Weaver plays Dian Fossey, the anthropologist whose defense of mountain gorillas from hunters led to her murder. Bryan Brown costars. **DR6, DR10, DR76**

Gorky Park (1983, C, 128m, R)
Three corpses found in Moscow's Gorky Park set a Russian police captain (William Hurt) off on a twisted case. Based on the bestseller by Martin Cruz Smith. Lee Marvin and Joanna Pacula costar. **DR31, DR43, MY6, MY20**

Gospel According to St. Matthew, The (1966, B&W, 135m, NR)
Low-key dramatization of the life of Christ, from Italian director Pier Paolo Pasolini. **FF2**

Gospel According to Vic, The (1985, C, 92m, PG)
A teacher at a Catholic school embarks on a skeptical inquiry into miracles that have been occurring at his school. Tom Conti and Helen Mirren star in this offbeat British comedy. **CO17**

Gotham (1988, C, 93m, NR)
A private eye (Tommy Lee Jones) is hired by a man who's certain that his dead wife (Virginia Madsen) is following him. Originally made for cable TV. **MY14**

Gothic (1987, C, 87m, R)
One dark and stormy night in the lives of writers Lord Byron, Percy Shelley, and Mary Shelley, as imagined by flamboyant director Ken Russell. Julian Sands, Gabriel Byrne, and Natasha Richardson star. **CU31, HO25**

Grace Quigley (1985, C, 87m, PG)
Katharine Hepburn plays an elderly woman who hires hit man Nick Nolte to kill her and other friends who would rather be dead. Also known as *The Ultimate Solution of Grace Quigley.* **CL16, CO12, DR44**

Graduate, The (1967, C, 105m, PG)
A naive college graduate (Dustin Hoffman) is seduced by a middle-aged woman (Anne Bancroft) but falls in love with her daughter (Katharine Ross). Director Mike Nichols won an Oscar for this brilliant comedy. **CO2, CO4, DR30, DR75, XT6** *Highly Recommended*

Graduation Day (1981, C, 96m, R)
Horror story about members of a high school track team who are brutally murdered a few days before graduation. **HO12**

Grand Canyon Trail (1948, B&W, 68m, NR)
Roy Rogers' mine may have him sitting pretty on pay dirt, or it could just be useless gravel. Only the town swindler knows for sure. **WE23**

Grand Highway, The (1988, C, 104m, NR)
French drama of a 9-year-old boy sent to live in a village in Brittany while mother has a baby. Directed by Jean-Loup Hubert, based on his own experiences. **FF1**

Grand Hotel (1932, B&W, 113m, NR)
Drama set in luxury hotel featuring a mind-boggling cast of MGM stars: Wallace Beery, Greta Garbo, John Barrymore, Joan Crawford, Lionel Barrymore, and Jean Hersholt, for starters. Grand, old-fashioned entertainment; winner of Best Picture Oscar. **CL28, CL50, CU17, XT1** *Highly Recommended*

Grand Illusion (1937, B&W, 111m, NR)
Director Jean Renoir's masterful anti-war drama, set in a World War I prisoner of war camp. Jean Gabin, Erich Von Stroheim, and Pierre Fresnay star. **AC7, CL53, FF12** *Highly Recommended*

Grand Prix (1966, C, 176m, NR)
Big-budget, all-star drama about racing on the European circuit. James Garner, Eva Marie Saint, Yves Montand, and Toshiro Mifune head the cast; John Frankenheimer directed. **AC10, DR22, FF28**

Grande Bourgeoisie, La (1974, C, 115m, NR)
Italian drama, based on true story, of a man who murders his sister's no-good husband. Giancarlo Giannini and Catherine Deneuve star. **FF2, FF27**

Grandview U.S.A. (1984, C, 97m, R)
Smalltown drama of kids trying to stay out of trouble, with C. Thomas Howell, Patrick Swayze, and Jamie Lee Curtis. **DR9, DR62**

Grapes of Wrath, The (1940, B&W, 129m, NR)
John Steinbeck story of a poor family in the midst of the Depression and their hopes for a better life in California. Henry Fonda stars; Oscars went to actress Jane Darwell and director John Ford. **CL8, CL24, CL24, CL34, XT5, XT6** *Recommended*

Grass Is Greener, The (1960, C, 105m, NR)
Cary Grant and Deborah Kerr play a British couple whose marriage is threatened by a handsome tourist (Robert Mitchum) in this comedy. Directed by Stanley Donen. **CL18, MU23**

Grateful Dead Movie, The (1977, C, 131m, NR)
Rock concert film starring those tie-dyed wonders of laid-back rock 'n' roll. Outstanding animated sequence opens the film. **MU10**

Graveyard Shift (1987, C, 89m, R)
Horror story about a New York cabbie with a deadly secret—he's a vampire who prefers a nip on the neck to a tip. **HO5**

Gray Lady Down (1978, C, 111m, PG)
A downed submarine is the object of a daring rescue mission in this adventure saga. Charlton Heston, David Carradine, Stacy Keach, Ned Beatty, and Ronny Cox star. **AC24**

Grease (1978, C, 110m, PG)
Olivia Newton-John and John Travolta star in this screen version of the long-running Broadway musical about high school life in the 1950s. In the supporting cast: Stockard Channing, Eve Arden, Edd Byrnes, and Frankie Avalon. **MU2, MU9**

Grease 2 (1982, C, 114m, PG)
More musical adventures of the students at Rydell High in the 1950s. Maxwell Caulfield and Michelle Pfeiffer star. **MU9**

Greased Lightning (1977, C, 94m, PG)
In a dramatic change of pace, Richard Pryor portrays Wendell Scott, the first black racing car driver. **CO29**

Great American Cowboy, The (1974, C, 90m, NR)
An Oscar-winning documentary about modern day rodeo cowboys. Narrated by Joel McCrea. **WE13**

The Great Battle *see* Battle Force

Great Caruso, The (1951, C, 113m, NR)
Ann Blyth and Mario Lanza star in this biographical film about the opera star's life. **MU1**

Great Day in the Morning (1956, C, 92m, NR)
In pre-Civil War Colorado, a separationist wants to finance the impending war with gold. Starring Robert Stack and Ruth Roman; directed by Jacques Tourneur. **HO37**

Great Dictator, The (1940, B&W, 128m, NR)
Charlie Chaplin's classic spoof of Hitler, as he plays "Adenoid Hynkel," dictator of Tomania. Jack Oakie costars as "Benzino Napaloni." **CL10, CO18** *Recommended*

Great Escape, The (1963, C, 168m, NR)
Superb drama of World War II POW's and a massive breakout from a Nazi prison, based on a true story. James Garner, Steve McQueen, Charles Bronson, Richard Attenborough, James Coburn, and Donald Pleasence head the cast. **AC7, AC28, AC29** *Highly Recommended*

Great Expectations (1946, B&W, 118m, NR)
David Lean directed this adaptation of Charles Dickens' story of a poor orphan who becomes a wealthy young gentleman, thanks to an unknown benefactor. John Mills, Alec Guinness (in his film debut), and Jean Simmons star. **CL1, DR50, DR63, FA3, XT10**

Great Gabbo, The (1929, B&W, 95m, NR)
Erich Von Stroheim plays a boastful ventriloquist in this backstage drama with musical numbers. **CL7, CL53**

Great Gatsby, The (1974, C, 144m, PG)
Robert Redford portrays the mysterious Jay Gatsby in this lavish adaptation of F. Scott Fitzgerald's novel of the Jazz Age. Mia Farrow, Sam Waterston, Bruce Dern, and Karen Black costar. **DR19, DR29**

Great Guns (1941, B&W, 74m, NR)
After their boss joins the army, a gardener and a chauffeur (Stan Laurel and Oliver Hardy) enlist, too. **CO20**

Great Guy (1936, B&W, 75m, NR)
James Cagney plays an inspector out to crack down on illegal dealings in the meat business. **CL22, DR60**

Great Locomotive Chase, The (1956, C, 85m, NR)
Disney adventure based on the true story of a Union spy who led a band of renegades in the theft of a train during the Civil War. Story previously filmed as *The General*. **FA1**

Great Lover, The (1949, B&W, 80m, NR)
Bob Hope plays a boy scout leader aborad a cruise ship with a lovely redhead (Rhonda Fleming) and a fugitive killer (Roland Young). **CO40**

Great McGinty, The (1940, B&W, 81m, NR)
Classic comedy of a bum maneuvered into the governor's mansion by a political machine, which finds to its dismay that their man is actually honest. Brian Donlevy and Akim Tamiroff star. Written and directed by Preston Sturges. **CO24**

Great McGonagall, The (1975, C, 95m, NR)
British comedy of a Scot trying to become poet laureate of England. Spike Mulligan stars, with Peter Sellers as Queen Victoria. **CO26**

Great Missouri Raid, The (1950, C, 83m, NR)
A Western tale that follows the legendary James and Younger boys to their eventual demise. Wendell Corey and MacDonald Carey star. **WE2**

Great Muppet Caper, The (1981, C, 90m, G)
Kermit, Fozzie, and Gonzo travel to London as newspaper reporters in search of jewel thieves. Miss Piggy is close on their heels to keep an eye on "Kermie." Featuring guest stars Diana Rigg and Charles Grodin. **FA15**

Great Northfield Minnesota Raid, The (1972, C, 91m, PG)
Western with cult following about Cole Younger (Cliff Robertson) and Jesse James (Robert Duvall) and their ill-fated attempt to rob a bank in the title town.

Written and directed by Philip Kaufman. **DR37, WE2, WE16**

Great Outdoors, The (1988, C, 90m, PG)
Comic tale of a family's vacation ruined by the arrival of obnoxious relatives. John Candy and Dan Aykroyd star; written by John Hughes. **CO5, CO13, CO14, CO47**

Great Race, The (1965, C, 150m, NR)
Blake Edwards directed this old-fashioned, big-budget comedy about an intercontinental road race. Jack Lemmon, Tony Curtis, and Natalie Wood star. **AC14, CO6, CO46, DR64, FA6**

Great Santini, The (1979, C, 116m, PG)
Portrait of a career Marine whose battles are mainly with his teenaged son. Robert Duvall, Michael O'Keefe, and Blythe Danner star. **DR8, DR37**

Great Scout and Cathouse Thursday (1976, C, 102m, PG)
Lee Marvin, Oliver Reed, and Robert Culp star as a crazy trio of gold prospectors who strike it rich in 1908 Colorado. **DR43, WE15**

Great Smokey Roadblock, The (1976, C, 84m, PG)
An aging truckdriver's rig is reposessed while he is in the hospital. He escapes, steals the truck, and decides to go across the country one last time. Henry Fonda stars, with Eileen Brennan and Susan Sarandon. **CL24**

Great Train Robbery, The (1979, C, 111m, PG)
Victorian England is the setting for this heist thriller, starring Sean Connery, Donald Sutherland, and Lesley-Anne Downe. **AC36, MY34**

Great Waldo Pepper, The (1975, C, 107m, PG)
Robert Redford stars as a barnstorming pilot of the 1920s in this affectionate comedy-drama about aerial daredevils. Susan Sarandon costars; directed by George Roy Hill. **AC11, DR29**

Great Ziegfeld, The (1936, B&W, 176m, NR)
Musical bio of the legendary showman, played by William Powell. Oscar winner for Best Picture and Actress (Luise Rainer). Also in the cast: Myrna Loy, Fanny Brice, and Ray Bolger. **CL15, CL46, MU5, MU7, XT1, XT3**

Greatest, The (1977, C, 101m, PG)
This screen biography of Muhammad Ali traces his life from boyhood in Louisville to his incredible achievements as heavyweight champ. Ali stars as himself, with support from Ernest Borgnine and Robert Duvall. **DR37**

Greatest Love, The *see* Europa '51

Greatest Show on Earth, The (1952, C, 153m, NR)
Oscar-winning drama about life in the circus, directed by Cecil B. DeMille, starring Charlton Heston, Betty Hutton, and James Stewart. **CL7, CL25, XT1**

Greatest Story Ever Told, The (1965, C, 196m, NR)
George Stevens directed this lavish epic detailing the life of Christ. Max von Sydow plays the lead, with guest appearances by many Hollywood stars. **CL13, CL42**

Greed (1925, B&W, 133m, NR)
Director Erich Von Stroheim's masterpiece, a searing version of the Frank Norris novel *McTeague*. A simple dentist (Gibson Gowland) and his wife (Zasu Pitts) become bitter enemies over money and her former suitor (Jean Hersholt). Video version contains new musical score by Carl Davis. **CL1, CL12, CL53** *Highly Recommended*

Green Berets, The (1968, C, 141m, NR)
John Wayne stars in and co-directed this Vietnam War drama that makes no apologies for American involvement in that conflict. **AC4, CL17**

Green Room, The (1978, C, 95m, PG)
A writer obsessed with World War I casualties builds a memorial in their honor. Adaptation of Henry James story directed by François Truffaut, who also stars. **FF13**

Greetings (1968, C, 88m, R)
Comedy of a trio of New Yorkers (Jonathan Warden, Robert DeNiro, Gerrit Graham) and their obsessions: women, ducking the draft, and the Kennedy assassination. Directed by Brian De Palma. Originally rated "X." **CU5, CU28, DR25**

Gregory's Girl (1981, C, 91m, PG)
A young Scottish goalie develops a crush on the new girl on the soccer team. Charming comedy from director Bill Forsyth. **CO17, CU36, FA7**

Gremlins (1984, C, 111m, PG)
A teenager's unusual pet produces offspring which turn violent when not properly cared for. Frantic horror comedy directed by Joe Dante. **CO11, CU40, HO16, HO24**

Grey Fox, The (1982, C, 92m, PG)
After thirty-three years in prison, a gentleman bandit (Richard Farnsworth) just can't go straight, so he stages a train robbery. Western drama filmed in Canada. **DR11, WE4, WE11, WE12**

Greyfriars Bobby (1961, C, 91m, NR)
Disney drama about a terrier who became a "community pet" in Edinburgh in the 19th century. **FA1**

Greystoke: The Legend of Tarzan (1984, C, 130m, PG)
This version of the Tarzan story starts at the very beginning when, as a baby, Greystoke's parents are shipwrecked in Africa and die, leaving the jungle apes to raise him. Christopher Lambert stars, with Ralph Richardson, Ian Holm, and Andie McDowell. **AC12, AC17**

Groove Tube, The (1972, C, 75m, R)
Chevy Chase stars in this wild collection of satirical skits about television. **CO13**

Ground Zero (1988, C, 99m, PG-13)
Australian drama, based on actual events, about a 1950s atomic test that turned disastrous, leading to a government coverup, which a camerman discovers thirty years later. Colin Friels stars. **FF5**

Group, The (1966, C, 150m, NR)
Film version of Mary McCarthy novel about a clique of Vassar students and their lives after college. Candice Bergen, Joanna Pettet, Joan Hackett, Elizabeth Hartman, Shirley Knight, Jessica Walter, Kathleen Widdoes, and Mary-Robin Redd star. Directed by Sidney Lumet. **DR10, DR19, DR58**

Guess Who's Coming to Dinner (1967, C, 108m, NR)
Spencer Tracy (in his last film) and Katharine Hepburn (an Oscar winner) team in this drama about a couple whose daughter tells them she's marrying a black doctor (Sidney Poitier). **CL15, CL16, CL19, DR7, DR38, XT3, XT11**

Gulliver's Travels (1939, C, 74m, NR)
Jonathan Swift's adventure comes to the screen in this full-length animated feature. **FA10**

Gumball Rally, The (1976, C, 107m, PG)
A variety of characters gather for a cross-country road race in this action-filled comedy. Michael Sarrazin, Tim McIntire, Raul Julia, and Gary Busey star. **AC10, CO9**

Gumshoe (1972, C, 88m, NR)
Albert Finney stars in this comic thriller about a man obsessed with Bogart who decides to solve a murder. Directed by Steven Frears. **CO17, MY15, MY19**

Gun Fury (1953, C, 83m, NR)
Rock Hudson plays a cowboy who tracks down the men who kidnapped his fiancée. Lee Marvin and Donna Reed costar. **DR43**

Gunfight, A (1971, C, 90m, PG)
Two aging gunslingers decide to sell tickets to a final shootout with themselves as the star attractions. Kirk Douglas, Raf Vallone, and Johnny Cash star. **MU12**

Gunfight at the O.K. Corral (1957, C, 122m, NR)
Burt Lancaster and Kirk Douglas join forces as Wyatt Earp and Doc Holliday in this western classic about the fabled Dodge City shootout. With Rhonda Fleming, Jo Van Fleet, John Ireland, Lee Van Cleef, and Dennis Hopper. **CU46, DR41, WE2**

Gunfighter, The (1950, B&W, 84m, NR)
Gregory Peck plays Johnny Ringo, a disillusioned gunslinger who feels it's time to hang up the holster. **WE2**

Gung Ho! (1943, B&W, 88m, NR)
Randolph Scott prepares Marine recruits for World War II action. **WE22**

Gung Ho (1986, C, 111m, PG-13)
The foreman of an auto plant about to go under persuades a Japanese car company to take over management of the factory. Michael Keaton stars in this comedy, with Gedde Watanabe, George Wendt, and Mimi Rogers. **CO2, CO45** *Recommended*

Gunga Din (1939, B&W, 117m, NR)
Rousing adventure classic about three British soldiers fighting the natives—and each other—in 19th-century India. Cary Grant, Douglas Fairbanks, Jr., and Victor McLaglen star. George Stevens directed this version of Kipling's tale. **AC13, CL18, CL42, FA4** *Highly Recommended*

Guns of Navarone, The (1961, C, 157m, NR)
Adventure yarn about a group of World War II commandoes out to destroy massive Nazi guns. Gregory Peck, David Niven, Anthony Quinn, and Stanley Baker star. **AC1**

Gus (1976, C, 96m, G)
This Disney comedy features a mule named Gus with a talent for kicking footballs. A group of evildoers plots to kidnap the talented animal for their own pur-

poses. Edward Asner, Don Knotts, and Tim Conway star. **FA1**

Guy Named Joe, A (1943, B&W, 120m, NR)
Spencer Tracy plays an angel who comes to earth to help a World War II soldier in trouble. Irene Dunne, Van Johnson, Esther Williams, and Lionel Barrymore costar. **CL19**

Guys And Dolls (1955, C, 150m, NR)
Frank Sinatra, Marlon Brando, and Jean Simmons star in this classic Damon Runyon story about a gambler and a missionary, set to a Frank Loesser score. Joseph L. Mankiewicz directed. **CL55, DR33, MU2, MU6, MU17, MU26**

Gymkata (1985, C, 90m, R)
Undercover agent competes in international gymnastic meet, with an eye toward recovering stolen U.S. documents. Kurt Thomas stars in this martial arts thriller. **AC26**

Gypsy (1962, C, 149m, NR)
Natalie Wood plays Gypsy Rose Lee in this musical account of the stripper's life, with Rosalind Russell as Mama Rose. **MU5**

HBO Comedy Club (1987, C, 60m each, NR)
This series of three tapes highlight the best of today's comedy. The first is *Howie From Maui,* featuring Howie Mandel in concert. The second, *Tenth Anniversary Young Comedians Special* is a reunion of comics featuring Robin Williams. The third, *Roseanne Barr,* stars the witty, sharp-tongued comedienne. **CO16**

H-Man, The (1958, C, 79m, NR)
Japanese science fiction story set in Tokyo with twin plots: radioactive substance causes havoc, while police and dope dealers battle it out. **FF4, SF18**

Hail! Hail! Rock 'n' Roll *see* Chuck Berry: Hail! Hail! Rock 'n' Roll

Hail Mary (1985, C, 107m, NR)
Director Jean-Luc Godard's controversial drama about a contemporary young woman's unexplained pregnancy. **CU8, FF14**

Hair (1979, C, 121m, R)
The Broadway musical about a group of New York hippies opposed to the Vietnam War. Treat Williams, John Savage, and Beverly D'Angelo star; Milos Forman directed. **DR57, MU2, MU9, XT9**

Hairspray (1988, C, 90m, PG)
Baltimore in the early 1960s: a TV teen dance show is disrupted when one of the "regulars" tries to bring her black friends to the show. A marvelously nostalgic comedy from director John Waters, starring Ricki Lake, Divine (in two roles), Jerry Stiller, Sonny Bono, Debby Harry, and Ruth Brown. **CO6, CU43, MU12** *Recommended*

Half Moon Street (1986, C, 90m, R)
Sigourney Weaver plays an American researcher in London who turns to prostitution to make ends meet, becomes involved in political intrigue. Michael Caine costars in this adaptation of Paul Theroux's novella. **DR76, MY6**

Half of Heaven (1987, C, 127m, NR)
Spanish drama, with elements of comedy and fantasy, starring Angela Molina as a woman who molds herself into a successful restaurant owner. Directed by Manuel Guttierez Aragon. **FF7**

Halloween (1978, C, 85m, R)
A young boy murders his teenaged sister, is locked up, and escapes years later, looking for more victims. Cult horror film was also a hit movie spawning dozens of imitators. Jamie Lee Curtis and Donald Pleasence star; John Carpenter directed. **CU4, CU29, HO9** *Recommended*

Halloween II (1981, C, 92m, R)
Terror continues as the killer stalks his victims on Halloween night, taking up where *Halloween* left off. Jamie Lee Curtis and Donald Pleasence return, too. **HO9**

Halloween III: Season of the Witch (1983, C, 96m, R)
A mad scientist hatches a plot to slaughter millions of children on Halloween. Not a sequel to earlier *Halloween films*. **HO20**

Halloween IV: The Return of Michael Myers (1988, C, 88m, R)
As the title suggests, the monstrous killer from the first two *Halloween* horrorfests is back, with the same good doctor (Donald Pleasence) in pursuit. **HO9**

Hambone and Hillie (1984, C, 89m, G)
Lillian Gish plays a woman who's separated from her beloved dog at an airport in this family drama. **CL49, FA5**

Hamburger Hill (1987, C, 104m, R)
War drama of American company caught up in bloody battle for a strategic position in Vietnam. Michael Dolan, Daniel O'Shea, and Dylan McDermott star. **AC4**

Hamlet (1948, B&W, 153m, NR)
Laurence Olivier directed and stars in this adaptation of the Shakespeare play about the tormented Danish prince. Jean Simmons and Peter Cushing costar. Winner of four Academy Awards, including Best Picture and Actor. **CL1, CL32, HO33, XT1, XT2** *Recommended*

Hamlet (1969, C, 114m, G)
Nicol Williamson stars in this version of Shakespeare's tragedy, with Gordon Jackson, Anthony Hopkins, and Marianne Faithfull (as Ophelia). Directed by Tony Richardson. **CL1, MU12**

Hammersmith Is Out (1972, C, 108m, R)
Elizabeth Taylor and Richard Burton team up in this story of a violent mental patient who is determined to escape from the hospital. **CL15, CL33**

Hammett (1983, C, 97m, PG)
Real-life author Dashiell Hammett gets involved in a real-life mystery. Based on Joe Gores' novel about Hammett's career as a Pinkerton detective. Frederic Forrest stars, with Peter Boyle, Marilu Henner, Elisha Cook, Samuel Fuller, and R.G.

Armstrong. Wim Wenders directed. **CU22, FF21, MY8** *Recommended*

Handful of Dust, A (1988, C, 118m, PG)
The Evelyn Waugh story of a failed marriage between a sensitive aristocrat (David Wilby) and his self-centered wife (Kristin Scott-Thomas). **DR1, DR19, DR23**

Handle With Care *see* Citizens Band

Hands Across the Border (1944, B&W, 54m, NR)
Roy Rogers does his bit to promote good relations between the U.S. and Mexico in this western adventure. **WE23**

Hang 'Em High (1968, C, 114m, NR)
A cowboy (Clint Eastwood) vows revenge on the men who tried to kill him in this American-made spaghetti western. With Inger Stevens, Ed Begley, Pat Hingle, Ben Johnson, and Dennis Hopper. **CU46, WE14, WE26**

Hanky Panky (1982, C, 105m, PG)
Comic thriller about a woman looking for the men who murdered her brother and involving an innocent bystander in her investigation. Gilda Radner and Gene Wilder star; directed by Sidney Poitier. **CO13, DR38**

Hanna K. (1983, C, 108m, R)
Jill Clayburgh plays a lawyer in Israel who is juggling a persistent ex-husband, an amorous district attorney, and a mysterious Arab defendant she is representing. Topical drama from director Costa-Gavras. **DR3, DR7, DR10**

Hannah and Her Sisters (1986, C, 106m, PG)
Woody Allen comedy-drama of a family of neurotic New Yorkers whose lives mingle over three Thanksgivings. Dianne Wiest and Michael Caine won Oscars, as did Allen's screenplay. With Mia Farrow and Barbara Hershey. **CO5, CO27, XT4, XT5, XT9** *Recommended*

Hannah's War (1988, C, 148m, PG-13)
True-life drama of a Hungarian woman
who worked for the Allies in World War
II on rescue missions. She was captured
and tortured by the Nazis. Maruschka
Dettmers stars, with Ellen Burstyn, An-
thony Edwards, and Donald Pleasence.
DR5

Hanoi Hilton, The (1987, C, 126m, R)
Drama of Vietnam War POWs; the title
refers to their sarcastic name for their
quarters. Michael Moriarty, Jeffrey
Jones, and Paul LeMat star. **AC7**

Hanover Street (1979,C, 109m, PG)
World War II romance between British
wife and American serviceman, starring
Harrison Ford and Lesley-Anne Downe.
DR1, DR32

Hans Christian Andersen (1954, C, 120m,
NR)
Danny Kaye stars in this family musical
about the famous storyteller. **CO41, FA9**

Hansel and Gretel (1984, C, 58m, NR)
Two hungry children (Ricky Schroder,
Bridgette Andersen) stop to snack on a
gingerbread house and almost become
dinner for the witch (Joan Collins) who
lives there. A Faerie Tale Theatre presentation. **FA12**

Happiest Millionaire, The (1967, C, 118,
NR)
This Disney musical features Fred
MacMurray and Greer Garson as an ec-
centric Philadelphia couple dealing with
life in the early 1900s. Geraldine Page and
Lesley Ann Warren costar. **FA1**

Happy Birthday to Me (1981, C, 107m, R)
Horror story of a high school student who
may be killing off her classmates in retribution for the accidental death of her
mother. **HO9**

Happy Ending, The (1969, C, 112m, PG)
Contemporary drama of a middle-aged
woman walking out on her marriage, starring Jean Simmons, with John Forsythe,

Lloyd Bridges, Shirley Jones, and Robert
(Bobby) Darin. **DR10, MU12**

Happy New Year (1973, C, 112m, PG)
A pair of jewel thieves plot a heist, only
to have one fall in love with the proprietor
of the store next to their target. French
comedy stars Lino Ventura, Françoise
Fabian, and Charles Gerard. U.S. remake
released in 1987. **FF1, FF36**

Happy New Year (1987, C, 85m, PG)
Remake of French comedy about two
jewel thieves and romantic complications,
starring Peter Falk, Wendy Hughes,
Charles Durning, and Tom Courtenay.
FF36

Hard Choices (1984, C, 90m, NR)
Drama of social worker and her teenaged
client, a juvenile offender, falling in love,
with her helping him to escape custody.
Gary McCleery and Margaret Klenck
star. **DR1, DR3**

Hard Day's Night, A (1964, B&W, 85m,
NR)
Richard Lester directed this brilliant rock
musical about a day in the life of The
Beatles, shot on location in London.
CU35, FA9, MU9, XT9 *Highly Recom-
mended*

Hard Rock Zombies (1987, C, 90m, R)
Four heavy metal musicians are murdered
but return from the grave for their scheduled concert as zombies. **HO6**

Hard Times (1975, C, 97m, R)
Drama about street fighter in Depression-
era New Orleans, starring Charles Bron-
son, James Coburn, and Strother Martin.
Directed by Walter Hill. **AC8, AC29,
CU27**

Hardcore (1979, C, 108m, R)
Religious father from the Midwest tries to
find runaway daughter in the midst of the
porno film and prostitution worlds.
George C. Scott stars; Paul Schrader
wrote and directed. **DR7** *Recommended*

Harder They Come, The (1973, C, 98m,
R)
A poor youth in Jamaica gains fame as
both a singer and an outlaw in this mid-

night movie classic starring Jimmy Cliff. Great reggae music soundtrack. **CU1, CU9, MU9** *Recommended*

Harder They Fall, The (1956, B&W, 109m, NR)
Humphrey Bogart's last screen appearance has him playing a press agent who befriends an exploited prizefighter. Rod Steiger costars. **CL20, DR22, XT11**

Hardly Working (1981, C, 91m, PG)
An unemployed circus clown (Jerry Lewis) stumbles through a series of odd jobs, all with disastrous results. Susan Oliver, Steve Franken, and Lewis J. Stone costar; Lewis directed. **CO25**

Harlan County, U.S.A. (1977, C, 103m, PG)
Oscar-winning documentary about a bitter and violent coal miner's strike in Kentucky. Directed by Barbara Kopple. **CU16**

Harold and Maude (1972, C, 90m, PG)
Offbeat romantic comedy about a suicidal rich boy (Bud Cort) and a life-loving 80-year-old (Ruth Gordon) finding romance. A cult favorite at midnight screenings. **CO12, CU1, CU5, CU17**

Harold Lloyd (1962, B&W, 80m, NR)
Compilation of the classic silent comedian's short films from the early 1920s, including his masterpiece, *Safety Last*. **CL11** *Recommended*

Harper (1966, C, 121m, NR)
Paul Newman plays detective Lew Harper, hired by a frustrated wife (Lauren Bacall) to find her missing husband. Janet Leigh, Robert Wagner, and Shelley Winters costar. Based on the Ross Mac-Donald novel, *The Moving Target*. **DR28, MY27**

Harry and Son (1984, C, 117m, PG)
Paul Newman cowrote, coproduced, directed, and stars in this tale of a strained relationship between a widowed construction worker and his idealistic son.

Robby Benson and Joanne Woodward costar. **DR28, DR67**

Harry and Tonto (1974, C, 115m, R)
Odyssey of a senior citizen and his pet cat on the road from New York to California, with Oscar winner Art Carney magnificent. Ellen Burstyn and Larry Hagman costar; directed by Paul Mazursky. **DR11, XT2** *Recommended*

Harry and Walter Go to New York (1976, C, 123m, PG)
Two unsuccessful vaudevillians (Elliott Gould, James Caan) resort to theft and land in jail in 1890s New York. Diane Keaton costars in this comedy. **CO6, DR40**

Harry Tracy (1982, C, 100m, PG)
A wanted criminal's exploits made him the envy of all and a folk hero to most. Bruce Dern and singer Gordon Lightfoot star in this Canadian-produced western. **MU12, WE4**

Harum Scarum (1965, C, 86m, NR)
Elvis Presley musical about a movie star who gets involved in an attempted assassination in the Middle East. **MU22**

Harvey Girls, The (1946, C, 101m, NR)
Judy Garland stars in this musical about a girl who travels west to work for Fred Harvey and his railroad-stop restaurants. Ray Bolger, Angela Lansbury, and Preston Foster costar. **MU6, MU21**

Hatari! (1962, C, 159m, NR)
John Wayne is the leader of a group of big-game stalkers who capture wild animals for zoos. Directed by Howard Hawks. **AC12, CL17, CL35**

Haunted Summer (1988, C, 106m, R)
Drama based on actual meeting of 19th-century English poets Lord Byron (Philip Anglim) and Percy Bysshe Shelley (Eric Stoltz). Laura Dern and Alice Krige costar. **DR5**

Haunted Honeymoon (1986, C, 82m, PG-13)
A recently married couple (Gene Wilder, Gilda Radner) spend their honeymoon in a haunted house. Dom DeLuise costars in this horror comedy. **CO13**

Haunted Strangler, The (1958, B&W, 81m, NR)
A mystery writer (Boris Karloff) investigates a series of murders which took place in London twenty years before, believing that an innocent man was hanged for the crimes. **HO27**

Haunting, The (1963, B&W, 113m, NR)
Two women who have had clairvoyant experiences are invited to a mysterious house where strange and terrifying events have occurred. Claire Bloom and Julie Harris star. Directed by Robert Wise. **CL58, HO1, HO2, HO3, HO19**

Haunting of Julia, The (1976, C, 96m, R)
Mia Farrow stars as a tormented woman who, after the death of her young daughter, moves to a house inhabited by a spirit. Keir Dullea and Tom Conti costar in this British horror film. **HO2, HO3, HO19, HO26**

Hawaii (1966, C, 171m, NR)
Missionaries try to bring Christianity to Hawaiian Islands in the 19th century. Julie Andrews, Max von Sydow, and Gene Hackman star. Directed by George Roy Hill, from the James Michener novel. **DR39**

Hawmps! (1976, C, 113m, G)
Camels are trained as army mounts for desert maneuvers in this comedy based on a true story. **FA6**

He Knows You're Alone (1981, C, 94m, R)
A mad killer is after women who are about to be married. Don Scardino and Caitlin O'Heaney star; watch for Tom Hanks in a small part. **CO44**

He Walked by Night (1948, B&W, 79m, NR)
Los Angeles homicide investigators are looking for a cop killer in this classic thriller. Anthony Mann co-directed, with Alfred Werker. **MY1, WE20**

Head (1968, C, 86m, G)
The Monkees made their film debut in this wild collection of skits, written by Jack Nicholson and directed by Bob Rafelson. **CU3, MU9**

Head Office (1986, C, 86m, PG-13)
A naive college graduate (Judge Reinhold) gets a job with a powerful conglomerate after his father pulls some strings. Comedy about big business also features Rick Moranis, Danny DeVito, Eddie Albert, and Jane Seymour. **CO14**

Head Over Heels *see* Chilly Scenes of Winter

Heart Beat (1980, C, 109m, R)
The life and times of Beat writer Jack Kerouac (John Heard) and his pal Neal Cassidy (Nick Nolte). Sissy Spacek plays Carolyn Cassidy and Ray Sharkey is very funny as Allen Ginsberg. **DR4, DR44, DR68**

Heart Is a Lonely Hunter, The (1968, C, 125m, G)
Heart-rending version of Carson McCullers novel about a young girl's coming of age in a small Southern town. Sondra Locke and Alan Arkin star, with Stacy Keach, Chuck McCann, and Cicely Tyson. **DR2, DR9, DR19, DR62**

Heart Like a Wheel (1983, C, 113m, PG)
The true story of Shirley Muldowney, the first woman to dent the all-male barrier in modern drag racing. Bonnie Bedelia, Beau Bridges, and Hoyt Axton star. **DR4, DR22** *Recommended*

Heart of the Golden West (1942, B&W, 54m, NR)
Roy Rogers comes to the rescue of Cherokee City ranchers. **WE23**

Heart of the Rio Grande (1942, B&W, 70m, NR)
Gene Autry sings his way out of the middle of a family feud. **WE24**

Heart of the Rockies (1951, B&W, 54m, NR)
Roy Rogers plays a highway engineer battling a crooked rancher in this contemporary western. **WE23**

Heartbeeps (1981, C, 79m, PG)
The ultimate futuristic romance: two robots fall in love. Andy Kaufman and Bernadette Peters star; Allan Arkush directed. **CU41, FA8, SF21**

Heartbreak Hotel (1988, C, 101m, PG-13)
To cheer up his widowed mother who's an avid Elvis Presley fan, her teen son and his buddies kidnap The King from his hotel and take him to their small Ohio town. Comedy, set in the early 1970s, stars Charlie Schlatter and Tuesday Weld, with David Keith as Elvis. **CO6**

Heartbreak Kid, The (1972, C, 104m, PG)
A Jewish man (Charles Grodin) marries, but has a change of heart when he meets a beautiful WASP (Cybill Shepherd) on his honeymoon. Elaine May directed, Neil Simon wrote this dark comedy with a cult following. Eddie Albert costars. **CO1, CO34, CU5** *Highly Recommended*

Heartbreak Ridge (1986, C, 130m, R)
A tough Army sergeant (Clint Eastwood) shapes up his young recruits for action in the Grenada invasion. Marsha Mason, Everett McGill, and Mario Van Peebles costar. **AC6, AC27**

Heartburn (1986, C, 108m, R)
Jack Nicholson and Meryl Streep are a seemingly happily married couple, until she learns during her pregnancy that he's having an affair. Directed by Mike Nichols from the novel by Nora Ephron. Filmed on location in Washington, D.C. **CO1, CO2, DR24, DR26, DR75, XT9**

Heartland (1979, C, 96m, PG)
A western woman's saga of life on the 1910 Wyoming frontier, based on a true story. Conchata Ferrell and Rip Torn star. **CU47, WE9** *Recommended*

Heartland Reggae (1980, C, 87m, NR)
Concert film shot in Jamaica in April 1978, featuring some of reggae's superstars, including Bob Marley and Peter Tosh. **MU10**

Hearts and Minds (1974, C, 110m, R)
Oscar-winning documentary explores America's involvment in the Vietnam War. Directed by Peter Davis. **CU16** *Recommended*

Hearts of Fire (1987, C, 95m, R)
Drama of a romantic triangle among pop singers, starring Bob Dylan, Fiona, and Rupert Everett. **DR12**

Hearts of the West (1975, C, 102m, PG)
Jeff Bridges plays an aspiring novelist in the 1930s who goes to Hollywood to work as a screenwriter, but winds up starring in cheap westerns. Offbeat comedy also stars Blythe Danner, Alan Arkin, and Andy Griffith. **CO6, CO8, DR71** *Recommended*

Hearts of the World (1918, B&W, 152m, NR)
Sentimental silent drama from director D.W. Griffith, made to persuade America to enter World War I. Robert Harron is the young man who goes off to fight; Lillian and Dorothy Gish costar. Erich Von Stroheim has a small role as a German soldier. **AC2, CL48, CL53, XT8**

Heat (1972, C, 100m, NR)
Andy Warhol-produced takeoff on *Sunset Boulevard,* with Joe Dallessandro and Sylvia Miles as the writer and faded star. Directed by Paul Morissey. **CU2, CU12, CU44**

Heat (1987, C, 101m, R)
Burt Reynolds is a mystery man based in Vegas, protecting the innocent, teaching a neophyte gambler the ropes. Written by William Goldman from his novel. **AC37**

Heat and Dust (1983, C, 130m, NR)
Two-pronged story of a pair of English-women (Greta Scacchi, Julie Christie) who a century apart journey to India and fall in love with the country and one of its natives. From the filmmaking team of producer Ismail Merchant, director James Ivory, and writer Ruth Prawer Jhabvala. **DR23**

Heat of Desire (1980, C, 90m, R)
A respectable professor is seduced by a free-spirited woman, and both his marriage and career are ruined. Patrick Dewaere, Clio Goldsmith, and Jeanne Moreau star. **FF1, FF26**

Heathers (1989, C, 103m, R)
Dark comedy starring Winona Ryder as a high school girl vying to be accepted into a clique of snotty princesses, until she meets rebel student Christian Slater. Murders trumped up to look like suicides are his specialty. **CO4, CO12, CO35, CU5** *Recommended*

Heatwave (1983, C, 99m, R)
A radical activist leads a fight against a multi-million dollar development which will destroy a neighborhood. Matters get complicated when she and the project architect fall in love. Australian drama starring Judy Davis. **FF5, MY20**

Heaven (1987, C, 80m, NR)
Diane Keaton directed this documentary about people's perceptions of heaven. Film alternates between clips of Hollywood movies on the subject and interviews. **DR40**

Heaven Can Wait (1978, C, 100m, PG)
Remake (and updating) of *Here Comes Mr. Jordan,* with Warren Beatty as a football player taken to heaven before his time and allowed to return to Earth. Julie Christie, Dyan Cannon, and Charles Grodin costar in this comedy, co-directed by Beatty and screenwriter Buck Henry. **CU18, DR34**

Heaven Help Us (1985, C, 104m, R)
A New York Catholic boy's school in the early 1960s is the setting for this coming of age comedy. Andrew McCarthy and Kevin Dillon are the students; Donald Sutherland, John Heard, and Wallace Shawn are in charge. **CO4, CO35** *Recommended*

Heavens Above (1963, B&W, 113m, NR)
A deeply devoted reverend wreaks havoc when he becomes a bishop on a nuclear missile base in outer space. Peter Sellers stars. **CO26**

Heaven's Gate (1980, C, 219m, R)
A sweeping, controversial epic of a war between immigrant settlers and cattle barons in Johnson County, Wyoming. Kris Kristofferson, Christopher Walken, Isabelle Huppert, and Jeff Bridges star. Michael Cimino directed. (Also available in a 149m version.) **DR71, MU12, WE1**

Heidi (1937, B&W, 88m, NR)
Shirley Temple stars as the little girl living in the Swiss Alps with her grandfather whose life turns upside down when she moves to the city to live with a wealthy invalid girl. **FA2, FA14**

Heiress, The (1949, B&W, 115m, NR)
The plain daughter of a wealthy doctor is threatened with disinheritance when she falls in love with a young social climber. Oscar winner Olivia de Havilland stars, with Ralph Richardson and Montgomery Clift. Directed by William Wyler; based on the Henry James novel, *Washington Square.* **CL1, CL4, CL6, CL38, DR19, XT3** *Recommended*

Hell Fighters, The (1969, C, 121m, NR)
John Wayne leads a team of brave men who put out oil well fires. Jim Hutton and Katharine Ross costar. **CL17**

Hell Night (1981, C, 101m, R)
Four girls pledging a sorority must spend the night in a haunted mansion supposedly occupied by the ghost of a killer. But as the night wears on, they're not sure he's really dead. **HO12**

Hell on Frisco Bay (1955, C, 98m, NR)
Gangster saga, set in contemporary San
Francisco, with good guy Alan Ladd
against baddie Edward G. Robinson.
With Joanne Dru, William Demarest, Fay
Wray, and Jayne Mansfield. **AC22, CL52**

Hell up in Harlem (1973, C, 96m, R)
Sequel to *Black Caesar* stars Fred Wil-
liamson as a vengeance-seeking gangster.
Directed by Larry Cohen. With Julius W.
Harris, Gloria Hendry, and Margaret Av-
ery. **CU30**

Hellbound: Hellraiser II (1988, C, 93m, R)
The demons who haunted the couple in
the first *Hellraiser* are back for more
sport, this time with the couple's daughter (Ashley Laurence). Available in an
unrated version with a 98m running time.
CU10, HO14

Helldorado (1946, B&W, 54m, NR)
Roy Rogers and Dale Evans travel to Las
Vegas for Nevada's Frontier Days. **WE23**

Heller in Pink Tights (1960, C, 100m, NR)
Sophia Loren travels the 1880s West with
a theatrical troupe, entertaining in the
face of Indian uprisings, bill collectors,
and thieves. With Anthony Quinn, Steve
Forrest, Eileen Heckart, Margaret
O'Brien, and Ramon Novarro. Directed
by George Cukor; based on a Louis L'A-
mour story. **CL9, CL39, FF31, WE9,
WE29** *Recommended*

Hello, Dolly! (1969, C, 146m, G)
In this screen version of the Broadway
smash, Barbra Streisand plays Dolly
Levi, a widowed matchmaker in old New
York who finds herself attracted to a
bachelor merchant (Walter Matthau). Di-
rected by Gene Kelly. **MU2, MU19,
MU27**

Hellraiser (1987, C, 94m, R)
Clive Barker wrote and directed this harrowing tale about a man whose dead
brother comes back to haunt him and his
family. **HO14**

Hell's Angels on Wheels (1967, C, 95m,
NR)
Low-budget nonsense about the infamous
motorcycle gang. Jack Nicholson stars as
a gas station attendant named Poet. **DR24**

Hell's House (1932, B&W, 72m, NR)
A young boy is sent to a reformatory after
he takes the blame for a crime to protect
someone else. Bette Davis appears in one
of her first film roles. **CL21**

Hellstrom Chronicle, The (1971, C, 90m,
G)
Oscar-winning documentary which pro-
poses that insects may take over the
world from man by weight of sheer numbers. **CU16**

Help! (1965, C, 90m, NR)
In their second film, The Beatles dodge a
crazy cult that's after a sacrificial ring
that Ringo possesses. Richard Lester directed. **CU35, FA9, MU9** *Highly Recommended*

Helter Skelter (1976, C, 194m, NR)
Chilling dramatization of the Charles
Manson murders and the subsequent
trials, based on prosecutor Vincent Bug-
liosi's book. Steve Railsback is a very
creepy Manson. Originally made for TV.
DR6, DR16 *Recommended*

Henry V (1945, C, 137m, NR)
Laurence Olivier produced, directed, and
stars in this colorful adaptation of Shake-
speare's classic. Olivier won a special
Oscar for his achievement. **CL1, CL9,
CL32** *Recommended*

Henry IV (1984, C, 95m, PG-13)
Marcello Mastroianni stars as a mad nobleman who believes he's Emperor
Henry IV in this version of the Pirandello
play, directed by Marco Bellochio. Claudia Cardinale costars. **FF2, FF24**

Her Alibi (1989, C, 94m, PG)
Comic mystery of a novelist (Tom Selleck) who's not sure if the lovely new
woman in his life (Paulina Porizkova) is

really guilty of murder. With William Daniels. **MY15, MY21**

Herbie Goes Bananas (1980, C, 93m, G)
Herbie, the magical Volkswagen from *The Love Bug,* travels to South America to enter a car race. Fourth in the series from the Disney studios. **FA1**

Herbie Goes to Monte Carlo (1977, C, 104, G)
Herbie gets involved in a Monte Carlo race and his driver (Dean Jones) is unaware that a spy ring has a diamond hidden in the gas tank. Third in the Disney series. **FA1**

Herbie Rides Again (1974, C, 88m, G)
This sequel to *The Love Bug* casts Helen Hayes as a woman trying to thwart a villain who wants to get his hands on Herbie. **FA1**

Hercules (1959, C, 107m, NR)
Strongman Steve Reeves plays the mighty warrior in this adventure that set off a wave of sequels and imitators. **FF2**

Here Come the Littles (1985, C, 72m, G)
Based on the children's books, this animated feature follows the adventures of the Littles, tiny people who live in the walls of people's houses. In this story, they get involved with a 12-year-old boy. **FA10**

Here Comes Mr. Jordan (1941, B&W, 93m, NR)
Classic fantasy of boxer taken to heaven before his time and returned to Earth in another man's body. Robert Montgomery, Claude Rains, Evelyn Keyes, and Edward Everett Horton star. Remade in 1978 as *Heaven Can Wait.* **SF2**

Hero and the Terror (1988, C, 97m, R)
Chuck Norris plays a cop who puts away a super-human killer, only to have the man escape, precipitating another manhunt led by you-know-who. **AC32**

Heroes (1977, C, 113m, PG)
A disturbed Vietnam vet (Henry Winkler) embarks on a cross-country trip and meets a confused young girl (Sally Field) along the way. Harrison Ford costars in this comedy-drama. **DR32, DR36**

Hester Street (1975, B&W, 92m, PG)
In turn-of-the-century New York, a young immigrant wife struggles to adapt to the ways of her new life. Carol Kane stars; Joan Micklin Silver directed. **DR5, DR15** *Recommended*

Hey Babu Riba (1986, C, 109m, NR)
Yugoslavian comedy centering on four men and their memories of youthful 1950s fascination with the same girl. Gala Videnovic plays the object of their desire. **FF7**

Hey There, It's Yogi Bear (1964, C, 89m, G)
Yogi Bear and Boo Boo star in this animated musical feature about life in Jellystone Park. As spring and picnic basket season approach, the bears try to outsmart Ranger Smith. **FA10**

Hidden, The (1987, C, 96m, R)
A police detective joins forces with an alien cop (in human form) to track a sinister force that possesses people and causes them to go berserk. Michael Nouri and Kyle MacLachlan star in this science fiction/action thriller. **AC8, SF17**

Hidden Fortress, The (1958, B&W, 139m, NR)
Japanese adventure starring Toshiro Mifune as the loyal companion to a spoiled princess making a dangerous journey with precious royal cargo. Directed by Akira Kurosawa. Video version is completely restored print. **CU10, FF9, FF28**

Hide in Plain Sight (1980, C, 98m, PG)
James Caan directed and stars in this story of a man who frantically searches for his children after they disappear with his ex-wife. Jill Eikenberry costars. **MY8**

Hideous Sun Demon, The (1959, B&W, 74m, NR)
Low-budget science fiction yarn about scientist exposed to radiation who turns into the title character in sunlight. Robert Clarke directed and stars. **SF10**

High and Low (1962, B&W, 142m, NR)
Akira Kurosawa directed this suspenseful study of a businessman (Toshiro Mifune) whose chauffeur's son is mistakenly kidnapped; he agrees to pay the ransom anyway. Deliberately paced, but exceptionally exciting. **FF9, FF24, MY20** *Recommended*

High Anxiety (1977, C, 94m, PG)
Mel Brooks directed and stars in this spoof of Hitchcock films, about a psychiatrist who finds trouble behind every door when he becomes the head of a sanitarium. Madeline Kahn, Harvey Korman, and Cloris Leachman costar. **CO7, CO28**

High Heels (1972, C, 100m, NR)
Jean-Paul Belmondo stars in this French comedy-mystery about a doctor who marries an unattractive woman and falls in love with her sister. Directed by Claude Chabrol; Mia Farrow and Laura Antonelli costar. **FF33**

High Noon (1952, B&W, 85m, NR)
Gary Cooper's performance as the honorable sheriff who faces a showdown with outlaws on his wedding day won him an Oscar. Grace Kelly costars, with Lon Chaney, Jr., Thomas Mitchell, Katy Jurado, and Lloyd Bridges. Directed by Fred Zinnemann. **CL26, CL31, CL57, HO30, WE2, WE25, XT2**

High Noon, Part II: The Return of Will Kane (1980, C, 100m, NR)
Lee Majors plays a retired marshal who takes the law into his hands when he returns to find a corrupt sheriff in his town. **WE2**

High Plains Drifter (1973, C, 105m, R)
Clint Eastwood stars in and directed this spooky, violent western tale about a mys-terious character in a strange frontier town. **WE6, WE26**

High Road to China (1983, C, 106m, PG)
A soldier of fortune agrees to fly a spoiled young woman on a rescue mission to help her father out of China. Tom Selleck and Bess Armstrong star. **AC11, AC14, AC21**

High School Confidential (1958, B&W, 85m, NR)
Camp cult classic which opens with Jerry Lee Lewis singing the title tune (on the back of a flatbed truck) and goes downhill from there. Story has Russ Tamblyn as an undercover agent investigating widespread marijuana use by teens. Also in the cast: Mamie Van Doren, Jackie Coogan, Charlie Chaplin, Jr., and Michael Landon. **CU2**

High Sierra (1941, B&W, 100m, NR)
Humphrey Bogart plays a gangster running from the police, with the help of his girl friend (Ida Lupino). Written by John Huston; Raoul Walsh directed. **AC22, CL20, MY1** *Recommended*

High Society (1956, C, 107m, NR)
In this musical remake of *The Philadelphia Story*, Grace Kelly is a wealthy socialite trying to avoid nosy reporters (Frank Sinatra, Celeste Holm) and her ex-husband (Bing Crosby) on the eve of her wedding. Louis Armstrong appears as himself. **CL31, MU1, MU14, MU25, MU26** *Recommended*

High Spirits (1988, C, 99m, PG-13)
Peter O'Toole plays an impoverished nobleman who claims his castle is haunted, to attract American tourists Steven Guttenberg and Beverly D'Angelo for a paying visit. Daryl Hannah costars as a real live ghost in this comedy. **CO11, DR45**

High Tide (1987, C, 120m, PG-13)
Australian drama of a woman whose aimless life on the road with musical groups is changed when she's reunited with the daughter she abandoned many years ago. Judy Davis stars; Gillian Armstrong directed. **DR9, DR10, FF5** *Recommended*

High Voltage (1929, B&W, 57m, NR)
A bus is stranded in a mountain snow-storm and its passengers seek help from a lineman, who is in reality a fugitive from justice. William Boyd, Owen Moore, and Carole (billed as "Carol") Lombard star. **CL48**

Higher and Higher (1943, B&W, 90m, NR)
Frank Sinatra made his starring debut in this musical about a down-on-his-luck gentleman who conspires with his servants to raise money. **MU26**

Highlander (1986, C, 111m, R)
Adventure tale of an ancient Scottish warrior who pursues his arch-rival to contemporary Manhattan. Christopher Lambert stars, with Sean Connery. Music by Queen. **AC36, SF4, XT9**

Highpoint (1980, C, 88m, PG)
An innocent man gets involved in a murder after he begins working for a wealthy family in this comedy/thriller. Richard Harris, Christopher Plummer, and Beverly D'Angelo star. **MY9**

Hillbillys in a Haunted House (1967, C, 88m, NR)
A group of country singers get stranded at a haunted house during a storm in this comic horror story. Lon Chaney, Jr. and Basil Rathbone star. **HO30**

Hills Have Eyes, The (1977, C, 89m, R)
Horror film about family stranded in the desert, attacked by crazed "family" of mutants. Wes Craven directed this cult film. **CU4, HO14**

Hills of Utah, The (1951, B&W, 70m, NR)
Gene Autry uncovers the truth about his father's death when he visits his hometown. **WE24**

Himatsuri (1984, C, 120m, NR)
Japanese drama of a man who renounces modern ways for Shinto way of life, winds up killing his family and himself. **FF4**

Hindenburg, The (1975, C, 125m, PG)
Drama centering on the disastrous crash in 1937 of the famed German dirigible, starring George C. Scott, Anne Bancroft, William Atherton, Charles Durning, and Burgess Meredith. Directed by Robert Wise. **AC16, AC23, CL58**

Hired Hand, The (1971, C, 93m, PG)
Peter Fonda directed this western drama set in 1880s New Mexico. He plays a cowhand who returns to work for the woman he abandoned years earlier. Warren Oates costars. **CU48, WE16**

Hiroshima, Mon Amour (1960, B&W, 88m, NR)
Groundbreaking drama about an affair between French woman and Japanese man, with echoes of atomic bomb catastrophe lurking in the background. French-language film directed by Alain Resnais. **FF1**

His Double Life (1933, B&W, 67m, NR)
When a famous but retiring artist is thought dead, he happily accepts oblivion to marry a spinster. Roland Young and Lillian Gish star. **CL49**

His Girl Friday (1940, B&W, 92m, NR)
Cary Grant is a newspaper editor whose star reporter and ex-wife (Rosalind Russell) is planning to remarry. Ralph Bellamy costars in this breakneck comedy based on the play *The Front Page*. Written by Ben Hecht and Charles Lederer; Howard Hawks directed. **CL10, CL18, CL35** *Highly Recommended*

His Kind of Woman (1951, B&W, 120m, NR)
Robert Mitchum plays a fall guy for a criminal (Raymond Burr) who wants to re-enter the country from Mexico. Jane Russell and Vincent Price costar. **HO31, MY1**

History of the World—Part I (1981, C, 92m, R)
Mel Brooks directed and stars in this zany revisionist view of human history, starting with prehistoric times. Gregory

Hines, Dom DeLuise, Madeline Kahn, Harvey Korman, and Sid Caesar costar. **CO28**

Hit and Run (1982, C, 93m, NR)
A cabdriver's involvement with a mysterious woman leads to murder. **MY7**

Hit List (1989, C, 87m, R)
✓ Jan-Michael Vincent and Rip Torn star in this action drama of an innocent man whose best friend and son are victimized by a Mob hit man. **CU47**

Hit the Deck (1955, C, 112m, NR)
MGM musical of fun-loving sailors on shore leave, starring Jane Powell, Tony Martin, Debbie Reynolds, Ann Miller, and Vic Damone. **MU1**

Hit the Ice (1943, B&W, 82m, NR)
Abbott and Costello are newspaper photographers who get involved with a gangster and his minions at the winter resort of Sun Valley. **CO23**

Hitler: The Last Ten Days (1973, C, 108m, PG)
Alec Guinness stars in this recreation of the dying days of the Third Reich. **DR63**

Hobbit, The (1978, C, 76m, NR)
Based on the J.R.R. Tolkien fantasy novel, this animated feature deals with a magical hobbit named Bilbo Baggins. **FA8, FA10, SF13**

Hobson's Choice (1954, B&W, 107m, NR)
A bootshop owner (Charles Laughton) in 1890s Britain decides whom his daughters shall marry, despite their objections. Directed by David Lean. **CO17, DR50**

Hobson's Choice (1983, C, 100m, NR)
TV movie remake of the classic comedy about a shopowner's attempts to control his daughters' lives. Richard Thomas, Sharon Gless, Jack Warden, and Lillian Gish star. **CL49**

Holcroft Covenant, The (1985, C, 112m, R)
A former henchman for Hitler leaves his son (Michael Caine) a fortune intended to make amends for Nazi atrocities. Thriller based on the bestseller by Robert Ludlum. **MY6, MY32**

Hold That Ghost (1941, B&W, 86m, NR)
Abbott and Costello are bumbling gas station attendants who inherit a gangster's mysterious mansion. **CO23**

Holiday (1937, B&W, 93m, NR)
Bright comedy about a nonconformist (Cary Grant) who becomes engaged to the daughter of a high society family, then falls for her sister (Katharine Hepburn). Directed by George Cukor. **CL10, CL16, CL18, CL39** *Recommended*

Holiday Inn (1942, B&W, 101m, NR)
Bing Crosby breaks with show-biz partner and rival Fred Astaire to run a Connecticut inn which only opens on holidays. This film introduced the Irving Berlin songs "White Christmas" and "Easter Parade." **MU4, MU6, MU18, MU25**

Hollywood Boulevard (1976, C, 83m, R)
Determinedly low-budget, intentionally sleazy comedy about a young girl trying to "make it" in movies, with dozens of inside gags, especially about filmmaking for producer Roger Corman. Paul Bartel stars; Joe Dante and Allan Arkush directed. **CO8, CU5, CU14, CU40, CU41, CU42**

Hollywood or Bust (1956, C, 95m, NR)
Jerry Lewis plays a zealous movie fan who wins a car in a raffle and travels to Hollywood with a gambler (Dean Martin) to meet his idol, Anita Ekberg. Martin and Lewis's last film. **CO8, CO25, FA6**

Hollywood Shuffle (1987, C, 82m, R)
A young black actor (Robert Townsend) tries to make an impression in Hollywood, but runs into stereotyping everywhere he goes. Robert Townsend directed and co-wrote this comedy. **CO8**

Hollywood Vice Squad (1986, C, 100m, R)
Episodic action thriller set on the mean
streets of Hollywood, starring Ronny
Cox, Carrie Fisher, Frank Gorshin, and
Leon Isaac Kennedy. **AC9**

Holocaust (1978, C, 450m, NR)
Meryl Streep, Fritz Weaver, and Michael
Moriarty star in this gripping account of
the Nazis' efforts to exterminate all European Jews, and the effects on one family. Originally made for TV. **DR26**

Hombre (1967, C, 111m, NR)
A white man (Paul Newman) raised by
Indians is the victim of prejudice in fron-
tier Arizona. Fredric March, Richard
Boone, Martin Balsam, and Diane Cil-
ento costar. Based on a story by Elmore
Leonard. **DR28, MY26, WE8**

Home and the World, The (1984, C, 130m,
NR)
From Indian director Satyajit Ray, a
drama about a woman caught up in the
political turmoil that swept her country in
the first decade of the 20th century. **FF23**

Home for the Holidays (1972, C, 74m, NR)
An elderly man, threatened by a killer, is
protected by his four daughters. Eleanor
Parker, Sally Field, Jessica Walter, Julie
Harris, Jill Haworth, and Walter Brennan
star. Originally made for TV. **DR36**

Home in Oklahoma (1947, B&W, 54m,
NR)
Roy Rogers plays a newspaper editor,
Dale Evans a reporter; they're investigat-
ing a shifty rancher. **WE23**

Home Is Where the Heart Is *see* Square
Dance

Home Movies (1979, C, 90m, PG)
An egotistical film director (Kirk Douglas) gives the star treatment to a nerd,
who then decides to pursue his brother's
girlfriend. Comedy about show-biz life
directed by Brian DePalma. **CO8, CU28**

Home of the Brave (1949, B&W, 85m, NR)
A black G.I. is abused by his fellow soldiers during World War II in this classic
drama about the effects of racism. James
Edwards stars. **AC1, CL8**

Home Sweet Home (1914, B&W, 62m, NR)
D.W. Griffith directed this silent drama
inspired by the work of poet and composer John Howard Payne. Dorothy and
Lillian Gish star. **CL36, XT8**

Home to Stay (1978, C, 74m, NR)
A young girl runs away from home with
her elderly grandfather (Henry Fonda) to
avoid her family sending him to a nursing
home. Originally made for TV. **CL24**

Honeymoon (1985, C, 98m, R)
A French woman marries a man in order
to stay in the America, only to find that
he's a psychotic killer. Nathalie Baye and
John Shea star. **HO9**

Honeymoon Killers, The (1969. B&W,
103m, R)
Cult drama, based on fact, about a nurse
and her lover posing as brother and sister
to lure lonely, rich women to their deaths.
Shirley Stoler and Tony LoBianco star;
Leonard Kastle directed, his only credit
behind the camera. **CU15, DR6, DR16**
Recommended

Honeysuckle Rose (1980, C, 119m, PG)
Willie Nelson plays a country singer who
romances one of his back-up singers,
much to his wife's dismay. With Amy
Irving, Dyan Cannon, and Slim Pickens.
Willie sings "On the Road Again" and
many of his hits. **DR12**

Honkytonk Man (1982, C, 122m, PG)
Clint Eastwood stars in this drama set in
the Depression about a broken-down
country singer who won't get off the
road. Eastwood's son Kyle plays his son
on screen. **AC27, DR12, XT8**

Honor Among Thieves (1968, C, 115m, R)
Charles Bronson and Alain Delon star in
this action drama of French mercenaries
in Marseilles with a big heist in their
plans. Also known as *Farewell, Friend*.
AC29

Hooper (1978, C, 100m, PG)
Burt Reynolds portrays an aging Hollywood stuntman who is challenged by a young maverick to perform a dangerous stunt. Sally Field and Jan-Michael Vincent costar. **AC37, DR36**

Hoosiers (1986, C, 114m, PG)
Drama about a middle-aged man who accepts a job coaching basketball in small-town Indiana in the 1950s. He meets opposition from the townspeople for his methods, until the school begins winning. Barbara Hershey and Dennis Hopper costar in this drama based on a true story. **CU46, DR22, DR39** *Recommended*

Hope and Glory (1987, C, 113m, PG-13)
A young boy suddenly becomes the man of the house when his father goes off to war. John Boorman wrote, produced, and directed this nostalgic, comic view of Britain during World War II. Sebastian Rice-Edwards and Sarah Miles star. **CO5, CO6, CO17, CU32** *Highly Recommended*

Hopscotch (1980, C, 104m, R)
A CIA man who's been phased out of The Company decides to get revenge on his boss by publishing his memoirs. Walter Matthau, Glenda Jackson, and Ned Beatty star in this comedy. **CO10**

Horror Express (1972, C, 88m, NR)
A frozen monster thaws out and comes to life on train traveling through Asia, while two anthropologists (Peter Cushing, Christopher Lee) lock horns. **HO8, HO32, HO33**

Horror Hotel (1960, B&W, 76m, NR)
The spirit of a witch burned at the stake in the 17th century lives at a Massachusetts inn. Several young people who stay there become human sacrifices to the Devil. Christopher Lee stars. **HO32**

Horror of Dracula (1958, C, 82m, NR)
This British film from the famed Hammer studios features Christopher Lee as the cursed count. Peter Cushing costars as Professor Van Helsing. **HO1, HO5, HO26, HO32, HO33**

Horror of Frankenstein (1970, C, 95m, R)
A self-destructive doctor does away with his father, best friend, and wife while creating a monster. This British version of the classic horror tale is strictly tongue-in-cheek. **HO26**

Horse Feathers (1932, B&W, 67m, NR)
The Marx Brothers matriculate at Huxley College, and campus life will never be the same again. Thelma Todd costars. Highlights: the speakeasy "password" scene and the football game. **CO21, CO35** *Recommended*

Horse in the Gray Flannel Suit, The (1968, C, 113m, G)
An advertising executive (Dean Jones) designs a campaign to take advantage of his daughter's love for horses. Diane Baker costars in this Disney comedy. **FA1**

Horse Soldiers, The (1959, C, 119m, NR)
Set during the Civil War, this western drama stars John Wayne as a soldier who leads his cavalry troops into Confederate territory. Directed by John Ford; William Holden costars. **CL51, WE5, WE7, WE17, WE18**

Horse's Mouth, The (1958, C, 93m, NR)
Alec Guinness plays a iconoclastic British painter who doesn't need a canvas to work on. Guinness also wrote this comedy, based on the Joyce Cary novel. **CO17, DR63**

Hospital, The (1971, C, 103m, PG)
This offbeat comedy casts George C. Scott as a disillusioned doctor who gets involved with a nutty girl (Diana Rigg) and her father amid the sloppy workings of an inner-city hospital. **CO12**

Hot Lead and Cold Feet (1978, C, 90m, G)
Disney western features a ranching patriarch and his two sons, a gunfighter and his timid twin, all played by Jim Dale. **FA1**

Hot Rock, The (1972, C, 105m, PG)
A group of thieves blunder their way through a jewel heist. Robert Redford and

George Segal star; based on Donald West-lake's novel. **AC9, CO10, DR29, MY34**

Hot Shot (1986, C, 94m, PG)
Rich American boy runs off to Brazil to meet his idol, soccer superstar Pele (playing himself). Jim Youngs stars in this family drama. **DR22, FA7**

Hot Spell (1958, B&W, 86m, NR)
Anthony Quinn stars as an unfaithful husband whose breakup with his nagging wife (Shirley Booth) has a strong impact on their recently jilted daughter (Shirley MacLaine). **DR42**

Hotel Colonial (1987, C, 104m, R)
International intrigue, involving an Italian man's journey to Colombia to investigate the death of his brother. John Savage stars, with Rachel Ward and Robert Duvall. **DR37**

Hotel New Hampshire, The (1984, C, 110m, R)
This film version of John Irving's bestselling novel deals with an unusual family's sexual and social adventures. Rob Lowe, Nastassja Kinski, Jodie Foster, and Beau Bridges head the cast. **CO5**

Hotel Terminus (1988, C/B&W, 267m, NR)
Oscar-winnning documentary from director Marcel Ophuls which explores the trial in Lyons, France, of Nazi torture specialist Klaus Barbie. **CU16**

Hound of the Baskervilles, The (1938, B&W, 80m, NR)
A wealthy British family is cursed by a violent hound until Sherlock Holmes (Basil Rathbone) solves the mystery. The first of the series starring Rathbone and Nigel Bruce. **MY10**

Hound of the Baskervilles, The (1959, C, 84m, NR)
Peter Cushing portrays Sherlock Holmes in this remake of the Conan Doyle novel. Produced by Hammer Films; costarring Christopher Lee. **HO32, HO33, MY10**

Hound of the Baskervilles, The (1977, C, 84m, PG)
Sherlock Holmes spoof starring Peter Cook as the great detective, Dudley Moore as Watson (and Holmes' mother), plus Denholm Elliott, Joan Greenwood, Spike Milligan, and Roy Kinnear. Directed by Paul Morissey. **CO31, CU44, MY10**

Hour of the Star (1985, C, 96m, NR)
A 19-year-old girl from the impoverished northern region of Brazil holds fast to her dream of some day breaking out of her dreary surroundings. **FF6**

House (1986, C, 93m, R)
A novelist (William Katt), plagued by the break-up of his marriage and the disappearance of his son, moves to a house where his late aunt hung herself. **HO3, HO19**

House by the River, The (1950, B&W, 88m, NR)
Melodrama of a dishonest man who commits a crime and gets his wife and brother involved. Louis Hayward, Jane Wyatt, and Lee Bowman star. Directed by Fritz Lang. **CL43**

House Calls (1978, C, 98m, PG)
A widowed doctor (Walter Matthau), who enjoys the single life, meets an opinionated divorcee (Glenda Jackson), who wants a commitment. Art Carney costars in this romantic comedy. **CO1**

House of Fear (1945, B&W, 69m, NR)
Sherlock Holmes (Basil Rathbone) and Dr. Watson (Nigel Bruce) investigate a murder at Drearcliff, a club whose members are being killed off one at a time. **MY10**

House of Games (1987, C, 102m, R)
A psychologist (Lindsay Crouse) whose patient is a compulsive gambler seeks out the con men who have set him up. Fascinated by their techniques, she lets herself get used by them, then seeks revenge. Written and directed by David Mamet. **DR15**

House of the Long Shadows (1983, C, 96m, PG)
Four notable horror film stars, Vincent Price, Peter Cushing, John Carradine, and Christopher Lee, have small roles in this tale of a mystery writer (Desi Arnaz, Jr.) spending the night with his girlfriend at mysterious mansion. **HO19, HO31, HO32, HO33**

House of Usher *see* The Fall of the House of Usher

House of Wax (1953, C, 88m, PG)
A vengeful sculptor (Vincent Price), disfigured by a fire, rebuilds his gallery by using human corpses as wax statues. Frank Lovejoy and Charles Buchinski (Charles Bronson) costar. Remake of *Mystery of the Wax Museum*. **AC29, CU18, HO1, HO19**

House on Carroll Street, The (1988, C, 111m, PG-13)
Thriller set in 1950s New York, with a photo researcher uncovering a plot to smuggle Nazis into the country. Kelly McGillis, Jeff Daniels, and Mandy Patinkin star. **MY3, MY6**

House on Haunted Hill (1958, B&W, 75m, NR)
Vincent Price plays a wealthy eccentric who offers a group of people $50,000 each if they'll spend the night in a mansion with a history of murder. **HO3, HO19, HO31**

House That Dripped Blood, The (1971, C, 101m, NR)
Christopher Lee, Peter Cushing, and Denholm Elliot star in this four-part horror story about a new owner of a mysterious looking mansion who has doubts about living there. **HO23, HO32, HO33**

House 2: The Second Story (1987, C, 88m, PG-13)
Sequel in name only to *House,* with another young man discovering evil that lurks behind the walls of a creepy piece of real estate. **HO3**

House Where Evil Dwells, The (1982, C, 88m, R)
An American family moves into a house in Japan, ignoring warnings that the house is dominated by the ghosts of a 19th-century love affair that ended in tragedy. **HO3**

Houseboat (1958, C, 110m, NR)
A Washington, D.C. widower (Cary Grant) with three children hires a housekeeper (Sophia Loren), and romance blossoms. **CL18, FF31, XT9**

Housekeeping (1987, C, 117m, PG)
Two orphaned sisters are taken in by their loony aunt in this drama set in Montana in the 1940s. Christine Lahti stars; Bill Forsyth directed. Based on a novel by Marilynne Robinson. **CU36, DR9, DR10, DR19** *Recommended*

How I Won the War (1967, C, 109m, PG)
A man recalls his career in World War II with hilariously exagerrated details. Michael Crawford and John Lennon star in this dark comedy from director Richard Lester. **CO6, CO12, CO17, CO38, CU35, MU12** *Recommended*

How the West Was Won (1963, C, 165m, G)
Spencer Tracy narrates this monumental drama about the men and the women who explored and settled the great American West. John Wayne, Henry Fonda, and James Stewart costar. John Ford directed one of the four segments. **CL19, CL24, CL25, WE1, WE7, WE17**

How to Beat the High Cost of Living (1980, C, 105m, PG)
Susan Saint James, Jane Curtin, and Jessica Lange play three fed-up housewives who plan a robbery at a local shopping mall. **CO13, DR74, MY34**

How to Marry a Millionaire (1953, C, 95m, NR)
Marilyn Monroe, Betty Grable, and Lauren Bacall are the man-hungry young women in pursuit of rich husbands in this comedy. **CL29**

How to Succeed in Business Without Really Trying (1967, C, 121m, NR)
Title says it all, in this Broadway musical starring Robert Morse as the aspiring window washer making good in Rudy Vallee's conglomerate. Michele Lee costars. **MU2**

Howard the Duck (1986, C, 111m, PG)
A duck from another planet comes to Earth and saves the planet from alien invaders. Spoofy special effects comedy. Lea Thompson stars. **CO9, CO37**

Howards of Virginia, The (1940, B&W, 140m, NR)
Cary Grant plays a colonial during the Revolutionary War, caught between his father-in-law's loyalist views and his own principles. **CL18**

Howie From Maui *See* HBO Comedy Club

Howling, The (1981, C, 90m, R)
Gory tale of a news reporter who is sent to a California retreat after she experiences a sexual trauma. She comes to realize that everyone there is a werewolf. Joe Dante directed; memorable transformation scenes, plenty of in-jokes about other horror movies. **CU40, HO4, HO17** *Recommended*

Howling II, The (1985, C, 98m, R)
After the death of his sister, a law officer discovers that she may have been the victim of a werewolf. Christopher Lee stars. **HO4, HO32**

Howling III: The Marsupials (1987, C, 94m, R)
Australia is the setting for this horror tale about a scientist's investigation into a new breed of werewolf. Barry Otto stars. **HO4**

Howling IV, The (1988, C, 92m, R)
Fourth installment in werewolf series has lovely writer on a woodsy retreat, with predictable results. **HO4**

Hud (1963, B&W, 112m, NR)
In contemporary Texas, an arrogant cattleman plays by his own set of rules—and gets away with it. Paul Newman and Oscar winners Patricia Neal and Melvyn Douglas star. Based on Larry McMurtry's novel, *Horseman, Pass By*. **DR28, WE13, XT3, XT4** *Recommended*

Human Condition, The
Part I (1958, B&W, 200m, NR)
Part II (1959, B&W, 180m, NR)
Part III (1961, B&W, 190m, NR)
Epic Japanese tale of a pacifist's wartime experiences. In Part I, Kaji (Tatsuya Nakadai) is sent to Manchuria to supervise mine workers; he is betrayed by his enemies and is eventually served with a draft notice. Part II (originally titled *Road to Eternity*) finds Kaji at the front, where he distinguishes himself in battle. In Part III (original title: *A Soldier's Prayer*), Kaji is thrown into despair during the final days of the war, as he comes to understand the true madness of the conflict. Directed by and co-written by Masaki Kobayashi. **FF4**

Human Desire (1954, B&W, 90m, NR)
Drama of weak-willed man involved with a married woman, who'd like to be rid of her husband. Glenn Ford, Gloria Grahame, and Broderick Crawford star; Fritz Lang directed. Remake of Jean Renoir's *La Bête Humaine*. **CU18, CL43, FF36**

Human Monster, The (1939, B&W, 73m, NR)
Bela Lugosi plays the evil owner of a home for blind men. He persuades them to buy more life insurance, then plots to kill them off. **HO9, HO28**

Human Vapor, The (1964, B&W, 79m, NR)
Japanese science fiction drama of an experiment which transforms a man into a gaseous, deadly monster. **FF5, SF18**

Humanoids From the Deep (1980, C, 80m, R)
A seaside village is menaced by mutated sea monsters who rape women to produce their offspring. Doug McClure, Vic Mor-

row, and Ann Turkel star. Trashy fun.
HO16, HO25 *Recommended*

Hunchback of Notre Dame, The (1923, B&W, 93m, NR)
Lon Chaney, Sr. portrays the Parisian hunchback in this first film version of the Victor Hugo novel. **HO29**

Hunchback of Notre Dame, The (1939, B&W, 115m, NR)
Charles Laughton plays the handicapped bell-ringer, who is attracted to a beautiful gypsy girl (Maureen O'Hara) in this version of Victor Hugo's classic. Cedric Hardwicke costars. **CL1** *Recommended*

Hunger, The (1983, C, 97m, R)
A 2000-year old vampire (Catherine Deneuve) searches for fresh blood in a new lover to replace her old one (David Bowie), who is aging rapidly. Susan Sarandon costars. **FF27, HO5, MU12**

Hunter, The (1980, C, 97m, PG)
Steve McQueen stars as contemporary bounty hunter Pappy Thorson in this action thriller set in Chicago. Eli Wallach, Kathryn Harrold, and LeVar Burton costar. **AC8, AC28**

Hunter's Blood (1987, C, 102m, R)
Five city boys hunting in the country run afoul of some nasty poachers. Sam Bottoms, Kim Delaney, and Clu Gulager star in this survival adventure. **AC24**

Hurricane, The (1937, B&W, 102m, NR)
John Ford directed this tale of a South Seas island and its inhabitants being tormented by a vindictive governor. Climactic storm scenes will blow you away. Dorothy Lamour, Jon Hall, and Mary Astor star; John Ford directed. **AC13, AC23, CL34**

Hush . . . Hush, Sweet Charlotte (1965, B&W, 133m, NR)
Bette Davis plays a victimized Southern woman who cannot live down a scandal from her past. Olivia de Havilland and Joseph Cotten costar in this camp cult favorite. **CL21, CU2**

Hustle (1975, C, 120m, R)
Burt Reynolds stars as a detective who gets involved with a call girl (Catherine Deneuve) while investigating a suicide. Directed by Robert Aldrich. **AC9, AC37, FF27, MY2** *Recommended*

Hustler, The (1961, B&W, 135m, NR)
Paul Newman plays Fast Eddie Felson, a jaded drifter with a talent for shooting pool who challenges the champ, Minnesota Fats (Jackie Gleason). George C. Scott and Piper Laurie costar in this superb drama from writer-director Robert Rossen. **DR22, DR28** *Highly Recommended*

I Am a Fugitive From a Chain Gang (1932, B&W, 93m, NR)
Powerful story of an innocent man (Paul Muni) who is sentenced to prison, victimized by the system. **CL8**

I Am the Cheese (1983, C, 95m, PG)
Drama of a young boy who witnesses his parent's deaths, and the fantasies he imagines while under a doctor's care. **FA7**

I Am the Law (1938, B&W, 83m, NR)
Edward G. Robinson plays a law professor hired to clean up a corrupt city government. Otto Kruger and Wendy Barrie costar. **CL52**

I Confess (1953, B&W, 95m, NR)
Montgomery Clift portrays a priest who hears a confession of murder and becomes the prime suspect due to his vows of silence. Directed by Alfred Hitchcock. **MY7, MY22**

I Could Go On Singing (1963, C, 99m, NR)
In her final film, Judy Garland plays an American singer on tour in London battling personal problems. Dirk Bogarde costars. **DR12, MU21**

I Dream Too Much (1935, B&W, 95m, NR)
Henry Fonda plays an American composer having marital problems with his lovely opera star wife. **CL24**

I Love You (1981, C, 104, R)
Brazilian drama of a man with nothing left to lose, who finds love. Sonia Braga stars. **FF6, FF34**

I Love You, Alice B. Toklas (1968, C, 93m, R)
Peter Sellers plays a successful Los Angeles lawyer who becomes involved with a lovely flower child (Leigh-Taylor Young) in this comedy co-written by Paul Mazursky. **CO2, CO26**

I Married a Monster From Outer Space (1958, B&W, 78m, NR)
Newlywed can't figure out her husband's strange behavior. Tom Tryon and Gloria Talbot star in this classic of 1950s science fiction. **SF1, SF9** *Recommended*

I Married a Witch (1942, B&W, 77m, NR)
Fantasy comedy about a pesky sorceress (Veronica Lake) determined to make mischief on the descendants of the Puritan (Fredric March) who had her burned at the stake 300 years ago. **SF2**

I Married an Angel (1942, B&W, 84m, NR)
Nelson Eddy and Jeanette MacDonald's swan song as a screen team, the lighthearted tale of a playboy and the heavenly lady who tames him. **CL15**

I Never Sang for My Father (1970, C, 93m, PG)
A middle-aged man (Gene Hackman) takes the responsibility of caring for his elderly, stubborn father (Melvyn Douglas) after his mother dies. **DR39**

I Ought to Be in Pictures (1982, C, 107m, PG)
A young New Yorker (Dinah Manoff) travels to Los Angeles to make it in the movies, but her real ambition is to find her father (Walter Matthau). Based on the Neil Simon play. **CO5, CO34**

I Remember Mama (1948, B&W, 134m, NR)
George Stevens directed this heartwarming film of an immigrant family from Nor-

way adjusting to life in San Francisco. Irene Dunne and Barbara Bel Geddes star. **CL42**

I Sent a Letter to My Love (1981, C, 96m, PG)
A woman and her invalid brother unknowingly begin a romance in a newspaper personals column. Simone Signoret and Jean Rochefort star in this French drama. **FF1**

I Shot Jesse James (1949, B&W, 81m, NR)
The true tale of Bob Ford, the man who killed the West's most famous desperado. Director Sam Fuller's first film. **CU22, WE2**

I Stand Condemned (1935, B&W, 75m, NR)
An officer gets framed by his superior as a spy in a fit of jealousy over a woman. Laurence Olivier stars in one of his early films. **CL32**

I, the Jury (1982, C, 111m, R)
Hard-boiled detective Mike Hammer is played by Armand Assante in this Mickey Spillane mystery. **MY30**

I Wake Up Screaming (1941, B&W, 82m, NR)
An actress' agent (Victor Mature) is the prime suspect in her murder, and he turns to her sister (Betty Grable) for help in clearing his name. With Laird Creagar and Carole Landis. **MY1, MY7**

I Walked With a Zombie (1943, B&W, 69m, NR)
Classic horror tale of nurse coming to Haiti to treat victim of coma-like state, discovering voodoo rituals. Directed by Jacques Tourneur; produced by Val Lewton. **CU4, HO1, HO6, HO36, HO37** *Recommended*

I Wanna Hold Your Hand (1978, C, 104m, PG)
Charming comedy about a group of teenagers who use every trick they can think of to get tickets to the Beatles' debut on *The Ed Sullivan Show* in 1964. Robert

Zemeckis directed a lively cast, including Nancy Allen, Bobby DiCicco, Mark Mc-Clure, Wendy Jo Sperber, Eddie Deezen, and, as Sullivan, Will Jordan. **CO6** *Recommended*

I Want to Live! (1958, B&W, 122m, NR)
This classic prison drama deals with the story of Barbara Graham, who was framed for murder and sent to the gas chamber. Susan Hayward won an Academy Award for her performance, directed by Robert Wise. **CL58, DR18, XT3**

I Will Fight No More Forever (1975, C, 100m, NR)
Historical account of Chief Joseph, who led his tribe on a 1600 mile trek to Canada to avoid a U. S. Cavalry battle. James Whitmore stars. **WE8**

I Will, I Will . . . For Now (1976, C, 110m, R)
Diane Keaton and Elliott Gould play a couple who are bored with their ten-year marriage. They try every means, including therapy and a sex clinic to rekindle the spark. **DR40**

Ice Pirates, The (1984, C, 93, PG)
Science fiction comedy about band of lovable cutthroats out to hijack a drought-stricken galaxy's water supply. Robert Urich, Mary Crosby, and Anjelica Huston star. **SF21**

Idaho (1943, B&W, 70m, NR)
Roy Rogers and Smiley Burnette clear a judge who's been framed for murder. **WE23**

Idiot's Delight (1939, B&W, 105m, NR)
Clark Gable is a song and dance man and Norma Shearer is his former love. Both are stranded in a hotel in the Italian Alps at the outset of World War II. Comedy-drama features Gable performing "Puttin' on the Ritz." **CL23, MU17**

Idolmaker, The (1980, C, 119m, PG)
This fictionalized biography of music producer Bob Marcucci shows how he pushed rock singers Frankie Avalon and Fabian to the top of the charts in the early days of rock 'n' roll. Ray Sharkey stars; Taylor Hackford directed. **DR12, MU4, MU9**

if . . . (1969, C/B&W, 111m, R)
Rebellious boys at a British boarding school finally resort to violence in this drama with darkly comic overtones. Malcolm McDowell stars; Lindsay Anderson directed. **DR9, DR61** *Recommended*

Ikiru (1952, B&W, 143m, NR)
Japanese drama of a bureaucrat who finds that he has terminal cancer and searches for a sense of purpose in his life. Akira Kurosawa directed; Takashi Shimura stars. **FF9** *Recommended*

I'll Cry Tomorrow (1956, B&W, 120m, NR)
Susan Hayward plays singer-actress Lillian Roth, whose battles with the bottle were the stuff of show-biz legend. **CL2, CL5**

Ill Met by Moonlight (1957, B&W, 93m, NR)
World War II drama, set in Nazi-occupied Crete, about British commandos kidnapping a German general. Michael Powell directed. Also known as *Night Ambush.* **CU19**

I'm All Right, Jack (1960, B&W, 104m, NR)
British comedy of a factory owner's elaborately crooked schemes being upset by the arrival of his strait-laced nephew. Ian Carmichael and Peter Sellers star. **CO17, CO26**

I'm Dancing as Fast as I Can (1982, C, 106m, PG)
TV producer gets hooked on pills and tries to quit cold turkey, with nearly disastrous results. Jill Clayburgh stars in this true story. **DR10**

I'm Gonna Git You Sucka (1989, C, 89m, R)
Spoof of blaxploitation films, starring Ivory Keenen Wayans (who wrote and directed), with Bernie Casey, Antonio

Fargas, Jim Brown, and Isaac Hayes. **CO7** *Recommended*

Imagine: John Lennon (1988, C, 103m, R)
Documentary tribute to the late musician, singer, and activist, with rare footage from his Beatle days and subsequent years of marriage to Yoko Ono. **MU11**

Imitation of Life (1959, C, 124m, NR)
This glossy tear jerker deals with a white actress, her black housekeeper, and the conflicts they share with their teenage daughters. Lana Turner and Sandra Dee star; Douglas Sirk directed. **CL6, CU24, DR2**

Immortal Sergeant, The (1943, B&W, 91m, NR)
Henry Fonda plays an inexperienced corporal who has to take command of the troops after their sergeant dies. **CL24**

Importance of Being Earnest, The (1952, C, 95m, NR)
Based on the Oscar Wilde play, this comedy of manners set in Victorian England stars Michael Redgrave and Margaret Rutherford. **CL1**

In a Lonely Place (1950, B&W, 93m, NR)
Humphrey Bogart is a frustrated screenwriter in this moody drama from director Nicholas Ray. Gloria Grahame costars. **CL20, CU23**

In a Shallow Grave (1988, C, 91m, R)
Low-key drama of a scarred war veteran's passion for the girl he left behind but couldn't forget. Michael Biehn and Patrick Dempsey star in this adaptation of the James Purdy novel. **DR1**

In Cold Blood (1967, B&W, 134m, NR)
Drama based on Truman Capote's famed "non-fiction novel" about the senseless murder of a Kansas family by two drifters. Scott Wilson and Robert Blake star; Richard Brooks wrote and directed. **DR6, DR16** *Recommended*

In Harm's Way (1965, B&W, 165m, NR)
All-star cast in standard World War II yarn of Navy heroics in the South Pacific, with John Wayne, Henry Fonda, Kirk Douglas, Patricia Neal, George Kennedy, and Slim Pickens. Directed by Otto Preminger. **AC1, CL17, CL24**

In Name Only (1939, B&W, 94m, NR)
Cary Grant plays a married man trying to escape a loveless marriage for his beautiful mistress (Carole Lombard). **CL6, CL18, CL48**

In Old Amarillo (1951, B&W, 68m, NR)
During a drought, a courageous cowboy (Roy Rogers) organizes local ranchers. **WE23**

In Old Caliente (1939, B&W, 54m, NR)
A cowpoke (Roy Rogers) is framed for theft by an evil half-breed. With Gabby Hayes. **WE23**

In Old California (1942, B&W, 88m, NR)
A young Boston pharmacist (John Wayne) goes West during the California gold rush. **WE17**

In Old Santa Fe (1934, B&W, 60m, NR)
Gene Autry helps veteran plainsman Ken Maynard recover his horse from bandits. **WE24**

In Search of the Castaways (1962, C, 80m, NR)
An expedition looks for a missing sea captain, and along the way encounters many hardships. Hayley Mills, Maurice Chevalier, and George Sanders star in this Disney adventure based on a Jules Verne story. **FA1, SF27**

In the Good Old Summertime (1948, C, 102m, NR)
Judy Garland and Van Johnson star in this musical remake of *The Shop Around The Corner,* about two coworkers who unknowingly become pen pals. **MU14, MU21**

In the Heat of the Night (1967, C, 109m, NR)
Oscar winner Rod Steiger plays a small-town Southern sheriff who unwillingly receives help from a black police detective (Sidney Poitier) in a murder case. With Warren Oates and Lee Grant. Winner of four other Oscars, including Best Picture. **CU48, DR38, MY14, XT1, XT2**

In the Mood (1987, C, 100m, PG-13)
Comedy based on the true story of Sonny Wisecarver, a 1940s teenager who ran away to marry an older woman and became known as The Woo-Woo Kid. **CO6**

In the Shadow of Kilimanjaro (1986, C, 97m, R)
During a severe drought in the African bush country, herds of baboons begin attacking humans. **HO16**

In Which We Serve (1942, B&W, 115m, NR)
World War II drama of men on board a British battleship recalling the events that shaped their lives. Written by Noel Coward, who also stars and co-directed (with David Lean). John Mills, Celia Johnson, and Richard Attenborough costar. **AC1, DR50**

Incredible Invasion: *see* Sinister Invasion

Incredible Journey, The (1963, C, 80m, NR)
Two dogs and a cat make a 250-mile journey across Canada to be reunited with their human owners in this Disney adventure. **FA1, FA5**

Incredible Sarah, The (1976, C, 105m, PG)
Glenda Jackson plays famed stage and silent screen actress Sarah Bernhardt. Daniel Massey costars. **DR4, DR12**

Incredible Shrinking Man, The (1957, B&W, 81m, NR)
A radioactive mist has a terrifying effect on an ordinary man, who's soon battling a spider five times his size. Classic 1950s science fiction with cult following, directed by Jack Arnold. **CU4, FA8, SF1**
Recommended

Incredible Shrinking Woman, The (1981, C, 88m, PG)
This take-off on *The Incredible Shrinking Man* stars Lily Tomlin as a housewife who begins to shrink after exposure to household products. Charles Grodin and Ned Beatty costar. **CO11, SF21**

Incredibly Strange Creatures Who Stopped Living and Became Mixed-up Zombies, The (1963, C, 82m, NR)
Cult horror story of sideshow proprietor who disfigures patrons and puts them on display in his show. Moody cinematography, atrocious acting and dialogue. **CU4**

Independence Day (1983, C, 110m, R)
Small-town woman with big ambitions yearns to break free, but is held back in part by a romance with a local mechanic. Kathleen Quinlan and David Keith star. **DR1, DR10, DR62**

Indestructible Man, The (1956, B&W, 70m, NR)
A thief returns from the dead to get revenge on his cohorts who betrayed him during a robbery. Lon Chaney, Jr. stars. **HO30**

Indiana Jones and the Temple of Doom (1984, C, 118m, PG)
This prequel to *Raiders of the Lost Ark* follows the 1930s archeologist as he tries to save a group of children from a murderous cult. Harrison Ford and Kate Capshaw star. Directed by Steven Spielberg. **AC21, DR32, SF24**

Indiscreet (1958, C, 100m, NR)
Cary Grant is a playboy who romances a famous actress (Ingrid Bergman) and realizes he may be falling seriously in love. Directed by Stanley Donen. **CL18, CL27, MU23**

Informer, The (1935, B&W, 91m, NR)
Victor McLaglen won an Oscar for his portrayal of a drunk who turns on a friend to collect reward money during the Irish

Rebellion. Oscar-winning direction by John Ford. **CL34, XT2, XT6**

Inherit the Wind (1960, B&W, 127m, NR)
Spencer Tracy, Fredric March, and Gene Kelly star in this drama of the Scopes Monkey Trial of 1925, in which a schoolteacher was indicted for teaching Darwin's theory of evolution. Based on the play by Jerome Lawrence and Robert E. Lee; directed by Stanley Kramer. **CL19, DR17, MU19**

Inheritance, The (1976, C, 105m, R)
A dying patriarch plans to disinherit his entire family, save his lovely daughter-in-law, with whom he's having an affair. Italian drama starring Anthony Quinn and Dominique Sanda. **FF2**

Inheritors, The (1984, C, 89m, NR)
German drama of an impressionable youth caught up in a neo-Nazi movement. Directed by Walter Bannert. **FF3**

Initiation of Sarah (1978, C, 96m, NR)
When she pledges a sorority, a young girl with telepathic powers falls under the spell of a witch. **HO7**

In-Laws, The (1979, C, 103m, PG)
A quiet, unassuming dentist (Alan Arkin) gets involved in the bizarre schemes of his daughter's father-in-law (Peter Falk), a bumbler claiming to be a CIA agent. Zany comedy written by Andrew Bergman. **CO10** *Recommended*

Inn of the Sixth Happiness, The (1958, C, 158m, NR)
A missionary (Ingrid Bergman) leads children through enemy territory in pre-World War II China. Robert Donat co-stars. **CL27**

Innerspace (1987, C, 120m, PG)
Dennis Quaid plays a cocky Navy test pilot who is miniaturized for an experiment but is accidentally injected into the body of a timid grocery store clerk (Martin Short). Joe Dante directed. **CO9, CO11, CO14, CU40, SF3, SF21**

L'Innocente (1979, C, 115m, R)
A faithless Sicilian husband finds that his lovely wife has her own lovers, too. Giancarlo Giannini and Laura Antonelli star; director Luchino Visconti's last film. **FF3**

Inside Man, The (1984, C, 90m, NR)
Spy drama, made in Sweden, with agents vying for submarine-detecting device. Dennis Hopper stars. **CU46**

Inside Moves (1980, C, 113m, PG)
A suicide survivor (John Savage) who was left cripped gets involved with a group of handicapped men at a local bar. Through these friends and his love for basketball, he regains his self esteem. **DR22**

Insignificance (1985, C, 105m, R)
"Historical" drama about chance encounters between a scientist, a senator, a lovely movie star, and her baseball player husband—resembling Albert Einstein, Joseph McCarthy, Marilyn Monroe, and Joe DiMaggio. Michael Emil, Tony Curtis, Theresa Russell, and Gary Busey star; Nicolas Roeg directed. **CU34**

Inspector General, The (1949, C, 102m, NR)
Musical comedy featuring Danny Kaye as a man who impersonates a bureaucrat in an Eastern European village. **CO41**

Instant Justice (1986, C, 101m, R)
A marine swears vengeance on the drug smugglers who killed his sister. Michael Pare and Tawny Kitaen star. **AC19, AC25**

Interiors (1978, C, 93m, PG)
Woody Allen wrote and directed this drama of a guilt-ridden family trying to come to terms with each other. Geraldine Page, Diane Keaton, E.G. Marshall, Maureen Stapleton, and Mary Beth Hurt star. **CO27, DR8, DR40**

Intermezzo (1939, B&W, 70m, NR)
A married violinist (Leslie Howard) falls in love with his musical protege (Ingrid Bergman). **CL4, CL27**

International House (1933, B&W, 70m, NR)
W.C. Fields stars with Burns & Allen in this comedy set in a hotel in China, where a scientist has invented television and assorted people come from all over the world to buy the rights. **CO22**

International Velvet (1978, C, 127m, PG)
This sequel to *National Velvet* follows a grown Velvet Brown as she primes her niece to take her place as a champion rider. Tatum O'Neal, Nanette Newman, and Christopher Plummer star. **FA5**

Into the Night (1985, C, 115m, R)
An insomniac finds himself involved with a beautiful girl, who is being chased by killers. Michelle Pfeiffer and Jeff Goldblum star in this comic thriller, with cameos by many film directors and pop music stars, including Paul Mazursky, Jonathan Demme, David Bowie, and Carl Perkins. **AC14, CU17, MU12**

Intolerance (1916, B&W, 123m, NR)
Four stories about man's inhumanity to man, stretching from ancient times to modern day, are interwoven in this silent classic directed by D.W. Griffith. Lillian Gish, Robert Harron, Mae Marsh, Norma Talmadge, and Bessie Love star; watch for Erich Von Stroheim. **CL12, CL14, CL36, CL49, CL53** *Highly Recommended*

Invaders From Mars (1953, C, 78m, NR)
Small-town boy sees invasion of aliens who brainwash adults, but he can't get anyone to believe him. Classic 1950s science fiction drama, starring Helena Carter, Arthur Franz, and Jimmy Hunt. **SF1, SF9**

Invaders From Mars (1986, C, 100m, PG)
Karen Black, Hunter Carson, and Laraine Newman star in this remake of the 1953 science fiction thriller. **CO13, SF9**

Invasion of the Bee Girls (1973, C, 85m, R)
Cult science fiction film about sinister alien force that turns women in a small town into sexually ravenous creatures. **CU4**

Invasion of the Body Snatchers (1956, B&W, 80m, NR)
Pods from outer space begin duplicating humans in zombie-like form. Classic science fiction with political overtones for the 1950s, starring Kevin McCarthy, directed by Don Siegel. **CU4, SF1, SF9** *Highly Recommended*

Invasion of the Body Snatchers (1978, C, 115m, PG)
Remake of the sci-fi classic, updated to 1970s San Francisco, with pointed commentary on self-help trends. Donald Sutherland and Brooke Adams star, with Jeff Goldblum, Veronica Cartwright, and Leonard Nimoy. Directed by Philip Kaufman. **CU4, CU18, CU50, SF9, XT9** *Highly Recommended*

Invasion U.S.A. (1985, C, 107m, R)
Chuck Norris does his very best to thwart a Russian-backed invasion of America. **AC20, AC32**

Invisible Ghost, The (1941, B&W, 64m, NR)
A man commits murder after his domineering wife hypnotizes him. Bela Lugosi stars. **HO28**

Invisible Man, The (1933, B&W, 71m, NR)
Claude Rains' debut, as he stars in the H. G. Wells story of the mad scientist who makes himself invisible and causes great problems in a small British town. Directed by James Whale. **HO1, HO20, HO34, SF26, XT10** *Recommended*

Invisible Ray, The (1936, B&W, 81m, NR)
Boris Karloff plays a man whose exposure to radiation during an experiment slowly destroys his mind. Bela Lugosi costars. **HO21, HO27**

Invitation to the Dance (1957, C, 93m, NR)
Gene Kelly directed and stars in this trio of stories told in dance. **MU1, MU19**

Ipcress File, The (1965, C, 108m, NR)
Michael Caine stars in the first of his
three films as Harry Palmer, a British
crook who becomes a spy. Based on the
character created by Len Deighton. **MY6**

Irma La Douce (1963, C, 142m, NR)
A Paris policeman (Jack Lemmon) falls
for a prostitute (Shirley MacLaine), and
tries hard to keep her for himself. Comedy directed by Billy Wilder. **CL37,
DR42, DR64**

Iron Eagle (1986, C, 117m, PG-13)
When an Air Force officer is taken hostage by terrorists in Northern Africa, his
teenaged son and another officer commandeer two jets and attempt a daring
rescue mission. Jason Gedrick and Louis
Gossett, Jr. star. **AC11**

Iron Eagle II (1988, C, 105m, PG)
More aerial action with Louis Gossett,
Jr.. teaming up with the Soviets to wipe
out a Middle East nuclear missile instal-
lation. Rock soundtrack features Alice
Cooper's version of ''I Got a Line on
You.'' **AC11**

Iron Triangle, The (1988, C, 94m, R)
Vietnam war drama, told from Vietcong
point of view, of American officer's capture and treatment by the enemy. Beau
Bridges stars, with Haing S. Ngor. **AC4**

Ironweed (1987, C, 143m, R)
Jack Nicholson and Meryl Streep star as
alcoholic outcasts weathering the storm
of the Great Depression. Based on the
novel by William Kennedy. Tom Waits
costars. **DR19, DR24, DR26, MU12**

Irreconcilable Differences (1984, C, 117m,
PG)
A young girl sues her selfish, materialistic
parents for divorce in this modern comedy-drama. Ryan O'Neal, Shelley Long,
and Drew Barrymore star. **CO5, DR8**

Isadora (1969, C, 153m, PG)
Vanessa Redgrave plays Isadora Duncan,
who was as famous for her free-spirited
lifestyle as she was for her influence on

modern dance. Jason Robards and James
Fox costar. Video version restores some
footage cut after original theatrical release. **CU10, DR4, DR65** *Recommended*

Ishtar (1987, C, 107m, PG)
Warren Beatty and Dustin Hoffman play
two untalented singer-songwriters who
can only get a gig in a war-torn North
African kingdom. Charles Grodin and Isabelle Adjani costar. Written and directed
by Elaine May. **CO3, DR30, DR34**

Island, The (1962, B&W, 96m, NR)
Japanese drama, with no dialogue, about
family's struggle to survive on a rocky
island. Directed by Kaneto Shindo. **FF4**

Island at the Top of the World (1974, C,
93m, G)
An arctic expedition uncovers a Viking
civilization thought to be extinct. Adventure from the Disney studios. **FA1**

Island Monster (1953, B&W, 87m, NR)
A group of cut-throat drug smugglers
elude the law. Boris Karloff stars. **HO27**

Island of Dr. Moreau, The (1977, C, 104m,
PG)
Burt Lancaster plays a mad doctor who
creates ''humanimals'' in his island laboratory. Based on an H. G. Wells story;
Michael York and Barbara Carrera costar. **DR41, HO20, SF26**

Island of the Blue Dolphins (1964, C, 93m,
NR)
Family adventure set in the 19th century,
about a young Indian girl abandoned on a
desert island and befriended by a pack of
wild dogs. Celia Kaye stars. **FA4**

Islands in the Stream (1977, C, 105m, PG)
Drama based on Ernest Hemingway
novel about an artist living in the Caribbean and his relationships with his three
sons. George C. Scott stars. **DR8, DR19**

Isle of the Dead (1945, B&W, 72m, NR)
Boris Karloff stars in this tale about a
group of mysterious people stranded on a

quarrantined Greek Island. Produced by Val Lewton. **HO6, HO27, HO36**

It (1927, B&W, 72m, NR)
Clara Bow plays the "it" girl, a gold-digger who has designs on her boss, in this silent comedy. Gary Cooper has a small role. **CL11, CL26**

It Came From Beneath the Sea (1955, B&W, 80m, NR)
Science fiction monster story of massive octopus wreaking havoc in San Francisco. Kenneth Tobey and Faith Domergue star; special effects by Ray Harryhausen. **SF10**

It Came From Hollywood (1982, C, 80m, PG)
Comedy stars, including Gilda Radner, Dan Aykroyd, and Cheech & Chong, introduce scenes from some of Hollywood's worst science fiction and horror films. **CO13, CO32**

It Came From Outer Space (1953, B&W, 81m, NR)
Classic 1950s science fiction from director Jack Arnold, about an alien spaceship crashing in the desert and its passengers assuming human identities. Richard Carlson and Barbara Rush star. **SF1, SF9** *Recommended*

It Happened at the World's Fair (1963, C, 105m, NR)
Elvis Presley plays a pilot who finds romance during the Seattle World's Fair. **MU22**

It Happened One Night (1934, B&W, 105m, NR)
Clark Gable is a newspaper reporter who meets an heiress (Claudette Colbert); she's running away from her father who is against her marriage. This classic comedy was an Academy Award winner for Best Actor, Best Actress, Best Picture, and Best Director (Frank Capra). **CL10, CL23, CL40, XT1, XT2, XT3, XT6** *Highly Recommended*

It Lives Again (1978, C, 91m, R)
Sequel to *It's Alive,* featuring more mayhem, this time by three demonic infants. Frederic Forrest and Kathleen Lloyd star. Directed by Larry Cohen. **CU30, HO13**

It Should Happen to You (1954, B&W, 81m, NR)
Judy Holliday plays an unemployed actress who uses her savings to buy New York City billboards to publicize her name. This comedy marked Jack Lemmon's film debut; directed by George Cukor. **CL39, CO42, DR64, XT9**

It Takes Two (1988, C, 79m, PG-13)
Comedy about a young couple about to be married, only he's getting cold feet. His solution—buy the sportscar of his dreams and ride off for a fling. George Newbern and Leslie Hope star. **CO1**

It's a Gift (1934, B&W, 73m, NR)
W.C. Fields plays a grocer bedeviled by insomnia, clumsy blind men, and an indifferent family. A classic comedy, perhaps Fields' funniest. **CL10, CO22, CU5** *Highly Recommended*

It's a Mad Mad Mad Mad World (1963, C, 154m, NR)
Comedy featuring a truly all-star cast of comic performers, with police detective Spencer Tracy watching a frantic group of people search for stolen bank money. Jonathan Winters, Sid Caesar, Dick Shawn, Phil Silvers, Ethel Merman, and Mickey Rooney are among the treasure hunters. **CO9, CL19, CU17, FA6**

It's a Wonderful Life (1946, B&W, 129m, NR)
George Bailey (Jimmy Stewart) wishes he had never been born, and an angel shows him what life in his hometown would have been like without him. Donna Reed and Lionel Barrymore costar; Frank Capra directed. **CL6, CL25, CL40, FA13**

It's Alive! (1974, C, 91m, PG)
Newborn baby turns into rampaging demon in this cult horror film. Directed by

Larry Cohen. Sequel: *It Lives Again.* **CU30, HO13**

It's Always Fair Weather (1955, C, 105m, NR)
Gene Kelly, Dan Dailey, and Michael Kidd are three wartime buddies who meet ten years later, only to find that they have nothing in common. Musical written by Betty Comden and Adolph Green, directed by Kelly and Stanley Donen. **MU19, MU23**

It's an Adventure, Charlie Brown (1983, C, 50m, NR)
The whole Peanuts gang joins in for these six vignettes about a boy named Charlie Brown. **FA10**

It's in the Bag (1945, B&W, 87m, NR)
Rare film outing for comic Fred Allen, as the proprietor of a flea circus in search of a hidden inheritance. His encounter with archrival Jack Benny is a classic bit. **CL10**

It's My Turn (1980, C, 91m, R)
A young woman (Jill Clayburgh) tries to have it all as a career woman and a lover. Michael Douglas and Charles Grodin co-star. **CO1, CO2, DR70**

Ivan the Terrible, Part One (1943, B&W, 96m, NR) **Part Two** (1946, C, 84m, NR)
Russian director Sergei Eisenstein's historical epic about Czar Ivan IV is packed with mesmerizing imagery and music by Sergei Prokofiev. Tapes are available separately or in one package. **FF22** *Highly Recommended*

Ivanhoe (1952, C, 106m, NR)
Elizabeth Taylor and Robert Taylor star in this family adventure of knights and their ladies fair, based on the Sir Walter Scott novel. **AC13, CL33, FA4**

I've Heard the Mermaids Singing (1987, C, 81m, PG)
Comedy-drama, with cult following, about an aimless young woman who finally finds happiness working at a trendy art gallery. Sheila McCarthy stars. **CO12**

Jabberwocky (1977, C, 100m, PG)
This black comedy about the Middle Ages, directed by Terry Gilliam, stars Terry Jones and Michael Palin, also from the Monty Python troupe. **CO15**

Jack and the Beanstalk (1952, B&W/C, 87m, NR)
Abbott and Costello star in a version of the children's fairy tale. **CO23**

Jack and the Beanstalk (1983, C, 60m, NR)
Dennis Christopher stars as the young boy who trades a cow for magic beans, climbs a beanstalk, and encounters a husband/wife giant team (Jean Stapleton, Elliott Gould) in this classic story from the Faerie Tale Theatre collection. **FA12**

Jack the Ripper (1980, C, 82m, R)
Klaus Kinski plays the notorious lady-killer of Victorian London. **FF30, HO9**

Jackie Chan's Police Force (1987, C, 90m, PG-13)
Martial arts thriller about a cop framed for murder. Jackie Chan stars. **AC9, AC26**

Jackie Mason on Broadway (1988, C, 60m, NR)
Highlights from the veteran comic's one-man Broadway show, *The World According to Me.* **CO16** *Recommended*

Jacknife (1989, C, 102m, R)
A Vietnam veteran (Robert DeNiro) tries to pull his one-time war buddy (Ed Harris) out of postwar trauma. Kathy Baker costars in this topical drama. **DR7, DR25**

Jack's Back (1988, C, 97m, R)
Mystery set in contemporary Los Angeles, where a killer is imitating Jack the Ripper's crimes on their 100th anniversary. James Spader plays a young intern who discovers the killer's identity. Cynthia Gibb is one of the potential victims. **MY3, MY7, MY17** *Recommended*

Jagged Edge (1985, C, 108m, R)
Glenn Close plays an attorney who gets romantically involved with her client (Jeff

Bridges), a newspaper publisher accused of murdering his heiress wife. Peter Coyote and Robert Loggia costar. **DR3, DR17, DR71, DR72, MY3, MY5**

Jaguar Lives (1979, C, 91m, PG)
A karate expert is hired to travel all over the world to track down narcotics kingpins. Joe Lewis, Christopher Lee, and Barbara Bach star. **HO32**

Jail Bait (1954, B&W, 70m, NR)
From cult director Ed Wood, Jr. comes the tragic tale of a youth led into a crime and then forced to alter his face through plastic surgery to avoid capture. Timothy Farrell, Lyle Talbot, and Steve Reeves star. **CU45**

Jailhouse Rock (1957, B&W, 96m, NR)
Elvis Presley musical about a young man who learns to play the guitar while in jail and becomes a successful rock star after his release. **MU22** *Recommended*

Jake Speed (1986, C, 104m, PG)
A fictional adventure hero and his trusty companion come to life to rescue a lady in distress. Michael Crawford and Dennis Christopher star as the heroes; John Hurt is the villain. **AC21**

Jamaica Inn (1939, B&W, 98m, NR)
Alfred Hitchcock directed this version of Daphne du Maurier's novel about an orphan girl (Maureen O'Hara) who gets involved with a band of smugglers. Charles Laughton costars. **MY3, MY22, MY36**

Jamaica Inn (1985, C, 200m, NR)
New version of the du Maurier classic of a lovely lass in distress at the hands of her evil uncle. Jane Seymour stars, with Patrick McGoohan, John McEnery, and Billie Whitelaw. Originally made for TV. **MY3, MY36**

James Dean Story, The (1957, B&W, 82m, NR)
Documentary about the legendary movie star, co-directed by Robert Altman. **CU25**

Jane Doe (1983, C, 103m, NR)
Karen Valentine plays an amnesiac stalked by a killer who wants her dead before she can incriminate him. Originally made for TV. **MY3**

Janis (1975, C, 97m, NR)
Documentary about the short life and career of blues/rock singer Janis Joplin; includes extensive concert footage. **MU11**

January Man, The (1989, C, 122m, R)
Kevin Kline is a suspended New York cop on the trail of a serial killer in this crime drama with comic overtones. With Susan Sarandon, Harvey Keitel, and Rod Steiger. **AC9**

Jason and the Argonauts (1963, C, 104m, NR)
Jason sets out to find the Golden Fleece in order to regain his rightful place on the throne, and encounters many obstacles along the way. Great special effects highlight this fantasy. **AC18, FA8**

Jaws (1975, C, 124m, PG)
Blockbuster horror film about a great white shark's attacks on swimmers at a New England beach. Steven Spielberg directed; Richard Dreyfuss, Roy Scheider, and Robert Shaw star. **HO16, SF24** *Highly Recommended*

Jaws 2 (1978, C, 117m, PG)
The saga of the great white shark continues, with Roy Scheider and his wife in Florida, where they're bedeviled by further attacks. **HO16**

Jaws 3 (1983, C, 98m, PG)
In the third chapter, personnel at a sea world park in Florida are under siege from a shark enraged that its offspring has been captured. Dennis Quaid, Bess Armstrong, and Louis Gossett, Jr. star. **HO16**

Jaws: The Revenge (1987, C, 87m, PG-13)
Lorraine Gary, who played Roy Scheider's wife in the first and second installments, is back to battle another mam-

moth shark, this time in the Caribbean. Michael Caine costars. **HO16**

Jazz Singer, The (1980, C, 115m, PG)
This remake of the classic melodrama stars Neil Diamond as the son of a Jewish cantor (Laurence Olivier); Neil breaks with family tradition to become a rock star. **CL32, MU4**

Jean de Florette (1986, C, 122m, PG)
French drama, based on Marcel Pagnol's tale, about a scheming landowner who conspires with his dim-witted nephew to deprive their new neighbor of water for his crops. Yves Montand, Daniel Auteil, and Gerard Depardieu are the principals. Directed by Claude Berri. Story concludes in *Manon of the Spring*. **FF1, FF29** *Recommended*

Jennifer (1978, C, 90m, PG)
A shy girl is ostracized when she moves to a new school, and her telekinetic powers allow her to unleash deadly snakes on those who snubbed her. **HO7**

Jeremiah Johnson (1972, C, 107m, PG)
A mountain man (Robert Redford) who has turned his back on civilization goes to war with the Crow Indians who killed his family. Directed by Sydney Pollack. **DR29, DR56**

Jerk, The (1979, C, 94m, R)
Steve Martin stars as the title character, a stupid young man who attempts to adjust to life in the "normal" world. **CO33**

Jerry Lewis Live (1985, C, 77m, NR)
This live concert, filmed in Las Vegas, includes many of Jerry Lewis's zaniest routines. **CO25**

Jesse James (1939, C, 105m, NR)
A biography of the famed outlaw starring Henry Fonda, Tyrone Power, and Randolph Scott. **CL24, WE2, WE4, WE22**

Jesse James at Bay (1941, B&W, 54m, NR)
Roy Rogers and Gabby Hayes team up in a saga of the notorious outlaw's battles with the railroads. **WE2, WE23**

Jesus Christ, Superstar (1973, C, 103m, G)
Screen version of the successful Broadway rock opera portrays the last seven days in the life of Christ. Ted Neeley, Carl Anderson, and Yvonne Elliman star. **FA9, MU9**

Jesus of Nazareth (1977, C, 371m, NR)
The life of Christ, portrayed by Robert Powell, features an all-star supporting cast, including Laurence Olivier and Anne Bancroft. Directed by Franco Zeffirelli; originally made for TV. **CL13, CL32**

Jet Benny Show, The (1986, C, 77m, NR)
Science fiction spoof featuring a character who resembles Jack Benny. Steve Norman and Kevin Dees star. **SF21**

Jewel of the Nile (1985, C, 104m, PG)
Kathleen Turner, Michael Douglas, and Danny DeVito return in this sequel to *Romancing the Stone,* set in a North African kingdom. Author Joan Wilder is kidnapped by a mad prince, and soldier of fortune Jack Colter is off to the rescue. **AC14, AC21, DR46, DR70**

Jezebel (1938, B&W, 103m, NR)
Bette Davis plays a willful Southern belle who defies social customs to make her fiance (Henry Fonda) jealous. Davis and supporting actress Fay Bainter both won Oscars under William Wyler's direction. **CL3, CL21, CL24, CL38, XT3, XT5**

Jigsaw Man, The (1984, C, 91m, PG)
A British agent (Michael Caine) who defected to Russia comes back to Britain for a final mission. Laurence Olivier costars. **CL32, MY6**

Jimi Hendrix (1973, C, 102m, NR)
This documentary on rock's greatest guitarist features interviews with his friends and musical associates, plus rare concert footage. **MU11** *Recommended*

Jimi Plays Berkeley (1973, C, 55m, NR)
Master musician Jimi Hendrix in concert. **MU10**

Jimmy the Kid (1983, C, 85m, PG)
A stuffy young boy, the child of wealthy parents, is kidnapped by a group of bumblers who teach him how to be a kid. Gary Coleman and Paul LeMat star. **FA7**

Jinxed! (1982, C, 103m, R)
Dark comedy of shady doings in Las Vegas involving a lounge singer (Bette Midler), her obnoxious lover (Rip Torn), and a handsome young blackjack dealer (Ken Wahl). **CU47, MU12**

Jo Jo Dancer, Your Life Is Calling (1986, C, 97m, R)
Richard Pryor stars in this semi-autobiographical story of a comedian who nearly dies from drug abuse. He reflects on his past, starting with his youth in his grandmother's brothel. Debbie Allen, Art Evans, Barbara Williams, Carmen McRae, and Billy Eckstine costar. Pryor co-wrote and directed. **CO29, DR12, DR14, MU12**

Joan of Arc (1948, C, 100m, NR)
Ingrid Bergman portrays the tragic heroine in this adaptation of the Maxwell Anderson play. **CL2, CL27**

Jocks (1987, C, 91m, R)
Teen comedy about a traveling tennis team whose hijinks in Las Vegas overshadow their tennis tournament. Look for Christopher Lee and Richard Roundtree in small roles. **HO32**

Joe Cocker: Mad Dogs and Englishmen (1971, C, 119m, NR)
This documentary features highlights of Joe Cocker's 1970 American tour, with outstanding performances by Cocker and Leon Russell. **MU10**

Joe Kidd (1972, C, 88m, PG)
Clint Eastwood is hired on the wrong side of a land war between Mexican natives and American land owners. Robert Duvall costars. **DR37, WE26**

Joe Piscopo New Jersey Special (1986, C, 60m, NR)
This TV special shows funny man Piscopo kidding his home state with guest star Danny DeVito. **CO16**

Joe Piscopo Video, The (1984, C, 60m, NR)
Saturday Night Live alumnus does it all in this one-man show, highlighting many of his famous impressions. **CO16**

Johnny Be Good (1988, C, 91m, R)
A high school quarterback is the object of a mad scramble among unscrupulous recruiters. Anthony Michael Hall and Robert Downey, Jr. star in this comedy. Rated PG-13 in its theatrical release; video version contains additional footage to earn the "R" rating. **CO4, CO34, CU10**

Johnny Belinda (1948, B&W, 103m, NR)
Jane Wyman's Oscar-winning performance highlights this tale of a deaf-mute and the doctor (Lew Ayres) who comes to her aid. **XT3**

Johnny Dangerously (1984, C, 90m, PG-13)
Spoof of Prohibition-era gangster movies, starring Michael Keaton, Joe Piscopo and Danny DeVito. **CO7, CO10, CO13, CO45**

Johnny Guitar (1954, C, 110m, NR)
Offbeat western with women in the two leads: Joan Crawford as a tough saloon owner who learns her wealth can't buy everything, and Mercedes McCambridge as her rival. Sterling Hayden costars; Nicholas Ray directed. **CL50, CU17, CU23, WE9, WE16** *Recommended*

Johnny Tremain (1957, C, 80m, NR)
Based on the Esther Forbes novel, this Disney film deals with a young boy's involvement in the Revolutionary War. **FA1**

Jolson Sings Again (1949, C, 96m, NR)
This sequel to *The Jolson Story* continues the success story of American entertainer Al Jolson. Larry Parks stars; Jolie supplied the vocals. **MU5**

Jolson Story, The (1946, C, 128m, NR)
Larry Parks plays Al Jolson in this biographical film tracing his rise to stardom.
MU5

Jonathan Winters: On the Ledge (1987, C, 60m, NR)
One of America's premier funnymen stars in this series of sketches, also featuring Robin Williams and Milton Berle. **CO16**

Jour de Fête (1949, B&W, 70m, NR)
Comedy from French director Jacques Tati about a postman's bizarre attempts to mechanize mail delivery, with hilarious results. **FF16**

Jour Se Leve, Le (1939, B&W, 85m, NR)
Classic French drama of a factory worker driven to murder, trying to sort out his life before he's captured. Jean Gabin stars; Marcel Carné directed. **FF1**

Journey Back to Oz (1974, C, 90m, G)
This animated sequel to *The Wizard of Oz* features the voices of Liza Minnelli, Mickey Rooney, Margaret Hamilton (the witch from the original), and Milton Berle. **FA10**

Journey Into Fear (1942, B&W, 69m, NR)
An American armaments smuggler (Orson Welles) flees from Turkey in this World War II thriller, adapted from an Eric Ambler novel. Joseph Cotten costars; he and Welles wrote the screenplay. **CL41, MY1, MY6**

Journey of Natty Gann, The (1985, C, 101m, PG)
During the Depression, a young girl travels cross-country to see her father and is protected along the way by a pet wolf. John Cusack and Meredith Salenger star in this Disney family adventure. **FA1, FA4**

Journey Through Fairyland (1989, C, 95m, NR)
Animated adventure for children about a brave hero's exciting travels, featuring many classical music pieces on the soundtrack. **FA10**

Journey to the Center of the Earth (1959, C, 132m, NR)
Jules Verne fantasy tale of 19th-century expedition, packed with perils and wonders. James Mason, Arlene Dahl, Pat Boone, and Diane Baker star. **FA4, SF1, SF3, SF13, SF27**

Journey to the Far Side of the Sun (1969, C, 99m, G)
British science fiction adventure, with space voyagers finding a hidden planet. Roy Thinnes, Lynn Loring, and Herbert Lom star. **SF3, SF19**

Joy House (1964, B&W, 98m, NR)
A playboy (Alain Delon) with a secret past stumbles into a mansion in France run by two American women. Jane Fonda stars. **DR27**

Joy of Sex, The (1984, C, 93m, R)
A high school girl, thinking she has only weeks to live, decides to experience it all before it's too late. Michelle Meyrink and Christopher Lloyd star in this comedy. **CO4**

Juarez (1939, B&W, 132m, NR)
This biographical drama stars Paul Muni as Mexican leader Juarez, with Bette Davis as Carlotta. **CL2, CL21**

Jubal (1956, C, 101m, NR)
A rancher becomes jealous of his best friend, who he thinks is having an affair with his lovely wife. Ernest Borgnine and Glenn Ford star, with Valerie French, Rod Steiger, and Charles Bronson. **AC29**

Judge Priest (1934, B&W, 80m, NR)
John Ford directed this humorous tale of a controversial judge (Will Rogers) in a small town. **CL34**

Judgment at Nuremberg (1961, B&W, 178m, NR)
Spencer Tracy plays an American judge who presides over the Nuremberg war crimes trials. Outstanding supporting performances by Burt Lancaster, Judy Garland, Montgomery Clift, and Maximilian Schell, who won an Academy Award as

the German defense attorney. **CL8, CL19, CL47, DR17, DR41, MU21, XT2**

Juggernaut (1937, B&W, 64m, NR)
A doctor (Boris Karloff) is hired by a woman to murder her husband. But he doesn't stop with one corpse, as he continues to poison people. **HO27**

Juggernaut (1974, C, 109m, PG)
A madman plants four bombs aboard an ocean liner and demands blackmail money from the shipping company. First-rate adventure, with touches of sly wit, starring Richard Harris, Anthony Hopkins, and Shirley Knight. Directed by Richard Lester. **AC23, CU35** *Highly Recommended*

Jules and Jim (1961, B&W, 104m, NR)
Director François Truffaut's modern classic: two men try to share the same free-spirited woman. Jeanne Moreau, Oskar Werner, and Henri Serre star. **FF13, FF26** *Highly Recommended*

Julia (1977, C, 118m, PG)
True story of how writer Lillian Hellman got involved with World War II Resistance movement in Europe, thanks to a courageous friend. Jane Fonda and Oscar winner Vanessa Redgrave star; Jason Robards also won an Oscar for playing Dashiell Hammett. Meryl Streep debuted in a small role. Directed by Fred Zinnemann. **CL57, DR4, DR26, DR27, DR65, XT4, XT5** *Recommended*

Julia and Julia (1988, C, 98m, R)
Kathleen Turner stars as a woman whose husband is killed on their wedding day; years later, he returns with their six-year-old son. She's unable to sort reality from fantasy, which creates tension with her new lover (Sting). **DR46**

Juliet of the Spirits (1965, C, 148m, NR)
Director Federico Fellini's dream-movie about the fantasies of an ordinary housewife (Giulietta Masina) who's afraid that her husband is cheating on her. **FF10**

Julius Caesar (1953, B&W, 123m, NR)
The Shakespeare drama of power politics in ancient Rome, with Marlon Brando as Mark Anthony, and James Mason, John Gielgud, Louis Calhern, and Deborah Kerr. Joseph L. Mankiewicz directed. **CL1, CL55, DR33** *Recommended*

Julius Caesar (1970, C, 117m, G)
An all-star cast, including Charlton Heston, Jason Robards, Diana Rigg, and Christopher Lee, is featured in this adaptation of Shakespeare's play about political intrigue in Rome. **CL1, HO32**

Jumbo (1962, C, 125m, NR)
Rodgers & Hart songs and Busby Berkeley choreography highlight this circus musical starring Doris Day, Stephen Boyd, Jimmy Durante, and Martha Raye. Also known as *Billy Rose's Jumbo*. **MU20**

Jumpin' Jack Flash (1986, C, 100m, R)
Whoopi Goldberg plays a computer programmer who gets involved in international intrigue when a spy contacts her on her computer screen. Jim Belushi co-stars. **CO10, CO13**

June Night (1940, B&W, 90m, NR)
Ingrid Bergman stars in this melodrama, made in Sweden before her Hollywood career began, about a woman trying to escape her scandalous past. Also known as *A Night in June*. **CL27, FF7**

Jungle Book, The (1942, C, 109m, NR)
Colorful live action fantasy about a boy raised by wolves in the jungle. Great family entertainment, based on the Kipling book. **FA4**

Jungle Raiders (1985, C, 102m, PG-13)
Adventure story featuring Captain Yankee, a fearless soldier of fortune who's off in search of the Ruby of Gloom. Christopher Connelly and Lee Van Cleef star. **AC21**

Junior Bonner (1972, C, 103m, PG)
Steve McQueen plays an ex-rodeo star determined to be in the spotlight again. Ida Lupino and Robert Preston costar.

Sam Peckinpah directed. **AC28, WE13, WE19** *Recommended*

Just a Gigolo (1979, C, 98m, R)
Atmospheric drama of Prussian war veteran (David Bowie) adrift in Berlin. Sydne Rome, Kim Novak, and David Hemmings costar; Marlene Dietrich makes a brief appearance. **CL47, MU12**

Just Around the Corner (1938, B&W, 70m, NR)
Shirley Temple teams with Bill "Bojangles" Robinson for some of their best musical numbers, as Shirley puts an end to the Depression by persuading an elderly tycoon to create more jobs. Bert Lahr and Joan Davis costar. **FA14**

Just Between Friends (1986, C, 110m, PG-13)
When a woman's husband is killed in an accident, she learns a terrible secret about her new best friend. Mary Tyler Moore and Christine Lahti star; Ted Danson and Sam Waterston offer support. **DR10**

Just Tell Me What You Want (1980, C, 112m, R)
A business executive (Alan King) unknowingly pushes his mistress (Ali MacGraw) into the arms of a younger man (Peter Weller), then does everything in his power to get her back. Slam-bang New York comedy directed by Sidney Lumet. With Myrna Loy and Dina Merrill. **CL46, DR58, XT9**

Justine (1969, C, 116m, NR)
A banker's wife (Anouk Aimee) gets involved with politicians from the Middle East. Adaptation of the Lawrence Durrell novel also stars Dirk Bogarde, Robert Forster, and Michael York. Directed by George Cukor. **CL39, DR19**

K-9 (1989, C, 102m, PG-13)
James Belushi plays a cop whose new partner is a German shepherd in this action comedy. **CO13**

Kagemusha (1980, C, 159m, PG)
Epic adventure tale of thief who assumes identity of dead warlord, directed by Japan's premier filmmaker, Akira Kurosawa. Tatsuya Nakadai stars. **FF9** *Recommended*

Kameradschaft (1931, B&W, 89m, NR)
Classic German drama of post-World War I enmity between Germans and French forgotten during mining disaster rescue. Directed by G.W. Pabst. **FF3**

Kamikaze '89 (1982, C, 106m, NR)
Thriller set in futuristic Germany about a detective (Rainer Werner Fassbinder) foiling a bomb plot. **FF3, FF20**

Kanal (1956, B&W, 90m, NR)
From Polish director Andrzej Wajda, a drama of the Polish Resistance fighters taking their last stand against the Nazis during the Warsaw Uprising. **FF7** *Recommended*

Kangaroo (1986, C, 105m, R)
Australian drama, based on D.H. Lawrence's autobiographical novel, of a writer scorned in his native England. He and his German-born wife emigrate to Australia, where they become involved with a band of Fascists. Colin Friels and Judy Davis star. **FF5**

Kansas (1988, C, 111m, R)
Two aimless young men (Matt Dillon, Andrew McCarthy) pull off an impromptu bank robbery. One hides the money, and his partner comes looking for him. **DR16**

Karate Kid, The (1984, C, 126m, PG)
The new kid in town is the punching bag for neighborhood bullies until a kindly handyman teaches him self-defense. Ralph Macchio and Noriyuki "Pat" Morita star. **DR9, DR22, FA7**

Karate Kid II, The (1986, C, 113m, PG)
Further adventures of the young karate student, now in Japan for martial arts tournament, and his kindly teacher. **DR9, DR22, FA7**

Katherine (1975, C, 100m, NR)
Sissy Spacek plays a young woman who turns from political activist to terrorist. Art Carney and Henry Winkler costar. Originally made for TV. **DR7, DR68**

Keeper, The (1984, C, 96m, NR)
The patients at an insane asylum are tortured by their sadistic keeper. Christopher Lee stars in this horror drama. **HO32**

Keeping Track (1986, C, 107m, R)
A newsman and a bank teller become pawns in a game of international intrigue after $5 million falls into their laps. Michael Sarrazin and Margot Kidder star. **MY6**

Kelly's Heroes (1970, C, 145m, PG)
A gang of GIs plan a daring robbery behind enemy lines during World War II. Clint Eastwood stars in this comedy-adventure, with Telly Savalas, Donald Sutherland, Carroll O'Connor, and Harry Dean Stanton. **AC27, CO38, CU49**

Kennel Murder Case, The (1933, B&W, 73m, NR)
William Powell plays Philo Vance, the sophisticated detective, as he investigates a murder in New York City. **MY14**

Kentuckian, The (1955, C, 104, NR)
Burt Lancaster directed and starred in this western about a man starting life over with his son in 1820s Texas. Diana Lynn and Walter Matthau costar. **DR41**

Kermit and Piggy Story, The (1985, C, 57m, NR)
The rags-to-riches show biz saga of The Muppets' Miss Piggy, as told by Cheryl Ladd, Raquel Welch, and Tony Randall. **FA15**

Key, The (1958, B&W, 134m, NR)
In World War II London, a woman whose apartment key has passed from one sea captain to another, in a series of affairs, finally finds true love with a Canadian officer. Sophia Loren and William Holden star. **CL51, FF31**

Key Largo (1948, B&W, 101m, NR)
A gangster (Edward G. Robinson) holds people captive in a Florida hotel during a hurricane. Humphrey Bogart and Lauren Bacall star, with Claire Trevor, who won an Oscar for Best Supporting Actress. Directed by John Huston. **CL15, CL20, CL44, CL52, MY1, XT5** *Recommended*

Kid, The/Idle Class, The (1921, B&W, 85m, NR)
In his first feature-length film, Charlie Chaplin plays The Little Tramp, who adopts an orphan (Jackie Coogan). Also included on this tape is the Chaplin short, *The Idle Class.* **CO18** *Highly Recommended*

Kid From Brooklyn, The (1946, C, 113m, NR)
Danny Kaye comedy about a milkman turned pugilist, with Virginia Mayo, Vera-Ellen, and Eve Arden. **CO41**

Kid Galahad (1962, C, 95m, NR)
Elvis Presley plays a successful boxer who would rather be a mechanic. Charles Bronson has a small role. **AC29, MU22**

Kidnapped (1960, C, 97m, NR)
Disney adaptation of Robert Louis Stevenson's book, about a young heir who looks for his uncle, only to be abducted along the way and sold into slavery. Peter Finch and James MacArthur star, with Peter O'Toole. **DR45, FA1**

Kids Are Alright, The (1979, C, 108m, NR)
Documentary on the British rock group The Who, concentrating on the group's memorable concert performances. **MU11**

Kid's Auto Race/Mabel's Married Life (1914/1915, B&W, 21m, NR)
Charlie Chaplin stars in two of his most famous short films. The first deals with a kiddie-car contest. The second focuses on two married people who flirt in the park. **CO18**

Kill and Kill Again (1981, C, 100m, R)
Sequel to *Kill or Be Killed,* with karate
star James Ryan foiling the plans of an
evil scientist. **AC26**

Kill or Be Killed (1980, C, 90m, PG)
Karate champ James Ryan stars in a
drama about an ex-Nazi and his Japanese
counterpart from World War II meeting
years later in a martial arts tournament.
AC26

Killer Bats (1941, B&W, 67m, NR)
A cosmetics manufacturer deprives his
partner (Bela Lugosi) of his share of the
profits, and the partner plots revenge.
Also known as *The Devil Bat.* **HO28**

Killer Elite, The (1975, C, 122m, R)
A tale of two professional assassins
(James Caan, Robert Duvall) who end up
stalking each other. Sam Peckinpah directed. **AC8, AC19, DR37, MY6, WE19**

Killer Force (1975, C, 100m, PG)
A diamond mine in South Africa is the
scene for skullduggery in this action-
adventure story, starring Peter Fonda and
Telly Savalas, with Hugh O'Brian, Christopher Lee, and O. J. Simpson. **HO32**

Killer Inside Me, The (1976, C, 99m, R)
Stacy Keach plays a deputy sheriff who
is near the breaking point. Based on a
novel by Jim Thompson. **MY17, MY29**

Killer Party (1986, C, 92m, R)
A trio of sorority pledges are special
guests at an April Fool's party held in an
abandoned fraternity house. Horror
drama starring Elaine Wilkes, with Paul
Bartel. **CU42, HO12**

Killers, The (1964, C, 95m, NR)
Thriller, loosely based on Hemingway
short story, about hit men learning about
their victim's past. Lee Marvin, Angie
Dickinson, John Cassavetes, and Ronald
Reagan (in his last film) star. Cult reputation for Reagan's role as sadistic hoodlum. **CU2, DR19, DR43**

Killing, The (1956, B&W, 83m, NR)
Breakthrough film for director Stanley
Kubrick, a classic tale of a gang pulling
off a complex robbery at a racetrack.
Sterling Hayden stars, with Coleen Gray,
Vince Edwards, Elisha Cook, Jr., and
Timothy Carey. **DR53, MY1, MY34**

Killing Fields, The (1984, C, 142m, R)
Fact-based drama about *New York Times*
reporter escaping Cambodia during Vietnam War and his subsequent reunion with
his translator. Sam Waterston and Oscar
winner Haing S. Ngor star. **DR6, XT4**
Recommended

Killing of Angel Street, The (1981, C,
101m, PG)
A political activist and a geologist team
up to halt greedy real estate developers
who are forcing residents to sell their
homes. Australian drama stars Liz Alexander and John Hargreaves. **FF5**

Killing of Sister George, The (1968, C,
138m, R)
A middle-aged British actress loses her
job on a popular TV series and is also in
danger of losing her young female lover
to another woman. Beryl Reid, Susannah
York, and Coral Browne star; Robert Aldrich directed this drama. **DR3**

Killings at Outpost Zeta, The (1980, C,
92m, NR)
Science fiction mystery about team of
scientists and soldiers investigating murders at a remote planet. **SF17**

Killjoy (1981, C, 100m, NR)
Whodunit about a murdered woman and
the many possible suspects. Robert Culp
and Kim Basinger star. **MY16**

Kim (1950, C, 113m, NR)
Rudyard Kipling's tale of British soldiers
fighting against fierce tribesmen in India,
starring Errol Flynn and Dean Stockwell.
AC13, AC34, FA4

Kind Hearts and Coronets (1949, B&W, 104m, NR)
The black sheep of a wealthy family decides to kill them off. Alec Guinness plays all eight victims in this comic British mystery. **CL10, CL17, DR63, MY19, MY21** *Recommended*

Kindred, The (1987, C, 92m, R)
A young man discovers that he has been the guinea pig for an experiment combining his tissue with that of a sea monster. Rod Steiger and Kim Hunter star. **HO13**

King and I, The (1956, C, 133m, NR)
Yul Brynner won an Oscar for his performance as the King of Siam in this version of the Rodgers and Hammerstein Broadway musical. Deborah Kerr stars as Anna, the governess hired to teach his many children. **FA9, MU2, MU7, XT2**

King Creole (1958, B&W, 116m, NR)
A night-club singer (Elvis Presley) with a troubled past gets involved with criminals in New Orleans. **MU22**

King in New York, A (1957, B&W, 105m, NR)
Charlie Chaplin comedy about a European monarch who visits America during the McCarthy witch hunts and gets a strong taste of American morality. **CO18**

King Kong (1933, B&W, 100m, NR)
The granddaddy of all monster movies, with the big hairy ape terrorizing Skull Island and then demolishing Manhattan. Robert Armstrong, Bruce Cabot, and Fay Wray star. **CU4, FA8, HO1, HO16, SF2, SF10, SF13, SF16** *Highly Recommended*

King Kong (1976, C, 134m, PG)
Jeff Bridges and Jessica Lange star in this remake of the classic story about a gigantic ape who captures a young woman and terrorizes Manhattan. **CU18, DR71, DR74, HO16**

King Lear (1971, B&W, 137m, PG)
Shakespeare's tragedy of a lonely monarch, starring Paul Scofield, Irene Worth, and Jack MacGowran; directed by Peter Brook. **CL1**

King Lear (1987, C, 91m, PG)
The title is Shakespeare, but the director is French iconoclast Jean-Luc Godard, who "updates" the tale in his own way. Peter Sellars, Burgess Meredith, and Molly Ringwald head the cast, with appearances by Woody Allen and Norman Mailer. **CL1, CO27, FF14**

King of Comedy (1983, C, 109m, PG)
A stand-up comic kidnaps a popular talk-show host in hopes of getting a shot at the big time. Dark comedy about success and fame, starring Robert DeNiro and Jerry Lewis, with Sandra Bernhard. Directed by Martin Scorsese. **CU5, CO2, CO12, CO25, DR25, DR52** *Recommended*

King of Hearts (1966, C, 102m, NR)
Midnight movie classic, a fantasy about a World War I soldier separated from his division and coming upon a town occupied only by inmates escaped from an asylum. Alan Bates and Genevieve Bujold star. **CU1, CU5**

King of Jazz, The (1930, C, 93m, NR)
This revue features a cartoon sequence by Walter Lantz, plus Bing Crosby and The Rhythm Boys, and a performance of Gershwin's "Rhapsody in Blue." **MU15**

King of Kings (1961, C, 168m, NR)
Nicholas Ray directed this epic drama centering on the life of Christ. Jeffrey Hunter, Robert Ryan, Rip Torn, and Hurd Hatfield star. **CL13, CU23**

King of the Cowboys (1943, B&W, 67m, NR)
Roy Rogers fights contemporary saboteurs who are plotting to destroy a defense installation. With Smiley Burnette. **WE23**

King of the Grizzlies (1970, C, 93m, G)
In this Disney film, an Indian youth befriends a bear cub, only to grow up to face the same animal as a full-grown grizzly. **FA1**

King of the Kongo, The (1929, B&W, 213m, NR)
Silent serial starring Boris Karloff in a tale of ivory thieves in Africa. **HO27**

King of the Mountain (1981, C, 90m, PG)
A mechanic and his pals spend their spare time racing on Los Angeles' winding Mulholland Drive. Harry Hamlin stars, with Joseph Bottoms, Deborah Van Valkenburgh, and Dennis Hopper as the one-time King of the Mountain. **CU46**

King Rat (1965, B&W, 133m, NR)
In a Japanese POW camp during World War II, an American hustler inspires envy and grudging admiration from his fellow captives. George Segal stars, with Tom Courtenay and James Fox. **AC7** *Recommended*

King Solomon's Mines (1937, B&W, 80m, NR)
First screen version of classic tale of African exploration, starring Paul Robeson, Cedric Hardwicke, and Roland Young. **AC12, AC13, AC21**

King Solomon's Mines (1950, C, 103m, NR)
Second and most memorable version of the H. Rider Haggard tale of African adventure, starring Stewart Granger and Deborah Kerr. **AC12, AC13, AC21, FA4**

King Solomon's Mines (1985, C, 101m, PG-13)
Richard Chamberlain stars as the classic British adventurer, Allan Quartermain, as he plunges into deepest, darkest Africa in search of a fabled treasure. **AC12, AC21**

Kings of the Road (1976, B&W, 176m, NR)
Rambling drama from director Wim Wenders about two drifters making their way through the contemporary German landscape. **FF21**

King's Row (1942, B&W, 127m, NR)
Drama of small town life in the years prior to World War I. Ronald Reagan and Robert Cummings star. **CL6**

Kinjite: Forbidden Subjects (1988, C, 97m, R)
A Los Angeles cop (Charles Bronson) with a grudge against Orientals must change his tune when he must track down the kidnapped daughter of a visiting Japanese businessman. **AC29**

Kismet (1955, C, 113m, NR)
Howard Keel and Ann Blyth star in this colorful musical based on the Broadway show about the Arabian Nights. Directed by Vincente Minnelli. **MU1, MU2, MU8, MU24**

Kiss and Kill *see* Against All Odds (1969)

Kiss Me Goodbye (1982, C, 101m, PG)
Sally Field plays a young New York socialite visited by the ghost of her dead husband (James Caan) just as she's about to marry another man (Jeff Bridges). Loosely based on *Doña Flor and Her Two Husbands*. **DR36, DR71, FF36**

Kiss Me Kate (1953, C, 109m, NR)
Cole Porter's musical version of *The Taming of the Shrew* stars Howard Keel, Kathryn Grayson, and Ann Miller. Watch for Bob Fosse. **MU1, MU2, MU14, MU28**

Kiss of the Spider Woman (1985, C, 119m, R)
Oscar winner William Hurt stars with Raul Julia and Sonia Braga in this drama of cellmates, one a political prisoner, the other a homosexual with his film fantasies. Directed by Hector Babenco. **DR18, DR31, FF6, FF34, XT2**

Kiss Tomorrow Goodbye (1950, B&W, 102m, NR)
James Cagney plays the most ruthless of all criminals in one of his last tough-guy roles. **CL22**

Kissin' Cousins (1964, C, 96m, NR)
Elvis Presley in a dual role: a military officer and his down-home relative. The army man is trying to persuade the hick to sell his farm as a site for a missile base. **MU22**

Kitty Foyle (1940, B&W, 107m, NR)
Ginger Rogers won an Academy Award for her performance as a working-class girl who falls in love with her boss. **CL5, CL6, XT3**

Klute (1971, C, 114m, R)
Oscar winner Jane Fonda stars as a New York call girl who is being threatened by sadistic phone calls. She attracts the attention of Klute (Donald Sutherland), a small-town detective searching for a missing friend. **DR27, MY3, MY5, MY14, XT3** *Recommended*

Knife in the Water (1962, B&W, 94m, NR)
Director Roman Polanski's drama of a couple who pick up a hitchhiker and invite him on a boating holiday. In Polish. **DR54, FF7** *Recommended*

Knight Without Armor (1937, B&W, 101m, NR)
Robert Donat is the secret agent who helps Russian noblewoman Marlene Dietrich escape vengeful revolutionaries. **CL47**

Knightriders (1981, C, 145m, R)
George Romero wrote and directed this unusual drama about a traveling motorcycle gang who stage medieval fairs in which knights joust on cycles. Ed Harris stars. **HO38**

Knights and Emeralds (1986, C, 94m, PG)
Racial tension develops when white musician Christopher Wild befriends black musicians in this British drama-musical. **DR23**

Knights of the City (1985, C, 87m, R)
Action drama set on the mean streets of Miami, where a street gang tries to go straight and start a career in the music industry. Leon Isaac Kennedy, Nicholas Campbell, and singer Smokey Robinson star. **AC8**

Knights of the Round Table (1953, C, 115m, NR)
Robert Taylor, Ava Gardner, and Mel Ferrer star in this lavish drama of the King Arthur legend. **AC13**

Knock on Any Door (1949, B&W, 100m, NR)
Humphrey Bogart plays a prominent attorney who defends a young hoodlum accused of killing a cop. Directed by Nicholas Ray. **CL8, CL20, CU23, MY1**

Knockout, The/Dough and Dynamite (1914, B&W, 54m, NR)
Charlie Chaplin stars in both these comedy shorts, featuring some of his most famous routines. *The Knockout* features Chaplin as referee of a big fight. *Dough and Dynamite* is about a strike at a bakery where Chaplin works. **CO18**

Knute Rockne—All American (1940, B&W, 96m, NR)
Pat O'Brien plays the legendary Notre Dame football coach and Ronald Reagan is his star player, George Gipp. **CL2, DR22**

Kotch (1971, C, 113m, G)
Walter Matthau plays an elderly man who resists his family's attempts to write him off. Jack Lemmon directed this comedy-drama. **DR11, DR64**

Koyaanisqatsi (1983, C, 87m, NR)
Impressions of nature and man-made structures blend together in this one-of-a-kind documentary meditation on contemporary life. Directed by Godfrey Reggio; music by Philip Glass. **CU16**

Kramer vs. Kramer (1979, C, 105m, PG)
Drama of a marriage breakup and the father's learning to care for his young son, starring Dustin Hoffman, Meryl Streep, and Justin Henry. Written and directed by Robert Benton. Oscar winner for Best Picture, Actor, Supporting Actress, and Director. **DR8, DR17, DR26, DR30, DR55, XT1, XT2, XT5, XT6** *Recommended*

Kriemhilde's Revenge (1924, B&W, 95m, NR)
This silent film, directed by Fritz Lang, is the sequel to *Siegfried,* based on a popular legend of German mythology. **CL43, FF3**

Kronos (1957, B&W, 78m, NR)
A metallic monster from outer space crash-lands off the coast of Mexico and begins absorbing all the Earth's energy. Science fiction drama stars Jeff Morrow, Barbara Lawrence, and John Emery. **SF1**

Krull (1983, C, 117m, PG)
Sword & sorcery adventure of young man in search of a lost jewel, starring Ken Marshall and Lysette Antony. Lavish production values. **AC18**

Kwaidan (1964, C, 164m, NR)
A quartet of horror stories from Japan, based on works by Lafcadio Hearn. Imaginative use of color; directed by Masaki Kobayashi. **FF4**

La Bamba (1987, C, 103m, PG-13)
Biography of rock 'n' roll's first Hispanic star, Ritchie Valens, starring Lou Diamond Phillips. Esai Morales costars. Los Lobos performs Valens' music on the soundtrack. **MU5** *Recommended*

Labyrinth (1986, C, 101m, PG)
A young girl wishes her brother would be captured by goblins—and when her wish comes true, she sets out to rescue him. Family adventure starring Jennifer Connelly and David Bowie, with Terry Jones. **CO15, FA8, MU12, SF13**

Ladies Club, The (1986, C, 86m, R)
Frustrated with the criminal justice system, a policewoman, a rape victim, and several other angry women set out to get justice their own way. **AC19**

Lady and the Tramp (1955, C, 75m, G)
Classic Disney animated feature about a pampered cocker spaniel and her romance with a street mutt. **FA2** *Highly Recommended*

Lady Caroline Lamb (1972, C, 118m, PG)
True story of wife of British politician and her open affair with poet Lord Byron. Sarah Miles, Peter Finch, and Richard Chamberlain form the romantic triangle; Laurence Olivier costars. **CL32**

Lady Eve, The (1941, B&W, 94m, NR)
A preoccupied scientist (Henry Fonda) is thoroughly confused and fleeced by a smooth con woman (Barbara Stanwyck) in this classic comedy from writer-director Preston Sturges. **CL10, CL24, CL45, CO24** *Highly Recommended*

Lady for a Night (1941, B&W, 87m, NR)
Gambling boat owner tries marriage to a wealthy man but is framed for murder. Joan Blondell and John Wayne star in this drama. **CL17**

Lady From Louisiana (1941, B&W, 82m, NR)
John Wayne plays a crusading lawyer in old New Orleans who falls in love with the daughter of a gambling boss he wants to put behind bars. **CL17**

Lady From Shanghai, The (1948, B&W, 87m, NR)
Orson Welles directed and stars in this bizarre thriller about a sailor's infatuation with the lovely wife (Rita Hayworth) of a sleazy lawyer. Famous climax in house of mirrors. **CL41, MY1** *Recommended*

Lady Ice (1973, C, 93m, PG)
An insurance investigator tracks a gang of jewel thieves in this caper mystery. Donald Sutherland, Jennifer O'Neill, and Robert Duvall star. **DR37**

Lady in a Cage (1964, B&W, 93m, NR)
Olivia De Havilland stars in a thriller about a woman trapped in her home and terrorized by hoodlums. James Caan costars. **MY3**

Lady in White (1988, C, 113m, PG-13)
In 1962, a ten-year-old boy, locked in a school coatroom, witnesses a murder which took place ten years before. A ghost story with plenty of scares but very

little violence. Lukas Haas stars. **HO2, HO19**

Lady Jane (1985, C, 140m, PG-13)
The true story of the 16th-century teen-aged Queen of England, her dramatic rise to the throne, and her sudden downfall. Helena Bonham Carter and Cary Elwes star in this lavish historical drama. **DR5**

Lady of Burlesque (1943, B&W, 91m, NR)
Barbara Stanwyck plays detective when a murderer begins eliminating strippers in this comic mystery. **CL45, MY21**

Lady of the Evening (1979, C, 110m, PG)
Italian comedy features Sophia Loren and Marcello Mastroianni as a prostitute and a crook who become partners. **FF24, FF31**

Lady on the Bus (1978, C, 102m, R)
A new bride finds her husband unattractive in bed but learns that she is attracted to nearly every other man in sight. Sexy comedy from Brazil starring Sonia Braga. **FF34**

Lady Sings the Blues (1972, C, 144m, R)
Diana Ross plays famed singer Billie Holiday, who fought a losing battle with drug addiction. Billy Dee Williams and Richard Pryor costar. **CO29, DR14, MU5**

Lady Takes a Chance, The (1943, B&W, 86m, NR)
John Wayne is a rodeo star and Jean Arthur is the city girl he tames in this light-hearted western. **WE13, WE15, WE17**

Lady Vanishes, The (1938, B&W, 97m, NR)
Hitchcock mystery set aboard a speeding train with a disappearing lady, lots of suspects, sly comedy. Margaret Lockwood, Michael Redgrave and Dame May Whitty star. **MY19, MY22** *Highly Recommended*

Lady Vanishes, The (1979, C, 99m, PG)
Remake of Hitchcock's classic thriller, starring Cybill Shepherd, Elliott Gould, and Angela Lansbury. **CU18**

Lady Windermere's Fan (1925, B&W, 80m, NR)
Silent screen version of the Oscar Wilde play of blackmail, deception, and infidelity among British nobility. Ronald Colman, Irene Rich, and May McAvoy star. Ernst Lubitsch directed. **CL54**

Ladyhawke (1985, C, 121m, PG-13)
A magician's spell has doomed a knight (Rutger Hauer) and his maiden fair (Michelle Pfeiffer) always to be apart—until they meet a young pickpocket (Matthew Broderick). **AC14, AC18**

Ladykillers, The (1955, C, 90m, NR)
Classic British comedy about a bungling band of crooks and a little, old (but quite resourceful) lady. Alec Guinness and Peter Sellers head the cast. **CL10, CO10, CO17, CO26, CU5, DR63, MY19, MY21** *Recommended*

Lair of the White Worm (1988, C, 93m, R)
Director Ken Russell takes on a story by Bram Stoker, about a sexy female vampire. Amanda Donohoe, Catherine Oxenberg, and Sammi Davis star. **CU31, HO5, HO25**

Land Before Time, The (1988, C, 66m, G)
Animated feature set in prehistoric times, with cute dinosaur and his friends undergoing many adventures. **FA10**

Land of Faraway, The (1988, C, 95m, PG)
Family fantasy of an 11-year-old boy who becomes a knight when he releases a spirit in a bottle. Christian Bale stars, with Timothy Bottoms, Susannah York, and Christopher Lee. **FA8, HO32, SF13**

Land of the Minotaur (1976, C, 88m, PG)
A devil-worshipping cult in Greece kidnaps tourists for their bizarre rituals. Donald Pleasence and Peter Cushing star. **HO11, HO33**

Land That Time Forgot, The (1975, C, 90m, PG)
Science fiction fantasy about Germans and Americans discovering a prehistoric

land in Latin America. Doug McClure stars. **SF4**

Land Without Bread (1932, B&W, 28m, NR)
Director Luis Buñuel's searing documentary about Las Hurdes, one of the poorest regions of rural Spain. **FF11** *Recommended*

Laserblast (1978, C, 82m, PG)
A young boy finds a laser gun left behind by aliens and uses it to get even with his tormentors. Family science fiction drama. **SF13**

Lassie Come Home (1943, C, 88m, NR)
Family classic of a collie who is separated from the family who loves him and embarks on a dramatic journey to return to them. Roddy McDowall, Donald Crisp, Dame Mae Whitty, and Edmund Gwenn star, with a young Elizabeth Taylor in a small role. **CL33, FA5**

Lassiter (1984, C, 110m, R)
A handsome cat burglar is forced to go undercover for Scotland Yard against the Nazis. Tom Selleck stars, with Lauren Hutton, Jane Seymour, and Bob Hoskins. **AC14**

Last American Hero, The (1973, C, 100m, PG)
Jeff Bridges plays a moonshine runner whose driving skills catapult him to fame on the stock-car racing circuit. Valerie Perrine, Geraldine Fitzgerald, and Gary Busey costar. Loosely based on the life of Junior Johnson. **DR22, DR71** *Recommended*

Last Angry Man, The (1959, B&W, 100m, NR)
An elderly doctor who has devoted his life to patients in a Brooklyn slum finds himself the unwilling subject of a TV documentary. Paul Muni stars, with Luther Adler, Betsy Palmer, Godfrey Cambridge, Billy Dee Williams, and Cicely Tyson. **CL8**

Last Chase, The (1981, C, 101m, R)
In the future, an oil shortage has virtually doomed auto travel—until one man reassembles his Porsche and leads police on a cross-country chase. Lee Majors stars. **AC10, SF11**

Last Command, The (1928, B&W, 88m, NR)
An expatriate Russian general is reduced to playing out his life as a Hollywood extra. Oscar winner Emil Jannings stars, with Evelyn Brent and William Powell. Josef von Sternberg directed this silent classic. **CL7, CL12, CL56, XT2** *Recommended*

Last Days of Man on Earth, The (1973, C, 79m, R)
British science fiction, with comic overtones, about an impudent scientist who creates a "new messiah" as the world comes to an end. Jon Finch stars. **SF19, SF21**

Last Detail, The (1973, C, 105m, R)
Jack Nicholson stars in this comedy-drama about a pair of Navy "lifers" transporting a young seaman to the brig. Otis Young and Randy Quaid costar. Written by Robert Towne. **DR24** *Recommended*

Last Dragon, The (1985, C, 108, PG-13)
Kung Fu meets Motown in this martial arts adventure with musical numbers. Taimak provides the kicks and Vanity the music. **AC26**

Last Embrace (1979, C, 101m, R)
A CIA agent's wife is murdered and he believes the killers are after him, too. Roy Scheider and Janet Margolin star in this thriller from director Jonathan Demme. **CU39, MY4, MY6** *Recommended*

Last Emperor, The (1987, C, 160m, R)
Winner of 9 Oscars (including Best Picture and Director), this lavish drama tells the incredible story of Pu Yi, the Chinese emperor set adrift in the currents of 20th-century history. John Lone stars, with Peter O'Toole and Joan Chen. Bernardo

Bertolucci directed. A visual treat. **DR4, DR45, FF18, XT1, XT6** *Recommended*

Last Flight of Noah's Ark, The (1980, C, 97m, G)
Disney adventure about a pilot, a female missionary, two young stowaways, and a pair of Japanese soldiers converting a crippled plane into a boat. Elliott Gould and Genevieve Bujold star. **FA1**

Last Four Days, The (1977, C, 91m, PG)
Drama recounting the final days of Italian dictator Benito Mussolini. Rod Steiger and Henry Fonda star. **CL24**

Last House on the Left (1972, C, 91m, R)
Two teenaged girls are tortured and murdered by a sadistic gang, and one girl's father exacts his own revenge. Cult horror film directed by Wes Craven. A loose remake of *The Virgin Spring*. **FF36, HO12**

Last Hurrah, The (1958, B&W, 121m, NR)
Spencer Tracy stars as a Boston Irish politican in the twilight of his career. Directed by John Ford. **CL19, CL34**

Last Laugh, The (1924, B&W, 77m, NR)
Classic silent drama from Germany about a doorman at a hotel and his meager existence, starring Emil Jannings. Directed by F. W. Murnau. **FF3, CL12** *Recommended*

Last Man on Earth, The (1964, B&W, 86m, NR)
Vincent Price plays the sole survivor of a world-wide plague who must fight nightly battles against blood-seeking victims. **HO31**

Last Metro, The (1980, C, 133m, PG)
Director François Truffaut's drama of a theater troupe in occupied Paris. Gerard Depardieu and Catherine Deneuve co-star. **FF13, FF27, FF29**

Last Movie, The (1971, C, 108m, R)
Offbeat drama about an American film company shooting on location in a poor village in Peru. Director Dennis Hopper

stars, with Peter Fonda and Kris Kristofferson. **CU46, DR13, MU12**

Last Night at the Alamo (1983, B&W, 80m, NR)
The denizens of a Houston bar that's about to be demolished gather for one last stand in this comedy about urban cowboys. **WE13**

Last of Sheila, The (1973, C, 120m, PG)
A yacht party featuring a mystery game turns into something more serious when the hostess is found murdered. James Coburn, Dyan Cannon, James Mason, and Joan Hackett star. Anthony Perkins and Stephen Sondheim wrote the script. **MY9, MY16**

Last of the Mohicans, The (1936, B&W, 91m, NR)
Randolph Scott stars in this adaptation of James Fenimore Cooper's adventure of the French and Indian War. **AC13, WE22**

Last of the Pony Riders (1953, B&W, 80m, NR)
Gene Autry saddles up for his last feature film, with sidekick Smiley Burnette. **WE24**

Last of the Red Hot Lovers, The (1972, C, 98m, PG)
Neil Simon comedy about a married man's inept attempts at various romantic affairs. Alan Arkin, Sally Kellerman, and Paula Prentiss star. **CO34**

Last Ride of the Dalton Gang, The (1979, C, 150m, NR)
The story of the Old West's notorious gang of outlaws. Cliff Potts and Randy Quaid star, with Jack Palance and Dale Robertson. Originally made for TV. **WE15**

Last Rites (1988, C, 103m, R)
A mysterious woman, seeking sanctuary in a New York church, draws a young priest into a story of murder and revenge. Tom Berenger and Daphne Zuniga star. **DR16**

Last Starfighter, The (1984, C, 100m, PG)
A video game whiz is recruited into an interplanetary war. Science fiction adventure starring Lance Guest, Robert Preston, and Dan O'Herlihy. **SF8, SF13**

Last Tango in Paris (1973, C, 129m, X)
Controversial drama about a casual affair involving an American whose wife has just committed suicide and a free-spirited young Frenchwoman. Marlon Brando and Maria Schneider star; Bernardo Bertolucci directed. **CU6, CU13, DR1, DR3, DR33, FF18, XT9** *Recommended*

Last Temptation of Christ, The (1988, C, 160m, R)
Director Martin Scorsese's controversial adaptation of the Nikos Kazantzakis novel about Christ's human side. Willem Dafoe stars, with Barbara Hershey, Harvey Keitel, Harry Dean Stanton, John Lurie, and David Bowie. **CU49, DR52, MU12** *Recommended*

Last Time I Saw Paris, The (1954, C, 116m, NR)
Elizabeth Taylor and Van Johnson star in this drama, loosely based on an F. Scott Fitzgerald story, about Americans adrift in late 1940s Paris. **CL33**

Last Tycoon, The (1976, C, 125m, PG)
F. Scott Fitzgerald's final novel, the story of a driven movie executive and the people who support and oppose his power. Robert DeNiro stars, with a supporting cast headed by Jack Nicholson, Jeanne Moreau, and Robert Mitchum. Written by Harold Pinter; directed by Elia Kazan. **CU17, DR13, DR19, DR24, DR25, DR59, FF26** *Recommended*

Last Unicorn, The (1982, C, 95m, PG)
Animated story about a mythical beast trying to survive in an unfriendly world. Voices supplied by Alan Arkin, Jeff Bridges, and Mia Farrow. **FA10**

Last Waltz, The (1978, C, 117m, PG)
Concert film of rock group The Band's farewell performance, featuring many of their hits, plus performances by Bob Dylan, Neil Young, Eric Clapton, Muddy Waters, Van Morrison, Joni Mitchell, and many more. Directed by Martin Scorsese. **DR52, MU10** *Highly Recommended*

Last War, The (1962, C, 79m, G)
From Japan, a science fiction drama about a future conflict that escalates into nuclear annihilation. **FF4, SF18**

Last Wave, The (1977, C, 106m, PG)
Richard Chamberlain stars in this Australian drama about a lawyer who gets more than he bargained for in defending an aborigine on a murder charge. Directed by Peter Weir. **FF5**

Last Year at Marienbad (1962, B&W, 93m, NR)
Cryptic, hypnotic film about a young man's attempts to seduce an attractive but enigmatic woman. Directed by Alain Resnais. **FF1**

Late Show, The (1977, C, 94m, R)
Art Carney plays a private eye who gets help from a kooky woman (Lily Tomlin) in solving the murder of his ex-partner. An offbeat, likable mystery from writer-director Robert Benton. **DR55, MY14** *Recommended*

Laughing Policeman, The (1974, C, 111m, R)
San Francisco police track down a crazed killer who has shot up a busload of people. Walter Matthau, Bruce Dern, and Louis Gossett, Jr. star. **AC9, XT9**

Laura (1944, B&W, 88m, NR)
Classic mystery starring Gene Tierney as supposed victim, Dana Andrews as sleuth, Clifton Webb as key to crime. Vincent Price costars; Otto Preminger directed. **HO31, MY1, MY3, MY5** *Recommended*

Laurel and Hardy Comedy Classics (9 volumes: each B&W, 70-90m, NR)
Each volume of this series contains several short films by the great comedy duo. **CO20** *Recommended*

Lavender Hill Mob, The (1951, B&W, 82m, NR)
A caper comedy from Britain starring Alec Guinness as a bank clerk who masterminds a safe-cracking scheme. Watch for Audrey Hepburn in a brief appearance. **CL30, CO10, CO17, DR63, MY19, MY21, MY34**

Law of Desire (1986, C, 100m, NR)
Comedy from Spanish director Pedro Almodóvar about a homosexual director of adult movies, his transsexual sister, and their various liaisons. Carmen Maura and Eusebio Poncala star. **FF7**

Lawrence of Arabia (1962, C, 222m, G)
Peter O'Toole's stunning star debut as T.E. Lawrence, the Englishman who led Arab tribesmen against the Turks in the 1920s. With Omar Sharif, Alec Guinness, Anthony Quinn, Arthur Kennedy, Stanley Baker, and Jack Hawkins. Directed by David Lean. Now available in a newly restored, letterbox-format version. **CL2, CU10, DR45, DR50, DR63, XT1, XT6, XT10** *Highly Recommended*

Lean on Me (1989, C, 104m, PG-13)
Real-life story of New Jersey high school principal Joe Clark, who brought order to an inner-city school plagued by crime and dropouts. Morgan Freeman stars. **DR6, DR61**

Learning Tree, The (1969, C, 107m, PG)
Gordon Parks directed this version of his autobiographical novel about a young black boy growing up in 1920s Kansas. **DR14**

Left Hand of God, The (1955, C, 87m, NR)
A priest is caught in the political turbulence of post-World War II China. Humphrey Bogart, Gene Tierney, and Lee J. Cobb star. **CL20**

Left-Handed Gun, The (1958, B&W, 102m, NR)
Paul Newman plays Billy the Kid in this psychological study of the Kid's outlaw ways. Based on Gore Vidal's TV play. **DR28, WE2, WE4**

Legacy, The (1979, C, 100m, R)
Two Americans are kidnapped and taken to a British mansion where a secret cult prepares to deal with them. Katharine Ross and Sam Elliott star. **HO11**

Legal Eagles (1986, C, 116m, PG)
When an attorney is caught in a compromising situation with his female client who's suspected of murder, he calls on a female lawyer for help. Robert Redford, Debra Winger, and Daryl Hannah star in this comedy-mystery. **DR29, DR47, MY21**

Legend (1986, C, 89m, PG)
A young hermit living in a magical forest sets off to rescue a lovely maiden from the forces of evil. Tom Cruise stars in this lavishly produced adventure fantasy. Ridley Scott directed. **AC18, CU33, DR73, SF13, SF14**

Legend of Frenchie King, The (1971, C, 97m, NR)
Brigitte Bardot stars in a western comedy about female outlaws in New Mexico. Claudia Cardinale costars. Dubbed in English. **FF32**

Legend of Hell House, The (1973, C, 95m, PG)
Horror tale of researchers spending a week in a haunted house. Roddy McDowall and Pamela Franklin star; Richard Matheson wrote the screenplay. **HO1, HO3**

Legend of Lobo, The (1962, C, 67m, NR)
Family drama about a wild wolf from his days as a pup. Disney production features songs by the Sons of the Pioneers. **FA5**

Legend of Sleepy Hollow, The (1949, C, 49m, G)
Washington Irving's fantasy about Ichabod Crane and the Headless Horseman comes to life in this Disney animated feature. Narrated and sung by Bing Crosby. **FA2**

Legend of the Werewolf (1975, C, 87m, R)
A Parisian zoo worker has a hairy problem when the moon is full. Peter Cushing stars as the investigator on his trail. **HO4, HO33**

Lemon Drop Kid, The (1951, B&W, 91m, NR)
Bob Hope is in hock to a gangster and tries to use his prowess at the racetrack to make the payment. **CO40**

Lenny (1974, B&W, 112m, R)
Dustin Hoffman plays controversial comic Lenny Bruce, whose life was plagued by troubles with the law and drugs. Valerie Perrine costars; Bob Fosse directed. **DR4, DR30, MU28**

Lenny Bruce (1967, B&W, 60m, NR)
The only filmed performance of the controversial stand-up comic. **CU16** *Recommended*

Leonor (1975, C, 90m, NR)
Liv Ullmann stars in this strange drama about a woman who makes herself mistress to the Devil. **FF25**

Leopard Man, The (1943, B&W, 66m, NR)
Horror film about a small desert town terrorized by what it thinks is an escaped animal. Directed by Jacques Tourneur; produced by Val Lewton. **HO16, HO36, HO37**

Lepke (1975, C, 110m, R)
Tony Curtis plays real-life gangster Louis Lepke Buchalter, the head of Murder Inc., in this violent crime saga. **AC22**

Les Girls (1957, C, 114m, NR)
A star of a variety show (Gene Kelly) romances three dancing girls (Taina Elg, Kay Kendall, Mitzi Gaynor). Cole Porter score; Orry-Kelly won an Oscar for his costumes. George Cukor directed. **CL39, MU1, MU19**

Less Than Zero (1987, C, 98m, R)
A wealthy young crowd in Los Angeles hops from party to party and drug to drug. Adapted from the bestselling novel; Andrew McCarthy, Jami Gertz, and Robert Downey, Jr. star. **DR9**

Lesson in Love, A (1954, B&W, 95m, NR)
From director Ingmar Bergman, the story of a married couple's separate affairs. Gunnar Bjornstrand and Eva Dahlbeck star. **FF8**

Let It Be (1970, C, 80m, G)
Documentary chronicles the Beatles' recording one of their last albums. Some memorable musical moments and insight into why the band broke up. **MU11**

Let There Be Light (1945, B&W, 60m, NR)
Director John Huston's documentary about the psychological effects of World War II combat. **CU16, CL44**

Lethal Weapon (1987, C, 110m, R)
Mel Gibson and Danny Glover are cop partners on the trail of vicious drug smugglers. Gary Busey costars in this urban action thriller. **AC9, DR69**

Lethal Weapon 2 (1989, C, 113m, R)
More buddy-cop action with Mel Gibson and Danny Glover, with the latter marked for murder by South African government agents. **AC9, DR69**

Let's Dance (1950, C, 112m, NR)
Fred Astaire and Betty Hutton star in this musical tale of former dance partners fighting for custody of her young son. **MU18**

Let's Do It Again (1975, C, 112m, PG)
Sequel to *Uptown Saturday Night* has Sidney Poitier and pal Bill Cosby as wacky lodge brothers hoping to cash in on a "hypnotized" boxer (Jimmie Walker). **DR38**

Let's Get Harry (1986, C, 98m, R)
An American businessman is kidnapped by terrorists in South America, and a soldier of fortune leads his buddies on a

rescue mission. Robert Duvall heads the expedition; Gary Busey and Glenn Frey follow his orders. **AC20, DR37, MU12**

Let's Make Love (1960, C, 118m, NR)
Yves Montand plays a millionaire who falls for Marilyn Monroe in this show-biz saga. Bing Crosby, Milton Berle, and Gene Kelly have bit parts. George Cukor directed. **CL29, CL39, MU19, MU25**

Let's Spend the Night Together (1982, C, 94m, PG)
Concert film of the Rolling Stones' 1981 tour. **MU10**

Letter, The (1940, B&W, 95m, NR)
Bette Davis stars in the Somerset Maugham drama of a woman who claims self-defense in a twisted murder case. Directed by William Wyler. **CL5, CL21, CL38**

Letter From an Unknown Woman (1948, B&W, 90m, NR)
Joan Fontaine stars as a woman hopelessly in love with a dashing musician (Louis Jourdan). Directed with great style by Max Ophuls; written by Howard Koch. **CL4, CL6, CU20** *Recommended*

· **Letter to Brezhnev** (1985, C, 95m, NR)
Comedy about two Liverpool working-class girls who meet a pair of lonely Russian sailors, with love unexpectedly blossoming between one couple. Alexandra Pigg and Peter Firth star. **CO17**

Lianna (1983, C, 110m, R)
A married woman finds herself attracted to another woman in this drama from writer-director John Sayles. Linda Griffiths and Jane Hallaren star. **DR3**

Liberation of L. B. Jones, The (1970, C, 102m, R)
A hotly contested divorce case threatens to blow the lid off simmering race relations in a small Southern town. Lee J. Cobb stars in this drama from director William Wyler. **CL38, DR14**

Lt. Robin Crusoe, USN (1966, C, 110m, G)
Navy pilot Dick Van Dyke makes the most of his being stranded on a desert island in a family comedy from the Disney studios. **FA1**

Life and Death of Colonel Blimp, The (1943, C, 115m, NR)
Epic drama of British soldier through many campaigns and personal crises, starring Roger Livesey and Deborah Kerr (in four roles). Directed by Michael Powell. Original running time: 163m. **CU19**

Life and Times of Grizzly Adams, The (1976, C, 93m, G)
Family adventure about a fur trapper and his unlikely friendship with a bear. Dan Haggerty stars. **FA4**

Life and Times of Judge Roy Bean, The (1972, C, 124m, PG)
An offbeat western drama from director John Huston, about the famous hanging judge of Texas. Paul Newman heads the cast, which includes Jacqueline Bisset, Stacy Keach, and Ava Gardner. **CL44, DR28, WE16**

Life of Emile Zola, The (1937, B&W, 116m, NR)
Classic biography of French writer, highlighted by his role in the Dreyfus scandal. Paul Muni stars, with Oscar winner Joseph Schildkraut as Dreyfus. Film won Best Picture Oscar as well. **CL2, XT1, XT4**

Life of Oharu, The (1952, B&W, 146m, NR)
From Japan, the story of a woman banished because of her forbidden love for a samurai warrior (Toshiro Mifune). Kenji Mizoguchi directed. **FF4, FF28**

Life With Father (1947, C, 118m, NR)
Long-running Broadway comedy about colorful family headed by a strong patriarch, in turn-of-the-century New York City. William Powell, Irene Dunne, and Elizabeth Taylor star. **CL33**

Lifeboat (1944, B&W, 96m, NR)
The survivors of a German submarine attack struggle to survive in a small boat. Alfred Hitchcock thriller starring Tallulah Bankhead, Walter 'Slezak, and William Bendix. **MY22**

Lifeforce (1985, C, 100m, R)
Astronauts return to Earth as blood-sucking vampires in this horror-science fiction film from director Tobe Hooper. **HO5, HO40, SF20**

Lift, The (1985, C, 95m, R)
From Holland, a horror film about an elevator that begins attacking its passengers. **HO22**

Light at the Edge of the World (1971, C, 126m, PG)
Jules Verne saga of lighthouse keeper (Kirk Douglas) and pirate (Yul Brynner) battling for possession of an island and a lovely woman (Samantha Eggar). **SF27**

Light in the Forest, The (1958, C, 93m, NR)
Disney adventure of a white boy raised by Indians and returned to his original family. James MacArthur, Carol Lynley, and Fess Parker star. **FA1**

Light of Day (1987, C, 107m, PG-13)
A factory worker and his single-parent sister spend their evenings performing in a bar band in Cleveland. Michael J. Fox, Joan Jett, and Gena Rowlands star in this drama about a family in crisis. **DR8**

Lighthorsemen, The (1987, C, 111m, PG)
Australian adventure tale of a company of horse soldiers and their disastrous World War I campaign against the Turks. Directed by Simon Wincer. **AC2, FF5**

Lightning Over Water (1980, C, 91m, NR)
A heartfelt documentary portrait of American film director Nicholas Ray, by his German colleague Wim Wenders. Shot during the final days of Ray's life. **CU23, FF21**

Lightning: The White Stallion (1986, C, 93m, PG)
A horse trainer has his prize stallion stolen and recovers it with the help of two youngsters. Mickey Rooney stars in this family adventure. **FA1, FA4**

Lights of Old Santa Fe (1944, B&W, 79m NR)
A rodeo trick rider leaves the big time to help a struggling friend's show. Roy Rogers stars, with Dale Evans and Gabby Hayes. **WE23**

Lightship, The (1985, C, 89m, R)
A trio of crooks lay siege to a lightship in this offbeat thriller starring Robert Duvall and Klaus Maria Brandauer. **DR37**

Lili (1952, C, 81m, G)
Leslie Caron plays a teenaged orphan who joins a circus and helps a bitter puppeteer (Mel Ferrer) see the good things in life. The theme song, "Hi Lili, Hi Lo," helped the film score to win an Oscar. **MU1**

Lilies of the Field (1963, B&W, 93m, NR)
Sidney Poitier won an Oscar for his performance as a handyman who comes to the aid of a group of German nuns trying to build a chapel in the Arizona desert. **DR38, XT2**

Lilith (1964, B&W, 114m, NR)
Warren Beatty plays a naive young therapist who falls under the spell of one of his patients. Jean Seberg, Peter Fonda, and Gene Hackman costar. Directed by Robert Rossen. **DR34, DR39** *Recommended*

Limelight (1952, B&W, 120m, NR)
Charlie Chaplin's sentimental drama of a washed-up comedian who's given inspiration by a young ballerina (Claire Bloom). Buster Keaton appears as a colleague of Chaplin's in one unforgettable scene. **CO18, CO19**

Link (1986, C, 103m, R)
A crazed scientist and his lovely assistant are endangered species when his experimental chimps launch a revolt. Terence

Stamp and Elisabeth Shue star. **HO16, HO19, HO20**

Lion in Winter, The (1968, C, 134m, PG)
Katharine Hepburn is Eleanor of Aquitaine, Peter O'Toole is Henry II in this drama of familial and political intrigue in medieval England. Hepburn won her third Oscar for her performance. **CL16, DR5, DR45, XT3**

Lion, the Witch, and the Wardrobe, The (1983, C, 95m, NR)
When four children walk through a magic wardrobe closet, they're transported into a magical land and meet an evil witch and a kindly lion. An animated adventure based on C.S. Lewis's *Narnia* tales. **FA10**

Liquid Sky (1983, C, 112m, R)
Cult science fiction film about aliens who land in New York in the middle of the punk-downtown scene. Anne Carlisle plays a male and female role in this highly original film. **CU4, CU6, SF22, XT9** *Recommended*

List of Adrian Messenger, The (1963, B&W, 98m, NR)
Whodunit set on an Irish estate during hunting season, with guest stars in disguise as the suspects. George C. Scott plays detective; Kirk Doulgas, Frank Sinatra, Tony Curtis, and Burt Lancaster are the guest stars. Directed by John Huston. **CL44, DR41, MY16**

Lisztomania (1975, C, 105m, R)
A stylized, anything-goes biography of composer Franz Liszt, starring rock singer Roger Daltrey, directed by Ken Russell. Not for viewers with tender sensibilities. **CU31, MU5**

Little Big Man (1970, C, 150m, PG)
The tall tale of Jack Crabbe, a 130-year-old man who claims he was the only white to survive Custer's Last Stand. Dustin Hoffman, Faye Dunaway, and Chief Dan George head the cast of this epic. **DR30, DR35, WE1, WE2, WE8**

Little Boy Lost (1953, B&W, 95m, NR)
A journalist travels to post-World War II France to find his orphaned son. Bing Crosby stars. **MU25**

Little Caesar (1930, B&W, 80m, NR)
Edward G. Robinson plays Rico, the mob boss modeled on Al Capone, in this early gangster classic. **AC22, CL52** *Highly Recommended*

Little Colonel, The (1935, B&W, 80m, NR)
In the Reconstruction South, a little girl reunites her feuding mother and grandpa. Shirley Temple, Lionel Barrymore, and Bill Robinson star. **FA14**

Little Dorritt (1988, C, 360m, G)
Epic version of the Charles Dickens novel about the trials and tribulations of a young girl and her father. Divided into two films: "Nobody's Fault" (177m) and "Dorritt's Story" (183m). Derek Jacobi and Sarah Pickering star, with Alec Guinness. **CL1, DR23, DR63**

Little Drummer Girl, The (1984, C, 130m, R)
From John LeCarre's novel, the story of a British actress recruited by Israeli intelligence to trap a terrorist. Diane Keaton and Klaus Kinski star. **DR40, FF30, MY33** *Recommended*

Little Foxes, The (1941, B&W, 116m, NR)
Lillian Hellman drama about the collapse of a Southern family, starring Bette Davis in one of her showcase performances. Herbert Marshall and Teresa Wright co-star. Directed by William Wyler.**CL21, CL38**

Little Girl Who Lives Down the Lane, The (1976, C, 94m, PG)
Subtle horror mystery about a strange girl whose father has been missing for a long time and a menacing man with a special interest in her. Jodie Foster and Martin Sheen star. **HO13**

Little Gloria. . . Happy at Last (1982, C, 200m, NR)
True story of bitter custody fight over young Gloria Vanderbilt, with Bette Davis, Angela Lansbury, and Christopher Plummer. Originally made for TV. **CL21**

Little Lord Fauntleroy (1936, B&W, 98m, NR)
Freddie Bartholomew plays the young American who suddenly finds himself a British lord in this adaptation of the classic children's story. C. Aubrey Smith and Mickey Rooney costar. **FA3**

Little Lord Fauntleroy (1980, C, 100m, NR)
TV movie remake of the children's classic about an American lad in Britain. Ricky Schroder and Alec Guinness star. **FA3, DR63**

Little Mermaid, The (1984, C, 55m, NR)
A Faerie Tale Theatre presentation of the Hans Christian Andersen tale. A lovely sea creature (Pam Dawber) has to choose between her home in the ocean and life on land with a sailor (Treat Williams). **FA12**

Little Minister, The (1934, B&W, 110m, NR)
Katharine Hepburn plays a gypsy girl who falls in love with a Scottish minister. **CL16**

Little Miss Broadway (1938, B&W, 70m, NR)
Shirley Temple stars in a musical about a theatrical boarding house. George Murphy and Jimmy Durante are on hand, too. **FA14**

Little Miss Marker (1980, C, 103m, PG)
Comedy set in the 1930s about a little girl being left with a bookie as an IOU. Walter Matthau, Julie Andrews, Bob Newhart, and Sara Stimson star. **FA6**

Little Murders (1971, C, 110m, PG)
Dark comedy, written by cartoonist Jules Feiffer, about life in a New York City where random killings are the order of the day. Elliott Gould and Marcia Rodd star, with Vincent Gardenia, Elizabeth Wilson, Donald Sutherland, and Alan Arkin, who directed. **CO2, CO12, CU5**

Little Night Music, A (1978, C, 124m, PG)
Stephen Sondheim musical, based on Ingmar Bergman's comedy *Smiles of a Summer Night*, about summertime romance among the rich and beautiful people. Elizabeth Taylor and Diana Rigg star. Musical highlight: "Send in the Clowns." **CL33, MU2, MU17**

Little Nikita (1988, C, 98m, PG)
F.B.I. agent has the tough task of telling an American teen that his parents are Soviet agents. Sidney Poitier and River Phoenix star. **DR38**

Little Prince, The (1974, C, 88m, G)
Unusual musical based on children's book about a young boy and his friendship with an aviator. Richard Kiley, Bob Fosse, Gene Wilder, and Steven Warner star. Stanley Donen directed. **MU16, MU23, MU28**

Little Princess, The (1939, B&W#, C, 93m, NR)
Shirley Temple stars as a Victorian waif searching for her soldier father. Cesar Romero and Arthur Treacher costar. **FA14**

Little Red Riding Hood (1985, C, 60m, NR)
This Faerie Tale Theatre presentation features Mary Steenburgen as the unsuspecting girl and Malcolm McDowell as the evil wolf. **FA12**

Little Romance, A (1979, C, 108m, PG)
Laurence Olivier plays matchmaker in Paris to a young American girl (Diane Lane) and her new French boyfriend (Thelonius Bernard) **CL32, CO4, XT9**

Little Shop of Horrors, The (1960, B&W, 70m, NR)
Low-budget horror comedy (supposedly filmed in 3 days) about a man-eating plant and its nerdy keeper. Jack Nicholson has

a small part as a pain-loving dental patient. **CU4, DR24, HO24**

Little Shop of Horrors (1986, C, 88m, PG-13)
Musical version of the horror comedy about a man-eating plant named Audrey II. Rick Moranis and Steve Martin star. Bill Murray, John Candy, and Jim Belushi make brief appearances. **CO14, CO33, MU8, MU14, MU16**

Little Treasure (1985, C, 95m, R)
An American stripper journeys to Mexico to visit her father but winds up searching for treasure with an amiable adventurer. Margot Kidder, Burt Lancaster, and Ted Danson are the stars. **DR41**

Little Women (1933, B&W, 115m, NR)
Louisa May Alcott's classic novel of a family full of varied sisters, starring Katharine Hepburn and Joan Bennett. Directed by George Cukor. **CL1, CL16, CL39**

Little Women (1949, C, 121m, NR)
All-star MGM cast is featured in this version of Louisa May Alcott's book, with June Allyson, Margaret O'Brien, Elizabeth Taylor, and Peter Lawford leading the way. **CL1, CL33**

Littlest Horse Thieves, The (1977, C, 104m, G)
Three children attempt to save a herd of abused ponies who work in the mines. Disney drama set in turn-of-the-century England. **FA1**

Littlest Outlaw, The (1955, C, 75m, NR)
A Mexican boy, fearful that a horse will be destroyed, runs away with it. Disney family drama. **FA1**

Littlest Rebel, The (1935, B&W, 70m, NR)
A little girl saves her father from prison during the Civil War by pleading directly to President Lincoln. Shirley Temple stars; Bill Robinson adds a few dance steps. **FA14**

Live a Little, Love a Little (1968, C, 90m, NR)
Elvis Presley plays a photographer who moonlights at a second job—and manages to fit in a little singin' as well. Michele Carey and Rudy Vallee costar. **MU22**

Live and Let Die (1973, C, 121m, PG)
Roger Moore's debut as James Bond has 007 chasing down a madman who's distributing drugs as part of his scheme to take over the world. Yaphet Kotto costars. **AC35**

Lives of a Bengal Lancer, The (1935, B&W, 109m, NR)
Gary Cooper heads the cast of this classic adventure tale about a British regiment on patrol in India. **AC13, CL26, FA4**

Living Daylights, The (1987, C, 130m, PG)
Timothy Dalton takes over the James Bond role in this story of a rogue Soviet general (Jeroen Krabbe) and a crooked international arms dealer (Joe Don Baker). Maryam D'Abo and John Rhys-Davies costar. **AC35**

Living Desert, The (1953, C, 73m, G)
Oscar-winning documentary about flora and fauna in the American desert, from the Disney studios. **FA1**

Living Free (1972, C, 91m, G)
Sequel to *Born Free* features more action with Elsa and her cubs in the African wilderness. Susan Hampshire and Nigel Davenport star. **FA5**

Local Hero (1983, C, 111m, PG)
Charming, original comedy about an American oil company trying to buy a Scottish fishing village as a site for a refinery. Peter Riegert and Burt Lancaster star; Bill Forsyth directed. Music by Mark Knopfler. **CO2, CO17, CU36, DR41**
Highly Recommended

Lodger, The (1926, B&W, 125m, NR)
Silent thriller from Alfred Hitchcock, his first foray into suspense, about a mysterious man suspected of committing a se-

ries of murders in London. Ivor Novello stars. **MY17, MY22**

Logan's Run (1976, C, 120m, PG)
Science fiction adventure about a society of unlimited pleasures but extermination at the age of 30, and one man's attempt to escape that fate. Michael York and Jenny Agutter star. The special effects won an Oscar. **SF8, SF15**

Lola (1969, C, 88m, PG)
A teenager (Susan George) and a middle-aged writer (Charles Bronson) fall in love. Also known as *Twinky*. **AC29**

Lola Montes (1955, C, 110m, PG-13)
The story of a famed circus performer and her many affairs with European nobility. A cult favorite, directed by Max Ophuls. **CL14, CU20**

Lolita (1962, B&W, 152m, NR)
Dark comedy about a middle-aged man's obsession with a sexy teenager. James Mason, Sue Lyon, Peter Sellers, and Shelley Winters star; Stanely Kubrick directed. Vladimir Nabokov adapted his novel. **CO12, CO26, DR19, DR53** *Recommended*

Lone Wolf McQuade (1983, C, 107m, PG)
Chuck Norris, as a Texas Ranger, and David Carradine, as a drug lord, square off in this modern-day western with plenty of martial arts thrown in. **AC32**

Lonely Are the Brave (1962, B&W, 107m, NR)
In the contemporary West, a rebellious cowboy leads a posse on a wild chase. Kirk Douglas and Walter Matthau star. **WE13** *Recommended*

Lonely Guy, The (1983, C, 91m, R)
When Steve Martin's girl friend walks out on him, he joins the official ranks of America's lonely guys in this contemporary comedy. Charles Grodin costars. **CO33**

Lonely Hearts (1981, C, 95m, R)
A romantic drama from Australia about the unlikely pairing of a piano tuner and an awkwardly shy office worker. Wendy Hughes and Norman Kaye star. **FF5**

Lonely Lady, The (1983, C, 92m, R)
A screenwriter claws (and sleeps) her way to the top of the Hollywood heap. This adaptation of the Harold Robbins novel stars Pia Zadora and virtually defines the word "trash." **CU2**

Lonelyhearts (1958, B&W, 101m, NR)
A reporter takes on his newspaper's advice to the lovelorn column and begins to take his readers' problems to heart. Montgomery Clift stars in this version of Nathanael West's novel, with Robert Ryan, Myrna Loy, and Maureen Stapleton. **CL46, DR19**

Long, Dark Hall, The (1951, B&W, 96m, NR)
Rex Harrison is accused of murder, but his wife (Lilli Palmer) stands by his claims of innocence. **MY19**

Long Day's Journey Into Night (1962, B&W, 170m, NR)
Eugene O'Neill's famous autobiographical play about a family in turmoil, starring Katharine Hepburn, Ralph Richardson, Jason Robards, and Dean Stockwell. Directed by Sidney Lumet. **CL16, DR8, DR20, DR58** *Highly Recommended*

Long Gone (1987, C, 113m, NR)
Comedy-drama of life in baseball's minor leagues, starring William Petersen and Virginia Madsen. Originally made for cable TV. **DR22**

Long Good Friday, The (1980, C, 114m, R)
A British gangster saga, with Bob Hoskins superb as a London crime boss whose empire suddenly begins to crumble. Helen Mirren costars. **AC22, DR23, XT9** *Highly Recommended*

Long Riders, The (1980, C, 100m, R)
The story of the James Brothers and their friends and enemies, with four real-life sets of brothers (Carradine, Quaid, Keach, and Guest) starring. Directed by Walter Hill; music by Ry Cooder. **CU27, WE2, WE4, XT8**

Long Voyage Home, The (1940, B&W, 105m, NR)
Drama of Swedish seamen, starring John Wayne, Thomas Mitchell, and Barry Fitzgerald. Adapted from Eugene O'Neill plays; directed by John Ford. **CL17, CL34**

Longest Day, The (1962, B&W, 180m, NR)
Mammoth recreation of the Normandy Invasion, featuring an all-star, nearly all-male cast, including John Wayne, Henry Fonda, Richard Burton, Sean Connery, and many more. **AC1, AC36, CL17, CL24** *Recommended*

Longest Yard, The (1974, C, 123m, R)
Prison comedy-drama, with an ex-pro football star (Burt Reynolds) leading the cons in a rousing game against the vicious guards and their tyrannical warden. Eddie Albert is the warden; among the players are Michael Conrad, Ed Lauter, and Richard Kiel. **AC37, CO36, DR18**

Longshot, The (1985, C, 110m, PG)
Tim Conway—Harvey Korman comedy set at a racetrack, directed by Paul Bartel. **CU42**

Look Back in Anger (1958, B&W, 99m, NR)
Classic contemporary British drama of angry young man (Richard Burton) lashing out at society for all its injustices. Mary Ure and Claire Bloom costar; Tony Richardson directed on location in London. **DR23, XT9** *Recommended*

Looker (1981, C, 94m, PG)
A plastic surgeon uncovers a corporate plot to reproduce female models by computer image and eliminate the real people. Albert Finney, James Coburn, and Susan Dey star in this science fiction mystery. **SF5**

Looking for Mr. Goodbar (1977, C, 135m, R)
Schoolteacher Diane Keaton prowls singles bars at night, with disastrous consequences. Drama based on a true story costars Richard Gere and Tom Berenger. **DR3, DR7, DR40**

Looking Glass War, The (1970, C, 108m, PG)
John LeCarre thriller about a photographer out to get picture of a secret rocket in East Berlin. Christopher Jones, Ralph Richardson, and Anthony Hopkins star. **MY33**

Looney, Looney, Looney Bugs Bunny Movie, The (1981, C, 79m, G)
Bugs and all his pals, from Yosemite Sam to Daffy Duck and Porky Pig, are on hand for this collection of Warner Bros. cartoons. **FA11**

Loot . . . Give Me Money, Honey! (1972, C, 101m, PG)
Dark comedy, based on Joe Orton play, about a pair of bank robbers who hide their stash in a coffin. Lee Remick and Richard Attenborough star. **CO12, CO17**

Lord Jim (1965, C, 154m, NR)
Peter O'Toole stars in Joseph Conrad's tale of a British sailor living with guilt over a single act of cowardice. James Mason, Curt Jurgens, and Eli Wallach costar. **DR45**

Lord of the Flies (1963, B&W, 90m, NR)
After an atomic holocaust, a planeload of young boys escaping the devastation crashes on a jungle island. This unusual story of survival was adapted from William Golding's bestselling novel. **DR19, SF12**

Lord of the Rings (1978, C, 133m, PG)
The first of the famous J.R.R. Tolkien books about the fantastic characters of Middle Earth to be filmed. An animated feature for the entire family. **FA8, FA10, SF13**

Lords of Flatbush, The (1974, C, 88m, PG)
Comedy about a gang of fun-loving guys living in Brooklyn in the 1950s. Sylvester Stallone, Henry Winkler, and Perry King star. **AC31**

Losin' It (1983, C, 104m, R)
A trio of teens make their way to Tijuana for a wild weekend. Tom Cruise, Jackie Earle Haley, and John Stockwell star, with Shelley Long. **DR73**

Lost Angels (1989, C, 116m, R)
An institution for the children of wealth with emotional problems is the setting for this drama of life in Los Angeles, starring Adam Horovitz (of the rap group The Beastie Boys) and Donald Sutherland. **DR9, MU12**

Lost Boys, The (1987, C, 97m, R)
Horror story of two teenaged brothers up against a gang of teen vampires in a small town. Kiefer Sutherland, Corey Haim, and Jason Patric star. **HO5, HO13**

Lost Command (1966, C, 130m, NR)
Combat action between French and Algerian forces, starring Anthony Quinn, Alain Delon, George Segal, and Claudia Cardinale. **AC6**

Lost Honor of Katharina Blum, The (1975, C, 97m, R)
A political thriller from Germany about a woman who's persecuted by officials after she spends the night with a suspected terrorist. Directed by Volker Schlöndorff. **FF3**

Lost Horizon (1937, B&W, 132m, G)
Director Frank Capra's classic fable about a group of stranded travelers who stumble onto the kingdom of Shangri-la. Ronald Colman, Jane Wyatt, Thomas Mitchell, and Sam Jaffe star. The video version restores about 15 minutes of footage from the film's original release. **CL40, CU10, SF2**

Lost in America (1985, C, 91m, R)
Albert Brooks directed and stars in this brilliant satire about a middle-class cou-
ple who decide to quit their jobs and take to the great American road. Julie Hagerty costars. **CO2** *Highly Recommended*

Lost in the Stars (1974, C, 114m, NR)
Musical based on South African novel *Cry, the Beloved Country,* about a minister's trials and tribulations under apartheid. Brock Peters heads the all-black cast. **MU13**

Lost Patrol, The (1934, B&W, 74m, NR)
A British army patrol is stranded in the African desert, and Arab tribesmen pick them off one by one. Classic adventure directed by John Ford, starring Victor McLaglen and Boris Karloff. **AC13, CL34, HO27** *Recommended*

Lost Squadron, The (1932, B&W, 79m, NR)
Hollywood story of former World War I aces working as stunt pilots. Richard Dix stars, with Mary Astor, Joel McCrea, and Erich Von Stroheim as an egomaniacal director. **CL7, CL53**

Lost Weekend, The (1945, B&W, 101m, NR)
Ray Milland plays an alcoholic who lives only for his next drink in this drama. Oscar winner for Best Picture, Actor, and Director (Billy Wilder). **CL8, CL37, XT1, XT2, XT6**

Lost World, The (1925, B&W, 77m, NR)
Classic silent adventure about a modern expedition stumbling onto a prehistoric region. One of the first films to make extensive use of special effects techniques. **AC13, SF4, SF16**

Lots of Luck (1985, C, 88m, NR)
An unlucky family find their fortunes reversed when they win a lottery. Unfortunately, they also lose all claims to privacy. This Disney comedy stars Martin Mull, Annette Funicello, and Fred Willard. Originally made for cable TV. **FA1**

Louisiana Story (1948, B&W, 79m, NR)
Classic documentary, directed by Robert Flaherty, centering on the arrival of an

oil-drilling operation in the Louisiana bayou. Made on commission from Standard Oil Company. Music by Virgil Thomson. **CU16** *Recommended*

Love Among the Ruins (1975, C, 100m, NR)
An aging actress hires a barrister to defend her, unaware that the two were one time lovers. Katharine Hepburn and Lawrence Olivier star; George Cukor directed. Originally made for TV. **CL17, CL32, CL39** *Recommended*

Love and Anarchy (1973, C, 108m, R)
From Italian director Lina Wertmüller, a drama of an Italian peasant's plan to assassinate Mussolini. Giancarlo Giannini stars. **FF2**

Love and Bullets (1979, C, 95m, PG)
Charles Bronson plays an F.B.I. agent assigned to retrieve a mobster's girl friend from Switzerland; instead, he falls in love with her. **AC29**

Love and Death (1975, C, 82m, PG)
Woody Allen spoofs foreign movies, Russian literature, Napoleon, and more. Diane Keaton and Alfred Lutter costar. **CO27, DR40**

Love at First Bite (1979, C, 96m, PG)
Comic twist on the Dracula story has George Hamilton as a lovesick vampire, traveling to New York to meet (and nip on) the girl of his dreams. **CO7, HO5, HO24**

Love Bug, The (1968, C, 108m, G)
Herbie is a Volkswagen with a mind of his own in this popular Disney comedy that spun off many sequels. Dean Jones and Michelle Lee costar. **FA1**

Love From a Stranger (1947, B&W, 81m, NR)
Agatha Christie story of a woman (Sylvia Sidney) who learns that her husband is a killer. John Hodiak and John Howard costar. **MY23**

Love Happy (1949, B&W, 91m, NR)
Late Marx Brothers film about putting on a show. Marilyn Monroe has a small part. **CL29, CO21**

Love in the Afternoon (1957, B&W, 130m, NR)
Romance blossoms between Gary Cooper and Audrey Hepburn in this comedy set in Paris. Billy Wilder directed. **CL26, CL30, CL37**

Love in the City (1953, B&W, 90m, NR)
Six Italian directors demonstrate different aspects of love in Rome. Contributors include Federico Fellini and Michelangelo Antonioni. **FF10, FF17, XT9**

Love Is a Many Splendored Thing (1955, C, 102m, NR)
Glossy romantic drama, with a Eurasian woman (Jennifer Jones) and American reporter (William Holden) learning the meaning of the title. Drama set in Hong Kong during the Korean War. **CL4, CL51**

Love Me or Leave Me (1955, C, 122M, NR)
Musical drama about real life singer Ruth Etting and her affair with a domineering gangster. Doris Day and James Cagney star. **CL22, MU5**

Love Me Tender (1956, B&W, 89m, NR)
Elvis Presley made his film debut in this Civil War western about family conflicts. **MU22, WE7**

Love on the Run (1979, C, 93m, PG)
The fifth installment in French director François Truffaut's series of films about Antoine Doinel, starring Jean-Pierre Léaud. **FF13**

Love Songs (1986, C, 108m, NR)
A woman is deserted by her husband and is uncertain of her new-found freedom. Drama from France, starring Catherine Deneuve. **FF27**

Love Story (1970, C, 99m, PG)
The contemporary classic about a Harvard student (Ryan O'Neal) and his short-lived marriage to a working-class girl (Ali MacGraw). **DR2**

Love With the Proper Stranger (1963, B&W, 100m, NR)
New York is the setting for this romance between a jazz musician (Steve McQueen) and working girl (Natalie Wood). **AC28, DR1, XT9**

Lovers, The (1959, B&W, 90m, NR)
Jeanne Moreau plays a bored wife who finds true love with an overnight guest and runs away with him. Louis Malle directed. **FF26**

Lovers and Liars (1979, C, 96m, R)
Marcello Mastroianni and Goldie Hawn are the frantic lovers in this dark comedy made in Italy. **CO30, FF2, FF24**

Lovers and Other Strangers (1970, C, 106m, PG)
Comedy centering around the wedding of a young couple, with the impending ceremony bringing out the best—and worst—in both families. Michael Brandon, Bonnie Bedelia, Bea Arthur, Richard Castellano, and Gig Young star. Diane Keaton's film debut. **DR40**

Loves of a Blonde (1965, B&W, 88m, NR)
Boy meets girl, Czech style, in this poignant drama from director Milos Forman. **DR57, FF7**

Lovesick (1983, C, 95m, PG)
Psychiatrist falls in love with his own patient and calls on Sigmund Freud for advice. Dudley Moore, Elizabeth McGovern, and Alec Guinness star in this romantic comedy. **CO31, DR63**

Loving Couples (1980, C, 97m, PG)
Mate-switching comedy starring Shirley MacLaine, James Coburn, Susan Sarandon, and Stephen Collins. **DR42**

Loving You (1957, C, 101m, NR)
Elvis Presley's second film finds him playing a gas jockey whose singing doesn't go unnoticed by a talent scout (Lizabeth Scott). **MU22**

Lower Depths, The (1957, B&W, 125m, NR)
Japanese version of the famed Maxim Gorky play, directed by Akira Kurosawa. Toshiro Mifune plays a thief whose life is changed by an itinerant priest. **FF9, FF28**

Lucas (1986, C, 100m, PG-13)
A sixteen-year-old boy tries out for the school football team, despite his lack of size, to impress his first love. Corey Haim, Charlie Sheen, and Keri Green star in this family drama. **DR9, FA7**

Lucky Luciano (1974, C, 110m, R)
Drama depicting the final years of the deported crime kingpin, starring Gian-Maria Volonte, Rod Steiger, and Edmond O'Brien. **AC22**

Lulu in Berlin (1985, C/B&W, 50m, NR)
Documentary portrait of actress Louise Brooks, featuring a rare interview plus generous clips from *Pandora's Box, Diary of a Lost Girl,* and her other films. Directed by Richard Leacock and Susan Woll. **CU16** *Recommended*

Lumiere (1976, C, 95m, R)
French actress Jeanne Moreau directed and stars in this drama about four women and their friendships. **FF1, FF26**

Lunatics and Lovers (1975, C, 93m, PG)
Italian comedy about a man with an imaginary wife. Marcello Mastroianni stars, with Claudia Mori. **FF24**

Lust for a Vampire (1971, C, 95m, R)
An all-girls' boarding school is really a haven for vampires in this sexy horror tale. **HO5, HO25, HO26**

Lust for Life (1956, C, 122m, NR)
Biography of tormented painter Vincent Van Gogh (Kirk Douglas), directed by Vincente Minnelli, with an Oscar-winning performance by Anthony Quinn as Paul Gauguin. Outstanding color photography. **CL2, CL9, MU24, XT4**

Lust in the Dust (1985, C, 85m, R)
Spoof of westerns has Divine and Lainie Kazan playing saloon singers with different parts of a treasure map tattooed on their posteriors. Tab Hunter costars. **CO7, CU42**

Lusty Men, The (1952, B&W, 113m, NR)
Susan Hayward, Robert Mitchum, and Arthur Kennedy star in this contemporary western drama about the men who tour the rodeo circuit. Directed by Nicholas Ray. **CU23, WE13**

Luv (1967, C, 95m, NR)
In this comedy, Jack Lemmon plays a would-be suicide who is "saved" by a pal (Peter Falk) who persuades him to take his wife (Elaine May) off his hands. **DR64**

M (1931, B&W, 99m, NR)
Classic German drama about a child molester (Peter Lorre) who's hunted down by criminal gangs. Directed by Fritz Lang. **CL43, FF3, HO1, MY17** *Highly Recommended*

M*A*S*H (1970, C, 116m, R)
Uproarious military comedy about a trio of fun-loving surgeons and their operating procedures during the Korean War. Donald Sutherland, Elliott Gould, Tom Skerritt, and Robert Duvall star; Robert Altman directed. **AC3, CO6, CO12, CO38, CU25, DR37** *Highly Recommended*

MUSE Concert: No Nukes, The (1980, C, 103m, NR)
Concert film, shot at benefit rally opposing nuclear power, includes performances by Bruce Springsteen, James Taylor, Carly Simon, Jackson Browne, and Crosby, Stills & Nash. Also known as *No Nukes*. **MU10**

Macabre Serenade (1969, C, 89m, NR)
Boris Karloff stars in this horror film, one of his last, about a wicked toymaker whose creations are deadly weapons. **HO27**

Macao (1952, B&W, 80m, NR)
Robert Mitchum and Jane Russell star in an adventure yarn set in the exotic title port. Josef von Sternberg directed. **CL56**

Macaroni (1985, C, 104m, PG)
Marcello Mastroianni and Jack Lemmon are the stars of this comedy about an American returning to the Italian village where he served in World War II. **CO3, DR64, FF2, FF24**

MacArthur (1977, C, 130m, PG)
Gregory Peck plays the fabled general who led the U.S. to victories in World War II but clashed with President Truman over how to wage the Korean War. **DR4**

Macbeth (1948, B&W, 111m, NR)
Orson Welles directed and stars in Shakespeare's play of a suspicious Scottish lord and his scheming wife. **CL1, CL41**

Macbeth (1971, C, 140m, R)
Director Roman Polanski's version of the Shakespeare play of political intrigue in Scotland. Jon Finch and Francesca Annis star. **CL1, DR54**

McCabe and Mrs. Miller (1971, C, 121m, R)
Warren Beatty is a gambler, Julie Christie a frontier madam in this low-key but richly textured western set in the Pacific Northwest. With Rene Auberjonois, Keith Carradine, Bert Remsen, Shelley Duvall, Michael Murphy, and Hugh Millais. Directed by Robert Altman; songs by Leonard Cohen. **CU25, DR34, WE9, WE11, WE12, WE16** *Highly Recommended*

Macho Callahan (1970, C, 99m, R)
David Janssen plays a prison escapee in a Civil War western about revenge. **WE6, WE7**

Mack, The (1973, C, 110m, R)
An Oakland pimp just released from prison finds that his old territory has been taken over. Urban action starring Max Julien, Richard Pryor, and Roger E. Mosley. **AC8, CO29**

Mackenna's Gold (1969, C, 128m, PG)
Western saga of the search for a lost canyon filled with gold, starring Gregory Peck, Omar Sharif, Telly Savalas, Edward G. Robinson. **WE1**

Mackintosh Man, The (1973, C, 105m, PG)
Espionage thriller about the elimination of a double agent, starring Paul Newman and James Mason, directed by John Huston. **CL44, DR28, MY6**

McQ (1974, C, 116m, PG)
John Wayne takes to the streets of Seattle as a veteran cop out to avenge the murder of his partner. **CL17**

McVicar (1980, C, 111m, R)
True-life story of England's most dangerous criminal and his escape from prison. Roger Daltrey stars. **MU12**

Mad Dog Morgan (1976, C, 102m, R)
Fact-based story of a 19th-century outlaw who terrorized the Australian countryside and outwitted the law, starring Dennis Hopper. **CU46, FF5, WE4**

Mad Max (1979, C, 93m, R)
In the near future, a gang of cyclists rule the outback roads of Australia, and only a fearless cop can stop them. Mel Gibson stars; George Miller directed this non-stop action adventure. **AC10, AC25, CU7, FF5, DR69** *Highly Recommended*

Mad Max Beyond Thunderdome (1985, C, 106m, PG-13)
In the third Mad Max adventure, Mel Gibson squares off against Tina Turner and her mangy minions in a desert battle to the death. **AC10, AC24, AC25, DR69, FF5, MU12**

Mad Miss Manton, The (1938, B&W, 80m, NR)
A mystery comedy, with socialite Barbara Stanwyck and her society pals involved. Henry Fonda costars. **CL24, CL45, MY21**

Mad Monster Party? (1967, C, 94m, NR)
Animated children's feature, with Frankenstein announcing his retirement at a gathering of famous monsters. Features the voice of Boris Karloff. **FA10, HO27**

Madame Bovary (1949, B&W, 115m, NR)
The Flaubert story of a woman's sacrifice for her husband, lushly told by director Vincente Minnelli. Jennifer Jones and James Mason star. **CL1, CL5, MU24**

Madame Rosa (1977, C, 105m, NR)
Oscar-winning French drama of a madam (Simone Signoret) who shelters the children of prostitutes. **FF1, XT7**

Madame Sin (1971, C, 73m, NR)
Bette Davis stars as an evil foreign agent out to make trouble for the U.S. Navy. Robert Wagner costars. Originally made for TV. **CL21**

Madame Sousatzka (1988, C, 121m, PG-13)
Shirley MacLaine plays an eccentric Russian piano teacher in this drama, with Navin Chowdhry, Twiggy, and Peggy Ashcroft. **DR42**

Madame X (1966, C, 100m, NR)
The classic soap story about a woman accused of murder, defended by a man who has no idea she is really his mother. Lana Turner stars. **CL5, CL6, DR2**

Made for Each Other (1939, B&W, 93m, NR)
Young marrieds James Stewart and Carole Lombard have their ups and downs, mainly the latter, in this classic melodrama. **CL6, CL25, CL48**

Made in Heaven (1987, C, 103m, PG)
Two souls meet in heaven and begin a romance that is interrupted when one of them is sent down to earth. Timothy Hutton and Kelly McGillis star in this romantic drama from director Alan Rudolph. Debra Winger has a small role. **CU26, DR1, DR47**

Mademoiselle Striptease (1957, B&W, 99m, NR)
Brigitte Bardot stars in this caper comedy about the theft of a rare art book. Also known as *Please! Mr. Balzac*. **FF32**

Madigan (1968, C, 101m, NR)
A police detective (Richard Widmark) and his commissioner boss (Henry Fonda) disagree on how to keep the peace in New York. **AC9, CL24** *Recommended*

Madigan's Millions (1967, C, 86m, NR)
Comedy about an incompetent U.S. Treasury agent sent to Italy to recover stolen funds belonging to a late gangster. Dustin Hoffman stars; made before *The Graduate* but released only after its success. **DR29**

Madman (1979, C, 92m, PG)
A Russian Jew survives years of forced confinement in an asylum and swears revenge. Sigourney Weaver, Michael Beck, and F. Murray Abraham star. **DR76**

Maedchen in Uniform (1931, B&W, 90m, NR)
Once considered daring, this German drama takes place in an oppressive girls' school, where one student and her teacher form a lesbian relationship. Dorothea Wieck and Hertha Thiele star; Leontine Sagan directed. **FF3**

Magic (1978, C, 106m, R)
A high-strung ventriloquist lets his dummy take over his life. Anthony Hopkins and Ann-Margret star. **HO8, HO19**

Magic Christian, The (1970, C, 93m, PG)
Far-out Terry Southern comedy about the world's wealthiest man testing to see just what people will do for money. Peter Sellers and Ringo Starr lead the cast, which also includes Graham Chapman, John Cleese, Christopher Lee, and Richard Attenborough. **CO12, CO15, CO17, CO26**

Magic Flute, The (1974, C, 134m, G)
A change of pace from director Ingmar Bergman: a delightful screen version of Mozart's classic opera. **FF8**

Magic of Lassie, The (1978, C, 100m, G)
Remake of *Lassie Come Home*, with the popular collie the object of a custody battle. James Stewart stars—and even sings, too. **CL25, FA5**

Magic Sword, The (1962, C, 80m, NR)
Adventure film about a young knight's quest to rescue a princess from an evil sorcerer. Basil Rathbone stars. **AC18**

Magical Mystery Tour (1967, C, 60m, NR)
The Beatles' legendary "home movie," originally made for TV, is a loosely connected series of skits incorporating songs from their album of the same name. A midnight movie favorite. **CU1, MU9**

Magician, The (1959, B&W, 102m, NR)
A magician (Max von Sydow) has more than simple tricks up his sleeve in this somber drama from director Ingmar Bergman. **FF8**

Magnificent Ambersons, The (1942, B&W, 88m, NR)
Orson Welles' second film as a director (he narrates but does not appear on screen) is a rich portrait of a turn-of-the-century Midwest family resisting the modern era. Tim Holt, Joseph Cottten, and Agnes Moorehead star. **CL14, CL41** *Recommended*

Magnificent Matador, The (1955, C, 94m, NR)
An aging bullfighter grooms his young protege for a future in the bull ring. Anothy Quinn stars. Directed by Budd Boetticher. **WE28**

Magnificent Obsession (1954, C, 108m, NR)
A playboy carelessly blinds a woman in an auto accident and decides to become a surgeon to restore her sight. Rock Hudson and Jane Wyman star in this tearjerker from director Douglas Sirk. **CL6, CU24**

Magnificent Seven, The (1960, C, 126m, NR)
Seven cowboys assemble to help a Mexican village besieged by bandits. Yul Brynner heads the cast of future stars, including Steve McQueen, Charles Bronson, Robert Vaughn, and James Coburn. A remake of the Japanese classic, *The Seven Samurai*. **AC28, AC29, CU17, CU18, FF36, WE1** *Recommended*

Magnifique, Le (1976, C, 84m, NR)
A novelist falls in love with a young student, who admires one of his super hero creations. Jean-Paul Belmondo and Jacqueline Bissett star in this French comedy. **FF33**

Magnum Force (1973, C, 124m, R)
The second Dirty Harry adventure, with Clint Eastwood hunting down a band of rogue cops trying to dispense justice their own way. **AC9, AC27**

Mahler (1974, C, 115m, PG)
Director Ken Russell's dramatic portrait of the great composer: his torments, his relationship with his lovely wife, and his triumphs. Robert Powell stars. **CU31, MU5**

Mahogany (1975, C, 109m, PG)
Diana Ross plays a fashion designer with love life problems in this soap opera costarring Billy Dee Williams and Anthony Perkins. **DR14**

Main Event, The (1979, C, 112m, PG)
Barbra Streisand comedy has her playing a business executive who decides to manage a luckless prizefighter (Ryan O'Neal). Patti D'Arbanville costars. **MU27**

Major Dundee (1965, C, 124m, NR)
Civil War western about a ragged band of Confederate soldiers at war with the Apaches and French troops. Charlton Heston and Richard Harris star, with Jim Hutton, James Coburn, Warren Oates, Ben Johnson, and Slim Pickens. Sam Peckinpah directed. **CU48, WE7, WE19**

Major League (1989, C, 107m, R)
The new owner of the Cleveland Indians baseball team wants to move the franchise to Miami, so she assembles a ragtag collection to ensure that attendance figures will justify the move. The plan backfires when the misfits are inspired by a flaky pitcher (Charlie Sheen) and veteran catcher (Tom Berenger). David S. Ward wrote and directed this comedy. **CO36**

Make Mine Mink (1960, B&W, 80m, NR)
Terry-Thomas heads a gang of fur thieves in this British comedy. Original running time: 100m. **CO17**

Making Contact (1985, C, 80m, PG)
After his father's death, a nine-year-old boy finds he has new powers which he uses to thwart demons from another dimension. **SF13**

Making Love (1982, C, 113m, R)
A married doctor discovers his true sexual identity when he is attracted to one of his male patients. Michael Ontkean, Harry Hamlin, and Kate Jackson star. **DR3**

Making Mr. Right (1987, C, 100m, PG-13)
Comedy about a hip public relations expert (Ann Magnusson) hired to "sell" a mandroid astronaut to the public. John Malkovich plays the mandroid and his scientist creator. Directed by Susan Seidelman. **CO2** *Recommended*

Malcolm (1986, C, 96, PG-13)
A kooky inventor teams up with a larcenous couple to pull off a heist in this Australian comedy. **CO12, FF5, MY34**

Malice in Wonderland (1985, C, 100m, NR)
Elizabeth Taylor and Jane Alexander play Louella Parsons and Hedda Hopper, the feuding gossip columnists of 30s and 40s Hollywood. Originally made for TV. **CL33**

Malicious (1973, C, 97m, R)
Laura Antonelli plays a lusty housekeeper who's the love object of both a

father and his teenaged son in this Italian comedy. **FF2**

Malone (1987, C, 92m, R)
An ex-C.I.A. agent blows into a small town Western town, discovers it's dominated by a rich racist and his hate organization. Burt Reynolds and Cliff Robertson star. **AC37**

Malta Story, The (1953, B&W, 98m, NR)
World War II action with British air forces, starring Alec Guinness and Jack Hawkins. **AC1, DR63**

Maltese Falcon, The (1941, B&W, 100m, NR)
Classic detective story of Sam Spade (Humphrey Bogart) and "the stuff that dreams are made of"—the statue of a black bird. Sydney Greenstreet, Mary Astor, and Peter Lorre costar; written and directed by John Huston. **CL20, CL44, MY1, MY28** *Highly Recommended*

Mame (1974, C, 131m, PG)
Broadway musical version of the *Auntie Mame* tale of a grande dame taking in her impressionable nephew. Lucille Ball and Robert Preston star. **MU2, MU14**

Man and a Woman, A (1966, C, 102m, NR)
Romantic drama about a widow and widower finding that love is even better the second time around. Anouk Aimee and Jean-Louis Trintignant star. Oscar winner for Best Foreign Language Film. **FF1, XT7**

Man and a Woman: Twenty Years Later, A (1986, C, 112m, PG)
Sequel to the popular romantic drama, with the same stars (Anouk Aimee and Jean-Louis Trintignant) continuing their love affair. **FF1**

Man Betrayed, A *see* Wheel of Fortune

Man Called Horse, A (1970, C, 114m, PG)
Richard Harris as an English aristocrat captured by Indians and initiated into their tribal ways. Followed by two sequels: *Return of . . and Triumphs of . . .* **WE8**

Man Facing Southeast (1986, C, 105m, R)
From Argentina, a science fiction drama about a man who mysteriously appears in a mental hospital, claiming to be an alien. **FF6, SF19**

Man for all Seasons, A (1966, C, 120m, NR)
Paul Scofield plays Thomas More, the cleric who defied Henry VIII at the risk of execution. Robert Shaw, Wendy Hiller, Vanessa Redgrave, and Orson Welles costar in this Oscar winner for Best Picture, Actor, and Director (Fred Zinnemann). **CL41, CL57, DR5, DR65, XT1, XT2, XT6**

Man for all Seasons, A (1988, C, 168m, NR)
Charlton Heston heads the cast of this adaptation of Robert Bolt's life of Thomas More. Vanessa Redgrave and John Gielgud costar. Originally made for cable TV. **DR5, DR65**

Man Friday (1976, C, 109m, R)
The Robinson Crusoe story, with a contemporary race relations angle emphasized. Peter O'Toole and Richard Roundtree star. **AC24, DR45**

Man From Cheyenne (1942, B&W, 54m, NR)
A government agent (Roy Rogers) investigates a rustling ring run by a lovely lady. Gabby Hayes costars. **WE23**

Man From Colorado, The (1949, C, 99m, NR)
William Holden stars in a western drama of a cowboy forced to deal with an old Civil War comrade (Glenn Ford) who has become a judge dispensing a brutal form of frontier justice. **CL51**

Man From Laramie, The (1955, C, 104m, NR)
Western revenge drama, with James Stewart out to bring in the men who murdered his brother. Anthony Mann directed. **CL25, WE20**

Man From Music Mountain, The (1938, B&W, 54m, NR)
Gene Autry and partner Smiley Burnette foil the plans of a swindler. **WE24**

Man From Snowy River, The (1982, C, 104m, PG)
Australian adventure about a pack of wild horses and the young cowboy who would capture them. Kirk Douglas stars as twin brothers in this family film. Sequel: *Return to Snowy River, Part II.* **AC12, FF5**

Man From the Alamo, The (1953, C, 79m, NR)
Glenn Ford plays a Texan who escapes from the carnage at the Alamo to warn others but is accused of desertion. Directed by Budd Boetticher. **WE28**

Man in a Cocked Hat *see* Carlton Browne of the F.O.

Man in the Iron Mask, The (1939, B&W, 110m, NR)
Adventure tale of twin brothers, one ascending to royalty, the other becoming a musketeer. Louis Hayward, Joan Bennett, and Warren William star; James Whale directed. **FA4, HO34**

Man in the White Suit, The (1952, B&W, 84m, NR)
Classic British comedy about an inventor (Alec Guinness) who comes up with a miracle fabric and is hounded by the clothing establishment. **CO17, DR63**

Man Like Eva, A (1983, C, 92m, NR)
A young woman impersonates film director Rainer Werner Fassbinder in this drama from Germany. **FF3**

Man of Flowers (1984, C, 91m, R)
Australian drama about a wealthy bachelor who pays an artist's model to take off her clothes for him. Norman Kaye stars; directed by Paul Cox. Werner Herzog plays Kaye's father in flashback scenes. **FF5, FF19**

Man of Iron (1980, C, 140m, PG)
Sequel to *Man of Marble*, this Polish drama follows a documentary filmmaker and her romance with the son of a worker-hero whose story she filmed. Andrzej Wajda directed. **FF7**

Man of La Mancha (1972, C, 130m, G)
Musical version of the classic novel *Don Quixote,* about a knight in search of his dream quest. Peter O'Toole and Sophia Loren head the cast. **DR45, FF31, MU2, MU17**

Man of Marble (1977, C, 160m, NR)
Epic Polish drama of a woman filmmaker shooting a documentary about the leader of a workers' uprising. Directed by Andrzej Wajda. **FF7**

Man of the Forest (1933, B&W, 62m, NR)
Randolph Scott western has him framed for murder by Noah Beery, Sr. Based on a Zane Grey novel. **WE22**

Man of the Frontier (1936, B&W, 60m, NR)
Early Gene Autry western, featuring the debut of his mighty horse, Champion. Also titled *Red River Valley.* **WE24**

Man They Could Not Hang, The (1939, B&W, 72m, NR)
A scientist is hung for his mad crimes but brought back to life for revenge on the judge and jury that convicted him. Boris Karloff stars. **HO20, HO27**

Man Who Could Work Miracles, The (1937, B&W, 82m, NR)
A shy bank clerk suddenly discovers he has the power to do anything he wants. Family fantasy film, based on an H.G. Wells story, stars Roland Young and Ralph Richardson. **SF13, SF26**

Man Who Fell to Earth, The (1976, C, 140m, R)
Science fiction drama about an alien (David Bowie) who comes to Earth in search of water for his parched planet but is unable to return home. Brilliantly directed by Nicolas Roeg. Candy Clark, Rip

Torn, and Buck Henry costar. **CU4, CU34, CU47, MU12, SF9** *Highly Recommended*

Man Who Haunted Himself, The (1970, C, 94m, PG)
Low-key horror film set in London about a man who begins seeing a double of himself after he's injured in a car crash. Roger Moore stars. **HO15**

Man Who Knew Too Much, The (1934, B&W, 75m, NR)
Hitchcock thriller about a couple who accidentally learn intelligence information, and their daughter is kidnapped by spies. Leslie Banks, Edna Best, and Peter Lorre star. **MY6, MY7, MY22**

Man Who Knew Too Much, The (1956, C, 120m, PG)
Hitchcock remade his own film, with the setting now North Africa. James Stewart plays the title character; Doris Day is his wife. **CL25, CU18, MY6, MY7, MY22**

Man Who Loved Cat Dancing, The (1973, C, 114m, PG)
Burt Reynolds and Sarah Miles are trail companions in this western about two people on their own quests. **AC37, WE9**

Man Who Loved Women, The (1977, C, 119m, R)
A man who simply loves all kinds of women tries to come to grips with his obsession by writing his life story. French comedy-drama directed by François Truffaut. American remake released in 1983. **FF13, FF36**

Man Who Loved Women, The (1983, C, 110m, R)
Burt Reynolds stars in a remake of the French comedy about a man with insatiable romantic tendencies. Julie Andrews plays his analyst; Kim Basinger, Marilu Henner, and Cynthia Sikes are the objects of his affections. Directed by Blake Edwards. **AC37, CO46, FF36**

Man Who Shot Liberty Valance, The (1962, C, 122m, NR)
A peace-loving lawyer confronts a violent outlaw. James Stewart, John Wayne, and Lee Marvin star in this western classic, directed by John Ford. **CL25, DR43, WE12, WE17, WE18** *Recommended*

Man Who Would Be King, The (1975, C, 129m, PG)
Sean Connery and Michael Caine star in the Rudyard Kipling story of two adventurers held captive by a mountain tribe who think one of them is a god. John Huston directed. **AC12, AC36, CL44** *Recommended*

Man With Bogart's Face, The (1980, C, 106m, PG)
Would-be detective has plastic surgery to resemble Bogart, goes on to solve comic caper. Robert Sacchi stars, with Michelle Phillips, Olivia Hussey, George Raft (in his last film), and Mike Mazurki in support. **MY21**

Man With One Red Shoe, The (1985, C, 92m, PG)
An innocent man is mistaken for a spy and is caught in a comic crossfire of international agents. Tom Hanks and Jim Belushi star. Remake of French film, *The Tall Blonde Man With One Black Shoe.* **CO10, CO13, CO44, FF36**

Man With the Golden Arm, The (1955, B&W, 119m, NR)
Classic drama of a drug addict (Frank Sinatra) and his desperate attempts to control his problem. Directed by Otto Preminger. **CL8, DR49**

Man With the Golden Gun, The (1974, C, 125m, PG)
James Bond (Roger Moore) takes on a vicious international assassin (Christopher Lee). Britt Ekland and Maud Adams costar. **AC35, HO32**

Man With Two Brains, The (1983, C, 90m, R)
Mad scientist Steve Martin marries a lovely but cold woman (Kathleen Turner);

his real love is another woman's brain, which he keeps in his laboratory. **CO7, CO33, DR46, SF21**

Man Without a Star (1955, C, 89m, NR)
Kirk Douglas is the gunslinger who helps a farm woman (Jeanne Crain) in distress. **WE3**

Manchurian Candidate, The (1962, B&W, 126m, PG)
Intelligent, stylish political thriller about a war hero (Laurence Harvey) programmed by communists to be an assassin. Frank Sinatra, Angela Lansbury, and Janet Leigh also star. Adapted by George Axelrod from Richard Condon's novel. Directed by John Frankenheimer. **CU9, DR21, DR49, MY2, MY6** *Highly Recommended*

Mango Tree, The (1977, C, 93m, NR)
Drama set in Australia around the time of World War I about a young man's coming of age in a small town. Michael Pate and Geraldine Fitzgerald star. **FF5**

Manhattan (1979, B&W, 95m, R)
Woody Allen's comedy about the endless possibilities of love—and heartbreak—in the Big Apple. Diane Keaton, Mariel Hemingway, and Meryl Streep costar as the women in Woody's life. **CO1, CO2, CO27, DR26, DR40, XT9** *Recommended*

Manhattan Merry-Go-Round (1938, B&W, 80m, NR)
A gangster takes control of a record company—but the story is just an excuse to present musical numbers by the likes of Gene Autry, Cab Calloway, Louis Prima, and (believe it or not) Joe DiMaggio. **WE24**

Manhattan Project, The (1986, C, 117m, PG-13)
A teenager creates a unique science project with stolen plutonium. Drama starring Christopher Collet, John Lithgow, and Jill Eikenberry. **DR9**

Manhunter (1986, C, 119m, R)
An F.B.I. agent comes out of retirement to catch a vicious serial killer by imagining how the psycho must plan his crimes. Superb suspense drama, based on Thomas Harris' novel *Red Dragon*. William Petersen stars, with Kim Greist, Brian Cox, Joan Allen, and Dennis Farina. **MY2, MY9, MY17** *Recommended*

Maniac (1980, C, 88m, R)
Extremely graphic horror film about a homicidal killer with a talent for mutilation. Joe Spinell stars. **CU7, HO18**

Manon of the Spring (1987, C, 116m, PG)
Concluding chapter of Marcel Pagnol story, begun with *Jean de Florette*: daughter of wronged French landowner seeks revenge on the neighbors responsible. Emmanuelle Beart, Yves Montand, and Daniel Auteil star. Directed by Claude Berri. **FF1** *Recommended*

Man's Favorite Sport? (1964, C, 120m, NR)
Phony fishing expert (Rock Hudson) is forced to enter an angling competition in this comedy from director Howard Hawks. Paula Prentiss costars. **CL35**

Manxman, The (1929, B&W, 90m, NR)
Hitchcock's last silent film, a drama about two best friends, a lawyer and fisherman, who love the same woman. **MY22**

Marat/Sade (1967, C, 115m, NR)
Harrowing version of the stage hit about the Marquis de Sade directing his fellow lunatic asylum inmates in a play about the French Revolution and the murder of Jean-Paul Marat. Patrick Magee is a magnetic de Sade, Glenda Jackson is Charlotte Corday. Full title: *The Persecution and Assassination of Jean-Paul Marat by the Inmates of the Asylum of Charenton Under the Direction of the Marquis de Sade*. **DR5, DR20, DR23** *Recommended*

Marathon Man (1976, C, 125m, R)
Thriller about an innocent New Yorker caught up in international intrigue set in motion by the murder of his secret agent

brother. Dustin Hoffman, Laurence Olivier, and Roy Scheider star. **CL32, DR30, MY7**

March or Die (1977, C, 104m, PG)
Old-fashioned adventure tale of the French Foreign Legion, starring Gene Hackman, Terence Stamp, Max von Sydow, and Catherine Deneuve. **AC12, DR39, FF27**

Marie (1985, C, 113m, PG-13)
The true story of a woman who blew the whistle on corruption in the highest levels of Tennessee state government. Sissy Spacek and Jeff Daniels star. **DR6, DR10, DR68**

Marius (1931, B&W, 125m, NR)
French comedy-drama of life in the Provence region, written by Marcel Pagnol. Pierre Fresnay plays the title character, a man torn between his love for Fanny (Orane Demazis) and life at sea. The first of a trilogy, followed by *Fanny* and *Cesar*. **FF1**

Marjoe (1972, C, 88m, PG)
Documentary portrait of pseudo-evangelist Marjoe Gortner. **CU16**

Marjorie Morningstar (1958, C, 123m, NR)
Natalie Wood plays a naive young girl with great ambitions; Gene Kelly is her summer lover. **MU19**

Mark of the Hawk, The (1957, C, 83m, NR)
Sidney Poitier drama set in contemporary Africa, centering on the debate over the means of achieving racial equality. With Eartha Kitt, Juano Hernandez, and John McIntire. **DR14, DR38**

Mark of the Vampire (1935, B&W, 61m, NR)
Bela Lugosi and his *Dracula* director, Tod Browning, are reunited for more bloodsucking thrills. Lionel Barrymore costars. **HO5, HO28, HO35**

Marked Woman (1937, B&W, 99m, NR)
Crusading district attorney (Humphrey Bogart) persuades four women to testify against their gangster boss. Bette Davis costars. **CL20, CL21**

Marlene (1986, C/B&W, 96m, NR)
Actor Maximilian Schell's documentary about fabled performer Marlene Dietrich, filmed with her very reluctant cooperation. **CL47, CU16** *Recommended*

Marnie (1964, C, 129m, NR)
A compulsive thief is caught by her boss, who has fallen in love with her. She agrees to marry him to avoid prosecution. Hitchcock thriller starring Tippi Hedren and Sean Connery. **AC36, MY5, MY22**

Marooned (1969, C, 134m, PG)
A group of astronauts is trapped in space, unable to return to Earth, in this science fiction thriller. Gregory Peck, Richard Crenna, and Gene Hackman costar; special effects won an Oscar. **DR39, SF3, SF15**

Marriage of Maria Braun, The (1978, C, 120m, R)
In postwar Germany, a war widow builds a financial empire. Acclaimed drama from director Rainer Werner Fassbinder. Hanna Schygulla stars. **FF20** *Recommended*

Married to the Mob (1988, C, 103m, PG)
Wacky crime comedy set in New York and Miami Beach, with a Mafia hit man's widow pursued by her late husband's boss (and killer), *his* jealous wife, and a bumbling F.B.I. agent. Michelle Pfeiffer stars, with Dean Stockwell, Mercedes Ruehl, and Matthew Modine. Witty direction by Jonathan Demme. **CO10, CU39, XT9** *Recommended*

Married Woman, A (1965, B&W, 94m, NR)
Director Jean-Luc Godard's study of a marriage in crisis, with a bored wife taking on a lover. **FF14**

Marseillaise, La (1938, B&W, 130m, NR)
From director Jean Renoir, a drama about the turbulent times of the French Revolution. **FF12**

Martin (1978, C, 95m, R)
A teenaged vampire struggles with his terrible secret in this cult horror film from director George Romero. **CU4, HO5, HO38** *Recommended*

Marty (1955, B&W, 91m, NR)
Oscar-winning story of an ordinary Joe, a Bronx butcher, who unexpectedly finds love. Star Ernest Borgnine, director Daniel Mann, and writer Paddy Chayevsky all won Oscars. **CL4, XT1, XT2, XT6**

Mary of Scotland (1936, B&W, 123m, NR)
Katharine Hepburn plays the doomed 16th-century queen. Fredric March co-stars; John Ford directed. **CL3, CL16, CL34**

Mary Poppins (1964, C, 139m, G)
Classic Disney musical about a nanny with magical powers. Oscar winner Julie Andrews (in her movie debut) and Dick Van Dyke star in this brilliant combination of live action and animation. **FA1, FA9, MU7, MU8, XT3, XT10**

Masculine-Feminine (1966, B&W, 103m, NR)
A love affair between a journalist and a would-be rock star is the springboard for director Jean-Luc Godard's exploration of mid-60s Paris. Jean-Pierre Leaud stars. **FF14, XT9**

Mask (1985, C, 120m, PG-13)
True story about a mother's patient love for her teenaged son, whose face is disfigured by an incurable disease. Cher and Eric Stoltz star in this heart-wrenching drama. **DR2, DR6, DR8, DR9, MU12**

Masks of Death, The (1980, C, 80m, NR)
Peter Cushing plays Sherlock Holmes in this mystery about three unidentified corpses found in London's North End. **HO33, MY10**

Masque of the Red Death, The (1964, C, 86m, NR)
Vincent Price stars as evil Prince Prospero, the madman who throws a massive ball in his castle while a plague sweeps the land. Roger Corman directed this adaptation of two Edgar Allan Poe stories. **HO1, HO31, HO41**

Masquerade (1988, C, 91m, R)
A shy young heiress meets a handsome stranger shortly after her mother's mysterious death. Is her stepfather using the man to romance her out of her money? Meg Tilly, Rob Lowe, and John Glover star in this thriller. **MY3**

Mass Appeal (1984, C, 100m, PG)
Conflict between an eager young priest and a veteran pastor forms the basis of this comedy starring Jack Lemmon and Zeljko Ivanek. **DR64**

Massacre at Fort Holman (1974, C, 92m, NR)
A Civil War western involving the bloody battle for a heavily fortified position. James Coburn and Telly Savalas lead the opposing armies. **WE7**

Massacre in Rome (1973, C, 103m, PG)
During World War II, a Vatican priest pleas for the lives of 300 villagers condemned by Hitler's orders. Richard Burton and Marcello Mastroianni star. **FF2, FF24**

Master of the House (1925, B&W, 81m, NR)
Silent comedy from Danish director Carl Dreyer, with a woman deserting her abusive husband, returning when he has learned his lesson at the hands of an old nurse. **FF35**

Master of the World (1961, C, 104m, NR)
Vincent Price wants to rule the world from his zeppelin in this science fiction adventure. Charles Bronson costars; based on several Jules Verne stories. **AC29, HO31, SF27**

Masters of the Universe (1987, C, 106m, PG)
A science fiction adventure tale based on the popular children's toys. Dolph Lundgren stars. **AC17, FA8, SF13**

Matewan (1987, C, 130m, PG-13)
Drama based on events surrounding a bitter and bloody coal miner's strike in 1920 West Virginia. Chris Cooper and James Earl Jones star. Written and directed by John Sayles. **DR5** *Recommended*

Matilda (1978, C, 103m, G)
Family comedy about a boxing kangaroo, starring Elliott Gould, Robert Mitchum, and Lionel Stander. **FA6**

Matter of Time, A (1976, C, 99m, PG)
Liza Minnelli and Ingrid Bergman star in this drama about a chambermaid taught lessons in life by a daft noblewoman. Director Vincente Minnelli's last film. **CL27, MU24**

Maurice (1987, C, 100m, NR)
Drama based on E. M. Forster's novel about a young Englishman's gradual awakening to his homosexual nature. Produced by Ismail Merchant; directed by James Ivory. **DR3, DR19**

Mausoleum (1983, C, 96m, R)
A housewife is possessed by a demon from the 17th century in this horror film starring Marjoe Gortner. **HO8**

Maverick Queen, The (1956, C, 92m, NR)
Barbara Stanwyck plays a lady outlaw who falls for a lawman in this western drama. **CL45, WE9**

Max Dugan Returns (1983, C, 98m, PG)
From Neil Simon, a comedy about a schoolteacher whose ex-con father turns up one day with gifts to charm her and her teenaged son. Marsha Mason, Jason Robards, and Matthew Broderick star. **CO5, CO34**

Max Headroom (1986, C, 60m, NR)
Comic adventure about a computer-created character and his alter ego, a TV news reporter. The original episode of the TV series. Matt Frewer and Amanda Pays star. **CO2, CO11** *Recommended*

Maxie (1985, C, 90m, PG)
Glenn Close stars in this fantasy-comedy about a contemporary San Francisco woman possessed by the spirit of a Roaring 20s flapper. Mandy Patinkin costars, with Ruth Gordon. **CO37, DR72**

Maximum Overdrive (1986, C, 97m, R)
Horror tale directed by Stephen King, based on one of his stories, about the passing of a comet and its effects on all the machinery at a truck stop in the South. Emilio Estevez stars. **HO22, HO42**

Mayerling (1936, B&W, 89m, NR)
Classic story of doomed love, with Charles Boyer as Crown Prince Rudolph of Austria, Danielle Darrieux as the commoner who wins his heart. **CL4, DR3**

Maytime (1937, B&W, 132m, NR)
Nelson Eddy and Jeanette MacDonald team for this love story about a married opera star and poor singer; John Barrymore plays the jealous husband. **CL15**

Mean Frank and Crazy Tony (1975, C, 85m, R)
Lee Van Cleef and Tony LoBianco play a mob boss and a street punk who break out of prison together in this crime thriller from Italy. **AC22, FF2**

Mean Machine, The (1973, C, 89m, R)
Chris Mitchum plays a man with a mission—he's out to get even with the Mob. **AC19**

Mean Streets (1973, C, 112m, R)
In New York's Little Italy, a young hood tries to rise within the organization while keeping his crazy cousin out of trouble. Brilliant portrait of modern urban life, directed by Martin Scorsese, starring Harvey Keitel and Robert DeNiro, with Richard Romanus, David Proval, and Amy Robinson. **DR15, DR16, DR25, DR52, XT9** *Highly Recommended*

Meatballs (1979, C, 92m, PG)
Bill Murray stars as an amiable camp counselor in this comedy. **CO13**

Mechanic, The (1972, C, 100m, R)
Hit man Charles Bronson passes on his knowledge to understudy Jan-Michael Vincent. **AC29**

Medium Cool (1969, C, 110m, R)
Intense, original drama set in Chicago, during the 1968 Democratic National Convention. An apolitical TV reporter is galvanized by the turmoil in the city. Robert Forster, Verna Bloom, and Peter Bonerz star; Haskell Wexler directed. **DR7, XT9** *Highly Recommended*

Meet John Doe (1941, B&W, 132m, NR)
A sleazy politician hires a naive ex-baseball player to persuade the public that they never had it so good. Gary Cooper and Barbara Stanwyck star in this comedy directed by Frank Capra. **CL26, CL40, CL45**

Meet Me in St. Louis (1944, C, 113m, NR)
Musical glimpse into the life of a family visiting the 1903 World's Fair. Judy Garland and Margaret O'Brien, who won a special Academy Award, star; Vincente Minnelli directed. **FA9, MU1, MU6, MU21, MU24** *Recommended*

Melody Ranch (1940, B&W, 80m, NR)
Unusual Gene Autry western, mainly because of his costars: Jimmy Durante and Ann Miller. Otherwise, it's business as usual for the singing cowboy. **WE24**

Melvin and Howard (1980, C, 95m, R)
Comedy based on the true story of Melvin Dummar, the gas station owner who claimed to be an heir to billionaire Howard Hughes. Paul LeMat, Jason Robards, and Oscar winner Mary Steenburgen star in this satirical look at fame and fortune from director Jonathan Demme. **CO2, CU39, XT5** *Highly Recommended*

Member of the Wedding, The (1952, B&W, 91m, NR)
Poignant story of 12-year-old Frankie, a young girl confused by her brother's upcoming marriage. Julie Harris stars, with Ethel Waters and Brandon de Wilde. Fred Zinnemann directed this adaption of Carson McCullers' play. **DR9**

Memories of Me (1988, C, 103m, PG-13)
A surgeon suffers a heart attack and while recovering decides to seek a reconciliation with his estranged father, who works as a professional extra in Hollywood. Billy Crystal and Alan King star in this drama, with JoBeth Williams. **CO13, DR8**

Men (1986, C, 99m, R)
From Germany, a comedy about a business executive who becomes buddies with his wife's lover, an artist. **FF3**

Men, The (1950, B&W, 85m, NR)
Marlon Brando made his film debut in this drama about handicapped World War II veterans trying to adjust to their disabilities. Teresa Wright and Jack Webb costar. Directed by Fred Zinnemann. **CL8, CL57, DR33, XT10** *Recommended*

Men in War (1957, B&W, 104m, NR)
Korean War drama starring Robert Ryan, Aldo Ray, and Vic Morrow; directed by Anthony Mann. **AC3, WE20**

Men Who Tread on the Tiger's Tail, The (1945, B&W, 58m, NR)
Early film from Japanese director Akira Kurosawa, based on a historical incident: a medieval general flees with his retinue, disguised as priests, from his rival brother. Also known as *They Who Step on the Tiger's Tail*. **FF9**

Mephisto (1981, C, 135m, NR)
Oscar-winning Hungarian drama of a vain actor throwing in with the Nazis during the Occupation, paying a terrible price. Klaus Maria Brandauer stars. **FF7, XT7**

Mephisto Waltz, The (1971, C, 108m, R)
A journalist falls in with a satanic cult after meeting a renowned concert pianist.

Alan Alda stars in this horror film, with Jacqueline Bisset, Curt Jurgens, and Barbara Parkins. **HO10, HO11**

Merry Christmas, Mr. Lawrence (1983, C, 122m, R)
Prisoner-of-war drama, with British captives Tom Conti and David Bowie locked in struggle against two Japanese officers (Ryuichi Sakamoto and Takeshi). In English and Japanese; directed by Nagisa Oshima. **AC7, FF4, MU12**

Merry Widow, The (1934, B&W, 88m, NR)
Operetta, starring Jeanette MacDonald and Maurice Chevalier, of a rich widow's courtship in Paris. Directed by Ernst Lubitsch. Original running time: 99m. **CL54**

Messenger of Death (1988, C, 92m, R)
Charles Bronson plays an investigative reporter looking into a mass murder which may be linked to a splinter sect of Mormons. **AC29**

Metalstorm—The Destruction of Jared-Syn (1983, C, 84m, PG)
A peacekeeping ranger is assigned to destroy the evil Jared-Syn, who holds the planet of Lemuria under his tyrranical reign. Adventure fantasy with plenty of swordplay and special effects. **AC18**

Meteor (1979, C, 103m, PG)
A runaway meteor threatens destruction of the earth in this all-star disaster adventure. Sean Connery, Natalie Wood, and Henry Fonda head the cast. **AC23, AC36, CL24, SF7**

Metropolis (1926, B&W, 120m, NR)
Director Fritz Lang's legendary science fiction drama takes place in an underground city, whose workers are enslaved by a cruel dictatorship. Re-released in 1984 in an 87-minute version with some color tinting and a rock music score composed by Giorgio Moroder. Both editions available on home video. **CL12, CL43, FF3, SF2, SF5, SF14, SF16** *Highly Recommended* (both editions)

Micki and Maude (1984, C, 117m, PG-13)
Dudley Moore stars as a man whose wife and mistress both announce they're pregnant—and they have the same doctor. Frantic comedy from director Blake Edwards costars Ann Reinking and Amy Irving. **CO1, CO31, CO46**

Microwave Massacre (1983, C, 75m, NR)
Comedian Jackie Vernon stars in this horror comedy about man and his mysterious oven. **HO24**

Midnight *see* Call It Murder

Midnight Cowboy (1969, C, 113m, R)
Naive young man comes to New York and falls in with a hustling vagrant. Jon Voight and Dustin Hoffman star in this drama which won Oscars for Best Picture and Director (John Schlesinger). **DR15, DR30, XT1, XT6, XT9** *Recommended*

Midnight Crossing (1987, C, 96m, R)
Intrigue, double cross, and murder aboard a charter boat on a voyage from the Florida Keys to recover a stolen fortune. Daniel J. Travanti and Faye Dunaway star. **DR35**

Midnight Express (1978, C, 121m, R)
Billy Hayes, an American visiting Turkey, is caught at the airport trying to smuggle drugs out of the country and is thrown into a barbaric prison. Brad Davis, Randy Quaid, and John Hurt star in this true story. **DR6, DR18**

Midnight Girl, The (1925, B&W, 84m, NR)
Silent drama starring Lila Lee as a Russian immigrant in New York and Bela Lugosi as a sophisticated suitor. **HO28**

Midnight Lace (1960, C, 108m, NR)
Thriller set in London with a wife (Doris Day) the victim of anonymous threats that may be coming from her husband (Rex Harrison). With John Gavin, Myrna Loy, and Roddy McDowall. **CL46, MY3, XT9**

Midnight Run (1988, C, 125m, R)
A bounty hunter (Robert DeNiro) accompanies a former Mob accountant (Charles Grodin) on a cross-country journey, with the F.B.I., Mafia hit men, and a rival bountry hunter all in pursuit. Action comedy also featurs Yaphet Kotto, Dennis Farina, and John Ashton. **CO9, DR25**

Midsummer Night's Dream, A (1935, B&W, 132m, NR)
Shakespeare's classic comedy, with an all-star cast, including Mickey Rooney, James Cagney, Dick Powell, and Olivia de Havilland. **CL1, CL22**

Midsummer Night's Sex Comedy, A (1982, C, 88m, PG)
Sex and romance at a country estate in this Woody Allen comedy set at the turn of the century. The lovers include Mia Farrow, Jose Ferrer, Julie Hagerty, Mary Steenburgen, and Tony Roberts. **CO1, CO27**

Midway (1976, C, 132m, G)
Drama centering on the key naval battle of World War II, using many clips from previous war films and documentary footage. Charlton Heston heads the cast, which also includes Henry Fonda and Toshiro Mifune. **AC1, CL24, FF28**

Mighty Quinn, The (1989, C, 98m, R)
Mystery on a Caribbean island, with murdered white businessman, black police chief, and his boyhood friend (and prime suspect) the main ingredients. Denzel Washington and Robert Townsend star, with James Fox, Mimi Rogers, and M. Emmet Walsh. **MY20**

Mike's Murder (1984, C, 97m, R)
After her boyfriend is murdered, a young woman decides to investigate and finds that he has been involved with drug dealers. Debra Winger and Paul Winfield star. **DR47, MY15**

Mikey and Nicky (1976, C, 119m, R)
Drama about the friendship of two hoods, one of whom may be setting up his buddy for a rubout. Peter Falk and John Cassavetes star; Elaine May wrote and directed. **DR16**

Milagro Beanfield War, The (1988, C, 118m, R)
Comedy-drama set in a small New Mexico town, whose citizens are up in arms over water rights and a new recreation development. Robert Redford directed; the cast is headed by Chick Vennera, with Sonia Braga, John Heard, Ruben Blades, Melanie Griffith, Daniel Stern, Freddy Fender, and Christopher Walken. Based on John Nichols' novel. **CO2, DR19, DR29, FF34, MU12**

Mildred Pierce (1945, B&W, 109m, NR)
Joan Crawford's classic role (an Oscar winner, too), as a woman whose success in business can't disguise her problems with headstrong daughter Ann Blyth. Based on the James M. Cain novel. **CL5, CL6, CL50, MY1, MY25, XT3**

Miles From Home (1988, C, 108m, R)
When a bank forecloses on their family farm, a pair of brothers burn the house and flee the law. Soon, they're regarded as folk heroes. Richard Gere and Kevin Anderson star, with John Malkovich. **DR7, DR16**

Milky Way, The (1970, C, 105m, NR)
Director Luis Buñuel's meditations on the history of Christianity. A funny, irreverent film from the master of surrealistic movie art. **FF11**

Millhouse: A White Comedy (1971, B&W, 93m, NR)
A scathing documentary about Richard Nixon, using extensive and by now famous clips from his checkered career. Directed by Emile de Antonio. **CU16** *Recommended*

Million Dollar Duck, The (1971, C, 92m, G)
Disney comedy about a duck exposed to radiation that lays eggs with gold yolks. Dean Jones and Sandy Duncan play the lucky owners. **FA1**

Mind Snatchers, The (1972, C, 94m, PG)
An American soldier in Germany is admitted to a mental hospital, where he discovers that a mad doctor is conducting thought-control experiments on his patients. Christopher Walken stars. **HO20**

Mines of Kilimanjaro, The (1987, C, 88m, PG-13)
A soldier of fortune swears revenge on the Nazis who murdered his professor. Their trail leads to Africa, where he encounters many unexpected adventures. Christopher Connelly stars. **AC21**

Miracle Down Under (1986, C, 107m, NR)
Loose adaptation of Dickens' *Christmas Carol*, set in frontier Australia, as a small boy warms a miser's heart. Dee Wallace Stone, John Waters, and Charles Tingwell star. **FA13, FF5**

Miracle of Morgan's Creek, The (1944, B&W, 99m, NR)
Wacky comedy about a girl who attends an all-night party, gets pregnant, but isn't sure who's the father. Betty Hutton, Eddie Bracken, and William Demarest star; Preston Sturges wrote and directed. **CO24**

Miracle of the Bells, The (1948, B&W, 120m, NR)
When a famous movie star is buried in her hometown, it sets off an unexplained chain of miracles. Frank Sinatra stars as a priest in this drama. **DR49**

Miracle of the White Stallions, The (1963, C, 117m, NR)
True adventure of the evacuation of prized horses from Vienna during World War II. Family fare from the Disney studios. **FA1, FA5**

Miracle on 34th Street (1947, C, 96m, NR)
Classic holiday story of a department store Santa proving to a little girl (and the world) that Mr. Claus (and the spirit he embodies) lives. Oscar winner Edmund Gwenn and Natalie Wood star. **FA13, XT4**

Miracle Worker, The (1962, B&W, 107m, NR)
Oscar winners Patty Duke and Anne Bancroft play Helen Keller and her teacher Anne Sullivan in this vivid recreation of their relationship. Directed by Arthur Penn, from the play by William Gibson. **DR4, DR20, XT3, XT5**

Mirror Crack'd, The (1980, C, 105m, PG)
Agatha Christie whodunit, with Angela Lansbury as Miss Marple. Elizabeth Taylor, Rock Hudson, Kim Novak, and Tony Curtis are among the suspects. **CL33, MY23**

Misadventures of Merlin Jones, The (1964, C, 88m, NR)
A college whiz kid shows off his powers of mind-reading and hypnotism in this Disney comedy starring Tommy Kirk. **FA1**

Misfits, The (1961, B&W, 124m, NR)
Clark Gable and Marilyn Monroe star in this drama (the last film for both) about horse trappers in modern Nevada. Montgomery Clift, Eli Wallach, and Thelma Ritter costar. Written by Arthur Miller; John Huston directed. **CL23, CL29, CL44, WE9, WE13, XT11**

Mishima (1985, C/B&W, 120m, R)
The turbulent life of Japan's controversial novelist and self-styled samurai is told in this stylized film from American director Paul Schrader. Award-winning cinematography, production design, and musical score. **FF4** *Recommended*

Miss Annie Rooney (1942, B&W, 84m, NR)
Shirley Temple gets her first screen kiss (from Dickie Moore) in this tale of a poor girl in love with a boy from a wealthy family. **FA14**

Miss Firecracker (1989, C, 102m, PG)
Zany comedy set in Yazoo City, Mississippi, about a local beauty contest and its eccentric entrants. Holly Hunter stars, with Mary Steenburgen, Alfred Woodard, Tim Robbins, and Scott Glenn. Beth Hen-

ley adapted her play, *The Miss Fire-cracker Contest*. **CO12, DR20**

Miss Mary (1986, C, 100m, R)
A drama set in Argentina about a British governess (Julie Christie) and her strange relationship to her family of employers. **FF6**

Miss Sadie Thompson (1953, C, 91m, NR)
Musical remake of Somerset Maugham's *Rain*, with Rita Hayworth as the South Seas lady of the night who seduces a respectable minister. **MU14**

Missing (1982, C, 122m, R)
Fact-based drama about an American in a Latin American country who's abducted by state police, with his wife and father desperate to find his whereabouts. Jack Lemmon and Sissy Spacek star; Costa-Gavras directed. **DR6, DR64, DR68**
Recommended

Missing In Action (1984, C, 112m, R)
Chuck Norris stars as a former P.O.W. who returns to Vietnam to free more Americans being held captive. **AC4, AC32**

Missing in Action 2: The Beginning (1985, C, 96m, R)
In this sequel to *Missing in Action,* the story of Chuck Norris' captivity in Vietnam and his escape are told. **AC7, AC32**

Mission, The (1986, C, 126m, PG)
The true story of missionaries in 17th-century South America clashing with slave traders. Robert DeNiro and Jeremy Irons star. Oscar-winning cinematography by Chris Menges; directed by Roland Joffe. **DR5, DR25**

Missionary, The (1982, C, 90m, R)
Comedy about a cleric just back from Africa who is assigned to run a home for women of weak virtue. Michael Palin and Maggie Smith star. **CO15**

Mississippi Burning (1988, C, 125m, R)
The 1964 murder of three civil rights workers is the jumping-off point for this melodrama about the subsequent F.B.I.

investigation. Gene Hackman and Willem Dafoe star, with Frances McDormand and Brad Dourif. **DR6, DR7, DR39**

Missouri Breaks, The (1975, C, 126m, PG)
Bounty hunter Marlon Brando squares off against reformed outlaw Jack Nicholson in a leisurely western drama. Harry Dean Stanton, Dennis Quaid, and Kathleen Lloyd costar. Written by Tom McGuane; directed by Arthur Penn. **CU49, DR24, DR33, WE4, WE16**

Mrs. Miniver (1942, B&W, 134m, NR)
Classic story of the effects of World War II on a middle-class British family. Winner of seven Oscars, including Best Picture, Director (William Wyler), Actress (Greer Garson), and Supporting Actress (Teresa Wright). Walter Pidgeon costars. **CL8, CL38, XT1, XT3, XT5, XT6**

Mrs. Soffel (1984, C, 113m, PG-13)
Prison warden's wife falls in love with a convict and helps him and his brother escape. True-life romantic drama, starring Diane Keaton, Mel Gibson, and Matthew Modine. Directed by Gillian Armstrong. **DR1, DR16, DR40, DR69**
Recommended

Mrs. Wiggs of the Cabbage Patch (1934, B&W, 80m, NR)
A poor woman raising five children on her own finds time to play matchmaker to a spinster. Pauline Lord stars, with ZaSu Pitts and W. C. Fields as the matched couple. **CO22**

Mr. and Mrs. North (1941, B&W, 67m, NR)
Screen version of popular radio show, with fun-loving couple solving murder mystery. Gracie Allen stars. **MY21**

Mr. and Mrs. Smith (1941, B&W, 95m, NR)
Alfred Hitchcock takes a break from thrillers to make a comedy about a couple who find that their marriage was never legal. Robert Montgomery and Carole Lombard star. **CL48, MY22**

Mr. Arkadin (1955, B&W, 99m, NR)
Twisted tale of mystery millionaire, directed by and starring Orson Welles. **CL41, DR60**

Mr. Blandings Builds his Dream House (1948, B&W, 94m, NR)
New York couple decide to buy their dream home in the Connecticut countryside; the fun begins when they decide to fix it up "a little." Cary Grant, Myrna Loy, and Melvyn Douglas star in this classic comedy. **CL10, CL18, CL46** *Recommended*

Mr. Deeds Goes to Town (1936, B&W, 115m, NR)
Director Frank Capra won an Oscar for this comedy about an ordinary guy who inherits a fortune and decides to give it all away. Gary Cooper and Jean Arthur star, with George Bancroft and Lionel Stander. **CL26, CL40, XT6**

Mr. Halpern and Mr. Johnson (1983, C, 57m, NR)
Modest drama of two men meeting after the funeral of one's wife, the second revealing a longtime secret friendship with the woman. Originally made for cable TV. Laurence Olivier and Jackie Gleason star. **CL32**

Mr. Hobbs Takes a Vacation (1962, C, 116m, NR)
Family comedy about a father who's put through the wringer on a summer vacation. James Stewart and Maureen O'Hara star. **CL25**

Mr. Hulot's Holiday (1953, B&W, 86m, NR)
The first film about M. Hulot, the comic Frenchman with a knack for getting into the strangest situations. Director Jacques Tati also plays the lead role. **FF16** *Recommended*

Mr. Klein (1977, C, 122m, PG)
In Nazi-occupied France, an art dealer exploiting Jews finds himself confused with another man who's a Jew and under scrutiny from the Germans. Alain Delon

and Jeanne Moreau star; Joseph Losey directed. **FF1, FF26**

Mr. Lucky (1943, B&W, 100m, NR)
Cary Grant stars as the dashing owner of a gambling ship out to bilk Laraine Day, who charms him into respectability. **CL18**

Mr. Majestyk (1974, C, 103m, PG)
A Colorado melon grower (Charles Bronson) won't knuckle under to the Mob, which decides to have him eliminated. Adapted by Elmore Leonard from his own novel. **AC29, MY26**

Mr. Mom (1983, C, 92m, PG)
When an executive loses his job and his wife goes to work, their roles are reversed and their lives turned upside-down. Comedy starring Michael Keaton, Teri Garr, and Martin Mull. Written by John Hughes. **CO2, CO5, CO37, CO45, CO47**

Mr. North (1988, C, 90m, PG)
Gentle comic fable, set in 1920s Newport, Rhode Island, about an extraordinary young man who charms society with his very "electric" personality. Anthony Edwards stars, with Robert Mitchum, Harry Dean Stanton, Anjelica Huston, and Lauren Bacall. Based on a novel by Thornton Wilder. **CO6, CU49**

Mister Roberts (1955, C, 123m, NR)
Classic comedy-drama about World War II shipboard battle between high-strung captain (James Cagney) and determined first mate (Henry Fonda). With Oscar winner Jack Lemmon (as Ensign Pulver) and William Powell (in his last film). Co-directed by John Ford. **CL10, CL22, CL24, CL34, DR64, XT4, XT11** *Recommended*

Mr. Skeffington (1944, B&W, 140m, NR)
Bette Davis and Claude Rains star as a New York society couple whose loveless marriage warms with the passing years. The video version restores 13 minutes of footage from the film's original release. **CL4, CL5, CL21, CU10**

Mr. Smith Goes to Washington (1939, B&W, 129m, NR)
James Stewart plays an idealistic young Congressman in conflict with the Old Guard in the Nation's Capital. Jean Arthur, Thomas Mitchell, and Claude Rains costar; Frank Capra directed. **CL25, CL40, XT9**

Mr. Winkle Goes to War (1944, B&W, 80m, NR)
Comedy-drama of a mild-mannered man (Edward G. Robinson) who's accidentally drafted and winds up becoming a war hero. **CL52**

Mr. Wong, Detective (1939, B&W, 69m, NR)
Boris Karloff plays an Oriental detective in this low-budget mystery. **HO27**

Mr. Wong in Chinatown (1939, B&W, 70m, NR)
Boris Karloff's third appearance as the wily Oriental detective has him on the trail of the murderer of a Chinese princess. **HO27**

Misunderstood (1984, C, 92m, PG)
Gene Hackman stars in this drama about a family torn apart when the wife dies and the son (Henry Thomas) retreats into a world of his own. With Rip Torn and Susan Anspach. **CU47, DR8, DR39**

Mixed Blood (1985, C, 98m, R)
A comedy-drama about a gang of Brazilian toughs trying to muscle in on New York's drug trade, thwarted by romance between their leader and the daughter of a rival boss. Directed by Paul Morissey. **CU44**

Moby Dick (1956, C, 116m, NR)
Screen version of Herman Melville's classic tale of Captain Ahab (Gregory Peck) and his obsession with the white whale. Directed by John Huston; Orson Welles has one memorable scene as a priest. **CL1, CL41, CL44**

Modern Problems (1981, C, 91m, PG)
Chevy Chase stars in this comedy about an air traffic controller who discovers he has telekinetic powers. **CO11, CO13**

Modern Romance (1981, C, 93m, R)
A film editor drives his girlfriend crazy with his obsessive behavior about their relationship. Albert Brooks directed and stars, Kathryn Harrold plays the object of his affections. **CO1**

Modern Times (1936, B&W, 89m, G)
Charlie Chaplin's sublime comedy of contemporary man bedeviled by machines. Paulette Goddard costars in this silent, which features music composed by Chaplin. **CL11, CO18** *Highly Recommended*

Moderns, The (1988, C, 126m, R)
Drama set in 1926 Paris, amid the art and literary world of expatriate Americans, including Ernest Hemingway and Gertrude Stein. Keith Carradine plays an art forger, Wallace Shawn a columnist, John Lone a wealthy art collector, Linda Fiorentino his wife and Carradine's former lover. With Geraldine Chaplin and Genevieve Bujold. Alan Rudolph directed. **CU26, DR5**

Mogambo (1953, C, 115m, NR)
Remake of classic adventure story *Red Dust*, with Clark Gable once again the plantation foreman caught between advances of Ava Gardner and Grace Kelly. John Ford directed on location in Africa. **AC12, AC14, CL23, CL31, CL34, CU18**

Mohawk (1956, C, 79m, NR)
An Indian war is prevented by a white man (Scott Brady) and a lovely Indian (Rita Gam). **WE8**

Molly Maguires, The (1970, C, 123m, PG)
In 19th-century Pennsylvania, striking coal miners are betrayed by a union-busting spy. Sean Connery, Richard Harris, and Samantha Eggar star in this historical drama. **AC36, DR5**

Mommie Dearest (1981, C, 129m, PG)
Movie star and (according to her daughter) monster mom Joan Crawford is portrayed by Faye Dunaway in this highly charged drama. **CU2, DR12, DR35**

Mon Oncle *see* My Uncle

Mon Oncle d'Amerique (1980, C, 123m, PG)
From French director Alain Resnais, a comedy about modern life, focusing on the work habits of three individuals. Gerard Depardieu stars. **FF1, FF29**

Mona Lisa (1986, C, 104m, R)
In London, a hood just out of jail agrees to return to work for his old boss, chauffeuring (and spying on) a black prostitute who's suspected of pocketing her earnings. Bob Hoskins, Michael Caine, and Cathy Tyson star. **DR16, DR23, XT9** *Recommended*

Mondo Trasho (1969, B&W, 95m, NR)
Director John Waters presents a self-described "gutter film" about one day in the life of a hit-and-run driver, played by the inimitable Divine. A cult favorite. **CU12, CU43**

Money Pit, The (1986, C, 91m, PG)
A young married couple (Tom Hanks, Shelley Long) discover that the house of their dreams needs more than a "little" fixing up. Maureen Stapleton and Alexander Gudonov costar. **CO44**

Monkey Business (1952, C, 97m, NR)
Cary Grant plays a scientist looking for a youth serum in this zany comedy from director Howard Hawks. Ginger Rogers and Marilyn Monroe costar. **CL18, CL29, CL35**

Monkey Shines (1988, C, 115m, R)
A quadriplegic is helped by a trained monkey, who performs daily tasks for him. Trouble develops when the animal, injected with human brain cells, begins acting strangely. Directed by George Romero. **HO16, HO38**

Monkeys, Go Home! (1967, C, 101m, G)
American inherits an olive farm in France and trains a group of monkeys to pick his harvest. Disney comedy starring Dean Jones and Maurice Chevalier (in his last film). **FA1**

Monkey's Uncle, The (1965, C, 87m, NR)
Sequel to Disney comedy *The Misadventures of Merlin Jones* has college brain Tommy Kirk inventing a flying machine. **FA1**

Monsieur Verdoux (1947, B&W, 123m, NR)
Charlie Chaplin's dark comedy about a man who marries, then murders, a string of women for their money. Martha Raye costars. **CO18** *Recommended*

Monster Club, The (1980, C, 97m, PG)
Vincent Price plays a vampire who narrates three tales of terror, all revolving around a Transylvanian disco. **HO23, HO31**

Monster in the Closet (1986, C, 87m, PG)
A comic tribute to 1950s sci-horror films, about a gang of monsters which hide in closets and kill people. Donald Grant stars, with Claude Akins, Henry Gibson, Howard Duff, Paul Dooley, and John Carradine. **SF21**

Monster Squad, The (1987, C, 82m, PG-13)
A gang of plucky kids meet up with every monster imaginable, from Frankenstein and Dracula to the Wolf Man and the Mummy, in this horror comedy. **HO24**

Monte Walsh (1970, C, 99m, PG)
Oldtime cowboys Lee Marvin and Jack Palance won't face the fact that the frontier is closing down. Jeanne Moreau costars. **DR43, FF26, WE12**

Montenegro (1981, C, 98m, R)
A bored housewife discovers a new way to approach life when she begins an affair with a Yugoslavian worker. Susan Anspach stars; Dusan Makavejev directed. **FF7**

Monterey Pop (1969, C, 72m, NR)
Concert film of ground-breaking 1967 California pop festival, featuring Jimi Hendrix, Janis Joplin, Otis Redding, The Who, Ravi Shankar, Simon & Garfunkel, The Mamas and the Papas, and more. **MU10** *Highly Recommended*

Monty Python and the Holy Grail (1974, C, 90m, PG)
The boys from TV's most wickedly funny program take on the King Arthur legends. **CO7, CO15**

Monty Python's Flying Circus (17 volumes: all C, 60m, NR)
Each tape in this series contains two half-hour programs from the deliriously silly TV program starring John Cleese, Eric Idle, Graham Chapman, Michael Palin, Terry Jones, and Terry Gilliam. **CO15** *Highly Recommended*

Monty Python's Life of Brian (1979, C, 90m, R)
Britain's bad boys of humor tell their own version of the Messiah story in this irreverent spoof of religious epics. **CO7, CO15**

Monty Python's The Meaning of Life (1983, C, 107m, R)
More madness from the Python troupe, as they attempt to answer some of life's great questions in this series of bawdy and naughty sketches. **CO15**

Moon in the Gutter, The (1983, C, 126m, R)
Gerard Depardieu and Nastassja Kinski star in this stylized thriller about a man in search of the thug who brutalized his sister. **FF1, FF29**

Moon Is Blue, The (1953, B&W, 95m, NR)
A young woman's virginity is at stake in this comedy, considered daring in its day. William Holden, David Niven, and Maggie McNamara star; Otto Preminger directed. **CL51**

Moon Over Parador (1988, C, 93m, PG-13)
An American movie actor, on location in a Latin American country, is forced to impersonate the land's dictator after the despot suffers a fatal heart attack. This comedy, directed by Paul Mazursky, stars Richard Dreyfuss, with Sonia Braga, Raul Julia, and Jonathan Winters. Watch for appearances by Sammy Davis, Jr., Charo, and Dick Cavett. **CO2, CO8, CO37, FF34**

Moon Pilot (1962, C, 98m, G)
Just before he blasts off, an astronaut meets a lovely alien. Disney comedy starring Tom Tryon, Brian Keith, and Dany Saval. **FA1**

Moon-Spinners, The (1964, C, 118m, NR)
Hayley Mills stars in a Disney mystery about an innocent tourist in Crete becoming involved with a smuggling operation. **FA1**

Moonlighting (1982, C, 97m, PG)
Jeremy Irons plays the foreman of a gang of Polish workmen in London on a temporary construction job. He tries to keep news of political turmoil back home from his co-workers. **FF7**

Moonlighting (1985, C, 97m, NR)
A classy fashion model and a hip investigator team up to run a detective agency. Cybill Shepherd and Bruce Willis star in this mystery-comedy, originally the pilot for a TV series. **CO10** *Recommended*

Moonraker (1979, C, 126m, PG)
James Bond blasts into outer space to take on a madman and his steel-toothed henchman. Roger Moore, Michael Lonsdale, and Richard Kiel star. **AC35**

Moon's Our Home, The (1936, B&W, 76m, NR)
Margaret Sullavan and Henry Fonda star in this romantic comedy about the up-and-down relationship between a movie star and a New York writer. **CL24**

Moonstruck (1987, C, 102m, PG)
A young Italian-American widow, set to marry a second time, falls in love with her fiance's younger brother in this romantic comedy set in Brooklyn. Cher and Olympia Dukakis won Oscars for their performances as the widow and her mother. Costarring Nicolas Cage, Vincent Gardenia, and Danny Aiello. **CO1, XT3, XT5** *Recommended*

More Ripping Yarns *see* Ripping Yarns (series)

Morgan: A Suitable Case for Treatment (1966, B&W, 97m, NR)
Madcap British comedy about a loony artist (David Warner) who's obsessed with apes and his ex-wife (Vanessa Redgrave). **CO17, CU5, DR65** *Recommended*

Morgan Stewart's Coming Home (1987, C, 92m, PG-13)
Hip prep school student (Jon Cryer) shows his uptight parents (Lynn Redgrave, Nicholas Coster) how to loosen up in this comedy. **CO5**

Morituri (1965, B&W, 123m, NR)
Marlon Brando plays a German who helps British forces capture a cargo ship in World War II. Yul Brynner costars, with Trevor Howard, Janet Margolin, and Wally Cox. Also known as *Saboteur: Code Name Morituri.* **DR33**

Morning After, The (1986, C, 103m, R)
Jane Fonda stars in this mystery about an alcoholic actress who wakes up one morning next to a corpse—and can't remember what happened the night before. Jeff Bridges costars; Sidney Lumet directed. **DR27, DR58, DR71, MY3, MY5**

Morning Glory (1933, B&W, 74m, NR)
Katharine Hepburn won the first of her four Oscars for her role as an aspiring young actress in this drama. Adolphe Menjou and Douglas Fairbanks, Jr. costar. **CL5, CL16, XT3**

Morocco (1930, B&W, 92m, NR)
Marlene Dietrich's first American film has her succumbing to the charms of legionnaire Gary Cooper. Directed by Josef von Sternberg. **CL26, CL47, CL56**

Moscow Does Not Believe in Tears (1980, C, 152m, R)
Oscar-winning drama from the Soviet Union about a trio of women who emigrate to the capital city in the 1950s to seek their fortunes. **FF7, XT7**

Moscow on the Hudson (1984, C, 115m, R)
A Soviet saxophonist defects—in the middle of Bloomingdale's—in this comedy-drama starring Robin Williams. Paul Mazursky directed. **CO37, CO43, DR15, XT9**

Moses (1975, C, 141m, PG)
Burt Lancaster stars as the Biblical prophet in this condensed version of the 6-hour TV miniseries. **DR41**

Mosquito Coast, The (1986, C, 119m, PG)
An eccentric inventor (Harrison Ford) moves his family from New England to the jungles of Central America to escape the evil influences of "civilization." River Phoenix and Helen Mirren costar. Peter Weir directed; based on Paul Theroux's novel. **DR8, DR32**

Most Dangerous Game, The (1932, B&W, 78m, NR)
Classic adventure saga, based on famous short story about a man and woman pursued for sport by a mad big game hunter. Joel McCrea and Fay Wray star. **AC24**

Motel Hell (1980, C, 102m, R)
Horror film, played for laughs, about a brother and sister whose motel swallows up tourists and recycles them into a popular brand of sausage. Rory Calhoun stars. **HO24**

Mother, Jugs & Speed (1976, C, 95m, R)
Darkly comic adventures of city ambulance drivers, starring Bill Cosby, Raquel Welch, and Harvey Keitel, with Larry Hagman. **CO2**

Mother's Day (1980, C, 98m, NR)
A trio of women out for a hike are brutalized by two backwoods brothers, but the women have the final say in this gruesome horror story. **CU7, HO18**

Mothra (1962, C, 100m, NR)
Japanese monster movie about gigantic flying creature whose destructive ways can be checked only by two tiny twin sisters. **FF4, SF18**

Motown 25: Yesterday, Today, Forever (1983, C, 130m, NR)
Celebration of the black pop music label that recorded such great performers as Stevie Wonder, Marvin Gaye, The Supremes, The Four Tops, The Temptations, and The Jackson 5. Originally shown on TV. **MU10** *Recommended*

Mouse That Roared, The (1959, C, 83m, NR)
Peter Sellers plays three roles in this British comedy about a tiny, mythical kingdom declaring war on America so they can be eligible for generous foreign aid. **CO17, CO26**

Movers and Shakers (1985, C, 79m, PG)
Hollywood screenwriter tries to sell script called "Love in Sex" in this satire of the contemporary movie scene. Walter Matthau and Charles Grodin star; guest appearances by Steve Martin and Gilda Radner. **CO8, CO13, CO33**

Movie Movie (1978, C/B&W, 107m, PG)
Spoof of 1930s movies contains two films, one a boxing drama called *Dynamite Hands*, the other a big-budget musical called *Bathing Beauties of 1933*. George C. Scott heads the cast; Stanley Donen directed. **CO7, MU23**

Moving (1988, C, 89m, R)
Richard Pryor stars in this comedy about a man whose transfer from New Jersey to Idaho is one disaster after another. Dave Thomas costars. **CO14, CO29**

Ms. Don Juan (1973, C, 87m, R)
Brigitte Bardot plays a temptress whose conquests include her cousin, a priest. With Maurice Ronet, Robert Hossein, and Jane Birkin. Directed by Roger Vadim. **FF32**

Ms. 45 (1981, C, 84m, R)
In New York City, a mute seamstress is raped twice and goes on a killing spree in revenge. Zoe Tamerlis stars in this action film with a cult following. **AC19, CU7, MY3**

Multiple Maniacs (1971, B&W, 90m, NR)
Cult favorite, described by its creator, director John Waters, as a "celluloid atrocity." Divine stars as the proprietor of a "Cavalcade of Perversions," a carnival at which customers are robbed and beaten. **CU12, CU43**

Mummy, The (1932, B&W, 72m, NR)
Boris Karloff plays the Egyptian wrapped in bandages in the classic horror film. Directed by Karl Freund. **HO1, HO27** *Recommended*

Mummy, The (1959, C, 88m, NR)
British remake of the horror fable of the cursed Egyptian's tomb, starring Christopher Lee and Peter Cushing. **HO26, HO32, HO33**

Muppet Moments (1985, C, 56m, NR)
A collection of musical numbers and comedy skits from the popular TV series. Guest stars include Lena Horne, Liza Minnelli, Pearl Bailey, and Zero Mostel. **FA15**

Muppet Movie, The (1979, C, 94m, G)
The Muppets' feature film debut, in a comedy loaded with human stars as well: Orson Welles, Mel Brooks, Steve Martin, and Richard Pryor head the list. **CL41, CO28, CO29, CO33, FA15**

Muppet Revue, The (1985, C, 56m, NR)
More sketches and songs from the hit TV series, with guest stars Harry Belafonte, Linda Ronstadt, and Rita Moreno. **FA15**

Muppet Treasures (1985, C, 56m, NR)
Kermit, Miss Piggy, and friends welcome human stars Loretta Lynn, Ethel Merman, Peter Sellers, and Paul Simon in this collection of funny moments from the TV series. **FA15**

Muppets Take Manhattan, The (1984, C, 94m, G)
Broadway-bound frog, pig, and friends take the Great White Way by storm. Liza Minnelli, Joan Rivers, Brooke Shields, Elliott Gould, Art Carney, and Dabney Coleman lend support. **FA15, XT9**

Murder (1930, B&W, 108m, NR)
Herbert Marshall stars in this Hitchcock thriller about a jury member who has second thoughts about a condemned woman. **MY22**

Murder at the Baskervilles *see* The Silver Blaze

Murder at the Vanities (1934, B&W, 89m, NR)
Combination mystery and musical, with detective Victor McLaglen investigating backstage killing. Duke Ellington and his band are among the performers. **MU16, MY16**

Murder by Death (1976, C, 94m, PG)
Mystery comedy featuring an all-star collection of detectives (Charlie Chan, Sam Spade, Miss Marple) attempting to solve a whodunit in the mansion of Truman Capote. Peter Sellers, Peter Falk, and Alec Guinness head the cast. Written by Neil Simon. **CO7, CO10, CO26, CO34, DR63, MY21**

Murder by Decree (1979, C, 121m, PG)
Sherlock and Dr. Watson track Jack the Ripper. Christopher Plummer and James Mason star. **MY10**

Murder by Natural Causes (1979, C, 100m, NR)
The unfaithful wife of a mentalist tries to scare her husband to death, with unexpected results. Katharine Ross and Hal Holbrook star; written by William Levin-son and Richard Link. Originally made for TV. **MY18**

Murder by Television (1935, B&W, 60m, NR)
Low-budget mystery about the murder of a professor working on early TV technology; Bela Lugosi plays his assistant, the prime suspect. **HO28**

Murder Is Announced, A (1984, C, 153m, NR)
Joan Hickson stars as Miss Marple, Agatha Christie's intrepid sleuth, in this whodunit involving a murder that is advertised ahead of schedule in the classified ads of a newspaper. Originally made for British TV. **MY16, MY23**

Murder My Sweet (1944, B&W, 95m, NR)
Dick Powell plays Raymond Chandler's famous detective Philip Marlowe in this version of *Farewell, My Lovely*. Filmed under the original title in 1975. **MY1, MY24**

Murder on the Orient Express (1974, C, 127m, PG)
Agatha Christie's master sleuth Hercule Poirot solves the killing of a rich American aboard the famous luxury train. Albert Finney plays Poirot; among the suspects are Oscar winner Ingrid Bergman, Lauren Bacall, Sean Connery, and Vanessa Redgrave. Sidney Lumet directed. **AC36, CL27, DR58, DR65, MY16, MY23, XT5**

Murder Over New York (1940, B&W, 64m, NR)
Ace detective Charlie Chan (Sidney Toler) attends a police convention and comes up against saboteurs who are crippling the Allied air effort. **MY35**

Murders in the Rue Morgue (1971, C, 87m, PG)
Horror story, based on Edgar Allan Poe tale, of Parisian murders by a most mysterious assailant. Jason Robards and Herbert Lom star. **HO41**

Murphy's Law (1986, C, 100m, R)
Charles Bronson plays a police detective
framed for murder by an ex-con (Carrie
Snodgress). **AC29**

Murphy's Romance (1986, C, 107m, PG-
13)
A newly divorced mother moves to a
small Arizona town hoping for a new life,
and she falls in love with the town drug-
gist. Sally Field and James Garner star.
CO1, DR36, DR62

Murphy's War (1971, C, 108m, PG)
Peter O'Toole stars in this drama of a
British seaman who survives a Nazi at-
tack and swears revenge. **DR45**

Music Box, The/Helpmates (1932, B&W,
50m, NR)
Two classic Laurel and Hardy shorts; the
first, about an inept piano-moving team,
won them their only Oscar. **CO20**

Music Man, The (1962, C, 151m, G)
A con man charms the people of River
City, Iowa, in this all-American musical
starring Robert Preston and Shirley
Jones. Songs includes "Till There Was
You" and "76 Trombones." **FA9, MU2,
MU6** *Recommended*

Mutant (1984, C, 100m, R)
A chemical plant's deadly toxic waste
finds its way into the town's water supply,
turning everyone into a horrible monster.
Wings Hauser, Bo Hopkins, and Jennifer
Warren star. **HO21**

Mutilator, The (1985, C, 90m, R)
Five teens at a remote beach house are
stalked by a mad killer out for revenge in
this horror film. **HO12**

Mutiny on the Bounty, The (1935, B&W,
132m, NR)
The great sea adventure of Captain Bligh
(Charles Laughton) and his rebellious
first mate Fletcher Christian (Clark Gable). Oscar winner for Best Picture.
AC12, AC13, AC16, CL3, CL23, XT1 *Recommended*

Mutiny on the Bounty (1962, C, 177m,
NR)
Remake of the true-life sea story, with
Marlon Brando as Christian and Trevor
Howard as Captain Bligh. **AC12, AC16,
DR33**

My Beautiful Laundrette (1985, C, 93m,
R)
A young Pakistani emigre living in Lon-
don borrows money from a wealthy uncle
to open his own business. He also begins
a secret affair with a white British youth.
Perceptive comedy-drama originally
made for British TV. Directed by Stephen
Frears; written by Hanif Kureishi. **DR3,
DR7, DR23, XT9** *Recommended*

My Bodyguard (1980, C, 96m, PG)
When bullies harass a small high school
student, he hires a very large friend to
protect him. Comedy-drama starring
Chris Makepeace, Adam Baldwin, and
Matt Dillon. **CO4**

My Brilliant Career (1979, C, 101m, G)
In turn-of-the-century Australia, a young
woman finds her headstrong ways are getting her into loads of trouble. Judy Davis
stars in this superb drama from director
Gillian Armstrong. **FF5** *Recommended*

My Darling Clementine (1946, B&W, 97m,
NR)
Henry Fonda is Wyatt Earp, Victor Mature is Doc Holliday in this classic telling
of the gunfight at the O. K. Corral, directed by John Ford. **CL24, WE2, WE6,
WE9, WE18** *Highly Recommended*

My Demon Lover (1987, C, 90m, PG-13)
Romantic comedy about a guy who has a
problem around girls: whenever he gets
turned on, he's transformed into a hideous beast. Scott Valentine and Michelle
Little star. **CO11**

My Dinner With Andre (1981, C, 110m,
NR)
A New York playwright (Wallace Shawn)
and director (Andre Gregory) share a
meal and talk about their separate life
experiences. A cult comedy, with the per-

formers more or less playing themselves and improvising their dialogue. **CO12, CU5**

My Fair Lady (1964, C, 107m, G)
Hit Broadway musical about a Cockney flower girl learning her manners from stuffy professor. Audrey Hepburn, Rex Harrison, and a great Lerner and Loewe score share the spotlight. Oscar winner for Best Picture, Actor, and Director (George Cukor). **CL30, CL39, FA9, MU2, MU7, MU17, XT1, XT2, XT6**

My Favorite Brunette (1947, B&W, 87m, NR)
Bob Hope comedy about a photographer involved with mobsters, costarring Dorothy Lamour, Peter Lorre, and Lon Chaney, Jr. **CO40, HO30**

My Favorite Wife (1940, B&W, 88m, NR)
A woman thought dead returns from a desert island to find her husband has remarried. Irene Dunne, Cary Grant, and Randolph Scott star in this comedy. **CL10, CL18, WE22**

My Favorite Year (1982, C, 92m, PG)
A young writer for a popular 1950s TV program is assigned to keep watch over a tipsy Hollywood star who's to appear live on the show. A nostalgic comedy starring Peter O'Toole, Mark-Linn Baker, and Joseph Bologna. **CO6, CO8, DR45** *Recommended*

My First Wife (1984, C, 95m, NR)
Intense drama from Australian director Paul Cox of a man trying to cope when his wife leaves him after ten years of marriage. **FF5**

My Life as a Dog (1987, C, 101m, NR)
Swedish boy becomes too much for his ill mother to handle, so he's sent to live with relatives in a village. Gentle comedy about pains and pleasures of growing up. (Available in both subtitled and dubbed versions.) **CO4**

My Life to Live (1962, B&W, 85m, NR)
Director Jean-Luc Godard's portrait of a Parisian prostitute (Anna Karina) is the subject of this groundbreaking experimental film. **FF14**

My Little Chickadee (1940, B&W, 83m, NR)
Mae West and W.C. Fields team up to tame the Old West in this classic spoof. **CL10, CO22, CO39, WE15**

My Little Pony: The Movie (1986, C, 90m, G)
Animated feature film starring the beautiful Little Ponies, who befriend humans and fight against evil in the world. **FA10**

My Man Godfrey (1936, B&W, 95m, NR)
Classic comedy of Depression era, with wealthy man turning hobo and becoming butler to a Park Avenue family of eccentrics. William Powell and Carole Lombard star, with Gail Patrick, Eugene Pallette, and Alice Brady. **CL10, CL48, CO37**

My Name Is Nobody (1974, C, 115m, PG)
In this spaghetti western, Henry Fonda plays an aging gunfighter who's idolized by a young cowpoke (Terence Hill). **CL24, WE14**

My New Partner (1985, C, 104m, R)
A French comedy about a veteran cop (Philippe Noiret) training his young partner in the fine art of selective law enforcement. **FF1**

My Night at Maud's (1970, B&W, 105m, PG)
An upright, uptight Catholic intellectual is fascinated by an attractive woman. Jean-Louis Trintignant stars in this French comedy from director Eric Rohmer. **FF15**

My Pal Trigger (1946, B&W, 79m, NR)
Roy Rogers and his faithful horse ride the range in search of adventure. **WE23**

My Pet Monster (1986, C, 60m, NR)
A boy under a mysterious spell turns into a monster every time he gets hungry in this family adventure. **FA4**

My Science Project (1985, C, 94m, PG)
A group of high school students cook up something in their lab that could destroy the whole school. A comedy with plenty of special effects action. John Stockwell stars, with Danielle Von Zerneck and Dennis Hopper. **CO11, CU46**

My Stepmother Is an Alien (1988, C, 108m, PG-13)
A widowed scientist is romanced by a sexy blonde—who is in reality an alien assigned to enlist his help in saving her imperiled planet. Dan Aykroyd and Kim Basinger star. **CO11, CO13**

My Uncle (1958, C, 116m, NR)
Jacques Tati's Oscar-winning film about the misadventures of M. Hulot (Tati), whose simple life is in contrast to his sister and brother-in-law's gadget-filled home. Also known as *Mon Oncle*. **FF16, XT7**

Myra Breckenridge (1970, C, 94m, R)
Cult movie about decadent Hollywood scene, based on Gore Vidal's novel. Raquel Welch, Mae West, and John Huston star. **CL44, CU1, CU2**

Mysterians, The (1959, C, 85m, NR)
Japanese science fiction drama about highly evolved aliens trying to take over our planet. **FF4, SF18**

Mysterious Island (1961, C, 101m, NR)
Jules Verne's tale of prison escapees landing on an island inhabited by gigantic animals. Michael Craig, Joan Greenwood, and Michael Callan star; special effects by Ray Harryhausen. **FA3, FA4, SF10, SF27**

Mysterious Mr. Wong (1935, B&W, 56m, NR)
Oriental sleuth (Bela Lugosi) uncovers a deadly mystery in Chinatown involving the 13 Coins of Confucious. **HO28**

Mystery of Kasper Hauser, The *see* Every Man for Himself and God Against All

Mystery of the *Mary Celeste*, The: The Phantom Ship, (1937, B&W, 63m, NR)
Mystery story, based on fact, about a ship found in mid-ocean with no one aboard. Bela Lugosi stars. **HO28**

Mystery of the Wax Museum, The (1933, C, 77m, NR)
Classic horror film about a mad doctor (Lionel Atwill) dipping his victims in wax and putting them on display. One of the early films shot in Technicolor. Fay Wray costars. **HO1**

Mystic Pizza (1988, C, 101m, R)
In a seaside Connecticut town, three young women who work at a pizza restaurant try to figure what to do with the rest of their lives. Julia Roberts, Annabeth Gish, and Lili Taylor star, with Vincent Philip D'Onofrio, Conchata Farrell, Adam Storke, and William R. Moses. **DR10**

Nadine (1987, C, 83m, PG)
Austin, Texas, 1954: Vernon and Nadine are about to get divorced, but first there's this matter of some risqué photos, a dead photographer, and a sleazy gangster. Comedy from writer-director Robert Benton, starring Jeff Bridges, Kim Basinger, and Rip Torn. **CO6, CU47, DR55, DR71** *Recommended*

Naked and the Dead, The (1958, C, 131m, NR)
From Norman Mailer's first novel, a drama of men at war—often with each other—in the South Pacific. Aldo Ray and Cliff Robertson star. **AC1**

Naked Civil Servant, The (1980, C, 80m, NR)
John Hurt portrays Quentin Crisp, a British advocate of rights for homosexuals in the 30s and 40s, in this drama. **DR4**

Naked Face, The (1985, C, 103m, R)
A psychiatrist, accused of murdering his own patient, turns detective to find the

real killer. Roger Moore, Rod Steiger, and Elliott Gould star. **MY15**

Naked Gun, The (1988, C, 85m, R)
Spoof of cop movies, with Leslie Nielsen a poker-faced detective investigating a plot to assassinate Queen Elizabeth at a California Angels baseball game. With O.J. Simpson and Reggie Jackson. **CO7**

Naked in the Sun (1957, C, 79m, NR)
Seminole Indians battle slave traders in this western tale, based on a true story. **WE8**

Naked Jungle, The (1954, C, 95m, NR)
Charlton Heston is a South American plantation owner whose property and life are threatened by a mammoth army of ravenous red ants. **AC12, AC24**

Naked Night, The *see* Sawdust and Tinsel

Naked Prey, The (1966, C, 94m, NR)
Cornel Wilde directed and stars in this adventure story of a Britisher pursued by murderous African tribesmen. **AC12, AC24** *Recommended*

Naked Spur, The (1953, C, 91m, NR)
Bounty hunter James Stewart and fugitive Robert Ryan play a cat-and-mouse game in this classic western. Directed by Anthony Mann. **CL25, WE20**

Naked Truth, The (1957, B&W, 92m, NR)
British comedy about an assortment of people united in their desire to do away with the sleazy editor of a pornographic magazine. Terry-Thomas and Peter Sellers star. Also known as *Your Past Is Showing*. **CO26**

Name of the Rose, The (1986, C, 130m, R)
Sean Connery stars as a monk in 14th-century Italy who solves a bizarre series of murders in a monastery. Based on Umberto Eco's bestselling novel. **AC36, MY15**

Nanook of the North (1922, B&W, 69m, NR)
Pioneering documentary, directed by Robert Flaherty, about the daily lives of an Eskimo family. **CU16** *Recommended*

Napoleon (1927, B&W/C, 235m, G)
Grand, epic telling of the life of France's great emperor. This silent film, directed by Abel Gance, features tinted scenes and a Polyvision, three-screen sequence that was far ahead of its time. **CL1, CL12, FF1** *Highly Recommended*

Napoleon (1955, C, 115m, NR)
Orson Welles and Erich Von Stroheim head the cast of this French-made drama about the famed emperor's life. **CL41, CL53**

Napoleon and Samantha (1972, C, 92m, G)
A pair of young children runs off with a pet lion in this Disney drama. Johnny Whitaker, Jodie Foster, and Michael Douglas star. **DR70, FA1**

Nashville (1975, C, 159m, R)
Multi-character study of the music scene in Nashville and its connection to a political candidate. Henry Gibson, Karen Black, Ronee Blakley, Keith Carradine, Lily Tomlin, Michael Murphy, and Ned Beatty head the cast. Robert Altman directed. **DR12, CU25, MU6**

Nasty Habits (1977, C, 96m, PG)
Dark comedy about political machinations inside a convent that mirror the Watergate affair. Glenda Jackson, Geraldine Page, Melina Mercouri, and Sandy Dennis star, with Rip Torn, Edith Evans, Jerry Stiller, and Eli Wallach. **CO12, CU47**

Nate and Hayes (1983, C, 100m, PG)
Swashbuckling story of a pirate pair who roam the Caribbean in search of treasure and lovely women. Tommy Lee Jones and Michael O'Keefe star. Written by John Hughes. **AC15, CO47**

National Lampoon's Animal House (1978, C, 109m, R)
The groundbreaking comedy about life in the Delta House, the fraternity where disorder always reigns. John Belushi stars, with Tim Matheson, Peter Riegert, Thomas Hulce, and Bruce McGill. **CO4, CO13, CO35** *Recommended*

National Lampoon's Class Reunion (1982, C, 84m, R)
A psycho killer stalks a high school reunion party in this comedy written by John Hughes. Gerrit Graham stars. **CO35, CO47**

National Lampoon's European Vacation (1985, C, 94m, PG-13)
The wacky family from *National Lampoon's Vacation* invades the continent for more misadventures in tourism. Chevy Chase, Beverly D'Angelo, and Eric Idle star. Written by John Hughes. **CO5, CO13, CO15, CO47**

National Lampoon's Vacation (1983, C, 98m, R)
Chevy Chase and family take off for the summer and travel every back road in America on their way to mythical Wally World. Beverly D'Angelo, Christie Brinkley, John Candy, and Eugene Levy costar. Written by John Hughes; directed by Harold Ramis. **CO5, CO13, CO14, CO47**

National Velvet (1944, C, 124m, G)
Classic story of a girl and the horse she must ride in the Grand National—even if it means disguising herself as a boy. Elizabeth Taylor and Mickey Rooney star, with Oscar winner Anne Revere. **CL33, FA5, XT5**

Native Son (1986, C, 112m, PG)
In 1940, a young black chauffeur accidentally murders the daughter of his employer and becomes the center of a highly publicized trial. Adapted from Richard Wright's novel. Victor Love, Elizabeth McGovern, and Oprah Winfrey star. **DR14, DR19**

Natural, The (1984, C, 134m, PG)
Robert Redford is baseball star Roy Hobbs, the man with a mysterious past. Glenn Close, Robert Duvall, Barbara Hershey, and Kim Basinger costar. Adapted from the novel by Bernard Malamud. **DR2, DR19, DR22, DR29, DR37, DR72**

Naughty Marietta (1935, B&W, 106m, NR)
Nelson Eddy and Jeanette MacDonald debuted together in this operetta about a runaway princess and dashing Indian scout. Songs include "Ah, Sweet Mystery of Life." **CL14**

Naughty Nineties, The (1945, B&W, 76m, NR)
Abbott and Costello play a couple of riverboat gamblers in this comedy which includes their unforgettable "Who's on First?" routine. **CO23**

Nazarin (1961, B&W, 92m, NR)
From director Luis Buñuel, the story of a Mexican priest and his unsuccessful attempts to bring the word of God to the peasants. **FF11**

Near Dark (1987, C, 94m, R)
A teenaged boy in Oklahoma is kidnapped by a family of vampires who roam the roads of the Midwest by night. Atmospheric horror story with modern twists; music by Tangerine Dream. **HO5** *Recommended*

Neighbors (1981, C, 94m, R)
Placid suburban man is bedeviled by rude and lewd new next-door neighbors—but is he imagining it all? John Belushi and Dan Aykroyd star in this offbeat comedy, based on Thomas Berger's novel. **CO12, CO13**

Nelson Mandela 70th Birthday Tribute (1988, C, 120m, NR)
Highlights from a benefit concert held at London's Wembley Stadium to honor the jailed South African activist. Among the performers: George Michael, The Eurythmics, Al Green, Tracy Chapman, Peter Gabriel, Whitney Houston, Stevie

Wonder, Dire Straits, and Eric Clapton. **MU10**

Neptune's Daughter (1949, C, 93m, NR)
Esther Williams plays a bathing suit designer in this aquatic MGM musical costaring Red Skelton, Betty Garrett, and Mel Blanc. **MU1**

Nest, The (1988, C, 88m, R)
A scientific experiment gone wrong results in a breed of giant cockroaches. Robert Lansing, Lisa Langlois, and a lot of bugs star. **HO16**

Network (1976, C, 121m, R)
An aggressive programmer (Faye Dunaway) at a major TV network clashes with a veteran producer (William Holden) and an unstable anchorman (Peter Finch, in his last film). With Beatrice Straight, Robert Duvall, and Ned Beatty. Directed by Sidney Lumet; written by Paddy Chayevsky. Finch, Dunaway, and Straight won Oscars. **CL51, DR12, DR35, DR37, DR58, XT2, XT3, XT5, XT11** *Recommended*

Nevada Smith (1966, C, 135m, NR)
Steve McQueen is an obsessed cowboy out to avenge the murders of his parents. **AC28, WE4, WE6**

Never a Dull Moment (1968, C, 100m, G)
A TV star accidentally becomes involved with gangsters. Disney comedy starring Dick Van Dyke and Edward G. Robinson. **CL52, FA1**

Never Cry Wolf (1983, C, 105m, PG)
Based on a true story, this adventure drama follows a naturalist as he braves Arctic conditions to study wolves up close. Charles Martin Smith stars in this family film. **AC12, AC24, FA4** *Recommended*

Never Give a Sucker an Even Break (1941, B&W, 71m, NR)
W. C. Fields' last feature film appearance is a zany free-for-all of vintage Fields bits. Margaret Dumont costars. **CO22**

Never Let Go (1963, B&W, 90m, NR)
Rare dramatic outing for Peter Sellers, as he plays a gangster involved with car thefts. **CO26**

Never Love a Stranger (1958, B&W, 91m, NR)
A young hood finds himself caught between his boyhood friends on the right side of the law and his colleagues in the Mob. John Drew Barrymore stars; Steve McQueen has a small supporting role. **AC28**

Never on Sunday (1960, B&W, 91m, NR)
An American visiting Greece tries to "educate" a carefree prostitute, who turns the tables on him. Melina Mercouri and husband Jules Dassin star; Dassin directed. **CO1**

Never Say Never Again (1983, C, 134m, PG)
Sean Connery's return as an older but no less crafty James Bond is a remake of *Thunderball*. Klaus Maria Brandauer is the villain, Kim Basinger and Barbara Carrera are the ladies. **AC35, AC36**

Never So Few (1959, C, 124m, NR)
Frank Sinatra leads a guerrilla band against the Japanese in World War II Burma. Steve McQueen and Charles Bronson head the supporting cast. **AC1, AC28, AC29, DR49**

Never Steal Anything Small (1959, C, 94m, NR)
James Cagney plays a union boss in this offbeat musical comedy-drama. **CL22**

NeverEnding Story, The (1984, C, 92m, PG)
A young boy imagines that the fantasy story he is reading comes true—and he becomes part of a fabulous adventure. **FA8, FF3, SF13**

New Adventures of Pippi Longstocking, The (1988, C, 100m, G)
The children's book heroine embarks on more adventures with her friends Tommy and Annika. Tami Erin stars, with Eileen

Brennan, Dennis Dugan, and Dick Van Patten. See also: *Pippi Longstocking* series. **FA4**

New Kids, The (1984, C, 90m, R)
A brother and sister off to live with their uncle suddenly find themselves confronted by a neighborhood gang. Shannon Presby, Lori Loughlin, and Eric Stoltz star in this drama. **DR9**

New Leaf, A (1971, C, 102m, PG)
Elaine May directed and stars in this comedy about a frumpy scientist who's wooed strictly for her money by an unscrupulous playboy (Walter Matthau). **CO12**

New Life, A (1988, C, 104m, PG-13)
The comic mishaps of a New York couple who divorce and encounter the world of singles and "dating." Alan Alda and Ann-Margret star, with Hal Linden, Veronica Hamel, and John Shea. Alda wrote and directed. **CO1, CO2**

New Moon (1940, B&W, 105m, NR)
Jeanette MacDonald-Nelson Eddy musical set in Louisiana. Songs include "Softly as in a Morning Sunrise" and "Stout-Hearted Men." **CL15**

New York, New York (1977, C, 163m, R)
Drama set at the end of the Big Band era, centering on the stormy romance between a hot-tempered musician (Robert DeNiro) and a rising singer (Liza Minnelli). Martin Scorsese directed. The video version contains the "Happy Endings" production number, which did not appear in the original release of the film. **CU10, DR12, DR25, DR52, MU4, MU6**

New York Stories (1989, C, 123m, PG)
A trio of tales set in contemporary Manhattan. In "Life Lessons," directed by Martin Scorsese, a temperamental artist (Nick Nolte) tries to prevent his protegé-lover (Rosanna Arquette) from leaving him. Francis Ford Coppola's "Life Without Zoe" focuses on the adventures of a girl who lives in a luxurious hotel while her parents are away tending to their sep-arate careers. "Oedipus Wrecks" features director-star Woody Allen as a Jewish attorney whose dominating mother (Mae Questel) ruins his relationship with a Gentile woman (Mia Farrow). **CO2, CO27, DR1, DR9, DR15, DR44, DR51, DR52, XT9** *Recommended*

Newsfront (1978, C, 110m, PG)
Behind-the-scenes drama of the people who made newsreels in Australia during the 1940s and 1950s. **FF5** *Recommended*

Next Year, If All Goes Well (1981, C, 95m, R)
French comedy of a couple (Isabelle Adjani, Thierry Lhermitte) who can't decide if they're really in love, even after conceiving a child. **FF1**

Niagara (1953, C, 89m, NR)
Marilyn Monroe stars in this thriller about a woman planning to murder her new husband on their honeymoon. Joseph Cotten costars. **CL29, MY4**

Nice Dreams (1981, C, 89m, R)
Cheech and Chong, those spaced-out L.A. hipsters, use their ice cream truck as a front for selling marijuana. Stacy Keach and Timothy Leary costar. **CO32**

Nicholas and Alexandra (1971, C, 183m, PG)
Epic tale of the final days of Czar Nicholas of Russia and his wife, with court intrigue aplenty. Michael Jayston and Janet Suzman star; Laurence Olivier heads the supporting cast. **CL32, DR5**

Night Ambush *see* Ill Met by Moonlight

Night and Day (1946, C, 128m, NR)
Cary Grant plays composer Cole Porter in this dramatic biography. Eve Arden and Alexis Smith costar; many Porter tunes on the soundtrack. **CL18, MU5**

Night and Fog (1955, B&W, 34m, NR)
Classic documentary about the horrors of the Nazi death camps, directed by Alain Resnais. **CU16** *Recommended*

Night at the Opera, A (1935, B&W, 92m, NR)
The Marx Bros. journey to America, demolish a production of *Il Travatore*. Margaret Dumont takes a dim view of it all. Stateroom scene an all-time crowd pleaser. Kitty Carlisle and Allan Jones offer a few songs. **CO21** *Recommended*

Night Before, The (1988, C, 90m, PG-13)
Comedy of errors, set during a teenaged boy's prom night, starring Keanu Reeves, Lori Loughlin, and Trinidad Silva. Songs by George Clinton, who appears in a nightclub scene. **CO4**

Night Call Nurses (1972, C, 85m, R)
Sexy comedy about wild goings-on at a hospital. Produced by Roger Corman; directed by Jonathan Kaplan. **CU14**

Night Crossing (1981, C, 106m, PG)
True-life drama about two families escaping from East Berlin in a hot-air balloon. John Hurt, Jane Alexander, and Glynnis O'Connor star in this Disney production. **FA1**

Night Flight From Moscow (1973, C, 113m, PG)
A Russian diplomat attempts to defect to the West. Spy thriller starring Yul Brynner, Henry Fonda, and Dirk Bogarde. **CL24**

Night Force (1986, C, 82m, R)
A strike force composed of young recruits engages terrorist during a rescue mission in the jungles of Southeast Asia. Linda Blair is in command. **AC20**

Night Gallery (1969, C, 98m, NR)
Trio of creepy stories, narrated by Rod Serling, each originating with a separate painting. Roddy McDowall, Ossie Davis, and Joan Crawford are among the stars; Steven Spielberg directed the segment with Crawford. Originally made for TV. **CL50, HO23, SF24**

Night in Casablanca, A (1946, B&W, 85m, NR)
The Marx Brothers turn a Moroccan hotel upside-down in search of Nazi spies. **CO21**

Night in June, A *see* June Night

Night in the Life of Jimmy Reardon, A (1988, C, 90m, R)
The comic misadventures of a sexually precocious young man, set in 1962 suburban Chicago. River Phoenix stars, with Ann Magnuson, Meredith Salenger, and Ione Skye. **CO4**

Night Is My Future (1947, B&W, 87m, NR)
Early film from director Ingmar Bergman about a blind veteran who is taken in by a caring housekeeper. Mai Zetterling stars. **FF8**

'night, Mother (1986, C, 97m, PG-13)
A drama about a woman's determination to end her life and her mother's attempts to talk her out of suicide. Sissy Spacek and Anne Bancroft star. **DR8, DR20, DR68**

Night Moves (1975, C, 95m, R)
Detective, hired to find runaway rich girl, uncovers bizarre mystery plot centering on a smuggling ring in the Florida Keys. Clever thriller, starring Gene Hackman, with Jennifer Warren, Melanie Griffith, and James Woods. Directed by Arthur Penn; written by Alan Sharp. **DR39, MY2, MY14** *Highly Recommended*

Night of the Comet (1984, C, 95m, PG-13)
The passing of a strange comet over the skies of Los Angeles leaves two air-head sisters as survivors to battle zombie victims. Tongue-in-cheek science fiction, starring Catherine Mary Stewart and Kelli Maroney. **SF12, SF21, XT9** *Recommended*

Night of the Creeps (1986, C, 89m, NR)
An alien organism is released through a human carrier, creating monsters and havoc. **HO21**

Night of the Generals, The (1967, C, 148m, NR)
Someone is murdering the generals of the Third Reich in this mystery/war drama. Peter O'Toole, Omar Sharif, and Tom Courtenay star. **DR45**

Night of the Ghouls *see* Revenge of the Dead

Night of the Hunter (1955, B&W, 93m, NR)
Moody thriller about two children fleeing from murderous preacher. Robert Mitchum, Lillian Gish, and Shelley Winters star. The only film directed by actor Charles Laughton; a cult favorite. **CL49, CU15, MY1** *Recommended*

Night of the Iguana, The (1964, B&W, 93m, NR)
Tennessee Williams drama about a minister in Mexico and his worldly temptations. Richard Burton stars, with Ava Gardner, Deborah Kerr, and Sue Lyon as the temptations. John Huston directed. **CL44**

Night of the Living Dead (1969, B&W, 96m, NR)
Low-budget horror classic about ghouls returning from the grave to feed on the living. George Romero directed this midnight movie staple. **CU1, CU4, CU7, HO6, HO18, HO38** *Highly Recommended*

Night of the Shooting Stars, The (1982, C, 106m, R)
During the final days of World War II, the residents of an Italian village try to survive the Nazi retreat. Directed by Paolo and Vittorio Taviani. **FF2** *Recommended*

Night Porter, The (1974, C, 115m, R)
A former concentration camp official and the prisoner he once abused meet years after the war and resume a bizarre sexual relationship. Dirk Bogarde and Charlotte Rampling star in this drama. **CU6**

Night Shift (1982, C, 106m, R)
A nerd and a fast-talking hustler who work nights together at the New York City morgue decide to go into the call girl business. Sweet comedy starring Henry Winkler, Michael Keaton, and Shelley Long. Directed by Ron Howard. **CO1, CO2, CO45** *Recommended*

Night Stage to Galveston (1952, B&W, 61m, NR)
Gene Autry and pal Pat Buttram are working to uncover corruption in the ranks of the Texas Rangers. Clayton Moore (TV's Lone Ranger) costars. **WE24**

Night They Raided Minsky's, The (1968, C, 99m, PG)
Comedy set in burlesque era in New York, with Quaker girl (Britt Ekland) meeting baggy-pants comic (Jason Robards). Narrated by Rudy Vallee. **CO6**

Night Time in Nevada (1948, C, 67m, NR)
A western town is caught in the grip of a pair of cattle thievin', embezzlin' varmints, and it's Roy Rogers to the rescue. With Andy Devine and Bob Nolan. **WE23**

Night to Remember, A (1942, B&W, 91m, NR)
Comic mystery about a suspense novelist (Brian Aherne) and his wife (Loretta Young) solving a real murder case. **MY15, MY21**

Night to Remember, A (1958, B&W, 123m, NR)
Dramatic recreation of the infamous sinking of the *Titanic*. Kenneth More and David McCallum head the cast of this disaster adventure. **AC23, CL3, DR5**

Night Visitor, The (1970, C, 106m, PG)
Liv Ullmann and Max von Sydow star in this suspense drama about a man who escapes from a mental institution intent on revenge. English-language film, shot in Denmark and Sweden. **FF25, HO9**

Night Watch (1973, C, 105m, R)
A wealthy widow claims she witnessed a murder, but police can find no evidence a crime has been committed. Elizabeth

Taylor and Laurence Harvey star in this thriller. **CL33, MY3**

Nightbreaker (1989, C, 99m, NR)
During the 1950s, the U.S. government deliberately exposes thousands of soldiers to an atomic bomb test to determine the effects of radiation. Emilio Estevez and Martin Sheen (son and father in real life) star, with Lea Thompson. Originally made for cable TV. **DR7, XT8**

Nightcomers, The (1972, C, 96m, R)
Prequel of sorts to the ghost tale *Turn of the Screw* tries to imagine how the children of that story came to be haunted. Marlon Brando stars. **DR33**

Nighthawks (1981, C, 99m, R)
Two New York police detectives (Sylvester Stallone and Billy Dee Williams) comb Manhattan for a cold-blooded terrorist (Rutger Hauer). **AC9, AC31**

Nightingale, The (1985, C, 60m, NR)
Mick Jagger stars in this Faerie Tale Theatre presentation of the story of a powerful emperor and a magical bird. Barbara Hershey and James Edward Olmos co-star. **FA12**

Nightmare on Elm Street (series)
Nightmare on Elm Street (1984, C, 92m, R)
Nightmare 2: Freddy's Revenge (1986, C, 87m, R)
Nightmare 3: Dream Warriors (1987, C, 97m, R)
Nightmare 4: The Dream Master (1988, C, 93m, R)
Quartet of horror tales about teenagers with horrible dreams featuring the same demented, scarred killer. Robert Englund stars as the evil Freddy Krueger in all four films. **HO12, HO18**

Nightmare Weekend (1985, C, 88m, R)
Three college coeds answer an ad for an experimental weekend in the country, only to find themselves captives of a professor's crazed assistant. **HO20**

Nightmares (1983, C, (99m, R)
Four-story horror film, starring Emilio Estevez, Christina Raines, and William Sanderson. **HO23**

Nights of Cabiria (1957, B&W, 110m, NR)
A prostitute in Rome dreams of a better life for herself in this Oscar-winning drama from director Federico Fellini. Giulietta Masina (his real-life wife) stars. **FF10, XT7**

Nightwing (1979, C, 105m, PG)
Horror drama, set in Arizona, about killer vampire bats. David Warner, Kathryn Harrold, and Strother Martin star. **HO16**

Nijinsky (1980, C, 125m, R)
True-life drama of relationship between famed Russian dancer Nijinsky and impressario Sergei Diaghliev. George de la Pena and Alan Bates star, with Leslie Browne, Alan Badel, and Jeremy Irons. **DR3, DR4, DR12**

Nikki, Wild Dog of the North (1961, C, 74m, NR)
Disney adventure about a Canadian wolf-dog and his master. **FA1, FA5**

9 1/2 Weeks (1986, C, 117m, R)
Drama of an intense love affair between two modern New Yorkers, with overtones of sadism and masochism. Mickey Rourke and Kim Basinger star. **CU6, DR3, DR48**

9 to 5 (1980, C 110m, PG)
Comedy about three long-suffering secretaries (Jane Fonda, Lily Tomlin, and Dolly Parton) who take out their frustrations on their loutish boss (Dabney Coleman). **CO3, DR27**

1918 (1984, C, 94m, NR)
Matthew Broderick stars in this drama about a small Texas town devastated by the famous influenza epidemic. **DR5, DR62**

1984 (1984, C, 117m, R)
Screen version of the George Orwell novel about life under a future dictator-

ship. John Hurt and Richard Burton (in his last film) star. **DR19, SF11**

1941 (1979, C, 118m, PG)
Panic erupts in Southern California when residents believe a Japanese attack is imminent. Steven Spielberg directed this comedy with a huge cast that includes John Belushi, Dan Aykroyd, Toshiro Mifune, Warren Oates, Christopher Lee, and Slim Pickens. **CO6, CO13, CU48, FF28, HO32, SF24**

1900 (1977, C, 255m, R)
From director Bernardo Bertolucci, the epic story of two friends, one a landowner, the other a peasant, and how they're affected by the rise of fascism. Robert DeNiro, Gerard Depardieu, Burt Lancaster, and Dominique Sanda star. **DR25, DR41, FF2, FF18, FF29** *Recommended*

92 in the Shade (1975, C, 93m, R)
Bizarre goings-on in the Florida Keys in this comedy about rival fishing guides and their wacky women. Peter Fonda, Warren Oates, Margot Kidder, and Elizabeth Ashley star, with William Hickey, Burgess Meredith, and Joe Spinell. Tom McGuane directed and wrote; based on his own novel. **CO12, CU48, DR19** *Recommended*

Ninotchka (1939, B&W, 110m, NR)
Greta Garbo is the Russian agent who falls for suave Melvyn Douglas in one of Garbo's rare comic outings. With Bela Lugosi. Directed by Ernst Lubitsch; co-written by Billy Wilder. **CL10, CL28, CL54, HO28** *Highly Recommended*

No Deposit, No Return (1976, C, 112m, G)
Two clever kids stage their kidnapping, just to get some attention. David Niven and Darren McGavin star as villains in this Disney comedy. **FA1**

No Man of Her Own (1932, B&W, 85m, NR)
Clark Gable and Carole Lombard costar in this drama of a no-good guy and the woman who sets him straight. **CL23**

No Mercy (1986, C, 108m, R)
A Chicago cop (Richard Gere) travels to New Orleans to nab the gangster who killed his partner. Kim Basinger and Jeroen Krabbe costar. **AC19, MY5**

No Nukes *see* The MUSE Concert: No Nukes

No Retreat, No Surrender (1985, C, 85m, PG)
A karate student squares off against a Russian bully. **AC26**

No Way Out (1987, C, 116m, R)
A naval aide to the Secretary of Defense finds himself incriminated in the death of the Secretary's mistress. Kevin Costner, Gene Hackman, and Sean Young star in this political thriller filmed on location in Washington, D.C. **DR21, DR39, MY2, MY5, MY6, XT9** *Recommended*

No Way to Treat a Lady (1968, C, 108m, NR)
An actor with a mother fixation dons disguises to commit his crimes against women. Rod Steiger, George Segal, and Lee Remick star. **MY17**

Nobody's Fault *see* Little Dorritt

Nomads (1986, C, 95m, R)
A scientist discovers a secret cult of ghosts living in modern-day Los Angeles. Horror thriller stars Pierce Brosnan, Lesley-Anne Down, and Adam Ant. **HO11, MU12**

Nomads of the North (1920, B&W, 109m, NR)
In the wilderness of northern Canada, a lovely young woman is forced into marriage with a villain to absolve her father's debts. Silent melodrama starring Lon Chaney, Sr. **HO29**

None but the Lonely Heart (1944, B&W, 113m, NR)
Rare drama for Cary Grant as a Cockney trying to do right by his dying mother (Oscar winner Ethel Barrymore). Grant's only Oscar nomination. **CL18, XT5**

Norma Rae (1979, C, 113m, PG)
Sally Field won an Oscar for her portrayal of a Southern working woman who helps organize a union against enormous pressures. **DR10, DR36, XT3**

Norte, El (1984, C, 141m, R)
Heartrending story of a brother and sister fleeing their Latin American country because of political persecution and heading for the United States, where they encounter a different set of problems. Directed by Gregory Nava; produced by Anna Thomas. **DR7** *Recommended*

North Avenue Irregulars, The (1979, C, 99m, G)
A young priest and some of his female parishioners take on local criminals in this Disney comedy. Edward Herrmann, Barbara Harris, and Susan Clark star. **FA1**

North by Northwest (1959, C, 136m, NR)
Hitchcock chase drama, with innocent businessman Cary Grant mistaken for government agent. Many memorable scenes, with exciting climax on Mount Rushmore. Eva Marie Saint and James Mason costar. **CL18, MY7, MY22** *Highly Recommended*

North Dallas Forty (1979, C, 119m, R)
A pro football player finds his love of the game soured by the win-at-all-costs attitudes of his team's coaches and management. A devastating (and often funny) portrait of modern professional sports, starring Nick Nolte and Mac Davis. **CO36, DR44** *Highly Recommended*

North of the Great Divide (1950, C, 67m, NR)
Roy Rogers stars in this western about a Canadian Mountie and an Indian agent joining forces against a corrupt cannery owner. **WE11, WE23**

North Shore (1987, C, 96m, PG)
Matt Adler and Gregory Harrison star in this drama about surfers living for the big wave on the California coast. **DR22**

North Star (1943, B&W, 105m, NR)
World War II drama set in a Russian village, with noble townspeople resisting the German army. Anne Baxter, Dana Andrews, Walter Huston, and Erich Von Stroheim star. Written by Lillian Hellman; directed by Lewis Milestone. A few years after its release, Cold War politics forced scenes especially sympathetic to the Soviets to be cut; film was retitled *Armored Attack*. **AC1, CL53, CU8**

North to Alaska (1960, C, 122m, NR)
Golddiggers on the northern frontier battle the elements and each other. John Wayne, Stewart Granger, and Fabian star. **MU12, WE11, WE17**

Northern Pursuit (1943, B&W, 94m, NR)
Errol Flynn plays a Canadian Mountie tracking a downed Nazi spy pilot. **AC34**

Northwest Passage (1940, C, 125m, NR)
Spencer Tracy stars in this colorful historical drama about Roger's Rangers, a group of scouts in Colonial America. Robert Young and Walter Brennan costar. **CL3, CL19**

Nosferatu (1922, B&W, 63m, NR)
Silent film version of the Dracula story, directed by F.W. Murnau, is a classic of mood and atmosphere rather than blood and gore. **HO1, HO5** *Recommended*

Nosferatu the Vampyre (1979, C, 107m, PG)
Effective remake of the classic vampire tale, starring Klaus Kinski and Isabelle Adjani, directed by Werner Herzog. **CU18, HO5, FF19, FF30** *Recommended*

Not for Publication (1984, C, 88m, PG)
Comedy about a reporter who moonlights as a campaign worker for a zany mayor and her romance with a photographer. Nancy Allen and David Naughton star; Paul Bartel directed. **CU42**

Nothing in Common (1986, C, 119m, PG)
After a hip advertising executive sees his parents' long-standing marriage fall apart, he finds that his ailing father is now de-

pendent on him. Tom Hanks, Jackie Gleason, and Eva Marie Saint star in this comedy-drama set in Chicago. **CO44, DR8, DR60, XT9** *Recommended*

Nothing Sacred (1937, C, 75m, NR)
Smooth-talking reporter gets fictional scoop on a Vermont girl supposedly dying of radium poisoning and turns her into a national celebrity. Fredric March and Carole Lombard star in this comedy written by Ben Hecht. **CL10, CL48**

Notorious (1946, B&W, 101m, NR)
Hitchcock's classic mixture of suspense and passion, with American agent Cary Grant forcing Ingrid Bergman to spy on neo-Nazi Claude Rains. **CL4, CL18, CL27, MY3, MY5, MY6, MY22** *Highly Recommended*

Now and Forever (1983, C, 93m, R)
An Australian couple's happiness is shattered when he's falsely accused of rape and sent to prison. Cheryl Ladd stars. **FF5**

Now, Voyager (1942, B&W, 117m, NR)
Classic Bette Davis tearjerker about a spinster's romance. Paul Henreid and Claude Rains costar. **CL4, CL5, CL21**

Now You See Him, Now You Don't (1972, C, 88m, G)
College student Kurt Russell invents a spray that makes him invisible and is pursued by crooks who want the formula. Disney comedy also stars Cesar Romero and Jim Backus. **FA1**

Nowhere to Hide (1987, C, 100m, R)
Amy Madigan is a Marine whose husband, also a member of the Corps, is murdered by assassins. She uses her training to protect herself and her small son. **AC25**

Nuit de Varennes, La (1982, C, 133m, R)
This historical drama has Casanova and Thomas Paine sharing a coach during the violent days of the French Revolution. Marcello Mastroianni, Harvey Keitel, and Hanna Schygulla star. **FF2, FF24**

Number 17 (1932, B&W, 83m, NR)
Light-hearted Hitchcock thriller about a hobo who gets mixed up with gang of jewel thieves. **MY19, MY22**

Nun's Story, The (1959, C, 149m, NR)
Audrey Hepburn stars as a young sister who serves as a missionary in Africa and later decides to leave her order. Peter Finch costars; Fred Zinnemann directed. **CL30, CL57**

Nuts (1987, C, 116m, R)
A prostitute on trial for murdering a customer must battle her own lawyer and the legal system which wants to declare her insane. Barbra Streisand and Richard Dreyfuss star in this adaptation of the award-winning play. **DR10, DR17, DR20, MU27**

Nutty Professor, The (1963, C, 107m, NR)
Comic variation on the Dr. Jekyll and Mr. Hyde story, with Jerry Lewis as the supremely nerdy scientist and his alter ego, suave crooner Buddy Love. Stella Stevens costars. **CL14, CO25, CO35**

O. C. and Stiggs (1987, C, 109m, R)
Comedy about two teenagers determined one summer to wreak havoc on their neighborhood. Dan Jenkins and Neill Barry star, with Paul Dooley, Dennis Hopper, and Jon Cryer. Robert Altman directed. **CU25, CU46**

O Lucky Man! (1973, C, 173m, R)
Epic adventures of a plucky young Britisher (Malcolm McDowell) who becomes top coffee salesman, suffers humiliating failure, only to land on his feet again. Unique musical interludes featuring composer Alan Price. Directed by Lindsay Anderson. **DR23** *Recommended*

Oblong Box, The (1969, C, 91m, PG)
Vincent Price and Christopher Lee star in this horror story of two brothers, one a respectable British aristocrat, the other his disfigured, reclusive brother. Based on an Edgar Allan Poe tale. **HO14, HO31, HO32, HO41**

Obsession (1976, C, 98m, PG)
Years after his wife and daughter are kidnapped and disappear, a New Orleans businessman meets a young woman with an uncanny resemblance to his wife. Cliff Robertson, Genevieve Bujold, and John Lithgow star in this thriller from director Brian DePalma. **CU28, MY5**

Ocean's Eleven (1960, C, 127m, NR)
Frank Sinatra heads a gang of thieves with plans to rob five Las Vegas casinos at one time. Dean Martin, Sammy Davis, Jr., Peter Lawford, and Angie Dickinson costar in this comic caper. **DR49**

Octagon, The (1980, C, 103m, R)
Chuck Norris plays a bodyguard whose client is in danger from an army of Ninja assassins. **AC32**

Octopussy (1983, C, 130m, PG)
James Bond (Roger Moore) travels to India to tangle with a deadly female assassin (Maud Adams) and her cult. **AC35**

Odd Angry Shot, The (1979, C, 90m, R)
A group of Australian soldiers try to cope with combat life during the Vietnam War. John Hargreaves and Bryan Brown star. **FF5**

Odd Couple, The (1968, C, 105m, G)
Classic Neil Simon comedy about two newly divorced men (Walter Matthau and Jack Lemmon) sharing a New York apartment despite their totally incompatible lifestyles. **CO3, CO34, DR64, XT9**

Odd Man Out (1947, B&W, 113m, NR)
James Mason plays a wounded Irish gunman on the lam, with no one to shelter him, in this classic thriller. Directed by Carol Reed. **MY19** *Recommended*

Odd Obsession (1959, C, 96m, NR)
In this Japanese drama, an elderly man persuades his wife to take up with a younger man, with disastrous consequences. **FF4**

Odessa File, The (1974, C, 128m, PG)
Frederick Forsyth thriller about a German reporter tracking ex-Nazis in 1963 Berlin. Jon Voight and Maximillian Schell star. **MY6, MY31**

Of Human Bondage (1934, B&W, 83m, NR)
Classic Somerset Maugham story of a crippled man's infatuation with a scornful waitress, starring Bette Davis and Leslie Howard. **CL21**

Of Mice and Men (1939, B&W, 107m, NR)
Drama, based on John Steinbeck novel, about clever George (Burgess Meredith) and dim-witted Lenny (Lon Chaney, Jr.) and the tragic event that leads to their separation. **DR19, HO30**

Of Unknown Origin (1983, C, 88m, R)
Horror story of a New York businessman doing battle in his home with a gigantic rodent. Peter Weller stars. **HO16**

Off Limits (1953, B&W, 89m, NR)
Service comedy, with Bob Hope and Mickey Rooney trying to put one (or two) over on the brass. **CO38, CO40**

Off Limits (1988, C, 110m, R)
A pair of American police detectives track down a killer in 1968 Saigon. Willem Dafoe and Gregory Hines star, with Amanda Pays, Fred Ward, and Scott Glenn. **AC9, MY20**

Officer and a Gentleman, An (1982, C, 126m, R)
Romance blossoms between a headstrong naval pilot-in-training and a girl who works at a local factory. Richard Gere and Debra Winger star; Oscar winner Louis Gossett, Jr. lends support. **DR1, DR47, XT4**

Official Story, The (1985, C, 110, R)
Oscar-winning film from Argentina about a woman who discovers that the parents of her adopted daughter may be among the "missing" persons executed by the secret police. Norma Aleandro stars. **FF6, XT7**

Offspring, The (1986, C, 99m, R)
A quartet of horror tales, narrated by an old man (Vincent Price) who lives in a mysterious small town. **HO23, HO31**

Oh! Calcutta! (1972, C, 105m, NR)
Long-running Broadway musical, actually a series of sketches about sexuality, in which the actors wear no clothes. **MU2**

Oh, God! (1977, C, 104m, PG)
A supermarket manager strikes up a friendship with the earthly presence of the Supreme Being. John Denver and George Burns star in this family comedy. **FA6**

Oh, God! Book II (1980, C, 94m, PG)
George Burns returns as the Man Upstairs. This time, he's using a little girl to get out the word that reports of his demise have been greatly exaggerated. **FA6**

Oh, God! You Devil (1984, C, 96m, PG)
The third in the series finds George Burns playing both title roles in the story of a singer who sells his soul to you-know-who for fame and fortune. Ted Wass co-stars. **FA6**

Oh! Heavenly Dog (1980, C, 104m, PG)
A private eye (Chevy Chase) is reincarnated in the body of a lovable dog (Benji) in this family comedy. **CO13, FA5**

Oklahoma! (1955, C, 145m, G)
Classic Rodgers and Hammerstein musical about settlers in the Sooner State, starring Gordon MacRae, Shirley Jones, and Rod Steiger. Songs include "Oh, What a Beautiful Mornin' " and "People Will Say We're in Love." Directed by Fred Zinnemann. **CL57, FA9, MU2, MU6**

Oklahoma Kid, The (1939, B&W, 85m, NR)
Unusual casting in this western featuring Humphrey Bogart and James Cagney as the villain and lawman in a revenge struggle. **CL20, CL22, WE16**

Old Barn Dance, The (1938, B&W, 58m, NR)
Singing cowboy Gene Autry exposes some evil businessmen in this modern-day western. Roy Rogers is in the supporting cast under the name Dick Weston. **WE23, WE24**

Old Boyfriends (1979, C, 103m, R)
Drama about a woman who looks up her former lovers to try to understand herself better. Talia Shire stars; John Belushi, Richard Jordan, and Keith Carradine play the title roles. **CO13**

Old Corral, The (1936, B&W, 56m, NR)
Contemporary cowboy Gene Autry battles gangsters on the range. The Sons of the Pioneers (featuring Roy Rogers) harmonize; Lon Chaney, Jr. costars. **HO30, WE23, WE24**

Old Ironsides (1926, B&W, 111m, NR)
A trio of sailors ship out in search of adventure in this silent adventure classic, starring Wallace Beery, Boris Karloff, and Charles Farrell. **CL12, HO27**

Old Maid, The (1939, B&W, 95m, NR)
Bette Davis and Miriam Hopkins play cousins at war over Davis's illegitimate daughter in this classic soap opera. **CL5, CL21**

Old Yeller (1958, C, 84m, G)
A Texas pioneer family in the 1860s adopts a lovable stray dog in this Disney western drama. Fess Parker, Dorothy McGuire, and Tommy Kirk star. **FA1, FA5**

Oldest Living Graduate, The (1982, C, 75m, NR)
Henry Fonda plays an alumnus of a Texas school who is in conflict with his son. Videotape of a stage performance, originally shown on public TV. **CL24**

Oldest Profession, The (1967, C, 97m, NR)
A comic look at prostitution through the ages, from the viewpoint of six directors, including Jean-Luc Godard. **FF14**

Oliver! (1968, C, 153m, G)
Musical version of the Dickens story about an orphan's adventures in London won six Oscars, including Best Picture and Director (Carol Reed). Ron Moody, Oliver Reed, and Mark Lester star; songs include "As Long as He Needs Me."
CL1, FA9, MU2, MU7, XT1, XT6

Oliver and Company (1988, C, 72m, G)
Disney animated feature, loosely based on Dickens' *Oliver Twist*, with a kitten adopted by a streetwise pack of dogs in New York City. Among the character voices: Billy Joel, Bette Midler, Richard "Cheech" Marin, and Dom Deluise.
CL1, FA2

Oliver Twist (1922, B&W, 77m, NR)
Silent version of the Charles Dickens tale of orphans and thieves, starring Jackie Coogan and Lon Chaney, Sr. **CL1, FA3, HO29**

Oliver Twist (1933, B&W, 70m, NR)
The Dickens classic of an orphan caught up in a world of thieves, starring Dickie Moore. **CL1, FA3**

Oliver Twist (1948, B&W, 116m, NR)
Director David Lean's version of the Dickens classic, starring Alec Guinness, Robert Newton, and Anthony Newley. **CL1, DR50, FA3**

Olvidados, Los (1950, B&W, 88m, NR)
Drama about the street boys of Mexico City is one of the most powerful films on the subject of rebellious youth. Luis Buñuel directed. **FF1** *Highly Recommended*

Olympia (1938, B&W, 215m, NR)
Legendary documentary of the 1936 Olympic Games, directed by Leni Riefenstahl. Available on two tapes: Part I, *The Festival of the People*, runs 119m; Part II, *The Festival of Beauty*, runs 96m. **CU16** *Highly Recommended*

Omen, The (1976, C, 111m, R)
The American ambassador to England finds out that his step-child is actually the "anti-christ" incarnate. Horror drama

starring Gregory Peck, Lee Remick, and David Warner. **HO10, HO13**

On a Clear Day You Can See Forever (1970, C, 129m, PG)
Musical fairy tale about a woman whose psychiatrist discovers she has lived a previous life. Barbra Streisand and Yves Montand star; Jack Nicholson has a small role. Directed by Vincente Minnelli.
DR24, MU8, MU24, MU27

On Any Sunday (1971, C, 91m, G)
Documentary on the thrills and spills of motorcycle racing, featuring Steve McQueen. **AC28**

On Golden Pond (1981, C, 109m, PG)
Katharine Hepburn won her fourth Oscar, Henry Fonda his first (and in his last film) in this sentimental drama about an elderly couple and their clashes with their headstrong daughter (Jane Fonda). **CL16, CL24, DR11, DR27, XT2, XT3, XT8, XT11**

On Her Majesty's Secret Service (1969, C, 140m, PG)
James Bond not only takes on archenemy Ernst Stavro Blofeld, but he also decides to marry a contessa. George Lazenby (in his only 007 film) stars, with Telly Savalas and Diana Rigg. **AC35**

On the Beach (1959, B&W, 133m, NR)
After the superpowers destroy one another with atomic weapons, a group of survivors in Australia await the deadly radiation clouds. Classic 1950s science fiction, starring Gregory Peck, Ava Gardner, and Fred Astaire. **MU18, SF1, SF12**

On the Edge (1985, C, 92m, PG)
Bruce Dern plays a middle-aged runner training for a grueling race that could turn his life around. **DR22**

On the Nickel (1980, C, 96m, R)
Drama about street persons in Los Angeles, starring Ralph Waite and Donald Moffat, directed by Waite. **DR15**

On the Right Track (1981, C, 98m, PG)
Gary Coleman stars in this family comedy about a shoeshine boy who lives in a train station locker. **FA6**

On the Town (1949, C, 98m, NR)
Musical about three sailors (Gene Kelly, Frank Sinatra, Jules Munshin) on shore leave in New York City trying to see all they can in 24 hours. Directed by Gene Kelly and Stanley Donen. **MU1, MU6, MU19, MU23, MU26, XT9** *Recommended*

On the Waterfront (1954, B&W, 108m, NR)
Drama of life on the New Jersey docks, with Marlon Brando the former prizefighter caught between his fellow workers and his brother, who works for the crooked union boss. Eva Marie Saint, Rod Steiger, and Lee J. Cobb costar; directed by Elia Kazan. Oscar winner for Best Picture, Actor, Supporting Actress, and Director. **CL8, DR33, DR59, XT1, XT2, XT5, XT6** *Highly Recommended*

On the Yard (1979, C, 102m, R)
Prison drama about young convict making the big mistake of taking on the top con in the joint. John Heard and Thomas Waites star. **DR16**

On Top of Old Smoky (1953, B&W, 59m, NR)
Gene Autry is in hot water when he's mistaken for an outlaw. Smiley Burnette adds comic relief. **WE24**

On Valentine's Day (1986, C, 106m, PG)
A young woman from a small southern town shocks her family by marrying a man with few prospects. Matthew Broderick and Hallie Foote star. Horton Foote wrote this drama about his parents' marriage; sequel to *1918*. **DR5**

Once Upon a Honeymoon (1942, B&W, 117m, NR)
Ginger Rogers marries a man she does not know is a Nazi officer; Cary Grant comes to the rescue. Walter Slezak costars in this comedy. **CL18**

Once Upon a Time in America (1984, C, 225m, R)
Rich, powerful, gangster epic about two Jewish buddies who grow up in New York and turn rivals as adults. Robert DeNiro and James Woods star; Sergio Leone directed. (Also available in a 143-minute version) **AC22, DR25, WE27** *Highly Recommended*

Once Upon a Time in the West (1968, C, 166m, PG)
The ultimate spaghetti Western—maybe the ultimate Western, with Henry Fonda (as a villain) pitted against Jason Robards and a vengeful Charles Bronson. Claudia Cardinale costars. Sensational photography; lovely score by Ennio Morricone. Directed by Sergio Leone. **AC29, CL14, CL24, WE1, WE6, WE16, WE27** *Highly Recommended*

One and Only Genuine Original Family Band, The (1968, C, 117m, G)
Disney comedy about a musical family from the Dakota Territories who lend their talents to the 1888 Presidential campaign. Walter Brennan stars; Goldie Hawn debuts in a small role. **CO30, FA1**

One Body Too Many (1944, B&W, 75m, NR)
Jack Haley plays a salesman forced to solve a crime when he's mistaken for a detective. Comedy-mystery costars Bela Lugosi. **HO28**

One Crazy Summer (1987, C, 94m, PG)
Life on Nantucket Island during the tourist season is the basis for this freewheeling comedy, starring John Cusack, Demi Moore, and Joe Flaherty. **CO14**

One Deadly Summer (1983, C, 133m, R)
Isabele Adjani stars in this French thriller about a young girl whose eccentric manner disguises an intricate revenge plan. Also known as *L'Ete Meurtrier*. **MY20**

One-Eyed Jacks (1961, C, 141m, NR)
Marlon Brando stars in this western tale (which he directed) about an outlaw left for dead by his partner. Karl Malden co-

stars as the object of Brando's vengeance. **CU15, DR33, WE6, WE16** *Highly Recommended*

One-Eyed Swordsman, The (1963, C, 95m, NR)
Japanese samurai action drama starring Tetsuro Tanba. **FF4**

One Flew Over the Cuckoo's Nest (1975, C, 129m, R)
A misfit decides to get himself committed to a mental hospital for "a little rest." But he doesn't anticipate clashing with a strong head nurse. Adaptation of the Ken Kesey novel won Oscars for Best Picture, Actor (Jack Nicholson), Actress (Louise Fletcher), and Director (Milos Forman). **DR19, DR24, DR57, XT1, XT2, XT3, XT6** *Highly Recommended*

One From the Heart (1982, C, 100m, R)
From director Francis Ford Coppola, a stylized musical drama about a couple in Las Vegas who split up and find other momentary partners. Teri Garr, Frederic Forrest, Raul Julia, and Nastassja Kinski star, with Harry Dean Stanton. Songs by Tom Waits, sung by Waits and Crystal Gayle. **CU49, DR51, MU16**

100 Rifles (1960, C, 110m, PG)
A deputy sheriff pursues a gun thief into Mexico, where the lawman falls in love with a lovely revolutionary. Burt Reynolds, Jim Brown, and Raquel Welch star. **AC37, WE8, WE10**

One Magic Christmas (1985, C, 88m, G)
A modern Christmas fable about a harried mother (Mary Steenburgen) who learns the true meaning of the season from a special angel (Harry Dean Stanton). **CU49, FA13**

One Million B.C. (1940, B&W, 80m, NR)
Life in prehistoric times, with cavemen battling dinosaurs. Victor Mature and Lon Chaney, Jr. star. **HO30**

One Minute to Zero (1952, B&W, 105m, NR)
Korean War drama starring Robert Mitchum, with Ann Blyth, William Talman, and Richard Egan. **AC3**

One of Our Aircraft Is Missing (1941, B&W, 106m, NR)
Drama about British pilots who crash during war mission over Holland and try to make their way home. Michael Powell directed. **CU19**

One on One (1977, C, 98m, R)
A heavily recruited high school basketball player finds he's just another player on the team at a big university. Robby Benson is the struggling jock; Annette O'Toole is his academic tutor. **DR22**

One-Trick Pony (1980, C, 98m, R)
A rock star tries to juggle the demands of his marriage and his changing audience. Paul Simon, Blair Brown, and Rip Torn star. **CU47, DR12, MU9**

One, Two, Three (1961, B&W, 108m, NR)
James Cagney plays a fast-talking American Coca-Cola executive caught up in some hilarious Cold War complications in Berlin. Billy Wilder directed. **CL10, CL22, CL37, CO2** *Highly Recommended*

One Woman or Two (1985, C, 97m, PG-13)
A comedy about a French scientist (Gerard Depardieu) and his relationship with the American woman (Sigourney Weaver) who finances his work. **DR76, FF29**

Onion Field, The (1979, C, 122m, R)
True story, based on Joseph Wambaugh book, about a Los Angeles policeman whose partner is murdered by two punks and how he deals with the consequences. John Savage, James Woods, and Ted Danson star. **DR6, DR16** *Recommended*

Only Angels Have Wings (1939, B&W, 121m, NR)
Superbly realized buddy adventure of mail pilots working the dangerous routes through the Andes. Cary Grant stars, with Jean Arthur and Rita Hayworth as

the women in his life, Richard Barthelmess, Thomas Mitchell, and Noah Beery, Jr. as the fliers. Howard Hawks directed. **AC11, AC13, CL18, CL35** *Highly Recommended*

Only the Valiant (1951, B&W, 105m, NR)
Western drama of courageous army man (Gregory Peck) battling Indians. Lon Chaney, Jr. costars. **HO30**

Only When I Laugh (1981, C, 120m, R)
Change of pace for Neil Simon in this drama about an actress who's a recovering alcoholic and her relationship with her teenaged daughter. Marsha Mason, Kristy McNichol, Joan Hackett, and James Coco star. **CO34**

Open City (1946, B&W, 105m, NR)
Influential Italian drama about the tense days of Rome's occupation during World War II. Directed by Roberto Rossellini. **WW2**

Operation C.I.A. (1965, B&W, 90m, NR)
Saigon-based thriller with Burt Reynolds as an American agent trying to prevent an assassination. **AC37**

Operation Petticoat (1959, C, 124m, NR)
Cary Grant and Tony Curtis star in this service comedy set aboard a submarine. Directed by Blake Edwards. **CL18, CO38, CO46**

Operation Thunderbolt (1977, C, 125m, PG)
Drama about the Entebbe hijack rescue by Israeli commandoes on July 4, 1976. This film was officially approved by the Israeli government. Klaus Kinski stars. **FF30**

Opposing Force (1986, C, 99m, R)
During a war games maneuver on a remote Pacific island, two officers discover that a third is waging war for real. Tom Skerritt and Lisa Eichorn star. **AC20, AC24**

Orca (1977, C, 92m, PG)
A giant whale goes on a rampage when bounty hunters murder his mate. Horror/disaster story starring Richard Harris and Charlotte Rampling. **HO16**

Ordeal by Innocence (1984, C, 87m, PG-13)
Agatha Christie tale of injustice in a small English town and the amateur sleuth who rights the wrong. Donald Sutherland, Faye Dunaway, and Christopher Plummer star. **MY23, DR35**

Ordet (1955, B&W, 125m, NR)
Danish director Carl Dreyer's classic story of feuding families who must resolve their religious differences when a love affair between one son and daughter of each clan is revealed. **FF35**

Ordinary People (1980, C, 123m, R)
A family is torn apart over the death of its oldest son in this drama. Donald Sutherland, Mary Tyler Moore, and Timothy Hutton (in his debut) star; Robert Redford directed. The film, Redford, and Hutton each won Oscars. **DR2, DR8, DR9, DR29, XT1, XT4, XT6** *Recommended*

Organization, The (1971, C, 107m, PG)
Sidney Poitier returns for his third stint as Detective Virgil Tibbs in this drama about a dope-smuggling operation. **DR38**

Orphans of the Storm (1922, B&W, 125m, NR)
Silent drama from director D.W. Griffith set amid the turbulence of French Revolution, involving sisters unfairly separated. Lillian and Dorothy Gish costar. **CL36, CL49, XT8**

Oscar, The (1966, C, 119m, NR)
Behind-the-scenes soap opera centering on the annual Hollywood Academy Awards show. Eleanor Parker, Stephen Boyd, Elke Sommer, and Ernest Borgnine star. **DR12**

Osterman Weekend, The (1983, C, 102m, R)
A talk show host is persuaded that several of his best friends are Soviet agents. A convoluted thriller, based on the Robert Ludlum novel. John Hurt, Rutger Hauer, and Burt Lancaster star, with Craig T. Nelson, Dennis Hopper, and Helen Shaver. Director Sam Peckinpah's final film. **CU46, DR41, MY6, MY32, WE19**

Other, The (1972, C, 100m, PG)
Thriller, based on Thomas Tryon's novel, about young twin boys, one good, one evil. Uta Hagen, Diana Muldaur, and Chris and Martin Udvarnoky star. **HO15**

Other Side of Midnight, The (1977, C, 165m, R)
Epic soap opera, from the Sidney Sheldon bestseller, about a woman's ruthless climb to the top of the show business world. Marie-France Pisier, Susan Sarandon, and John Beck star. **DR2**

Our Daily Bread (1934, B&W, 74m, NR)
During the Depression, a couple living on a dilapidated farm invite homeless people to work their land and form a commune of sorts. Classic drama of hard-times 1930s, directed by King Vidor. **CL8**

Our Little Girl (1935, C, 65m, NR)
Shirley Temple plays a girl who tries to bring her feuding parents (Rosemary Ames, Joel McCrea) together. **FA14**

Our Relations (1936, B&W, 74m, NR)
Laurel and Hardy comedy in which the boys play two sets of twins, one set happy-go-lucky sailors, the others peacable married men. **CO20**

Our Town (1940, B&W, 90m, NR)
Thronton Wilder's classic play about life in a small New England town stars William Holden, Martha Scott, and Thomas Mitchell. **CL51, DR20, DR62**

Out of Africa (1985, C, 161m, PG)
Meryl Streep plays writer Isak Dinesen, who journeyed from her native Denmark to live on a plantation in Africa and write about her experiences there. Robert Redford and Klaus Maria Brandauer costar; Sydney Pollack directed this drama, which won 7 Academy Awards, including Best Picture and Director. **DR4, DR26, DR29, DR56, XT1, XT6** *Recommended*

Out of Bounds (1986, C, 93m, R)
A young man visting Los Angeles from Iowa is mistaken for a drug courier in this thriller starring Anthony Michael Hall. **MY7**

Out of Control (1985, C, 78m, R)
A group of high school students are trapped on a desert island and forced to battle a ruthless gang of smugglers for survival. Martin Hewitt stars. **AC24**

Out of the Blue (1980, C, 94m, R)
A teenager tries to deal with the problems of her parents, an ex-con and a drug addict, but finally loses control of her life, too. Linda Manz stars with Dennis Hopper (who directed) and Sharon Farrell. **CU46, DR8**

Out of the Past (1947, B&W, 97m, NR)
Classic film noir about an ex-con up to his neck in trouble from his former boss and a no-good woman. Robert Mitchum, Kirk Douglas, and Jane Greer are the points in the deadly triangle. Jacques Tourneur directed. **HO37, MY1, MY5** *Highly Recommended*

Out of Towners, The (1970, C, 97m, PG)
Jack Lemmon and Sandy Dennis play a couple of Ohio tourists who encounter every nightmare situation possible on a trip to New York City. Written by Neil Simon. **CO34, DR64, XT9**

Outland (1981, C, 111m, R)
Sean Connery is an outer space lawman in this futuristic thriller about drug smuggling at a space station. Peter Boyle costars. **AC36, SF17**

Outlaw, The (1943, B&W, 103m, NR)
Cult western, initially banned in some cities, about Billy the Kid and Doc Holliday, was controversial for its allegedly

steamy scenes with Jane Russell (in her film debut). Directed by Howard Hawks and Howard Hughes. **CU8, WE2, WE4, WE16, WE21**

Outlaw Josey Wales, The (1976, C, 137m, PG)
Clint Eastwood stars in and directed this western saga of a man consumed with hatred for the Union soldiers who killed his family. **WE4, WE7, WE26** *Recommended*

Outrageous! (1977, C, 100m, R)
A lonely young woman and a female impersonator strike up a friendship in this cult comedy starring Craig Russell and Hollis McLaren. **CO12, CU1**

Outrageous Fortune (1987, C, 100m, R)
Bette Midler and Shelley Long play two women who track down the man that two-timed them. Wild chase comedy costars Peter Coyote and George Carlin. **CO2, MU12**

Outside the Law (1921, B&W, 77m, NR)
Lon Chaney, Sr. and director Tod Browning's first collaboration is this silent melodrama with Chaney playing two roles: Black Mike, the slimy hoodlum, and Ah Wing, the faithful Chinese retainer to the story's heroine. **HO29, HO35**

Outsiders, The (1983, C, 91m, PG)
Three teenaged brothers try to get through life without parents in this drama adapted from S.E. Hinton's novel. C. Thomas Howell, Ralph Macchio, Patrick Swayze, and Matt Dillon star, with Rob Lowe, Emilio Estevez, Diane Lane, and Tom Cruise; Francis Ford Coppola directed. **CU17, DR9, DR19, DR51, DR73**

Over the Edge (1979, C, 95m, R)
In a suburban community, a group of bored, restless teens clash with parents and law enforcement officials. Provocative, disturbing drama starring Michael Kramer and Matt Dillon. Written by Tim Hunter and Charlie Haas; directed by Jonathan Kaplan. **DR9** *Recommended*

Over the Top (1986, C, 94m, PG)
Sylvester Stallone is a trucker involved in a custody battle and the national arm-wrestling championships. **AC31, DR22**

Overboard (1987, C, 112m, PG)
Goldie Hawn plays a snob who suffers amnesia when she falls off her yacht, and Kurt Russell is the carpenter who claims her for his wife in this comedy. **CO30**

Owl and the Pussycat, The (1970, C, 95m, R)
Barbra Streisand and George Segal star in this romantic comedy about a sassy New York prostitute and a fussy, would-be writer. Written by Buck Henry. **CO1, MU27** *Recommended*

Ox-Bow Incident, The (1943, B&W, 75m, NR)
Western tale of injustice, about the lynching of a trio of cowboys who turn out to be innocent. Henry Fonda stars. **CL24** *Recommended*

Oxford Blues (1984, C, 98m, PG-13)
An American rower enrolls at Oxford to compete with the best that Britain has to offer. Rob Lowe, Ally Sheedy, and Amanda Pays star. **DR22**

P.O.W. The Escape (1986, C, 90m, R)
David Carrdine plays a hard-bitten officer determined to lead a group of American prisoners out of Vietnam. **AC7**

Pack, The (1977, C, 99m, R)
Wild dogs attack two families in this horror tale starring Joe Don Baker and R.G. Armstrong. **HO16**

Pack Up Your Troubles (1932, B&W, 68m, NR)
Laurel and Hardy enlist in the army to fight in World War I. The Germans almost die laughing. **CO20**

Padre Padrone (1977, C, 114m, NR)
Based on a true story, this Italian drama portrays the bitter childhood of a peasant boy who grows up to be a renowned

scholar. Directed by Paolo and Vittorio Taviani. **FF2**

Pain in the A—, A (1974, C, 90m, PG)
A hit man and a would-be suicide wind up sharing the same hotel room in this dark comedy from France. American remake: *Buddy, Buddy*. **FF1, FF36**

Paint Your Wagon (1969, C, 166m, G)
Lavish musical about the gold rush in California, starring Clint Eastwood, Lee Marvin, and Jean Seberg. **AC27, DR43, MU6, MU17**

Painted Desert, The (1931, B&W, 75m, NR)
Western drama about two feuding families. Clark Gable's talking pictures debut; he plays a baddie. **CL23**

Paisan (1946, B&W, 90m, NR)
Classic drama of Italian life during World War II, directed by Roberto Rossellini and cowritten by Federico Fellini. **FF2**

Pajama Game, The (1957, C, 101m, NR)
Doris Day and John Raitt square off in this Broadway musical about labor troubles, directed by Stanley Donen and George Abbott. With Carol Haney; choreography by Bob Fosse. **MU2, MU23, MU28**

Pale Rider (1985, C, 113m, R)
Clint Eastwood directed and stars in this western story of a mysterious lone gunfighter who comes to the aid of persecuted prospectors. **WE3, WE26**

Paleface, The (1948, C, 91m, NR)
Bob Hope is the world's biggest dude, Jane Russell is his straight-shooting sidekick in this western comedy. **CO40, WE15**

Palm Beach Story, The (1942, B&W, 90m, NR)
Classic comedy about a wife deciding to divorce her inventor husband because her tastes are too rich for them. Claudette Colbert, Joel McCrea, and Rudy Vallee star; Preston Sturges wrote and directed. **CL10, CO24** *Highly Recommended*

Pancho Villa (1972, C, 92m, PG)
Telly Savalas plays the legendary Mexican bandit/revolutionary in this western adventure. **WE10**

Pandora's Box (1928, B&W, 110m, NR)
Classic silent drama of Lulu, the bewitching woman who casts an irresistible spell on all men. Louise Brooks gives a dynamic, sexy performance. Directed by G. W. Pabst. **FF3, CU6, CL12** *Highly Recommended*

Paper Chase, The (1973, C, 111m, PG)
Portrait of a first-year Harvard Law School student (Timothy Bottoms) and his affair with the daughter of his most feared professor (John Houseman, in an Oscar-winning performance). **DR61, XT4**

Paper Lion (1968, C, 107m, G)
Writer George Plimpton (Alan Alda) goes on assignment with pro football's Detroit Lions, training with the team and quarterbacking in one exhibition game. Alex Karras, then a star lineman, steals the film. Also in the cast: Lauren Hutton, Sugar Ray Robinson, and (in a small part) Roy Scheider. **CO36**

Paper Moon (1973, B&W, 102m, PG)
Depression-era comedy about a con man (Ryan O'Neal) and his daughter (Oscar winner Tatum O'Neal) traveling through Middle America with a bible selling routine. **CO6, XT5, XT8**

Paper Tiger (1976, C, 99m, PG)
David Niven plays the cowardly tutor to a Japanese diplomat's son who musters all his courage when he and the boy are kidnapped. Toshiro Mifune costars in this family drama. **FF28**

Papillon (1973, C, 151m, PG)
True story of Henri Charrière, played by Steve McQueen, and his dramtic escape from Devil's Island prison. Dustin Hoffman costars. **AC24, AC28, DR30**

Paradine Case, The (1948, B&W, 116m, NR)
Alfred Hitchcock courtroom drama, starring Gregory Peck and Valli. **DR17, MY22**

Paradise Alley (1978, C, 109m, PG)
Sylvester Stallone directed and stars in this comedy of three New York brothers and their dreams for fame and fortune, with one going for a career as a pro wrestler. Armand Assante costars. **AC31**

Paradise, Hawaiian Style (1966, C, 91m, NR)
Elvis Presley returns to the islands after his success with *Blue Hawaii* for some more ukulele strumming and romancing with the local ladies. **MU22**

Parallax View, The (1974, C, 102m, R)
Reporter Warren Beatty uncovers a complex political conspiracy in this very contemporary thriller. Directed by Alan J. Pakula. Photographed by Gordon Willis. **CU9, DR21, DR34, MY6, MY15** *Recommended*

Pardon Mon Affaire (1977, C, 105m, PG)
A happily married man is nevertheless fascinated by a gorgeous model he spots in a parking garage. This French comedy was remade in the U.S. as *The Woman in Red*. **FF1, FF36**

Pardon Us (1931, B&W, 55m, NR)
Laurel and Hardy are shipped off to prison for making homemade brew during the height of Prohibition. **CO20**

Parent Trap, The (1961, C, 127m, NR)
Hayley Mills plays twin sisters who are separated when their parents divorce and meet years later at a summer camp. Disney comedy costars Brian Keith and Maureen O'Hara. **FA1**

Parents (1989, C, 83m, R)
Dark comedy set in the 1950s, featuring a seemingly normal couple whose young son begins to suspect that their dinners are composed of human meat. Randy Quaid and Marybeth Hurt star. **CO5, CO6, CO12**

Paris Blues (1961, B&W, 98m, NR)
Quartet of Americans in Paris—two jazz musicians, two female tourists—are the focus of this drama. Paul Newman, Sidney Poitier, Joanne Woodward, and Diahann Carroll star; Louis Armstrong makes an appearance. **DR28, DR38, DR67, XT9**

Paris Express, The (1953, C, 83m, NR)
A shy bookkeeper uncovers embezzling by his boss and follows him to Paris, where he's accused of the thief's murder. Claude Rains stars. **MY7**

Paris Holiday (1958, C, 100m, NR)
Bob Hope plays an American in Paris looking to purchase a screenplay, involved in misunderstandings and mix-ups. Fernandel and Anita Ekberg costar; watch for writer-director Preston Sturges in a rare acting role. **CO24, CO40**

Paris, Texas (1984, C, 150m, R)
Drama of two brothers reunited years after one deserted his son and wife. Harry Dean Stanton, Nastassja Kinski, and Dean Stockwell star; directed by Wim Wenders and written by Sam Shepard. **CU49, DR8, FF21**

Paris When It Sizzles (1964, C, 110m, NR)
An American screenwriter and his secretary are in Paris trying to work on a script in this comedy starring William Holden and Audrey Hepburn. Marlene Dietrich is among the stars who appear in cameos. **CL30, CL47, CL51**

Party Line (1988, C, 91m, R)
A brother and sister, unhinged by their mother's suicide and father's abuse, turn killers, using special telephone party lines to lure their victims. Leif Garrett and Greta Blackburn star. **MY18**

Pascali's Island (1988, C, 106m, PG-13)
British period drama set on a Mediterranean outpost, where a Turkish intelligence officer is frustrated in both his professional and love life. Ben Kingsley stars, with Helen Mirren and Charles Dance. **DR23**

Passage to India, A (1984, C, 163m, PG)
From director David Lean comes this screen version of the E.M. Forster novel about an impressionable Englishwoman's tragic experiences in India. Judy Davis, Victor Bannerjee, Alec Guinness, and Oscar winner Peggy Ashcroft star. **DR19, DR50, DR63, XT5**

Passage to Marseilles (1944, B&W, 110m, NR)
Escape drama set on infamous Devil's Island, starring Humphrey Bogart, Claude Rains, Sydney Greenstreet, and Peter Lorre. **CL20**

Passenger, The (1975, C, 119m, PG)
A journalist in North Africa assumes the identity of a man he finds dead in a hotel room. Jack Nicholson stars in this drama from director Michelangelo Antonioni. **DR24, FF17**

Passion (1919, B&W, 135m, NR)
Silent version of *Madame du Barry*, starring Pola Negri and Emil Jannings and directed by Ernst Lubitsch. **FF3, Cl2, CL54**

Passion (1954, C, 84m, NR)
Western drama of revenge set in California, starring Cornel Wilde, Yvonne De Carlo, and Lon Chaney, Jr. **HO30**

Passion of Joan of Arc, The (1928, B&W, 114m, NR)
Director Carl Dreyer's austere, gripping recreation of the young martyr's trial and execution. A silent film classic. Maria Falconetti gives a mesmerizing performance. **CL12, FF1, FF35** *Recommended*

Pat and Mike (1952, B&W, 96m, NR)
Spencer Tracy—Katharine Hepburn comedy of a hustling sports promoter and his latest find, a superb female athlete. Directed by George Cukor; written by Garson Kanin and Ruth Gordon. Watch for Charles Bronson (billed as Charles Buchinski). **AC29, CL10, CL15, CL16, CL19, CL39, CO36** *Recommended*

Pat Garrett and Billy the Kid (1973, C, 106m, R)
The tragic tale of the famous outlaw and his sheriff friend who gunned him down. James Coburn and Kris Kristofferson star, with Richard Jaeckel, Katy Jurado, Jason Robards, Rita Coolidge, Slim Pickens, and Harry Dean Stanton. Directed by Sam Peckinpah; music by Bob Dylan, who also has a small role. Also available in a 122m version that restores the director's original footage. **CU10, CU49, MU12, WE2, WE4, WE16, WE19** *Recommended*

Paternity (1981, C, 94m, PG)
The manager of New York's Madison Square Garden decides to look for the perfect woman to father his first child. Burt Reynolds stars in this comedy, with Beverly D'Angelo, Elizabeth Ashley, and Lauren Hutton. **AC37**

Paths of Glory (1957, B&W, 86m, NR)
World War I drama about a French general who orders his men on a suicide mission, then has three survivors court-martialed and executed. Powerful anti-war statement from director Stanley Kubrick. Kirk Douglas stars. **AC2, DR53** *Highly Recommended*

Patrick (1978, C, 96m, PG)
A young murderer in a coma uses his telekinetic powers to further destroy those around him. A horror drama from Australia, directed by Richard Franklin. **FF5, HO7**

Patsy, The (1964, C, 101m, NR)
Nerdy bellhop agrees to impersonate a dead comedian so that the star's hangers-on can keep the money rolling in. Jerry Lewis stars. **CO25**

Patton (1970, C, 169m, PG)
George C. Scott won an Oscar (which he refused to accept) for his performance as the legendary U.S. Army general with a controversial record in Europe during World War II. The film and its director, Franklin Schaffner, also won Academy

Awards. **AC1, DR4, XT1, XT2, XT6** *Recommended*

Patty Hearst (1988, C, 100m, R)
True story of publishing heiress kidnapped by political radicals and brainwashed into joining them in a crime spree. Natasha Richardson and William Forsythe star. Paul Schrader directed. **DR6, DR16**

Pauline at the Beach (1983, C, 94m, R)
From French director Eric Rohmer, a comedy about a teenaged girl's experiences during a summer of growing up at a resort. **FF15**

Pawnbroker, The (1965, B&W, 116m, NR)
Rod Steiger stars as a Jewish survivor of the Nazi death camps who runs a pawn shop in Harlem, fighting against his horrible memories. Sidney Lumet directed. **DR15, DR58, XT9**

Payday (1973, C, 103m, R)
A country singer pushes himself—and everyone around him—to the brink with his rowdy, uninhibited ways. Rip Torn is the magnetic star of this cult favorite. **CU47, DR12** *Recommended*

Peanut Butter Solution, The (1985, C, 96m, PG)
An 11-year-old boy with a very vivid imagination finds himself in a strange house with more adventures than he ever dreamed of. Family comedy. **FA6, FA7**

Pearl of Death (1944, B&W, 69m, NR)
Sherlock Holmes adventure starring Basil Rathbone and Nigel Bruce. They're out to find a killer who calls himself The Creeper. **MY10**

Pee-wee's Big Adventure (1985, C, 92m, PG)
Pee-wee Herman discovers that his favorite bicycle has been stolen, and he embarks on a cross-country mission to recover it. Silly fun for kids of all ages. **CO11, CO12, CU5, FA6** *Recommended*

Peeping Tom (1960, C, 109m, R)
Legendary cult film, censored and banned in its original release, about a murderous cinematographer who films his crimes. Michael Powell directed. **CU8**

Peggy Sue Got Married (1986, C, 103m, PG-13)
At her 20th anniversary high school reunion, a woman passes out and wakes up to find herself in high school again. Will she marry the same no-good guy? Kathleen Turner and Nicolas Cage star in this comedy from director Francis Ford Coppola. **CO6, CO37, DR46, DR51**

Pelle the Conqueror (1988, C, 138m, PG-13)
Oscar-winning drama from Denmark, starring Max von Sydow as an impoverished Swedish widower who moves to Denmark to begin a new life with his son. **FF7, XT7**

Pendulum (1969, C, 106m, PG)
Police detective is framed for murder and must clear himself. George Peppard and Jean Seberg star. **MY7**

Pennies From Heaven (1981, C, 107m, R)
One-of-a-kind musical about a Depression-era sheet music salesman who sings his way through his various troubles. Filled with lavish production numbers, brilliantly photographed by Gordon Willis. Steve Martin, Bernadette Peters, and Christopher Walken star. **CO33, MU3, MU16** *Recommended*

Penny Serenade (1941, B&W, 125m, NR)
Cary Grant and Irene Dunne star in this tearjerker about a couple who decide to adopt a baby. **CL6, CL18, CL42**

People That Time Forgot, The (1977, C, 90m, PG)
Sequel to *The Land That Time Forgot*, with more adventures in ancient world populated by fierce dinosaurs. Doug McClure stars. **SF4**

Pepe LePew's Skunk Tales (1960, C, 56m, NR)
A collection of Warner Bros. cartoons featuring that misunderstood and amorous skunk. Includes the Oscar-winning cartoon, *For Scent-imental Reasons.* **FA11**

Perfect! (1985, C, 120m, R)
Reporter John Travolta is supposed to do an exposé on fitness clubs as a place to pick up dates; he finds himself falling for aerobics instructor Jamie Lee Curtis. Laraine Newman costars. **CO13**

Perfect Furlough, The (1958, B&W, 93m, NR)
Romantic comedy of a young soldier (Tony Curtis) wooing a military psychiatrist (Janet Leigh). Directed by Blake Edwards. **CO46**

Performance (1970, C, 105m, R)
A London gangster on the lam hides out in the home of a reclusive rock star, and their lives begin to intertwine. James Fox and Mick Jagger star in this cult drama, co-directed by Nicolas Roeg and Donald Cammell. **CU1, CU3, CU34, DR16, MY2** *Recommended*

Permanent Record (1988, C, 91m, PG-13)
A teenager who seems to have it all— good grades, popularity, girl friends— commits suicide, leaving his friends to wonder why. Alan Boyce stars, with Keanu Reeves and Richard Bradford. **DR9**

Persecution and Assassination of Jean-Paul Marat as Performed by the Inmates of the Asylum of Charenton Under the Direction of the Marquis de Sade, The *see* Marat/ Sade

Persona (1966, B&W, 81m, NR)
Hypnotic drama from director Ingmar Bergman about the relationship between an actress and a nurse. Liv Ullmann and Bibi Andersson star. **FF8, FF25** *Recommended*

Personal Best (1982, C, 124m, R)
A pair of women runners, competing for a place on the Olympic team, become lovers. Mariel Hemingway, Patrice Donnelly, and Scott Glenn star. **DR22**

Personal Services (1987, C, 104m, R)
Julie Walters stars as a London working-class girl who stumbles into running a brothel and soon becomes very successful at it. This saucy comedy was directed by Terry Jones of the Monty Python troupe. **CO15, CO17**

Pet Sematary (1989, C, 102m, R)
Stephen King horror tale of an ancient burial ground with powers that can bring dead animals back to life. Dale Midkiff and Fred Gwynne star. King adapted his novel and has a small role as a minister. **HO16, HO42**

Pete Kelly's Blues (1955, C, 95m, NR)
Drama revolving around the jazz scene of the 1920s, starring Jack Webb as a trumpet player and featuring real-life music stars Peggy Lee and Ella Fitzgerald. Janet Leigh and Lee Marvin costar. **DR12, DR43**

Pete 'n' Tillie (1972, C, 100m, PG)
Walter Matthau and Carol Burnett star in this romantic comedy-drama about a couple who meet and marry late in life. Co-starring Geraldine Page, Barry Nelson, and Rene Auberjonois. Based on Peter DeVries' novella, *Witch's Milk.* **CO1, DR1**

Pete's Dragon (1977, C, 105m, G)
An orphan is befriended by a large and very friendly dragon in this Disney musical. Helen Reddy, Jim Dale, and Mickey Rooney star. **FA1**

Petrified Forest, The (1936, B&W, 83m, NR)
Escaped convict Humphrey Bogart holds waitress Bette Davis and drifter Leslie Howard hostage in this classic melodrama. **CL20, CL21**

Petulia (1968, C, 105m, PG)
Drama set in 1967 San Francisco about a divorced surgeon (George C. Scott) and his affair with a restless newlywed (Julie Christie). Powerful portrait of late-60s America is brilliantly told through multiple flashbacks. With Richard Chamberlain, Arthur Hill, and musical appearances by The Grateful Dead and Big Brother & the Holding Company. Directed by Richard Lester; photographed by Nicolas Roeg. **CL14, CU35, DR7, DR15, XT9** *Highly Recommended*

Phantom Creeps, The (1939, B&W, 75m, NR)
Condensed version of serial adventure about the evil Dr. Zorka (Bela Lugosi) and his robot and mechanical spider. **HO28**

Phantom Empire (1935, B&W, 245m, NR)
A 12-chapter western serial starring Gene Autry, as he battles the "Thunder Riders" from an underworld kingdom beneath his ranch. Also available in an 80-minute version titled *Radio Ranch*. **WE24**

Phantom of Liberty, The (1974, C, 104m, R)
Director Luis Buñuel presents a series of surrealistic sketches, loosely connected, all designed to satirize contemporary society's claims to freedom. Jean-Claude Brialy, Monica Vitti, and Michel Piccoli star. **FF1**

Phantom of the Opera, The (1925, B&W, 79m, NR)
Lon Chaney, Sr. silent version of the horror classic can't be beat for chills; unmasking scene still an all-time movie highlight. **HO1, HO9, HO29** *Highly Recommended*

Phantom of the Opera (1943, C, 92m, NR)
Second version of horror classic adds brilliant color photography and set design (both Oscar winners). Claude Rains, Susanna Foster, and Nelson Eddy star. **CL9, CU18, HO9**

Phantom of the Paradise (1974, C, 92m, PG)
Rock 'n' roll version of *Phantom of the Opera,* with a little Faust thrown in. Paul Williams, William Finley, Jessica Harper, and Gerrit Graham star; Brian DePalma directed. **CU28, MU4, MU9**

Phantom Ship *see* The Mystery of the Mary Celeste

Phantom Tollbooth, The (1969, C, 90m, G)
Live action and animation blend in this version of the classic children's book about a boy's adventures in a land of numbers and letters. Animation directed by Chuck Jones. **FA8**

Phar Lap (1984, C, 107m, PG)
In 1932, Phar Lap became a national hero, a pug ugly horse from New Zealand that won 37 races in Australia. Tom Burlinson stars in this horse lover's drama. **DR22, FA5**

Phase IV (1974, C, 86m, PG)
Science fiction/horror story of three scientists at remote outpost beset by mutant ants. Clever photography and special effects. **SF20** *Recommended*

Philadelphia Experiment, The (1984, C, 102m, PG)
Two American sailors fall through a time warp in 1943 and wind up in 1984. After one disappears, the other discovers he's part of a secret government experiment. Michael Pare, Nancy Allen, and Bobby Di Cicco star. **SF4**

Philadelphia Story, The (1940, B&W, 112m, NR)
Witty story of spoiled society girl (Katharine Hepburn) who dumps one husband (Cary Grant), tries to marry another man, falls in love with a third (Oscar winner James Stewart). Directed by George Cukor. **CL4, CL16, CL18, CL25, CL39, XT2** *Highly Recommended*

Philby, Burgess and MacLean: Spy Scandal of the Century (1986, C, 83m, NR)
Dramatization of Britain's major spy scandal, involving three college chums recruited by the Russians and working undetected for thirty years. Anthony Bates, Derek Jacobi, and Michael Culver star. **MY6, MY8, MY19**

Phobia (1980, C, 91m, R)
John Huston directed this mystery about a doctor whose patients, all victims of various phobias, are being murdered one by one. **CL44**

Phone Call From a Stranger (1952, B&W, 96m, NR)
The survivor of a plane crash decides to visit the families of some of the victims. Gary Merrill and Bette Davis star, with Shelley Winters and Michael Rennie. **CL21**

Physical Evidence (1988, C, 99m, R)
Burt Reynolds is a suspended cop framed for murder whose only hope for acquittal is a snotty public defender (Theresa Russell). **AC37**

Pick-up Artist, The (1987, C, 81m, R)
A young New York schoolteacher spends his spare time roaming the streets of the city, hitting on women. He meets his match when an attractive young woman accepts his offer for casual sex, then spurns him. Robert Downey, Jr. and Molly Ringwald star, with Dennis Hopper and Harvey Keitel. **CU46, XT9**

Picnic at Hanging Rock (1975, C, 110m, PG)
Atmospheric drama set in turn-of-the-century Australia: a girls' school outing to the Outback turns tragic when three students and their teacher disappear. Rachel Roberts stars; Peter Weir directed. Based on a true story. **FF5**

Picture of Dorian Gray, The (1945, B&W, 111m, NR)
Oscar Wilde story of a man who never ages, despite a wild and carefree life. Hurd Hatfield, Angela Lansbury, and

George Sanders star. Several short sequences in color. **CL1, HO1, HO26**

Piece of the Action, A (1977, C, 135m, PG)
Con men Sidney Poitier and Bill Cosby are roped into helping a social worker and her young charges in this comedy. James Earl Jones costars. **DR38**

Pied Piper of Hamelin, The (1985, C, 60m, NR)
Eric Idle plays both the title role and poet Robert Browning in this Faerie Tale Theatre version of Browning's classic. **CO15, FA12**

Pillow Talk (1959, C, 105m, NR)
Doris Day and Rock Hudson share a party line, can't stand each other on the phone, but fall in love when they meet. Fluffy romantic comedy costarring Tony Randall and Thelma Ritter. **CO1**

Pin (1988, C, 103m, R)
Horror tale of a young boy's fascination with his physician father's anatomical dummy, which comes to life for him. **HO16**

Pink Flamingos (1972, C, 95m, NR)
Director John Waters' look at the cheap and disgusting lives of certain denizens of Baltimore, Maryland. Divine stars in this midnight movie classic. **CU1, CU12, CU43**

Pink Floyd: The Wall (1982, C, 99m, R)
Gloomy rock musical, based on album by British rock group, about the decay of modern society. Bob Geldof and Bob Hoskins star. **MU9, MU16**

Pink Panther, The (1964, C, 113m, NR)
The comedy that gave the madcap Inspector Clouseau (Peter Sellers) to the world. The theft of a rare jewel (the title reference) is the object of his investigation. David Niven, Capucine, and Robert Wagner costar; Blake Edwards directed. **CO26, CO46**

Pink Panther Strikes Again, The (1976, C, 103m, PG)
The fifth in the series about the inept Inspector Clouseau (Peter Sellers) has his ex-boss gone loony and attempting to (dare we say it?) rule the world. Herbert Lom costars. Directed by Blake Edwards. **CO26, CO46**

Pinocchio (1940, C, 87m, G)
Disney animated feature about a marionette who wants to become a boy and must learn some hard lessons about telling the truth. One of the great cartoon features of all time. **FA2** *Highly Recommended*

Pinocchio (1984, C, 60m, NR)
Paul Reubens (better known as Pee-wee Herman) stars as the marionette who wants to be a boy in this Faerie Tale Theatre presentation. **FA12**

Pippi Longstocking (series)
Pippi Longstocking (1974, C, 99m, G)
Pippi in the South Seas (1974, C, 99m, G)
Pippi Goes on Board (1975, C, 84m, G)
Pippi on the Run (1978, C, 99m, G)
The adventures of a daring little Swedish girl who inherits her spunk from her sea captain father. See also: *The New Adventures of Pippi Longstocking.* **FA4**

Piranha (1978, C, 92m, R)
Horror-movie spoof about a resort lake invaded by tiny but deadly fish. Joe Dante directed. **CU4, CU40, HO16, HO24**

Pirate, The (1948, C, 102m, NR)
Judy Garland believes that Gene Kelly is a famous pirate in this colorful musical directed by Vincente Minnelli. **CL9, MU1, MU19, MU21, MU24**

Pirate Warrior (1964, C, 86m, NR)
Low-budget movie about fierce buccaneers, starring Ricardo Montalban and Vincent Price. **HO31**

Pirates (1986, C, 117m, PG-13)
A colorful adventure tale starring Walter Matthau as a one-legged rascal seeking revenge on the crew that set him adrift. Directed by Roman Polanski. **AC15, DR54**

Pit and the Pendulum, The (1961, C, 80m, NR)
Vincent Price stars in this adaptation of the Edgar Allan Poe story of an evil torturer. Directed by Roger Corman. **HO31, HO41**

Pixote (1981, C, 127m, NR)
Powerful drama set on the streets of Rio de Janeiro about a homeless boy's daily struggle for survival. Directed by Hector Babenco. **FF6** *Highly Recommended*

Place in the Sun, A (1951, B&W, 122m, NR)
Montgomery Clift is an ambitious man trapped in a dead-end affair with a factory worker (Shelley Winters) and really in love with a society girl (Elizabeth Taylor). Adapted from Theodore Dreiser's *An American Tragedy.* Directed by Oscar winner George Stevens. **CL4, CL6, CL8, CL33, CL42, DR19, XT6** *Recommended*

Places in the Heart (1984, C, 113m, PG)
Heartfelt drama of a farm woman in Texas during the 1930s and her valiant attempts to bring in the harvest after her husband dies. Oscar winner Sally Field stars, with Danny Glover, Lindsay Crouse, and John Malkovich in support. Written and directed by Robert Benton. **DR2, DR5, DR8, DR36, DR55, XT3**

Plainsman, The (1936, B&W, 113m, NR)
With this lavish western, director Cecil B. DeMille manages to pack Buffalo Bill, Annie Oakley, Wild Bill Hickok, and George Armstrong Custer into one story. Gary Cooper and Jean Arthur star. **WE1, WE2, WE9, WE25**

Plan 9 From Outer Space (1959, B&W, 79m, NR)
Notoriously awful film (and, therefore, a cult classic) from director Ed Wood, Jr. about aliens raising the dead. Bela Lugosi's last film. **CU11, CU45, HO28**

Planes, Trains, and Automobiles (1987, C, 93m, R)
Comedy about the agonies of holiday travel, starring Steve Martin and John Candy as unwilling companions trying to get from New York to Chicago for Thanksgiving. Directed by John Hughes. **CO2, CO3, CO14, CO33, CO47**

Planet of the Apes (1968, C, 112m, PG)
Science fiction adventure about astronauts landing on a planet inhabited by a race of intelligent apes—which hold humans captive as beasts. Charlton Heston stars. First film in long-running series; see **SF23** for a complete list of titles. **FA8, SF8, SF12, SF13, SF23**

Platoon (1986, C, 120m, R)
A young recruit is pitched into the horrors of combat in Vietnam. Charlie Sheen, Willem Dafoe, and Tom Berenger star. Oscar winner for Best Picture and Director (Oliver Stone, who also scripted). **AC4, XT1, XT6** *Recommended*

Play It Again, Sam (1972, C, 87m, PG)
Woody Allen stars in this adaptation of his play about a lovelorn New Yorker with a Humphrey Bogart hang-up. Diane Keaton and Tony Roberts costar. Directed by Herbert Ross. **CO1, CO27, DR40**

Play Misty for Me (1971, C, 102m, R)
Clint Eastwood plays a disc jockey whose one-night stand with a fan (Jessica Walter) turns into a nightmare when the woman relentlessly pursues him. Eastwood's first film as a director. **AC27, MY17** *Recommended*

Playing for Time (1980, C, 150m, NR)
Drama set in a Nazi concentration camp, where certain prisoners played in an orchestra while others met their deaths. Originally made for TV; Emmys to stars Vanessa Redgrave and Jane Alexander, plus writer Arthur Miller. **DR5, DR65**

Playtime (1967, C, 108m, NR)
Jacques Tati directed and stars in this comedy about M. Hulot, the perpetually befuddled Parisian who is trying to keep an important appointment. **FF16**

Plaza Suite (1971, C, 115m PG)
Trio of Neil Simon playlets about goings-on at famous hotel in New York City. Walter Matthau stars in all three episodes; Maureen Stapleton, Lee Grant, and Barbara Harris costar. **CO34**

Please! Mr. Balzac *see* Mademoiselle Striptease

Plenty (1985, C, 119m, R)
Meryl Streep plays a British woman whose teenaged act of heroism during World War II makes the rest of her life seem dull and unrewarding. Charles Dance, Tracey Ullman, John Gielgud, and Sting costar in this adaptation of David Hare's play. **DR10, DR20, DR26, MU12**

Ploughman's Lunch, The (1983, C, 100m, R)
Dark view of British society and journalism in particular, focusing on the conduct of a reporter (Jonathan Pryce) and colleagues during the Falklands war. **DR23**

Plumber, The (1980, C, 76m, NR)
An overbearing plumber destroys a young couple's bathroom in this comic thriller from Australian director Peter Weir. **FF5, HO24, MY3, MY20**

Pocketful of Miracles (1961, C, 136m, NR)
Bette Davis is Apple Annie, a street-corner vendor of the Depression who's turned into a real lady by a producer (Glenn Ford). Directed by Frank Capra. **CL21, CL40**

Pocketful of Rye, A (1984, C, 102m, NR)
Miss Marple, the indefatigable sleuth created by Agatha Christie, comes to the help of a protege in this whodunit. Joan Hickson stars; originally made for British TV. **MY16, MY23**

Point Blank (1967, C, 92m, NR)
Stylized, violent thriller about a man with a mission: to recover money his partner stole during a heist at abandoned Alcatraz

Prison. Lee Marvin stars, with John Vernon, Keenan Wynn, Lloyd Bochner, and Angie Dickinson. Directed with great flair by John Boorman on locations in San Francisco and Los Angeles. **AC8, AC19, AC25, CU7, CU32, DR16, DR43, XT9** *Highly Recommended*

Poker Alice (1987, C, 109m, NR)
Elizabeth Taylor plays a New Orleans gambler who makes her mark in a frontier saloon. George Hamilton and Tom Skerritt costar in this western originally made for cable TV. **CL33, WE9**

Pollyanna (1960, C, 134m, NR)
An orphan comes to live with her aunt in a small town in New England and her good spirits soon affect everyone around her. Disney classic, starring Hayley Mills, Jane Wyman, and Karl Malden. **FA1**

Poltergeist (1982, C, 115m, PG)
Suburban family is haunted by ghosts through their TV set, with youngest daughter kidnapped into another dimension. Craig T. Nelson and JoBeth Williams star; Tobe Hooper directed and Steven Spielberg produced. **HO2, HO3, HO19, HO40**

Poltergeist II (1986, C, 91m, PG-13)
Same family, different house, as Craig T. Nelson, JoBeth Williams and children undergo more hauntings. **HO2, HO3**

Poltergeist III (1988, C, 97m, PG-13)
Heather O'Rourke, the young star of the first two chapters, is still in contact with otherworldly demons, while living with her aunt and uncle (Nancy Allen, Tom Skerritt). **HO2**

Polyester (1981, C, 86m, R)
Suburban Baltimore housewife Francine Fishpaw is romanced by drive-in movie theater owner Todd Tomorrow in this comedy from cult director John Waters. Divine and Tab Hunter star. **CU12, CU43**

Pony Express (1953, C, 101m, NR)
Western drama about the founding of the famous mail route that helped to open the West. Buffalo Bill and Wild Bill are among the historical figures portrayed. Charlton Heston and Rhonda Fleming star. **WE2**

Poor Little Rich Girl (1936, B&W, 72m, NR)
Shirley Temple is a runaway who teams up with a vaudeville couple in this show-business musical. Alice Faye and Jack Haley costar. **FA14**

Pope of Greenwich Village, The (1984, C, 120m, R)
A pair of smalltime New York hoods (Mickey Rourke and Eric Roberts) decide to challenge the neighborhood crime boss. **DR15, DR48**

Popeye (1980, C, 114m, PG)
Live action musical of the famous cartoon and comic strip sailor with a taste for spinach. Robin Williams stars, with Shelley Duvall as Olive Oyl, Paul Dooley as Wimpy. Directed by Robert Altman; songs by Harry Nilsson. **CO43, CU25, FA9**

Pork Chop Hill (1959, B&W, 97m, NR)
Korean War action centering on battle for a strategic position. Gregory Peck, Harry Guardino, and Rip Torn star. **AC3, CU47**

Porky Pig and Daffy Duck Cartoon Festival (1981, C, 57m, NR)
A collection of Warner Bros. cartoons from the 1940s starring that st-st-stuttering pig and his foolish fowl of a friend. **FA11**

Porky's (series)
Porky's (1981, C, 94m, R)
Porky's II: The Next Day (1983, C, 100m, R)
Porky's Revenge (1985, C, 95m, R)
These comedies depict the zany and raunchy misadventures of a gang of teenagers at a Florida high school in the 1950s. **CO4, CO35**

Port of Call (1948, B&W, 99m, NR)
In a Swedish port town, a young outcast
and a seaman strike up a friendship. Directed by Ingmar Bergman. **FF8**

Poseidon Adventure, The (1972, C, 117m,
PG)
When a cruise ship is capsized by a tidal
wave, a group of passengers engage in
desperate battle for escape and survival.
Gene Hackman stars, with Ernest Borg-
nine, Red Buttons, Stella Stevens, and
Shelley Winters. **AC23, DR39**

Positive I.D. (1987, C, 96m, R)
A housewife victimized by a rapist learns
that he's being released from jail. Written
and directed by Andy Anderson. **MY3**

Possessed (1931, B&W, 72m, NR)
Joan Crawford stars in this melodrama of
a woman's sacrifice for the man she loves.
Clark Gable costars. **CL23, CL50**

Postman Always Rings Twice, The (1946,
B&W, 113m, NR)
First screen version of the James M. Cain
story of adultery and murder, with Lana
Turner (in all-white outfits) and John Gar-
field the amorous killers. **DR3, MY1,
MY5, MY25** *Recommended*

Postman Always Rings Twice, The (1981,
C, 123m, R)
Jack Nicholson and Jessica Lange are the
lovers in this version of James M. Cain's
classic tale of adultery and murder.
CU18, DR3, DR24, DR74, MY5, MY25

Pot o' Gold (1941, B&W, 86m, NR)
James Stewart and Paulette Goddard star
in this musical about a boy who wrangles
a spot on his uncle's radio show. **CL25**

Potemkin (1925, B&W, 65m, NR)
Classic film based on real-life sailors' mu-
tiny and subsequent massacre of citizens
in 1905 Russia. Brilliant editing and im-
agery give this silent film, directed by
Sergei Eisenstein, real emotional power.
Also known as *Battleship Potemkin*. **CU9,
CL12, FF22** *Highly Recommended*

Power (1928, B&W, 60m, NR)
Early talkie about a pair of rival dam
workers and their love affairs. William
Boyd, Alan Hale, Carole Lombard, and
Joan Bennett star. **CL48**

Power (1986, C, 111m, R)
A Washington political consultant finds
himself representing a mysterious client
with some nasty secrets. Richard Gere,
Gene Hackman, and Julie Christie star;
Sidney Lumet directed. **DR21, DR39,
DR58, XT9**

Power Play (1978, C, 102m, PG)
A group of military officers plot a coup in
a country ruled by a dictatorship and
secret police. Peter O'Toole and David
Hemmings star. **DR45**

Prairie Moon (1938, B&W, 58m, NR)
Gene Autry is saddled with three young
children after their father dies in this
light-hearted western. **WE24**

Pray for Death (1985, C, 93m, R)
Sho Kosugi stars in this action drama
about a former Ninja who reverts to his
training when he and his family are
threatened by mobsters. **AC26**

Prayer for the Dying, A (1987, C, 107m,
R)
A gunman for the Irish Republican Army
decides to escape the country. But before
he can, he has to carry out a hit for a
ruthless mobster. Mickey Rourke, Alan
Bates, and Bob Hoskins star. **DR48**

Predator (1987, C, 107m, R)
Arnold Schwarzenegger and his jungle
combat buddies are being picked off one
by one by an alien creature. **AC24, AC25,
AC30**

Premature Burial, The (1962, C, 81m,
NR)
Ray Milland plays a medical student with
an obsession that he'll be buried alive.
Roger Corman directed this loose adap-
tation of Edgar Allan Poe's story. **HO41**

Premonition (1971, C, 83m, PG)
Drama about three drug-using college students who all experience the same forebodings of death. Directed by Alan Rudolph. **CU26**

Presenting Lily Mars (1943, B&W, 104m, NR)
Early Judy Garland musical about a young singer trying to make it big on Broadway. **MU21**

President's Analyst, The (1967, C, 104m, NR)
James Coburn stars as the title character, a man who knows so many intimate details about the Chief Executive that every spy in the world is after him. Satirical comedy costars Godfrey Cambridge and William Daniels. **CO2**

President's Plane Is Missing, The (1971, C, 100m, NR)
Thriller, adapted from Robert Serling bestseller, about an attempted overthrow of the U.S. government. Buddy Ebsen, Arthur Kennedy, and Peter Graves star, with Rip Torn, Raymond Massey, and Mercedes McCambridge. Originally made for TV. **CU47, MY6**

Presidio, The (1988, C, 97m, R)
A San Francisco police detective (Mark Harmon) and an army officer (Sean Connery) clash over the investigation of a murder on the latter's base. Meg Ryan costars. **AC9, AC36, XT9**

Pretty Baby (1978, C, 110m, R)
In New Orleans, around the time of World War I, a strange photographer asks permission of a madam to take pictures of her prostitutes. Based on the true story of E.J. Bellocq. Keith Carradine, Brooke Shields, and Susan Sarandon star; Louis Malle directed. **DR5, XT9**

Pretty in Pink (1986, C, 96m, PG-13)
A girl from the wrong side of the tracks and a guy from a wealthy family fall in love and defy their respective crowds at the high school prom. Molly Ringwald and Andrew McCarthy star, with Harry

Dean Stanton. John Hughes produced. **CO47, CU49, DR9**

Prick up Your Ears (1987, C, 111m, R)
The life of British playwright Joe Orton, who authored several hit comedies before he was murdered by his homosexual lover. Gary Oldman and Alfred Molina star, with Vanessa Redgrave. **DR3, DR4, DR23, DR65**

Pride and Prejudice (1940, B&W, 118m, NR)
Jane Austen's classic comedy of manners features Greer Garson and Laurence Olivier as romantic sparring partners in 19th-century England. **CL1, CL32**

Pride and the Passion, The (1957, C, 132m, NR)
War drama set in 19th-century Spain, focusing on the capture of a mammoth cannon. Cary Grant, Frank Sinatra, and Sophia Loren star. **CL18, DR49, FF31**

Pride of the Yankees, The (1942, B&W, 119m, NR)
Gary Cooper plays New York Yankees star Lou Gehrig, whose brilliant career was cut short by a mysterious disease. **CL2, CL26, DR22**

Prime Cut (1972, C, 91m, R)
Rival mobsters Gene Hackman and Lee Marvin duke it out over the Kansas City meat packing business. Sissy Spacek's film debut. **AC22, DR39, DR43, DR68** *Recommended*

Prime of Miss Jean Brodie, The 1969, C, 116m, PG)
Maggie Smith's Oscar-winning performance highlights this drama of an unconventional teacher in a girls' school. **DR61, XT3**

Prince and the Pauper, The (1937, B&W, 120m, NR)
Screen version of Mark Twain's story of royal son and commoner who trade places. Errol Flynn stars, with real-life twins Billy and Bobby Mauch. **AC34, CL1, FA3**

Prince and the Pauper, The (1978, C, 113m, PG)
Remake of the Twain tale of prince and his subject. Mark Lester, Oliver Reed, Raquel Welch, George C. Scott, and Charlton Heston star. Also known as *Crossed Swords*. **CL1, FA3**

Prince and the Showgirl, The (1957, C, 117m, NR)
Unique pairing of Laurence Olivier and Marilyn Monroe in this comedy: title says it all. Olivier directed. **CL29, CL32**

Prince of Darkness (1988, C, 102m, R)
A group of students and scientists discover an ancient cannister in a church, and the contents reap terrifying results. Horror drama from director John Carpenter. **CU29**

Prince of Pennsylvania, The (1988, C, 90m, R)
Family troubles in a working class suburb of Pittsburgh, with teen genius son (Keanu Reeves) hatching a plot to kidnap his father (Fred Ward). Bonnie Bedelia and Amy Madigan costar. **DR8**

Prince of the City (1981, C, 167m, R)
True-life drama of New York City cop persuaded by special investigators to go undercover and expose corruption in the force. Treat Williams stars; Sidney Lumet directed. **DR6, DR16, DR58, XT9** *Recommended*

Princess and the Pea, The (1985, C, 60m, NR)
Liza Minnelli, Tom Conti, and Pat McCormick star in this Faerie Tale Theatre presentation of the children's classic. **FA12**

Princess and the Pirate, The (1944, C, 94m, NR)
Pirate comedy with Bob Hope ducking bucaneers Victor McLaglen and Walter Brennan. Virginia Mayo costars. **CO40**

Princess Bride, The (1987, C, 98m, PG)
A fairy tale story for both grownups and kids, with a lovely princess (Robin Wright) tricked by an evil prince (Chris Sarandon) into believing that her lover (Cary Elwes) is dead. The supporting cast includes Mandy Patinkin, Wallace Shawn, Andre the Giant, and Billy Crystal. **AC14, AC15, CO13**

Princess Who Never Laughed, The (1984, C, 60m, NR)
A Faerie Tale Theatre presentaiton of the Brothers Grimm classic, starring Howie Mandel, Ellen Barkin, and Howard Hesseman. **FA12**

Principal, The (1987, C, 90m, R)
At an inner-city school, a new principal finds that discipline is his most important subject. Jim Belushi and Louis Gossett, Jr. star in the action drama. **CO13, DR61**

Prisoner, The (1955, B&W, 91m, NR)
Alec Guinness stars in this British drama, set in an Eastern Bloc country, about a cardinal interrogated by a brutal official (Jack Hawkins). **CL8, DR63**

Prisoner of Second Avenue, The (1975, C, 105m, PG)
Neil Simon comedy-drama about an unemployed executive in Manhattan who can't cope with his troubles. Jack Lemmon and Anne Bancroft star. **CO34, DR64**

Prisoner of Zenda, The (1937, B&W, 101m, NR)
First-rate version of the classic adventure tale of commoner filling in for regal relative, gaining revenge. Ronald Colman, Douglas Fairbanks, Jr., and Madeleine Carroll star. **AC13, FA4** *Recommended*

Prisoner of Zenda, The (1952, C, 101m, NR)
The classic swashbuckler about a commoner mistaken for a king. Stewart Granger crosses swords with everyone in sight; Deborah Kerr is his lady love. **AC13**

Prisoner of Zenda, The (1979, C, 108m, PG)
Comic version of the classic swashbuckler, with Peter Sellers in the lead. **CO26**

Private Benjamin (1980, C, 100m, R)
A pampered young Jewish woman, widowed on her wedding night, enlists in the army and learns a few lessons in life. Goldie Hawn and Eileen Brennan star, with Armand Assante, Harry Dean Stanton, and Albert Brooks in this comedy. **CO2, CO30, CO38, CU49**

Private Files of J. Edgar Hoover, The (1977, C, 112m, PG)
Melodramatic recreation of the life of famed F.B.I. chief, starring Broderick Crawford as the man with the goods on everyone in Washington. Dan Dailey, José Ferrer, and Rip Torn costar. Directed by Larry Cohen. **CU2, CU30, CU47, DR4**

Private Function, A (1985, C, 93m, R)
During the late 1940s, when meat rationing was still in force in Britain, an illegal pig becomes the focus of deception and double-dealing. This comedy stars Michael Palin and Maggie Smith. **CO6, CO15**

Private Life of Henry VIII, The (1933, B&W, 97m, NR)
Oscar winner Charles Laughton stars as the much-married King of England, with Elsa Lanchester as one of his unfortunate brides. **CL2, XT2**

Private Life of Sherlock Holmes, The (1970, C, 125m, PG)
As the title implies, not your everyday Homes mystery. Robert Stephens, Colin Blakely, and Christopher Lee star in this film from writer-director Billy Wilder with a strong cult following. **CL37, HO32, MY10**

Private Lives of Elizabeth and Essex, The (1939, C, 106m, NR)
Historical drama of the political—and personal—relationship of Queen Elizabeth I (Bette Davis) and the dashing Earl of Essex (Errol Flynn). Vincent Price costars. **AC34, CL2, CL3, CL21, HO31**

Privates on Parade (1982, C, 100m, PG-13)
Comedy about a special theatrical unit performing for British troops in the Pacific during World War II, starring John Cleese. **CO6, CO15, CO38**

Prize Fighter, The (1979, C, 99m, PG)
Family comedy about a lame-brained boxer and his mouthy manager, starring Don Knotts and Tim Conway. **FA6**

Prizzi's Honor (1985, C, 130m, R)
A pair of professional killers fall in love, even though one has been assigned to "hit" the other. Jack Nicholson and Kathleen Turner star in this darkly comic tale, based on Richard Condon's novel. Oscar winner Anjelica Huston heads the supporting cast. John Huston directed. **CL44, DR16, DR24, DR46, XT5**

Producers, The (1968, C, 88m, PG)
Mel Brooks' debut as a writer-director is a daring comedy about an unscrupulous Broadway producer's attempts to intentionally make a flop and walk away with his investors' money. Zero Mostel, Gene Wilder, and Dick Shawn star. **CO28** *Recommended*

Professionals, The (1966, C, 117m, NR)
In this western drama, a wealthy man hires four soldiers of fortune to recapture his wife, who has been kidnapped by a Mexican bandit. Burt Lancaster, Lee Marvin, and Robert Ryan star. **DR41, DR43, WE10** *Recommended*

Project X (1987, C, 107m, PG)
An Air Force enlisted man is assigned to a project involving chimpanzees and soon discovers the deadly secret behind the experiments. Matthew Broderick stars. **DR2, DR7**

Promised Land (1988, C, 101m, R)
Story of three small-town high school friends whose lives after graduation diverge and then converge, disastrously. Kiefer Sutherland, Jason Gedrick, and Tracy Pollan star, with Meg Ryan. **DR7, DR62**

Promoter, The (1952, B&W, 88m, NR)
Alec Guinness plays a brash young opportunist in this British comedy, costarring Glynis Johns. Written by Eric Ambler. **DR63**

Proof of the Man (1984, C, 100m, NR)
An American found murdered in Tokyo is the key to a mystery with international implications. Toshiro Mifune, George Kennedy, and Broderick Crawford star. **FF28**

Prophecy (1979, C, 95m, PG)
A doctor and his pregnant wife investigate mercury poisoning in Maine streams and come face to face with a mutant monster. Talia Shire, Robert Foxworth, and Armand Assante star in this science fiction/horror tale. **SF10**

Protector, The (1985, C, 94m, R)
Martial arts star Jackie Chan plays a New York City cop who's after a drug kingpin. **AC26**

Protocol (1984, C, 95m, PG)
Goldie Hawn stars in this comedy about a know-nothing who's given a do-nothing job in the State Department—and winds up involved in serious foreign relations matters. **CO30**

Proud Rebel, The (1958, C, 103m, NR)
Alan Ladd plays a proud man seeking help for his mute son (David Ladd, the star's real-life son). Olivia de Havilland costars, with Dean Jagger, John Carradine, and (Harry) Dean Stanton. **CU49, XT8**

Providence (1977, C, 104m, R)
From French director Alain Resnais, an English-language film about an aging writer (John Gielgud), his attempts to finish his last novel, and his relationships with his family. Ellen Burstyn and David Warner costar. **DR8, FF1** *Recommended*

Psych-Out (1968, C, 82m, NR)
In late-60s San Francisco, a young deaf runaway tries to locate her brother and falls in with a local rock band. Susan Strasberg, Bruce Dern, and Jack Nicholson star in this relic from the psychedelic era. **DR24**

Psycho (1960, B&W, 109m, R)
Hitchcock's most memorable shocker, about a woman thief, a shabby motel, a shy clerk, and a murderous mother. Anthony Perkins and Janet Leigh star. **HO1, HO9, MY22** *Highly Recommended*

Psycho II (1983, C, 113m, R)
Norman Bates is out of prison for his fiendish crimes, but he just can't stay away from the Bates Motel. Anthony Perkins and Meg Tilly star; Richard Franklin directed. **HO9**

Psycho III (1986, C, 93m, R)
The third entry in the saga of Norman has director-star Anthony Perkins playing the horror more for laughs. **HO9**

Psycho Sisters (1972, C, 76m, PG)
A woman whose husband has just died goes to live with her sister, recently released from an insane asylum. Horror fare starring Susan Strasberg and Faith Domergue. **HO14**

Psychomania (1971, C, 95m, R)
A British motorcycle gang returns from the dead after making a special deal in this adult horror film. George Sanders stars. **HO6**

Psychos in Love (1985, C, 88m, NR)
Horror comedy about a romance between a pair of demented killers. **HO24**

Puberty Blues (1981, C, 86m, R)
Two young girls experience the joys and pains of adolescence while they hang out with the surfing crowd in Sydney, Australia. Directed by Bruce Beresford. **FF5**

Public Enemy, The (1931, B&W, 84m, NR)
James Cagney rose to stardom with this film; he's a tough-talking gangster who packs a mean wallop, especially with a grapefruit in his hand. **AC22, CL22** *Highly Recommended*

Puff the Magic Dragon (1985, C, 45m, NR)
Based on the children's song, this is an animated feature about a lonely boy and his gigantic fire-breathing friend. **FA10**

Pumping Iron (1976, C, 85m, PG)
Documentary about the world of weight-lifters and professional bodybuilders, featuring Arnold Schwarzenegger and Lou Ferrigno. **AC30, CU16**

Pumping Iron II: The Women (1985, C, 107m, NR)
Sequel to *Pumping Iron* concentrates on the female bodybuilders. Bev Francis is the star. **CU16**

Pumpkinhead (1988, C, 87m, R)
Horror story of a vengeance-seeking father who summons a legendary demon to deal with his son's murderers but cannot control it once the killing begins. **HO14**

Punch Line (1988, C, 123m, R)
Tom Hanks and Sally Field play stand-up comics; he's the cynical veteran of the club scene, she's a housewife trying to break into the biz. Jerry Belson directed this drama. **CO44, DR12, DR36**

Purlie Victorious (1963, C, 97m, NR)
Musical fable about a black preacher standing up to a wicked plantation owner. Written by and starring Ossie Davis; Ruby Dee, Sorrell Booke, and Godfrey Cambridge costar. **MU2**

Purple Hearts (1984, C, 115m, R)
A Navy medic and a nurse fall in love against the backdrop of the war in Vietnam. Cheryl Ladd and Ken Wahl star. **AC4**

Purple Rain (1984, C, 113m, R)
The movie debut of rock star Prince, as he plays a character named The Kid, a rocker battling rival musicians, his own band members, and family problems. **DR12, MU9**

Purple Rose of Cairo, The (1985, C, 84m, PG)
During the Depression, a waitress trapped in a loveless marriage imagines her favorite movie star has come off the screen to romance her. Mia Farrow and Jeff Daniels star in this comedy written and directed by Woody Allen. **CO8, CO27**

Pursued (1947, B&W, 101m, NR)
Robert Mitchum is a cowboy out to find his father's killers. **WE6**

Pursuit of D.B. Cooper, The (1981, C, 100m, PG)
The tale of the legendary airline bandit who parachuted from the sky with thousands in ransom. Treat Williams and Robert Duvall star. **DR37**

Pursuit of the Graf Spee (1957, C, 106m, NR)
Michael Powell directed this World War II drama about the British attempts to sink a German battleship. John Gregson, Anthony Quayle, and Christopher Lee star. **CU19, HO32**

Pursuit to Algiers (1945, B&W, 65m, NR)
Sherlock Holmes mystery, starring Basil Rathbone and Nigel Bruce, has the famous detective and his companion accompanying an heir to a foreign throne on a voyage. Not based on any Arthur Conan Doyle story. **MY10**

Puss 'n' Boots (1984, C, 60m, NR)
Ben Vereen and Gregory Hines star in this Faerie Tale Theatre presentation of the beloved children's story. **FA12**

Putney Swope (1969, C/B&W, 88m, R)
Satirical comedy about a black man taking over a prestigious New York advertising agency and renaming it Truth and Soul, Inc. Arnold Johnson stars; Mel Brooks has a small part. Directed by Robert Downey. **CO2, CO12, CO28**

Pygmalion (1938, B&W, 95m, NR)
The George Bernard Shaw play about a professor's gamble that he can turn a Cockney flower girl into a lady of culture.

Leslie Howard and Wendy Hiller star in this comedy that was the basis for *My Fair Lady*. **CL1**

Q Planes *see* Clouds Over Europe

Q: The Winged Serpent (1982, C, 93m, R)
Horror comedy about a monster from Mexican legend terrorizing Manhattan, nesting on top of the Chrysler Building. Michael Moriarty, Richard Roundtree, and David Carradine star; Larry Cohen directed. **CU30, HO16**

Quackbusters (1989, C, 76m, G)
Feature-length cartoon, spoofing *Ghostbusters*, starring Daffy Duck as a spook-hunting detective. **FA10**

Quackser Fortune Has a Cousin in the Bronx (1970, C, 90m, R)
Gene Wilder plays an amiable Irishman who collects horse manure from the streets of Dublin and sells it to gardeners. Margot Kidder plays an American student who falls in love with him. **CO1**

Quadrophenia (1979, C, 115m, R)
Musical drama about a young Briton in the early l960s with four separate personalities, based on the rock album by The Who. Superb marriage of music and imagery; directed by Franc Roddam. Phil Daniels stars, with Sting in a small role. **MU9** *Recommended*

Quality Street (1937, B&W, 84m, NR)
A woman pretends to be her own niece in order to woo a flame she hasn't seen in ten years. Katharine Hepburn and Franchot Tone star in this comedy; George Stevens directed. **CL16, CL42**

Quartet (1949, B&W, 120m, NR)
W. Somerset Maugham introduces four of his short stories, each with its own cast. Among the players: Mai Zetterling, Ian Fleming, and Dirk Bogarde. Sequels: *Trio* and *Encore*. **DR19**

Quatermass Conclusion, The (1980, C, 107m, NR)
British science fiction adventure about a professor who is the key to stopping a deadly ray from destroying the planet. John Mills stars. Originally made for TV. **SF19**

Que Viva Mexico! (1932, B&W, 85m, NR)
Russian director Sergei Eisenstein's legendary, unfinished documentary about life in Mexico. **FF22**

Queen Kelly (1929, B&W, 95m, NR)
Director Erich Von Stroheim's bizarre tale of a young girl's odyssey from a convent school to a brothel. Gloria Swanson stars in this reconstruction of a long-lost and never-finished classic silent drama. **CL12, CL53**

Querelle (1982, C, 120m, R)
Director Rainer Werner Fassbinder's last film, about a sailor's discovery of his homosexual nature. Brad Davis and Jeanne Moreau star. **FF20, FF26**

Quest, The (1986, C, 93m, PG)
A young boy learns of an ancient myth in the Australian outback and confronts the source in this adventure. Henry Thomas stars. **FA4, FF5**

Quest for Fire (1981, C, 97m, R)
A drama of life in prehistoric times, filmed on several continents, with special languages and body movements designed for the film. Everett McGill, Ron Perlman, and Rae Dawn Chong star. **AC12, AC24, FF1**

Quick and the Dead, The (1987, C, 93m, NR)
Sam Elliott stars in this Louis L'Amour western of a homesteading family falling under the protection of a mysterious stranger. Kate Capshaw and Tom Conti costar. Originally made for cable TV. **WE29**

Quiet Cool (1986, C, 80m, R)
A New York cop brings his special brand of street smarts to a small California town

being overrun by a gang of pot growers. James Remar and Nick Cassavetes star. **AC9**

Quiet Earth, The (1985, C, 91m, R)
Only three people are left on Earth after a top-secret project goes haywire. Science fiction drama from New Zealand. **SF12**

Quiet Man, The (1952, C, 129m, NR)
American prizefighter returns to his native Ireland and courts local lass in this rollicking comedy from Oscar-winning director John Ford. John Wayne and Maureen O'Hara star, with Victor McLaglen and Barry Fitzgerald. Gorgeous, Oscar-winning color cinematography. **CL9, CL17, CL34, XT6** *Recommended*

Quiller Memorandum, The (1966, C, 105m, NR)
An American agent in Britain hunts down ex-Nazis in this spy thriller starring George Segal, Alec Guinness, and Max von Sydow. Written by Harold Pinter. **MY6, DR63**

Quintet (1979, C, 118m, R)
Science fiction drama about a frozen city of the future and its few inhabitants who play a bizarre game for survival. Paul Newman stars; Robert Altman directed. **CU25, DR28, SF8**

Rabbit Test (1978, C, 86m, R)
Billy Crystal stars in a comedy about the world's first pregnant man. Joan Rivers directed. **CO13**

Rabid (1977, C, 90m, R)
From horror director David Cronenberg, the story of a woman who develops a thirst for human blood after she's had plastic surgery. Not for the squeamish. Marilyn Chambers stars. **HO18, HO39**

Race With the Devil (1975, C, 88m, PG)
Two couples on vacation tangle with some devil worshippers in this action thriller that features lots of motorcycle and car chases. Peter Fonda and Warren Oates costar. **AC10, CU48, HO11**

Rachel and the Stranger (1948, B&W, 93m, NR)
A romantic triangle, western-style, featuring Loretta Young, William Holden, and Robert Mitchum. **CL51, WE9**

Rachel, Rachel (1968, C, 101m, R)
Joanne Woodward stars in this drama about a lonely schoolteacher looking for love in her mid-thirties. Estelle Parsons and James Olson costar; Paul Newman directed. **DR10, DR28, DR67**

Racing With the Moon (1984, C, 108m, PG)
Nostalgic drama set in small California coastal town in the early 40s about the romance between a poor boy and a servant's daughter he mistakenly thinks is wealthy. Sean Penn, Elizabeth McGovern, and Nicolas Cage star. **DR1**

Racketeer (1929, B&W, 68m, NR)
A gangster tries to go straight for the love of a young woman. Robert Armstrong and Carole Lombard star. **CL48**

Rad (1986, C, 95m, PG)
Family drama centering on the world of BMX bike racing. Bill Allen is the kid with the hot wheels; Talia Shire, Ray Walston, and Jack Weston are the adults on the sidelines. **AC10, FA7**

Radio Days (1986, C, 85m, PG)
Woody Allen directed this affectionate portrait of New York in the early 1940s, when everyone listened to the nightly radio programs of adventure, romance, and mystery. Mia Farrow heads the large cast; Diane Keaton has a small role as a band singer. **CO5, CO6, CO8, CO27, DR40, XT9** *Highly Recommended*

Radio Ranch *see* Phantom Empire

Rafferty and the Gold Dust Twins (1975, C, 92m, PG)
A nerdy driving instructor is forced by a pair of kooky women to drive them from Los Angeles to New Orleans. Alan Arkin, Sally Kellerman, and Mackenzie Phillips star, with Harry Dean Stanton. **CU49**

Rage at Dawn (1955, C, 87m, NR)
Randolph Scott and his saddle buddies
hunt down an outlaw gang. **WE22**

Rage of Angels (1983, C, 192m, NR)
Sidney Sheldon soaper about a lovely
lawyer (Jaclyn Smith) torn between two
lovers: a married politician (Ken Howard)
and a mob lawyer (Armand Assante).
Originally made for TV. **DR2**

Raggedy Man (1981, C, 94m, PG)
Sissy Spacek stars as a widow in a small
Texas town during the 1940s who has a
romance with a sailor (Eric Roberts) on
leave. Sam Shepard costars. **DR10, DR68**

Raging Bull (1980, B&W/C, 129m, R)
Robert DeNiro won an Oscar for his portrayal of boxer Jake LaMotta, as brutal
outside the ring as in it. Cathy Moriarty
and Joe Pesci costar. Martin Scorsese
directed; photographed by Michael Chapman and edited by Oscar winner Thelma
Schoonmaker. **DR4, DR22, DR25, DR52,
XT2** *Highly Recommended*

Ragtime (1981, C, 156m, PG)
Epic panorama of turn-of-the-century
America, adapted from E.L. Doctorow
bestseller. James Cagney, Mary Steenburgen, Howard Rollins, and Elizabeth
McGovern head a large cast; Milos Forman directed. **CL22, DR5, DR57**

Raid on Entebbe (1977, C, 150m, NR)
Drama about the July 4, 1976 rescue by
Israeli commandos of hostages held in
Uganda by terrorists. Charles Bronson
and Peter Finch star. Originally made for
TV. **AC29, DR6**

Raiders of the Lost Ark (1981, C, 115m,
PG)
Steven Spielberg's modern tribute to the
old-fashioned movie serials, with Harrison Ford as the bullwhip-toting professor,
Karen Allen as his companion, and plenty
of hair-raising escapes and breath-taking
chases. **AC14, AC21, DR32, SF24** *Recommended*

Railroaded (1947, B&W, 71m, NR)
Gangster John Ireland makes life miserable for Sheila Ryan in this thriller. Directed by Anthony Mann. **WE20**

The Railrodder *see* Buster Keaton Rides
Again/The Railrodder

Railway Children, The (1972, C, 102m, G)
From Britain, a family adventure about a
trio of plucky children determined to
clear their father of false charges of espionage. Dinah Sheridan and Bernard Crib-
bins star. **FA4**

Rain (1932, B&W, 93m, NR)
Joan Crawford and Walter Huston square
off in this version of W. Somerset Maugham's tale of a lady of ill repute and a
reform-minded preacher. **CL50**

Rain Man (1988, C, 140m, R)
Cross-country odyssey of two brothers,
one a sharp hustler, the other a long-
institutionalized autistic savant. Oscar
winner for Best Picture, Actor (Dustin
Hoffman), and Director (Barry Levinson). Tom Cruise costars. **DR8, DR30,
DR73, XT1, XT2, XT6** *Recommended*

Rain People, The (1969, C, 102m, R)
A housewife deserts her family and takes
to the road for an odyssey of self-discovery. Francis Ford Coppola directed this
drama starring Shirley Knight, James
Caan, and Robert Duvall. **DR10, DR37,
DR51**

Rainbow, The (1989, C, 112m, R)
D.H. Lawrence's story of young love
awakening, focusing on a female character who later appeared in *Women in Love*.
Stars Sammi Davis, Paul McGann, and
Amanda Donohoe, with Glenda Jackson
and David Hemmings. Written and directed by Ken Russell. **CU31, DR1, DR19,
DR23**

Rainmaker, The (1956, C, 121m, NR)
Katharine Hepburn stars as a spinster
living in a parched Southwest town who's
wooed by a smooth-talking con man.
(Burt Lancaster). **CL16, DR41**

Raintree County (1957, C, 168m, NR)
Elizabeth Taylor is the selfish Southern belle, Montgomery Clift the schoolteacher she ruins in this historical drama of the Confederacy. Lee Marvin costars. **CL3, CL33, DR43**

Raise the Titanic! (1980, C, 112m, PG)
Big-budget version of bestselling novel about the salvage job of a lifetime, starring Jason Robards, with Richard Jordan, David Selby, and Alec Guinness. **DR63**

Raisin in the Sun, A (1961, B&W, 128m, NR)
Drama of black family life in Chicago, adapted from Lorraine Hansberry's play. Sidney Poitier, Claudia McNeil, Ruby Dee, and Louis Gossett, Jr. star. **DR8, DR14, DR20, DR38**

Raising Arizona (1987, C, 94m, PG-13)
A childless couple decide to kidnap one of a set of quintuplets in this frantic action comedy starring Nicolas Cage and Holly Hunter. **CO5, CO9, CO10**

Rambo: First Blood Part II (1985, C, 95m, R)
Sylvester Stallone is the Special Forces maverick with a mission: to free Americans still held captive in Vietnam. **AC4, AC25, AC31**

Rambo III (1988, C, 101m, R)
In this installment, John Rambo travels to Afghanistan to rescue his old commander from the Soviet invaders. Sylvester Stallone and Richard Crenna star. **AC25, AC31**

Ran (1985, C, 161m, R)
A Japanese version of Shakespeare's King Lear, with samurai warriors, Oscar-winning costumes, and some of the greatest battle scenes ever filmed. Directed by Akira Kurosawa. **FF9** *Highly Recommended*

Rancho Notorious (1952, C, 89m, NR)
Cowboy Arthur Kennedy, seeking revenge for a murder, winds up at a strange hideout for outlaws run by Marlene Dietrich. Directed by Fritz Lang. **CL43, CL47, WE6, WE16**

Random Harvest (1942, B&W, 127m, NR)
Romantic drama of a wartime amnesia victim (Ronald Colman) and the woman (Greer Garson) whose love leads him to recovery. **CL4**

Ranger and the Lady, The (1938, B&W, 54m, NR)
Roy Rogers finds romance in the Old West. Gabby Hayes costars—not as the love interest! **WE23**

Rape and Marriage: The Rideout Case (1980, C, 96m, NR)
True story of the landmark court case in which a woman charged her estranged husband with rape. Mickey Rourke and Linda Hamilton star, with Rip Torn. Originally made for TV. **CU47, DR48**

Rape of Love (1977, C, 117m, NR)
French drama of a nurse who's sexually assaulted and then undergoes a worse ordeal in the criminal justice system. Nathalie Neil stars. **FF1**

Rapunzel (1983, C, 60m, NR)
The fairy tale of the girl with long flowing locks, presented by Faerie Tale Theatre. Shelley Duvall, Jeff Bridges, and Gena Rowlands star. **FA12**

Rare Breed, The (1966, C, 108m, NR)
James Stewart stars in this western drama; Maureen O'Hara can't decide between him and Brian Keith. **CL25**

Rashomon (1951, B&W, 88m, NR)
Classic Japanese drama of a criminal act in a forest and the various versions the story takes in the retelling. Toshiro Mifune stars; Akira Kurosawa directed. Winner of an Oscar for Best Foreign Language Film. **FF9, FF28, XT7** *Recommended*

Raven, The (1935, B&W, 62m, NR)
Boris Karloff and Bela Lugosi star in the bizarre tale of a mad doctor, who's ob-

sessed with Edgar Allan Poe, and one of his victims. **HO1, HO27, HO28**

Raven, The (1963, C, 86m, NR)
A trio of magicians square off in this horror comedy, starring Vincent Price, Peter Lorre, and Boris Karloff. Jack Nicholson costars; Roger Corman directed. **DR24, HO27, HO31, HO41**

Ravishing Idiot (1965, B&W, 110m, NR)
Comedy about an inept crook who's out to steal some important NATO documents. Anthony Perkins and Brigitte Bardot star. **FF32**

Raw Deal (1986, C, 97m, R)
Arnold Schwarzenegger plays a special F.B.I. agent assigned to clean up Mob activity in Chiago as only he can. **AC25, AC30**

Razorback (1984, C, 95m, R)
A wild hog terrorizes the Australian outback. Gregory Harrison stars. **FF5, HO16**

Razor's Edge, The (1946, B&W, 146m, NR)
Tyrone Power stars in this version of the Somerset Maugham story of a man's disillusionment after his experiences in World War I. Oscar winner Anne Baxter and Gene Tierney costar. **DR19, XT5**

Razor's Edge, The (1984, C, 129m, PG-13)
Bill Murray plays it straight in this second screen version of the Somerset Maugham story of a man looking for inner peace. Theresa Russell costars. **CO13, DR19**

Real Bruce Lee, The (1980, C, 108m, R)
Highlights of martial arts star Bruce Lee in action from four of his early films. **AC33**

Real Genius (1985, C, 108m, PG)
Comedy about a group of college whiz kids getting revenge on their professor for using their research on a death-dealing government project. Val Kilmer and William Atherton star. **CO2, CO4, CO35** *Recommended*

Real Life (1979, C, 99m, PG)
Pushy documentary filmmaker (Albert Brooks) invades home of typical family to make a movie about them. Brooks also directed this comedy, costarring Charles Grodin. **CO8** *Recommended*

Real Men (1987, C, 86m, R)
Jim Belushi and John Ritter star in this action comedy about a CIA agent and a civilian caught up in a dangerous game of international intrigue. **CO13**

Really Weird Tales (1986, C, 85m, NR)
Spoof of *Twilight Zone*-style TV shows, with three episodes starring John Candy, Martin Short, and Catherine O'Hara. **CO14, SF21**

Re-Animator (1985, C, 86m, NR)
Extremely gory horror film with cult following about a young doctor's experiments reviving the dead. Jeffrey Combs and Barbara Crampton star. (Also available in an R-rated version with some of the gore trimmed.) **CU4, CU7, HO18, HO20**

Reap the Wild Wind (1942, C, 124m, NR)
Adventure tale of 19th-century salvagers working off the Georgia coast, starring John Wayne, Ray Milland, and Paulette Goddard. Directed by Cecil B. DeMille. Oscar-winning special effects. **AC12, AC13, SF15**

Rear Window (1954, C, 112m, PG)
Classic Hitchcock thriller about a photographer spying on his neighbor, who may have murdered his wife. James Stewart, Grace Kelly, and Thelma Ritter star. **CL25, CL31, MY15, MY22** *Highly Recommended*

Rebecca (1940, B&W, 130m, NR)
Daphne du Maurier story, directed by Alfred Hitchcock, about a young woman's marriage to a widower whose former wife dominates everything around them. Laurence Olivier and Joan Fontaine star. Winner of the Best Picture Oscar. **CL32, MY22, MY36, XT1**

Rebecca of Sunnybrook Farm (1938, B&W, 80m, NR)
Shirley Temple stars in this musical about a young radio star. Randolph Scott and Gloria Stuart add some romance. **FA14, WE22**

Rebel (1973, C, 80m, PG)
Sylvester Stallone plays a student radical in this drama made several years before his success with *Rocky*. **AC31**

Rebel (1986, C, 93m, R)
Matt Dillon is an American G.I. deserter adrift in World War II Australia. Bryan Brown costars in this drama. **FF5**

Rebel Rousers (1967, C, 78m, NR)
Low-budget melodrama about motorcycle gangs, famous mainly for prestardom pairing of Jack Nicholson and Bruce Dern. With (Harry) Dean Stanton. **CU49, DR24**

Rebel Without a Cause (1955, C, 111m, NR)
Vintage 1950s drama of misunderstood teens, with James Dean, Natalie Wood, and Sal Mineo a trio of outcasts. With Jim Backus, Corey Allen, and Dennis Hopper. Directed by Nicholas Ray. **CL8, CU23, CU46, DR9** *Highly Recommended*

Reckless (1983, C, 93m, R)
Straight-arrow student Daryl Hannah falls for moody rebel Aidan Quinn. Stylish high school romance, directed by James Foley. **DR9**

Red Badge of Courage, The (1951, B&W, 70m, NR)
The classic Civil War story (from Stephen Crane's novel) about a young soldier's initiation into the horrors of combat. Audie Murphy stars; John Huston directed. **AC5, CL1, CL44**

Red Beard (1965. B&W, 185m, NR)
Toshiro Mifune stars as a crusty doctor who tries to impart his knowledge to a young, more kindly intern. Epic drama from director Akira Kurosawa. **FF9, FF28**

Red Dawn (1984, C, 114m, PG-13)
When Soviet-backed troops invade a small town in the American Southwest, a band of teenagers takes to the hills and wages a guerrilla war. Patrick Swayze and C. Thomas Howell star, with Powers Boothe, Ben Johnson, and Harry Dean Stanton. **AC20, CU49**

Red Desert (1964, C, 116m, NR)
Director Michelangelo Antonioni's drama of a woman alienated from modern urban life, on the brink of a breakdown. Monica Vitti and Richard Harris star. **FF17**

Red Dust (1932, B&W, 83m, NR)
A romantic triangle on a rubber plantation: Clark Gable has to pick between lusty Jean Harlow and demure Mary Astor. Classic romantic adventure, remade as *Mogambo*. **AC13, AC14, CL23** *Highly Recommended*

Red Headed Stranger, The (1987, C, 108m, NR)
Willie Nelson stars in this western story based on his classic album about a preacher who swears revenge on an unfaithful wife. **MU12, WE3, WE6**

Red Heat (1988, C, 106m, R)
Soviet cop and his Chicago counterpart team to catch a Russian drug dealer on the lam in the Windy City. Arnold Schwarzenegger and Jim Belushi star; Walter Hill directed. **AC9, AC30, CO13, CU27, XT9**

Red House (1947, B&W, 100m, NR)
Melodrama of simple farmer (Edward G. Robinson) and his fear of a certain house and its mysterious occupants. With Lon McAllister, Judith Anderson, Rory Calhoun, and Julie London. **CL52**

Red Lion (1969, C, 115m, NR)
Toshiro Mifune stars in an action drama about a soldier confronting the corrupt officials in his home town. **FF4, FF28**

Red Pony, The (1949, B&W, 89m, NR)
Drama of young boy's love for his horse and the escape it offers him from family

problems. Adapted from the John Steinbeck novel; Robert Mitchum, Myrna Loy, and Peter Miles star. **CL46, DR19, FA5**

Red Pony, The (1973, C, 101m, NR)
Latest version of the Steinbeck story, starring Henry Fonda, Maureen O'Hara, Ben Johnson, and Clint Howard. Originally made for TV. **CL24, DR19, FA5**

Red River (1948, B&W, 133m, NR)
This classic cattle-drive story features John Wayne and Montgomery Clift as a feuding father and son. Directed by Howard Hawks. **WE1, WE17, WE21** *Recommended*

Red River Valley *see* Man of the Frontier

Red Scorpion (1989, C, 102m, R)
Body builder Dolph Lundgren plays a Russian special services officer assigned to kill the rebel leader of an African freedom movement. **AC20, AC25**

Red Shoes, The (1948, C, 133m, NR)
Ballerina must choose between her devoted lover and a hard-driving impressario who knows "what's best" for her career. Director Michael Powell's film won Oscars for photography and art direction. Moira Shearer, Anton Walbrook, and Marius Goring star in this cult favorite. **CL6, CL7, CL9, CU19, MU3**

Red Sonja (1985, C, 89m, PG-13)
Arnold Schwarzenegger and Brigitte Nielsen team up as warriors in a land of sacred talismans and magic. **AC18, AC30**

Red Sun (1972, C, 112m, R)
An international cast is featured in this western about a gunslinger and a samurai joining forces. Charles Bronson, Toshiro Mifune, and Ursula Andress star. **AC29, FF28**

Red Tent, The (1971, C, 121m, G)
Based on a true story, this adventure saga dramatizes an ill-fated 1928 expedition to the frozen Arctic led by General Nobile

(Peter Finch). Sean Connery costars. **AC12, AC24, AC36**

Reds (1981, C, 195m, PG)
Epic story of John Reed, American journalist and adventurer who chronicled the Mexican and Russian Revolutions. Star Warren Beatty won an Oscar for his direction; Diane Keaton, Jack Nicholson, Gene Hackman, and Oscar winner Maureen Stapleton head the supporting cast. Narrative is interspersed with interviews with "witnesses," contemporaries of Reed who offer their impressions of him. **DR4, DR24, DR34, DR39, DR40, XT5, XT6** *Recommended*

Reefer Madness (1936, B&W, 67m, NR)
Cheaply made melodrama warning audience of the dangers of marijuana "addiction." A cult favorite at midnight showings in the 1960s. **CU1, CU11**

Reflections in a Golden Eye (1967, C, 108m, NR)
The dark side of life on a Southern military base, adapted from Carson McCullers' novel. Marlon Brando, Elizabeth Taylor, Brian Keith, and Julie Harris star; John Huston directed. **CL33, CL44, DR19, DR33**

Reflections of Murder (1974, C, 100m, NR)
Remake of French thriller *Diabolique*, about a neglected wife and scorned mistress conspiring to murder a schoolteacher. Tuesday Weld, Joan Hackett, and Sam Waterston star. Written by William Levinson and Richard Link; originally made for TV. **MY18**

Rehearsal for Murder (1982, C, 100m, NR)
Backstage mystery: star of new Broadway show is killed on opening night. Robert Preston and Lynn Redgrave star. Written by William Levinson and Richard Link; originally made for TV. **MY16**

Reivers, The (1969, C, 107m, PG)
Comedy set in turn-of-the-century Mississippi about a young boy's friendship

with his family's ne'er-do-well chauffeur. Steve McQueen stars in this adaptation of the William Faulkner novel. **AC28, DR19**

Rent-a-Cop (1988, C, 95m, R)
Burt Reynolds is the title character, Liza Minnelli the prostitute he's protecting from a serial killer. **AC37**

Repo Man (1984, C, 93m, R)
Offbeat comedy about a punked-out kid falling in with a band of car repossessors in Los Angeles and learning the "repo" way of life. Emilio Estevez and Harry Dean Stanton star in this cult movie. **CO2, CO12, CU5, CU49, XT9** *Recommended*

Repos du Guerrier, Le (1962, C, 100m, NR)
Brigitte Bardot stars in this French drama about a woman involved with a suicidal lover. Directed by Roger Vadim. Also known as *Warrior's Rest*. **FF32**

Repulsion (1965, B&W, 105m, NR)
An unstable young woman, left alone in her sister's apartment, descends into madness. Catherine Deneuve stars in this disturbing psychological study from director Roman Polanski. **DR54, FF27** *Recommended*

Rescue, The (1988, C, 98m, PG)
A band of teens whose U.S. Navy fathers are being held captive in North Korea launch a mission to bring them home. Kevin Dillon, Marc Price, and Christina Howard star. **AC20**

Resurrection (1980, C, 102m, PG)
Ellen Burstyn plays a woman who recovers from an auto accident to learn that she has been endowed with powers of healing. A drama of faith and courage costarring Sam Shepard. **DR2**

Retreat, Hell! (1952, B&W, 95m, NR)
Korean War drama about U.S. withdrawal from the Changjin Reservoir, starring Frank Lovejoy, Richard Carlson, and Russ Tamblyn. **AC3**

Return Engagement (1978, C, 76m, NR)
A lonely professor (Elizabeth Taylor) falls in love with one of her students (Joseph Bottoms). **CL33**

Return From Witch Mountain (1978, C, 93m, G)
Bette Davis and Christopher Lee play kidnappers in this family adventure from the Disney studios. Sequel to *Escape From Witch Mountain*. **CL21, FA1, HO32**

Return of a Man Called Horse, The (1976, C, 129m, PG)
In this sequel to *A Man Called Horse*, Richard Harris again stars as the aristocrat who learns the ways of the Sioux Indians. **WE8**

Return of Captain Invincible, The (1983, C, 90m, PG)
A superhero who has turned into a broken-down drunk is persuaded to don his costume once again to save the world. Bizarre comedy, with musical numbers, stars Alan Arkin and Christopher Lee. **HO32**

Return of Chandu, The (1934, B&W, 206m, NR)
Serial starring Bela Lugosi as a mysterious magician who uses his powers to rescue a maiden from a cat-worshiping cult. **HO28**

Return of Frank James, The (1940, C, 92m, NR)
Henry Fonda plays the outlaw Jesse James's brother, looking to avenge his brother's murder. Gene Tierney costars; Fritz Lang directed. **CL24, CL43, WE6**

Return of Martin Guerre, The (1982, C, 111m, PG-13)
French peasant disappears; years later a man (Gerard Depardieu) turns up, claiming to be the missing man. Nathalie Baye costars in this mystery based on a true story. **FF1, FF29**

Return of the Bad Men (1948, B&W, 90m, NR)
Randolph Scott has his hands full with outlaws including Billy the Kid, The Sundance Kid, and The Dalton Gang. **WE2, WE22**

Return of the Dragon (1973, C, 91m, R)
Bruce Lee and Chuck Norris match kicks in this action drama about a Chinese in Rome protecting his family from mobsters. **AC32, AC33**

Return of the Fly (1959, B&W, 80m, NR)
Sequel to *The Fly* has son following in his father's footsteps to duplicate dangerous experiment, with dire results. Vincent Price stars. **HO31**

Return of the Jedi (1983, C, 133m, PG)
The third in the *Star Wars* trilogy finds Luke Skywalker, Han Solo, and Princess Leia teaming with the Ewoks to do battle with Darth Vader and his minions. Harrison Ford, Mark Hamill, and Carrie Fisher star. **DR32, FA8, SF11, SF13, SF23**

Return of the Living Dead, The (1985, C, 91m, R)
Horror spoof, with plenty of gore, about zombies terrorizing group of people trapped in a mortuary. Clu Gulager and James Karen star. **HO6, HO18, HO24** *Recommended*

Return of the Pink Panther, The (1975, C, 113m, G)
The fourth installment in the comedy series about the bumbling Inspector Clouseau (Peter Sellers), as he matches what few wits he has with a master thief (Christopher Plummer). Directed by Blake Edwards. **CO26, CO46**

Return of the Secaucus 7 (1980, C, 100m, NR)
A reunion of 1960s pals who once got arrested in New Jersey on their way to a protest rally is the framework for this entertaining, insightful comedy-drama. John Sayles wrote, directed, and plays a small role. **DR7** *Recommended*

Return of the Seven (1966, C, 96m, NR)
Sequel to *The Magnificent Seven* has Yul Brynner rounding up a new collection of cowboys (including Warren Oates, Robert Fuller, and Jordan Christopher) to fight more Mexican bandits. **CU48**

Return of the Soldier, The (1981, C, 101m, NR)
Alan Bates stars as a World War I veteran trying to put the pieces of his life back together. Glenda Jackson, Julie Christie, and Ann-Margret are the women who offer to help him. **DR5**

Return of the Vampire, The (1943, B&W, 69m, NR)
Bela Lugosi plays a Rumanian vampire who's dead and buried in London—until German bombs disturb his grave. Then he's back to work, with the help of a werewolf assistant. **HO5, HO28**

Return to Macon County (1975, C, 90m, PG)
Action and suspense down in Dixie, with two young hotheads ready for hot rod thrills. Don Johnson and Nick Nolte (in his film debut) star. **DR44**

Return to Oz (1985, C, 109m, PG)
Dorothy, the brave heroine of the Oz tales, goes back to the magic kingdom for a new set of adventures. Fairuza Balk stars, with support from Nicol Williamson, Jean Marsh, and Piper Laurie. Imaginative special effects. **FA4, SF13**

Return to Snowy River, Part II (1988, C, 97m, PG)
Sequel to *The Man From Snowy River*, with same young stars (Tom Burlinson, Sigrid Thornton), same great wild horse action and lovely Australian scenery. **AC12, FF5**

Reuben, Reuben (1983, C, 101m, R)
Tom Conti stars in this offbeat comedy as a lecherous poet who finds true love with Kelly McGillis. Adapted from the Peter DeVries novel by Julius Epstein. **CO1, DR19** *Recommended*

Revenge of the Dead (1960, B&W, 69m, NR)
A "bad" horror movie classic, directed by the legendary Ed Wood, Jr. Narrated by the psychic Criswell—from a coffin. And that's just for starters. Also known as *Night of the Ghouls*. **CU45**

Revenge of the Nerds (1984, C, 90m, R)
Social outcasts at a university get revenge on the snooty fraternity that runs the school. Robert Carradine stars. **CO4, CO35**

Revenge of the Pink Panther, The (1978, C, 99m, PG)
Peter Sellers' final film as Inspector Clouseau has him in Hong Kong investigating his own murder. Dyan Cannon, Herbert Lom, and Robert Webber costar. Directed by Blake Edwards. **CO26, CO46**

Revenge of the Zombies (1943, B&W, 61m, NR)
Low-budget horror film about a mad doctor (John Carradine), his zombie wife, and Nazis lurking in the background. **HO6**

Revolt of Job, The (1983, C, 97m, NR)
In Hungary, a Jewish couple adopt a Gentile boy in the shadow of the Holocaust. **FF7**

Revolution (1985, C, 123m, PG)
A lavishly produced drama about the American colonists' fight for independence from the British. Al Pacino, Nastassja Kinski, and Donald Sutherland star. **AC6, DR5, DR66**

Rhinestone (1984, C, 111m, PG)
Sylvester Stallone and Dolly Parton star in this comedy about a country singer's bet that she can turn a New York cabbie into a singing sensation. **AC31**

Rich and Famous (1981, C, 117m, R)
Jacqueline Bissett and Candice Bergen play friends/rivals over a 20-year period in this modern soap opera. Directed by George Cukor. **CL39, DR10**

Rich and Strange (1932, B&W, 92m, NR)
Early Hitchcock drama, produced in Great Britain, concerning a couple whose boredom is alleviated by a sudden inheritance. Henry Kendall and Joan Barry star. **MY22**

Rich Kids (1979, C, 101m, PG)
Two teenagers from wealthy New York families find comfort in their friendship as their parents' marriages break up. Trini Alvarado, Jeremy Levy, and John Lithgow star in this comedy-drama. **CO4**

Richard Pryor (concert films)
Live and Smokin' (1971, C, 47m, NR)
Live in Concert (1979, C, 78m, R)
Live on the Sunset Strip (1982, C, 82m, R)
Here and Now (1983, C, 83m, R)
Pryor's no-holds-barred monologues on race, sex, and life's crazy moments. **CO29**

Richard III (1956, C, 155m, NR)
Laurence Olivier directed and stars in this version of Shakespeare's tragedy of the misshapen British monarch and his political problems. This full-length version contains newly restored footage. **CL1, CL32**

Richard's Things (1980, C, 104m, R)
Liv Ullmann plays a widow who is seduced by her late husband's girl friend. English-language film shot in Great Britain. **FF25**

Ride in the Whirlwind (1966, C, 82m, NR)
A case of mistaken identity has three cowboys fleeing from the law in this cult western. Jack Nicholson and Harry Dean Stanton star. Monte Hellman directed. **CU49, DR24, WE16**

Ride, Ranger, Ride (1936, B&W, 56m, NR)
Gene Autry joins the cavalry and prevents an Indian war. **WE24**

Ride the High Country (1962, C, 94m, NR)
Two aging gunfighters agree to team up for one last (honest) ride. Sam Peckinpah

directed; Joel McCrea and Randolph Scott (in his last movie) star, with Mariette Hartley, R.G. Armstrong, and Warren Oates. **CU48, WE12, WE19, WE22, XT11** *Highly Recommended*

Rider on the Rain (1970, C, 115m, PG)
A woman is attacked by a mysterious stranger, whom she manages to kill—but there's another man following her, too. Charles Bronson stars in this thriller made in France. **AC29, FF1, MY3**

Riders of Death Valley (1941, B&W, 195m, NR)
Western serial about a trio of peacemakers patrolling a crime-riddled mining area. Buck Jones, Dick Foran, and Leo Carillo star; Lon Chaney, Jr. heads the supporting cast. **HO30**

Riders of the Storm (1986, C, 92m, R)
A pair of loony Vietnam veterans (Dennis Hopper, Michael J. Pollard) run a pirate TV station from their vintage aircraft in this satirical comedy. **CU46**

Riders of the Whistling Pines (1949, B&W, 70m, NR)
Gene Autry rescues a girl about to be swindled out of her land. Jason Robards, Sr. and Clayton Moore (TV's Lone Ranger) costar. **WE24**

Ridin' Down the Canyon (1942, B&W, 62m, NR)
Roy Rogers thwarts a band of horse rustlers who are gumming up the war effort. With Gabby Hayes. **WE23**

Ridin' on a Rainbow (1941, B&W, 79m, NR)
In this western, Gene Autry spends almost as much time singing on a showboat as he does riding the range to nab some outlaws. **WE24**

Rififi (1954, B&W, 115m, NR)
Four French jewel thieves decide to pull off the ultimate caper, but there is immediate mistrust and suspicion in the gang. Directed by Jules Dassin. **FF1, MY20**

Right of Way (1983, C, 106m, NR)
Bette Davis and James Stewart play an elderly couple who decide to end their lives rather than suffer the indignities of age and illness. Originally made for cable TV. **CL21, CL25, DR11**

Right Stuff, The (1983, C, 193m, PG)
Epic saga of the first Americans in space, adapted from the Tom Wolfe bestseller. Sam Shepard stars as Colonel Chuck Yeager; the large cast also includes Dennis Quaid, Scott Glenn, Ed Harris, Levon Helm, and Barbara Hershey. Photographed by Caleb Deschanel; directed by Philip Kaufman. **AC11, CU50, DR6, MU12** *Recommended*

Rikisha-Man (1958, B&W, 105m, NR)
From Japanese director Hiroshi Inagaki, a drama of urban life starring Toshiro Mifune. **FF28**

Rikky and Pete (1988, C, 107m, R)
Australian comedy about brother and sister misfits and their adventures in an isolated mining town. Directed by Nadia Tass; written and photographed by her husband, David Parker, who also designed Pete's wacky inventions. **FF5**

Ring of Bright Water (1969, C, 107m, G)
Family adventure about a man's friendship with his pet sea otter. Bill Travers and Virignia McKenna star. **FA4**

The Rink/The Immigrant (1917, B&W, 79m, NR)
Two Charlie Chaplin shorts. In the first, he plays a waiter in a wacky restaurant; in the second, he's a friendly immigrant who meets a young mother and her child on a boat to America. **CO18**

Rio Bravo (1959, C, 141m, NR)
A cult favorite of westerns fans, starring John Wayne, Dean Martin, and Rick Nelson as a trio trying to uphold the law in a small town. Directed by Howard Hawks. **CL14, CU13, MU12, WE16, WE17, WE21**

Rio Grande (1950, B&W, 105m, NR)
Life in a cavalry outpost in the days after the Civil War. John Wayne stars; John Ford directed. **WE5, WE17, WE18**

Rio Lobo (1970, C, 114m, G)
For Civil War veteran John Wayne, the war isn't over until he's dealt out his own brand of justice. Director Howard Hawks' last film. **WE17, WE21**

Riot in Cell Block 11 (1954, B&W, 80m, NR)
Classic prison drama of convicts taking over, using the press to convey their demands. Neville Brand stars; Don Siegel directed. **DR16** *Recommended*

Rip Van Winkle (1985, C, 48m, NR)
The classic tale of the world's greatest sleeper, presented by Faerie Tale Theatre. Harry Dean Stanton stars. Francis Ford Coppola directed. **DR51, FA12**

Ripping Yarns (series) (1979, C, 90m each, NR)
Three volumes (*Ripping Yarns*, *More Ripping Yarns*, and *Even More Yarns*) of parodies of schoolboy adventure tales, created by Monty Python's Michael Palin and Terry Jones. **CO15**

Risky Business (1983, C, 99m, R)
Suburban Chicago high school student, left alone by traveling parents, becomes involved with call girl and her nasty pimp. Tom Cruise and Rebecca DeMornay star in this comedy with real bite. Written and directed by Paul Brickman; music by Tangerine Dream. **CO4, DR73, XT9** *Highly Recommended*

Rita, Sue and Bob Too (1986, C, 95m, R)
Raunchy British comedy about two teen babysitters involved in a menage à trois with the husband of the couple they work for. Siobahn Finneran, Michelle Holmes, and George Costigan star. **CO4, CO17**

Ritz, The (1976, C, 91m, R)
Comedy about a man on the run hiding out in gay baths. Jack Weston, Rita Moreno, and Jerry Stiller star; Richard Lester directed. **CU35**

River, The (1951, C, 99m, NR)
Drama, adapted from a Rumer Godden novel, of English children growing up in India. Directed by Jean Renoir, with superb Technicolor cinematography. Patricia Walters, Nora Swinburne, and Adrienne Cori star. **CL9, FF12**

River, The (1984, C, 120m, PG-13)
A contemporary farm couple fight to save their land from developers, led by the woman's ex-boyfriend. Sissy Spacek, Mel Gibson, and Scott Glenn star. **DR7, DR68, DR69**

River Niger, The (1976, C, 105m, R)
The intertwined lives of a black family living in Harlem are dramatized in this film version of the award-winning play. **DR8, DR14, DR20**

River of No Return (1954, C, 91m, NR)
Western drama has Robert Mitchum caring for abandoned Marilyn Monroe in Indian-infested wilderness. Tommy Rettig and Rory Calhoun costar. Directed by Otto Preminger. **CL29**

River's Edge (1987, C, 99m, R)
True-life drama about a group of alienated high school kids, one of whom murders his girl friend, none of whom will report the crime. Crispin Glover and Dennis Hopper star. Directed by Tim Hunter. **DR9** *Recommended*

Road Games (1981, C, 100m, PG)
A trucker and a lovely hitch-hiker join forces to solve murders occurring on lonesome highways in the Australian outback. Stacy Keach and Jamie Lee Curtis star. **MY20**

Road Runner vs. Wile E. Coyote: The Classic Chase (1985, C, 54m, NR)
A collection of superb cartoons, directed by Chuck Jones, about that lovable roadrunner and his inept adversary. **FA11** *Recommended*

Road to Bali (1952, C, 90m, NR)
Bing Crosby and Bob Hope hit the high-way for the Far East, with Dorothy La-mour along for laughs and songs. **CO40, MU25**

Road to Eternity *see* Human Condition, Part II, The

Road to Rio (1947, B&W, 100m, NR)
Bob Hope and Bing Crosby are out to rescue Dorothy Lamour from her evil aunt (Gale Sondergaard). The Andrews Sisters show up for one number. **CO40, MU25**

Road to Salina (1971, C, 96m, R)
Drifter returns home to mother, proceeds to begin an affair with young girl who may be his sister. Offbeat thriller starring Robert Walker, Jr., Mimsy Farmer, and Rita Hayworth. **MY18**

Road to Utopia (1945, B&W, 90m, NR)
Bob Hope and Bing Crosby travel to Alaska in search of gold and Dorothy Lamour, not necessarily in that order. Robert Benchley offers color commen-tary. **CO40, MU25**

Road Warrior, The (1982, C, 95m, R)
The second Mad Max adventure takes place in a post-apocalypse world where fuel is the most valuable commodity. Mel Gibson stars; the final chase sequence is a classic. Directed by George Miller. **AC10, AC24, AC25, DR69, FF5** *Highly Recommended*

Roadie (1980, C, 105m, PG)
A Texas beer truck driver aspires to meet his rock 'n' idol, Alice Cooper, in this zany comedy from director Alan Ru-dolph. Meat Loaf (himself a rock singer) stars, with Kaki Hunter and Art Carney. Appearances by music stars Debby Harry & Blondie, Roy Orbison, Asleep at the Wheel, and Hank Williams, Jr. **CO8, CU26, MU9** *Recommended*

Roaring Twenties, The (1939, B&W, 104m, NR)
James Cagney and Humphrey Bogart trade punches and bullets in this classic saga of Prohibition and the gangsters who profited from it. **AC22, CL20, CL22** *Rec-ommended*

Robbery (1967, C, 114m, NR)
Dramatic account of famous Great Train Robbery in 1963 Britain, starring Stanley Baker and Joanna Pettet. **MY8, MY19, MY34**

Robe, The (1953, C, 135m, NR)
Epic religious drama about the Roman centurion who carried out the execution of Christ. Richard Burton and Victor Ma-ture star. **CL13**

Robert Klein: Child of the 60s, Man of the 80s (1984, C, 60m, NR)
Comic monologues from the comedian who waxes nostalgic about those golden days of protest. **CO16**

Robert Klein on Broadway (1986, C, 60m, NR)
More comic observations about modern life from the stand-up comic. **CO16**

Roberta (1935, B&W, 105m, NR)
Fred Astaire and Ginger Rogers sparkle in this musical which features "Smoke Gets in Your Eyes" and "I Won't Dance." Irene Dunne and Randolph Scott costar. **CL15, MU18, WE22**

Robin and Marian (1976, C, 112m, PG)
The Robin Hood-Maid Marian story, con-tinued: Robin and Little John return from the Crusades to find that Marian has joined a convent. Sean Connery and Au-drey Hepburn star, with Nicol William-son and Robert Shaw. Richard Lester directed this bittersweet romance. **AC14, AC15, AC36, CL30, CU35, DR1** *Highly Recommended*

Robin and the Seven Hoods (1964, B&W, 103m, NR)
Gangster spoof starring Frank Sinatra and his Rat Pack pals (Dean Martin, Sammy

Davis, Jr., et al.), plus Bing Crosby. Frank sings "My Kind of Town." **MU25, MU26**

Robin Hood (1973, C, 83m, G)
Disney animated version of the classic tale, with animals playing the parts. **FA2**

Robin Hood and the Sorcerer (1983, C, 115m, NR)
Michael Praed stars as the legendary bandit of Sherwood Forest; here, his opponent is not the Sheriff of Nottingham, but a wicked magician. **AC18**

Robin Hood of Texas (1947, B&W, 71m, NR)
Gene Autry is accused of bank robbery and must clear his name to avoid the law. **WE24**

Robin Williams Live! (1986, C, 65m, NR)
From the famed stage of New York's Metropolitan Opera House comes this fast-paced, free-wheeling comic monologue from one of the funniest men alive. **CO16, CO43** *Highly Recommended*

Robinhood of the Pecos (1941, B&W, 56m, NR)
Roy Rogers plays a Confederate veteran battling Northern politicians. **WE23**

Robocop (1987, C, 96m, R)
In the Detroit of the future, a critically wounded policeman is transformed into an impervious robot, who goes after the crooks who assaulted him. Peter Weller and Kurtwood Smith star. **AC9, AC25**

Robot Monster (1953, B&W, 63m, NR)
Cult "bad" movie about an alien (actually, a gorilla with a diving helmet) terrorizing the last remaining family on Earth. **CU11**

Rock Music With the Muppets (1985, C, 54m, NR)
The Muppets get down with Alice Cooper, Debbie Harry, Paul Simon, Linda Ronstadt, and Helen Reddy. **FA15**

Rock 'n' Roll High School (1979, C, 93m, PG)
Riff Randell, a student at Vince Lombardi High, would rather listen to punk group The Ramones than attend classes. This spoof of teen exploitation movies, directed by Allan Arkush, has become a midnight movie staple. P.J. Soles and Paul Bartel star. **CO35, CU1, CU41, CU42, MU9**

Rock, Pretty Baby (1956, B&W, 89m, NR)
High school rock band competes in a talent contest in this early rock musical. Sal Mineo, John Saxon, Rod McKuen, and Fay Wray star. **MU9**

Rock, Rock, Rock (1956, B&W, 83m, NR)
Tuesday Weld tries to raise money to buy a prom dress, but the story's a flimsy excuse to showcase a long list of rock and pop performers. Chuck Berry, Frankie Lymon and the Teeenagers, and La Vern Baker perform. **MU9**

Rocket Gibraltar (1988, C, 100m, PG)
Family drama centering on the 77th birthday celebration of a patriarch (Burt Lancaster). **DR8, DR41**

Rocket Ship X-M (1950, B&W, 77m, NR)
A spaceship is struck by a meteor and forced to land on Mars, where astronauts find a planet ravaged by nuclear war and inhabited by mutant monsters. One of the first postwar sci-fi films. Stars Lloyd Bridges and Hugh O'Brian. **SF1, SF3**

Rocky (series)
Rocky (1976, C, 119m, PG)
Rocky II (1981, C, 119m, PG)
Rocky III (1982, C, 99m, PG)
Rocky IV (1985, C, 91m, PG)
Sylvester Stallone plays Rocky Balboa, the prizefighter who rises from obscurity to the heavyweight championship in these four dramas. Talia Shire and Carl Weathers costar. First installment won Best Picture and Director (John G. Avildsen) Oscars. **AC31, DR22, XT1, XT6** (*Rocky* only for last two lists)

Rodan (1957, C, 70m, NR)
Fire-breathing creature threatens to incinerate Tokyo. **FF4, SF18**

Rodney Dangerfield: It Ain't Easy Bein' Me (1987, C, 59m, NR)
The comic that gets no respect hosts this collection of stand-up routines from some of America's brightest young comics, including Robert Townsend. **CO16**

Roger Corman: Hollywood's Wild Angel (1978, C, 58m, NR)
Documentary about the producer/director/talent maven who gave career starts to many great directors and made scores of low-budget classics. Includes appearances by Corman alumni Jonathan Demme, Allan Arkush, and Joe Dante. **CU16** *Recommended*

Rollerball (1975, C, 128m, R)
In the near-future, a corporate dictatorship puts on brutal "games" for the masses, and one contestant decides to defy the system. James Caan and John Houseman star. **SF11**

Rollercoaster (1977, C, 119m, PG)
Madman threatens to destroy popular amusement park ride. George Segal, Timothy Bottoms, and Henry Fonda star. **CL24**

Rolling Thunder (1977, C, 9m,R)
A Vietnam veteran swears revenge on the thugs who killed his family and mutilated him. William Devane and Tommy Lee Jones star in this violent action drama. **AC19**

Rollover (1981, C, 118m, R)
When a multimillionaire is murdered, his widow and a financial troubleshooter sort out the financial conspiracy that caused his death. Jane Fonda and Kris Kristofferson star. **DR27, DR60, MU12**

Roman Holiday (1953, B&W, 119m, NR)
Audrey Hepburn won an Oscar for her first starring role, as a princess on the run from stuffy royal life, in love with an American reporter (Gregory Peck). Directed by William Wyler. **CL30, CL38, XT3, XT9, XT10**

Roman Scandals (1933, B&W, 92m, NR)
Eddie Cantor dreams he's back in ancient Rome in this musical romp. Choreography by Busby Berkeley. **MU20**

Roman Spring of Mrs. Stone, The (1961, C, 104m, NR)
A middle-aged American actress in Rome falls in love with a young Don Juan in this adaptation of a Tennessee Williams short novel. Vivien Leigh and Warren Beatty star. **DR1, DR34, XT9**

Romance and Riches *see* Amazing Adventure

Romance on the Range (1942, B&W, 54m, NR)
Roy Rogers captures a gang of fur thieves as well as the heart of a lovely lady. **WE23**

Romancing the Stone (1984, C, 105m, PG)
A romance writer finds herself living out one of her stories when her sister is kidnapped in South America. Kathleen Turner and Michael Douglas star in this rousing romantic adventure. Directed by Robert Zemeckis. **AC14, AC21, DR46, DR70** *Recommended*

Romantic Comedy (1983, C, 102m, PG)
Dudley Moore and Mary Steenburgen are a playwright team with a good professional relationship—but he's looking to get personal. **CO31**

Romantic Englishwoman, The (1975, C, 115m, R)
Romantic triangle involving a British novelist, his restless wife, and a German houseguest. Michael Caine, Glenda Jackson, and Helmut Berger star; Joseph Losey directed. **DR1, DR23** *Recommended*

Romeo and Juliet (1936, B&W, 126m, NR)
Classic Hollywood production of the Shakespeare tragedy, with Norma Shearer and Leslie Howard starring. **CL1, DR3**

Romeo and Juliet (1968, C, 138m, PG)
Director Franco Zeffirelli's version of
Shakespeare's classic love story, with
Leonard Whiting and Olivia Hussey the
doomed young lovers. **CL1, DR3, FF2**

Ronde, La (1950, B&W, 97m, NR)
Director Max Ophuls spins a romantic
web about the interlocking lives and loves
of a group of people in Vienna. **CU20,
FF1** *Recommended*

Rooftops (1989, C, 98m, R)
Drama of contemporary gangs in New
York living on the tops of buildings. Jason
Gedrick stars. Directed by Robert Wise.
CL58, XT9

Room Service (1938, B&W, 78m, NR)
The Marx Brothers play a trio of penni-
less producers trying to stay one step
ahead of their creditors and their hotel
management, which wants them evicted.
CO21

Room With a View, A (1985, C, 115m,
NR)
In the early 1900s, a young Englishwoman visits Florence, and despite her
chaperone's best efforts, falls in love with
a dashing Englishman. This adaptation of
the E.M. Forster novel stars Helena Bonham Carter, Maggie Smith, and Julian
Sands. **DR19**

Rooster Cogburn (1975, C, 107m, PG)
John Wayne recreates his Oscar-winning
role from *True Grit* in this western romp
with Katharine Hepburn. **CL16, WE3,
WE17**

Rootin' Tootin' Rhythm (1938, B&W, 55m,
NR)
Gene Autry and Smiley Burnette settle a
range war before things get out of hand.
WE24

Rope (1948, C, 80m, PG)
Hitchcock drama of two murderers who
brazenly throw a party in the room where
they've hidden the corpse. James Stewart
plays the guest who unravels the crime.

Farley Granger and John Dall costar.
CL25, MY9, MY15, MY22

Rose, The (1979, C, 134m, R)
Bette Midler plays a rock singer whose
hard-living lifestyle is about to catch up
with her. Alan Bates, Frederic Forrest,
and Harry Dean Stanton costar. **CU49,
DR12, MU4, MU9**

Rose Marie (1936, B&W, 110m, NR)
An opera singer (Jeanette MacDonald)
searches for her brother (James Stewart)
who is also being pursued by a Mountie
(Nelson Eddy). The singer and the
Mountie fall in love and sing "Indian
Love Call." **CL15, CL25, MU1**

Roseanne Barr *see* HBO Comedy Club

Rosemary's Baby (1968, C, 136m, R)
The wife of a New York actor suspects
that her pregnancy may not be normal.
Mia Farrow, John Cassavetes, and Oscar
winner Ruth Gordon star in this modern
horror classic from director Roman Polanski. **DR54, HO10, HO11, HO19, XT5,
XT9** *Highly Recommended*

Rough Cut (1980, C, 112m, R)
A jewel thief and a female agent from
Scotland Yard fall in love in this caper
comedy. Burt Reynolds and Lesley-Anne
Downe star. **AC37**

Rough Riders' Roundup (1939, B&W,
58m, NR)
Early Roy Rogers western, with plenty of
action and some singing as well. Raymond Hatton plays Roy's sidekick. **WE23**

Round Midnight (1986, C, 132m, R)
In the 1950s, an American jazz musician
moves to Paris, hoping to find and peace
and respect. Based loosely on the lives of
jazz greats Bud Powell and Lester Young,
this drama stars saxophonist Dexter Gordon. Martin Scorsese has a small role.
Directed by Bertrand Tavernier. **DR12,
DR52** *Recommended*

Round-up Time in Texas (1937, B&W, 58m, NR)
One of Gene Autry's early films, featuring sidekick Smiley Burnette and the usual singing and light gunplay. **WE24**

Roustabout (1964, C, 110m, NR)
Elvis Presley musical has The King going to work in a carnival run by Barbara Stanwyck. **CL45, MU22**

Rowlf's Rhapsodies With the Muppets (1985, C, 56m, NR)
Bloopers from the popular TV show, with guests stars Steve Martin, Peter Sellers, Marisa Berenson, and George Burns. **FA14**

Roxanne (1987, C, 107m, PG)
In this modern remake of *Cyrano de Bergerac*, Steve Martin plays a small-town fire chief with two problems: a large nose and unrequited love for visiting astronomer Daryl Hannah. **CO1, CO33** *Recommended*

Royal Wedding (1951, C, 93m, NR)
A brother and sister dance team (Fred Astaire, Jane Powell) perform in London during the wedding festivities of Princess Elizabeth and Prince Phillip. Directed by Stanley Donen. **MU1, MU18, MU23**

Ruby Gentry (1952, B&W, 82m, NR)
Jennifer Jones plays a Southern temptress who marries an older man to spite her real love (Charlton Heston) in this melodrama. **CL5**

Rude Boy (1980, C, 123m, NR)
Documentary-style drama of an English lad working as a roadie for rock band The Clash. Plenty of concert footage in this midnight movie favorite. **CU1**

Ruggles of Red Gap (1935, B&W, 92m, NR)
A butler finds that he has been won in poker game by a rude rancher in this comedy western. Charles Laughton stars. **WE15**

Rules of the Game (1939, B&W, 105m, NR)
Director Jean Renoir's classic study of the subtle relationship of the aristocratic class and their servants during a weekend in the country. **FF12**

Ruling Class, The (1972, C, 154m, PG)
Zany British comedy about a wacky heir to British lordship (Peter O'Toole) who's convinced that he's Jesus Christ. Irreverent, to say the least, with a cult following. **CO17, CU5, DR45**

Rumblefish (1983, B&W, 94m, R)
Matt Dillon stars as a restless teen, coping with his alcoholic father (Dennis Hopper), idolizing his older brother (Mickey Rourke). Moody, stylized drama from director Francis Ford Coppola, based on a novel by S.E. Hinton. **CU46, DR9, DR19, DR48, DR51**

Rumpelstiltskin (1985, C, 60m, NR)
A Faerie Tale Theatre presentation of the classic story of a dwarf who forces a young maiden to spin gold out of straw. Shelley Duvall and Herve Villechaize star. **FA12**

Run of the Arrow (1957, C, 86m, NR)
A Confederate veteran decides to throw in with the Sioux Indians after the Civil War. Rod Steiger and Charles Bronson star; Samuel Fuller directed. **AC29, CU22, WE7, WE8**

Run Silent, Run Deep (1958, B&W, 93m, NR)
Submarine action during World War II, starring Clark Gable and Burt Lancaster as clashing officers. Directed by Robert Wise. **AC1, CL23, CL58, DR41**

Runaway (1985, C, 99m, PG-13)
Futuristic cops-and-robbers story about a mad inventor unleashing deadly robots on an unsuspecting policeman. Tom Selleck and Gene Simmons star. **MU12, SF6, SF17**

Runaway Barge, The (1975, C, 78m, NR)
A trio of hard-living guys try to eke out a living as riverboat men in modern society. Bo Hopkins, Tim Matheson, and Nick Nolte star. Originally made for TV. **DR44**

Runaway Train (1985, C, 112m, R)
Two escaped convicts (Jon Voight and Eric Roberts) are trapped aboard a speeding train whose engineer has died of a heart attack. Shot on location in the Alaskan wilderness; Rebecca DeMornay costars. **AC24**

Running Brave (1983, C, 106, PG)
True story of Billy Mills, the native American who ran for a Gold Medal in the 1964 Olympics. Robby Benson stars. **DR22**

Running Man (1987, C, 101m, R)
Arnold Schwarzenegger plays a cop of the future who's sentenced by the dictatorship to be a contestant on a deadly quiz show—a test of skill only the strongest survive. **AC30, SF11**

Running on Empty (1988, C, 16m, PG)
A teenager with ambitions to become a music student is torn by loyalty to his fugitive parents, former antiwar activists still purused by the F.B.I. River Phoenix stars, with Christine Lahti, Judd Hirsch, and Martha Plimpton. Directed by Sidney Lumet. **DR7, DR8, DR58**

Running Out of Luck (1986, C, 88m, R)
Mick Jagger stars in this musical adventure, based on songs from his album, *She's the Boss.* Shot in South America, it's about a rock star abandoned and left for dead. Dennis Hopper, Jerry Hall, and Rae Dawn Chong costar. Directed by Julien Temple. **CU46, MU9**

Running Scared (1986, C, 106m, R)
Chicago cops Billy Crystal and Gregory Hines are ready to retire to Florida—but they'd like to nab just one more scumbag. An action film with comedy, too. **AC9, CO3, CO13**

Running Wild (1927, B&W, 68m, NR)
Silent comedy starring W.C. Fields as his usual put-upon family man. **CL11, CO22**

Russians Are Coming! The Russians Are Coming!, The (1966, C, 120m, NR)
When a Russian submarine runs aground off the New England coast, the locals are thrown into total panic. Satirical comedy about the Cold War stars Alan Arkin, Brian Keith, Carl Reiner, and Jonathan Winters. **CO2**

Rust Never Sleeps (1979, C, 103m, NR)
Concert film featuring rocker Neil Young and his band, Crazy Horse. Songs include "Down by the River" and "My, My, Hey, Hey." **MU10**

Rustler's Rhapsody (1985, C, 88m, PG)
Tom Berenger stars as Rex O'Herlihan, the last of the singing cowboys. This comedy costars Andy Griffith and Marilu Henner. **CO17, WE15**

Ruthless Four, The (1968, C, 96m, NR)
Western drama about four partners in a gold mine, starring Van Heflin, Gilbert Roland, Klaus Kinski, and George Hilton. **FF30**

Ruthless People (1986, C, 93m, R)
A desperate couple kidnap a wealthy businessman's wife, just as he's about to bump her off so that he can run off with his mistress, who is two-timing him. Frantic comedy starring Bette Midler and Danny DeVito. **CO10, MU12**

Rutles, The *see* All You Need Is Cash

Ryan's Daughter (1970, C, 176m, R)
In Ireland, a young woman trapped in a loveless marriage to a middle-aged schoolteacher embarks on a scandalous affair with a British soldier. Sarah Miles, Robert Mitchum, Christopher Jones, and Oscar winner John Mills star. Directed by David Lean. **DR3, DR50, XT4**

S.O.B. (1981, C, 121m, R)
Broad lampoon of modern Hollywood, with frantic director trying to talk his

actress wife into doing a nude scene to rescue his latest bomb. Blake Edwards wrote and directed; the cast includes Julie Andrews, William Holden (in his last film), Robert Preston, Richard Mulligan, Shelley Winters, and Robert Vaughn. **CL51, CO8, CO46, XT11** *Highly Recommended*

S.O.S. Coastguard (1937, B&W, 195m, NR)
Serial adventure about a Coast Guard commander who must stop a mad scientist (Bela Lugosi) from delivering a disintegrating gas to enemies of America. **HO28**

Sabotage (1936, B&W, 76m, NR)
Early Alfred Hitchcock thriller has a woman suspecting that her husband is secretly a mad bomber terrorizing London. Sylvia Sidney and Oscar Homolka star. **MY6, MY19, MY22**

Saboteur (1942, B&W, 108m, NR)
Robert Cummings plays the typical Alfred Hitchcock hero: the man accused of a crime he didn't commit, in this case, sabotage in the munitions industry. Classic finale atop the Statue of Liberty. **MY6, MY7, MY22**

Saboteur: Code Name Morituri *see* Morituri

Sabrina (1954, B&W, 113m, NR)
Audrey Hepburn is a chauffeur's daughter romanced by two brothers, played by Humphrey Bogart and William Holden. Sparkling comedy directed by Billy Wilder. **CL20, CL30, CL37, CL51** *Recommended*

Sacco and Vanzetti (1971, C, 120m, PG)
The story of the infamous trial of two Italian anarchists in the 1920s, with the worldwide protests that arose over their conviction and execution. Gian Maria Volonte stars. **FF2**

Sacketts, The (1979, C, 200m, NR)
Western drama, adapted from two novels by Louis L'Amour, about a trio of broth-ers (Sam Elliott, Tom Selleck, Jeff Osterhage) making their fortunes on the post-Civil War frontier. Originally made for TV. **WE29**

Sacrifice, The (1986, C, 145m, NR)
Soviet director Andrei Tarkovsky's final film, produced in Sweden, deals with nuclear annihilation and the choices it forces on an aging intellectual. Erland Josephson stars. **FF7**

Safari 3000 (1982, C, 91m, PG)
Action in the wilds of Africa, as an ex-stuntman tries to win an international car race. David Carradine stars, with Stockard Channing and Christopher Lee. **AC10, HO32**

Safety Last *see* Harold Lloyd

Saga of Death Valley (1939, B&W, 56m, NR)
Roy Rogers battles an outlaw with a hidden identity. Gabby Hayes and Don "Red" Barry costar. **WE23**

Saga of the Vagabonds, The (1959, C, 115m, NR)
Japanese adventure drama of a band of bandits distributing money to overtaxed peasants. Toshiro Mifune stars. **FF28**

Saginaw Trail (1953, B&W, 56m, NR)
Gene Autry and old pal Smiley Burnette are reunited for this tuneful western. **WE24**

Sahara (1943, B&W, 97m, NR)
During World War II, an Allied battalion is stranded in the desert without supplies or hope of reinforcements. Humphrey Bogart and Dan Duryea star. **CL20**

The Saint (series)
The Saint in New York (1938, B&W, 71m, NR)
The Saint in London (1939, B&W, 72m, NR)
The Saint Strikes Back (1939, B&W, 67m, NR)

The Saint Takes Over (1940, B&W, 69m, NR)
The Saint's Vacation (1941, B&W, 60m, NR)
Series of detective films based on the debonair sleuth created by Leslie Charters. Louis Hayward played the lead in *New York,* Hugh Sinclair in *Vacation;* George Sanders starred in the other films. Note: *The Saint Strikes Back* is packaged with a second feature, *Criminal Court;* see separate entry. **MY12**

St. Elmo's Fire (1985, C, 107m, R)
Melodramatic look at a group of friends fresh out of Georgetown University, trying to get on with their lives. Andrew McCarthy, Ally Sheedy, Rob Lowe, Demi Moore, Judd Nelson, Emilio Estevez, and Mare Winningham star. **DR7, XT9**

St. Ives (1976, C, 94m, PG)
A writer (Charles Bronson) becomes a pawn in a millionaire's international conspiracy plot. John Houseman and Jacqueline Bisset costar. **AC29**

St. Valentine's Day Massacre (1967, C, 100m, NR)
Jason Robards portrays Al Capone in this recreation of the events leading up to the famous gangster massacre. George Segal costars; Roger Corman directed. **AC22**

Sakharov (1984, C, 118m, NR)
Drama about the Soviet scientist and dissident who was imprisoned for many years for defying authorities. Jason Robards and Glenda Jackson star; originally made for TV. **DR6**

Salamander, The (1981, C, 101m, NR)
Political intrigue in Italy, as a band of neo-Fascists plot a coup. Franco Nero stars, with Anthony Quinn, Martin Balsam, Christopher Lee, and Claudia Cardinale. Based on Morris West's novel. **HO32, MY6**

Salem's Lot (1979, C, 112m, PG)
A sinister antiques dealer (James Mason) is the protector of a vampire who takes over a small New England village. It is up to a writer (David Soul) and a teenager (Lance Kerwin) to stop him. Based on the Stephen King novel; directed by Tobe Hooper. A shorter version of the movie made originally for TV, with violent scenes added. **HO5, HO40, HO42**

Sally of the Sawdust (1925, B&W, 91m, NR)
Silent comedy starring W. C. Fields as a con man with a soft heart for a young girl who is an outcast of polite society. Directed by D.W. Griffith. **CL36, CO22**

Salome's Last Dance (1988, C, 90m, R)
Outrageous depiction of imagined night in the life of notorious playwright Oscar Wilde, as a theatrical troupe performs the title play in a brothel before its author. Directed by Ken Russell; Glenda Jackson stars, with Nicholas Grace as Wilde. **CU31**

Salt of the Earth (1953, B&W, 94m, NR)
Cult drama of New Mexico miners' strike, made when the director and major stars were blacklisted in Hollywood during the Red Scare. Will Geer stars; Herbert Biberman directed. **CU9**

Salute to Chuck Jones, A (1985, C, 57m, NR)
The Oscar-winning creator of Wile E. Coyote, the Road Runner, and Pepe Le Pew is showcased in eight cartoons, including the classics *For Scentimental Reasons, One Froggy Evening,* and *What's Opera, Doc?* **FA11** *Highly Recommended*

Salute to Friz Freleng, A (1985, C, 57m, NR)
The veteran animator, winner of six Academy Awards, is represented here by eight of his major Warner Bros. cartoons, including *Birds Anonymous, Speedy Gonzales,* and *Knighty Knight Bugs.* **FA11**

Salute to Mel Blanc, A (1985, C, 58m, NR)
Mel, the man of more than 400 voices, is at his most vocal in the eight cartoons in this compilation, including *Robin Hood Daffy, Bad Ol' Putty Tat,* and *The Rabbit of Seville.* **FA11** *Recommended*

Salvador (1985, C, 123m, R)
American journalist and his wacked-out buddy travel to El Salvador in search of a story and cheap thrills; they get both as they witness the horrors of civil war raging there. Powerful performance by James Woods; James Belushi and John Savage costar. Written and directed by Oliver Stone. **CO13, DR7** *Recommended*

Salvation (1986, C, 80m, R)
Offbeat, timely comedy about a lustful preacher whose financial empire is threatened by blackmailers. Stephen McHattie stars; directed by Beth B. **CO12**

Sammy and Rosie Get Laid (1987, C, 100m, NR)
Drama set in contemporary London about a Pakistani whose son and daughter-in-law are caught up in political and sexual escapades. Shashi Kapoor, Frances Barber, Claire Bloom, and Ayub Khan Din star. Written by Hanif Kureishi and directed by Stephen Frears. **DR23, XT9**

Sam's Song *see* The Swap

Samson and Delilah (1949, C, 128m, NR)
Cecil B. DeMille's Biblical spectacular about the strongman and his downfall at the hands of a temptress. Victor Mature and Hedy Lamarr star, with George Sanders, Angela Lansbury, and Henry Wilcoxon. Spectacular finale. **CL13**

Samurai *see* The Seven Samurai

Samurai Saga (1959, C, 112m, NR)
Swordplay and a romantic triangle are the ingredients of this Japanese action drama, starring Toshiro Mifune and Yoko Tsukasa. Hiroshi Inagaki directed. **FF28**

Samurai Trilogy, The
Samurai I (1955, C, 92m, NR)
Samurai II (1955, C, 102m, NR)
Samurai III (1956, C, 102m, NR)
Epic adventure story of Musashi Miyamoto, a warrior who must come to grips with defeat before he can taste true vic-

tory. Toshiro Mifune stars; Hiroshi Inagaki directed. **FF28**

San Francisco (1936, B&W, 116m, NR)
Clark Gable, Spencer Tracy, and Jeanette MacDonald star in this lavish portrait of early 20th-century San Francisco. Highlight is recreation of the infamous earthquake of 1906. **AC13, AC23, CL3, CL19, CL23**

Sand Pebbles, The (1966, C, 179m, NR)
Steve McQueen is an American sailor assigned to a U.S. gunboat anchored in the Yangtze River during the 1926 Chinese Revolution. Candice Bergen, Richard Crenna, and Richard Attenborough costar in this epic adventure, directed by Robert Wise. **AC6, AC28, CL58** *Recommended*

Sandpiper, The (1965, C, 116m, NR)
A free-spirited artist (Elizabeth Taylor) and married minister (Richard Burton) have an affair. Theme song "The Shadow of Your Smile" won an Oscar. Charles Bronson costars; directed by Vincente Minnelli. **AC29, CL15, CL33, MU24**

Sands of Iwo Jima, The (1949, B&W, 110m, NR)
John Wayne earned an Oscar nomination for his portrayal of a tough Marine sergeant whose men are responsible for the recapturing of a strategic island during World War II. **AC1, CL17**

Sanjuro (1962, B&W, 96m, NR)
Sequel to *Yojimbo* follows further adventures of scruffy samurai sword-for-hire (Toshiro Mifune). Akira Kurosawa directed. **FF9, FF28**

Sanshiro Sugata (1943, B&W, 82m, NR)
Debut of Japanese director Akira Kurosawa, with the story of a youth trained in the art of judo matched against a jujitsu master. **FF9**

Sansho the Bailiff (1954, B&W, 132m, NR)
Classic drama of Japanese family broken up by a feudal lord and how the son and daughter struggle for survival in a slave

labor camp. Directed by Kenji Mizoguchi. **FF4**

Santa Claus, The Movie (1985, C, 112m, PG)
This comedy about St. Nick has an evil toymaker out to steal away his business. David Huddleston plays the title role; John Lithgow and Dudley Moore costar. **CO31, FA13**

Santa Fe Trail (1940, B&W, 110m, NR)
Civil War Western dramatizing the pursuit of fanatic John Brown, played by Raymond Massey. Ronald Reagan costars as George Armstrong Custer. **AC34, WE2, WE7**

Saps at Sea (1940, B&W, 57m, NR)
Laurel and Hardy comedy, with Ollie trying to relax on a boat trip, Stanley making his life miserable. **CO20**

Saturday Night Fever (1977, C, 119m, R)
A working class Brooklyn youth (John Travolta) becomes the dancing king at the local disco on Saturday nights. Also available in a PG-rated version. **MU3, XT9**

Saturn 3 (1980, C, 88m, R)
Two research scientists (Farrah Fawcett, Kirk Douglas) create a Garden of Eden on their outpost. Their ideal life is threatened when a strange man (Harvey Keitel) and his killer robot arrive. Directed by Stanley Donen. **MU23, SF3, SF6**

Satyricon (1970, C, 129m, R)
Director Federico Fellini's lavish look at the decadence of ancient Rome, starring Martin Potter and Hiram Keller as a pair of pleasure-seeking young men. Also known as *Fellini Satyricon.* **FF10**

Savage Sam (1963, C, 103m, NR)
In this sequel to *Old Yeller,* two brothers are kidnapped by Indians and their father sets out to rescue them. Brian Keith and Tommy Kirk star. **FA1**

Savage Streets (1984, C, 93m, R)
A nice high school girl turns vigilante to avenge the rape of her sister. Linda Blair stars. **AC8**

Savannah Smiles (1982, C, 107m, PG)
A little runaway hooks up with two criminals and through her love she reforms them. Mark Miller and Donovan Scott star. **FA7**

Save the Tiger (1973, C, 101m, R)
Oscar-winning performance by Jack Lemmon highlights this drama of a dress manufacturer disillusioned with his life, longing for the sweet pleasures of his youth. **DR60, DR64, XT2**

Sawdust and Tinsel (1953, B&W, 92m, NR)
A romantic triangle, set in a traveling circus, is the basis for director Ingmar Bergman's observations on life and love. Also known as *The Naked Night.* **FF8**

Say Amen, Somebody (1983, C, 100m, G)
Documentary celebrating gospel music and its two guiding lights, Rev. Thomas Dorsey and Willie Mae Ford Smith. **CU16** *Recommended*

Say Anything (1989, C, 100m, PG-13)
Romantic comedy-drama of an energetic high school senior (John Cusack) who woos the class valedictorian (Ione Skye), despite the misgivings of her father (John Mahoney). **CO1, CO4**

Sayonara (1957, C, 147m, NR)
Romance blossoms between an Air Force pilot and a Japanese entertainer in this version of James Michener's novel. Marlon Brando and Miiko Taka star, with Oscar winners Red Buttons and Miyoshi Umeki. **DR33, XT4, XT5**

Scalpel (1976, C, 96m, R)
A plastic surgeon, desperate for a family inheritance, transforms a young woman into the image of his late daughter. Robert Lansing stars. **MY18**

Scandal (1989, C, 105m, R)
Ture-life story of the John Profumo—
Christine Keeler affair which rocked 1963
Britain and helped bring down that coun-
try's Conservative government. John
Hurt, Joanne Whalley-Kilmer, Bridget
Fonda, and Ian McKellen star. Also avail-
able in an unrated version; running time:
115m. **CU10, DR6, DR21, DR23** *Recom-
mended*

Scandalous (1983, C, 93m, PG)
Comic thriller starring Robert Hays as a
nosy reporter up to his ears in spies and
skullduggery. Pamela Stephenson and
John Gielgud costar. **MY21**

Scanners (1981, C, 102m, R)
A small group of people have the ability
to read minds; one uses his power for evil
and kills innocent people by making their
heads explode. A good scanner tracks the
evil one to stop him. Cult horror film
directed by David Cronenberg. **CU4,
CU7, HO7, HO39**

Scaramouche (1952, C, 110m, NR)
Swashbuckler classic, with Stewart
Granger as the 18th-century swordsman
memorably dueling with villainous Mel
Ferrer. Eleanor Parker and Janet Leigh
costar. **AC13, FA4**

Scarecrow (1973, C, 115m, R)
Gene Hackman and Al Pacino play a pair
of drifters in this episodic comedy-drama
costarring Dorothy Tristan, Eileen Brennan, and Ann Wedgeworth. **DR39, DR66**

Scared to Death (1947, C, 65m, NR)
All those who accuse a woman (Joyce
Compton) of murder wind up dead. Bela
Lugosi stars. **HO28**

Scarface (1932, B&W, 90m, NR)
Paul Muni stars as a gangster whose career is loosely based on Al Capone. Boris
Karloff, George Raft, and Ann Dvorak
costar; Howard Hawks directed this classic. **AC22, CL35, HO27** *Highly Recommended*

Scarface (1983, C, 170m, R)
Remake and updating of classic gangster
drama, with Al Pacino a Cuban immigrant
rising to the top of the Miami drug trade.
Michelle Pfeiffer, Steven Bauer, Mary
Elizabeth Mastrantonio, and Robert Loggia costar. Exceptionally violent film directed by Brian DePalma. **AC22, CU7,
CU18, CU28, DR66**

Scarlet Claw, The (1944, B&W, 74m, NR)
Sherlock Holmes mystery set in Canada,
involving the gruesome murder of a
noblewoman. Basil Rathbone and Nigel
Bruce star. **MY10**

Scarlet Letter, The (1980, C, 90m, NR)
German director Wim Wenders' version
of the classic Hawthorne tale of sin and
redemption. **FF21**

Scarlet Pimpernel, The (1934, B&W, 96m,
NR)
A British aristocrat becomes the savior of
French royalty during the French Revo-
lution. Leslie Howard and Merle Oberon
star. **AC13, FA4**

Scarlet Street (1945, B&W, 103m, NR)
A meek, middle-aged man is seduced into
a life of crime by a shady lady and her
no-good boyfriend. Edward G. Robinson,
Joan Bennett, and Dan Duryea star; Fritz
Lang directed this classic thriller. **CL43,
CL52, MY1, MY4** *Recommended*

Scars of Dracula (1970, C, 94m, R)
A man and woman must fight the legendary Dracula (Christopher Lee) while
searching for the man's missing brother.
HO5, HO26, HO32

Scene of the Crime (1986, C, 90m, NR)
An escaped convict kidnaps a young boy
and forces the child's mother to help him
hide from the police. Catherine Deneuve
stars in this French-made thriller. **FF27**

Scenes From a Marriage (1973, C, 168m,
NR)
Director Ingmar Bergman's portrait of a
marriage in crisis, starring Liv Ullmann
and Erland Josephson. Originally made
for Swedish TV and edited into a theatrical film by the director. **FF8, FF25**

Scenes From the Class Struggle in Beverly Hills (1989, C, 102m, R)
Comedy from cult director Paul Bartel concerning the sexual appetites of the filthy rich and their servants in a Southern California community. Jacqueline Bisset, Ray Sharkey, Robert Beltran, and Mary Woronov star, with Ed Begley, Jr., Wallace Shawn, Paul Mazursky, and Bartel. **CU42**

Schizoid (1980, C, 91m, R)
A psychiatrist's female patients are being killed. The killer tells an advice columnist of the murders and threatens her. Klaus Kinski and Marianne Hill star. **FF30, HO9**

School Daze (1988, C, 120m, R)
One-of-a-kind film, set in an all-black college, combines comedy and drama with musical numbers to cover variety of subjects, mainly racial identity. Spike Lee wrote and directed and stars as a young fraternity pledge. Uneven, but rewarding for its best segments. **CO2, DR14** *Recommended*

Scott of the Antarctic (1948, C, 110m, NR)
An account of the fateful Robert Scott expedition to the South Pole. Christopher Lee costars. **HO32**

Scream and Scream Again (1970, C, 95m, PG)
A mad scientist attempts to create a master race of unemotional beings. Vincent Price, Christopher Lee, and Peter Cushing star. **HO20, HO26, HO31, HO32, HO33**

Scream of Fear (1961, B&W, 81m, NR)
A wheelchair-bound young woman (Susan Strasberg) visits her father's Riviera villa, only to be told he's away. When she catches glimpses of his corpse, she begins to suspect her stepmother (Ann Todd) of foul play. British thriller costars Christopher Lee. **HO32, MY3, MY19**

Screamers (1980, C, 89m, R)
A group of convicts escapes to an island that's inhabited by a mad scientist who has created sub-human creatures. Barbara Bach and Joseph Cotten star. **HO20**

Scrooge (1970, C, 118m, G)
A musical adaptation of *A Christmas Carol*. Albert Finney stars, with Alec Guinness, Edith Evans, and Kenneth More. **CL1, DR63, FA13, MU14**

Scrooged (1988, C, 101m, PG-13)
Contemporary version of Dickens' *Christmas Carol*, with Bill Murray a callous TV executive brought to his senses by a series of wacky angels. With Carol Kane, John Forsythe, Karen Allen, John Glover, Bobcat Goldthwaite, David Johansen, Robert Mitchum, and Alfre Woodard. **CL1, CO2, CO13, FA13**

Scruffy (1985, C, 72m, NR)
An orphaned puppy searches for a home and is befriended by a stray. **FA10**

Sea Gypsies, The (1978, C, 101m, G)
A man, his daughters, a journalist, and a runaway go on a sailing expedition and learn survival techniques when they are shipwrecked. **FA4**

Sea Hawk, The (1940, B&W, 110m, NR)
A buccaneer is given approval by Queen Elizabeth I to wreak havoc on the Spanish fleet and their cities in the New World. Errol Flynn and Flora Robson star. Directed by Michael Curtiz. Home video version contains restored footage of scenes intended to boost British wartime morale. **AC13, AC34, CU10**

Sea Wolves, The (1980, C, 120m, PG)
Two British intelligence officers recruit a retired fighting unit for a top secret mission against the Nazis. Roger Moore, Gregory Peck, and David Niven star. **AC1**

Seance on a Wet Afternoon (1964, B&W, 115m, NR)
Suspense drama about a shady medium and her husband bilking a couple. Kim Stanley, Richard Attenborough, and Patrick Magee star. **DR23, MY19**

Searchers, The (1956, C, 119m, NR)
John Wayne spends years tracking down the Indians who kidnapped his niece (Natalie Wood). A cult favorite, directed by John Ford. **CU13, CL14, WE6, WE8, WE16, WE17, WE18** *Recommended*

Season of the Witch (1972, C, 89m, R)
A housewife develops an interest in witchcraft and joins a coven. Directed by George Romero. **HO38**

Second Chorus (1940, B&W, 83m, NR)
Fred Astaire and Burgess Meredith compete for Paulette Goddard in this musical featuring Artie Shaw and his Orchestra. **MU18**

Secret Agent, The (1936, B&W, 86m, NR)
Madeleine Carroll and John Gielgud are spies posing as man and wife to track down an enemy agent in Switzerland. Directed by Alfred Hitchcock. **MY6, MY19, MY22**

Secret Beyond the Door (1948, B&W, 98m, NR)
Joan Bennett stars in this thriller as a woman who suspects that her husband is a killer. Michael Redgrave costars; Fritz Lang directed. **CL43, MY3**

Secret Ceremony (1968, C, 109m, R)
A woman who grieves over her dead daughter forms a strange relationship with a girl whose mother is dead. Elizabeth Taylor and Mia Farrow star in this offbeat drama. **CL33**

Secret Diary of Sigmund Freud, The (1984, C, 129m, PG)
Comedy about the early days of the world's first therapist, starring Bud Cort, Carol Kane, Klaus Kinski, and Carroll Baker. **FF28**

Secret Honor (1984, C, 90m, NR)
Philip Baker Hall stars in this one-man show as Richard Nixon in all his paranoid glory. Directed by Robert Altman; originally made for cable TV. **CU25**

Secret Life of Walter Mitty, The (1947, C, 105m, NR)
A timid man (Danny Kaye) escapes his dull job and nagging mother through elaborate fantasies. Boris Karloff costars in this adaptation of the James Thurber story. **CO41, HO27**

Secret of My Success, The (1987, C, 110m, PG-13)
An ambitious young man from Iowa climbs the corporate ladder in a New York firm run by his uncle, whose wife has romantic designs on her nephew. Michael J. Fox stars in this comedy, with Richard Jordan, Margaret Whitton, and Helen Slater. **CO2, CO37**

Secret of NIMH, The (1982, C, 83m, G)
Animated adventure about a widowed mouse who seeks help in keeping her home and comes across a secret society of rats. Featuring the voices of Elizabeth Hartman, Derek Jacobi, and Peter Strauss. **FA10**

Secret Policeman's Other Ball, The (1982, C, 91m, R)
Concert film, derived from two London benefits for Amnesty International. Featured are members of the Monty Python troupe doing some of their best routines, plus musical performances by Eric Clapton, Pete Townshend, Jeff Beck, and other British rock stars. **CO15** *Recommended*

Secret Policeman's Private Parts, The (1984, C, 77m, R)
Concert footage from an Amnesty International benefit show starring members of Monty Python, plus Peter Cook and singers Phil Collins, Pete Townshend, and Donovan. **CO15**

Secret War of Harry Frigg, The (1968, C, 110m, NR)
Paul Newman stars as an Army hustler in this World War II comedy about a plot to free five kidnapped U.S. generals. **CO38, DR28**

Secrets of Life (1956, C, 75m, NR)
This Disney documentary, part of the True-Life Adventure series, looks at natural wonders and sea, plant, and insect life. **FA1**

Secrets of Women (1952, B&W, 114m, PG-13)
Three wives at a summer house compare notes on their relationships with their husbands in this comedy-drama from director Ingmar Bergman. **FF8**

Seduction of Joe Tynan, The (1979, C, 107m, PG)
United States Senator tries his best to resist temptations of political corruption, is less successful at resisting an affair. Alan Alda, Meryl Streep, Barbara Harris, Rip Torn, and Melvyn Douglas star. **CU47, DR21, DR26, XT9**

Seduction of Mimi, The (1974, C, 82m, R)
Italian comedy of a working class man (Giancarlo Giannini) and his problems, especially with women. Lina Wertmuller directed. Remade in the U.S. as *Which Way Is Up?* **FF2, FF36**

See No Evil (1971, C, 89m, PG)
A blind woman is stalked by a mad killer, who has already murdered her entire family at a secluded farm. Mia Farrow stars. **MY3**

See No Evil, Hear No Evil (1989, C, 103m, R)
Richard Pryor (as a blind man) and Gene Wilder (as a deaf man) team up in this comedy of mistaken identity: they're accused of a murder and must find the real culprit. **CO3, CO10, CO29**

See You in the Morning (1989, C, 119m, PG-13)
Drama of a second marriage and how the husband's ties to his first wife and set of children complicate his life. Jeff Bridges stars, with Alice Krige and Farrah Fawcett. Written and directed by Alan J. Pakula. **DR8, DR71**

Seems Like Old Times (1980, C, 121m, PG)
Neil Simon comedy about a well-meaning lawyer (Goldie Hawn) whose first husband (Chevy Chase) keeps popping up in her life, much to the annoyance of Husband #2 (Charles Grodin). **CO13, CO30, CO34**

Seize the Day (1986, C, 93m, NR)
Screen version of Saul Bellow's novel about a loser (Robin Williams) desperately trying to stay out of debt and in his father's good graces. Joseph Wiseman co-stars. **CO43, DR19** *Recommended*

Seizure (1974, C, 93m, R)
Horror tale of a novelist plagued by a trio of evildoers who put him and his family through hellish tortures—although they may exist only in his imagination. Jonathan Frid stars, with Martine Beswick, Troy Donahue, Herve Villechaize, and Mary Woronov. Written and directed by Oliver Stone. **HO14**

Semi-Tough (1977, C, 108m, R)
Comedy poking fun at professional sports and self-help groups, among other modern institutions, starring Burt Reynolds, Jill Clayburgh, and Kris Kristofferson. **AC37, CO2, MU12**

Senator Was Indiscreet, The (1947, B&W, 81m, NR)
The revelations in a lawmaker's diary are the cause for much scandal in this satiric comedy starring William Powell and Ella Raines. Playwright George S. Kaufman directed, his only stint behind the camera. **CL10, CU15**

Sense of Loss, A (1972, C, 135m, NR)
Documentary detailing the terrible toll that the Catholic-Protestant conflict in Northern Ireland takes on citizens. Directed by Marcel Ophuls. **CU16**

Senso (1954, C, 90m, NR)
An aristocratic woman takes a young, poor man for her lover, with tragic consequences. Classic story of infidelity and

obsession, directed by Luchino Visconti.
FF2

Separate Peace, A (1972, C, 104m, PG)
Screen version of John Knowles' popular
novel about friendship between two prep
school students during the 1940s. Parker
Stevenson and William Roerick star.
DR19

Separate Tables (1958, B&W, 99m, NR)
All-star drama set at English resort, with
intertwining stories of guests. Burt Lancaster, Rita Hayworth, David Niven,
Deborah Kerr, and Wendy Hiller are the
featured players; Niven and Hiller won
Oscars. **DR41, XT2, XT5**

September (1987, C, 82m, PG)
Woody Allen directed this somber drama
about a faded movie actress, her daughter, and their tangled lives. Elaine Stritch
and Mia Farrow star, with Denholm Elliott, Dianne Wiest, Sam Waterston, and
Jack Warden. **CO27**

Sgt. Pepper's Lonely Hearts Club Band
(1978, C, 111m, PG)
Peter Frampton and the Bee Gees create
a fantasy world from the songs on the
Beatles album of the same name. Steve
Martin costars. **CO33, MU8, MU16**

Sergeant Ryker (1968, C, 85m, NR)
Lee Marvin is on trial for treason during
the Korean War. Bradford Dillman and
Vera Miles costar. **AC3, DR43**

Sergeant York (1941, B&W, 134m, NR)
Gary Cooper won an Oscar for his por-
trayal of World War I hero Alvin York;
Howard Hawks directed. **AC2, CL2,
CL26, CL35, XT2**

Serial (1980, C, 86m, R)
Comedy about an affluent California suburb which embraces each new trend as it
comes along. Martin Mull, Tuesday Weld,
and Christopher Lee star. **CO2, HO32**

Serpent and the Rainbow, The (1988, C,
98m, R)
An American scientist travels to Haiti to
invesitgate voodoo drugs and rituals that
turn humans into zombies. Bill Pullman,
Cathy Tyson, and Paul Winfield star. Directed by Wes Craven. **HO6**

Serpent's Egg, The (1978, C, 120m, R)
Director Ingmar Bergman's grim drama
of Jews in pre-World War II Germany and
the humiliation they suffer in order to
survive. David Carradine and Liv Ullmann star. **FF8, FF25**

Serpico (1973, C, 129m, R)
True story of undercover New York cop
who blew the whistle on corruption in the
department and was nearly murdered for
his honesty. Al Pacino stars; Sidney Lumet directed. **DR6, DR16, DR58, DR66**

Servant, The (1963, B&W, 115m, NR)
From writer Harold Pinter and director
Joseph Losey, the contemporary tale of a
manservant (Dirk Bogarde) turning the
tables on his decadent master (James
Fox). Sarah Miles and Wendy Craig costar. **DR23**

Sesame Street Presents Follow That Bird
see Follow That Bird

Set-Up, The (1949, B&W, 72m, NR)
Gritty drama of a faded boxer asked to
take a fall for gamblers but defying them
at the last minute. Robert Ryan stars;
Robert Wise directed. **CL58, DR22, MY1**
Recommended

Seven Beauties (1976, C, 115m, R)
From Italian director Lina Wertmüller,
the tragicomic story of a man who will do
anything to survive in a prisoner-of-war
camp during World War II. Giancarlo Giannini stars. **FF2**

Seven Brides For Seven Brothers (1954, C,
103m, G)
When Howard Keel weds Jane Powell, his
six brothers decide to follow suit by kidnapping six townsgirls. Rousing musical
western based on Stephen Vincent Be-

net's "Sobbin' Women." Directed by Stanley Donen. **MU1, MU3, MU6, MU23**

Seven Days in May (1964, B&W, 118m, NR)
U.S. President is threatened when one of his high-ranking generals plots a coup. First-rate political thriller. Burt Lancaster, Kirk Douglas, Fredric March, Ava Gardner, and Edmond O'Brien star. Written by Rod Serling; directed by John Frankenheimer. **DR21, DR41** *Recommended*

7 Faces of Dr. Lao, The (1964, C, 101m, NR)
A traveling circus weaves magic and stories to show the inhabitants of a western town the truly important things in life. Tony Randall stars. Directed by George Pal. **FA8, SF13**

Seven Little Foys, The (1955, C, 95m, NR)
When Eddie Foy's wife dies, he is left alone to take care of his seven children. He adds them to his vaudeville act and they become stars. Bob Hope stars with a special appearance by James Cagney as George M. Cohan. **CL7, CL22, CO40, MU5**

Seven Percent Solution, The (1976, C, 113m, PG)
Sherlock Holmes tale, with the famous detective traveling to Vienna for treatment by a certain Dr. Freud for a drug habit. Sounds spoofy, but it's played straight, with a superb cast including Nicol Williamson, Robert Duvall (as Watson), Alan Arkin, Vanessa Redgrave, and Laurence Olivier. **CL32, DR37, DR65, MY10** *Recommended*

Seven Samurai, The (1954, B&W, 200m, NR)
A diverse collection of swordsmen come to the aid of villagers who are being ravaged by bandits. Akira Kurosawa directed; Toshiro Mifune stars. Oscar winner for Best Foreign Language Film under the title *Samurai*. Also available in a 141m version. U.S. remake: *The Mag-*

nificent Seven. **AC13, FF9, FF28, FF36, XT7** *Highly Recommended*

Seven Sinners (1940, B&W, 87m, NR)
Marlene Dietrich is a South Seas chanteuse, John Wayne her smitten protector in this melodrama. **CL17, CL47**

Seven-Ups, The (1973, C, 103m, PG)
Roy Scheider heads a special police task force against mobsters that is brutally efficient. Follow-up to *The French Connection*. **AC9**

Seven Year Itch, The (1955, C, 105m, NR)
A married man, with his wife and kids out of town for the summer, gets ideas about a beautiful blonde who has rented the apartment above his. Marilyn Monroe and Tom Ewell star. Directed by Billy Wilder. **CL29**

1776 (1972, C, 141m, G)
John Adams, Benjamin Franklin, and the rest of the first American Congress sing and dance their way to independence. William Daniels and Howard Da Silva recreate their Broadway roles. **FA9, MU2, MU16**

Seventh Seal, The (1956, B&W, 96m, NR)
Classic allegory from director Ingmar Bergman of medieval knight (Max von Sydow) and his search for truth and beauty. Bibi Andersson costars. **FF8** *Recommended*

7th Voyage of Sinbad, The (1958, C, 87m, G)
Sinbad must accomplish several tasks to save a princess who has been miniaturized by an evil magician. Kerwin Matthews and Kathryn Grant are the leads, but the real star is Ray Harryhausen and his special effects. **AC18, FA8, SF13** *Highly Recommended*

Sex Shop, Le (1973, C, 92m, R)
The owner of a book shop finds his business multiplying when he begins selling pornographic material. A light, naughty comedy from France. **FF1**

Sex With a Smile (1976, C, 100m, R)
Five episodes in this Italian comedy demonstrate how funny good, clean sex can be. Marty Feldman stars. **FF2**

Sextette (1978, C, 91m, R)
Mae West's last film, based on her play, about a woman's eventful honeymoon—her ex-husbands keep making appearances. A movie with "camp" written all over it. **CO39, CU2**

Shack Out on 101 (1955, B&W, 80m, NR)
Mind-blowing thriller set in a hash house on California's coastal highway, about espionage and thwarted romance. Lee Marvin is the cook named Slob who's really a Russian spy, Terry Moore is the lusted-after waitress, Frank Lovejoy is the professor working on a top-secret project. A camp classic. **CU2, DR43, MY1** *Recommended*

Shadow Box, The (1980, C, 100m, NR)
Dramatic story of a trio of terminally ill patients at a rural California hospice, adapted by Michael Cristofer from his play. Paul Newman directed; Joanne Woodward, Christopher Plummer, and James Broderick star. Originally made for TV. **DR7, DR20, DR28, DR67** *Recommended*

Shadow of a Doubt (1943, B&W, 108m, NR)
Hitchcock thriller set in a small town, where a young girl (Teresa Wright) suspects her kindly uncle (Joseph Cotten) of murder. Screenplay co-written by Thorton Wilder **DR62, MY18, MY22** *Recommended*

Shadow of the Thin Man (1941, B&W, 97m, NR)
Fourth Thin Man mystery, with sleuthing couple Nick and Nora Charles at the racetrack, betting on losers but picking the right murder suspect. William Powell and Myrna Loy star. **CL15, CL46, MY13, MY21, MY28**

Shadows (1922, B&W, 85m, NR)
A woman, who believes her nasty first husband is dead, remarries and starts a family. Soon after, she starts receiving blackmail threats from her first husband. Lon Chaney, Sr. stars in this silent drama. **HO29**

Shadows of Forgotten Ancestors (1964, B&W, 99m, NR)
Drama set in rural Russia of the early 20th century, about the trials and tribulations of a peasant (Ivan Mikolaychuk). **FF7**

Shaggy D.A., The (1976, C, 91m, G)
In this sequel to *The Shaggy Dog*, a lawyer (Dean Jones) who's just been elected District Attorney turns into a sheepdog when an ancient spell is read. Suzanne Pleshette and Tim Conway costar. **FA1**

Shaggy Dog, The (1959, B&W, 104m, G)
A young boy whose father hates dogs discovers his older brother turns into a sheepdog when an ancient spell is read. Fred MacMurray and Tommy Kirk star in this classic Disney comedy. **FA1**

Shaka Zulu (1985, C, 300m, NR)
The true story of Shaka, a tribal leader who united the Zulu nation against the British in Africa during the 1900s. Trevor Howard and Chistopher Lee star. Originally made for TV. **HO32**

Shakedown (1988, C, 90m, R)
A crusading lawyer (Peter Weller) and an undercover cop (Sam Elliott) team to clean up the New York Police Department of corruption. Patricia Charbonneau co-stars. Plenty of wild chases. **AC9**

Shalako (1968, C, 113m, NR)
Western drama about a hunting party of Europeans in New Mexico being attacked by Apaches. Sean Connery and Brigitte Bardot star. **AC36, FF32**

Shall We Dance (1937, B&W, 116m, NR)
A Russian ballet dancer (Fred Astaire) and an American musical performer (Ginger Rogers) marry as a publicity stunt and

end up falling in love. **CL15, MU18** *Recommended*

Shame (1988, C, 95m, R)
Australian drama set in a small town which holds a terrible secret: a gang of young men have been attacking women without fear of interference from the community or its law officers. A female barrister, stranded in the town, tries to persuade one of the victims to press charges. **DR62, FF5**

Shampoo (1975, C, 112m, R)
A Beverly Hills hairdresser tries to satisfy his customers in the shop and after hours. Warren Beatty, Julie Christie, Goldie Hawn, and Oscar winner Lee Grant star in this satiric comedy, set around the 1968 Presidential election. Written by Beatty and Robert Towne; directed by Hal Ashby. **CO1, CO2, CO30, DR34, XT5, XT9** *Recommended*

Shamus (1973, C, 106m, R)
Burt Reynolds plays a private eye with some offbeat detection methods in this mystery. Dyan Cannon costars. **AC37, MY14**

Shane (1953, C, 118m, NR)
Alan Ladd plays the lone gunman squared off against evil Jack Palance in this classic western. With Van Heflin, Jean Arthur (in her last film), and Brandon de Wilde. Directed by George Stevens. **CL42, WE3, XT11** *Recommended*

Shanghai Gesture, The (1941, B&W, 106m, NR)
Josef von Sternberg directed this murky tale of a man who discovers his daughter working in an Oriental den of iniquity. Walter Huston, Gene Tierney, and Victor Mature star. **CL56**

Shanghai Surprise (1986, C, 97m, PG13)
Pop star Madonna plays a missionary in 1930s China. Sean Penn plays a soldier of fortune who helps her out of a tight spot. **AC21, MU12**

Sharad of Atlantis see Undersea Kingdom

Shark! (1969, C, 92m, PG)
Burt Reynolds stars in this underwater adventure of treasure divers encountering toothy creatures of the deep. Directed by Samuel Fuller. **AC37, CU22**

Sharkey's Machine (1981, C, 119m, R)
An Atlanta cop's vendetta against a mobster gets personal when he becomes romantically involved with one of the crime boss's working girls. Burt Reynolds and Rachel Ward star, with Vittorio Gassman, Brian Keith, Bernie Casey, and Charles Durning. **AC9, AC37**

She (1985, C, 90m, NR)
A warrior woman must stop an expedition that is searching for the Flame of Eternal Life. Based on a novel by H. Rider Haggard. Sandahl Bergman stars. **AC18**

She Done Him Wrong (1933, B&W, 66m, NR)
Mae West is Diamond Lil; she invites Cary Grant to come up sometime and see her. **CL18, CO39**

She Wore a Yellow Ribbon (1949, C, 103m, NR)
John Wayne is a retiring cavalry officer with one more Indian battle to fight. Directed by John Ford. **AC5, WE5, WE17, WE18** *Recommended*

She's Having a Baby (1988, C, 106m, PG-13)
Comedy-drama from writer-director John Hughes, about the second thoughts of a young husband and father-to-be. Kevin Bacon and Elizabeth McGovern star. **CO1, CO47**

Sheena (1984, C, 117m, PG)
A white orphan raised by an African tribe has the ability to communicate with animals. Tanya Roberts stars in this adventure tale. **AC17**

Shenandoah (1965, C, 105m, NR)
A Virginia farmer tries to stay neutral during the Civil War, but his family soon drags him into the fray. James Stewart stars. **AC5, CL25, WE7**

Sherlock Holmes and the Secret Weapon (1942, B&W, 68m, NR)
Basil Rathbone and Nigel Bruce star in this contemporary Holmes case set during World War II, involving the disappearance of an inventor and his important discovery. Lionel Atwill costars as Professor Moriarty. **MY10**

Sherlock Holmes and the Spider Woman
see Spider Woman

Sherlock Holmes and the Voice of Terror (1942, B&W, 65m, NR)
More Holmes detection updated, with the detective battling Nazis who make their terrorist demands over the airwaves. Basil Rathbone and Nigel Bruce star. **MY10**

Sherlock Holmes Faces Death (1943, B&W, 68m, NR)
Basil Rathbone and Nigel Bruce are back for more deducing, this time to solve what appears to be a ritual murder. **MY10**

Sherlock Holmes in Washington (1943, B&W, 71m, NR)
Further adventures of the great detective in the World War II era, this time chasing spies in the Nation's Capital. Basil Rathbone and Nigel Bruce star. **MY10**

She's Gotta Have It (1986, B&W, 84m, R)
Sexy comedy from director Spike Lee (who also stars as hip messenger boy Mars) about a free-spirited woman (Tracy Camila-Johns) with three lovers and no qualms about keeping all of them. **CO1, CO2, CU6, DR14**

Shinbone Alley (1971, C, 85m, G)
Animated adventures of an independent alley cat and a poet cockroach who strike up an unusual friendship. Featuring the voices of Eddie Bracken, Carol Channing, and John Carradine. **FA10**

Shine On Harvest Moon (1938, B&W, 60m, NR)
Roy Rogers preserves the peace in the Old West against a gang of desperadoes. **WE23**

Shining, The (1980, C, 142m, R)
Writer agrees to stay at a deserted hotel for the winter with his wife and son, but the solitude (and other forces) prove too much for him. Jack Nicholson stars in this version of Stephen King's novel, directed by Stanley Kubrick. **DR24, DR53, HO2, HO3, HO42**

Ship of Fools (1965, B&W, 149m, NR)
Drama set aboard an ocean liner in the dark days just before World War II, with international assortment of characters. Based on Katherine Anne Porter's bestseller. Lee Marvin, Vivien Leigh, Oskar Werner, Simone Signoret, George Segal, Elizabeth Ashley, and Michael Dunne star. **DR5, DR19, DR43**

Shoah (1986, C, 570m, NR)
Monumental documentary about the effects of the Holocaust on its survivors and the townspeople who lived near the death camps. Relies almost exclusively on interview material, with almost no footage of the atrocities themselves. Directed by Claude Lanzmann. **CU16** *Recommended*

Shock, The (1923, B&W, 96m, NR)
A mobster sends a hired gun to a small town to kill a rival banker. The gunman falls in love with a sweet young girl and decides to reform. Lon Chaney, Sr. stars in this silent drama. **HO29**

Shock (1946, B&W, 70m, NR)
Vincent Price and his gang plan to kill a girl who witnessed one of their crimes. **HO31**

Shock Waves (1977, C, 86m, PG)
A Nazi scientist creates androids to man the Fuerher's submarines. Peter Cushing stars. **HO33**

Shoes of the Fisherman, The (1968, C, 152m, G)
A drama about the election of the first Russian Pope and its effect on world peace. Anthony Quinn and Laurence Olivier star. **CL32**

Shogun Assassin (1981, C, 90m, R)
A swordsman travels the Japanese countryside, wheeling his son in a baby carriage, taking on all comers in this extremely violent action saga. Video version of this cult favorite is dubbed in English. **CU7, FF4**

Shoot Loud, Louder. . .I Don't Understand (1966, C, 100m, NR)
Crazy-quilt comedy from Italy about an antiques dealer (Marcello Mastroianni) and his loony adventures with a lovely woman (Raquel Welch) and some bumbling gunmen. **FF24**

Shoot the Living, Pray for the Dead (1973, C, 90m, NR)
Klaus Kinski stars in a western drama about a killer who promises his guide a share in stolen gold. **FF30**

Shoot the Moon (1982, C, 123m, R)
A husband's infidelity leads to the painful breakup of his marriage, with a devastating effect on his three daughters. Albert Finney and Diane Keaton star; Alan Parker directed. **DR8, DR40**

Shoot the Piano Player (1962, B&W, 85m, NR)
A Parisian musician is torn between his musical ambitions and his relationships with gangsters. Moving drama from director François Truffaut, starring Charles Aznavour. **FF13, XT9** *Recommended*

Shoot to Kill (1988, C, 110m, R)
An F.B.I. agent (Sidney Poitier) and mountain guide (Tom Berenger) team to track a fugitive killer who has kidnapped the guide's girlfriend (Kirstie Alley). **AC12, DR38**

Shooting, The (1967, C, 82m, NR)
Cult western starring Jack Nicholson and Warren Oates in a convoluted tale of revenge. Monte Hellman directed. **CU48, DR24, WE16**

Shooting Party, The (1984, C, 108m, NR)
Weekend in the British countryside in 1913, with various personalities, class conflicts, romantic entanglements. James Mason, Dorothy Tutin, Edward Fox, and John Gielgud star. **DR23**

Shootist, The (1976, C, 99m, PG)
In his last film, John Wayne plays a once-famous gunfighter who finds that he has cancer. Lauren Bacall and James Stewart costar. **CL25, WE3, WE12, WE17, XT11**

Shop Around the Corner, The (1940, B&W, 97m, NR)
Romantic comedy of two shopworkers (James Stewart, Margaret Sullavan) who become unwitting lovers through correspondence. Directed by Ernst Lubitsch. **CL4, CL25, CL54**

Shop on Main Street, The (1965, B&W, 128m, NR)
Oscar-winning drama from Czechoslovakia about the relationship between an elderly Jewish woman and the man who takes over her business during World War II. **FF7, XT7**

Short Circuit (1986, C, 98m, PG)
A robot escapes from its military keepers and is taken in by a lovely young animal lover. Gentle comedy with special effects humor, starring Ally Sheedy, Steve Guttenberg, and Austin Pendleton. **CO11**

Short Circuit 2 (1988, C, 110m, PG)
More adventures of Johnny 5, the playful robot. Fisher Stevens, Michael McKean, and Cynthia Gibb are the human costars. **CO11**

Short Eyes (1977, C, 104m, R)
Prison drama of a child molester's fate at the hands of fellow cons. Rewarding drama, but not for the faint of heart. Bruce Davison, José Perez, and Miguel Piñero star; based on Piñero's play. **DR18** *Recommended*

Short Films of D.W. Griffith, The: Volume 1 (1911-12, B&W, 59m, NR)
Three early short films directed by D.W. Griffith. *The Battle* is a Civil War tale about a boy who shows signs of cowardice, then becomes a hero; Charles West

and Blanche Sweet star. *The Female of the Species (A Psychological Tragedy)* is a tale of three women who become friends after facing a series of hardships; Mary Pickford stars. *The New York Hat* is about small town hypocrisy and the damage of gossip; Mary Pickford stars. **CL36**

Short Fuse (1987, C, 91m, R)
A Washington, D.C. journalist (Art Garfunkel) investigates a murder in the funky "go-go" clubs of the Nation's Capital. Plenty of music from Chuck Brown & the Soul Searchers, Trouble Funk, and other groups. Released theatrically as *Good to Go*. **AC8, MU12, XT9**

Shot in the Dark, A (1964, C, 101m, NR)
Second (and arguably funniest) Pink Panther adventure has Inspector Clouseau trying to prove that a lovely young woman is innocent of murder. Peter Sellers is in top form, as is Elke Sommer; Herbert Lom, George Sanders, and Bert Kwouk are all hilarious. Directed by Blake Edwards. **CO26, CO46** *Highly Recommended*

Shout, The (1979, C, 87m, R)
A man who believes he can kill people by shouting terrorizes a young couple. Alan Bates, John Hurt, and Susannah York star in this strange drama directed by Jerzy Skolimowski. **HO7**

Shout at the Devil (1976, C, 119m, PG)
Action drama, set in pre-World War I Africa, about a poacher recruiting an Englishman in a plot to blow up a German ship. Lee Marvin and Roger Moore star. **DR43**

Show Boat (1952, C, 107m, NR)
The naive daughter (Kathryn Grayson) of the owners of a show boat falls in love with a gambler (Howard Keel). Ava Gardner costars in the Jerome Kern-Oscar Hammerstein musical. **MU1, MU6**

Show People (1928, B&W, 81m, NR)
Silent comedy set in Hollywood, with Marion Davies as an actress who lets success go to ther head. Watch for cameos by Charlie Chaplin, Douglas Fairbanks, and other Movie Town notables of the period. Carl Davis composed a musical score for the video version. **CL7, CL11** *Recommended*

Showdown at Boot Hill (1958, B&W, 76m, NR)
Charles Bronson is a bounty hunter out to collect his money in this western drama. **AC29**

Shy People (1988, C, 188m, R)
A New York journalist (Jill Clayburgh) travels with her daughter to the Louisiana bayou to meet a cousin (Barbara Hershey) as a subject for a story. **DR8, DR10**

Sicilian, The (1987, C, 146m, NR)
True story of Salvatore Giuliano, the Sicilian bandit who defied the wealthy landowners and gave the peasants a hero to look up to. This is the European cut with footage unseen in the American release. The 115m American version is also available. Christopher Lambert stars. Directed by Michael Cimino. **AC16, CU10, DR5**

Sid and Nancy (1986, C, 111m, R)
The heartbreaking story of English punk rocker Sid Vicious and Nancy Spungen, his American lover and partner in drug addiction. An instant midnight movie classic with stunning performances by Gary Oldman and Chloe Webb. **CU1, DR6, DR12** *Recommended*

Sidney Sheldon's Bloodline (1979, C, 116m, R)
Audrey Hepburn stars in this sudsy thriller about a woman who inherits a cosmetics company and is immediately plunged into danger and mystery. Also known as *Bloodline*. **CL30, MY3**

Siege of Firebase Gloria, The (1989, C, 95m, R)
Vietnam War drama centering on combat action at the time of the 1968 Tet Offensive. Wings Hauser and Lee Ermey star. **AC4**

Siegfried (1924, B&W, 100m, NR)
Fritz Lang directed this silent classic, based on the Teutonic legends. **CL43, FF3**

Sign o' the Times (1987, C, 85m, PG-13)
Controversial rock star Prince in concert; also features Sheila E. and Sheena Easton. **MU10**

Signal 7 (1983, C, 92m, NR)
Low-key drama about cabdrivers in San Francisco. Director Rob Nilsson encouraged his actors to improvise their dialogue. **DR15, XT9**

Signs of Life (1989, C, 91m, PG-13)
Drama set in a seaside Maine village, where a boat builder is going out of business. Arthur Kennedy stars, with Kevin J. O'Connor, Vincent Philip D'Onofrio, and Michael Lewis. **DR62**

Silent Movie (1976, C, 86m, PG)
Mel Brooks' tribute to the early days of film comedy: a movie with no dialogue, only music and sound effects. Mel's costars are Marty Feldman, Dom DeLuise, Sid Caesar; watch for guest cameos from Paul Newman, Anne Bancroft, and Burt Reynolds. **CO7, CO12, CO28**

Silent Night, Deadly Night (1984, C, 79m, R)
A man becomes a homicidal maniac when forced to wear a Santa suit. **HO9**

Silent Partner, The (1978, C, 103m, R)
Thriller about a bank clerk who's tipped off in advance to a robbery and neatly transfers the "stolen" money into his own account. Then the robber comes after him, and things get very nasty. Elliott Gould and Christopher Plummer star. **MY9** *Recommended*

Silent Rage (1982, C, 105m, R)
Chuck Norris battles a killer who has been rendered virtually indestructible by a scientific experiment. **AC32**

Silent Running (1972, C, 90m, G)
By the 21st century pollution has killed off all the vegetation on Earth. On a spe-cially designed spacecraft, the only botanical specimens left are carefully tended in hopes that one day they can be replanted on Earth. Bruce Dern stars in this science fiction drama directed by Douglas Trumbull. **SF3**

Silent Scream (1984, C, 60m, NR)
A former commandant of a concentration camp collects a variety of animals, including humans. Peter Cushing stars. **HO33**

Silk Stockings (1957, C, 117m, NR)
A cold Russian emissary (Cyd Charisse) visiting Paris warms up to the attentions of a playboy (Fred Astaire). Rouben Mamoulian directed this musical remake of *Ninotchka*. **CU18, MU1, MU14, MU18**

Silkwood (1983, C, 131m, R)
Meryl Streep plays Karen Silkwood, the factory worker who tried to expose safety practices in her nuclear plant and died in a mysterious car accident. Kurt Russell and Cher costar; Mike Nichols directed. **DR6, DR26, DR75, MU12** *Recommended*

Silver Blaze, The (1937, B&W, 60m, NR)
Arthur Wontner stars as Sherlock Holmes in this mystery about a missing racehorse. Also titled *Murder at the Baskervilles*. **MY10**

Silver Bullet (1985, C, 95m, R)
A deranged killer is terrorizing a small town and only a crippled boy (Corey Haim) and his irresponsible uncle (Gary Busey) realize the killer is really a werewolf. Based on a Stephen King novella. Directed by Dan Attias. **HO4**

Silver Chalice, The (1954, C, 144m, NR)
Drama of ancient Greece, about a sculptor who fashions cup for The Last Supper. Paul Newman's film debut; Virginia Mayo, Pier Angeli, and Jack Palance star. **CL13, DR28**

Silver Spurs (1943, B&W, 54m, NR)
A ranch foreman (Roy Rogers) rides to stop a villainous landgrabber (John Carradine). **WE23**

Silver Streak (1976, C, 113m, PG)
Comic thriller, set aboard a speeding train, with innocent editor (Gene Wilder) becoming involved with murder plot and lovely passenger (Jill Clayburgh). Richard Pryor costars. **CO3, CO10, CO29**

Silverado (1985, C, 132m, PG-13)
A trio of cowboys ride out to protect the persecuted settlers of a prairie town. Kevin Kline, Scott Glenn, and Danny Glover star. The supporting cast includes Brian Dennehy, Linda Hunt, Rosanna Arquette, Jeff Goldblum, and John Cleese. Written and directed by Lawrence Kasdan. **CO15, WE1**

Simon (1980, C, 97m, PG)
A group of scientists brainwash a man into believing he is an alien. Alan Arkin and Madeline Kahn star in this comedy. Written and directed by Marshall Brickman. **SF21**

Simon & Garfunkel: The Concert in Central Park (1982, C, 87m, NR)
Paul Simon and Art Garfunkel sing together for the first time in eleven years. **MU10**

Simon of the Desert (1965, B&W, 45m, NR)
Director Luis Buñuel's sly comedy about a real-life holy man who supposedly spent many years perched on top of a pillar. Claudio Brook and Silvia Pinal star. **FF11** *Recommended*

Simple Story, A (1978, C, 110m, NR)
Romy Schneider is a woman at the crossroads of her life in this French drama. **FF1**

Sin of Harold Diddlebock, The (1947, B&W, 90m, NR)
Harold Lloyd stars in his last sound comedy, about a timid bookkeeper and his first brush with alcohol. Directed by Preston Sturges. **CO24**

Sinbad and the Eye of the Tiger (1977, C, 113m, G)
Sinbad goes on another adventure with a beautiful princess and an evil witch. Special effects by Ray Harryhausen. Patrick Wayne and Jane Seymour star. **FA8**

Sincerely, Charlotte (1986, C, 92m, NR)
A singer is a suspect in her boyfriend's murder and flees from the police with the help of an old lover. Isabelle Huppert stars in this French thriller; her sister Caroline directed. **FF1, MY20**

Sincerely Yours (1955, C, 115m, NR)
Liberace stars as a pianist whose music is an inspiration to all around him. Written by Irving Wallace. As bad as it sounds—but revered by fans of campy movies. **CU2**

Singe en Hiver, Un (1962, B&W, 105m, NR)
An aging alcoholic gets a new lease on life when a young stranger enters his world. Jean Gabin and Jean-Paul Belmondo star in this French drama. **FF33**

Singin' in the Rain (1952, C, 102m, G)
Grand musical comedy set at the time when sound pictures came to Hollywood. Gene Kelly, Debbie Reynolds, and Donald O'Connor star. Directed by Stanley Donen and Gene Kelly. Many musical highlights, including Kelly's title tune dance, O'Connor's "Make 'Em Laugh." **FA9, MU1, MU4, MU19, MU23** *Highly Recommended*

Sinister Invasion (1970, C, 95m, NR)
A crazed scientist (Boris Karloff) creates a death ray. Also known as *Incredible Invasion*. **HO27**

Sinister Urge, The (1961, B&W, 75m, NR)
A pair of cops set out to break up a porno movies ring in this low-budget, brain-dead drama from director Ed Wood, Jr. **CU45**

Sioux City Sue (1946, B&W, 69m, NR)
Gene Autry is in Hollywood to try his
hand at show business, but there are rustlers even in the Hills of Beverly. **WE24**

Sirocco (1951, B&W, 98m, NR)
Humphrey Bogart plays a gunrunner during the 1920s. Lee J. Cobb and Zero Mostel costar in this thriller. **CL20**

Sister Kenny (1946, B&W, 116m, NR)
True-life story of courageous nurse and
her fight against polio. Rosalind Russell
stars. **CL2**

Sisters (1973, C, 93m, R)
Horror film about Siamese twins surgi-
cally separated at birth, one growing up
to become a homicidal maniac (Margot
Kidder). Jennifer Salt and William Finney
costar; Brian DePalma directed. **CU28,
HO15** *Recommended*

Six Weeks (1982, C, 107m, PG)
Tearjerker about a politician's friendship
with a little girl dying of cancer and her
mother. Dudley Moore, Mary Tyler
Moore, and Katherine Healy star. **DR2,
CO31**

Sixteen Candles (1984, C, 93m, PG)
A girl's 16th birthday is nearly ruined by
her family's distractions over her older
sister's wedding and her inability to get
the attention of a special boy. Molly Ringwald stars; John Hughes wrote and directed. **CO4, CO47**

Skin Deep (1989, C, 101m, R)
The comic dilemmas of a compulsive la-
dies' man (John Ritter) in contemporary
Los Angeles. Written and directed by
Blake Edwards. **CO1, CO46**

Skin Game, The (1931, B&W, 87m, NR)
Early Hitchcock film about a family resorting to blackmail to thwart a neighbor's plans. Edmund Gwenn stars. **MY22**

Skin Game, The (1971, C, 102m, PG)
Comedy about a pair of con men—one
black, the other white—traveling through
the Civil War South. James Garner and

Louis Gossett, Jr. star. **CO6, WE7, WE16**
Recommended

Sky Is Gray, The (1980, C, 46m, G)
Drama of black child in rural South and
his first encounters with racial injustices,
based on a story by Ernest Gaines. Olivia
Cole, James Bond III, and Cleavon Little
star. Originally made for TV. **DR14**

Sky's the Limit, The (1943, B&W, 89m,
NR)
A photographer (Joan Leslie) wants to
meet a heroic pilot (Fred Astaire). Complications arise when she does meet him,
but doesn't recognize him, as he is out of
uniform. Robert Benchley costars;
Astaire sings "One For My Baby." **CL18,
MU18**

Slap Shot (1977, C, 122m, R)
Broad, profane comedy about minor-
league hockey team and its aging player-
coach. Paul Newman stars, with Michael
Ontkean, Lindsay Crouse, Jennifer War-
ren, Melinda Dillon, and Strother Martin.
Directed by George Roy Hill. **CO36,
DR28**

Slapstick of Another Kind (1984, C, 82m,
PG)
Jerry Lewis comedy, based on Kurt Von-
negut, Jr. novel about deformed twins
who are really aliens with the solutions to
the world's problems. Madeline Kahn,
Marty Feldman, Samuel Fuller, and Jim
Backus costar. **CO25, CU22**

Slaughter in San Francisco (1981, C, 87m,
R)
Chuck Norris, in an early role, plays a
killer who is being sought by the police.
Originally filmed in 1973. **AC32**

Slaughterhouse (1987, C, 87m, R)
An old man with a retarded son doesn't
want to sell his slaughterhouse. Soon after the offer is made, people begin to die.
HO24

Slaughterhouse Five (1971, C, 104, R)
Screen version of the cult novel by Kurt
Vonnegut, Jr.: a man becomes unstuck in

time and exists where the past, present, and future occur in random order. His most vivid memory of the past is the firebombing of Dresden during World War II, which he and other American POWs survived. Michael Sacks, Valerie Perrine, and Ron Leibman star. **DR19, SF4**

Slave of Love, A (1978, C, 94m, NR)
Russian drama, set during the Revolution, of a love affair between a silent film actress and her cameraman. **FF7**

Slaves of New York (1989, C, 121m, R)
Tama Janowitz' collection of stories about the contemporary art scene in New York was adapted by the writer, concentrating on Eleanor (Bernadette Peters), a hat designer with a heartless painter (Adam Coleman Howard) for a lover. Also in the cast: Chris Sarandon, Mary Beth Hurt, and Mercedes Ruehl. Directed by James Ivory; produced by Ismail Merchant. **DR15, DR19, XT9**

Sleepaway Camp (1983, C, 90m, R)
A psychotic killer is brutally murdering the campers of Camp Arawat. **HO12**

Sleeper (1973, C, 90m, PG)
Woody Allen comedy about a man who is cryogenically frozen and revived two hundred years later to a vastly changed world. Diane Keaton costars. **CO7, CO27, DR40, SF4, SF21**

Sleeping Beauty (1959, C, 75m, G)
An evil witch places a curse on a princess, and it is up to her true love to save her. A classic of Disney animation. **FA2**

Sleeping Beauty (1985, C, 60m, NR)
From the Faerie Tale Theatre series, the tale about a princess who is cursed and her true love who can free her. Christopher Reeve, Bernadette Peters, and Beverly D'Angelo star. **FA12**

Sleeping Dogs (1977, C, 107m, R)
From New Zealand, a political drama of a workers' strike and one man caught between both sides. Sam Neill stars, with Warren Oates. **CU48**

Sleuth (1972, C, 138m, PG)
A vindictive mystery novelist lures his wife's lover into a deadly cat-and-mouse game at a deserted country house. Laurence Olivier and Michael Caine star; Joseph L. Mankiewicz directed from Anthony Shaffer's play. **CL32, CL55, DR20, MY9, MY19**

Slightly Pregnant Man, A (1973, C, 92m, NR)
Marcello Mastroianni plays the world's first man to suffer morning sickness in this comedy costarring Catherine Deneuve. **FF24, FF27**

Slightly Scarlet (1956, C, 99m, NR)
Thriller about political corruption involving a mayor's secretary and a gangster's secret affair. John Payne, Arlene Dahl, and Rhonda Fleming star. Based on a James M. Cain novel. **MY1, MY25**

Slithis (1979, C, 86m, PG)
Radiation leaks into the ocean and causes marine life to mutate, creating a horrifying monster. **HO21**

Slugger's Wife, The (1985, C, 105m, PG-13)
Portrait of a modern romance between a baseball star and a pop singer, whose separate careers threaten to ruin their new marriage. Michael O'Keefe and Rebecca DeMornay star. Written by Neil Simon. **CO34, DR1**

Slumber Party '57 (1980, C, 90m, R)
A group of sorority sisters gather to reveal how each lost her virginity. Debra Winger stars. **DR47**

Slumber Party Massacre (1982, C, 78m, R)
Teenaged girls are menaced by a killer with a power drill. Written by Rita Mae Brown; directed by Amy Jones. **HO9**

Small Change (1976, C, 104m, PG)
Director François Truffaut's loving tribute to children is a loosely connected series of episodes in the lives of youngsters in a French village. **FF13**

Smiles of a Summer Night (1955, B&W, 108m, NR)
A weekend at a Swedish country estate is the setting for Ingmar Bergman's peerless romantic comedy. **FF8** *Recommended*

Smith! (1969, C, 101m, G)
In this Disney western, a farmer stands up for the rights of an Indian accused of murder. Glenn Ford stars, with Warren Oates. **CU48, FA1, WE8**

Smithereens (1982, C, 90m, R)
Zany story about a New York hustler whose ambition is to manage a punk rock band. Susan Berman, Brad Rinn, and Richard Hell star; Susan Seidelman directed. **DR15, XT9**

Smokey and the Bandit (1977, C, 96m, PG)
Burt Reynolds' most popular good ol' boy comedy, about a bootlegger who delights in outwitting a numbskull sheriff (Jackie Gleason). Sally Field costars. **AC37, CO9, DR36**

Smokey and the Bandit II (1980, C, 104m, PG)
Follow-up to first *Smokey* film has Burt Reynolds and Sally Field transporting a pregnant elephant across the South, with sheriff Jackie Gleason in pursuit. **AC37, CO9, DR36**

Smokey and the Bandit 3 (1983, C, 98m, PG)
Third go-round for the action comedy series, with Jerry Reed now the good ol' boy foil for sheriff Jackie Gleason. **CO9**

Smooth Talk (1985, C, 92m, PG13)
A flirtatious adolescent (Laura Dern) meets a slick older man (Treat Williams). Levon Helm and Mary Kay Place costar. Originally made for TV. **DR9, MU12**

Smorgasbord *see* Cracking Up

Snake People, The (1968, C, 90m, NR)
A policeman investigates a series of murders on an island inhabited by a sect of voodoo snake worshipers. Boris Karloff stars. **HO27**

Snoopy Come Home (1972, C, 80m, G)
Snoopy runs away from home and the entire Peanuts gang searches for him in this animated feature. **FA10**

Snow Queen, The (1983, C, 60m, NR)
From the Faerie Tale Theatre series, the story of a queen who teaches a young boy about love and friendship and saves him from a cold curse. Lee Remick, Lance Kerwin, and Melissa Gilbert star. **FA12**

Snow White and the Seven Dwarfs (1983, C, 60m, NR)
Brothers Grimm tale about a beautiful princess helped by seven dwarfs and a handsome prince after her jealous stepmother tries to kill her. Elizabeth McGovern, Vanessa Redgrave, Vincent Price, and Rex Smith star in this Faerie Tale Theatre production. **FA12, HO31**

Snowball Express (1972, C, 92m, G)
An accountant (Dean Jones) inherits a hotel in Colorado and tries to turn it into a ski resort. Harry Morgan and Keenan Wynn costar in this Disney comedy. **FA1**

So Dear to My Heart (1948, C, 82m, NR)
A young boy tames a wild black sheep in hopes of winning a blue ribbon at the state fair. This Disney film incorporates some animation with live-action sequences. Burl Ives and Bobby Driscoll star. **FA1**

Sodom and Gomorrah (1963, C, 154m, NR)
Biblical spectacle of the twin cities of evil and their destruction. Stewart Granger stars, with Pier Angeli, Stanley Baker, and Anouk Aimee. Directed by Robert Aldrich. **CL13**

Soft Skin, The (1964, B&W, 120m, NR)
A married French businessman finds himself drawn into an affair with a stewardess in this drama from director François Truffaut. Françoise Dorleac stars. **FF13**

Soldier, The (1982, C, 90m, R)
A special agent is dispatched to the Middle East when Soviets hijack a truck packed with deadly plutonium. Ken Wahl

and Klaus Kinski star; James Glickenhaus directed. **AC25, FF30**

Soldier Blue (1970, C, 112m, R)
Violent and controversial Western focus-
ing on the brutal massacre of an entire
Indian village by U.S. cavalry soldiers.
Candice Bergen and Peter Strauss star.
WE5, WE8

Soldier in the Rain (1963, B&W, 88m, NR)
A conniving master sergeant (Jackie
Gleason) takes advantage of the G.I.
(Steve McQueen) who worships him.
Comedy-drama costars Tuesday Weld
and Tony Bill. **AC28, CO38**

Soldier of Orange (1979, C, 165m, R)
Epic story of six Dutch university stu-
dents who enlist when the Nazis invade
their homeland. Rutger Hauer and Jeroen
Krabbe star. Directed by Paul Verhoeven.
AC1

Soldiers of Fortune (1970, C, 97m, PG)
Action in war-torn Turkey of the 1920s,
with Charles Bronson and Tony Curtis as
mercenaries. Original title: *You Can't Win
'Em All*. **AC6, AC29**

Soldier's Prayer, A *see* Human Condition,
Part III, The

Soldier's Story, A (1985, C, 102m, PG)
On a segregated Army base during World
War II, an unpopular black officer is murdered, and another black officer is called
in to investigate. Howard E. Rollins,
Adolph Caesar, and Denzel Washington
star in this version of Charles Fuller's
play. **DR14, DR20**

Sole Survivor (1984, C, 85m, R)
The only survivor of a plane crash is
haunted by the victims of that disaster.
HO2

Some Came Running (1958, C, 136m, NR)
James Jones story set in a small town in
the Midwest, with characters whose lives
are going nowhere fast. Frank Sinatra,
Shirley MacLaine, and Dean Martin star.

Directed by Vincente Minnelli. **DR42,
DR49, DR62, MU24**

Some Kind of Hero (1982, C, 97m, R)
Comedy-drama about a Vietnam veteran
who gets a few surprises when he comes
home after six years' captivity as a POW.
Richard Pryor stars. **CO29**

Some Kind of Wonderful (1987, C, 93m,
PG-13)
Teen triangle of guy who loves rich girl,
is counseled by his best friend, a girl who
loves him. Eric Stoltz, Lea Thompson,
and Mary Stuart Masterson star. Produced by John Hughes. **CO4, CO47**

Some Like It Hot (1959, B&W, 119m, NR)
Hilarious comedy about a pair of musicians, on the lam from Al Capone, dressing up like women to join an all-girl jazz
band. Jack Lemmon, Tony Curtis, and
Marilyn Monroe star; Billy Wilder directed. **CL10, CL29, CL37, CO10, DR64**
Highly Recommended

Somebody Up There Likes Me (1956,
B&W, 113m, NR)
Bio of boxer Rocky Graziano, who
worked his way from the New York slums
and a criminal youth to become middle-
weight champion. Paul Newman stars,
with Pier Angeli, Everett Sloane, Sal
Mineo, and Robert Loggia. Watch for
Steve McQueen in a small role. **AC28,
DR22, DR28**

Someone Behind the Door (1971, C, 95m,
PG)
A psychiatrist (Anthony Perkins) discov-
ers that his amnesia patient (Charles
Bronson) is a killer and sets him up to kill
the psychiatrist's unfaithful wife. **AC29**

Someone to Love (1987, C, 111m, R)
Filmmaker Henry Jaglom invites friends
to a Valentine's Day party and records
their responses to his questions about
romance. Among the guests: Orson
Welles, Sally Kellerman, Michael Emil,
and Andrea Marcovici. **CL41, CO1**

Someone to Watch Over Me (1987, C, 106m, R)
Cop from Queens, New York, is assigned to protect Manhattan socialite threatened by murder suspect, and romance develops. Tom Berenger, Mimi Rogers, and Lorraine Braco star; Ridley Scott directed. **CU33, DR3, DR15, MY3, MY5, XT9**

Something for Everyone (1970, C, 112m, R)
Cult comedy about manipulative young man who sexually takes over the house of a poor noblewoman. Michael York and Angela Lansbury star; Harold Prince directed. **CU5, CU6**

Something of Value (1957, B&W, 113m, NR)
Drama set in Kenya during vicious Mau Mau uprising. Rock Hudson, Sidney Poitier, and Wendy Hiller star. **DR14, DR38**

Something to Sing About (1937, C, 82m, NR)
A bandleader goes Hollywood. James Cagney and William Frawley star. Original running time: 93m. **CL22**

Something Wicked This Way Comes (1983, C, 94m, PG)
The mysterious Mr. Dark and his Pandemonium Circus promise to make everyone's wishes come true—for a very high price. It's up to two small boys and an elderly man to stop him. Jason Robards and Jonathan Pryce star in this version of Ray Bradbury's story. **FA8, HO19, SF13**

Something Wild (1986, C, 116m, R)
Comedy-drama about an investment analyst "kidnapped" by a free-spirited woman. Jeff Daniels, Melanie Griffith, and Ray Liotta star; Jonathan Demme directed this one-of-a-kind movie. Director John Waters has a cameo role. **CO2, CO12, CU1, CU39, CU43** *Highly Recommended*

Sometimes a Great Notion (1971, C, 114m, PG)
Drama of logging family in the Pacific Northwest, adapted from Ken Kesey's novel, starring Paul Newman (who also directed), Henry Fonda, Lee Remick, and Richard Jaeckel. **CL24, DR8, DR28**

Somewhere in Time (1980, C, 103m, PG)
Time-travel romance about a man so enthralled by a dead woman's portrait that he wills himself into the past and into her life. Christopher Reeve and Jane Seymour star. **DR1**

Son of Dracula (1943, B&W, 78m, NR)
Classic horror tale with misleading title; it's about the count himself. He's traveling through the American South. Lon Chaney, Jr. stars, with Louise Albritton and Robert Paige. Directed by Robert Siodmak. **HO1, HO5, HO30**

Son of Flubber (1963, B&W, 100m, G)
Sequel to *The Absent Minded Professor*, with more inventions and trouble. Fred MacMurray and Keenan Wynn star. **FA1**

Son of Frankenstein (1939, B&W, 99m, NR)
The offspring of the famed scientist ressurects his father's creation, with the usual catastrophic results. Basil Rathbone stars, with Boris Karloff as The Monster and Bela Lugosi as Ygor. **HO1, HO20, HO27, HO28**

Son of Paleface (1952, C, 95m, NR)
Follow-up to *Paleface* finds Bob Hope reunited with Jane Russell. Roy Rogers joins in the fun in this western comedy. **CO40, WE15, WE23**

Son of Sinbad (1955, C, 88m, NR)
Sinbad's son carries on his father's legacy of adventure and romance. Vincent Price costars. **HO31**

Song of Arizona (1946, B&W, 67m, NR)
An outlaw entrusts his son with stolen money, and his gang set out after the boy. Only Roy Rogers can save the day. **WE23**

Song of Bernadette (1943, B&W, 156m, NR)
Jennifer Jones won an Oscar for her portrayal of the young French girl who saw a vision in Lourdes and was ostracized by her village, only to be vindicated years later by sainthood. William Eythe, Charles Bickford, and Vincent Price costar. **CL13, DR4, HO31, XT3**

Song of Nevada (1944, B&W, 75m, NR)
Roy Rogers and friends come to the aid of a girl who's being terrorized by outlaws. Dale Evans and Bob Nolan & the Sons of the Pioneers costar. **WE23**

Song of Norway (1970, C, 142m, G)
The life of Norwegian composer Edvard Grieg, starring Florence Henderson, Toralv Maurstad, and Edward G. Robinson. **CL52, MU5**

Song of Texas (1953, B&W, 54m, NR)
Roy Rogers helps an alcoholic cowboy sober up and regain his pride. Bob Nolan & the Sons of the Pioneers vocalize. **WE23**

Song of the Thin Man (1947, B&W, 86m, NR)
Sixth (and last) *Thin Man* film has Nick and Nora Charles aboard a gambling ship when a murder is committed. William Powell and Myrna Loy star; Dean Stockwell costars (as Nick, Jr.), with Keenan Wynn and Gloria Grahame. **CL15, CL46, MY13, MY21, MY28** *Recommended*

Song Remains the Same, The (1976, C, 136m, NR)
Led Zeppelin's "home movie" mixes concert footage with fantasy sequences. **MU11**

Song to Remember, A (1945, C, 113m, NR)
Cornel Wilde plays Frederic Chopin in this biography costarring Paul Muni and Merle Oberon (as George Sand). **MU5**

Songwriter (1984, C, 94m, R)
Two country singers plot to "sting" a greedy promoter in this amiable comedy starring Willie Nelson and Kris Kristofferson. With Lesley Anne Warren and Rip Torn. Plenty of fine music from both leads; directed by Alan Rudolph. **CO8, CU26, CU47** *Recommended*

Sons of Katie Elder, The (1965, C, 112m, NR)
Four brothers set out to avenge their mother's death in this spirited western starring John Wayne and Dean Martin, with Martha Hyer, Michael Anderson, Jr., George Kennedy, and Dennis Hopper. **CU46, WE6, WE17**

Sons of the Desert (1933, B&W, 69m, NR)
Classic Laurel and Hardy comedy, with the boys off to a convention for their lodge, then concocting a coverup story for their wives. **CL10, CO20** *Highly Recommended*

Sophia Loren: Her Own Story (1980, C, 150m, NR)
The international star plays herself (and her mother) in this biographical drama, costarring John Gavin as Cary Grant, Rip Torn as Carlo Ponti, and Edmund Purdom as Vittorio De Sica. Originally made for TV. **FF31**

Sophie's Choice (1982, C, 150m, R)
Intense drama, highlighted by Meryl Streep's Oscar-winning performance as a concentration camp survivor living in postwar Brooklyn. Kevin Kline and Peter MacNicol play the two men in her life. Adapted from William Styron's novel; directed by Alan J. Pakula. **DR1, DR2, DR19, DR26, XT3**

Sophie's Place *see* Crooks and Coronets

Sorority House Massacre (1986, C, 74m, R)
A madman preys on the snobby sisters of Theta Omega Theta, but his focus is on the newest pledge, an orphan who suffers from nightmares. **HO12**

Sorrow and the Pity, The (1970, B&W, 260m, PG)
Epic documentary portrait of France during the German Occupation and the aftershocks still felt today. Marcel Ophuls directed. **CU16** *Highly Recommended*

Sorrowful Jones (1949, B&W, 88m, NR)
Oft-filmed Damon Runyon story of Little Miss Marker, the orphan left with a racetrack hustler. Bob Hope stars, with Lucille Ball and William Demarest. **CO40**

Sorry, Wrong Number (1948, B&W, 89m, NR)
Barbara Stanwyck stars in this classic thriller about a woman who overhears her own murder being plotted but can't get anyone to believe her. Burt Lancaster costars. **CL45, DR41, MY1, MY3** *Recommended*

Soul to Soul (1971, C, 95m, NR)
A gathering of soul, jazz, and gospel stars to celebrate the 14th anniversary of Ghanian independence. Performers include Wilson Pickett, Roberta Flack, and Ike & Tina Turner. **MU10**

Sound of Music, The (1965, C, 174m, G)
A novice becomes the governess for the von Trapp children and teaches them and their widowed father the value of love. This film adaptation of the hit Broadway musical won five Academy Awards, including Best Picture and Director (Robert Wise). Julie Andrews and Christopher Plummer star. **CL58, FA9, MU2, MU5, MU7, XT1, XT6**

Sounder (1972, C, 105m, G)
Drama of a black family's struggle in the rural South to survive hardships and injustice, starring Paul Winfield, Cicely Tyson, and Kevin Hooks. **DR14**

South of Santa Fe (1942, B&W, 54m, NR)
Roy Rogers falls in love with a young woman who owns a gold mine. **WE23**

South of the Border (1939, B&W, 71m, NR)
Gene Autry and Smiley Burnette head off to Mexico for adventure and a few tunes, too. Duncan Renaldo (TV's Cisco Kid) costars. **WE24**

South Pacific (1958, C, 171m, NR)
Rodgers and Hammerstein's Broadway smash about Navy nurses on the Pacific Islands during World War II. Mitzi Gaynor, Rossano Brazzi, John Kerr, Ray Walston, and Juanita Hall star. **FA9, MU2**

Southern Comfort (1981, C, 105m, R)
Survival adventure of a Louisiana National Guard troop on weekend maneuvers, lost in the swamps, harassed by vengeful Cajuns. Powers Boothe, Keith Carradine, Fred Ward, and Peter Coyote star; Walter Hill directed. **AC24, CU27** *Highly Recommended*

Southerner, The (1945, B&W, 91m, NR)
Jean Renoir directed this drama of an American farm family struggling against all odds to make a living. Zachary Scott, Betty Field, and Beulah Bondi star. **FF12**

Southward Ho! (1939, B&W, 54m, NR)
Roy Rogers plays a cowpoke with an itchin' for the warmer climes. **WE23**

Soylent Green (1973, C, 97m, PG)
In the year 2022, a policeman (Charlton Heston) investigates the death of an executive whose company makes soylent green, the only foodstuff left on earth. Edward G. Robinson (in his last film) costars. **CL52, SF8**

Space Rage (1986, C, 78m, R)
A gang of convicts on a penitentiary planet stage a revolt. Skilled weapons specialists are called in to quell the disturbance. Richard Farnsworth and Michael Pare star. **SF17**

Space Raiders (1983, C, 82m, PG)
A young boy and a band of mercenaries battle an evil intergalactic dictator. Vince Edwards stars. **SF13**

Spaceballs (1987, C, 96m, PG13)
Mel Brooks parody of *Star Wars* and other science fiction films. An evil dictator plots to still the atmosphere of a neighboring planet. John Candy and Rick Moranis costar. **CO7, CO14, CO28, SF21**

SpaceCamp (1986, C, 107m, PG)
At an astronaut training school, a group of young students and their instructor are accidentally launched into space. Kate Capshaw and Lea Thompson star. **SF3**

Spacehunter: Adventures in the Forbidden Zone (1983, C, 90m, PG)
Science fiction adventure, starring Peter Strauss and Molly Ringwald, who rescue three beautiful women from the vicious half man/half machine, Overdog (Michael Ironside). **SF3, SF13**

Sparkle (1976, C, 100m, PG)
Three friends form a singing trio in this fictional story based on the early career of The Supremes. Irene Cara and Philip Michael Thomas star. **DR12, DR14, MU4**

Sparrows (1926, B&W, 75m, NR)
Silent melodrama starring Mary Pickford as the protector of a group of orphans. **CL12**

Spartacus (1960, C, 185m, NR)
Epic tale of the Roman gladiator who led a slave revolt and paid a dear price. Kirk Douglas, Jean Simmons, Laurence Olivier, Peter Ustinov (an Oscar winner), and Tony Curtis star; Stanley Kubrick directed. **CL32, DR5, DR53, XT4**

Special Bulletin (1983, C, 105m, NR)
Riveting drama, set up like a real TV news story with two studio anchors doing running commentary, about radicals engaged in dangerous protest against nuclear weapons. Ed Flanders, Kathryn Walker, Roxanne Hart, and Christopher Allport star. Originally made for TV. **DR7** *Recommended*

Special Day, A (1977, C, 106m, NR)
Sophia Loren and Marcello Mastroianni star in this bittersweet story of a house-wife and a homosexual and their chance encounter during World War II. **FF2, FF24, FF31**

Special Effects (1985, C, 106m, R)
A desperate movie producer intends to use footage from a real murder in his latest production, but the dead actress's husband is out for revenge. Zoe Tamerlis and Eric Bogosian star; Larry Cohen directed. **CU30**

Speckled Band, The (1931, B&W, 90m, NR)
Raymond Massey plays Sherlock Holmes, as the famed sleuth helps a girl whose sister has been murdered. Angela Baddely costars. **MY10**

Speed Zone (1989, C, 95m, PG)
In the grand tradition of the *Cannnonball Run* action comedies, here's more cross-country racing with an all-star cast. John Candy, Eugene Levy, Joe Flaherty, Tim Matheson, and Peter Boyle star, with cameo appearances from Brooke Shields (as herself), The Smothers Brothers, Carl Lewis, Michael Spinks, and Lee Van Cleef. **CO9, CO14**

Speedway (1968, C, 94m, NR)
Elvis Presley plays a singing race car driver who tries to romance his tax auditor (Nancy Sinatra). **MU22**

Spellbound (1945, B&W, 111m, NR)
A psychiatrist (Ingrid Bergman) and her patient (Gregory Peck) fall in love in this classic Hitchcock blend of suspense and romance. Leo G. Carroll costars; Salvador Dali contributed sketches for several dream sequences. **CL27, MY5, MY22**

Spetters (1980, C, 115m, R)
From Holland, a contemporary drama of aimless youth, with Rutger Hauer as a motorcycle racing champion. Paul Verhoeven directed. **FF7**

Spider Baby (1964, B&W, 80m, NR)
Lon Chaney, Jr. stars as the chauffeur for a family of cannibals in this horror tale. Lon warbles the title tune, too. **HO30**

Spider Woman (1944, B&W, 62m, NR)
Sherlock Holmes (Basil Rathbone) and
Dr. Watson (Nigel Bruce) take on a wily
adversary, a woman (Gale Sondergaard)
whose gang poisons wealthy businessmen
and disguises the crimes as suicides. Also
known as *Sherlock Holmes and the Spider Woman*. **MY10**

Spies (1928, B&W, 90m, NR)
A silent film classic from German director
Fritz Lang, about a government agent on
the trail of a master spy and his gang.
CL43, FF3

Spies Like Us (1985, C, 103m, PG)
Chevy Chase and Dan Aykroyd star as
two bumblers sent by the State Department on a diversionary mission. Features
many cameo appearances from directors,
as well as a special guest shot by Bob
Hope. **CO13, CU17**

Spike of Bensonhurst (1988, C, 101m, R)
Comic tale of a Brooklyn Romeo whose
exploits with two young ladies land him
in trouble with the local Mob boss. Sasha
Mitchell and Ernest Borgnine star, with
Sylvia Miles, Maria Pitillo and Talisa
Soto. Directed by Paul Morrissey. **CU44**

Spinout (1966, C, 90m, NR)
Elvis Presley at the racetrack, singing and
shifting gears (and women). Shelley Fabares and Diane McBain costar. **MU22**

Spiral Staircase, The (1946, B&W, 83m,
NR)
Dorothy McGuire plays a mute servant
who is sure there's a killer hiding in her
house but can't get anyone to believe her.
Directed by Robert Siodmak. **MY3**

Spirit of St. Louis, The (1957, C, 138m,
NR)
James Stewart plays Charles A. Lind-
bergh in this drama, which focuses on his
historic transatlantic solo flight. Billy Wilder directed. **AC11, CL2, CL25, CL37**

Spirit of the Beehive, The (1973, C, 95m,
NR)
Spanish drama of a little girl (Ann Tor-
rent) fascinated by the Frankestein monster after she sees the original Boris Karloff film. **FF7**

Spitfire (1934, B&W, 88m, NR)
Early Katharine Hepburn film has her
playing a naive girl in love with a married
man (Robert Young). **CL16**

Splash (1984, C, 109m, PG)
A mermaid falls for a young boy, con-
trives to meet him (on land) when they're
a bit older and really ready for love. Daryl
Hannah, Tom Hanks, John Candy, and
Eugene Levy star. Directed by Ron How-
ard on location in New York City. **CO1,
CO14, CO37, CO44, XT9** *Recommended*

Splendor in the Grass (1961, C, 124m, NR)
Tragic tale, set in a small town in the
1920s Midwest, about a thwarted love
affair that shatters the life of a young girl.
Starring Natalie Wood and Warren Beatty
(his film debut); Elia Kazan directed.
DR1, DR9, DR34, DR59, DR62, XT10

Split Decisions (1988, C, 95m, R)
Gene Hackman plays an ex-boxer with
two sons in the fight game: one has been
ordered by the Mob to throw a big fight,
while the other wants to go to college and
try out for the Olympics. **DR22, DR39**

Split Image (1982, C, 111m, R)
When an impressionable college athlete
joins a commune-like cult, his parents
have him kidnapped by a ruthless depro-
grammer. Michael O'Keefe, Karen Allen,
Brian Dennehy, James Woods, Peter
Fonda, and Elizabeth Ashley star. **DR8**

Spoilers, The (1942, B&W, 87m, NR)
Action on the Yukon frontier, with prospectors John Wayne and Randolph Scott
tussling over dancehall girl Marlene Dic-
trich. **CL47, WE11, WE17, WE22**

Spooks Run Wild (1941, B&W, 69m, NR)
The East Side Kids spend the night in a haunted mansion and run into Bela Lugosi. **HO28**

Springtime in the Rockies (1942, C, 91m, NR)
All-star, colorful musical about a Broadway couple's marital and professional ups and downs. Betty Grable and John Payne star, with Carmen Miranda, Cesar Romero, Jackie Gleason, and Harry James and His Band. **MU4**

Springtime in the Sierras (1947, B&W, 75m, NR)
Roy Rogers western, with villainous big-game poachers. Andy Devine provides the laughs. **WE23**

Spy in Black, The (1939, B&W, 82m, NR)
Espionage drama set in World War I Scotland, starring Conrad Veidt as a devious German. Directed by Michael Powell. **CU19, MY6, MY19**

Spy Who Loved Me, The (1977, C, 125m, PG)
James Bond (Roger Moore) and a sexy Russian agent (Barbara Bach) must join forces to stop a mad mastermind (Curt Jurgens) from destroying the world. Spectacular stunts, especially in the opening sequence. **AC35** *Recommended*

Square Dance (1987, C, 118m, PG-13)
A teenager leaves her granddaddy's Texas farm and strikes out for Ft. Worth and a reunion with her estranged mother. Winona Ryder, Jane Alexander, Rob Lowe, and Jason Robards star. Also known as *Home Is Where The Heart Is*. **DR9**

Squeeze, The (1987, C, 101m, R)
A con man and a debt collector team to solve a murder case involving the New York State Lottery. Michael Keaton and Rae Dawn Chong star in this comic mystery. **CO45**

Squirm (1976, C, 92m, PG)
During a storm, a high voltage tower falls to the ground and turns the worms into voracious eating machines who devour everything in their path, including humans. **HO16**

Squizzy Taylor (1982, C, 89m, NR)
True saga of an Australian gangster who rose to fame in 1920s Melbourne. David Atkins stars. **FF5**

Stacking (1987, C, 109m, PG)
Coming-of-age drama set in the rural West of the 1950s, starring Megan Follows, Christine Lahti, and Frederic Forrest. **DR9**

Stage Door (1937, B&W, 92m, NR)
A New York boardinghouse is the scene for this comedy-drama about young women with show-biz ambitions. Katharine Hepburn, Ginger Rogers, Lucille Ball, and Eve Arden star. **CL7, CL16** *Recommended*

Stage Door Canteen (1943, B&W, 132m, NR)
A fictional story of a romance between a G.I. and a hostess at the famous Stage Door Canteen is really an excuse to showcase a variety of stars, including Katharine Hepburn, Harpo Marx, Benny Goodman, Count Basie, and many more. **MU15**

Stage Fright (1950, B&W, 110m, NR)
An actress's husband is dead, and suspicion falls on a young drama student. Alfred Hitchcock thriller starring Jane Wyman and Marlene Dietrich. **CL47, MY22**

Stage Struck (1936, B&W, 86m, NR)
Busby Berkeley directed Dick Powell and Joan Blondell in this musical about life behind the scenes of a big show. **MU20**

Stage Struck (1958, C, 95m, NR)
Remake of *Morning Glory*, with Susan Strasberg playing Katharine Hepburn's role of the impressionable young actress. Henry Fonda costars; Sidney Lumet directed. **CL24, CU18, DR58**

Stagecoach (1939, B&W, 96m, NR)
The legendary western, starring John Wayne as the Ringo Kid, the outlaw who comes to the aid of a stagecoach in peril. Claire Trevor, Oscar winner Thomas Mitchell, Andy Devine, and John Carradine costar. Directed by John Ford. **WE4, WE17, WE18, XT4** *Highly Recommended*

Stakeout (1987, C, 115m, R)
Crime thriller with doses of comedy about two cops assigned to watch a waitress whose escaped con boyfriend may show up, with one cop falling in love with her. Richard Dreyfuss, Emilio Estevez, Madeleine Stowe, and Aidan Quinn star. **CO10** *Recommended*

Stalag 17 (1953, B&W, 120m, NR)
William Holden won an Academy Award for his portrayal of a cynical sergeant in a World War II POW camp. Outstanding supporting cast includes Don Taylor, Otto Preminger, Robert Strauss, Harvey Lembeck, and Peter Graves. Billy Wilder directed. **AC7, CL37, CL51, XT2** *Highly Recommended*

Stalking Moon, The (1969, C, 109m, G)
In the Old West, a woman who has been a captive of the Apaches escapes with her half-breed son and seeks protection from an Army scout. Eva Marie Saint and Gregory Peck star. **WE9**

Stand and Deliver (1988, C, 103m, PG)
True-life drama of a Los Angeles high school math teacher who inspired his underprivileged kids to study hard and perform beyond expectations on standardized tests. Edward James Olmos stars, with Lou Diamond Phillips and Rosana De Soto. **DR6, DR15**

Stand by Me (1986, C, 87m, R)
Comedy-drama of four smalltown pals (Wil Wheaton, River Phoenix, Corey Feldman, Jerry O'Connell) who strike out on an adventure to find a missing boy. Based on a story by Stephen King; directed by Rob Reiner. **DR9**

Stand Easy *see* Down Among the Z-Men

Stand-In (1937, B&W, 91m, NR)
Comedy poking fun at Hollywood, with Leslie Howard as a lawyer investigating Colossal Pictures, Joan Blondell as a perky stand-in, and Humphrey Bogart as a producer. **CL20, CO8**

Stand Up and Cheer (1934, B&W, 69m, NR)
Shirley Temple does her part to chase away the Depression blues in this musical comedy starring Warner Baxter, Madge Evans, and James Dunn. **FA14**

Star Chamber, The (1983, C, 109m, R)
Young judge learns of secret tribunal that dispenses its own justice to criminals who beat the legal system. Michael Douglas, Hal Holbrook, and Yaphet Kotto star in this drama. **DR16, DR70**

Star Crystal (1985, C, 93m, R)
A group of scientist astronauts unknowingly pick up a new lifeform which begins to stalk them. **SF20**

Star 80 (1983, C, 117m, R)
True story of model Dorothy Stratten and her murder by her manager-boyfriend. Mariel Hemingway and Eric Roberts star; Bob Fosse directed. **DR6, DR13, MU28**

Star Is Born, A (1937, C, 111m, NR)
Classic tale of Hollywood marriage between fading star (Fredric March) and rising one (Janet Gaynor). Screenplay co-written by Dorothy Parker; directed by William Wellman. **CL7, DR13**

Star Is Born, A (1954, C, 170m, G)
Judy Garland and James Mason star in this musical remake of the 1937 classic. Many outstanding numbers, including "The Man That Got Away." Directed by George Cukor. This version contains recently restored footage. A 154m version is also available. **CL7, CL39, DR13, MU4, MU14, MU21** *Highly Recommended*

Star Is Born, A (1976, C, 140m, R)
A rock 'n' roll remake of the familiar story. Kris Kristofferson plays a rock idol who marries Barbra Streisand, a promising singer, with tragic results. **CU18, MU4, MU9, MU27**

Star of Midnight (1935, B&W, 90m, NR)
Light-hearted mystery starring William Powell as a lawyer accused of murder, forced to prove his innocence. Ginger Rogers costars. **MY7, MY21**

Star Trek: The Motion Picture (1979, C, 143m, G)
The *Enterprise* crew is brought back together to battle a strange force field before it can reach Earth. William Shatner and Leonard Nimoy star. Directed by Robert Wise. Video version adds 12 minutes of new footage. **CL58, CU10, FA8, SF3, SF13, SF23**

Star Trek II: The Wrath of Khan (1982, C, 113m, PG)
Khan, a character introduced in the TV series, escapes from exile, looking to destroy Kirk and the rest of the universe. William Shatner and Ricardo Montalban star. **FA8, SF3, SF13, SF23**

Star Trek III: The Search for Spock (1984, C, 105m, PG)
Kirk and his crew head out to find Spock (who "died" at the end of *Star Trek II*) so they can restore him with the essence held in Dr. McCoy's body. Meanwhile, the Klingons decide to get revenge against Kirk by capturing his son. William Shatner and DeForest Kelly star. **FA8, SF3, SF13, SF23**

Star Trek IV: The Voyage Home (1986, C, 119m, PG)
A strange probe, which drains all energy, heads to Earth in search of whales, which are now extinct. Kirk and his crew decide to travel back to 1986 to retrieve a pair of whales, in order to save the Earth of their century. William Shatner and Leonard Nimoy star. **FA8, SF3, SF4, SF13, SF23**

Star Wars (1977, C, 121m, PG)
Science fiction adventure about a young man (Mark Hamill) who helps rescue a rebel princess (Carrie Fisher) from the clutches of the Empire and goes on to become a general in the rebel forces. An Oscar winner for special effects. Harrison Ford, Alec Guinness, and Peter Cushing costar. Directed by George Lucas. Two sequels: *The Empire Strikes Back* and *Return of the Jedi*. **DR32, DR63, FA8, HO33, SF11, SF13, SF15, SF16, SF23, SF25** *Recommended*

Starchaser: The Legend of Orin (1985, C, 107m, PG)
An animated tale about a young boy who leads a rebellion against an evil dictator. **FA10, SF13**

Stardust Memories (1980, B&W, 91m, PG)
Woody Allen comedy with very dark overtones, about a filmmaker who's frustrated with the demands of his fans, colleagues, and family. Echoes of *8 1/2* and other Fellini movies abound. Charlotte Rampling, Jessica Harper, Marie-Christine Barrault, Tony Roberts, and Daniel Stern head the very large supporting cast. **CO8, CO27** *Recommended*

Starman (1984, C, 115m, PG)
An alien crashlands in Wisconsin and retreats to a farm, where he transforms himself to look like a young widow's late husband. Karen Allen and Jeff Bridges star; John Carpenter directed. **CU29, DR1, DR71, SF9**

Stars and Bars (1988, C, 94m, R)
British satire of contemporary art scene and American eccentrics, with English gallery respresentative trying to track down a valuable painting purchased by a nouveau riche American. Daniel Day Lewis and Harry Dean Stanton head the cast. **CO2, CO17, CU49**

Starstruck (1982, C, 95m, PG)
An Australian musical comedy about a waitress with ambitions to be a famous singer. Directed by Gillian Armstrong. **FF5, MU4, MU9**

Start the Revolution Without Me (1970, C, 98m, PG)
Wild comedy set during the French Revolution involving two mismatched sets of twins (Gene Wilder and Donald Sutherland). Orson Welles narrates. **CL41, CO5** *Recommended*

Starting Over (1979, C, 106m, R)
A newly divorced man falls in love with a vulnerable single woman, although he has trouble shaking his obnoxious ex-wife. Burt Reynolds, Jill Clayburgh, and Candice Bergen star in this romantic comedy. Alan J. Pakula directed. **AC37, CO1** *Recommended*

State Fair (1962, C, 118m, NR)
The popular musical about an Iowa family's experiences at the title event. Pat Boone stars, with Bobby Darin, Pamela Tiffin, Ann-Margret, and Alice Faye. **FA9, MU6**

State of Siege (1973, C, 120m, NR)
Based on a true story, this political thriller concerns the kidnapping of an American diplomat in Latin America by guerrillas opposed to U.S. support of the country's secret police. Yves Montand stars; Costa-Gavras directed. **FF1**

State of the Union (1948, B&W, 124m, NR)
Katharine Hepburn-Spencer Tracy comedy about a Presidential candidate and his fiercely independent wife. Directed by Frank Capra; Angela Lansbury and Van Johnson costar. **CL15, CL16, CL19, CL40**

State of Things, The (1982, C, 120m, NR)
A comedy/mystery about a film crew on location in Portugal remaking the low-budget cult film, *The Day the World Ended*. Pointed behind-the-scenes look at today's filmmakers and their pretensions, directed by Wim Wenders. **CO8, FF21**

Stay As You Are (1978, C, 95m, NR)
Middle-aged man romances a teenager, who may be his illegitimate daughter. Marcello Mastroianni and Nastassja Kinski star. **FF24**

Stay Away, Joe (1968, C, 102m, NR)
Elvis Presley plays a Native American in this musical drama, costarring Burgess Meredith, Joan Blondell, and L.Q. Jones. **MU22**

Stay Hungry (1976, C, 103m, R)
A good ol' boy of the New South is torn between a career in real estate and his affection for a loony group of bodybuilders. Jeff Bridges, Sally Field, and Arnold Schwarzenegger star in this offbeat comedy. **AC30, CO2, DR36, DR71** *Recommended*

Staying Alive (1983, C, 96m, PG)
This sequel to *Saturday Night Fever* has John Travolta trying to make it as a Broadway dancer. Directed by Sylvester Stallone. **AC31, DR12, MU4**

Stealing Heaven (1989, C, 108m, R)
The Abelard & Heloise story, a forbidden affair between a teacher and his lovely young pupil, with Derek Van Lint and Kim Thomson. An unrated version is also available: running time is 115m. **CU10, DR3**

Steamboat Bill, Jr. (1928, B&W, 71m, NR)
Buster Keaton plays a young man who has to prove himself to his father, a riverboat captain, in this silent classic. Finale, with cyclone destroying a town, is a highlight. **CL11, CO19** *Recommended*

Steaming (1985, C, 95m, R)
The setting is a London steam bath for women, and the conversation is frank and revealing. Vanessa Redgrave, Sarah Miles, and Diana Dors star; director Joseph Losey's last film. **DR23, DR65**

Steel Helmet, The (1951, B&W, 84m, NR)
An American sergeant survives a massacre in North Korea and joins up with some other soldiers who have been cut off from their unit. Gene Evans stars; Samuel Fuller directed. **AC3, CU22**

Steele Justice (1987, C, 95m, R)
A Vietnam vet (Martin Kove) seeks revenge against a druglord who was a Viet-

cong general and the killer of the vet's best friend. Ronny Cox costars. **AC19**

Steelyard Blues (1973, C, 93m, PG)
Episodic comedy about a group of anti-Establishment types and their pranks, starring Jane Fonda, Donald Sutherland, and Peter Boyle. **DR27**

Stella Dallas (1937, B&W, 106m, NR)
Barbara Stanwyck stars in the classic soap opera of a woman who gives up everything for her daughter's happiness. **CL5, CL6, CL45**

Step Lively (1944, B&W, 88m, NR)
Musical remake of *Room Service,* starring George Murphy as a wheeler-dealer producer. Frank Sinatra, Adolphe Menjou, and Gloria DeHaven costar. **MU26**

Stepfather, The (1987, C, 89m, R)
A teenaged girl suspects her mother's new husband isn't entirely on the level, and she's right—he's a serial killer who sheds families and identities every few years. Terry O'Quinn and Jill Schoelen star. **MY17, MY18** *Recommended*

Steppenwolf (1974, C, 105m, R)
Moody drama of a suicidal writer and his involvement with a mysterious woman, based on Herman Hesse's cult novel. Max von Sydow, Dominique Sanda, and Pierre Clementi star. **DR19**

Sterile Cuckoo, The (1969, C, 107m, PG)
Story of young college boy's first romance, with a girl in desperate need of real affection. Liza Minnelli's film debut; Wendell Burton costars. Directed by Alan J. Pakula; adapted from John Nichols' novel. **DR1**

Steve Martin Live! (1986, C, 60m, NR)
Footage from a 1979 Martin concert, plus some of his classic bits, including "King Tut" and his Oscar-nominated short film, *The Absent-Minded Waiter.* **CO16, CO33**

Steven Wright Live (1985, C, 53m, NR)
The poker-faced comedian in concert. **CO16**

Stevie (1978, C, 102m, PG)
Glenda Jackson plays eccentric, reclusive British poet Stevie Smith in this unusual film biography. Mona Washbourne costars as Smith's addled aunt. **DR4, DR23**

Stick (1985, C, 109m, R)
Burt Reynolds is an ex-con who gets mixed up in the Miami drug dealing scene to avenge a friend's death. Candice Bergen, George Segal, and Dar Robinson costar. Based on Elmore Leonard's novel. **AC9, AC37, MY26**

Still of the Night (1982, C, 94m, PG)
Thriller borrowing heavily from Hitchcock has psychiatrist (Roy Scheider) and the girl friend of his murdered patient (Meryl Streep) falling in love. Robert Benton wrote and directed. **DR26, DR55, MY5**

Still Smokin' (1983, C, 91m, R)
Two-part Cheech and Chong comedy has them running wild at an Amsterdam film festival, plus extended concert footage. **CO32**

Sting, The (1973, C, 129m, PG)
Oscar-winning comedy about two Prohibition-era sharpies out to fleece a nasty gambler. Paul Newman and Robert Redford star; Robert Shaw and the music of Scott Joplin offer fine support. Directed by Oscar winner George Roy Hill. **CO6, DR28, DR29, XT1, XT6**

Stir Crazy (1980, C, 111m, R)
A pair of inept bank robbers make the most of their stay behind bars by joining the prison rodeo. Richard Pryor and Gene Wilder star; Sidney Poitier directed. **CO3, CO29, DR38**

Stolen Kisses (1968, C, 90m, NR)
The third in the Antoine Doinel series of films from star Jean-Pierre Léaud and director François Truffaut finds our hero getting his first taste of real romance. **FF13**

Stone Boy, The (1984, C, 93m, PG)
Montana family is torn apart when one son accidentally shoots and kills his brother. Robert Duvall, Glenn Close, and Frederic Forrest star. **DR8, DR37, DR72**

Stone Killer, The (1973, C, 95m, R)
A dedicated cop (Charles Bronson) works to solve a string of murders linked to organized crime. **AC29**

Stop Making Sense (1984, C, 99m, NR)
This Talking Heads concert film captures the essence of the band, thanks to director Jonathan Demme and his brilliant crew. Three songs added for video version. **CU10, CU39, MU10** *Highly Recommended*

Storm Boy (1976, C, 90m, NR)
From Australia, a family drama about a young boy learning about life from an elderly aborigine. **FF5**

Stormy Monday (1988, C, 93m, R)
Moody thriller set in English town of Newcastle, where an American developer (Tommy Lee Jones) puts the squeeze on a club owner (Sting). Melanie Griffith and Sean Bean costar. Written and directed by Mike Figgis, who also composed the music. **DR23, MU12, MY2, MY19** *Recommended*

Stormy Weather (1943, B&W, 77m, NR)
A musical that showcases many of the top black entertainers of the 1940s. Lena Horne, Bill Robinson, Fats Waller, Cab Calloway, and The Nicholas Brothers star. **MU3, MU4, MU13** *Recommended*

Story of Adele H,, The (1975, C, 97m, PG)
True tale of the daughter of French novelist Victor Hugo and her obsession with a young soldier. François Truffaut directed Isabelle Adjani in the title role. **FF13**

Story of Vernon and Irene Castle, The (1939, B&W, 93m, NR)
Fred Astaire and Ginger Rogers play the real-life husband and wife dance team in this musical biography. **CL15, MU4, MU5, MU18**

Stowaway (1936, B&W, 86m, NR)
A cute little stowaway on a cruise ship helps a young couple find romance. Shirley Temple, Alice Faye, and Robert Young star. **FA14**

Strada, La (1954, B&W, 115m, NR)
Oscar-winning drama from Federico Fellini about a traveling circus and three diverse characters: a lonely waif (Guilietta Masina), a strong man (Anthony Quinn), and an acrobat (Richard Basehart). **FF10, XT7**

Straight Shootin' (1917, B&W, 53m, NR)
This silent western was one of director John Ford's first films. It stars Hoot Gibson and Harry Carey. **WE18**

Straight Time (1978, C, 114m, R)
Ex-con tries to go straight, but is drawn inevitably into old bad habits. Dustin Hoffman, Theresa Russell, Gary Busey, and Harry Dean Stanton star in this underrated drama. **CU49, DR16, DR30** *Recommended*

Straight to Hell (1987, C, 86m, R)
The last word in western spoofs, with a hip cast that includes Dennis Hopper and rock stars Elvis Costello, Dick Rude, Grace Jones, and Joe Strummer. Directed by Alex Cox. **CU46, MU12, WE15**

Strait-Jacket (1964, B&W, 89m, NR)
Instant camp classic stars Joan Crawford as a just-released convict who served twenty years for ax-murdering her husband and his girl friend in front of her baby daughter. After she moves in with her grown daughter, a series of similar murders occur. **CL50, CU2, HO19**

Strange Brew (1983, C, 91m, PG)
Rick Moranis and Dave Thomas expand their McKenzie Brothers bit from *SCTV* into a feature-length comedy about those Canadian stooges and their search for the perfect beer. **CO14**

Strange Invaders (1983, C, 94m, PG)
Paul LeMat and Nancy Allen star in this gentle spoof of 50s sci-fi movies. An alien force is ready to return home after being on Earth for 25 years, and they want to take the pre-teen daughter of an alien-human union with them. **SF9, SF21**

Strange Love of Martha Ivers, The (1946, B&W, 117m, NR)
Barbara Stanwyck plays a woman with a past that haunts her in this classic film noir, costarring Van Heflin and Kirk Douglas. **CL45, MY1**

Stranger, The (1946, B&W, 95m, NR)
Ex-Nazi lives a second life in New England town until he's tracked down by a relentless pursuer. Orson Welles stars in and directed this thriller, with Loretta Young and Edward G. Robinson. **CL41, CL52, MY1, MY6** *Recommended*

Stranger and the Gunfighter, The (1976, C, 107m, PG)
A martial arts spaghetti western. Lee Van Cleef teams with Lo Lieh to track down a killer. **WE14**

Stranger Is Watching, A (1982, C, 92m, R)
A New York newscaster (Kate Mulgrew) and her daughter are abducted by a madman (Rip Torn). **CU47**

Stranger on the Third Floor, The (1940, B&W, 64m, NR)
A reporter's testimony helps convict an innocent man, but the journalist has second thoughts and decides to find the real killer. Peter Lorre stars. **MY7**

Stranger Than Paradise (1984, B&W, 90m, R)
Poker-faced comedy from director Jim Jarmusch about two New York goofs and a 16-year-old Hungarian girl. They sit around in New York apartments, they walk around in the snow in Cleveland, they drive to Florida. John Lurie, Richard Edson, and Eszter Balint star. **CO12, CU1, MU12**

Strangers *see* Voyage to Italy

Strangers Kiss (1984, C, 94m, R)
Drama about the making of a low-budget film whose director tries to encourage a behind-the-scenes romance between his stars to pump up their love scenes on camera. Peter Coyote, Blaine Novak, and Victoria Tennant star. **DR13**

Strangers on a Train (1951, B&W, 101m, NR)
Alfred Hitchcock classic about a psychotic (Robert Walker) trying to talk a tennis pro (Farley Granger) into a murder swap, then carrying out his end of the bargain. Lots of chills, even on repeated viewings; Walker is superb. **MY9, MY17, MY22** *Highly Recommended*

Strangers: The Story of a Mother and Daughter (1979, C, 100m, NR)
Bette Davis won an Emmy for her role as a widow whose daughter (Gena Rowlands) comes to visit after twenty years of separation. Originally made for TV. **CL21**

Strangers When We Meet (1960, B&W, 117m, NR)
Glossy romantic drama of an affair between a married man and woman, starring Kirk Douglas, Kim Novak, Ernie Kovacs, Barbara Rush, and Walter Matthau. **DR1**

Strategic Air Command (1955, C, 114m, NR)
James Stewart is a baseball player who puts away his mitt when he's called into the Air Force. Anthony Mann directed. **CL25, WE20**

Straw Dogs (1971, C, 113m, R)
An American academic visiting in rural England is harassed by local toughs and finally fights back in a violent confrontation. Dustin Hoffman stars; Sam Peckinpah directed. **DR30, WE19** *Recommended*

Strawberry Blonde, The (1941, B&W, 100m, NR)
A dentist (James Cagney) is infatuated with a golddigger (Rita Hayworth) but

marries a woman (Olivia de Havilland) who really loves him. **CL22**

Stray Dog (1949, B&W, 122m, NR)
In Tokyo, a police detective's gun is stolen and he has trouble persuading anyone that he's a cop. Toshiro Mifune stars; Akira Kurosawa directed. **FF9, FF28**

Streamers (1983, C, 118m, R)
Intense drama set in an Army barracks at the start of the Vietnam War, starring Matthew Modine, Michael Wright, and Mitchell Lichtenstein. Directed by Robert Altman; screenplay by David Rabe, from his own play. **CU25, DR7, DR20**

Street of Shame (1956, B&W, 96m, NR)
Japanese drama from director Kenji Mizoguchi (his last completed film), about prostitutes in a Tokyo brothel called Dreamland. Machiko Kyo stars. **FF4**

Street Smart (1987, C, 97m, R)
Hotshot reporter, on a tight deadline, concocts story about black pimp; the details happen to match a real pimp who's on trial for murder. Christopher Reeve and Morgan Freeman star in this story of contemporary ethics and life in the media spotlight. **DR7**

Streetcar Named Desire, A (1951, B&W, 122m, NR)
Classic version of Tennessee Williams play of brutal Stanley Kowalski (Marlon Brando), his tough wife Stella (Kim Hunter), and her fragile sister Blanche DuBois (Vivien Leigh). Both actresses and Karl Malden won Oscars; Elia Kazan directed. **DR20, DR33, DR59, XT3, XT4, XT5** *Highly Recommended*

Streets of Fire (1984, C, 93m, PG)
A rock singer is kidnapped by the leader of a biker gang, and her ex-boyfriend, a soldier of fortune, sets out to rescue her. Diane Lane, Willem Dafoe, and Michael Pare star in this self-proclaimed "rock 'n' roll fable" with music by Ry Cooder, The Blasters, and others. Rick Moranis and Amy Madigan costar. Directed by Walter Hill. **AC8, AC25, CO14, CU27**

Streets of Gold (1986, C, 94m, R)
Russian boxing coach defects to America, finds two fighters to train for international competition against you-know-who. Klaus Maria Brandauer stars. **DR22**

Streetwise (1984, C, 92m, NR)
Documentary portrait of homeless children in Seattle is a searing look at discarded youth. Directed by Martin Bell. **CU16** *Recommended*

Strike (1924, B&W, 70m, NR)
Director Sergei Eisenstein's dramatic account of a 1912 workers' clash with government police. Silent classic of political filmmaking. **CU9, FF22**

Strike Up the Band (1940, B&W, 120m, NR)
A high school band schemes to compete in a radio contest. Mickey Rooney and Judy Garland star; Busby Berkeley directed. **MU1, MU4, MU20, MU21**

Stripes (1981, C, 105m, R)
Old-fashioned service comedy with brand-new cast of comedians, featuring Bill Murray, Harold Ramis, and John Candy as the lovable losers, Warren Oates as their perplexed sergeant. **CO13, CO14, CO38, CU48**

Stripper, The (1963, B&W, 95m, NR)
Drama of a no-win love affair between an aging stripper (Joanne Woodward) and a teenager (Richard Beymer). Based on a play by William Inge. **DR67**

Stroker Ace (1983, C, 96m, PG)
Burt Reynolds vehicle has him once again playing the good ol' boy of the car racing circuit. Loni Anderson, Ned Beatty, and Jim Nabors costar. **AC37, CO36**

Stromboli (1950, B&W, 81m, NR)
Ingrid Bergman stars in this drama of a woman and her loveless marriage to an Italian fisherman. Directed by Roberto Rossellini. **CL27, FF2**

Studs Lonigan (1960, B&W, 95m, NR)
Drama of aimless Chicago youth in 1920s
and his inevitable fate. Based on James
T. Farrell's novel, starring Christopher
Knight, Frank Gorshin, and (in a small,
early role) Jack Nicholson. **DR19, DR24**

Study in Scarlet, A (1933, B&W, 70m,
NR)
Sherlock Holmes mystery which has
nothing to do with the story, the first in
the series, starring Reginald Owen. **MY10**

Study in Terror, A (1965, C, 94m, NR)
Sherlock Holmes (John Neville) takes on
Jack the Ripper in this British-made mystery. Donald Houston costars as Dr. Watson. **MY10**

Stuff, The (1985, C, 93m, R)
A popular new dessert is killing people.
A spoof of 1950's sci-fi/horror films. Mi-
chael Moriarty and Garrett Morris star;
Larry Cohen directed. **CO13, CU30,
HO24**

Stunt Man, The (1980, C, 129m, R)
Comedy-drama about filmmaker who offers a fugitive the most dangerous job in
movies after the film's stunt man is killed
in an accident. Peter O'Toole, Steve
Railsback, and Barbara Hershey star in
this dazzling look at the way movies create the illusion of reality. **DR13, DR45**
Recommended

Stunts (1977, C, 89m, PG)
When a stunt man is killed during filming,
his brother suspects foul play and decides
to investigate on his own. Robert Forster
stars. **MY15**

Suburbia (1984, C, 96m, R)
No-holds-barred drama of society's cas-
toffs, kids living in deserted tract houses,
stealing for food, drinking, and getting
high. Directed by Penelope Spheeris.
CU12, DR9 *Recommended*

Sudden Impact (1983, C, 117m, R)
Dirty Harry is on the trail of a woman
who is, one by one, killing the people
responsible for the gang rape she and her

sister suffered. Clint Eastwood and Sondra Locke star. **AC9, AC27**

Suddenly (1954, B&W, 77m, NR)
Thriller about a gang of thugs planning to
assassinate the President as he passes
through a small town. Frank Sinatra
stars. **DR16, DR49, MY1**

Suddenly, Last Summer (1959, B&W,
114m, NR)
Tennessee Williams drama of a young
girl's breakdown and her aunt's manipulative attempts to cure her. Elizabeth Taylor, Katharine Hepburn, and Montgomery Clift star; directed by Joseph L.
Mankiewicz. **CL16, CL33, CL55**

Sugarbaby (1985, C, 87m, R)
An odd-couple comedy from Germany
about a romance between a plump mortuary attendant and a wimpy subway conductor. **FF3**

Sugarland Express, The (1974, C, 109m,
PG)
Comedy-drama, based on a true story,
about a fugitive couple, their baby, and a
hostage state trooper pursued across
Texas by a small army of law enforcement
agents. Goldie Hawn, William Atherton,
and Michael Sacks star. Directed by
Steven Spielberg. **CO30, DR6, SF24** *Recommended*

Sullivan's Travels (1941, B&W, 91m, NR)
Writer-director Preston Sturges's satire
about a Hollywood director (Joel Mc-
Crea) who sets out to make a "serious"
film by bumming around the country. Ve-
ronica Lake, William Demarest, and Eric
Blore head the supporting cast. **CL10,
CO24, CO37** *Highly Recommended*

Summer (1986, C, 98m, R)
From French director Eric Rohmer, a
comedy about a Parisian secretary's attempts to escape the city during August.
FF15

Summer Camp Nightmare (1987, C, 87m, PG-13)
At a summer camp run by a strict counselor, the kids stage a revolt and imprison all the adults. **HO12**

Summer City (1976, C, 83m, NR)
A quartet of teens are out for a good-times weekend at a seaside resort but run into trouble with resentful locals. Mel Gibson stars in this Australian drama. **DR69, FF5**

Summer Interlude (1951, B&W, 90m, NR)
Early Ingmar Bergman drama about a woman sorting out the details of her relationship with a now-dead lover. Also known as *Illicit Interlude*. **FF8**

Summer Lovers (1982, C, 98m, R)
A young man and two attractive women enjoy a summer fling on a Greek island in this sexy movie with a cult following. Peter Gallagher, Daryl Hannah, and Valerie Quennessen star. **CU6**

Summer Magic (1963, C, 100m, NR)
Disney comedy-drama about a Maine widow raising her family on a meager income. Dorothy McGuire and Hayley Mills star. **FA1**

Summer Rental (1985, C, 87m, PG)
John Candy stars in this comedy about an air traffic controller's disastrous summer at the beach. Rip Torn and Richard Crenna costar. **CO14, CU47**

Summer School (1987, C, 98m, PG-13)
A laid-back physical education teacher is roped into teaching a summer course in history to a class of misfits. Mark Harmon stars with Kirstie Alley in this comedy. **CO35**

Summer Solstice (1981, C, 75m, NR)
An aging couple (Henry Fonda and Myrna Loy) return to the beach where they first met 50 years ago. Lindsay Crouse and Stephen Collins costar. Originally made for TV. **CL24, CL46**

Summer Stock (1950, C, 109m, NR)
Gene Kelly and his troupe invade Judy Garland's farm in order to rehearse their Broadway show. When the star of the show leaves, Judy fills in. Gene dances with newspapers and Judy sings "Get Happy." **MU4, MU19, MU21**

Summer Wishes, Winter Dreams (1973, C, 93m, PG)
Joanne Woodward plays a New York woman whose emotional distance from everyone around her frustrates her. Martin Balsam and Sylvia Sidney costar. **DR10, DR67**

Summertime (1958, C, 98m, NR)
Tearjerker about a spinster visiting Venice, falling in love with a married man. Katharine Hepburn and Rossano Brazzi star; David Lean directed. **CL4, CL6, CL16, DR50**

Sunday, Bloody Sunday (1971, C, 110m, R)
Romantic triangle, with middle-aged man and young woman competing for the same man. British drama stars Peter Finch, Glenda Jackson, and Murray Head. Screenplay by Penelope Gilliatt. **DR3, DR23**

Sunday in the Country, A (1984, C, 94m, G)
An aging painter invites his loved ones to spend a day at his rural estate. Bertrand Tavernier directed this French drama. **FF1**

Sundays and Cybelle (1962, B&W, 110m, NR)
A war veteran suffering from shell shock finds comfort in the friendship of a young girl. Oscar winner for Best Foreign-Language film. **FF1, XT7**

Sundowners, The (1960, C, 113m, NR)
Drama of Australian sheep herding family, starring Robert Mitchum, Deborah Kerr, and Peter Ustinov. Directed by Fred Zinnemann. **CL57**

Sunrise at Campobello (1960, C, 143m, NR)
Ralph Bellamy's famed portrait of Franklin D. Roosevelt, adapted from the Dore Schary stage hit. Greer Garson plays Eleanor; Hume Cronyn and Jean Hagen costar. **DR4**

Sunset (1988, C, 105m, PG-13)
In 1920s Hollywood, former Western lawman Wyatt Earp and cowboy movie star Tom Mix team to solve a murder mystery. James Garner and Bruce Willis star. Blake Edwards directed this nostalgic comedy, with plenty of detail about Hollywood in the Jazz Age. **CO6, CO8, CO46, MY21**

Sunset Boulevard (1950, B&W, 110m, NR)
Legendary look at the seamy underside of Hollywood, with reclusive former star (Gloria Swanson) taking in young screenwriter (William Holden). Erich von Stroheim costars; Billy Wilder directed. **CL7, CL37, CL51, CL53, DR13, MY1** *Highly Recommended*

Sunset in the West (1950, B&W, 67m, NR)
A deputy sheriff (Roy Rogers) battles gunrunners. **WE23**

Sunset on the Desert (1942, B&W, 53m, NR)
Roy Rogers action, with a man returning to his hometown to help his late father's partner out of a jam. **WE23**

Sunset Serenade (1942, B&W, 58m, NR)
Roy Rogers and Gabby Hayes step in the way of some dastardly villains intent on murder and thievery. Bob Nolan & the Sons of the Pioneers add some harmonizing. **WE23**

Sunshine Boys, The (1975, C, 111m, PG)
A pair of ex-vaudeville partners, not on speaking terms, are persuaded to reteam for a TV special. Neil Simon comedy stars Walter Matthau and Oscar winner George Burns. **CO3, CO34, XT4**

Superdad (1974, C, 96m, G)
A father (Bob Crane) challenges his daughter's fiance (Kurt Russell) to various competitions to test his worthiness in this Disney comedy. **FA1**

Supergirl (1984, C, 114m, PG)
Supergirl, cousin to Superman, is sent to Earth to recover the Omegahedron, a source of unlimited power, which has fallen into the hands of an evil witch. Helen Slater, Faye Dunaway, and Peter O'Toole star. **AC17, DR35, DR45, FA4**

Superman (1978, C, 143m, PG)
The history of Superman, from Krypton to Metropolis. The special effects won an Academy Award. Christopher Reeve stars, with Margot Kidder and Marlon Brando. **AC17, DR33, DR39, FA4**

Superman II (1980, C, 127m, PG)
Three villains from Krypton come to Earth with plans to rule the world. Christopher Reeve, Margot Kidder, and Terence Stamp star. Directed by Richard Lester. **AC17, CU35, DR39, FA4**

Superman III (1983, C, 123m, PG)
A master villain cons a computer genius to split Superman's personalities, one good, one bad. Christopher Reeve, Richard Pryor, and Robert Vaughn star. Richard Lester directed. **AC17, CO29, CU35, FA4**

Superman IV: The Quest for Peace (1987, C, 90m, PG)
Lex Luthor creates a monster to battle Superman, who has just rid the world of nuclear weapons. Christopher Reeve and Gene Hackman star. **AC17, DR39, FA4**

Supernaturals, The (1986, C, 85m, R)
A troop of new recruits on manuevers end up fighting for their lives when a ghost army of Confederate soldiers come to life seeking revenge. Maxwell Caulfield, LeVar Burton, and Nichelle Nichols star. **HO2**

Support Your Local Sheriff! (1969, C, 93m, PG)
An amiable western comedy, with James Garner as a peaceable lawman who has to bring in the bad guys without benefit of a six-shooter. **WE15**

Sure Thing, The (1985, C, 94m, PG-13)
Road comedy about two mismatched college students finding romance as they hitchhike cross-country. John Cusack and Daphne Zuniga star; directed by Rob Reiner. **CO1** *Recommended*

Surrender (1987, C, 95m, PG)
A much-divorced novelist and a struggling artist find romance. Michael Caine, Sally Field, and Steve Guttenberg star in this comedy. **DR36**

Survivors, The (1983, C, 102m, R)
Two unemployed men are fingered by the same hit man and flee for their lives to a survivalist commune. Comedy starring Walter Matthau and Robin Williams. **CO3, CO43**

Susana (1951, B&W, 87m, NR)
Director Luis Buñuel's study of a vagrant girl's alluring hold over a respectable Spanish family. Rosita Quintera stars, with Fernando Soler. **FF11**

Susanna Pass (1949, C, 67m, NR)
Roy Rogers and Dale Evans team up with Cuban star Estelita Rodriguez for western action and plenty of songs. **WE23**

Susannah of the Mounties (1939, B&W, 79m, NR)
Shirley Temple goes West in this sentimental tale of a Mountie (Randolph Scott) who adopts a girl orphaned in an Indian raid. **FA14, WE22**

Suspect (1987, C, 101m, R)
Drama set in Washington, D.C., about a public defender (Cher) whose client is accused of murder and a juror (Dennis Quaid) on the case who uncovers evidence that he decides to share with her. **DR17, MU12, XT9**

Suspicion (1941, B&W, 99m, NR)
Shy young woman is pursued by charming playboy and marries him, then immediately begins to suspect he's targeted her for murder. Classic Alfred Hitchcock suspense starring Oscar winner Joan Fontaine and Cary Grant. **CL18, MY3, MY5, MY22, XT3**

Suspicion (1987, C, 87m, NR)
Remake of the Alfred Hitchcock thriller about a woman who suspects her playboy husband of wanting to murder her, starring Jane Curtin and Anthony Andrews. Originally made for cable TV. **CO13, MY3, MY5**

Svengali (1983, C, 100m, NR)
The classic tale of a young woman's rise to fame and her manipulative benefactor, updated to star Jodie Foster as a rock singer and Peter O'Toole in the title role. Originally made for TV. **DR45**

Swamp Thing (1982, C, 91m, PG)
A research scientist who discovers a potion to end world hunger is covered with the substance and becomes a human vegetable. Adrienne Barbeau and Louis Jourdan star. Directed by Wes Craven. **HO16**

Swann in Love (1984, C, 110m, R)
A French aristocrat finds himself drawn to a woman of less than impeccable breeding in this adaptation of Marcel Proust's classic novel. Jeremy Irons and Ornella Muti star. **FF1**

Swap, The (1969, C, 90m, R)
Drama about a film editor's search for the killers of his brother, starring Robert DeNiro in an early screen appearance. Originally released in different form as *Sam's Song;* this version adds several new characters. **DR24**

Swarm, The (1978, C, 116m, PG)
Deadly killer bees attack an all-star cast which includes Michael Caine, Katharine Ross, Henry Fonda, and Richard Chamberlain. **CL24, HO16, SF7**

Swedenhielms (1935, B&W, 88m, NR)
Ingrid Bergman stars in this drama, made in Sweden before her emergence as a star in Hollywood. She's the girlfriend of a young man whose impoverished family is counting on their patriarch to win the Nobel Prize. **CL27, FF7**

Sweet Charity (1969, C, 133m, G)
A dancehall hostess wants a traditional wedding and marriage, but keeps falling in love with ne'er-do-wells who only want her money. The directorial debut of Bob Fosse. Shirley MacLaine stars. **DR42, MU2, MU3, MU14, MU28**

Sweet Dreams (1985, C, 115m, PG13)
Jessica Lange portrays legendary country singer Patsy Cline. Ed Harris costars; Cline's voice was used on the soundtrack recordings. **DR2, DR4, DR12, DR74, MU5**

Sweet Hearts Dance (1988, C, 101m, R)
A small Vermont town is the setting for this romantic comedy about a couple (Don Johnson, Susan Sarandon) whose shaky marriage isn't helped by his best buddy (Jeff Daniels). **CO1**

Sweet Liberty (1986, C, 107m, PG)
The author of a bestselling book on the American Revolution is apalled when a movie crew arrives in his hometown and begins filming a very loose adaptation of his work. Alan Alda stars, with Michael Caine, Michelle Pfeiffer, Bob Hoskins, and Lillian Gish. Alda also wrote and directed. **CL49, CO8**

Sweet Sixteen (1981, C, 90m, R)
As beautiful and promiscuous Melissa approaches her sixteenth birthday, her boyfriends start to die. Susan Strasberg and Bo Hopkins star. **HO7**

Sweet Smell of Success (1957, B&W, 96m, NR)
A ruthless New York gossip columnist (Burt Lancaster) uses his power to destroy anyone who doesn't curry favor with him. Tony Curtis costars as a sycophantic press agent. With Martin Milner and Susan Harrison. Superb screenplay by Ernest Lehman and Clifford Odets. **CL7, DR41** *Highly Recommended*

Sweet Sweetback's Badasssss Song (1971, C, 97m, R)
A black man kills two racist cops and flees for his life. Written and directed by Melvin Van Peebles, who also stars. **AC8, DR14**

Sweethearts (1938, C, 115m, NR)
Colorful show-biz saga of a Broadway couple (Nelson Eddy, Jeanette MacDonald) whose partnership is threatened when Hollywood beckons. **CL7, CL15**

Swept Away (1975, C, 116m, R)
An Italian comedy-drama about a shipwrecked odd couple—a snooty rich woman and a lusty sailor. Giancarlo Giannini and Mariangelo Meltao star; Lina Wertmuller directed. **FF2**

Swimmer, The (1968, C, 94m, PG)
Burt Lancaster stars in this drama about a suburbanite who swims through his neighbors' pools on his way home, recalling past experiences along the way. Based on a John Cheever story. **DR41**

Swimming to Cambodia (1987, C, 100m, NR)
Actor/monologist Spalding Gray recounts his experiences on location in Thailand for *The Killing Fields* in this mesmerizing one-man show. Directed by Jonathan Demme. **CO12, CU39** *Recommended*

Swing High, Swing Low (1937, B&W, 95m, NR)
Fred MacMurray is a trumpet player whose career hits every note on the scale. Carole Lombard costars. **CL7, CL48**

Swing Shift (1984, C, 100m, PG)
Goldie Hawn goes to work in a factory when her husband goes to fight in World War II. Christine Lahti, Kurt Russell, and Ed Harris star in this nostalgic drama from director Jonathan Demme. **CO30, CU39, DR3, DR5, DR10**

Swing Time (1936, B&W, 103m, NR)
A gambler falls in love with a dance teacher, even though he is engaged to another woman. Fred Astaire and Ginger Rogers star; George Stevens directed this classic musical. **CL15, CL42, MU4, MU18** *Highly Recommended*

Swiss Family Robinson (1960, C, 128m, G)
A shipwrecked family learn to survive on a deserted island. John Mills and Dorothy McGuire star in Disney's version of the family adventure classic. **FA1**

Swiss Miss (1938, B&W, 72m, NR)
Laurel and Hardy comedy, set in the Alps, with Ollie a love-smitten yodeler. **CO20**

Switching Channels (1988, C, 108m, PG)
Romantic comedy triangle composed of a TV news producer (Burt Reynolds), his star reporter and ex-wife (Kathleen Turner), and her fiance (Christopher Reeve). A loose remake of *The Front Page* and *His Girl Friday.* **AC37, CO1, CU18, DR46**

Sword and the Rose, The (1953, C, 93m, NR)
Mary Tudor works her charms on a knight, incurs the wrath of a duke, and is noticed by Henry the VIII. Disney version of *When Knighthood Was in Flower,* starring Glynis Johns and Richard Todd. **FA1**

Sword in the Stone, The (1963, C, 75m, G)
Disney animated feature about a young boy who is destined to be king of England and is helped by the wizard Merlin. **FA2**

Sword of Doom (1967, B&W, 120m, NR)
Tatsuya Nakadai stars in this adventure film as a samurai whose lust for action alienates even his own family. Toshiro Mifune appears in a small supporting role. **FF28**

Sword of the Valiant (1982, C, 101m, PG)
In order to become a knight, Gawain (Miles O'Keeffe) must battle the Green Knight (Sean Connery) and solve a rid-

dle. Trevor Howard and Peter Cushing costar. **AC36, FA4, HO33**

Sybil (1976, C, 132m, NR)
Famous case of woman with multiple personalities and the therapist who helped cure her. Sally Field stars, with Joanne Woodward. Originally made for TV with a running time of 198m. **DR6, DR36, DR67**

Sylvester (1984, C, 104m, PG)
Young woman trains her favorite show horse for competition. Melissa Gilbert stars. **DR22, FA5**

Sylvia and the Phantom (1945, B&W, 97m, NR)
French comedy of a teenaged girl's infatuation with the painting of a long-dead nobleman. Odette Joyeux stars, with Jacques Tati. **FF16**

Sylvia Scarlett (1935, B&W, 94m, NR)
Katharine Hepburn and Cary Grant star in this offbeat story of a traveling troupe of players; she's disguised as a boy and he doesn't suspect a thing—for a while. Directed by George Cukor; underappreciated until recent rediscovery. **CL14, CL16, CL18, CL39** *Highly Recommended*

Sympathy for the Devil (1970, C, 92m, NR)
French director Jean-Luc Godard alternates political rhetoric with shots of the Rolling Stone recording the title song. **CU9, FF14**

THX 1138 (1971, C, 88m, PG)
In the future, computers keep the humans drugged so they cannot think and feel for themselves. One man (Robert Duvall) and his roommate (Maggie McOmie) decide to stop taking the drugs and begin to feel human emotions. George Lucas directed. **DR37, SF11, SF25**

T-Men (1947, B&W, 96m, NR)
Undercover government agents try to expose a counterfeit ring. Suspenseful drama from director Anthony Mann, starring Dennis O'Keefe. **MY1, WE20**

T.N.T. Jackson (1974, C, 73m, R)
A female karate expert (Jeanne Bell) searches for her missing brother. **AC26**

Tai-Pan (1986, C, 127m, R)
Historical drama about the founding of modern Hong Kong, based on James Clavell's epic novel. Bryan Brown and Joan Chen star. **DR5**

Take a Hard Ride (1975, C, 103m, PG)
Jim Brown, Lee Van Cleef, and Fred Williamson head the cast of this western drama about a cowboy carrying a payroll shipment across the Mexico border. **WE10**

Take Me Out to the Ball Game (1949, C, 93m, NR)
Grand musical about a woman (Esther Williams) who takes over a winning baseball team. Gene Kelly and Frank Sinatra star; Busby Berkeley directed. **MU6, MU19, MU20, MU26**

Take the Money and Run (1969, C, 85m, PG)
Woody Allen's tale of an inept bank robber spoofs documentaries, crime movies, love stories—you name it. Janet Margolin costars. **CO7, CO10, CO27**

Taking of Pelham One Two Three, The (1974, C, 104m, PG)
A gang of hijackers hold the passengers of a New York subway car hostage. Walter Matthau is the cop on the case, Robert Shaw the lead baddie. **AC9, XT9**

Tale of the Frog Prince, The (1985, C, 60m, NR)
A spoiled princess is forced to look after a talented frog who turns out to be a cursed prince. Robin Williams and Teri Garr star in this presentation from Faerie Tale Theatre. **FA12**

Tale of Two Cities, A (1935, B&W, 121m, NR)
Charles Dickens' classic story of the French Revolution and one man's sacrifice for another on the guillotine. Ronald Colman, Elizabeth Allan, and Edna May Oliver star. **CL1** *Recommended*

Tales From The Crypt (1972, C, 92m, PG)
Five criminally minded people are trapped in the catacombs with a mind-reading monk. He shows each of them the consequences if they carry out the crimes they are plotting. Joan Collins and Peter Cushing star. **HO23, HO26, HO33**

Tales of Ordinary Madness (1983, C, 107m, NR)
Drama of hard-drinking poet who meets unusual assortment of women in his travels. Ben Gazzara, Ornella Muti, and Susan Tyrell star; based on stories by Charles Bukowski. **CU6**

Tales of Terror (1962, C, 90m, NR)
Three stories based on Edgar Allen Poe; "The Black Cat," "Morella," and "The Case of M. Valdemar." Vincent Price and Peter Lorre star. Directed by Roger Corman. **HO23, HO31, HO41**

Talk of the Town, The (1942, B&W, 118m, NR)
Classic comedy with Cary Grant a fugitive hiding out in boardinghouse run by Jean Arthur, debating fellow boarder Ronald Colman on the justice system. Directed by George Stevens. **CL10, CL18, CL42**

Talk Radio (1988, C, 110m, R)
Eric Bogosian plays a smart-mouthed radio talk show host whose personal life matches the turmoil he creates on the air. Oliver Stone directed; based on Bogosian's play and true incidents in the life of Alan Berg, a host who was assassinated by white supremacists. **DR6, DR7, DR12, DR20**

Tall Blonde Man With One Black Shoe, The (1972, C, 90m, PG)
From France, a spy spoof starring Pierre Richard as a man caught in the middle of a battle between espionage agents. U.S. remake: *The Man With One Red Shoe.* **FF1, FF36**

Tall Men, The (1955, C, 122m, NR)
After the Civil War, two Rebs sign on a cattle drive from Texas to Montana. Clark Gable and Robert Ryan star, with Jane Russell. **CL23**

Tamarind Seed, The (1974, C, 123m, PG)
Blake Edwards directed this story of romance and espionage, starring Omar Sharif and Julie Andrews. He's a Russian agent trying to recruit her at a Caribbean resort, but love intervenes. **CO46, MY5, MY6**

Taming of the Shrew, The (1967, C, 126m, NR)
Elizabeth Taylor-Richard Burton version of Shakespeare's classic comedy of a headstrong woman and her equallly stubborn suitor. Franco Zeffirelli directed. **CL1, CL15, CL33** *Recommended*

Tampopo (1987, C, 114m, NR)
Japanese comedy centering on a widow's attempts to open her own noodle restaurant, with a gruff truck driver coming to her rescue. Numerous subplots and sight gags revolve around the subject of food. Directed by Juzo Itami. **FF4** *Recommended*

Tank (1984, C, 113m, PG)
A teenager is arrested on trumped-up charges by a bigoted sheriff and his father decides to use a surplus tank to free him. James Garner and Shirley Jones star. **DR8**

Tanner '88 (1988, C, 120m, NR)
Witty look at contemporary politics, with fictional Presidential candidate slogging through primaries, dealing with ever-present media. Michael Murphy and Pamela Reed star. Written by Garry Trudeau; directed by Robert Altman. Originally a series made for cable TV. **CO2** *Recommended*

Tap (1989, C, 110m, PG-13)
Just out of jail, an ex-dancer is torn between continuing his life of crime and returning to his love of the stage. Gregory Hines stars, with Sammy Davis, Jr. and a host of exponents of old-time tap dancing. **DR12, MU3**

Tapeheads (1988, C, 93m, R)
Comedy about a pair of clumsy but with-it guys (Tim Robbins, John Cusack) trying to make it big in the rock music video biz. With Mary Crosby, Doug McClure, Connie Stevens, and real-life rockers Sam Moore and Junior Walker as a singing duo called The Swanky Modes. **CO8, MU9** *Recommended*

Taps (1981, C, 118m, R)
Timothy Hutton and George C. Scott star in this drama about a rebellious military school student and his commanding officer. Tom Cruise and Sean Penn costar. **DR9**

Target (1985, C, 117m, R)
When a businessman's wife is kidnapped on a trip to Europe, he's forced to admit to his son his association with the CIA. Gene Hackman and Matt Dillon star in this thriller. **DR39, MY6**

Targets (1968, C, 90m, PG)
Twin stories, which eventually intersect, about an aging horror film star (Boris Karloff) about to retire and a mad sniper. Peter Bogdanvich directed and costars. **DR13, HO27, MY17**

Tarzan, the Ape Man (1932, B&W, 98m, G)
Johnny Weissmuller's debut as the jungle hero. Maureen O'Sullivan costars. **AC13, FA4**

Taxi Driver (1976, C, 113m, R)
Riveting drama of a paranoid New York cab driver getting involved with a 12-year-old prostitute, whom he tries to "save" from the evils of the streets. Robert DeNiro, Cybill Shepherd, and Jodie Foster star; Martin Scorsese directed. Violent finale nearly got the film an "X" rating. **CU7, DR15, DR25, DR52, MY2, XT9** *Highly Recommended*

Taxing Woman, A (1988, C, 127m, NR)
Japanese comedy of a female tax collector who has to battle the prejudices of her male colleagues and the deceit of taxpayers. Directed by Juzo Itami. **FF4**

Teachers (1984, C, 106m, R)
Life at a big-city high school, where the students don't care and most of the teachers are just collecting a paycheck. Nick Nolte, JoBeth Williams, Ralph Macchio, and Richard Mulligan star. **DR44**

Teacher's Pet (1958, B&W, 120m, NR)
The editor of a newspaper (Clark Gable) enrolls in a night school class in journalism to make time with the teacher (Doris Day). Gig Young costars. **CL23**

Teddy Ruxpin: Teddy Outsmarts M.A.V.O. (1987, C, 75m, NR)
Animated adventure of Teddy and his friends pursued by the villainous members of M.A.V.O., who want a special crystal Teddy is carrying. **FA10**

Teen Wolf (1985, C, 91m, PG)
A teenager (Michael J. Fox) discovers he is descended from a family of werewolves and becomes popular at school when his classmates find out. **CO4, CO11, HO4**

Telefon (1977, C, 102m, PG)
Charles Bronson plays a Russian agent teaming up with the CIA to prevent an unhinged Soviet spy from unleashing a lethal army of hypnotized bombers. Lee Remick costars; Don Siegel directed. **AC29, MY6**

Tell Them Willy Boy Is Here (1969, C, 96m, G)
Robert Blake plays an Indian who kills a man in self-defense and is pursued by a large posse to his death. Based on a true story. Robert Redford stars as the sheriff out to get his man. **DR29, WE4, WE8, WE12**

10 (1979, C, 122m, R)
Comedy about middle-aged man who can't decide between marriage to his charming but predictable girlfriend and a wild fling with woman of his dreams. Dudley Moore, Julie Andrews, and Bo Derek star; Blake Edwards directed. **CO1, CO31, CO46**

Ten Commandments, The (1923, B&W, 146m, NR)
Cecil B. DeMille's silent classic, combining a modern tale of sin and redemption with the the story of Moses and the famous tablets. Theodore Roberts, Richard Dix, and Rod La Rocque star. **CL12, CL13**

Ten Commandments, The (1956, C, 220m, G)
Biblical epic about the life of Moses, from birth to his leading the Jews out of Egypt. All-star cast includes Charlton Heston, Yul Brynner, Anne Baxter, Debra Paget, Edward G. Robinson, and Vincent Price. Directed by Cecil B. DeMille; his last film. **CL9, CL13, CL52, HO31** *Highly Recommended*

Ten Days That Shook the World/October (1927, B&W, 104m, NR)
From director Sergei Eisenstein, a documentary of the events surrounding the 1917 Russian Revolution. **CU9, CU16, FF22**

Ten From Your Show of Shows (1973, B&W, 92m, NR)
Classic bits from the legendary TV show of the early 1950s, starring Sid Caesar, Imogene Coca, Carl Reiner, and Howard Morris. Sketch comedy at its absolute best. **CO16** *Highly Recommended*

Ten Little Indians (1975, C, 98m, PG)
Latest version of Agatha Christie's classic whodunit, with setting switched to a hotel in Iranian desert. Oliver Reed, Elke Sommer, and Herbert Lom head the list of victims/suspects. **MY16, MY23**

10 Rillington Place (1971, C, 111m, PG)
True story of the infamous John Christie murders in Britain, and how the real killer's testimony helped send the wrong man to the gallows. Richard Attenbor-

ough and John Hurt star. **DR6, DR16, MY7, MY8, MY19**

Ten to Midnight (1983, C, 100m, R)
Charles Bronson stars as a police detective tracking a psycho killer who has made the big mistake of harassing Bronson's daughter. **AC29, MY17**

Ten Wanted Men (1955, C, 80m, NR)
Randolph Scott western, with Richard Boone as a rival rancher who resorts to intimidation to get his way. **WE22**

Ten Who Dared (1960, C, 92m, NR)
Disney adventure, based on the exploits of Major John Wesley Powell (Brian Keith), who explored the uncharted Colorado River in 1869. With Ben Johnson, R.G. Armstrong, and L.Q. Jones. **FA1**

Tenant, The (1976, C, 125m, R)
Disturbed man moves into the Parisian apartment of a suicide victim, begins to assume her identity. Roman Polanski directed and stars in this psychological drama, with Isabelle Adjani, Shelley Winters, and Melvyn Douglas in the supporting cast. **DR54** *Recommended*

Tender Mercies (1983, C, 93m, PG)
A down-and-out country singer finds redemption in the love of a farm widow and her son. Oscar winner Robert Duvall stars; Tess Harper, Ellen Barkin, and Betty Buckley play the women in his life. **DR1, DR2, DR12, DR37, XT2**

Tentacles (1977, C, 90m, PG)
A giant octopus terrorizes a seaside community. Henry Fonda and Bo Hopkins star. **CL24**

Tenth Anniversay Young Comedians Special *see* HBO Comedy Club

Tenth Victim, The (1965, B&W, 92m, NR)
In a future society, killing humans is legal, with organized hunting. A science fiction spoof from Italy, starring Marcello Mastroianni and Ursula Andress. **FF2, FF24, SF21**

Tequila Sunrise (1988, C, 116m, R)
Romantic triangle involving an ex-drug dealer, a narcotics cop (who is also the ex-dealer's best friend), and the lovely owner of a posh Italian restaurant. Mel Gibson, Kurt Russell, and Michelle Pfeiffer star. Written and directed by Robert Towne. **DR1, DR69, MY2** *Recommended*

Terminal Choice (1985, C, 97m, R)
A series of mysterious deaths at a computerized hospital is the basis for this horror film. Joe Spano stars. **HO20**

Terminal Man, The (1973, C, 104m, PG)
A mini-computer is created to help control a person's psychopathic tendencies. When the computer is implanted in the brain of a test subject, it fails and turns him homicidal. George Segal stars. **SF4**

Terminator, The (1984, C, 108m, R)
A cyborg assassin from the year 2029 is sent to 1984 to kill the woman who will give birth to his opposition's leader. Arnold Schwarzenegger, Michael Biehn, and Linda Hamilton star; James Cameron directed. **AC25, AC30** *Recommended*

Terms of Endearment (1983, C, 132m, PG)
Shirley MacLaine and Debra Winger play a mother and daughter whose relationship virtually defines the phrase "love-hate" in this Oscar-winning drama. MacLaine and Jack Nicholson, writer-director James L. Brooks also won Oscars. **DR2, DR8, DR24, DR42, DR47, XT1, XT3, XT4, XT6** *Highly Recommended*

Terror, The (1963, C, 81m, NR)
A soldier in Napoleon's army (Jack Nicholson) follows a mysterious woman (Sandra Knight) to a castle owned by a sinister man (Boris Karloff). Directed by Roger Corman; footage from this film appears in *Targets*. **DR24, HO27**

Terror at Red Wolf Inn (1972, C, 90m, NR)
A student on vacation stays at an inn run by two very nice old people who have a retarded grandson. When several guests

disappear, she discovers that the proprietors are cannibals. **HO24**

Terror by Night (1946, B&W, 60m, NR)
Sherlock Holmes mystery starring Basil Rathbone and Nigel Bruce, set aboard a train, concerning a famous jewel and murders. **MY10**

Terror in the Wax Museum (1973, C, 93m, PG)
A girl inherits a wax museum where a grisly murder took place. When she moves into the apartment above the museum, she is terrorized by the wax figures of famous criminals. Ray Milland and Elsa Lanchester star. **HO26**

Terror of Mechagodzilla (1978, C, 79m, NR)
Aliens who want to invade Japan create a robot Godzilla monster to battle the real Godzilla, now the protector of Japan. **FF4, SF18**

Terror of Tiny Town, The (1938, B&W, 63m, NR)
A one-of-a-kind western drama, with an all-midget cast! This one has to be seen to be believed. **CU11, WE16**

Terror Train (1980, C, 97m, R)
A fraternity party aboard a train is plagued by a mad killer. Jamie Lee Curtis, Hart Bochner, Ben Johnson, and David Copperfield star. **HO12**

Terrorists, the (1975, C, 97m, PG)
Sean Connery plays a hostage negotiator in this thriller about an airline hijacking. **AC36**

Terrorvision (1986, C, 85m, R)
An alien emerges from a family's television set and wreaks havoc. **SF20**

Terry Fox Story, The (1983, C, 97m, NR)
True, heartfelt tale of a young Canadian runner who loses a leg to cancer and undertakes a cross-country run to raise funds to research his disease. Real-life amputee Eric Fryer stars, with Robert

Duvall. Originally made for cable TV. **DR6, DR37**

Tess (1979, C, 170m, PG)
Literate adaptation of the Thomas Hardy novel of a young girl twice wronged in love. Roman Polanski directed; Nastassia Kinski stars. **DR19, DR54** *Recommended*

Testament (1983, C, 89m, PG)
Jane Alexander tries to hold her family together after a nuclear attack, as they wait for the radiation approaching their small town. **DR7, DR10, SF12**

Testament of Dr. Mabuse, The (1933, B&W, 120m, NR)
A criminal kingpin controls his operations even while he's locked up in an insane asylum. Classic crime drama, with touches of the supernatural, from German director Fritz Lang. **CL43, FF3, SF2**

Tex (1982, C, 103m, PG)
Well-meaning but mischievous teenager (Matt Dillon) is raised by his older brother after their mother dies and father deserts them. Based on S.E. Hinton's novel. **DR9**

Texas (1941, B&W, 93m, NR)
William Holden and Glenn Ford plays pals competing for the same woman (Claire Trevor) in this western drama. **CL51**

Texas Chainsaw Massacre, The (1974, C, 83m, R)
A group of teenagers stumble onto a family of cannibals. Cult horror directed by Tobe Hooper. **CU1, CU4, CU7, HO12, HO40**

Texas Chainsaw Massacre II, The (1986, C, 95m, NR)
An ex-lawman (Dennis Hopper) swears revenge on the cannibal family who use human meat in their prize-winning chili. This sequel to *The Texas Chainsaw Massacre* was also directed by Tobe Hooper. **CU46, HO40**

Texas Lady (1955, C, 86m, NR)
Claudette Colbert stars in this low-key western about a newspaper editor battling injustice on the frontier. **WE9**

Texas Legionnaires (1943, B&W, 54m, NR)
Roy Rogers battles Axis spies in this western with a contemporary setting. **WE23**

Thank God, It's Friday (1978, C, 90m, PG)
Musical comedy centering on characters who hang out at a disco, starring Donna Summer and The Commodores, and featuring early screen appearances by Debra Winger and Jeff Goldblum. **DR47**

Thank Your Lucky Stars (1943, B&W, 127m, NR)
Eddie Cantor puts on a show to support the war effort and has many of Warner Bros.' dramatic stars doing musical and comedy sketches. Highlights include Bette Davis singing "They're Either Too Young or Too Old". Other appearances include Humphrey Bogart, Errol Flynn, and Olivia De Havilland. **AC34, CL20, CL21, MU15**

That Cold Day in the Park (1969, C, 113m, R)
Suspense drama about a spinster who takes in a young man and holds him prisoner. Sandy Dennis and Michael Burns star; Robert Altman directed. **CU25**

That Darn Cat (1965, C, 116m, G)
A pet cat leads the FBI to a gang of kidnappers. Hayley Mills and Dean Jones star in this Disney comedy. **FA1**

That Hamilton Woman (1941, B&W, 128m, NR)
Classic love story, based on historical events, of affair between Lord Nelson and Lady Hamilton. Laurence Olivier and Vivien Leigh costar; directed by Alexander Korda. **CL3, CL5, CL32**

That Obscure Object of Desire (1977, C, 103m, R)
A wealthy man with unconventional sexual ideas falls in love with a maid who accommodatingly teases him. Fernando Rey stars; Carole Bouquet and Angela Molina play the maid. Last film from director Luis Buñuel. **FF11**

That Sinking Feeling (1979, C, 92m, PG)
Comedy set in Glasgow, Scotland about a group of bored youths who turn to stealing sinks to pass the time. Directed by Bill Forsyth. **CO17, CU36**

That Touch of Mink (1962, C, 99m, NR)
Doris Day-Cary Grant romantic fluff about a playboy pursuing a determined woman of virtue. John Astin costars. **CL18, CO1**

That Uncertain Feeling (1941, B&W, 84m, NR)
Romantic comedy from director Ernst Lubitsch about a married couple (Merle Oberon, Melvyn Douglas) and their zany musician friend (Burgess Meredith). **CL54**

That Was Rock (1984, B&W, 92m, NR)
A compilation of rock and R&B performances from two films, *The TAMI Show* (1964) and *The TNT Show* (1966). Performers include Chuck Berry, James Brown, The Supremes, The Rolling Stones, and many more. Also known as *Born to Rock*. **MU10**

That Was Then, This Is Now (1985, C, 102m, R)
Drama about relationship between stepbrothers, one of whom is jealous of his brother's new girl friend. Emilio Estevez stars; he also wrote the screenplay, based on an S.E. Hinton novel. **DR9**

That'll Be the Day (1974, C, 90m, PG)
A British working class youth in the 1950s decides to become a rock star. David Essex stars, with Ringo Starr and Keith Moon. **MU4, MU9**

That's Dancing (1985, C/B&W, 105m, G)
A compilation of 50 years of dance numbers from MGM musicals, including a Ray Bolger/Scarecrow dance number that was cut from the final version of *The Wizard of Oz*. Fred Astaire, John Travolta, Gene Kelly, Liza Minnelli, and Sammy Davis, Jr. host. **MU1, MU3, MU15, MU18, MU19**

That's Entertainment (1974, C, 132m, G)
To mark its 50th anniversary, MGM produced this compilation of scenes from 100 of their musicals. **MU1, MU15, MU18, MU19, MU25, MU26** *Recommended*

That's Entertainment II (1976, C, 126m, G)
A sequel to *That's Entertainment*, this time including scenes from non-musical films as well as more classic MGM numbers. **MU1, MU15, MU18, MU19, MU25, MU26**

That's Life! (1986, C, 102m, R)
Jack Lemmon and Julie Andrews play a middle-aged couple preoccupied with their individual problems, less considerate of each other and their children. Drama from director Blake Edwards. Members of Lemmon's, Andrews', and Edwards' families play small roles. **CO46, DR8, DR64**

Theatre of Blood (1973, C, 104m, R)
A Shakespearean actor begins to kill off all his critics with methods from various Shakespeare plays. Vincent Price at his campy best. Diana Rigg costars. **CU4, HO24, HO26, HO31**

Theatre of Death (1967, C, 90m, NR)
The deaths on a Grand Guignol stage are no longer fake. Christopher Lee stars. **HO32**

Them! (1954, B&W, 93m, NR)
Classic 1950s science fiction thriller about giant ants, mutated by radiation. James Whitmore and James Arness star. **CU4, SF1, SF10, SF16** *Recommended*

There Was a Crooked Man (1970, C, 123m, R)
In the Old West, convict Kirk Douglas breaks out of prison and is pursued by greedy warden Henry Fonda to a cache of stolen money. With John Randolph, Hume Cronyn, and Warren Oates. Written by Robert Benton and David Newman; directed by Joseph L. Mankiewicz. **CL24, CL55, CU48, DR18, WE4, WE15, WE16** *Recommended*

There's a Girl in My Soup (1970, C, 95m, R)
Middle-aged businessman falls for flower child in this comedy starring Peter Sellers and Goldie Hawn. **CO26, CO30**

There's No Business Like Show Business (1954, C, 117m, NR)
A husband and wife vaudeville team return to the stage with their three children now in the act. Ethel Merman and Marilyn Monroe star. **CL29, MU4**

Thérèse (1987, C, 96m, NR)
True-life drama from French director Alain Cavalier about Thérèse Martin, a young nun whose devotion and patient suffering resulted in sainthood. **FF1**

These Three (1936, B&W, 92m NR)
Two teachers and a doctor have their professional and personal reputations ruined by the malicious stories of a spoiled little girl. Miriam Hopkins, Merle Oberon, Joel McCrea, and Bonita Granville star. Based on Lillian Hellman's play, *The Children's Hour;* directed by William Wyler. **CL38**

They All Laughed (1981, C, 115m, PG)
Amiable comedy about three New York private eyes and their various love lives. Ben Gazzara, John Ritter, and Blaine Novak are the gumshoes; Audrey Hepburn, Dorothy Stratten, Collen Camp, and Patti Hansen costar. Directed by Peter Bogdanovich. **CL30, CO10, XT9** *Recommended*

They Call Me MISTER Tibbs! (1970, C, 108m, PG)
Sidney Poitier plays his *In the Heat of the Night* character, Virgil Tibbs, in this

crime drama set in San Francisco. Barbara McNair and Martin Landau costar. **DR38**

They Call Me Trinity (1971, C, 109m, PG)
In this western spoof, Terence Hill and Bud Spencer play cowboys who agree to protect settlers from a band of Mexican marauders. **WE14, WE15**

They Came From Within (1975, C, 87m, R)
David Cronenberg directed this horrific tale of parasites who take over the residents of a high-rise apartment building. **HO39**

They Came to Cordura (1959, B&W, 123m, NR)
Gary Cooper stars in this western set in 1916 Mexico, about an officer accused of cowardice and determined to regain his pride. **WE10, WE25**

They Died With Their Boots On (1941, B&W, 138m, NR)
The story of George Armstrong Custer and his infamous Last Stand, with Errol Flynn as the notorious general. Olivia de Havilland costars. **AC24, WE2, WE5**

They Drive by Night (1940, B&W, 93m, NR)
A pair of brothers battle the crooked bosses running the trucking industry. Humphrey Bogart, George Raft, and Ann Sheridan star. **CL8, CL20**

They Got Me Covered (1943, B&W, 95m, NR)
Wartime spy comedy set in Washington, D.C., starring Bob Hope, Dorothy Lamour, and Otto Preminger. **CO40**

They Knew What They Wanted (1940, B&W, 96m, NR)
Romance by correspondence, as an Italian grape grower (Charles Laughton) falls in love with a lonely waitress (Carole Lombard). Garson Kanin directed. **CL48**

They Live (1988, C, 95m, R)
Aliens are taking over Earth, cleverly disguised and only detected through specially-made sunglasses. Roddy Piper stars; John Carpenter directed this low-budget science fiction drama. **CU29, SF9**

They Live by Night (1949, B&W, 95m, NR)
Depression-era tale of young lovers turned outlaws, starring Farley Granger and Cathy O'Donnell. Cult favorite, directed by Nicholas Ray. **CU23, MY1**

They Made Me a Criminal (1939, B&W, 92m, NR)
John Garfield stars in this thriller about a man on the run from the law for a crime he didn't commit. Claude Rains, May Robson, and the Dead End Kids costar. Directed by Busby Berkeley. **MU20, MY7**

They Might Be Giants (1971, C, 98m, PG)
Gentle comedy of a man who believes he's Sherlock Holmes and his female shrink, named Dr. Watson. George C. Scott and Joanne Woodward star. **DR67**

They Saved Hitler's Brain (1963, B&W, 74m, NR)
Classic "bad" movie about Nazi cult controlled by Der Fuehrer's still-living head. **CU11**

They Shoot Horses, Don't They? (1969, C, 121m, PG)
Grim drama centering on Depression marathon dance contest. Jane Fonda stars, with Michael Sarrazin, Susannah York, Red Buttons, Bruce Dern, Bonnie Bedelia, and Oscar winner Gig Young. Adapted from Horace McCoy's cult novel; directed by Sydney Pollack. **DR27, DR56, XT4** *Recommended*

They Went That-A-Way and That-A-Way (1978, C, 95m, PG)
Two amateur comedians, whose specialty is doing Laurel and Hardy impersonations, escape from prison. Tim Conway and Chuck McCann star. **FA6**

They Were Expendable (1945, B&W, 135m, NR)
American PT boats in the Pacific engage Japanese cruisers in battle. John Wayne and Robert Montgomery star. Directed by John Ford. **AC1, CL17, CL34**

They Who Step on the Tiger's Tail *see* Men Who Tread on the Tiger's Tail, The

They Won't Believe Me (1947, B&W, 79m, NR)
Robert Young plays a married man whose affairs lead only to tragedy in this thriller. Susan Hayward, Jane Greer, and Rita Johnson costar. **MY1, MY7**

They're Playing With Fire (1984, C, 96m, R)
A sexy teacher and her naive student lover plot a murder in this thriller starring Eric Brown and Sybil Danning. **NY5**

Thief (1981, C, 123m, R)
Drama about the world of a professional thief, starring James Caan and Tuesday Weld, with Robert Prosky and Willie Nelson. Directed by Michael Mann; music by Tangerine Dream. **AC8, MU12**

Thief of Bagdad, The (1924, B&W, 132m, NR)
A silent film version of the Arabian Nights tale of a professional thief who saves the Princess of Bagdad from an evil Mongol prince. Douglas Fairbanks stars. **AC13, CL12**

Thief of Bagdad, The (1940, C, 106m, NR)
Colorful fantasy from the Arabian Nights with a plucky native boy and a prince dueling a wicked sorcerer. Oscar winner for photography and special effects. Sabu, John Justin, and Conrad Veidt star; co-directed by Michael Powell. **AC13, CL9, CU19, FA4, FA8**

Thief of Hearts (1984, C, 100m, NR)
A burglar's haul includes a married woman's diary, which contains her secret sexual fantasies. The thief conspires to meet the woman and a romance soon develops. Steven Bauer and Barbara Williams star.

Some additional scenes were added for the home video version. **CU6, CU10, MY5**

Thief Who Came to Dinner, The (1973, C, 105m, PG)
Computer programmer turns to life of crime as a jewel thief in this comedy starring Ryan O'Neal, Jacqueline Bisset, Warren Oates, Jill Clayburgh, and Ned Beatty. **CO10, CU48**

Thin Blue Line, The (1988, C, 106m, NR)
Mesmerizing documentary study of a 1976 Dallas, Texas, murder case, for which the wrong man (Randall Dale Adams) was convicted and nearly executed. This film helped to reopen the case and eventually set Adams free. Directed by Erol Morris; music score by Philip Glass. **CU16, CU51, MY8** *Highly Recommended*

Thin Man, The (1935, B&W, 90m, NR)
First in the series of films about high society detectives Nick and Nora Charles, created by Dashiell Hammett. William Powell and Myrna Loy mix martinis and murder in a uniquely sophisticated kind of mystery. (For other series titles, see MY13.) **CL10, CL15, CL46, MY13, MY21, MY28** *Highly Recommended*

Thin Man Goes Home, The (1944, B&W, 100m, NR)
Fourth in the Nick and Nora Charles series has the high society duo returning to Nick's hometown with baby Nick, Jr. and solving a murder case. William Powell and Myrna Loy star. **CL15, CL46, MY13, MY21, MY28**

Thing, The (1982, C, 108m, R)
A group of researchers in the Antartic are terrorized by an alien creature who can transform itself into any living organism. Kirk Russell stars in this explicitly gory remake of the 1951 classic. John Carpenter directed. **CU18, CU29, HO17, SF9, SF20**

Thing (From Another World), The (1951, B&W, 86m, NR)
A U.S. outpost at the North Pole finds a crashed spaceship and manage to save its pilot. The alien is made of vegetable matter, feeds on blood, and intends to destroy the humans. Kenneth Tobey and James Arness (as the alien) star. **CU4, SF1, SF9** *Recommended*

Things Are Tough All Over (1982, C, 92m, R)
Cheech and Chong comedy, with the boys driving around around in a car with $5 million hidden in it. C&C also play two Arab brothers. **CO32**

Things Change (1988, C, 105m, PG)
Comic tale of an elderly shoemaker (Dom Ameche) persuaded to serve a short jail term for a crime boss he resembles. He and his "guard," a Mob flunky (Joe Mategna), take off for one last fling in Lake Tahoe. David Mamet directed; he and Shel Silverstein wrote the screenplay. **CO10, CO37** *Recommended*

Things To Come (1936, B&W, 91m, NR)
H.G. Wells wrote this science fiction drama about a war which nearly destroys the world and how the survivors try to construct a utopian society. Raymond Massey, Ralph Richardson, and Cedric Hardwicke star. **SF2, SF12, SF14, SF26**

Third Man, The (1949, B&W, 100m, NR)
Classic thriller set in postwar Vienna, with good guy Joseph Cotten finding out his old friend Harry Lime (Orson Welles) is working for the bad guys. Trevor Howard costars; Carol Reed directed. **CL41, MY6** *Highly Recommended*

Third Man on the Mountain (1959, C, 105m, NR)
A young man (James MacArthur) learns about life while attempting to climb the Matterhorn. Drama from the Disney studios. **FA1**

13 Ghosts (1960, B&W, 88m, NR)
A family inherits a haunted house and must solve several mysterious deaths in order to free the spirits. **HO2, HO3, HO19**

13 Rue Madeleine (1946, B&W, 95m, NR)
An Allied agent tries to locate a German missile site in World War II France. James Cagney stars. **CL22**

30 Is a Dangerous Age, Cynthia (1968, C, 98m, NR)
Dudley Moore plays a young man whose approaching 30th birthday is driving him loony with anxiety. Moore also co-wrote the screenplay and composed the music. **CO31**

39 Steps, The (1935, B&W, 87m, NR)
One of Alfred Hitchcock's best: innocent man Robert Donat becomes enmeshed in elaborate mystery involving spies and saboteurs. Madeleine Carroll is the woman he's handcuffed to. Many classic moments, including finale with "Mr. Memory." **MY6, MY7, MY19, MY22** *Highly Recommended*

39 Steps, The (1978, C, 102m, PG)
Remake of the Alfred Hitchcock classic, starring Robert Powell, David Warner, and Karen Dotrice. **CU18, MY6, MY7**

Thirty Seconds Over Tokyo (1944, B&W, 138m, NR)
Drama of America's first air raid on Japan during World War II. Spencer Tracy and Van Johnson star. **AC1, CL19**

This Gun for Hire (1942, B&W, 80m, NR)
Alan Ladd's first starring role, as a ruthless gunman, with Veronica Lake a lovely distraction. **MY1**

This Happy Feeling (1958, C, 92m, NR)
Debbie Reynolds plays a woman smitten by a vain actor (Curt Jurgens) and courted by an earnest young man (John Saxon). Comedy from director Blake Edwards. **CO46**

This Is Elvis (1981, C/B&W, 144m, PG)
A biography of The King combining documentary footage with recreated scenes from his life. Video version adds nearly 45 minutes of footage to theatrical release. **CU10, MU5, MU11** *Recommended*

This Is Korea/December 7th (1951/1943, C/B&W, 85m, NR)
John Ford directed these two propaganda documentaries for the Navy. *This Is Korea* praises the U.S. military effort in that conflict. *December 7th* recreates the bombing of Pearl Harbor and won an Academy Award for Best Documentary. **CL34, CU16**

This Is Spinal Tap (1984, C, 82m, R)
A British heavy metal group that's beginning to show some signs of rust tours America. Christopher Guest, Michael McKean, and Harry Shearer star in this hilarious parody of rock documentaries, directed by Rob Reiner. **CO7, MU11** *Recommended*

This Island Earth (1954, C, 86m, NR)
Inhabitants from Metaluna come to Earth hoping our scientists can help them find a new energy source before their home is destroyed. Jeff Morrow and Rex Reason star. **SF1, SF3, SF9**

This Land Is Mine (1943, B&W, 103m, NR)
Charles Laughton stars as a French schoolteacher who rises to acts of heroism under Nazi Occupation. Directed by Jean Renoir. **FF12**

This Man Must Die (1970, C, 115m, PG)
A man's son is killed by a hit-and-run driver and he becomes obsessed with exacting his own justice. A French thriller from director Claude Chabrol. **FF1**

This Property Is Condemned (1966, C, 109m, NR)
Adaptation of the Tennessee Williams play about a young woman (Natalie Wood) falling for a drifter (Robert Redford) who is staying at her mother's boarding house. Charles Bronson costars;

Sydney Pollack directed. **AC29, DR29, DR56**

This Sporting Life (1963, B&W, 129m, NR)
Drama of British rugby player whose star rises and falls quickly. Richard Harris and Rachel Roberts star; Lindsay Anderson directed. **DR22, DR23** *Recommended*

Thomas Crown Affair, The (1968, C, 102m, R)
A bored millionaire playboy (Steve McQueen) plots the perfect bank robbery. An insurance investigator (Faye Dunaway) is on the case, but she falls in love with the playboy. **AC28, DR35, MY5, MY34**

Those Calloways (1965, C, 130m, NR)
An eccentric New England family wants to build a bird sanctuary on some land near a lake and must battle some shady developers who want the land as a hunting resort. Brian Keith and Vera Miles star in this Disney film. **FA1**

Those Lips, Those Eyes (1980, C, 107m, R)
A young man working behind the scenes at a summer theater in Cleveland during the 1950s learns about the theater and love from two of the company's performers. Thomas Hulce, Frank Langella, and Glynnis O'Connor star. **CO6, CO8**

Those Magnificent Men in Their Flying Machines (1965, C, 123m, NR)
The early days of aviation races are the subject for this knockabout comedy starring Stuart Whitman, Sarah Miles, and James Fox. **CO6**

Thousand Clowns, A (1965, B&W, 118m, NR)
A carefree nonconformist and sometime TV writer has his life turned upside down when social workers try to wrest his nephew from his custody. Jason Robards stars, with Barbara Harris, William Daniels, Barry Gordon, and Oscar winner Martin Balsam. Shot on location in New

York City. **CO5, XT4, XT9** *Recommended*

Thousands Cheer (1943, C, 126m, NR)
A commander's daughter (Kathryn Grayson) falls in love with a private (Gene Kelly) and they decide to put on an all-star show for the troops. Mickey Rooney and Judy Garland costar, with appearances by many MGM musical stars. **MU15, MU19, MU21**

Thrashin' (1986, C, 90m, PG-13)
Drama about competitive downhill skateboarding, with Josh Brolin as the young contender for the championship. **DR22**

Threads (1984, C, 110m, NR)
The devastating aftermath of a nuclear attack and its effects on the lives of working class people in Sheffield, England, are dramatized in this British equivalent of *The Day After*. **SF12, SF19**

Three Ages, The (1923, B&W, 59m, NR)
Buster Keaton comedy spoofing historical epics (and especially D. W. Griffith's *Intolerance*), with segments taking place in prehistoric times, ancient Rome, and modern times. **CL11, CO19**

Three Amigos (1986, C, 105m, PG)
A trio of out-of-work movie actors in 1920s Hollywood are summoned to a Mexican village, which mistakenly thinks they are real cowboys, for a rescue mission. Steve Martin, Chevy Chase, and Martin Short star. **CO3, CO13, CO14, CO33**

Three Brothers (1980, C, 113m, PG)
A trio of Italian brothers return to their village for their mother's funeral, sparking many memories. Philippe Noiret stars; directed by Francesco Rosi. **FF2**

Three Caballeros, The (1945, C, 70m, NR)
Disney trip to Latin America mixes animation and live action, with Donald Duck hosting. **FA2** *Recommended*

Three Days of the Condor (1975, C, 117m, R)
A CIA researcher in New York survives an assassination attack which decimates his entire office, goes on the lam with almost no help from Washington. Robert Redford and Faye Dunaway star; Sydney Pollack directed. **DR29, DR35, DR56, MY6, MY7**

Three Faces West (1940, B&W, 79m, NR)
Unusual John Wayne vehicle has The Duke leading a group of Austrian refugees to Oregon during World War II. **WE13, WE17**

Three Fugitives (1989, C, 96m, PG-13)
Nick Nolte plays an ex-con who's kidnapped by a loony bank robber (Martin Short) in this chase comedy. **CO10, CO14, DR44**

Three Little Pigs, The (1985, C, 60m, NR)
From the Faerie Tale Theatre series, a look at three pigs who each build their own home and the wolf who wants to have them for dinner. Billy Crystal, Jeff Goldblum, Valerie Perrine, and Stephen Furst star. **FA12**

Three Little Words (1950, C, 102m, NR)
A film biography about songwriters Bert Kalmar and Harry Ruby. Fred Astaire, Red Skelton, Vera-Ellen, and Arlene Dahl star. **MU1, MU5, MU18**

Three Lives of Thomasina, The (1964, C, 98m, NR)
A mysterious woman brings Thomasina, a cat owned by a veternarian's daughter, back from the dead. Patrick McGoohan stars in this Disney fantasy. **FA1**

Three Men and a Baby (1987, C, 95m, PG)
Tom Selleck, Ted Danson, and Steve Guttenberg star as three bachelor roommates with a baby on their hands. American remake of *Three Men and a Cradle*. **CO2, FF36**

Three Men and a Cradle (1985, C, 100m, PG-13)
French comedy about a trio of bachelors who find themselves caring for an infant whom one of them has fathered. U.S. remake: *Three Men and a Baby.* **FF1, FF36**

Three Musketeers, The (1948, C, 125m, NR)
The Dumas tale of a farm boy (Gene Kelly) who wants to be a musketeer and gets caught up in court intrigues. Lana Turner, June Allyson, Van Heflin, and Vincent Price costar. **HO31, MU19**

Three Musketeers, The (1974, C, 107m, PG)
Swashbuckling adventure, romance, and splastick are brilliantly mixed in this adaptation of the Dumas tale. Oliver Reed, Richard Chamberlain, Michael York, Faye Dunaway, Christopher Lee, and Raquel Welch star. Directed by Richard Lester; followed by sequel, *The Four Musketeers.* **AC15, CU35, DR35, HO32** *Highly Recommended*

Three Sovereigns for Sarah (1985, C, 180m, NR)
Saga of Salem witch trials, starring Vanessa Redgrave, Phyllis Thaxter, and Kim Hunter. Originally made for public TV. **DR5, DR65**

Three Strange Loves (1949, B&W, 84m, NR)
Early drama from director Ingmar Bergman examines the lives of a trio of ballerinas. **FF8**

3:10 to Yuma (1957, B&W, 92m, NR)
A farmer tries to hold an outlaw captive until a prison train arrives. Western suspense starring Glenn Ford and Van Heflin. Based on a novel by Elmore Leonard. **MY26, WE16**

Threepenny Opera, The (1931, B&W, 112m, NR)
Film version of the famous Kurt Weill-Bertolt Brecht musical play about a gangster and his cronies. Rudolph Forster and Lotte Lenya star. **FF3**

Throne of Blood (1957, B&W, 105m, NR)
Japanese version of *Macbeth,* starring Toshiro Mifune as the ambitious nobleman. Stunning direction by Akira Kurosawa. **FF9, FF28** *Highly Recommended*

Through a Glass Darkly (1962, B&W, 91m, NR)
Ingmar Bergman's study of a woman recently released from a mental hospital and her relationships with her husband, father, and brother. Harriet Andersson stars in this Oscar-winning film. **FF8, XT7**

Throw Momma From the Train (1987, C, 90m, PG-13)
Comedy teaming Billy Crystal as a writing teacher with a grudge against his wife and Danny DeVito as his student with a monster for a mother (Anne Ramsey). DeVito hits on a "murder swap" scheme after seeing Hitchcock's *Strangers on a Train.* **CO3, CO10, CO13**

Thumbelina (1983, C, 60m, NR)
From the Faerie Tale Theatre series, a tale about a beautiful and kind princess who is only the size of a human thumb. Carrie Fisher, William Katt, and Burgess Meredith star. **FA12**

Thunder Bay (1953, C, 102m, NR)
Louisiana shrimp fisherman and oil drillers battle over Gulf waters. James Stewart stars; Anthony Mann directed. **CL25, WE20**

Thunder in the City (1937, B&W, 86m, NR)
Edward G. Robinson plays a brash American promoter who takes London by storm with a newly discovered mineral. **CL52**

Thunder Road (1958, B&W, 92m, NR)
Hot-rodding action with a family of moonshiners (Robert and Jim Mitchum) outrunning the feds and gangsters. The elder Mitchum sings the title tune. **AC10, XT8**

Thunderball (1965, C, 129m, PG)
James Bond (Sean Connery) battles a villain who wants to destroy Miami in this underwater adventure. Claudine Auger and Adolfo Celi costar. **AC35, AC36**

Thunderbolt and Lightfoot (1974, C, 115m, R)
A professional thief (Clint Eastwood) takes on an apprentice (Jeff Bridges) and, together with the thief's old partners, set out to recover money from a previous heist. George Kennedy and Geoffrey Lewis costar. Directed by Michael Cimino. **AC9, AC27, DR71, MY34**

Ticket to Heaven (1981, C, 107m, PG)
Canadian drama of young man lulled into joining a cult and his subsequent deprogramming experience. Nick Mancuso, Saul Rubinek, and R.H. Thomson star. **DR9**

Tickle Me (1965, C, 90m, NR)
A rodeo star (Elvis Presley) gets a job at an all-girl dude ranch, goes on a gold hunt, and finds love. **MU22**

Tiger Bay (1959, B&W, 105m, NR)
Hayley Mills stars as a child who witnesses a murder and is kidnapped by the killer (Horst Bucholz) in this classic British thriller. **FA7, MY19**

Tiger Town (1983, C, 95m, NR)
Young boy idolizes Detroit Tiger ballplayer, tries to help him through a slump. Justin Henry and Roy Scheider star. Originally made for cable TV. **DR22, FA7**

Tight Little Island see Whisky Galore

Tightrope (1984, C, 114m, R)
A New Orleans cop (Clint Eastwood) is searching for a sex murderer and uncovers some nasty truths about himself. Genevieve Bujold and Alison Eastwood (Clint's real-life daughter) costar. **AC9, AC27, XT8, XT9**

Till the Clouds Roll By (1946, C, 137m, NR)
Robert Walker plays songwriter Jerome Kern in this biography that's really a series of musical numbers. Songs performed by a variety of MGM's stable of stars, including Frank Sinatra and Judy Garland. **MU1, MU5, MU21, MU26**

Till the End of Time (1946, B&W, 105m, NR)
A trio of World War II veterans find heartbreak and frustration back in the States. Guy Madison, Robert Mitchum, and Bill Williams star, with Dorothy McGuire. **CL8**

Tillie's Punctured Romance (1914, B&W, 73m, NR)
First feature-length comedy, starring Charlie Chaplin as a swindler, Marie Dressler as his victim. Mabel Normand costars; Mack Sennet directed this silent film. **CO18**

Tim (1979, C, 108m, PG)
Australian drama of the friendship between a slightly retarded man (Mel Gibson) and an older woman (Piper Laurie). Based on a novel by Colleen McCullough. **DR69, FF5**

Time After Time (1979, C, 112m, PG)
H. G. Wells (Malcolm McDowell) invents a time machine that Jack the Ripper (David Warner) uses in order to escape from the police. Wells follows him to modern-day San Francisco where, with the help of a bank teller (Mary Steenburgen), he tries to stop the Ripper from launching another killing spree. Adapted from elements in several H. G. Wells stories. **AC14, SF4, SF26** *Recommended*

Time Bandits (1981, C, 110m, PG)
Six dwarfs and a British schoolboy in possession of a time map travel through history in an effort to escape the map's evil owner. Written by Terry Gilliam and Michael Palin; directed by Gilliam. Sean Connery, John Cleese, Michael Palin, Shelley Duvall, Ralph Richardson, David

Warner, and Ian Holm star. **AC36, CO15, FA8, SF4** *Recommended*

Time for Dying, A (1971, C, 87m, PG)
Audie Murphy stars in his last film, a western drama from director Budd Boetticher. **WE28**

Time Machine, The (1960, C, 103m, G)
An inventor constructs a time machine and, after stopping at various intervals, ends up in the year 802701. Based on a story by H. G. Wells. George Pal produced and directed. An Oscar winner for special effects. **FA8, SF4, SF13, SF15, SF26**

Time of Destiny, A (1988, C, 118m, PG-13)
Old-fashioned melodrama of revenge, with William Hurt as a World War II soldier pursuing fellow G.I. Timothy Hutton, whom Hurt blames for his father's death. Written by Gregory Nava and Anna Thomas; Thomas produced and Nava directed. **DR31**

Time of Indifference (1964, B&W, 84m, NR)
Social drama of a poor Italian family's struggles during the 1920s. Rod Steiger, Shelley Winters, Claudia Cardinale, and Paulette Goddard star. **FF2**

Time of Their Lives, The (1946, B&W, 82m, NR)
Abbott and Costello comedy, with Lou and Marjorie Reynolds as ghosts from the 18th century who are haunting a home inhabited by Bud and his pals. **CO23**

Time of Your Life, The (1948, B&W, 109m, NR)
William Saroyan's play about the diverse characters who hang out at a waterfront saloon. James Cagney stars. **CL22**

Time Stands Still (1981, C/B&W, 99m, NR)
Drama set in Hungary in the early 1960s about a group of bored, rebellious, and angry young men who idolize American pop culture heroes like Elvis Presley. **FF7**

Time to Love and a Time to Die, A (1958, C, 132m, NR)
Drama about German soldier who must return to battle after brief romance. John Gavin stars; Klaus Kinski has a small role. Directed by Douglas Sirk. **CU24, FF30**

Time Warp *see* The Day Time Ended

Timerider (1983, C, 93m, PG)
A motocross rider is caught in a government experiment and gets sent back in time to 1877. Fred Ward stars. **SF4**

Times of Harvey Milk, The (1984, C, 87m, NR)
Documentary about San Francisco's first gay public official and his assassination. Oscar winner directed by Robert Epstein. **CU16** *Recommended*

Times Square (1980, C, 111m, R)
Two runaways in New York get a helping hand from a deejay (Tim Curry) who makes them stars. **MU9**

Tin Drum, The (1979, C, 142m, R)
Adapted from Günter Grass's bestselling novel, this German drama traces a boy's bizarre adventures during the years of the Third Reich. Oscar winner for Best Foreign Language Film. David Bennent stars; directed by Volker Schlöndorff. **DR19, FF3, XT7** *Recommended*

Tin Men (1987, C, 110m, R)
Comic feud between two Baltimore aluminum-siding salesmen in the early 1960s, starring Richard Dreyfuss and Danny DeVito. Barbara Hershey costars; Barry Levinson directed. **CO3, CO6**

Tin Star, The (1957, B&W, 93m, NR)
A tenderfoot sheriff calls on a veteran bounty hunter for help. Anthony Perkins and Henry Fonda star. Anthony Mann directed. **CL24, WE3, WE20**

To Be or Not to Be (1943, B&W, 99m, NR)
Bold comedy, considering when it was released, about troupe of Polish actors defying Nazis with elaborate plan to pro-

tect a downed flier. Jack Benny and Carole Lombard star; Ernst Lubitsch directed. **CL10, CL14, CL48, CL54, CU5, XT11** *Highly Recommended*

To Be or Not to Be (1983, C, 107m, PG)
Remake of the Lubitsch classic, with Mel Brooks and Anne Bancroft in the leads. **CO28, CU18**

To Catch a Thief (1955, C, 103m, NR)
Colorful Alfred Hitchcock thriller, set on the French Riviera, about a suave cat burglar (Cary Grant) and the woman he intends to victimize (Grace Kelly). **CL18, CL31, MY22**

To Have and Have Not (1944, B&W, 100m, NR)
First teaming of Humphrey Bogart and Lauren Bacall in this loose adaptation of the Hemingway story about the French Resistance. Directed by Howard Hawks; co-written by William Faulkner. **CL15, CL20, CL35, DR19, MY4**

To Hell and Back (1955, C, 106m, NR)
Audie Murphy, America's most decorated World War II veteran, plays himself in this film based on his autobiography. **AC1**

To Kill a Mockingbird (1962, B&W, 129m, NR)
Small-town Southern lawyer (Gregory Peck, an Oscar winner) defends an innocent black man accused of rape. Each night, he tries to explain the case to his young children. Brock Peters, Mary Badham, Philip Alford, and Robert Duvall costar. **DR17, DR37, DR62, XT2** *Recommended*

To Live and Die in L.A. (1985, C, 116m, R)
A counterfeiter kills a Secret Service agent and the agent's partner does everything he can to get revenge. William L. Petersen and Willem Dafoe star. Directed by William Friedkin. **AC9, MY2, XT9** *Recommended*

To Paris With Love (1955, C, 78m, NR)
Alec Guinness stars in this British comedy of a father taking his son to France for a liberal education. **DR63**

To Sir, With Love (1967, C, 105m, NR)
Sidney Poitier plays a new teacher in London's East End who earns the respect of his rowdy class and teaches them how to get along in the world. Pop singers Lulu and Michael Des Barres play two of his students. **DR38, DR61, MU12**

To the Devil A Daughter (1976, C, 95m, R)
A satanist (Christopher Lee) and his followers pursue a young woman (Natassia Kinski) to force her to mate with the Devil. Her only hope is an occult expert (Richard Widmark). **HO10, HO26, HO32**

To the Last Man (1933, B&W, 74m, NR)
A family feud in Kentucky spills over to the frontier West. Randolph Scott stars in this drama; Shirley Temple has a small role. **FA14, WE22**

Toast of New York, The (1937, B&W, 109m, NR)
Colorful tale of turn-of-the-century businessman Jim Fiske, played by Edward Arnold, with Cary Grant as his partner; Frances Farmer costars. **CL18**

Toby Tyler (1960, C, 96m, NR)
At the turn of the century, a young boy runs away from home and joins the circus. Kevin Corcoran stars in this Disney drama. **FA1**

Tokyo Joe (1949, B&W, 88m, NR)
Humphrey Bogart plays a World War II veteran in search of his ex-wife and her child in postwar Japan. Sessue Hayakawa costars as a villainous Secret Service agent. **CL20**

Tom Brown's School Days (1940, B&W, 86m, NR)
A look into life at a boys' school during the Victorian era. Cedric Hardwicke and Freddie Bartholomew star. **FA2**

Tom Horn (1980, C, 98m, R)
Steve McQueen plays the legendary Wyoming outlaw and bounty hunter who was framed by the men who hired him. **AC28, WE4, WE12**

Tom Jones (1963, C, 129m, NR)
Oscar-winning comedy about a young British rake lusting his way through the 18th century countryside. Albert Finney stars, with Hugh Griffith, Edith Evans, Susannah York, Joyce Redmond, Diane Cilento, and David Warner in support. Based on the Henry Fielding novel; directed by Tony Richardson. **CO17, XT1, XT6** *Recommended*

tom thumb (1958, C, 98m, NR)
Children's musical fantasy of a tiny lad (Russ Tamblyn) who's taken in by a kindly couple, then exploited by a pair of crooks (Terry-Thomas, Peter Sellers). Special effects won an Oscar. **CO26, FA8, SF15**

Tomb of Ligeia (1965, C, 81m, NR)
The Edgar Allan Poe tale about a man's dead wife who comes back to haunt him when he remarries. Vincent Price stars; Roger Corman directed. **HO31, HO41**

Tommy (1975, C, 111m, PG)
A film adaptation of The Who's rock opera about a deaf, dumb, and blind boy's adventures. Roger Daltrey and Ann-Margret star, with special appearances by Elton John, Tina Turner, and Jack Nicholson. Directed by Ken Russell. **CU31, DR24, MU8, MU9**

Tomorrow (1972, C, 103m, PG)
Adaptation of William Faulkner story of farmer who takes in abandoned pregnant woman and learns to love her. Robert Duvall stars; written by Horton Foote. **DR19, DR37**

Toni (1934, B&W, 90m, NR)
Early film from director Jean Renoir is a realistic drama set in a French village involving love, jealousy, and murder. **FF12**

Tonight and Every Night (1945, C, 92m, NR)
As their contribution to the war effort, the London's Music Box Revue never misses a performance, not even for an air raid or personal tragedy. Rita Hayworth stars in this musical. **MU4**

Tonight for Sure (1961, B&W, 66m, NR)
Two men recall their various sexual experiences in this "nudie" film directed by a young Francis Ford Coppola. **DR51**

Tonio Kroger (1965, B&W, 92m, NR)
German drama about a young writer's loves and struggles to find his indentity as a man and an artist. Based on a novel by Thomas Mann. **FF3**

Too Late the Hero (1970, C, 133m, PG)
Two soldiers are sent on a suicide mission in the South Pacific during World War II. Michael Caine, Cliff Robertson, and Henry Fonda star. **CL24**

Tootsie (1983, C, 116m, PG)
An actor, desperate for a job, dresses up in drag and lands a part on a soap opera, where he becomes an overnight sensation. Dustin Hoffman stars in this smashing modern comedy, with Oscar winner Jessica Lange and Bill Murray in support. Directed by Sydney Pollack, who also plays Hoffman's agent. **CO2, CO8, CO13, DR30, DR56, DR74, XT5** *Highly Recommended*

Top Gun (1986, C, 109m, PG)
A hotshot student pilot enrolls in a Naval flying school, where he must compete with other pilots as skilled as he is. Tom Cruise, Kelly McGillis, and Val Kilmer star. **AC11, DR73**

Top Hat (1935, B&W, 99m, NR)
Fred Astaire falls for a divorcee Ginger Rogers who hates most men, particularly him. Then she dances with him . . . . **CL15, MU18.** *Highly Recommended*

Top Secret! (1984, C, 90m, PG)
An American rock singer touring East Germany ends up helping the French Resistance battle some neo-Nazis. A spy

spoof by the makers of *Airplane!* Val Kilmer stars, with Omar Sharif and Peter Cushing. **CO7, HO33**

Topaz (1969, C, 126m, PG)
Alfred Hitchcock Cold War thriller, with American and French spies hunting down a deadly double agent. John Forsythe stars. **MY6, MY22**

Topkapi (1964, C, 120m, NR)
Elaborate heist story featuring an odd assortment of crooks assembled to steal a jeweled sword from a Turkish museum. Melina Mercouri and Maximilian Schell star, with Oscar winner Peter Ustinov as the gang's designated bumbler. **MY34, XT4** *Recommended*

Topper (1937, B&W, 97m, NR)
A put-upon businessman is haunted by two delightful ghosts in this comedy classic. Roland Young stars, with Cary Grant and Constance Bennett the playful spirits. **CL18**

Tora! Tora! Tora! (1970, C, 143m, G)
Dramatic recreation of the events that led up to the attack on Pearl Harbor, as seen from both the American and Japanese points of view. Oscar-winning special effects. Martin Balsam, Jason Robards, and E. G. Marshall star. **AC1**

Torch Song Trilogy (1988, C, 120m, R)
Harvey Fierstein stars in this adaptation of his play about a gay man whose mother (Anne Bancroft) won't accept his lifestyle. Matthew Broderick and Brian Kerwin costar. **DR3, DR20**

Torment (1985, C, 85m, R)
A mid-mannered man on the surface, he's a killer with a hair-trigger temper beneath. Taylor Gilbert stars in this suspense movie about a man who has even his wife and daughter intimidated by his bizarre behavior. **MY18**

Torn Curtain (1966, C, 128m, NR)
Alfred Hitchcock thriller about an American scientist pretending to be a defector in Berlin. Paul Newman and Julie Andrews star. **DR28, MY6, MY22**

Tornado (1983, C, 90m, NR)
American soldiers fighting in Vietnam are pushed to the limit by a sadistic sergeant. **AC4**

Torpedo Alley (1953, B&W, 84m, NR)
Drama of submarine action during the Korean War, starring Dorothy Malone, Mark Stevens, and Bill Williams. **AC3**

Torture Chamber of Dr. Sadism, The (1967, C, 90m, NR)
A mysterious man (Christopher Lee) lures a couple to his castle and takes his revenge by torturing them. Based on Edgar Allan Poe's "The Pit and the Pendulum." **HO32, HO41**

Torture Garden (1968, C, 93m, NR)
A carnival sideshow mystic offers customers a look into their futures. Jack Palance and Peter Cushing star. **HO23, HO33**

Touch and Go (1980, C, 92m, R)
A group of respectable ladies resort to burglary to save their local kindergarten. Wendy Hughes stars in this comedy from Australia. **FF5**

Touch and Go (1986, C, 101m, R)
Michael Keaton plays a hockey star whose self-centered attitude is challenged when he falls in love with the mother of a troubled boy who tried to rob him. Maria Conchita Alonso costars. **CO45**

Touch of Class, A (1973, C, 105m, PG)
Married man is determined to have a carefree affair, even if it nearly kills him. Romantic comedy starring George Segal and Oscar winner Glenda Jackson. **CO1, XT3**

Touch of Evil (1958, B&W, 108m, NR)
Stylized thriller from Orson Welles, with the director playing a crooked border cop at odds with a Mexican police detective (Charlton Heston) over a car bombing. Janet Leigh, Akim Tamiroff, Marlene Dietrich, Dennis Weaver, and Mercedes McCambridge costar. Video version restores 15 minutes cut from original release. **CL14, CL41, CL47, CU10, MY1** *Highly Recommended*

Tough Enough (1983, C, 106m, R)
An aspiring country singer (Dennis Quaid) turns to amateur boxing in Tough

Man competitions. With Carlene Watkins, Stan Shaw, Pam Grier, and Warren Oates. **CU48**

Tough Guys (1986, C, 103m, PG)
Two train robbers, released after 30 years in prison, try to adjust to life in the 1980s in this comedy pairing Burt Lancaster and Kirk Douglas. **CO3, CO10, CO37, DR11, DR41**

Tougher Than Leather (1988, C, 92m, R)
Urban action drama of murder and revenge, featuring the rap music group Run-DMC in dramatic roles, with some musical interludes. **AC8**

Tower of London (1962, B&W, 79m, NR)
Political skullduggery with Richard III (Vincent Price) out to eliminate his enemies. Remake of 1939 film, in which Basil Rathbone played Richard and Price had a supporting role. **HO31**

Towering Inferno, The (1974, C, 165m, PG)
An all-star disaster film about a fire that engulfs the world's largest skyscraper. Steve McQueen and Paul Newman star, with William Holden, Faye Dunaway, Fred Astaire, Richard Chamberlain, Susan Blakely, Jennifer Jones, and O. J. Simpson. **AC23, AC28, CL51, DR28, DR35, MU18**

Town Like Alice, A (1980, C, 301m, NR)
Epic drama, based on Nevil Shute novel, of couple meeting in a World War II POW camp and reunited later to face a different set of hardships in the Australian outback. Bryan Brown and Helen Morse star. Originally a TV miniseries. **DR5, FF5**

Toxic Avenger (1985, C, 100m, R)
A harassed nerd falls into a vat of nuclear waste and becomes a mutated superhero. A gory spoof of horror films. **HO21, HO24**

Toy, The (1982, C, 99m, PG)
Rich man's son who has everything insists on "owning" a man he sees in a toy store, and Dad obliges. Richard Pryor and Jackie Gleason star. **CO29**

Toy Soldiers (1984, C, 91m, R)
Two mercenaries (Cleavon Little and Jason Miller) rescue a group of students from a Central American country in the midst of a revolution. **AC20**

Track 29 (1988, C, 90m, R)
Bizarre drama from director Nicolas Roeg, starring Theresa Russell as a woman trapped in a loveless marriage, obsessed with the child she had to give up for adoption when she was raped as a teenager. Gary Oldman, Christopher Lloyd, and Sandra Bernhard costar. Written by Dennis Potter. **CU34**

Tracks (1977, C, 90m, R)
Dennis Hopper stars as a Vietnam veteran whose cross-country train ride with the body of a fallen comrade proves to be too much for his fragile state of mind. With Taryn Power, Dean Stockwell, Zack Norman, and Michael Emil. **CU46**

Trading Places (1983, C, 118m, R)
A pair of wealthy brothers make a bet and force a black street hustler and white stockbroker to switch positions. Eddie Murphy, Dan Aykroyd, Ralph Bellamy, and Don Ameche star in this comedy from director John Landis. **CO3, CO13, CO37** *Recommended*

Trail of Robin Hood (1950, B&W, 67m, NR)
Roy Rogers hooks up with a collection of famous western stars to aid cowboy actor Jack Holt in delivering Christmas trees to orphans. Rex Allen heads the supporting cast. **WE23**

Trail of the Pink Panther (1982, C, 87m, PG)
The very *last* Pink Panther movie, made after the death of Peter Sellers, has a reporter doing a story on Inspector Clouseau—an excuse to show footage from previous films. David Niven, Herbert Lom, and Burt Kwouk costar; directed by Blake Edwards. **CO26, CO46**

Train, The (1965, B&W, 113m, NR)
French Resistance fighters rush to waylay a Nazi train loaded with art treasures. Burt Lancaster and Jeanne Moreau star. **FF26**

Train Robbers, The (1973, C, 92m, PG)
John Wayne and buddies try to help out a lovely widow (Ann-Margret) in this western drama. **WE17**

Tramp, The/A Woman (1915, B&W, 57m, NR)
Two early shorts from Charlie Chaplin. The first is considered to be his first short masterpiece. In the second, he does a hilarious bit in drag. **CO18** *Recommended*

Trancers (1985, C, 85m, PG13)
In the year 2247 an evil cult leader wants to rule the world. His plan is to travel back to 1985 to alter the future to his advantage. It's up to Jack Deth (Tim Thomerson) to follow and destroy him. Helen Hunt costars. **SF17**

Transatlantic Tunnel (1935, B&W, 70m, NR)
The trials and tribulations of building a tunnel under the Atlantic Ocean. Spectacularly convincing sets. **SF14**

Transformers: The Movie (1986, C, 86m, PG)
A feature-length film starring the television/toy superheroes battling an evil planet (voice provided by Orson Welles). **CL41, FA10, SF13**

Transmutations (1985, C, 100m, R)
A doctor (Denholm Elliott) has created a drug that mutates its users. Originally titled *Underworld*. **HO21**

Transylvania 6-5000 (1985, C, 93m, PG)
Horror movie spoof, with Jeff Goldblum and Ed Begley, Jr. as reporters snooping around a mad doctor's laboratory in modern-day Transylvania. Joseph Bologna, Carol Kane, Geena Davis, and John Byner costar. **CO7**

Trapeze (1956, C, 105m, NR)
Romantic triangle among circus performers, starring Burt Lancaster, Gina Lollabrigida, and Tony Curtis. **DR41**

Trash (1970, C, 110m, NR)
From director Paul Morrissey and producer Andy Warhol, the story of Joe (Joe Dallessandro) and Holly (Holly Woodlawn) and their Lower East Side adventures in the world of drug addiction and trash-can rummaging. **CU12, CU44**

Traveling North (1988, C, 97m, PG-13)
Australian drama of a May-September romance between a retiree (Leo McKern) and a younger woman (Julia Blake). **FF5**

Treasure Island (1934, B&W, 102m, NR)
An adaptation of Robert Louis Stevenson's story about a young boy who travels with pirates in search of treasure. Wallace Beery and Jackie Cooper star. **AC13, FA3**

Treasure Island (1950, C, 96m, G)
A Disney version of the Robert Louis Stevenson tale about a young boy's adventures with pirates. Bobby Driscoll and Robert Newton star. **FA1**

Treasure of the Four Crowns (1983, C, 97m, PG)
A soldier of fortune is hired to recover an ancient treasure, the source of mystical powers. Tony Anthony stars. **AC21**

Treasure of the Sierra Madre, The (1948, B&W, 125m, NR)
Three men in search of gold in Mexico form an uneasy partnership. Humphrey Bogart, Walter Huston, and Tim Holt star in this classic version of B. Traven's novel. Directed by John Huston, who also appears in a small role. Both Hustons won Oscars. **AC12, AC13, AC24, CL20, CL44, XT4, XT6, XT8** *Highly Recommended*

Tree Grows in Brooklyn, A (1945, B&W, 128m, NR)
Warm drama of a young girl's coming of age in turn-of-the-century New York. Dorothy McGuire and Peggy Ann Garner

star, with Oscar winner James Dunn. Directed by Elia Kazan. **DR59, XT4**

Trial, The (1963, B&W, 118m, NR)
The Franz Kafka story of a man accused of a crime he doesn't know by people he can never see. Directed by and starring Orson Welles, with Anthony Perkins, Jeanne Moreau, and Romy Schneider. **CL41, FF26**

Tribute (1980, C, 121m, PG)
Drama of a man dying with cancer who tries for reunion with his long-estranged son. Jack Lemmon and Robby Benson star. **DR8, DR64**

Trigger, Jr. (1950, C, 68m, NR)
Roy Rogers and his famous horse help to teach a young boy not to be afraid of animals—with the help of Trigger's son. Dale Evans costars. **WE23**

Trilogy of Terror (1975, C, 78m, NR)
Karen Black plays four different characters in three suspenseful tales. The best story is the third, in which a tiny warrior doll comes to life and tries to kill her. **HO23**

Trinity Is STILL My Name! (1972, C, 117m, PG)
Sequel to *My Name Is Trinity* features more western spoofing by Terence Hill and Bud Spencer. **WE14, WE15**

Trio (1950, B&W, 91m, NR)
Sequel to *Quartet* offers three more W. Somerset Maugham stories, starring Harold French, James Hayter, Michael Rennie, and Jean Simmons. **DR19**

Trip, The (1967, C, 85m, NR)
A TV director decides to experiment with LSD, and the results are both beautiful and horrifying. Peter Fonda, Bruce Dern, and Susan Strasberg star, with Dennis Hopper. Roger Corman directed and Jack Nicholson wrote the screenplay. **CU3, CU46**

Trip to Bountiful, The (1985, C, 105m, PG)
Geraldine Page won an Oscar for her performance as a lonely widow who returns to her small Texas hometown to find that it's completely deserted. Written by Horton Foote; John Heard, Carlin Glynn, and Rebecca DeMornay costar. **DR10, XT3**

Triumph of Sherlock Holmes, The (1935, B&W, 75m, NR)
Arthur Wontner stars as the legendary detective in this screen version of Arthur Conan Doyle's "Valley of Fear" tale. **MY10**

Triumph of the Will (1935, B&W, 110m, PG-13)
Infamous documentary, filmed at Hitler's behest, dramatizes the Nazi appeal to German people at 1934 Nuremberg rally. Directed by Leni Riefenstahl. Chilling content, but a stunning historical document nonetheless. **CU16** *Recommended*

Triumphs of a Man Called Horse (1983, C, 86m, PG)
The third installment in the *Man Called Horse* trilogy has Richard Harris and his half-breed Indian son battling for Indian rights. **WE8**

Trojan Women, The (1972, C, 105m, PG)
Classic Greek tragedy of the effects of war on the women of Troy, starring Katharine Hepburn, Irene Papas, Genevieve Bujold, and Vanessa Redgrave. **CL16, DR65**

Troll (1986, C, 86m, PG13)
An evil troll possesses the body of a little girl and sets out to transform her apartment building into a troll kingdom. Shelley Hack, Michael Moriarty, and Sonny Bono star. **HO16**

Tron (1982, C, 96m, PG)
The designer of a vast computer system is pulled into the computer and forced into a videogame competition with the computerized beings who want to overthrow the program that controls their lives. Jeff Bridges and Bruce Boxleitner

star. Groundbreaking use of computer animation. **FA1, SF11, SF13, SF16**

Trouble In Mind (1985, C, 111m, R)
Kris Kristofferson plays an ex-cop just released from prison who gets caught up with a naive girl and her hustler boyfriend. Alan Rudolph directed; Keith Carradine, Lori Singer, Genevieve Bujold, and Divine costar. **CU26, DR1, MU12** *Recommended*

Trouble With Angels, The (1966, C, 112m, NR)
Two students at a convent school create havoc with the Mother Superior. Hayley Mills, June Harding, and Rosalind Russell star in this Disney comedy. **FA1**

Trouble With Girls, The (1969, C, 104m, G)
Elvis Presley musical set in the 1920s, with El in charge of a Chautauqua company, a traveling medicine and educational show. With Marilyn Mason, Sheree North, Vincent Price, and John Carradine. **HO31, MU22**

Trouble With Harry, The (1955, C, 99m, PG)
The good folks of a New England village aren't sure just what to do with a dead body found in the woods. John Forsythe and Shirley MacLaine (her debut) star in this darkly comic mystery from Alfred Hitchcock. **CL14, CO10, CO12, DR42, MY21, MY22, XT10**

True Believers (1989, C, 103m, R)
A lawyer who was an anti-war radical in the 1960s now defends drug dealers. He gets a chance for redemption when he defends a convict on a jail murder charge. The lawyer soon realizes his client has been framed as part of a large-scale political conspiracy. James Woods stars, with Robert Downey, Jr. and Kurtwood Smith. **MY2, MY15**

True Confessions (1981, C, 108m, R)
A pair of brothers, one a priest (Robert DeNiro), the other a police detective (Robert Duvall), become enmeshed in a murder case in 1940s Los Angeles. Written by John Gregory Dunne and Joan Didion, based on Dunne's novel. **DR16, DR25, DR37, MY2, MY18, XT9** *Recommended*

True Grit (1969, C, 128m, G)
John Wayne won his only Oscar for his portrayal of Rooster Cogburn, the one-eyed sheriff on the trail of a gang of desperadoes. Glen Campbell and Kim Darby costar, with Robert Duvall and Dennis Hopper. **CU46, DR37, MU12, WE3, WE17, XT2**

True Heart Susie (1919, B&W, 93m, NR)
A plain farm girl raises the money to send her true love to college, where he repays her by falling in love with a beautiful and cruel city woman. Lillian Gish stars. Directed by D. W. Griffith. **CL36, CL49**

True West (1986, C, 110m, NR)
Sam Shepard's play about two brothers, one a petty thief, the other a respectable screenwriter, starring John Malkovich and Gary Sinise. Powerful drama; originally shown on public TV. **DR20** *Recommended*

Truite, La (1982, C, 105m, R)
French country girl (Isabelle Huppert) becomes emeshed in the shady world of high finance in this contemporary drama from director Joseph Losey. **FF1**

Tuck Everlasting (1980, C, 110m, NR)
An adaptation of Natalie Babbitt's novel about a magical family who never age or die. **FA8**

Tucker: The Man and His Dream (1988, C, 111m, PG)
The true story of Preston Tucker, the automobile creator who challenged Detroit's Big Three carmakers with his revolutionary designs. Jeff Bridges stars, with Martin Landau, Joan Allen, Frederic Forrest, Mako, Dean Stockwell (as Howard Hughes), Christian Slater, and Lloyd Bridges. Directed by Francis Ford Coppola. **DR4, DR51, DR60, DR71, XT8** *Recommended*

Tunes of Glory (1960, C, 106m, NR)
British army drama about the conflict between crusty officer and his replacement. Alec Guinness and John Mills star, with Susannah York. **DR63**

Turk 182 (1984, C, 96m, PG-13)
A New York fireman is injured on the job but can't collect compensation, so his younger brother, a graffiti artist, decides to use his talent to dramatize the predicament. Timothy Hutton and Robert Urich star in this drama. **DR15, XT9**

Turn of the Screw (1974, C, 120m, NR)
A governess (Lynn Redgrave) tries to save her two charges from the ghosts of their former governess and her lover. Based on a story by Henry James. **DR19, HO2, HO19, HO26**

Turning Point, The (1977, C, 119m, PG)
Shirley MacLaine and Anne Bancroft play former dance colleagues whose lives have gone in opposite directions in this drama. Tom Skerritt, Leslie Browne, and Mikhail Baryshnikov costar. **DR10, DR12, DR42**

Turtle Diary (1986, C, 96m, PG)
Unusual love story of two lonely souls in London who unite in a common cause: to kidnap a pair of giant sea turtles from a zoo and return them to their home in the sea. Glenda Jackson and Ben Kingsley star; screenplay by Harold Pinter. **DR1, DR23** *Recommended*

Twelve Angry Men (1957, B&W, 96m, NR)
Classic courtroom drama of lone juror holding out for acquittal of murder suspect. Henry Fonda stars; Lee J. Cobb, Jack Warden, Jack Klugman, and E. G. Marshall are among the other deliberators. Directed by Sidney Lumet. **CL8, CL24, DR17, DR58** *Recommended*

Twelve Chairs, The (1970, C, 94m, G)
Mel Brooks film, based on Russian story about the race to find one of a set of dining room chairs with a fortune hidden in the seat. Ron Moody, Dom DeLuise,

and Frank Langella star, with Brooks hilarious as an idiot servant. **CO6, CO28**

Twelve O'Clock High (1949, B&W, 132m, NR)
American bomber pilots stationed in Great Britain get a new commander (Gregory Peck) who nearly cracks under the responsibility. Gary Merrill and Oscar winner Dean Jagger costar. **AC1, AC11, XT4**

Twentieth Century (1934, B&W, 91m, NR)
Slam-bang comedy, set aboard the title train, involving a Broadway producer (John Barrymore) and the girl he makes a star (Carole Lombard). Both stars are outstanding under Howard Hawks' direction. **CL7, CL10, CL35, CL48** *Highly Recommended*

20,000 Leagues Under the Sea (1954, C, 118m, G)
The Jules Verne tale about Captain Nemo (James Mason), a 19th-century inventor who builds a nuclear-powered submarine which he uses to sink warships. Kirk Douglas, Paul Lukas, and Peter Lorre costar. The special effects in this Disney film won an Academy Award. **FA1, FA3, SF3, SF13, SF15, SF27** *Recommended*

Twice Dead (1988, C, 85m, R)
Haunted house story, with spirit of a dead movie star helping a family fend off a gang of punkers. Tom Breznahan and Jill Whitlow star. **HO3**

Twice in a Lifetime (1985, C, 117m, R)
A long-time marriage crumbles when the husband meets an attractive barmaid, leaving his wife confused and one of his grown daughters embittered. Gene Hackman, Ellen Burstyn, Ann-Margret, Amy Madigan, and Ally Sheedy star. **DR8, DR39**

Twice Told Tales (1963, C, 119m, NR)
Three stories based on works by Nathaniel Hawthorne; "Dr. Heidegger's Experiment," "Rapaccini's Daughter," and "The House of the Seven Gables." Vincent Price stars. **HO23, HO31**

Twilight Zone: The Movie (1983, C, 102m, PG)
Four tales of terror patterned after the famous TV show. Dan Aykroyd and Albert Brooks star in a witty prologue. Directed by Steven Spielberg, John Landis, Joe Dante, and George Miller. **CO13, CU40, HO23, SF24**

Twilight's Last Gleaming (1977, C, 146m, R)
Renegade American general seizes nuclear warhead facility, threatens to start World War III if his demands aren't met. Burt Lancaster, Paul Winfield, Richard Widmark, and Melvyn Douglas star. Directed by Robert Aldrich. **DR7, DR41**

Twinky see Lola

Twins (1988, C, 107m, PG)
Comedy of long-lost brothers reunited, one a gentle giant (Arnold Schwarzenegger), the other a pint-sized hustler (Danny DeVito). **AC30, CO3**

Twins of Evil (1972, C, 85m, R)
One of a set of beautiful twins (Mary and Madeleine Collinson) is a vampire. Peter Cushing costars. **HO15, HO33**

Twister (1989, C, 94m, PG-13)
Comic story set in Kansas about an odd family featuring a loony patriarch (Harry Dean Stanton) and his son and daughter (Crispin Glover, Suzy Amis). They're entertaining various relatives and friends during a storm. Adapted from Mary Robison's novel, *Oh!* **CO5, CU49, DR19**

Two Daughters (1961, B&W, 114m, NR)
From India, a drama in two parts: in "The Postmaster," a young servant girl learns obedience to her employer; in "The Conclusion," a new bride flees an arranged marriage but later returns. Directed by Satyajit Ray. **FF23**

Two English Girls (1972, C, 130m, NR)
French director François Truffaut's study of a romantic triangle involving a Frenchman and two very different British sisters. Jean-Pierre Léaud, Kika Markham,

and Stacey Tendeter star. Video version includes footage restored by the director in 1984. **CU10, FF13**

Two for the Road (1967, C, 112m, NR)
Literate comedy-drama of romance, marriage, and breakup of an attractive couple (Albert Finney, Audrey Hepburn). Written by Frederic Raphael; directed by Stanley Donen. **CL30, DR1, MU23** *Recommended*

200 Motels (1971, C, 98m, R)
Frank Zappa and the Mothers of Invention satirize suburban America. Ringo Starr, disguised as Zappa, narrates. **CU1, CU3, MU9**

Two Moon Junction (1988, C, 104m, R)
Steamy trash, with a modern Southern belle about to get married but attracted to an often shirtless carnival worker. Sherilyn Fenn and Richard Tyson star, with Louise Fletcher, Burl Ives, and Kristy McNichol. **CU6, DR3**

Two Mules for Sister Sara (1970, C, 105m, PG)
A prostitute disguised as a nun is befriended by an unsuspecting cowboy. Western action with Clint Eastwood and Shirley MacLaine. **DR42, WE9, WE26**

Two Rode Together (1961, C, 109m, NR)
James Stewart and Richard Widmark ride off on a rescue mission in this western directed by John Ford. **CL25, WE18**

2001: A Space Odyssey (1968, C, 139m, G)
Stanley Kubrick's masterpiece about the search for the aliens that have been helping humans develop throughout time. The special effects won an Oscar. Keir Dullea and a computer named HAL 9000 star. **CU3, CU4, DR53, SF3, SF6, SF15, SF16** *Recommended*

2010: The Year We Make Contact (1984, C, 114m, PG)
An American and Soviet space crew journey towards Jupiter in hopes of unraveling the mystery that began in *2001: A Space Odyssey*. Roy Scheider stars. **SF3**

Two Way Stretch (1960, B&W, 87m, NR)
Classic British comedy starring Peter Sellers as a convict who leads his cellmates on a robbery expedition outside the prison. **CO17, CO26**

Two Women (1961, B&W, 99m, NR)
Sophia Loren won an Oscar for her performance as a woman who is brutally attacked, along with her daughter, by soldiers during World War II. Jean-Paul Belmondo costars. **FF2, FF31, FF33, XT3**

Tycoon (1947, C, 128m, NR)
John Wayne stars in this drama about railroad builders; Laraine Day, Cedric Hardwicke, and Judith Anderson costar. **CL17**

UFOria (1986, C, 100m, PG)
Offbeat comedy about a grocery store clerk who is sure that aliens have contacted her. Cindy Williams, Harry Dean Stanton, Fred Ward, and Harry Carey, Jr. star. Made in 1980. **CO12, CU49**

U2: Live at Red Rocks "Under A Blood Red Sky" (1983, C, 55m, NR)
This Irish band in concert at a natural outdoor amphitheatre in Colorado. **MU10**

U2: Rattle and Hum (1988, B&W/C, 90m, PG-13)
Documentary focusing on the popular Irish rock band and their travels in America. One concert segment in color; the rest of the film was shot in B&W. **MU11**

Ugetsu (1953, B&W, 96m, NR)
From Japan, a classic drama of two peasants seeking their fortunes—one as a businessman in the city, the other as a samurai—and bringing disaster upon their families. Directed by Kenji Mizoguchi. **FF4** *Recommended*

Ugly American, The (1963, C, 120m, NR)
American diplomat in Southeast Asia is caught in political turmoil created by communist elements; he spearheads disastrous official reaction to those events. Marlon Brando stars in this adaptation of the Eugene Burdick's novel. **DR7, DR33**

Ultimate Solution of Grace Quigley, The
see Grace Quigley

Ulysses (1955, C, 104m, NR)
The classic Greek myth of the warrior who is destined to travel for seven years after the Trojan War before he can return home. Kirk Douglas stars. **AC18**

Ulzana's Raid (1972, C, 103m, R)
The U.S. Cavalry and Indian tribes battle it out in this violent Western tale. Burt Lancaster stars. Directed by Robert Aldrich. **DR41, WE5, WE8**

Umberto D (1952, B&W, 89m, NR)
Italian director Vittorio de Sica's acclaimed study of a retired bureaucrat and his struggle to maintain his dignity. **FF2**

Umbrellas of Cherbourg, The (1964, C, 91m, NR)
Musical drama (all the dialogue is sung) about two sisters and their umbrella shop in a French seaside resort. Catherine Deneuve stars. **FF1, FF27, MU16**

Unbearable Lightness of Being, The (1988, C, 172m, R)
Adaptation of Milan Kundera's novel of romance and betrayal set against the backdrop of the Czech reforms of 1968 and the Russian invasion of Prague. Daniel Day-Lewis, Lena Olin, and Juliette Binoche star; Philip Kaufman directed. **CU6, CU50, DR1, DR7, DR19**

Uncanny, The (1977, C, 85m, NR)
Peter Cushing plays an author who believes that household cats are responsible for a series of unsolved murders. **HO33**

Uncommon Valor (1983, C, 105m, R)
A retired colonel recruits some Vietnam vets to help him find his MIA son in Laos. Gene Hackman stars, with Robert Stack, Patrick Swayze, and Fred Ward. **AC4, AC20, DR39**

Undefeated, The (1969, C, 119m, G)
Western drama set in the aftermath of the Civil War, starring John Wayne and Rock Hudson as opposing colonels who must find a way to live in peace. **WE7, WE17**

Under California Skies (1948, B&W, 71m, NR)
When the famous stallion Trigger is kidnapped, Roy Rogers swings into action. Andy Devine and Bob Nolan & the Sons of the Pioneers costar. **WE23**

Under Capricorn (1949, C, 117m, NR)
Ingrid Berman plays the weak wife of Australian pioneer Joseph Cotten in this rare costume drama from Alfred Hitchcock. **CL27, MY22**

Under Fire (1983, C, 128m, R)
A trio of American journalists covering the downfall of dictator Somoza in Nicaragua get personally involved in a story. Powerfully made drama starring Nick Nolte, Gene Hackman, and Joanna Cassidy. Written by Ron Shelton. **DR7, DR21, DR39, DR44** *Recommended*

Under Milk Wood (1973, C, 90m, PG)
Drama, based on Dylan Thomas play, about the lives of people in a mythical Welsh town. Elizabeth Taylor, Richard Burton, and Peter O'Toole star. **CL15, CL33, DR45**

Under Nevada Skies (1944, B&W, 68m, NR)
Roy Rogers leads a band of friendly Indians against a gang of claim jumpers. **WE23**

Under the Rainbow (1981, C, 98m, PG)
Farce set in a hotel during the making of *The Wizard of Oz,* involving that film's midget actors, spies, and secret agents. Chevy Chase, Carrie Fisher, Eve Arden, and Billy Barty star. **CO8, CO13**

Under the Roofs of Paris (1930, B&W, 92m, NR)
This early sound film from France employs song and mime to tell the comic tale of a romantic triangle. Directed by René Clair. **FF1**

Under the Volcano (1984, C, 112m, R)
Somber drama, set in 1930s Mexico, of alcoholic British diplomat's final days. Albert Finney, Jacqueline Bisset, and Anthony Andrews star in this adaptation of the famed Malcolm Lowry novel. Directed by John Huston. **CL44, DR19**

Under Western Stars (1945, B&W, 83m, NR)
Roy Rogers stars in this tuneful western with his faithful steed Trigger and Smiley Burnette. **WE23**

Undersea Kingdom (1936, B&W, 223m, NR)
A serial about adventurers finding the lost kingdom of Atlantis. Lon Chaney, Jr. costars. Also known as *Sharad of Atlantis.* **HO30**

Underworld *see* Transmutations

Underworld, U.S.A. (1961, B&W, 99m, NR)
Young man swears revenge on the Mob after his father is murdered. Cliff Robertson stars; Samuel Fuller directed. **AC19, CU22**

Unfaithfully Yours (1948, B&W, 105m, NR)
An orchestra conductor is convinced that his lovely young wife is cheating on him with a musician, and he plots to do away with both of them. Classic comedy starring Rex Harrison, Linda Darnell, and Kurt Krueger; written and directed by Preston Sturges. **CO24**

Unfaithfully Yours (1984, C, 96m, PG)
Remake of the Preston Sturges classic, with Dudley Moore, Nastassja Kinski, and Armand Assante. **CO31**

Unforgiven, The (1960, C, 125m, NR)
Feuding in frontier Texas between two families and an Indian tribe, which claims a young woman (Audrey Hepburn) as one of theirs. Burt Lancaster stars, with Audie Murphy, Lillian Gish, and Charles Bickford; John Huston directed. **CL30, CL44, CL49, DR41, WE1, WE8, WE9, WE16**

Unholy, The (1988, C, 100m, R)
A priest in New Orleans investigates the murders of two fellow clerics—and comes up with a surprising revelation about himself. Horror story stars Ben Cross, Hal

Holbrook, Trevor Howard, and Ned
Beatty. **HO10**

Unidentified Flying Oddball (1979, C,
92m, G)
A Disney version of *A Conneticut Yankee
In King Arthur's Court*. A man gets sent
back to medieval times. Dennis Dugan
and Jim Dale star. **FA1**

Union City (1980, C, 87m, PG)
Debby Harry plays a housewife in this
thriller about paranoia and murder.
MU12, MY2

Union Station (1950, B&W, 80m, NR)
A madman (Lyle Bettger) kidnaps a blind
woman (Allene Roberts) and a police detective (William Holden) heads the manhunt. **CL51**

Unmarried Woman, An (1978, C, 124m,
R)
Middle-class Manhattan wife and mother
picks up the pieces after her husband
leaves her for another woman. Jill Clay-
burgh stars, with Michael Murphy and
Alan Bates. Directed and written by Paul
Mazursky. **DR10**

Unsinkable Molly Brown, The (1964, C,
128m, NR)
Debbie Reynolds plays a poor miner's
daughter who becomes a millionairess
and a heroine of the *Titanic* disaster in
this musical. Based on a true story.
Harve Presnell costars. **MU1, MU6**

Unsuitable Job for a Woman, An (1981, C,
94m, NR)
British private eye story with a twist: the
gumshoe's a woman (Pippa Guard) who's
investigating the suicide of her boss.
Based on a novel by P.D. James. **MY14,
MY19**

Until September (1984, C, 95m, R)
Love story set in Paris involving an
American woman (Karen Allen) and a
married French banker (Thierry L'Her-
mitte). **DR1**

Untouchables, The (1987, C, 119m, R)
In Prohibition-era Chicago, Al Capone
rules over all—until a determined government agent named Elliot Ness arrives in
town. Kevin Costner, Robert DeNiro, and
Oscar winner Sean Connery star in this
gangster saga. Written by David Mamet;
Brian DePalma directed. **AC22, AC36,
CU28, DR25, XT4**

Up in Arms (1944, C, 106m, NR)
A hypchondriac (Danny Kaye, in his film
debut) wreaks havoc on the Army. Constance Dowling and Dinah Shore costar.
CO38, CO41

Up in Smoke (1980, C, 87m, R)
The movie debut of Cheech and Chong,
those lovably stoned L.A. hipsters.
CO32, CU3

Up the Creek (1958, B&W, 83m, NR)
British service comedy set aboard a
mothballed ship, with the emphasis on
slapstick humor. David Tomlinson, Wil-
frid Hyde-White, and Peter Sellers star.
CO26, CO38

Up the Sandbox (1972, C, 97m, R)
Comedy-drama of a young New York wife
and mother whose overactive imagination
results in some bizarre fantasies. Barbra
Streisand stars. **CR10, MU27**

Uptown Saturday Night (1974, C, 104m,
PG)
Comedy starring Sidney Poitier and Bill
Cosby as a couple of screw-ups who are
after a valuable lottery ticket. Harry
Belafonte and Richard Pryor costar;
Poitier directed. **CO29, DR38**

Urban Cowboy (1980, C, 135m, R)
Set in contemporary Houston, this drama
centers on the life and loves of a young
hard-hat who hangs around the mammoth
honky-tonk bar, Gilley's. John Travolta
and Debra Winger star. **DR15, DR47,
WE13**

Used Cars (1980, C, 111m, R)
Wild comedy with cult following about
twin car dealer brothers (both played by

Jack Warden), one honest, the other totally unscrupulous. Kurt Russell stars in this contemporary slapstick classic. Written by Bob Gale and Robert Zemeckis; directed by Zemeckis. **CO12, CU5** *Recommended*

Utopia *see* Atoll K

Vagabond (1985, C, 105, R)
Moody, stylized story of a young woman's aimless wandering through the French countryside. Sandrine Bonnaire stars; Agnes Varda directed. **DR10, FF1** *Recommended*

Valley Girl (1983, C, 95m, R)
Romance blossoms between a San Fernando Valley mall rat and a punked-out dude from Los Angeles. Deborah Foreman and Nicolas Cage star; Martha Coolidge directed. **CO4** *Recommended*

Valley of Fire (1951, B&W, 63m, NR)
Gene Autry plays matchmaker for a lonely gang of prospectors. **WE24**

Vamp (1986, C, 94m, R)
Four college frat boys decide to hire a hooker for their party. They get more than they paid for when they hire a vampire. Grace Jones plays the prostitute with a taste for blood. **HO5, HO24, MU12**

Vampire Lovers (1971, C, 88m, R)
An erotic thriller from Britain's Hammer Studios about lesbian vampires. Peter Cushing costars. **HO5, HO25, HO33**

Vampyr (1932, B&W, 60m, NR)
Danish director Carl Dreyer's classic horror tale, full of rich imagery and atmosphere. **FF35, HO5**

Vanishing American, The (1925, B&W, 148m, NR)
Classic silent western about the mistreatment of Indians, based on a novel by Zane Grey. **WE8**

Vanishing Point (1971, C, 98m, PG)
A man is hired to drive a car from Denver to San Francisco. He decides to see if he can make the trip in 15 hours without stopping for anything, especially the police. Barry Newman and Cleavon Little star. **AC10**

Vanishing Prairie, The (1954, C, 75m, G)
This Disney documentary, part of the True-Life Adventure series, won an Academy Award for its look at animal life on the Great Plains. **FA1**

Vanity Fair (1932, B&W, 73m, NR)
Myrna Loy stars in this updated version of the William Thackeray novel about a young social climber. **CL1, CL46**

Variety (1925, B&W, 79m, NR)
Classic silent German drama about a love triangle in a circus mirroring the decadence of 1920s Germany. Emil Janings stars. **CL12, FF3**

Velvet Touch, The (1948, B&W, 97m, NR)
Rosalind Russell plays a stage actress who turns detective to solve a murder. With Leo Genn, Claire Trevor, and Sydney Greenstreet. **MY15**

Vengeance Valley (1951, C, 83m, NR)
Western drama about feuding brothers and their women, starring Burt Lancaster and Robert Walker. **DR41**

Venom (1982, C, 98m, R)
A black mamba, the world's deadliest snake, is loose in a London home whose residents are being held hostage by kidnappers. Klaus Kinski, Oliver Reed, and Nicol Williamson star. **FF30, HO16**

Vera Cruz (1954, C, 94m, NR)
In 1860s Mexico, two American cowboys become involved in revolutionary politics. Gary Cooper and Burt Lancaster star. Directed by Robert Aldrich. **DR41, WE10, WE25**

Verdict, The (1982, C, 128m, R)
A broken-down defense lawyer tries to rise to the occasion when he's involved in a complicated malpractice case against a skilled and well-funded legal team. Paul Newman, James Mason, Charlotte Ram-

pling, and Jack Warden star; Sidney Lumet directed. **DR17, DR28, DR58** *Recommended*

Vernon, Florida (1981, C, 60m, NR)
Documentary by Erol Morris depicts the lives of folk in a small town in Florida which seems to contain a high proportion of eccentrics. **CU16, CU51, DR62** *Recommended*

Vertigo (1958, C, 128m, PG)
Classic Alfred Hitchcock film, regarded by a growing cult as his best, about one man's obsession with a woman he thinks has died in a tragic fall. James Stewart and Kim Novak star. Shot on location in San Francisco. Music by Bernard Herrmann. **CL14, CU13, CL25, MY5, MY22, XT9** *Highly Recommended*

Very Curious Girl, A (1969, C, 105m, R)
From France, a comedy about a peasant girl who enjoys making love with the men in her village so much she decides to charge for her services. **FF1**

Very Edge, The (1963, B&W, 82m, NR)
British thriller about a pregnant woman (Anne Heywood) harassed by a sex criminal (Jeremy Brett). **MY3**

Very Private Affair, A (1962, C, 95m, NR)
Marcello Mastroianni and Brigitte Bardot star in this romantic drama in which a theater director gives shelter to a highstrung movie star. Directed by Louis Malle. **FF24, FF32**

Vibes (1988, C, 99m, PG)
Jeff Goldblum and Cyndi Lauper plays a pair of psychics in this adventure comedy about a treasure hunt in Peru. Peter Falk costars. **CO3, MU12**

Vice Squad (1982, C, 97m, R)
A man is mutilating prostitutes in Los Angeles, and a hooker helps a cop solve the case. Wings Hauser and Season Hubley star, with Wings Hauser as the memorable villain. **AC9**

Vice Versa (1988, C, 97m, PG0
A department store executive and his young son find their minds switched through the spell of a magic totem. Judge Reinhold and Fred Savage star. **CO5**

Victor/Victoria (1982, C, 133m, PG)
Farce of misunderstanding and sexual confusion, as a Paris nightclub singer (Julie Andrews) pretends to be a man impersonating a woman, much to the consternation of an American gangster (James Garner). Robert Preston, Lesley Anne Warren, and Alex Karas costar; Blake Edwards directed. **CO1, CO46**

Victory (1981, C, 110m, PG)
Allied personnel in a German POW camp challenge a Third Reich soccer team to a game. Michael Caine, Sylvester Stallone, and Pele star. Directed by John Huston. **AC31, CL44**

Videodrome (1983, C, 88m, R)
James Woods plays a cable TV programmer who stumbles onto a show that seduces and then ultimately controls its audience. Debbie Harry plays a kinky woman looking for the ultimate sexual thrill. Directed by David Cronenberg. **HO11, HO22, HO39, MU12**

Vietnam: In the Year of the Pig (1968, B&W, 115m, NR)
Director Emile De Antonio's documentary of the controversial war paints a bleak portrait of American policy and conduct. **CU16**

View to a Kill, A (1985, C, 131m, PG)
In this last James Bond film starring Roger Moore, 007 is up against a pair of villains (Christopher Walken, Grace Jones) who intend to create a devastating earthquake in Silicon Valley. **AC35, MU12**

Vigilante (1982, C, 90m, R)
An ex-cop joins a gang of vigilantes to avenge the brutal assault of his wife and child. Robert Forster and Fred Williamson star. **AC19**

Vikings, The (1958, C, 114m, NR)
Kirk Douglas and Tony Curtis terrorize the countryside as a pair of nasty Norsemen. Janet Leigh and Ernest Borgnine costar. Narrated by Orson Welles. **AC13, CL41**

Villa Rides (1968, C, 125m, PG)
Yul Brynner stars as the Mexican bandit and reolutionary, Pancho Villa. Robert Mitchum and Charles Bronson lead the supporting cast. **AC29, WE10**

Village of the Damned (1960, B&W, 78m, NR)
A strange mist covers an English village and everyone is rendered unconcious until the mist clears. Later, twelve woman discover they are pregnant and give birth to look-alike children with telepathic powers. George Sanders stars. **HO13, HO26, SF9, SF19**

Violent Years, The (1956, B&W, 60m, NR)
The king of no-budget trash, Ed Wood, Jr., strikes again with this drama of spoiled debutantes turning to robbery and rape. **CU45**

Violets Are Blue (1986, C, 88m, PG-13)
A successful photographer returns to her hometown and picks up with an old high school flame who's now married. Sissy Spacek and Kevin Kline star, with Bonnie Bedelia. **DR1, DR68**

Virgin and the Gypsy, The (1970, C, 92m, R)
D.H. Lawrence story of the daughter of a strict priest and her sexual awakening. Joanna Shimkus and Franco Nero star. **DR19**

Virgin Queen, The (1955, C, 92m, NR)
Bette Davis plays Queen Elizabeth I in this historical drama about her relationship with Sir Walter Raleigh. Richard Todd and Joan Collins costar. **CL3, CL21**

Virgin Spring, The (1959, B&W, 88m, NR)
Oscar-winning drama from director Ingmar Bergman: a woodsman seeks revenge on the men who raped and murdered his daughter. U.S. horror remake: *Last House on the Left*. **FF8, FF36, XT7**

Virginian, The (1929, B&W, 90m, NR)
Gary Cooper stars in one of his first westerns, based on the classic Owen Wister novel. **WE25**

Viridiana (1961, B&W, 90m, NR)
Controversial drama, banned for years in its native Spain, about a nun who is constantly thwarted in her attempts to do good in a world full of sinners. Luis Buñuel directed. **CU8, FF11** *Highly Recommended*

Virus (1980, C, 155m, PG)
A deadly manmade virus is accidentally unleashed, sparking a worldwide epidemic. The survivors (858 men and 8 women) must then try to restore civilization. Made in Japan, with a partly American cast that includes Chuck Connors, Glenn Ford, Olivia Hussey, and George Kennedy. **SF12**

Vision Quest (1984, C, 107m, R)
High school wrestler (Matthew Modine) embarks on ambitious training program for upcoming match, is distracted by the new female boarder (Linda Fiorentino) in his house. **DR9, DR22**

Vitelloni, I (1953, B&W, 104m, NR)
Comedy-drama from director Federico Fellini about five boys on the verge of adulthood. **FF10**

Viva Las Vegas (1964, C, 86m, NR)
Ann-Margret thinks Elvis Presley spends too much time with his sports car and sets out to win him over. **MU22**

Viva Zapata! (1952, B&W, 113m, NR)
Marlon Brando plays the legendary Mexican bandit who rose to political power. Oscar winner Anthony Quinn costars. Screenplay by John Steinbeck; directed by Elia Kazan. **DR33, DR59, WE10, XT4**

Vivacious Lady (1938, B&W, 90m, NR)
A professor (James Stewart) marries a fun-loving nightclub singer (Ginger Rogers), which takes his conservative family and his fiancee by surprise. Directed by George Stevens. **CL25, CL42**

Volunteers (1985, C, 107m, R)
An Ivy League student with gambling debts joins the Peace Corps to escape his creditors and winds up paired with a gung-ho boob. Tom Hanks and John Candy star. **CO3, CO14, CO44**

Von Ryan's Express (1965, C, 117m, NR)
World War II drama starring Frank Sinatra as a POW who commandeers a train in a bold escape plan. **DR49**

Voulez-Vous Danser Avec Moi? (1959, C, 90m, NR)
Brigitte Bardot stars in this comedy/mystery about a woman trying to clear her dance instructor husband of a murder charge. **FF32**

Voyage of the Damned (1976, C, 134m, PG)
Shipload of Jewish refugees fleeing Germany is denied permission to dock and forced to return to Germany. Drama, based on fact, with all-star cast, including Faye Dunaway, Max von Sydow, Oskar Werner, James Mason, and Orson Welles. **CL41, DR35**

Voyage to Italy (1953, B&W, 75m, NR)
A married couple (Ingrid Bergman, George Sanders) travel to Italy in an attempt to patch up their differences. Directed by Roberto Rosselini, then Bergman's husband. Also known as *Strangers*. Original running time: 97m. **CL27**

Voyage to the Bottom of the Sea (1961, C, 105m, NR)
An atomic powered submarine is on its maiden voyage beneath the Antarctic, when it is discovered that the polar cap is melting. Only the sub can save the Earth from destruction. Directed by Irwin Al-

len; starring Walter Pidgeon and Peter Lorre. **SF3**

W (1984, C, 90m, NR)
Drama of people trying to survive in a post-holocaust world. **SF8**

W. C. Fields Comedy Bag (1930/1932/1933, B&W, 56m, NR)
Three classic Fields shorts: *The Gold Specialist, The Dentist,* and *The Fatal Glass of Beer.* **CO22**

W. C. Fields Festival (1930, B&W, 56m, NR)
Further evidence of W. C. Fields' comic genius, in this collection of his early short films. **CO22**

Wackiest Ship in the Army, The (1960, C, 99m, NR)
The Army recruits Jack Lemmon for a top secret mission. On a schooner disguised as a Japanese fishing boat, he and first mate Ricky Nelson must rescue a spy. **CO38, DR64, MU12**

Wages of Fear, The (1952, B&W, 105m, NR)
Thriller about a quartet of desperate men who volunteer to drive two trucks loaded with explosives over dangerous mountain roads. Yves Montand stars. American remake: *Sorcerer*. Directed by Henri-Georges Clouzot. **AC13, FF1, MY20** *Highly Recommended*

Wagner (1983, C, 300m, NR)
The life and times of the famed composer, Richard Wagner. Richard Burton and Vanessa Redgrave star, with Ralph Richardson, Laurence Olivier, and John Gielgud. **CL32, DR65, MU5**

Wagonmaster (1950, B&W, 86m, NR)
Two cowboys join a group of pioneer Mormons and help them on their way to the promised land. Ben Johnson, Ward Bond, and Harry Carey, Jr. star. Directed by John Ford. **WE18**

Wait Until Dark (1967, C, 108m, NR)
A blind woman unknowingly possesses a doll stuffed with smuggled drugs, and a trio of nasty thugs harass her to get it back. Audrey Hepburn stars, with Alan Arkin, Richard Crenna, and Jack Weston. **CL30, MY3** *Recommended*

Wake of the Red Witch (1948, B&W, 106m, NR)
Adventure in the East Indies, starring John Wayne, Gail Russell, Luther Alder, and Gig Young. **CL17**

Walk, Don't Run (1966, C, 114m, NR)
In his last film, Cary Grant plays matchmaker to Samantha Eggar and Jim Hutton as the three share cramped quarters during the Tokyo Olympics. **CL18**

Walk in the Spring Rain, A (1970, C, 100m, PG)
Ingrid Bergman and Anthony Quinn star in this romantic drama of a married woman's unexpected love affair. **CL27, DR1**

Walk in the Sun, A (1945, B&W, 117m, NR)
Combat drama about an American infantry unit who are attacking a German stronghold in Italy. Dana Andrews stars. **AC1**

Walk Into Hell (1957, C, 91m, NR)
Adventure tale of an oil mining engineer and his lovely companion stranded in the New Guinea jungle. Chips Rafferty stars in this Australian film. **FF5**

Walk on the Wild Side (1962, B&W, 114m, NR)
A bordello in 1930s New Orleans is the setting for this drama of a drifter seeking his lost love. Laurence Harvey stars, with Barbara Stanwyck as the madam, and Capucine and Jane Fonda among her girls. **CL45, DR27**

Walking Tall (1973, C, 126m, R)
Joe Don Baker plays real life Tennessee sheriff Buford Pusser, who took on local corruption with a baseball bat. Directed by Phil Karlson. **AC9**

Walking Tall Part 2 (1975, C, 109m, PG)
Walking Tall: The Final Chapter (1977, C, 113m, R)
Bo Svenson takes over the role of Tennessee sheriff Buford Pusser in these two sequels to *Walking Tall*. **AC9**

Wall Street (1987, C, 124m, R)
Greed and manipulation in the stock market are the subjects of this topical drama, starring Oscar winner Michael Douglas and Charlie Sheen. With Daryl Hannah and Martin Sheen. Written and directed by Oliver Stone on location in New York City. **DR7, DR60, DR70, XT2, XT8, XT9**

Waltz of the Toreadors (1962, C, 105m, NR)
Peter Sellers stars as a retired military officer with an eye for the ladies in this British comedy classic. Margaret Leighton costar. **CO17, CO26**

Wanderers, The (1979, C, 113m, R)
Life on the Bronx streets, 1963, with four tough guys who name their mini-gang after the Dion song. Comedy-drama stars Ken Wahl, Karen Allen, and Linda Manz. Philip Kaufman directed and adapted Richard Price's novel. **CU50, DR15** *Recommended*

Wannsee Conference, The (1984, C, 87m, NR)
German drama, based on actual meeting in January 1942, in which Nazi officials discussed plans for the Final Solution. **FF3** *Recommended*

Wanted: Dead or Alive (1986, C, 104m, R)
Rutger Hauer plays a high-tech bounty hunter who must stop an international terrorist, played by Gene Simmons. **AC25, MU12**

War and Peace (1956, C, 208m, NR)
Leo Tolstoy's epic story of Russian society during the struggle against Napoleon, starring Henry Fonda, Audrey Hepburn, and Mel Ferrer. **CL1, CL3, CL24, CL30**

War and Peace (1968, C, 373m, NR)
Mammoth, Russian-made version of the Tolstoy classic, directed by Sergei Bondarchuk. Video is English-language dubbed version. Winner of Oscar as Best Foreign Language Film. **CL1, CL3, FF6, XT7**

War Lover, The (1962, B&W, 105m, NR)
While in the air, a hotshot pilot (Steve McQueen) is considered a good luck charm to the rest of the squad. On the ground, he antagonizes everyone, including his co-pilot (Robert Wagner). **AC1, AC11, AC28**

War of the Wildcats (1943, B&W, 102m, NR)
John Wayne is an oil wildcatter in frontier Oklahoma. Gabby Hayes and Dale Evans add support. **WE17**

War of the Worlds (1953, C, 85m, G)
Martian war machines invade Earth, intent on destroying all humans. Based on the H. G. Wells novel; produced by George Pal. Academy Award winner for special effects. Gene Barry stars. **FA8, SF1, SF7, SF9, SF13, SF26**

War Wagon, The (1967, C, 101m, NR)
John Wayne and Kirk Douglas pull off a gold heist in this light-hearted western. **WE17**

Wargames (1983, C, 114m, PG)
Computer whiz (Matthew Broderick) taps in accidentally to Pentagon system and precipitates a serious war exercise. Ally Sheedy, Dabney Coleman, and John Wood costar. **SF5, DR7**

Warlock (1959, C, 121m, NR)
Henry Fonda is the gunfighter, Anthony Quinn the gambler, and Richard Widmark the sheriff in this western drama that concentrates on character rather than action. **CL24, WE3**

Warlords of the 21st Century (1982, C, 91m, PG)
During an oil shortage after World War III an ex-commando decides to take a stand against an evil dictator. **SF8**

Warriors, The (1955, C, 85m, NR)
A British prince (Errol Flynn) defends a French village from mauraders. Peter Finch costars. Flynn's last swashbuckling film. **AC34**

Warriors, The (1979, C, 90m, R)
A New York City gang is falsely accused of murder and must fight its way across its rivals' turfs to get to safety. Michael Beck and James Remar star; Walter Hill directed. **AC8, DR15, CU7, CU27, XT9** *Recommended*

Warriors of the Wasteland (1983, C, 87m, R)
In a post-holocaust world three adventurers protect a band of settlers against the Templars, a gang of very nasty people. **SF8**

Warriors of the Wind (1985, C, 95m, PG)
An animated futuristic fantasy. **AC18**

Warrior's Rest *see* Repos du Guerrier, Le

Wasn't That a Time! (1982, C, 78m, PG)
A loving documentary about the 1980 reunion of The Weavers, a folk-singing group who were blacklisted during the McCarthy era. **MU4** *Recommended*

Watch on the Rhine (1943, B&W, 114m, NR)
Nazi agents harass a German (Paul Lukas, in an Oscar-winning performance) and his American wife (Bette Davis) who now live in Washington D.C. Geraldine Fitzgerald costars. **CL21, XT2**

Watcher in the Woods, The (1980, C, 84m, PG)
An American family moves into an English country house and the two children see visions of a missing girl. Bette Davis stars. **CL21, FA1, FA8, HO2, HO3, HO26, SF13**

Watchers (1988, C, 92m, R)
A government experiment goes haywire and unleashes a monster named Oxcom and a super-intelligent dog on an unsuspecting populace. Corey Haim stars, with Michael Ironside and Barbara Williams. **HO20**

Water Babies, The (1978, C, 92m, NR)
This undersea adventure mixes live action and animation. James Mason stars. **FA8**

Waterloo Bridge (1940, B&W, 103m, NR)
Vivien Leigh and Robert Taylor star in the classic romance about a ballet dancer and soldier falling in love during an air raid. **CL4**

Watership Down (1978, C, 90m, PG)
In this animated adventure, a warren of rabbits pursue freedom in the face of threats from humans, cats, dogs, and their own kind. Featuring the voices of John Hurt, Ralph Richardson, and Denholm Elliott. **FA10**

Wavelength (1983, C, 87m, PG)
A rock star (Robert Carradine) stumbles onto a government cover-up of aliens who crashed landed in California. **SF9**

Way Down East (1920, B&W, 107m, NR)
Classic silent melodrama, starring Lillian Gish, of a woman shunned because of her illegitimate baby. D.W. Griffith directed; the finale on the ice floes is breathtaking. **CL12, CL36, CL49** *Recommended*

Way Out West (1937, B&W, 65m, NR)
Laurel and Hardy star in this delightful comedy about the Old West. **CO20, WE15** *Recommended*

Way We Were, The (1973, C, 118m, PG)
Romantic drama about a Jewish political activist and WASP-y writer, following their lives from college in the 1930s to Hollywood and the blacklist in the 1950s. Barbra Streisand and Robert Redford star. Directed by Sydney Pollack. **DR1, DR13, DR29, DR56, MU27**

Way West, The (1967, C, 122m, NR)
The screen version of A.B. Guthrie's classic novel of pioneers in the Old West. Kirk Douglas, Robert Mitchum, and Richard Widmark star; Sally Field has a small role. **DR36, WE1**

We All Loved Each Other So Much (1977, C, 124m, NR)
From Italy, a comic story of friendship and love, about three pals who all lust for the same woman over a 30-year span. Federico Fellini and Marcello Mastroianni appear in bit parts as themselves. **FF2**

We of the Never Never (1983, C, 132m, G)
Visually rich adventure of first white woman to explore the Australian outback. Angela Punch McGregor and Arthur Dignam star. **FF5, AC12**

We Think the World of You (1989, C, 91m, R)
British comedy of a pair of male lovers (Alan Bates, Gary Oldman) who are separated when one goes to prison and the other has to care for his friend's dog. **CO17**

Wedding, A (1978, C, 125m, PG)
Comedy about variety of oddball family members and guests who show up at a suburban Chicago wedding. Robert Altman directed a diverse cast, including Carol Burnett, Desi Arnaz, Jr. Pat McCormick, Mia Farrow, Viveca Lindfors,

Weekend with Bernie

Paul Dooley, Lillian Gish, Lauren Hutton, Howard Duff, and Vittorio Gassman. **CL49, CO5, CU17, CU25** *Recommended*

Wedding in Blood (1973, C, 98m, PG)
Two lovers make plans to murder their respective spouses. A French thriller from director Claude Chabrol, starring Stephane Audran. **FF1, MY20**

Wedding March, The (1928, C, 113m, NR)
Silent classic, parts of which were restored for home video. Erich von Stroheim directed this drama of depravity set in pre-World War I Vienna. One of the earliest films shot in color. **CL12, CL53, CU10**

Wedding Party, The (1969, B&W, 92m, NR)
Comedy about preparations for marriage, starring Jill Clayburgh and Robert De-Niro, both in their first film. Brian De-Palma co-directed, with Cynthia Munroe and Wilford Leach. **CU28, DR25**

Wee Willie Winkie (1937, B&W, 100m, NR)
Rudyard Kipling tale of a British regiment in India and their mascot (Shirley Temple). Victor McLaglen costars; John Ford directed. **CL34, FA4, FA14**

Weeds (1987, C, 115m, R)
Nick Nolte stars in this drama based on fact, about a convict playwright who takes a troupe of his fellow prisoners on the road with his plays. **DR6, DR18, DR44**

Weekend of Shadows (1977, C, 94m, NR)
Australian drama of a Polish immigrant accused of murder, chased by an angry mob. **FF5**

Weird Science (1985, C, 94m, PG-13)
A pair of teen nerds create a lovely woman in their basement laboratory in this comedy. Anthony Michael Hall, Ilan Mitchell-Smith, and Kelly LeBrock star. Directed by John Hughes. **CO11, CO47**

Welcome to L.A. (1977, C, 106m, R)
Episodic drama about contemporary Californians and their aimless lives. Keith Carradine, Sally Kellerman, Geraldine Chaplin, Sissy Spacek, and Harvey Keitel star; Alan Rudolph directed. **CU26, DR68, XT9**

We're No Angels (1955, C, 103m, NR)
Three convicts escape from Devil's Island, hide out with a kind and understanding family, and get themselves into mischief. Humphrey Bogart stars in a rare comedy role, with Peter Ustinov and Basil Rathbone. **CL20**

Werewolf of Washington (1973, C, 90m, PG)
A personal friend of the President (Dean Stockwell) is bitten by a werewolf while in Budapest. When he returns to Washington as a werewolf, he begins to kill off all opponents of the administration. **HO4**

Werner Herzog Eats His Shoe (1980, C, 20m, NR)
The German director makes good on a bet involving colleague Erol Morris finishing a film. Directed by Les Blank. **FF19**

West Side Story (1961, C, 151m, G)
Broadway hit musical from Leonard Bernstein and Stephen Sondheim updates Romeo & Juliet story to contemporary New York. Winner of ten Oscars, including Best Picture, Supporting Actor and Actress (George Chakiris, Rita Moreno), and Director (Robert Wise). Wise and choreographer Jerome Robbins directed; Robbins was awarded a special Oscar. Natalie Wood, Russ Tamblyn, and Richard Beymer star. **CL58, FA9, MU2, MU3, MU6, MU7, MU14, XT1, XT4, XT5, XT6, XT9**

Westerner, The (1940, B&W, 100m, NR)
Gary Cooper gets involved in land feuds in this western, with Oscar winner Walter Brennan as Judge Roy Bean. Directed by William Wyler. **CL38, WE3, WE25, XT4**

Westfront 1918 (1930, B&W, 90m, NR)
Classic antiwar drama from German director G.W. Pabst; his first talking picture. **FF3**

Westworld (1973, C, 90m, PG)
An amusement park for the rich is populated by robots who look and act human. One day the robots rebel and slaughter all the human tourists—except one, who desperately tries to escape. Yul Brynner and Richard Benjamin star. **SF6**

Wetherby (1985, C, 97m, R)
British drama of stranger at a Yorkshire home committing suicide, leaving his hosts and others to sort it all out. Vanessa Redgrave, Joely Richardson, Judi Dench, and Ian Holm star. Written and directed by David Hare. **DR23, DR65**

Whales of August, The (1987, C, 91m, NR)
Screen legends Lillian Gish and Bette Davis star in this drama of two elderly sisters spending a summer on the coast of Maine. Vincent Price, Ann Sothern, and Harry Carey, Jr. costar. **CL21, CL49, DR11**

What Ever Happened to Baby Jane? (1962, B&W, 132m, NR)
An unbalanced ex-child star, Baby Jane Hudson (Bette Davis) terrorizes her crippled sister (Joan Crawford), a former movie idol. A camp classic. Directed by Robert Aldrich. **CL21, CL50, CU2, DR13, HO14**

What Have I Done to Deserve This! (1985, C, 100m, NR)
Comedy from Spanish director Pedro Almodóvar about a frantic housewife running a wild working-class family. Carmen Maura stars. **FF7**

What Price Glory (1952, C, 110m, NR)
James Cagney, Dan Dailey, and Robert Wagner are fighting in the French trenches during World War I. Directed by John Ford. **CL22, CL34**

What's New, Pussycat? (1965, C, 108m, NR)
Woman-crazy man consults loony shrink for help, which only makes his problems worse. Zany comedy starring Peter O'Toole and Peter Sellers, with Woody Allen (who wrote the screenplay), Romy Schneider, Capucine, Paula Prentiss, and Ursula Andress. **CO26, CO27, DR45** *Recommended*

What's Up, Doc? (1972, C, 94m, G)
Modern screwball comedy, set in San Francisco, with a free spirit (Barbra Streisand), a straight arrow (Ryan O'Neal), his uptight fiancee (Madeline Kahn), and assorted jewel thieves and other characters. Written by Robert Benton and David Newman; directed by Peter Bogdanovich. **MU27, XT9**

What's Up, Tiger Lily? (1966, C, 80m, NR)
Unique comic film co-written and "directed" by Woody Allen, who took a Grade B Japanese spy thriller called *Key of Keys* and dubbed in hilarious English dialogue. Silly fun. **CO7, CO27** *Recommended*

Wheel of Fortune (1941, B&W, 83m, NR)
John Wayne plays a country lawyer out to put a crooked politician behind bars—even though he loves the man's daughter. Frances Dee costars. Also known as *A Man Betrayed*. **CL17**

Wheels of Fire (1985, C, 81m, R)
A look into the future shows Earth as a wasteland and a car gang terrorizing the populace. **AC10**

When the Legends Die (1972, C, 105m, PG)
Richard Widmark and Frederic Forest star as a rodeo cowboy and his young Indian friend in this contemporary Western. **WE8, WE13**

When the North Wind Blows (1974, C, 113m, G)
A trapper in Siberia tries to protect snow tigers. Henry Brandon stars. **FA4**

When Time Ran Out (1980, C, 144m, PG)
A posh resort on a Polynesian island and its guests are in danger when a long-dormant volcano erupts. This video version has 20 minutes of additional footage not seen in the theatrical release. Paul Newman, William Holden, and Jacqueline Bisset head the cast. **AC23, DR28, CL51, CU10**

When Wolves Cry *see* Christmas Tree, The

When Worlds Collide (1951, C, 81m, G)
A small band of scientists and students who believe the Earth is on a collision course with a star race against time to build a space ark. Special effects won an Oscar; produced by George Pal. **SF1, SF7**

Where Are the Children? (1982, C, 97m, R)
Jill Clayburgh plays a woman under suspicion when children from her second marriage disappear (she was accused of murdering two children from a previous marriage but found innocent). Frederic Forrest costars in this thriller. **MY18**

Where Eagles Dare (1968, C, 158m, PG)
Richard Burton and Clint Eastwood go undercover to rescue a kidnapped general from a Nazi stronghold. **AC1, AC27**

Where the Buffalo Roam (1980, C, 96m, R)
The life and very hard times of gonzo journalist Hunter S. Thompson, as portrayed by Bill Murray. **CO13**

Where the Green Ants Dream (1984, C, 101m, NR)
An Australian uranium mining company comes into conflict with a local aborigine tribe when drilling begins on sacred tribal grounds. Bruce Spence stars; Werner Herzog directed. **FF19**

Where the Hot Wind Blows (1958, B&W, 120m, NR)
An all-star cast is featured in this drama set in an Italian seaport about a lusty young girl's many liaisions with the men of the village. Gina Lollabrigida, Marcello Mastroianni, Melina Mercouri, and Yves Montand star. **FF24**

Where the Red Fern Grows (1974, C, 90m, NR)
Family drama set in Depression-era Oklahoma, about a farm boy's devotion to two hunting dogs. **FA5**

Where the River Runs Black (1986, C, 96m, PG)
Young white boy reared in the Amazon jungle swears revenge on the hunters who killed his mother. **DR9, FA7**

Where Time Began (1978, C, 86m, G)
A group of adventurers travel to the center of the Earth and encounter a time warp. Loosely based on Jules Verne's *Journey To The Centre of the Earth*. Kenneth More stars. **SF4**

Where's Picone? (1984, C, 122m, NR)
Italian comedy about a tailor living on his wits in modern-day Naples. Giancarlo Giannini stars. **FF2**

Where's Poppa? (1970, C, 92m, R)
Comedy with cult following for its outrageous humor about a senile woman whose son is trying to scare her to death. Ruth Gordon and George Segal star; Carl Reiner directed. **CO5, CO12, CU5, CU12**

Which Way Is Up? (1977, C, 94m, R)
Richard Pryor plays three roles in this comedy about a farm worker mixed up in politics and woman troubles. Remake of Italian film *The Seduction of Mimi*. **CO26, FF36**

Which Way to the Front? (1970, C, 96m, G)
Jerry Lewis plays a World War II draftee who's declared 4-F but enlists a bunch of similar misfits to fight the Germans. Jan Murray, John Wood, and Kaye Ballard costar; Lewis directed. **CO25**

While the City Sleeps (1956, B&W, 100m, NR)
Fritz Lang directed this suspenseful tale of policemen and reporters looking for a serial killer. Dana Andrews, Ida Lupino, and Vincent Price star. **CL43, HO31, MY1**

Whisky Galore (1949, B&W, 82m, NR)
Classic British comedy about the efforts of island folk to recover booze from a sunken World War II ship. Basil Radford and Joan Greenwood star; Alexander

Mackendrick directed. Also known as *Tight Little Island*. **CO17**

Whistle Blower, The (1987, C, 99m, PG)
Michael Caine stars in this British thriller as a former intelligence agent with an idealistic son in a sensitive government job. Nigel Havers, Edward Fox, and John Gielgud costar. **MY19**

Whistle Down the Wind (1961, B&W, 99m, NR)
Three children find a murderer hiding in their barn and think he is Christ. Hayley Mills and Alan Bates star. **FA7**

White Christmas (1954, C, 120m, NR)
Two army buddies team up and become famous as a song and dance act. With the assistance of two singing sisters, they help out their old army commander, whose hotel is in financial trouble. Bing Crosby, Danny Kaye, Vera-Ellen, and Rosemary Clooney star. **CO41, MU4, MU6, MU25**

White Dawn (1974, C, 110m, PG)
Three whalers stranded in the Arctic take advantage of the Eskimos who rescue them. Warren Oates, Timothy Bottoms, and Louis Gossett, Jr. star. Directed by Philip Kaufman. **AC12, AC24, CU48, CU50**

White Heat (1949, B&W, 114m, NR)
James Cagney plays Cody Jarrett, the gangster with a mother fixation, in this crime drama with the explosive "top of the world" ending. Directed by Raoul Walsh. **AC22, CL22, MY1** *Highly Recommended*

White Lightning (1973, C, 101m, PG)
Moonshiner Burt Reynolds gets revenge on the lawman who killed his brother. **AC37**

White Mama (1980, C, 105m, NR)
A poor widow (Bette Davis) and a street-wise black kid (Ernest Harden) form an alliance for their mutual survival. Originally made for TV. **CL21**

White Mischief (1988, C, 106m, R)
British colony in 1940s Africa is rocked by scandal: the public affair between the young wife of a diplomat and an army officer, and the officer's mysterious murder. Based on real events, this drama stars Greta Scacchi and Charles Dance as the lovers, with Sarah Miles, Joss Ackland, and John Hurt. **DR5, DR23**

White Nights (1985, C, 135m, PG-13)
An airplane carrying a ex-Soviet dancer crashes in Siberia, and the Russians hold the man in detention, using a black Amercian defector as his guardian. Mikhail Baryshnikov and Gregory Hines are the dancers (and they do dance!); Jerzy Skolimowski and Isabella Rossellini costar. **DR21**

White of the Eye (1988, C, 113m, R)
Thriller set in Arizona, where a woman suspects her loving husband of being a vicious serial killer. Stylish drama, starring Cathy Moriarty and David Keith, directed by Donald Cammell. **MY17, MY18** *Recommended*

White Rose, The (1983, C, 108m, NR)
German drama about a small group of youths who defy Hitler. **FF3**

White Sheik, The (1951, B&W, 88m, NR)
Italian comedy about a couple on their honeymoon in Rome and the wife's adventures with a cartoon hero called The White Sheik. Alberto Sordi stars. Federico Fellini directed. **FF10**

White Wilderness (1958, C, 73m, G)
This Disney documentary, part of the True-Life Adventure series, goes to the Arctic to examine the animal and plant life there. **FA1**

White Zombie (1932, B&W, 73m, NR)
The owner of a sugar mill in Haiti cuts down on labor costs by using creating an army of zombies. Bela Lugosi stars. **HO1, HO6, HO28**

Who Am I This Time? (1982, C, 60m, NR) Charming comedy about a troupe of amateur actors in a small town and their bold, talented star—who's a painfully shy nerd off-stage. Christopher Walken and Susan Sarandon star. Directed by Jonathan Demme. **CO1, CU39** *Highly Recommended*

Who Done It? (1942, B&W, 77m, NR) Abbott and Costello comedy has the boys pretending to be detectives when they're really a couple of radio scriptwriters. William Bendix and Mary Wickes head the supporting cast. **CO23, MY21**

Who Framed Roger Rabbit (1988, C, 103m, PG) Mind-boggling combination of live action and animation in the story of a flesh-and-blood 1930s private eye (Bob Hoskins) investigating the murder of a movie studio executive, allegedly by one of his cartoon stars. Christopher Lloyd and Joanna Cassidy head the supporting cast, but the real stars are the cartoon characters, including many familiar faces in "cameo" appearances. Directed by Robert Zemeckis; animation supervised by Richard Williams. **CO8, CO10, CO11, FA6** *Highly Recommended*

Who Killed Baby Azaria (1983, C, 96m, NR) Australian drama based on the famous Lindy Chamberlain case, of a mother accused of murdering her baby girl. A better-known version of the same events is *A Cry in the Dark*. **FF5**

Who'll Stop the Rain? (1978, C, 126m, R) An American journalist in Vietnam persuades a Marine buddy to smuggle some heroin back to the States, where all hell breaks loose. Powerful thriller, with underlying commentary on effects of the war. Nick Nolte, Tuesday Weld, and Michael Moriarty star, with Anthony Zerbe and Richard Masur. Based on Robert Stone's novel, *Dog Soldiers*. **DR7, DR44, MY2** *Highly Recommended*

Wholly Moses (1980, C, 109m, R) Irreverent comedy about a nerd (Dudley Moore) who thinks God has picked him to lead the Jews to the Promised Land. Richard Pryor, Laraine Newman, Madeline Kahn, James Coco, Dom DeLuise, and John Houseman costar. **CO13, CO29, CO31**

Whoopi Goldberg Live (1986, C, 75m, NR) The stage show that launched Goldberg's film career, as she plays a wide variety of characters in a tour-de-force performance. **CO16**

Whoops Apocalypse (1981, C, 137m, NR) Britsh satire lampoons world politics and the news media, as the events leading up to World War III are chronicled. John Barron, John Cleese, and Richard Griffiths star. **CO2, CO15**

Who's Afraid of Virignia Woolf? (1966, B&W, 129m, NR) Elizabeth Taylor and Richard Burton in their best film, an adaptation of Edward Albee's play about a battlefield of a marriage. George Segal and Sandy Dennis costar; Mike Nichols directed. Taylor and Dennis won Oscars. **CL15, CL33, DR20, DR75, XT3, XT5** *Recommended*

Who's Harry Crumb? (1989, C, 91m, PG-13) John Candy plays a private eye who resorts to highly unorthodox methods to rescue a kidnap victim. Jeffrey Jones, Annie Potts, and Barry Corbin costar. **CO10, CO14**

Who's That Girl (1987, C, 94m, PG) Madonna plays a kook just released from prison for a crime she didn't commit. She involves an innocent lawyer (Griffin Dunne) in her zany schemes. **MU12**

Whose Life Is It Anyway? (1981, C, 118m, R) An artist, paralyzed from the neck down in a car accident, insists that he be allowed to end his life, against the wishes of his girl friend and doctor. Richard

Dreyfuss stars in this version of Brian Clark's play; Christine Lahti and John Cassavetes costar. **DR20**

Why Shoot the Teacher? (1977, C, 101m, PG)
Canadian drama, set during the Depression, about a young schoolteacher's experiences in a small town. Bud Cort and Samantha Eggar star. **DR61**

Wicked Lady, The (1983, C, 98m, R)
Campy version of the old highwayman tale, with sex change to Faye Dunaway as the robber. Alan Bates and John Gielgud costar. **CU2, DR35**

Wicker Man, The (1973, C, 95m, R)
While investigating the disappearance of a child, a policeman travels to a remote Scottish island and discovers pagan cultists. Edward Woodward, Christopher Lee, and Britt Ekland star. **CU4, HO11, HO32**

Wifemistress (1977, C, 110m, R)
A young woman's husband disappears and she discovers evidence that he has been less than faithful to her. Laura Antonelli and Marcello Mastroianni star in this Italian comedy. **FF2, FF24**

Wilby Conspiracy, The (1975, C, 101m, R)
Chase thriller set in Africa, where a black political activist (Sidney Poitier) is on the lam with a reluctant white journalist (Michael Caine). With Nicol Williamson. **DR38**

Wild Bunch, The (1969, C, 143m, R)
An aging band of outlaws is pursued across Mexico by a ragged band of bounty hunters. Director Sam Peckinpah's masterful and violent tale of the last days of the frontier stars William Holden and Robert Ryan, with Warren Oates, Ben Johnson, Strother Martin, L.Q. Jones, and Edmond O'Brien. **CL51, CU7, CU48, WE4, WE10, WE12, WE19** *Highly Recommended*

Wild Duck, The (1983, C, 96m, PG)
Updating of Henrik Ibsen play about a couple and their struggle to raise a blind child. Liv Ullmann and Jeremy Irons star. **FF25**

Wild Geese II (1985, C, 124m, R)
A group of mercenaries are hired to break Nazi Rudolph Hess out of Spandau Prison. Scott Glenn, Barbara Carrera, and Laurence Olivier star. **CL32**

Wild in the Country (1961, C, 114m, NR)
A backwoods boy (Elvis Presley) gets in trouble with the law; under a psychiatrist's care he is encouraged to write. Written by Clifford Odets. **MU22**

Wild in the Streets (1968, C, 97m, PG)
Satiric look at contemporary youth culture has a rock star elected President when the voting age is lowered to 14. Christopher Jones stars, with Shelley Winters, Diane Varsi, Hal Holbrook, and Richard Pryor. **CO26**

Wild Life, The (1984, C, 96m, R)
A high school graduate gets his first apartment and taste of freedom in this comedy about partying hearty. Christopher Penn, Eric Stoltz, and Rick Moranis star. **CO14**

Wild One, The (1954, B&W, 79m, NR)
Biker Marlon Brando and his gang (including Lee Marvin) roar into a small California town and terrorize the locals. Fifties scare movie that has since become a camp classic. **CU2, DR33, DR43**

Wild Orchids (1929, B&W, 102m, NR)
A married woman falls in love with another man while on a holiday. Greta Garbo, Lewis Stone, and Nils Asther star in this silent soap opera. **CL28**

Wild Party, The (1975, C, 95m, R)
Hollywood drama about fading film star trying to revive his career with major-league wing-ding. James Coco and Raquel Welch star; James Ivory directed. **DR13**

Wild Ride, The (1960, B&W, 63m, NR)
Early Jack Nicholson film has him playing
an amoral hotrodder not above murder or
stealing his best buddy's girl. **DR24**

Wild Rovers (1971, C, 138m, PG)
William Holden and Ryan O'Neal star as
saddle pals in this cult western drama
from director Blake Edwards. The video
version contains 29 minutes of footage
not included in the theatrical release.
CL51, CO46, CU10, WE16

Wild Strawberries (1957, B&W, 90m, NR)
An elderly professor, on his way to re-
ceive an honorary degree, recalls his
past, especially his disappointments. Victor Sjöstrom stars; Ingmar Bergman directed. **FF8** *Recommended*

Wild Style (1982, C, 82m, R)
A rappin' musical about a graffitti artist
in New York City. Lee Quinones stars.
MU9

Wildcats (1986, C, 104m, R)
A divorced mother badly in need of a job
agrees to coach an inner city high school
football team. Goldie Hawn stars in this
comedy, with James Keach, Swoosie
Kurtz, and Nipsey Russell. **CO30, CO36**

Wilderness Family Part 2, The (1978, C,
105m, G)
The family who left the city behind in *The
Adventures of the Wilderness Family* con-
tinue their lives in this sequel. Robert
Logan stars. **FA4**

Will Penny (1968, C, 109m, NR)
Western with cult following features
Charlton Heston as an aging saddlehand
befriending a settler (Joan Hackett) and
her young son. With Donald Pleasence,
Lee Majors, Bruce Dern, Ben Johnson,
Anthony Zerbe, and G.D. Spradlin.
WE16 *Recommended*

Willard (1971, C, 95m, PG)
A disturbed man (Bruce Davison) trains
his pet rats to attack all his enemies.
Sondra Locke and Ernest Borgnine costar. **HO16**

Willie Wonka and the Chocolate Factory
(1971, C, 100m, G)
A musical adaptation of Roald Dahl's
story, "Charlie and the Chocolate Factory." Charlie wins a trip to a chocolate
factory owned by a mysterious man.
Gene Wilder stars. **FA8, FA9**

Willow (1988, C, 126m, PG)
Lavish fantasy adventure revolving
around the efforts of a brave dwarf (War-
wick Davis) to protect an infant from the
clutches of an evil witch. Val Kilmer,
Joanne Whalley, and Jean Marsh costar.
Produced by George Lucas; directed by
Ron Howard. **AC18, FA8, SF13**

Winchester '73 (1950, B&W, 92m, NR)
James Stewart stars in this classic western drama of a man in search of his stolen
gun. Anthony Mann directed. **CL25,
WE2, WE20**

Wind, The (1928, B&W, 82m, NR)
Lillian Gish gives one of her finest per-
formances in this silent drama of a young
innocent and her hard life on the prairie.
Excellent direction by Victor Seastrom.
Video version features a new musical
score by Carl Davis. **CL5, CL12, CL49**
Recommended

Wind and the Lion, The (1975, C, 120m,
PG)
An American diplomat's wife (Candice
Bergen) and her son are kidnapped by a
Moroccan bandit (Sean Connery), and a
romance develops. Based on true events.
Brian Keith (as Theodore Roosevelt) and
John Huston costar. **AC12, AC14, AC16,
AC36, CL44**

Wind in the Willows, The (1982, C, 47m,
G)
An adaptation of Kenneth Grahame's
story about the tale of four gentlemen
friends, Mr. Badger, Mr. Mole, Mr.
Ratty, and Mr. Toad. Originally part of
the 1950 Disney animated feature, *Ichabod and Mr. Toad*. **FA2**

Windwalker (1980, C, 108m, PG)
An Indian patriarch returns to his tribe to prevent an act of revenge by his long-lost brother. Trevor Howard stars in this offbeat Western. **WE8**

Windy City (1984, C, 103m, R)
A reunion of old neighborhood chums in Chicago dramatizes their successes and failures as adults. John Shea, Kate Capshaw, and Josh Mostel star. **DR7**

Wings (1927, B&W, 139m, NR)
When the U.S. enters World War I, two friends in love with the same girl enlist in the Army Air Corps. This silent classic won the first Academy Award for Best Picture. Clara Bow, Buddy Rogers, and Richard Arlen star, with Gary Cooper. **AC2, AC11, CL12, CL26, XT1**

Wings of Desire (1988, B&W/C, 130m, NR)
From German director Wim Wenders, a captivating fantasy-drama focusing on the adventures of a pair of angels in contemporary Berlin. Bruno Ganz stars, with Otto Sander, Solveig Dommartin, and Peter Falk. Wenders and Peter Handke wrote the screenplay. **FF21** *Recommended*

Wings of the Morning (1937, C, 98m, NR)
Henry Fonda falls in love with a Gypsy while training a racehorse. The first British film shot in Technicolor. **CL24**

Winning (1969, C, 123m, PG)
Paul Newman plays a race car driver who's driven to become the best in this drama costarring Joanne Woodward and Robert Wagner. **DR22, DR28, DR67**

Winning of the West (1953, B&W, 57m, NR)
Gene Autry and Smiley Burnette ride together to help a crusading newspaper publisher in the Old West. **WE24**

Winter Kills (1979, C, 97m, R)
Political thriller about the brother of a slain President searching for the killers and uncovering a massive conspiracy.

Based on Richard Condon's novel. Jeff Bridges, John Huston, Toshiro Mifune, and Anthony Perkins head the cast; also in the cast are Belinda Bauer, Richard Boone, Sterling Hayden, Eli Wallach, and Elizabeth Taylor, who appears briefly. **CL33, CL44, CU9, CU17, DR21, DR71, FF28, MY6, MY18**

Winter Light (1962, B&W, 86m, NR)
A priest in a Swedish village wrestles with problems of faith in this Ingmar Bergman drama. Ingrid Thulin and Gunnar Bjornstrand star. **FF8**

Winter of Our Dreams, The (1981, C, 90m, R)
A married bookstore owner becomes involved with an embittered prostitute. Australian drama starring Bryan Brown and Judy Davis. **FF5**

Winter People (1989, C, 110m, PG-13)
In the 1934 North Carolina backwoods, romance blossoms between an unwed mother (Kelly McGillis) and a visiting widower (Kurt Russell). Lloyd Bridges costars. **DR1**

Wisdom (1986, C, 109m, R)
Emilio Estevez wrote, directed, and stars in this drama of a young man and his girl friend who take to robbing banks and redistributing the money to needy farmers. **DR16**

Wise Blood (1979, C, 108m, PG)
Bizarre, fascinating drama, populated by various Southern grotesques, including a young man claiming to be a preacher for The Church Without Christ. Brad Dourif, Daniel Shor, Amy Wright, Harry Dean Stanton, and Ned Beatty star; John Huston directed. Based on Flannery O'Connor's novel. **CL44, CU49, DR19** *Recommended*

Wise Guys (1985, C, 92m, R)
A pair of bumbling hit men are assigned to knock each other off in this comedy starring Joe Piscopo and Danny DeVito. Brian DePalma directed. **CO3, CO10, CO13, CU28**

Wish You Were Here (1987, C, 91m, R)
British comedy-drama about a teenager growing up in a stuffy small town in the 1950s, defying the locals with her sexy behavior. Emily Lloyd stars; written and directed by David Leland. **CO17**

Witches of Eastwick, The (1987, C, 118m, R)
A New England village becomes a battleground when three contemporary witches collide with a mysterious newcomer. Jack Nicholson, Cher, Michelle Pfeiffer, and Susan Sarandon star; George Miller directed from John Updike's novel. **DR19, DR24, MU12**

Withnail and I (1987, C, 110m, R)
Two unemployed actors in 1969 London decide to take a holiday in the country, with nearly disastrous results. Dark comedy starring Richard E. Grant, Paul McGann, and Richard Griffiths. Written and directed by Bruce Robinson. **CO17**

Without a Clue (1988, C, 107m, PG)
Sherlock Holmes played for laughs, with the famed detective (Michael Caine) a bungler and Dr. Watson (Ben Kingsley) the real brains of the operation. **MY10, MY21**

Without a Trace (1983, C, 120m, PG)
True story of a woman whose young son disappears in New York City and her frantic efforts to find him. Kate Nelligan and Judd Hirsch star. **MY8, MY18**

Without Reservations (1946, B&W, 107m, NR)
The author of a successful novel discovers the perfect man to play her hero in the movies. Claudette Colbert and John Wayne star in this romantic comedy, with cameos by several Hollywood stars. **CL17**

Witness (1985, C, 112m, R)
Drama of Amish boy witnessing murder on a visit to Philadelphia and the cop who befriends him and his mother. Harrison Ford, Kelly McGillis, Lukas Haas, and Danny Glover star; Peter Weir directed. **DR16, DR32**

Witness for the Prosecution (1957, B&W, 114m, NR)
Agatha Christie courtroomn drama, with Charles Laughton defending Tyrone Power on murder charge. Marlene Dietrich costars as Power's wife. Directed by Billy Wilder. **CL37, CL47, DR17, MY23** *Recommended*

Wiz, The (1978, C, 133m, G)
An update of *The Wizard of Oz,* based on the Broadway musical hit. Diana Ross stars, with Richard Pryor and Michael Jackson. Directed by Sidney Lumet. **CO29, DR58, FA9, MU2, MU8**

Wizard of Loneliness, The (1988, C, 110m, PG-13)
During World War II, a young boy is sent to live with his kindly but eccentric grandparents in a Vermont village. Lukas Haas stars in this drama, with Lea Thompson. Based on a novel by John Nichols. **DR9**

Wizard of Oz, The (1939, C/B&W, 101m, G)
A girl from Kansas discovers the power of friendship and love in a strange land over the rainbow. Judy Garland stars, with Ray Bolger, Bert Lahr, Jack Haley, and Margaret Hamilton. Available in a limited edition celebrating the 50th anniversary of the film's release, containing footage not used in the original release. **CU10, FA9, MU8, MU21, SF13** *Highly Recommended*

Wizard of Oz, The (1982, C, 78m, NR)
An animated adaptation of Frank L. Baum's classic story about a little girl and her dog and their adventures in the land over the rainbow. **FA10**

Wizards (1977, C, 80m, PG)
Animated adventure set in a world of magic. A good wizard rules his kingdom with kindness. His evil brother sets out to conquer the rest of the planet. **SF13**

Wizards of the Lost Kingdom (1985, C, 78m, PG)
Bo Svenson stars in this futuristic fantasy with plenty of swordplay. **AC18**

Wolf Man, The (1941, B&W, 70m, NR)
Lawrence Talbot (Lon Chaney, Jr.) is bitten by a werewolf (Bela Lugosi) and lives to carry on the curse. A horror classic. **HO1, HO4, HO17, HO28, HO30** *Recommended*

Wolfen (1981, C, 115m, R)
A New York detective (Albert Finney) discovers a race of wolf men living in the slums of the South Bronx. Spooky thriller with horror touches. Gregory Hines, Diane Venora, and James Edward Olmos costar. **HO4, HO16, XT9** *Recommended*

Woman Called Golda, A (1982, C, 195m, NR)
A look into the life of Israel's prime minister, Golda Meir. Ingrid Bergman won an Emmy for her portrayal of this courageous leader. Originally made for TV. **CL27**

Woman in Flames, A (1982, C, 106m, R)
A housewife deserts her husband and falls into a life of prostitution in this contemporary German drama. Gudrun Landgrebe stars; Robert Van Ackeren directed. **FF3**

Woman in Green, The (1945, B&W, 68m, NR)
Sherlock Holmes and Dr. Watson battle the nefarious Professor Moriarty in this tale of a murderer whose trademark is leaving corpses with one thumb missing. Basil Rathbone and Nigel Bruce star. **MY10**

Woman in Red, The (1984, C, 87m, PG-13)
Romantic comedy starring Gene Wilder as happily married man with hang-up on lovely woman he glimpsed one day in a parking garage. Kelly LeBrock costars, with Gilda Radner, Charles Grodin, and Judith Ivey. Remake of French film, *Pardon Mon Affaire*. **CO1, CO13, FF36**

Woman in the Dunes (1964, B&W, 123m, NR)
A scientist becomes trapped in a sandpit with a strange woman who lives there.

Offbeat drama from Japan, directed by Hiroshi Teshigahara. **FF4**

Woman in the Moon, The (1929, B&W, 146m, NR)
Fritz Lang directed this silent science fiction tale about the first expedition to the moon. **CL43**

Woman Next Door, The (1981, C, 106m, NR)
A married man's new neighbor, also married, is his ex-lover, and they resume their relationship. French drama from François Truffaut, starring Gerard Depardieu and Fanny Ardant. **FF13, FF29**

Woman of Paris, A (1923, B&W, 81m, NR)
This silent drama is about a woman pledged to marry who becomes a wealthy man's mistress through a series of misunderstandings. Edna Purviance, Adolphe Menjou, and Carl Miller star. A rare dramatic outing for director Charlie Chaplin, who has only a bit part as a railway porter. **CL12, CO18**

Woman of the Year (1942, B&W, 112m, NR)
First pairing of Katharine Hepburn and Spencer Tracy has her playing a political commentator, him a sportswriter. Written by Ring Lardner, Jr. and Michael Kanin (Oscar winners); directed by George Stevens. Sheer joy. **CL10, CL15, CL16, CL19, CL42** *Highly Recommended*

Woman Rebels, A (1936, B&W, 88m, NR)
Katharine Hepburn stars as a crusader for woman's rights in Victorian England. **CL5, CL16**

Woman Times Seven (1967, C, 99m, NR)
Shirley MacLaine plays seven roles in this series of comic sketches costarring Peter Sellers, Rossano Brazzi, and Vittorio Gassman. **CO26, DR42**

Woman Without Love, A (1951, C, 91m, NR)
Director Luis Buñuel's drama of infidelity, adapted from a Guy de Maupassant story. **FF11**

Woman's Face, A (1941, B&W, 105m, NR)
A woman with a disfigured face has plastic surgery which transforms her life as well as her face. Joan Crawford and Melvyn Douglas star. Directed by George Cukor. **CL39, CL50**

Women, The (1939, B&W, 132m, NR)
All-star comedy about a group of female friends (no men in the cast) and their love lives. Rosalind Russell, Joan Crawford, Norma Shearer, Paulette Goddard, and Joan Fontaine star. George Cukor directed. **CL5, CL39, CL50, CU2** *Highly Recommended*

Women in Love (1970, C, 129m, R)
D.H. Lawrence story of two love affairs, starring Alan Bates, Glenda Jackson (an Oscar winner), Oliver Reed, and Jennie Linden. Vigorous direction by Ken Russell. Prequel: *The Rainbow*. **CU31, DR1, DR19, DR23, XT3** *Recommended*

Women on the Verge of a Nervous Breakdown (1988, C, 88m, NR)
Spanish comedy from director Pedro Almodóvar, featuring an actress (Carmen Maura) who's trying to learn of her lover's infidelity. Zany look at how popular culture infects our lives. **FF7** *Recommended*

Wonder Man (1945, C, 98m, NR)
Danny Kaye plays twins, one a nightclub singer and one a scholar. The singer gets killed and his ghost pushes his brother into solving the murder. Virginia Mayo costars. **CO41, MU4**

Woodstock (1970, C, 184m, R)
Oscar-winning documentary about three days of peace, love, and music in August 1969. Among the musical highlights: The Who, Ritchie Havens, Joe Cocker, Santana, and Jimi Hendrix performing *The Star-Spangled Banner*. An exceptional filmmaking achievement, directed by Michael Wadleigh. **MU10** *Highly Recommended*

Words and Music (1948, C, 119m, NR)
This biography of songwriters Richard Rodgers and Lorenz Hart is really a showcase for 36 of their best songs. Mickey Rooney and Tom Drake star, with cameo appearances from many MGM musical stars, including Judy Garland, plus Gene Kelly and Vera-Ellen in an eight-minute ballet. **MU1, MU5, MU19, MU21**

Work/Police (1915/1916. B&W, 81m, NR)
Two early Charlie Chaplin short films. In the first, he's an inept paper hanger; in the second, he's an ex-con with a penchant for trouble. **CO18**

Working Girl (1988, C, 113m, R)
With her female boss laid up by a skiing injury, a bright, ambitious Wall Street secretary takes over a major deal—and falls in love with a handsome colleague. Melanie Griffith, Harrison Ford, and Sigourney Weaver star in this contemporary romantic comedy. Mike Nichols directed. **CO1, CO2, DR10, DR32, DR75, DR76, XT9** *Recommended*

Working Girls (1987, C, 93m, NR)
Vivid, sometimes comic portrait of everyday lives of several New York prostitutes, directed by Lizzie Borden. **DR10** *Recommended*

World According to Garp, The (1982, C, 136m, R)
Seriocomic adventures of a college professor and his family, adapted from the John Irving bestseller. Robin Williams stars, with Mary Beth Hurt, Glenn Close, John Lithgow, Hume Cronyn, and Jessica Tandy. **CO43, DR8, DR19, DR72**

World Apart, A (1988, C, 112m, PG)
South Africa is the setting for this drama of a young white girl whose mother neglects her to work in the anti-apartheid movement. Barbara Hershey and Jodhi May star. Shawn Slowo's script was based on her own experiences. **DR7, DR8**

World of Apu, The (1959, B&W, 103m, NR)
The concluding film in Indian director Satyajit Ray's classic *Apu* trilogy finds the young hero finally marrying and becoming a father. **FF23**

World of Henry Orient, The (1964, C, 106m, NR)
Two New York teenagers with a crush on a concert pianist make his life miserable by following him everywhere. Peter Sellers stars, with Tippy Walker and Merrie Spaeth. **CO4, CO26, XT9**

World of Suzie Wong, the (1960, C, 129m, NR)
An American artist living in Hong Kong falls in love with an Asian prostitute. William Holden and Nancy Kwan star. **CL51**

World's Greatest Athlete, The (1973, C, 93m, G)
A coach (John Amos) visiting Africa discovers a teenaged Tarzan (Jan-Michael Vincent) who's a super athlete, and takes him to America. Tim Conway costars in this Disney comedy. **FA1**

Wraith, The (1986, C, 91m, PG13)
A mysterious car begins to terrorize a group of teenagers. Charlie Sheen, Nick Cassavetes, and Randy Quaid star. **AC10**

Written on the Wind (1956, C, 99m, NR)
From director Douglas Sirk, a lush melodrama about an irresponsible playboy and his sister and their wasted lives. Robert Stack and Oscar winner Dorothy Malone star, with Rock Hudson and Lauren Bacall. **CL6, CU24, XT5**

Wrong Arm of the Law, The (1962, B&W, 94m, NR)
A trio of robbers find themselves pursued by crooks and cops in this British comic romp starring Peter Sellers. **CO26**

Wrong Box, The (1966, C, 105m, NR)
Zany British comedy, set in Victorian England, featuring skullduggery over immense inheritance. Great cast includes Ralph Richardson, John Mills, Dudley Moore, Peter Cook, Michael Caine, and Peter Sellers. **CO17, CO26, CO31** *Recommended*

Wrong Is Right (1982, C, 117m, R)
Satirical look at how modern news media shape political events, with Sean Connery hopscotching the world for news. Written for the screen and directed by Richard Brooks. With George Grizzard, Katharine Ross, Robert Conrad, Henry Silva, and Leslie Nielsen. **AC36**

Wrong Man, The (1956, B&W, 105m, NR)
Henry Fonda stars in this low-key Hitchcock thriller about a musician falsely accused of robbery, trying to overcome the system to prove he's innocent. Based on a true case. **CL24, MY7, MY8, MY22**

Wrong Move (1975, C, 103m, NR)
German drama of a young writer's odyssey toward self-discovery and experience. Directed by Wim Wenders. Ridgier Vogler, Hanna Schygulla, and Nastassia Kinski star. **FF21**

Wuthering Heights (1939, B&W, 104m, NR)
Laurence Olivier and Merle Oberon star in the beloved version of the Bronte novel. William Wyler directed this classic romantic drama, photographed by Gregg Toland. **CL1, CL4, CL6, CL32, CL38** *Recommended*

Wuthering Heights (1954, B&W, 90m, NR)
Director Luis Buñuel's version of the Bronte classic, filmed in Mexico, starring Iraseme Dilian and Jorge Mistral. **CL1, FF11**

X: The Man With the X-Ray Eyes (1963, C, 88m, NR)
Ray Milland invents eye drops to give him X-ray vision, which eventually leads to madness. Directed by Roger Corman. **SF5**

X: The Unheard Music (1985, C, 87m, R)
A documentary of the L.A.-based punk/country band, filmed between 1980 and 1985. **MU11**

X, Y, and Zee (1972, C, 110m, PG)
A woman (Elizabeth Taylor), her husband (Michael Caine), and his mistress (Susannah York) share each other in a triangular relationship. **CL33**

Xanadu (1980, C, 88m, PG)
An angel tries to help a roller-boogie boy achieve stardom. Olivia Newton-John stars, with a special appearance by Gene Kelly. **MU8, MU19**

Xtro (1983, C, 82m, R)
A man disappears and three years later returns to his son. It is then revealed that the man is an alien and that he intends to take his son to his home at any cost. **SF20**

Yakuza, The (1975, C, 112m, R)
Robert Mitchum returns to Japan to rescue Brian Keith's daughter from the Yakuza, the Japanese Mafia. Directed by Sydney Pollack; written by Paul Schrader. **AC22, DR56**

Yankee Doodle Dandy (1942, B&W, 126m, NR)
James Cagney won an Oscar for his irresistible portrayal of songwriter George M. Cohan. **CL22, FA9, MU5, MU6, MU7, XT2** *Recommended*

Year of Living Dangerously, The (1982, C, 115m, PG)
Romantic drama, set in turbulent Indonesia during the mid-1960s, about a naive Australian reporter (Mel Gibson) and a British embassy aide (Sigourney Weaver). Linda Hunt won an Oscar for her portrayal of a male photographer. Peter Weir directed. **DR21, DR69, DR76, FF5, XT5**

Year of the Dragon, The (1985, C, 136m, R)
Cynical police captain intrudes on gang warfare in New York's Chinatown. Mickey Rourke, Ariane, and John Lone star; directed by Michael Cimino. **DR48**

Year of the Quiet Sun, A (1984, C, 107m, PG)
Drama set in postwar Germany about an affair between an American soldier and a Polish war widow. Directed by Krzystoff Zanussi. **FF7**

Yearling, The (1946, C, 129m, NR)
Family living in the Florida swamps during the Depression find a hurt fawn and adopt it. Warm adaptation of the Marjorie Kinan Rawlings book, starring Gregory Peck, Jane Wyman, and Claude Jarman, Jr. Oscar winner for lovely color photography. **CL9, FA5**

Yellow Rose of Texas, The (1944, B&w, 55m, NR)
Roy Rogers goes undercover to catch some outlaws. Dale Evans costars, with vocal support from Bob Nolan & the Sons of the Pioneers. **WE23**

Yellow Submarine (1968, C, 85m, G)
The Beatles star in this surreal, animated tale about a band who set out to save Pepperland from the Blue Meanies. **CU3, MU8, MU9** *Recommended*

Yellowbeard (1983, C, 101m, PG)
Comic pirate movie with a boatload of stars, including Graham Chapman, Cheech & Chong, Marty Feldman, James Mason, Peter Cook, and Eric Idle. Co-written by Chapman and Cook. **CO15, CO32**

Yentl (1983, C, 134m, PG)
Barbra Streisand plays a Jewish woman living in 19th-century Eastern Europe who disguises herself as a male to obtain an education. The star, who also directed and co-wrote the script, sings a dozen soliloquy songs. With Mandy Patinkin, Amy Irving, and Steven Hill. **CO37, MU27**

Yesterday, Today and Tomorrow (1964, C, 119m, NR)
Oscar-winning comedy from Italy, a trio of tales about sex and money, starring Sophia Loren and Marcello Mastroianni. Vittorio de Sica directed. **FF2, FF24, FF31, XT7**

Yin and Yang of Mr. Go, The (1971, C, 89m, R)
Espionage drama, set in Hong Kong, with a CIA agent out to retrieve stolen military plans. Jeff Bridges stars, with James Mason, Burgess Meredith, and Broderick Crawford. **DR71**

Yojimbo (1961, B&W, 110m, NR)
Classic samurai adventure, exaggerated for comic effect, about a lone swordsman playing off two feuding families against one another. Toshiro Mifune stars; Akira Kurosawa directed. Loosely remade as *A Fistful of Dollars.* **AC13, FF9, FF28, FF36** *Recommended*

Yolanda and the Thief (1945, C, 108m, NR)
A con man tries to convince an heiress that he is her guardian angel. Fred Astaire stars in this colorful musical fantasy directed by Vincente Minnelli. **CL9, MU8, MU18, MU24**

You Can't Cheat an Honest Man (1939, B&W, 76m, NR)
W.C. Fields costars with Edgar Bergen and Charlie McCarthy in this comedy set in a circus. **CL10, CO22**

You Can't Win 'Em All *see* Soldiers of Fortune

You Only Live Once (1937, B&W, 86m, NR)
Henry Fonda and Sylvia Sidney are the couple on the run in this superb crime drama from director Fritz Lang. **CL24, CL43, MY1** *Recommended*

You Only Live Twice (1967, C, 116m, PG)
James Bond (Sean Connery) must outsmart Ernst Stavro Blofeld (Donald Pleasence) before the villain can cause the super powers to go to war. **AC35, AC36**

You Were Never Lovelier (1942, B&W, 97m, NR)
A hotel owner (Adolphe Menjou) allows a gambler (Fred Astaire) to work off his debts by trying to tame the man's headstrong daughter (Rita Hayworth). **MU18**

You'll Find Out (1940, B&W, 97m, NR)
Kay Kyser and his Orchestra spend the night at a haunted house. Boris Karloff, Bela Lugosi, and Peter Lorre costar. **HO27, HO28**

You'll Never Get Rich (1941, B&W, 88m, NR)
A choreographer (Fred Astaire) starts to romance a chorus girl (Rita Hayworth), then he's drafted. He is able to continue the romance when he arranges to put on a show at his base featuring her. **MU18**

Young and Innocent (1937, B&W, 80m, NR)
A fugitive from justice is aided by a young girl in proving his innocence. Directed by Alfred Hitchcock. **MY7, MY19, MY22**

Young and Willing (1943, B&W, 82m, NR)
Screen version of stage comedy *Out of the Frying Pan*, about the wacky world of show-biz hopefuls, starring William Holden, Eddie Bracken, and Barbara Britton. **CL7, CL51, DR20**

Young at Heart (1954, C, 117m, NR)
Frank Sinatra romances Doris Day in this musical about small-town life. **MU26**

Young Bill Hickok (1940, B&W, 54m, NR)
Roy Rogers plays the legendary Western scout, as Hickok matches wits with a pair of crafty outlaws. **WE2, WE23**

Young Buffalo Bill (1940, B&W, 54m, NR)
The Legend of the Plains is portrayed by Roy Rogers, who helps the U.S. Army put down an Indian uprising. **WE2, WE23**

Young Doctors in Love (1982, C, 95m, R)
Comedy set in a hospital where anything goes, starring Michael McKean, Sean Young, Harry Dean Stanton, Dabney Coleman, Pamela Reed, many others. **CU49**

Young Frankenstein (1974, B&W, 105m, PG)
Mel Brooks' parody of the great black-and-white monster movies from the 1930s, with Gene Wilder as the mad doctor, Peter Boyle as his creation, plus Marty Feldman, Teri Garr, Cloris Leachman, and (in a hilarious cameo) Gene Hackman. Brooks' best film. **CO7, CO28, DR39** *Highly Recommended*

Young Guns (1988, C, 107m, R)
Western tale of a youthful band of ruffians, led by Billy the Kid, out for revenge when their kindly rancher friend is murdered. Emilio Estevez stars as Billy, with Charlie Sheen, Kiefer Sutherland, Lou Diamond Phillips, Jack Palance, and Terence Stamp. **WE2, WE6, XT8**

Young Lions, The (1958, B&W, 167m, NR)
In this World War II drama, Marlon Brando plays a sensitive Nazi officer who questions the morality of his orders; Montgomery Clift is an American Jewish soldier contending with anti-Semitism within his unit. Dean Martin costars in this adaptation of Irwin Shaw's novel. **AC1, DR33**

Young Man With a Horn (1950, B&W, 112m, NR)
A talented trumpet player who dreams of the big time heads for destruction when he marries a socialite. Kirk Douglas, Lauren Bacall, and Doris Day star. **MU4**

Young Mr. Lincoln (1939, B&W, 100m, NR)
Henry Fonda plays the future President as a struggling lawyer in this classic directed by John Ford. **CL2, CL24, CL34** *Recommended*

Young Philadelphians, The (1959, B&W, 136m, NR)
Soap opera about an ambitious lawyer (Paul Newman) hoping to crack Philadelphia society with a socialite (Barbara Rush). **DR28**

Young Sherlock Holmes (1985, C, 109m, PG-13)
The movie that asks the question, What if Holmes and Watson had really met as prep school students? Nicholas Rowe and Alan Cox star as the future detective and his sidekick in this fanciful detective story. **FA4, MY10**

Young Winston (1972, C, 145m, PG)
The early days of Winston Churchill, from his schooling up to his first election to Parliament. Simon Ward, Anne Bancroft, Robert Shaw, and John Mills star; Richard Attenborough directed. **DR4**

Youngblood (1986, C, 111m, R)
Brash hockey player has a lot to prove to hard-driving coach, especially when he falls in love with the man's daughter. Rob Lowe, stars, with Patrick Swayze, Ed Lauter, and Cynthia Gibb. **DR22**

Your Past Is Showing *see* The Naked Truth

Your Ticket Is No Longer Valid (1979, C, 91m, R)
Melodrama of an impotent businessman (Richard Harris) and the Parisian madam (Jeanne Moreau) who tries to cure his problem. **FF26**

You're a Big Boy Now (1966, C, 96m, NR)
New York youth falls for a hard-hearted actress, against the wishes of his overbearing parents. Sweet, offbeat comedy from director Francis Ford Coppola, starring Peter Kastner, Elizabeth Hartman, Rip Torn, and Geraldine Page. **CO4, CU47, DR51, XT9**

Z (1969, C, 127m, PG)
Yves Montand stars as a popular politician whose murder by right-wing thugs sets off a major social movement in his country. Oscar winner for Best Foreign Language Picture; directed by Costa-Gavras. **FF1, MY20, XT7** *Recommended*

Zabriskie Point (1970, C, 112m, R)
Italian director Michelangelo Antonioni's impressions of life in late-1960s America (and particularly Los Angeles) are

wrapped around the story of a campus demonstrator on the run after shooting a policeman. Music by Pink Floyd, the Grateful Dead, Patti Page, and others. **CU3, DR7, FF17, XT9** *Recommended*

Zardoz (1974, C, 105m, R)
In the year 2293, the Brutals and the Exterminators are constantly at war, spurred on by the "god" Zardoz. Sean Connery stars; John Boorman directed. **CU4, CU32, SF8, SF19**

Zatoichi Meets Yojimbo (1970, C, 90m, NR)
Showdown between the fabled blind swordsman and mercenary in this action drama, starring Toshiro Mifune. **FF28**

Zelig (1983, C/B&W, 79m, PG)
Woody Allen spoofs newsreels and documentaries with his tale of the fictional Herbert Zelig, the man who knew every celebrity in the 20th century, from Babe Ruth to Adolf Hitler. Marvelous use of actual newsreel footage with Allen's character inserted. Mia Farrow costars. **CO7, CO12, CO27** *Recommended*

Zelly and Me (1988, C, 87m, PG)
Drama set in 1950s Virginia about a young orphan girl's relationship with her nanny. Alexandra Johnes is the little girl, Isabella Rossellini her nanny. With Glynis Johns, Joe Morton, and David Lynch. **CU38, DR9**

Zero for Conduct (1933, B&W, 44m, NR)
Hilarious, surreal comedy about life in a boys' boarding school from French director Jean Vigo. **DR61, FF1** *Highly Recommended*

Ziegfeld Follies (1945, C, 110m, NR)
A musical revue showcasing such talents as Judy Garland, Fred Astaire, Gene Kelly, Lena Horne, Esther Williams, and

many more. William Powell opens the show as Flo Ziegfeld in heaven. Directed by Vincente Minnelli. **MU1, MU4, MU18, MU19, MU21, MU24**

Ziggy Stardust and the Spiders From Mars (1983, C, 91m, PG)
An early David Bowie alter ego, Ziggy Stardust, filmed at a 1973 performance. **MU10**

Zombie (1979, C, 91m, NR)
The island of Matool is the setting for a zombie epidemic. **HO6, HO18**

Zombie High (1987, C, 91m, R)
All the students are well mannered and obedient at this school. A curious transfer student discovers why. Virginia Madsen stars. **HO12**

Zombie Island Massacre (1984, C, 95m, NR)
A group of tourists commit a sacrilege when they witness an ancient voodoo ceremony. They are then hunted and killed by the island inhabitants. Rita Jenrette stars. **HO6**

Zorba the Greek (1964, B&W, 146m, NR)
Anthony Quinn plays the title role, a peasant who teaches a visiting Britisher (Alan Bates) a thing or two about living. Lila Kedrova won an Oscar for her performance as a fatally ill prostitute. **XT5**

Zulu (1964, C, 138m, NR)
British soldiers hold off 4,000 Zulu warriors in this true story about the 1879 battle in Natal, South Africa. Michael Caine and Stanley Baker star. **AC6**

Zulu Dawn (1979, C, 117m, PG)
This follow-up to *Zulu* is actually about the events leading up to battle between the British Forces and the Zulu nation for control of Natal, South Africa. Peter O'Toole and Burt Lancaster star. **AC6, DR41, DR45**

CHECK LIST INDEX